THE SAYINGS
OF JESUS

THE SAYINGS
OF JESUS

AS RECORDED IN THE GOSPELS
ACCORDING TO ST. MATTHEW AND
ST. LUKE ARRANGED WITH INTRO-
DUCTION AND COMMENTARY BY

T. W. MANSON

SCM PRESS LTD
BLOOMSBURY STREET LONDON

The acknowledgements and thanks of the Author and Publishers of this work are due to the Delegates of the Oxford University Press for their kind permission to reprint the text of the Gospels from the Revised Version.

334 01441 7

First published as Part II of the Mission and Message of Jesus, 1937
Re-issued as a separate volume 1949
Reprinted 1950
Reprinted 1954
Reprinted 1957
Reprinted 1961
Reprinted 1964
Reprinted 1971

Reprinted by Offset Lithography in Great Britain by Billing & Sons Ltd, Guildford and London

Contents

CONTENTS

CONTENTS

Preface

The present volume was originally published in 1937 as the middle portion of a much larger work, *The Mission and Message of Jesus*, produced by Dr. H. D. A. Major, Dr. C. J. Wright, and myself, under the general editorship of Dr. Major. This larger book of almost 1,000 pages has been out of print for some years, and there seems to be no likelihood of its being reprinted as a whole in the near future. It is clear that there is a considerable demand for the work; and the immediate practical question has thus become whether this demand may not be met by the publication of the separate parts—whether, in short, one-third of a loaf is not better than no bread. On the one hand it has to be said that it is a pity that a piece of work that was planned as a single and complete commentary on the Four Gospels should be broken up. On the other hand there is the fact that the way in which the work was originally divided up by Dr. Major and the way in which it was carried out by the three contributors made it possible for each part to be complete in itself, and, if necessary, to stand by itself. In these circumstances I was very glad when the Student Christian Movement Press made the suggestion that they should publish my section as a separate volume, and I am very grateful to my colleagues, and particularly to Dr. Major, for agreeing to this being done.

As this edition can only be made by a photographic process, extensive alterations are impracticable. Nor, in fact, do I wish to make any. The work as originally carried out was the fruit of prolonged study of the text; and it was committed to paper in about a year. Further consideration of the text has not led me to any serious modification of the interpretation adopted; and I am not inclined to meddle with a piece of work that was conceived and executed in one sustained effort. I have, however, taken advantage of this reprinting to add a few notes on particular points and to make some additions to the Bibliography.

MANCHESTER.   T. W. M.
June, 1948

Introduction

1. *THE CHRISTIAN GOSPEL AND THE TEACHING OF JESUS*

HISTORIC Christianity is first and foremost a Gospel, the proclamation to the world of Jesus Christ and Him crucified. For the primitive Church the central thing is the Cross on the Hill rather than the Sermon on the Mount, and the characteristic Church act is the Communion rather than the conference. Christian doctrine and Christian ethics may be the inevitable corollaries of the Christian gospel; but they are corollaries. What is preached in the first instance is something that God has done for man in Christ. Only when this has been appropriated does the question arise how we are to think of the God who has done this great thing, or how we are now to order our lives as Christians.

Yet the problems of theology and ethics do arise very quickly in the Christian community. The earliest documents of the New Testament, the letters of St. Paul, are largely occupied with questions of Christian belief and Christian conduct. They presuppose groups of people who have already heard and responded to the preaching of the Gospel, who now require teaching about the truths implied in the Gospel, and the kind of life that ought to be lived by those who accept the gift of God in Christ. When such instruction has to be given the natural place to which the teacher turns is the source of the Gospel—Jesus Himself. In His life and words will be found the standard and norm of Christian behaviour.

The teaching of Jesus in the fullest and deepest sense is Jesus Himself, and the best Christian living has always been in some sort an imitation of Christ; not a slavish copying of His acts but the working of His mind and spirit in new contexts of life and circumstance. So we might be tempted to argue that all that is necessary is to have the Spirit and then all the details of belief and practice will settle themselves. The first epistle to the Corinthians is evidence that there were those in the Church there who took that view. It is also evidence that conversion did not at once make men and women infallible judges of what actually is the mind and spirit of Christ. Some objective test was required, and it was found in the recorded acts and words of Jesus.

Here, then, we have the chief motive for the preservation and collection of the sayings of Jesus: they were needed in the pastoral work, which followed necessarily on any successful missionary effort.

But while this was the principal factor, it was not the only one at work in the process which has given us the records of the teaching. It is possible to distinguish three other interests.

There is a personal interest in Jesus Himself. It is not a desire to write His biography—in the strict sense of the word there is no biography of Jesus—but rather a very natural instinct to treasure up characteristic words, words that revealed Him, sayings which, in their pointed brevity, told more about Him than many pages of description could tell. The interest of those who preserved and compiled these sayings is comparable to that which preserved the oracles of the Hebrew prophets long after the historical situations to which they were relevant were past. It is part of the devotion of the disciple to his Master, and it is not

9

difficult to believe that there were many among those who followed Jesus and heard His teaching, who pondered His sayings in their hearts, not with an eye to the future needs of the Church, but simply because they had known the author of them and loved Him.

Again, the sayings had a use in Christian propaganda in the Græco-Roman world. They did not constitute the Gospel. The Gospel meant primarily the story of the Passion and the Resurrection. But they provided, increasingly as time went on, a way of approach to those people in the Roman Empire who were in earnest with religion and morals. And these were not few. The world to which St. Paul brought the Gospel had its full measure of vices and iniquities; but it had its own virtues and, more important still, it had men and women who were seriously concerned to find the truth and to live the good life. The Stoic propaganda found a ready hearing for its exacting moral demands, and the Jewish synagogues of the Dispersion gathered round themselves a fringe of ' God-fearers,' men and women who were attracted by the pure monotheism and the high moral standards of Judaism, and only deterred from embracing the faith of Israel by those other requirements—circumcision, for example—which were necessary for full membership of the Jewish community. It was the religious and moral teaching of Judaism that attracted these Gentiles. How much more would they be attracted by the teaching of Jesus, claiming to express a righteousness higher than that of the Scribes and Pharisees and free from those features in Judaism which were naturally repugnant to Greek and Roman. The teaching of Jesus was singularly adapted to prepare the way for the Gospel. Hence we find that, when the Apologists set about their task of commending Christianity to the educated and influential classes in the Roman Empire, it was to the teaching of Jesus that they turned for evidence of the value of the new religion.

Finally, the teaching was important to the Palestinian Church in its relation to Palestinian Judaism, and especially to the Jewish Law. The teaching of Jesus was not given as a new Law, yet it did at many points touch both the written Law and the scribal tradition. Jesus Himself had, more than once, taken up an attitude to these standards that, from the point of view of orthodox Judaism, could only be described as heretical. Those who followed Him and accepted His teaching inevitably came under suspicion of heresy. It might be pleaded that the Teacher came not to destroy the Law but to fulfil it; but this plea would not be seriously considered by those in authority. Further, the natural tendency of hostile criticism would be —as it commonly is—to single out those features in the teaching which could be most readily attacked or misconstrued and to pass by the elements which were attractive. It was even possible for the teaching to be misrepresented in order to discredit the new heresy. It was therefore the more necessary that the Palestinian community should have some reliable and authoritative compilation of the teaching, first as a defence against Jewish misrepresentation and secondly for propaganda among Jewish scholars who might show some sympathy towards Christianity. That misrepresentation of the teaching was a real danger is shown by the story of Imma Shalom and Gamaliel (Klausner, *Jesus of Nazareth*, pp. 44 ff.).

We have thus four motives at work in the compilation of the teaching: the pastoral care of the churches, the personal interest of the disciple in the Master, the apologetic value of such teaching in the Gentile world, and the need of the Palestinian community to defend itself against the charge of uttering subversive doctrines. Of these the first was probably the most powerful. All four might be expected to make themselves felt at a very early stage in the history of the Church, and this expectation is confirmed by literary criticism of the Gospels. For it appears that both Matthew and Luke used a document consisting entirely of teachings of Jesus, and this document has a fair claim to be as old as, if not older than, the earliest written Gospel—that of Mark. We have in fact to recognise that in the earliest stages of the Christian tradition there are two streams which eventually unite to form the Gospel as we see it in Matthew or Luke The one has its source in the Passion and Resurrection: its story is the story of Him who came not to be ministered unto but to minister and to give His life a ransom for many. The other is the record of the sayings of a Teacher who astonished the multitudes because He taught with authority and not as their Scribes. It is this second stream of tradition whose history we must now attempt to trace.

2. THE HISTORY OF THE TRADITION

The ultimate source of all genuine matter in the teaching is the spoken word of Jesus Himself. The two most certain facts in the gospel tradition are that Jesus taught and that He was crucified. In Mark the verb ' teach ' occurs seventeen times, and in sixteen of these cases Jesus is the subject. In the same Gospel He is called ' teacher ' twelve times—four times by His disciples, once by Himself, five times by persons not of His circle but not hostile to Him, and twice *by His opponents*. Four times also in Mark He is called ' Rabbi,' the usual name for a Jewish teacher. The narrative parts of the Synoptic Gospels portray Him preaching and teaching in the synagogues and in the open air, instructing His followers in private, and discussing questions of belief and practice with the Jewish religious authorities.

The question now arises: granting that Jesus did teach, was He a teacher in the proper Jewish sense? Was He, so to speak, academically qualified for the title of Rabbi? Popular fancy has generally preferred to think of the simple carpenter of Nazareth, who, by His superior insight, confounds the learned. But such information as we have points rather in the opposite direction. The fact that He was addressed by His opponents as ' Teacher ' is difficult to explain unless He was in fact recognised by them as their equal in point of scholarship. The quotations from the Old Testament in His teaching show a close familiarity with the five books of the Law, most of the prophetic books, and Psalms, Job, and Daniel in the third division of the Hebrew canon. It is probable that He knew the Old Testament in Hebrew, and, I think, possible at least that He was acquainted with the Rabbinic Hebrew used in the schools of the Law. If Jesus used this language at all, it would be in His controversies with the learned. The impression left by the accounts of His dealings with these men is not that they saw in Him a village craftsman turned amateur theologian but rather a competent scholar who had developed heretical tendencies.

It may be taken as certain that the bulk of the teaching was spoken in Aramaic, the vernacular language of Palestine, and the only language in which the majority of the people were at home. It was their mother-tongue as it was the mother-tongue of Jesus, the language of His prayers—as is shown by His use of the word *Abba*—and the language which He used in speaking to ordinary folk—as we learn from the stories of the raising of Jairus' daughter and the healing of the deaf-mute (Mk. 5^{41}, 7^{34}). Besides this direct evidence we have the fact that many of the differences between Matthew and Luke in reporting the words of Jesus can be readily explained as due to translation—in a few cases, mistranslation—from Aramaic.

We have to think of the teaching being delivered in all kinds of circumstances to all kinds of people: in synagogues to congregations assembled for worship, or in the open air to crowds who had gathered, drawn by the reputation of Jesus, or again in chance encounters with individuals friendly or hostile, or in the intimate circle of the disciples, or in argument with more orthodox Jewish teachers. The scene constantly changes, and it can be shown that in some respects the form and content of the teaching vary with the kind of audience that is being addressed.[1]

There is no trace of evidence that Jesus Himself committed any of His teaching to writing. No book by Him has come down to us, nor any hint that such a book ever existed. All the evidence points in one direction, to the conclusion that in the earliest period we are dependent on oral tradition. The teaching was given by Jesus and passed on by word of mouth from those who first heard it. And at this time the number of such people must have been very great. In the second quarter of the first century there must have been literally thousands of people in Judæa and Galilee who had at one time or another seen Jesus, and could tell some story about Him or repeat some saying of His. The majority of these people would only have fragments of the whole story; but the tradition is made up by the piecing together of fragments. Some of these eye-witnesses must have become Christians and members of the Palestinian Church, and so their stories and sayings would find their way into the common stock of the community's story of its Founder.

Again, those who fell into argument with Jesus would carry away with them vivid memories of their encounters. His retorts to critics would not be easily forgotten, least of all by those who provoked them, and His counter-attacks on the scribal tradition may well have rankled in scribal memories. It has even been suggested, though it is never likely to be proved, that the criticisms made by Jesus may, at a later time when their origin was forgotten, have played some part in the development of the Jewish code as it took shape in the Mishnah and the Talmud.

The largest part of the tradition must, however, be credited to the disciples. They were most constantly with Jesus during the ministry. They heard what He said when He spoke to the multitudes or debated with Scribes and Pharisees, and they heard much besides that He taught them privately. They, more than anyone else, were in a position to know His mind on many points and to pass on their information to their fellow-Christians.

The importance of these considerations is that they remind us that in the first decades of the life of the original Palestinian community the tradition concerning the teaching of Jesus rested on a broader basis than we commonly imagine. We tend to think of it as being in the hands of a few distinguished persons who were

[1] For a fuller discussion of this point see my book *The Teaching of Jesus* (1931).

leaders of the Church, and to forget the common people who had heard Jesus gladly and who also had memories. When this is realised we can see that the Church's task in meeting the problems which arose in its own life and in its relations with the Jewish authorities was not that of creating words of Jesus applicable to these situations, but rather that of selecting what was relevant from the available mass of reminiscences.[1]

At this stage the tradition is still preserved in Aramaic and probably in the form of isolated sayings. Where sayings are already grouped together it will be because they happened to be spoken on the same occasion or on successive occasions; that is, the arrangement will be chronological. But when we consider the motives that led to the compilation of the teaching, it becomes obvious that a different kind of arrangement would be called for. For catechetical purposes what was required was a collection that would bring together all that Jesus had said on this or that important question of belief or practice: how far the Jewish Law was still binding on Christians, how one should think about demon-possession and exorcism, how members of the fellowship should behave towards one another, and the like. Study of the first three Gospels leads to the conclusion that such collections probably existed before the Gospels were written, and even before the compilation of the main sources used by the evangelists. Among such collections we should reckon the ' Little Apocalypse ' (Mk. 13[5-31]), which may well have had a separate existence before it came in to break the connexion between Mk. 13[1-4] and 13[32-37].[2] Similarly, Lk. 11[14-26] is a collection of sayings on demon-possession and exorcism. Strictly speaking, the reply to the charge of casting out demons by the aid of Beelzebul comes to an end at Lk. 11[20], and the essential refutation of the charge is given in Lk. 11[17f.], which is parallel to Mk. 3[23-26]. Now this section in Mk. is followed immediately by the saying about the ' strong man ' (Mk. 3[27]), and another version of this saying stands (11[21f.]) immediately after the Lucan reply to the charge. The natural inference is that this collocation is earlier than Mk. and Q (Luke is here dependent on Q).[3] Again, in Matthew's Sermon on the Mount we have a long section (Mt. 5[17-48]) dealing with the Jewish Law and contrasting it with the higher standard of righteousness demanded from followers of Jesus. As it stands, this section is composite; but here again it seems possible to separate out an original kernel older than the Gospel and probably older than the sources used by Matthew. To this original group of sayings we should probably assign vv. 17, 20; 21, 22a; 27, 28; 31, 32; 33, 34a (37a); 38, 39a; 43, 44a.[4]

In the cases just considered the grouping of the sayings is by subject. They are brought together by the fact that they give the answer to a single problem or show the mind of Jesus on a particular topic. This is not, however, the only method of grouping. We have also groups of sayings in which the connexion is not logical but simply by catchwords. This method, to which we can find parallels elsewhere in the New Testament, and frequently in the Talmud, is a simple way of ensuring that sayings will be remembered. Given the first link in

[1] See Vincent Taylor, *The Formation of the Gospel Tradition*, pp. 145 f.
[2] See my *Teaching of Jesus*, pp. 260-263.
[3] I think it possible to show that Mk. 3[20-35] formed a separate whole before the Gospel was written.
[4] See below, pp. 153-163.

the series, the others can be recollected by association of ideas. We have such a group of sayings in Mk. $9^{49 f.}$, where the link between them is the word ' salt.' Another is Lk. 11^{33-36}, where the catchword is ' light.'

So far we are dealing with the tradition of an Aramaic-speaking community, and the teaching naturally remains in the mother-tongue of the members. But Christianity is a missionary religion, and it was not long before the new faith began to spread beyond the borders of Palestine. It may be conjectured that it was at Antioch (Acts $11^{19 ff.}$), where Gentiles began to come into the Church in considerable numbers, that the need for a Greek version of the teaching first became pressing. Such a document would have to be sufficiently comprehensive in its scope to meet the needs of converts who had not been brought up in the Jewish tradition. Here, then, we have the incentive to bring together the smaller groups and the scattered individual sayings and to frame a larger Aramaic document which could then be translated into Greek.

Nor is this the only way in which a large collection of teaching could have been formed. The Palestinian community may well have felt the need for a full and comprehensive statement of the teaching for use in controversy with orthodox Judaism, as well as for the instruction of converts from Judaism, whether natives of Palestine or Greek-speaking Jews of the Dispersion who came into touch with Christianity when on pilgrimage to Jerusalem.

Such considerable bodies of teaching were certainly in existence at an early date. St. Paul appears to have had such a collection at his disposal when he wrote his first letter to the Corinthians (1 Cor. 7^{10}, 9^{14}), which would suggest that these compilations were already being made as early as the middle of the first century, and perhaps even earlier, certainly before the earliest of our Gospels was written. This is the stage in the history of the tradition to which we should assign the source Q and the source that lies behind matter peculiar to Matthew. Whether the special matter of Luke is derived from a written document or from oral tradition is a difficult matter to determine. Again it is a question whether there were not other collections of teaching of which we now know nothing, because they did not happen to be incorporated in one of the canonical Gospels. It may be, as Dibelius suggests,[1] that we have a remnant from such a collection in *I Clement* 13.

The final stage in the process, which we have been tracing, is the amalgamation of these sayings-collections with other material to form the canonical Gospels. Here it is Matthew and Luke that come specially into prominence. Both have drawn on the collection which we call Q and each has in addition another source containing teaching. For convenience we may use the symbols M and L to designate matter peculiar to Mt. and Lk. respectively. When the process which gave us the Gospels of Matthew and Luke was completed is still a matter of dispute. In any case, they are probably later than the date which we assign to Mk.; but if Streeter's Proto-Luke theory [2] is correct, the union of Q and L may easily antedate the writing of Mk.

Of more importance for our present purpose is the recognition of the editorial

---

[1] *Die Formgeschichte des Evangeliums*,[2] pp. 243f.
[2] See *The Four Gospels*, ch. viii.

methods of Matthew and Luke.   These can be determined with certainty from a study of their treatment of Mk., which both used and which itself survives for purposes of comparison.   The main conclusion to be drawn from this comparison is that Matthew conflates his sources, while Luke selects from them.   That is to say, where two sources overlap at a given point, Matthew makes a new story or a new version of a saying by combining the words and phrases of the original accounts.   Good examples of this are Mt. 12[31f]. (Mk. + Q) and 13[31f]. (Mk. + Q). In like circumstances Luke follows one of his sources and leaves the other on one side.   Another major difference between the two is that Matthew breaks up the material provided in his sources in order to compile long discourses.   Mt. 10 is a good example of the method, containing, as it does, material drawn from Mk. 6 and 13, from various parts of Q, and from the special source M.   Luke, on the other hand, tends to keep his sources separate, so that his Gospel consists of alternate layers of material from the different documents.   This means that it is much easier to disentangle the sources in Lk. than in Mt.; and it also makes it probable that the order in which we find the fragments of a source in Lk. is nearer to the original order than is the sequence of the corresponding fragments in Mt.   In the matter of verbal faithfulness to his sources Luke on the whole maintains a higher· standard than Matthew.   Bussmann,[1] who has recently studied the synoptic problem in great detail, comes to the conclusion that Luke's principal alterations are stylistic and that he is less prone to alter the spoken words of Jesus than to improve the style of the narrative portions.   There are other more detailed differences between the two evangelists in their editorial methods: these will be noticed as occasion offers in the commentary.[2]

3.   *THE SOURCES*

(a)   THE DOCUMENT Q

For teaching of the sort with which we are here concerned, namely religious and moral instruction suitable for those who have embraced Christianity, our principal source is the document now usually known as Q.   In the first instance Q is posited to account for the agreement of Mt. and Lk. in sections where they are not dependent on Mk., and on the whole this explanation of the phenomena has commended itself to scholars rather than the alternative hypotheses that Matthew has borrowed from Lk. or Luke from Mt. in these sections.   The exist-ence of a common source being granted, the next thing is to see what can be learnt about it, to attempt to restore it from the remains preserved in Mt. and Lk., to speculate about its probable date, authorship, place of origin, and the like.

From what has been said on the editorial methods of Luke it follows that his Gospel offers the most promising field for the restorer of Q, and it is usual now to make restorations in terms of Lk. rather than of Mt.   In such attempts as have been made in recent years there is a large measure of agreement, though no two restorations correspond exactly.   At the same time, the differences between scholars are on the fringes.   If we take what are perhaps the three most important

[1] *Synoptische Studien*, ii. pp. 106–109.
[2] Valuable studies in Scholten, *Das älteste Evangelium* (1869)—Matthew's treatment of Mk.; Hawkins, *Horæ Synopticæ* [2]; Cadbury, *Style and Literary Method of Luke*.

of modern restorations, those of Harnack, Streeter, and Bussmann, we find a large measure of agreement between them. The matter common to all three restorations is Lk. $3^{7\text{-}9}$, $4^{1\text{-}13}$, $6^{20\text{-}23,\ 27\text{-}33,\ 35\text{-}44,\ 46\text{-}49}$, $7^{1\text{-}10,\ 18\text{-}20,\ 22\text{-}35}$, $9^{57\text{-}60}$, $10^{2\text{-}16,\ 21\text{-}24}$, $11^{9\text{-}13,\ 29\text{-}35,\ 39,\ 41,\ 42,\ 44,\ 46\text{-}52}$, $12^{2\text{-}10,\ 22\text{-}31,\ 33,\ 34,\ 39,\ 40,\ 42\text{-}46,\ 51,\ 53,\ 58,\ 59}$, $13^{18\text{-}21,\ 24,\ 28,\ 29,\ 34,\ 35}$, $14^{26,\ 27,\ 34,\ 35}$, $16^{13,\ 16\text{-}18}$, $17^{1,\ 3,\ 4,\ 6,\ 23,\ 24,\ 26,\ 27,\ 33\text{-}35,\ 37}$. This represents the minimum to be assigned to Q. What more we shall add depends on the nice balancing of probabilities in particular cases. My reconstruction of Q is as follows. Brackets indicate doubt. Lk. $3^{7\text{-}9,\ 16,\ 17}$, $4^{1\text{-}13}$, $6^{20\text{-}49}$, $7^{(1\text{-}6a),\ 6b\text{-}9(10),\ 18\text{-}35}$, $9^{57\text{-}62}$, $10^{2,\ 3,\ 8\text{-}16,\ 21\text{-}24}$, $11^{9\text{-}26\ (27,\ 28),\ 29\text{-}36,\ (37\text{-}41),\ 42\text{-}52}$, $12^{(1),\ 2\text{-}12,\ 22\text{-}34,\ (35\text{-}38),\ 39\text{-}46,\ (47\text{-}50),\ 51\text{-}59}$, $13^{18\text{-}30,\ 34,\ 35}$, $14^{15\text{-}24,\ 26,\ 27,\ (34,\ 35)}$, $16^{13,\ 16\text{-}18}$, $17^{1\text{-}6,\ 22\text{-}37}$. This document begins and ends with the thought of the coming judgement. Its first sentences contain the eschatological preaching of John the Baptist; its closing paragraph consists mainly of a poem about the coming of the Son of Man. Is this deliberate? If it is, it is a strong argument in favour of the view, which I think antecedently probable, that in Mt. and Lk. we have preserved for us substantially all that Q ever contained.

An examination of the material shows that it consists entirely, or almost entirely, of teaching. The amount of narrative is negligible, and what there is shows so little agreement in the parallel versions of Mt. and Lk. that we may well doubt whether it is part of the original document.[1] Along with this goes the fact that there is no account of the Passion. Various reasons have been suggested for this remarkable omission. To Sir William Ramsay [2] it is an indication that the document was composed during the lifetime of Jesus. Professor Burkitt [3] thinks that Q did contain a Passion narrative in spite of the absence of non-Marcan material common to Mt. and Lk. in the relevant sections of those gospels. The most probable explanation is that there is no Passion-story because none is required, Q being a book of instruction for people who are already Christians and know the story of the Cross by heart.

A third striking feature in Q is the exceedingly small quantity of polemical matter which it contains. It records no disputes with Scribes and Pharisees such as we find in Mk. ($2^{1}\text{-}3^{6}$; $11^{27}\text{-}12^{34}$). At the same time, it contains a denunciation of Pharisaism (Lk. $11^{(37\text{-}41),\ 42\text{-}52}$). But ninety per cent. of the document is positive religious and moral teaching. This fact again is explicable on the assumption that the work was intended for use within the Christian community as a manual of instruction in the duties of the Christian life. If, as is possible, it was also intended to show the true nature of Christian beliefs and practices to the Jews, it may well be that the compiler thought that this purpose too would be better served by positive statement than by mere disputation.

So much we can learn from the document itself. The question now arises whether there is any external evidence which will throw light on its origin and history, and here we have to consider a much-discussed sentence from Eusebius. In his *Ecclesiastical History* (III. xxxix. 16), after quoting (§ 15) a tradition set forth by Papias, bishop of Hierapolis, concerning Mark the evangelist, he goes on:

---

[1] See my *Teaching of Jesus*, pp. 29 ff.
[2] *Luke the Physician*, p. 89.
[3] *Earliest Sources for the Life of Jesus*, pp. 103–106.

' Such then is Papias' account of Mark. But the following is the statement concerning Matthew: " So then, Matthew compiled the oracles in the Hebrew language; but everyone interpreted them as he was able." ' (Lawlor and Oulton's translation.)

Eusebius is here quoting from a work written by Papias early in the second century.[1] In this book he gave not only his own views, but also traditions which he had collected at an earlier date from leading men in the Church. The first point to be decided, therefore, is whether ' the statement concerning Matthew ' is Papias' own opinion or a piece of earlier tradition. The latter alternative is the more probable for the following reasons : (1) The immediately preceding statement about Mark is expressly said to be a tradition. We should expect Eusebius to give more of the same kind. (2) The form of the statement, its brevity, its categorical statements without argument, suggest that Papias is reporting evidence rather than airing his views. (3) Eusebius himself in this same chapter (§ 13) gives his opinion of Papias: ' He evidently was a man of exceedingly small intelligence, as one might say judging from his discourses.' It does not seem likely that Eusebius would have troubled to record the private opinion of Papias on such a question as this, if he had so poor an opinion of the bishop's mental powers. We may therefore conclude that the statement of Papias is material which he derived from an earlier generation. In that case, the statement is thrown back into the first century.

The next question is: if someone about A.D. 100 told Papias what Eusebius has reported, what did the statement mean? Before we discuss this question it should be noted that the Greek word rendered ' interpreted ' by Lawlor and Oulton could equally well mean ' translated,' and that this is the more probable rendering, as we shall see.

Short as it is, the Papias fragment makes four separate assertions:

(a) That a collection of oracles (logia) was put together.

(b) That it was composed in the Hebrew language. (This probably means the spoken language of the Palestinian Jews of the time, i.e. Aramaic[2]).

(c) That the composer of this work was named Matthew—presumably the Apostle is meant.

(d) That various people translated it as best they could—doubtless into Greek.

As applied to the Gospel of Matthew two of these propositions are demonstrably false (b and d); (c) is in the last degree improbable; and (a) a collection of oracles is a singularly inept description of the Gospel. It is true that the late Professor Bacon[3] argued that ' the Oracles ' was a perfectly legitimate designation of Mt., having regard to its five great discourses; but when it is observed that the discourses in question amount to scarcely more than one-third of the gospel the explanation becomes extremely forced. Further, the argument of Donovan[4] that

---

[1] The date of Papias is discussed by C. J. Cadoux in the *London Quarterly and Holborn Review*, July 1933, pp. 289–292. His conclusions demand careful consideration.
[2] Parallels for this use of ' Hebrew ' where ' Aramaic ' is meant in Dalman's *Grammatik* [2] § 1.
[3] *Studies in Matthew.*
[4] *The Logia in Ancient and Recent Literature* (1924).

the Greek *ta logia*, ' the oracles,' must in this context mean the canonical gospel of Matthew, rests on a series of misinterpretations of the term as used in the Septuagint, New Testament, and contemporary Jewish and early Christian writings. The use of the term ' oracles ' in the LXX can be very simply defined. In a general sense it means direct communications of God to man, notably those made through prophetic inspiration; and in particular it is applied to these communications considered as Divine commands or Divine promises. The ' oracles ' is the name, not of Scripture as a whole, but of certain things contained in Scripture, the things that God has said for the guidance or encouragment of Israel. It can be shown that this meaning for ' oracles ' fits perfectly in the places where the term occurs in the New Testament and other primitive Christian writings. Later the word came to be used in the sense ' Scripture,' and there is no doubt that Eusebius understood the statement of Papias to refer to the Gospel of Matthew; but at the time to which we refer the tradition (end of the first century) the original sense was still the proper and natural sense, as can be shown from the first epistle of Clement (*c.* A.D. 96).

The importance of this point is that it shows that the statement of Papias which cannot be made to fit the Gospel of Matthew except by a forced and unnatural interpretation, does, when taken in its simple and natural meaning, fit a document such as Q like a glove. For Q is a collection of Dominical oracles given for the guidance and encouragement of the New Israel. Just as to the Hebrew saints, whose piety found expression in the Psalter, ' the oracles ' meant the commands and promises of God under the Old Covenant, so to the Church ' the oracles ' meant the commands and promises of God under the New Covenant.

The statement that ' the oracles ' were composed in Hebrew (= Aramaic) and that various people translated them as best they could can be shown to be true in respect of Q. We have already seen that the tradition of the teaching circulated at first in Aramaic, and that probably the first considerable collections of it would be made in the original language. There is nothing improbable in the supposition that several Greek versions of such a document might be made. We know that at least four Greek versions of the Old Testament were made at various times and for various reasons. These, however, are possibilities: we must look now at the facts. We have two versions of Q—Q according to Matthew and Q according to Luke. The differences between them can be explained in part as editorial—stylistic or other ' improvements ' carried out by the Evangelists. But after we have allowed for these there is still a certain amount of difference in wording, and some of it at least can be explained on the supposition that we have before us two different renderings of a single Aramaic original. Such cases will be noted in the Commentary; here the point may be illustrated by a single example.

The Golden Rule is given by Matthew and Luke in almost identical words. The main difference is at the beginning. Here we have:

Mt. 7[12]. All things therefore whatsoever ye would that men . . .
Lk. 6[31]. And as ye would that men . . .

Now in the LXX version of Genesis 44[1] the Greek expression of Mt. rendered here by ' whatsoever ' is used to translate the Hebrew word *ka'ăsher*; and in

Genesis 41[13] the Greek word behind ' as ' in Lk. translates the same Hebrew word. In Aramaic the equivalent of the Hebrew *ka'ǎsher* is *kmā dě*. We may therefore legitimately regard Mt.'s ' whatsoever ' and Lk.'s ' as ' as alternative renderings of a common Aramaic original. This leaves Mt.'s ' all things ' in the air. This, however, is easily explained. In eleven places where Mt. is dependent on Mk. we find the word ' all ' in Mt. with nothing corresponding to it in the source. For example, in the Marcan account of the feeding of the 4,000 we read (8[8]): ' And they ate and were satisfied ': the Matthæan reproduction of this (15[37]) is: ' And they *all* ate and were satisfied.' That is to say, one of the literary habits of Matthew is to heighten the effects by inserting the word ' all ' from time to time. Finally, we have ' therefore ' in Mt. against ' and ' in Lk. Here we have to take account of Matthew's tendency to build up his material into discourses. The probability is that ' therefore ' is an attempt to provide a logical connexion between the Golden Rule and what has preceded it in the Sermon on the Mount. Luke's ' and ' represents the earlier state of the tradition. The result is that of the three differences between Mt. and Lk. in these few words, two can be put down to the editorial work of Matthew, while the third points to an Aramaic original behind the two variant renderings. There is a sufficient number of such translation variants to justify the belief that Q was originally an Aramaic document and that in Mt. and Lk. we have two renderings of it.

Thus three out of the four propositions contained in the Papias tradition tally with what can be discovered about Q. The tradition fits Q as it does not fit Mt.

The fourth proposition that ' the oracles ' were compiled by Matthew cannot be proved or disproved. All that can be said is that if at three points out of four this early tradition fits Q, there is a reasonable probability in favour of the fourth. If we wish to put an author's name on the title-page of Q, Matthew is the only candidate in the field: the tradition as we interpret it favours him, and there is nothing against the identification. It may be objected that if Q was a document of apostolic authorship, it is almost inconceivable that it should have been allowed to perish. To this it may be replied that the primitive Church was probably very little concerned about making archives for the use of scholars in the twentieth century. A community living in daily expectation of the end of the world does not pause to consider the literary requirements of a remote posterity. The wonder is not that some documents have perished, but that so many have been preserved. Further by the end of the first century an Aramaic original would be of interest only to a fraction of the Christian community. For the great majority the apostolic document *was* preserved in the only form in which it was of any use to them, in the Greek language. Again, the preservation or destruction of important documents is all too often determined by circumstances outside the control of the persons chiefly interested. Who can tell how much priceless evidence for the history of primitive Christianity perished in A.D. 70? Or, to come nearer home, it is to us almost inconceivable that the autographs of Shakespeare's plays should have been allowed to perish. Yet they were. Doubtless by about the middle of the second century an Aramaic document of apostolic origin giving the words of Jesus would have been a prized possession at Rome or Alexandria; but by that time it was probably too late. And even if such a document had survived till then its chances of falling into the hands of someone who would be able to identify it and appreciate its value are very remote. The history of priceless manuscripts in Eastern monasteries is a melancholy commentary on the survival-value of ancient documents, even in what might be considered favourable circumstances.[1]

Concerning the date and place of origin of Q we can do no more than make more or less probable conjectures. If it had its origin as a book of instruction for converts from Gentile paganism, it would be natural to connect it with Antioch, the first headquarters of the Gentile mission, and to date it about the middle of the first century, probably rather before than after A.D. 50. It is a point slightly in favour of this connexion with Antioch that Q, more than any other of the synoptic sources, shows a friendly attitude towards Gentiles. The Roman centurion, whose faith could not be paralleled in Israel; the people of Tyre and Sidon; the men of Nineveh, who were readier to repent than the Chosen People; and the Queen of Sheba, who was more eager for the wisdom of Solomon than the Jewish contemporaries of Jesus for the Kingdom of God—these are all Q characters: and to Q belongs the statement that people from all the ends of the earth will find their way into the Kingdom.

Additional Note

Dr. W. Bussmann, in the course of a very elaborate and painstaking study of the synoptic problem, has put forward the view (*Synoptische Studien*, ii) that Q can really be split up into two distinct sources. He starts from the fact that in some Q sections the agreement between Mt. and Lk. is very close while in others there is considerable difference. He lists the passages as follows:

I. Passages showing close agreements: Lk. 3^{7-9}, 4^{1-13}, $6^{31, \ 37-42}$, $7^{1-10, \ 18-35}$, 9^{57-62}, $10^{2-16, \ 21-24}$, 11^{33}, $12^{22-46, \ 51-56}$, 13^{18-35}, 16^{13}. This document he calls T.

II. Passages showing considerable variation: Lk. $6^{20-30, \ 32-36, \ 43-49}$, $11^{1-4, \ 9-13}$, $^{29-32, \ 34-36}$, $11^{37}-12^{12}$, 12^{57-59}, $14^{5, \ 6, \ 16-27, \ 34, \ 35}$, 15^{3-7}, 16^{16-18}, $17^{1-6, \ 22-37}$. This he calls R.

Working on this basis he finds a certain number of linguistic differences between R and T. These are given in *Synoptische Studien*, ii, pp. 124–126. In further investigation he thinks that he can detect differences of thought as well as of language between the two documents. Bussmann draws the conclusion that Matthew and Luke are dependent on the same Greek document for T. For R, on the other hand, they had (or made) separate Greek versions of an Aramaic original. R is the older of the two and is probably the *logia* of the Papias tradition.

An adequate treatment of this view will require as detailed and painstaking an examination of the material as Bussmann's own, and this cannot be undertaken here. But a few general observations may be made.

First, the outstanding feature of T is close agreement in wording between Mt. and Lk. Another characteristic of T, according to Bussmann, is that it contains a certain amount of narrative. But one of the features of the narrative settings of

[1] See, for example, the story of the discovery of *Codex Sinaiticus*, of which Tischendorf rescued portions from the monastic waste-paper basket.

sayings in Q is wide divergence between Mt. and Lk. In the story of the Centurion at Capernaum (Mt. 8^{5-13}; Lk. 7^{1-10}) the agreement between Mt. and Lk. begins and ends with the spoken words. The differences in the narrative setting are so great that it is difficult to suppose that the two evangelists are drawing on a common source in Greek or any other language; while the agreements in the dialogue are so close that here a common source seems to be necessary. This means that the two characteristics of T, close verbal agreement and the presence of narratives, are mutually inconsistent.

Further, the theory that only R shows unmistakable signs of being before us in two versions from Aramaic is seriously open to question. There are numerous examples in T of variants between Mt. and Lk. which are most probably to be regarded as translation variants. Not only so, but the general character of Bussmann's T sections is not inconsistent with the theory that they are translations from Aramaic. It is possible to compare theory with fact at this point. Certain chapters of the book of Daniel are written in Aramaic, and of this book we have two Greek versions, the LXX and the translation of Theodotion. Taking a passage at random from Daniel (Dan. 7^{9-14}), we find that it is turned into Greek by the LXX in 166 words, by Theodotion in 157. Comparing the two versions, we find complete agreement between them in 105 words and partial agreement in 12. Taking a passage of approximately equal length from Bussmann's T (Lk. $7^{24-28, \ 31-35}$ = Mt. $11^{7-11, \ 16-19}$), we get in Lk. 170 Greek words, in Mt. 158. There is complete agreement in 115 words and partial agreement in 20. That is to say, the features presented by Mt. and Lk. in a passage from T are very similar to those presented by LXX and Theodotion in what we know to be two translations from a common Aramaic original. Whether the similarity will hold over a larger range of passages is a matter for investigation.

So far as one can judge, Bussmann's case is not convincing, and if our view of Q is to be modified, it seems more likely that it will be in another direction, namely by recognition of the possibility of the overlapping of sources and so transferring passages, where verbal agreement between Mt. and Lk. is small, from Q to M or L. For the problem, which Bussmann tries to solve by his two-source hypothesis, namely the considerable difference in the measure of agreement between Mt. and Lk. in Q passages, is a real problem; and if we reject his solution, we are still left with the task of finding a better.

(b) THE MATTER PECULIAR TO MT.

The matter peculiar to Mt. falls into four groups: (i) Editorial additions and formulas; (ii) narratives; (iii) testimonia; (iv) teaching. Our chief concern will be with (iv); but we may note in passing that almost the whole of the narrative matter can be collected under two heads: birth and infancy stories and stories about the events in Jerusalem from the triumphal entry to the Resurrection. The fact that the special narrative contribution of Mt. to the story of the Ministry is mainly concerned with events in and about Jerusalem may well have some bearing on the question of the origin both of this material and of the special teaching peculiar to this Gospel. The testimonia, or illustrations of the fulfilment of Old

Testament prophecies in the life of Jesus, number eleven and are distributed through the Gospel from the birth narratives to the account of the arrest (Mt. $1^{22f.}$, $2^{5f.}$, ^{15}, $^{17f.}$, ^{23}, 4^{13-16}, 8^{17}, 12^{17-21}, 13^{35}, $21^{4f.}$, 27^9). The teaching proper is all contained in chapters 5–25 and is mostly arranged topically. The main sections are: Jesus' preaching (5–7), Mission charge to the disciples (10), Parables bearing on missionary work (13), Nature of the Christian fellowship (18), Conditions of service and reward (19, 20), The Refusers (21, 22), Against Pharisaism (23), Eschatology (25). Comparing this scheme with that of Q, it is important to note that the arrangement of this teaching material, which we shall call M, as given in Mt. corresponds at four points with the arrangement of the Q material *in Luke's order*.

Q	M
1. John's Preaching	——
2. The Temptations	——
3. Jesus' Preaching	1. Jesus' Preaching
4. Centurion of Capernaum	——
5. Jesus and John the Baptist	——
6. Mission Charge	2. Mission Charge
7. Beelzebul controversy	——
8. Refusal of a sign	——
——	3. Parables of missionary work
——	4. Nature of the Christian fellowship
——	5. Conditions of service and reward (cf. Q 10)
——	6. The Refusers (cf. Q 11)
9. Against Pharisaism	7. Against Pharisaism
10. Service, sacrifice, and reward (12) (cf. M 5)	——
11. Refusers (13, 14) (cf. M 6)	——
12. Eschatology	8. Eschatology

(*N.B.*—This table takes account only of considerable blocks of material. To avoid complication small pieces are omitted.)

The four points are Jesus' preaching, the mission charge, the speech against Pharisaism, and the eschatological speech. From this fact the inference is either that there is a scheme of the teaching older than M and Q, to which both conform, or that the M material has been incorporated into Q. The latter alternative would involve a kind of Proto-Matthew hypothesis; but the former seems the more probable view.

More than this coincidence in the general structure, there are also traces of coincidence in the structure of some of the speeches. If we compare the structure of the Q preaching of Jesus (Lk. 6^{20-49}) with those portions of the Sermon on the Mount that can most probably be assigned to M, we find a certain parallelism at four points.

Q		M
Lk. 6$^{20-23}$	Beatitudes . . .	Beatitudes Mt. 5$^{7-10}$
6$^{24-26}$	Woes	
	————	(Salt and Light 5$^{13-16}$)
6$^{27-36}$	The Law of the Christian life	The old Law and the new 5$^{17-24, \; 27-39a,}$ $^{43 \; (44a) \; (44b-48)}$
6$^{37-42}$	Against censoriousness	————
6$^{43-45}$	The test of true religion— character and life	The old piety and the new 6$^{1-4, \; 5-8, \; (9-15),}$ $^{16-18}$
	————	Some isolated sayings 6^{34}, 7$^{6, \; 13 f., \; 15,}$ $^{(16-20)}$
6^{46}	Why do you call me Lord, Lord . . .?	Self-deceivers and their fate 7$^{21-23}$
6$^{47-49}$	Parable of the two builders	————

(Brackets indicate a certain doubt as to whether the verses so enclosed belong to M.)

In the Mission Charge there are coincidences between Q and M at Lk. 10$^{8 \, f.}$|| Mt. 10$^{7 f.}$ and Lk. 10^{16}||Mt. 10$^{40 f.}$. In the speech against Pharisaism we may compare Lk. 11^{43} with Mt. 23^{7b}; Lk. 11^{44} with Mt. 23$^{27 f.}$; Lk. 11$^{47 f.}$ with Mt. 23^{30}. Similar in purport, though far apart in expression, are Lk. 11^{42} and Mt. 23^{24}.

We should not attempt to build too much on these parallelisms; but, such as they are, they allow us at least to entertain the supposition that there was a rough outline of the essentials of the teaching at an earlier stage of the tradition than is represented by Q and M. This outline, if it had a separate existence, dealt with essentials: the substance of the Christian life, the principles of Christian missionary propaganda, the defence of the new religion against Jewish attacks, and the hope of the future.[1]

The question whether there are any traces of earlier compilation within the sections, which go to make up M, is a difficult one. The most we can do is to indicate possibilities or probabilities. The most likely case occurs in the Sermon on the Mount. Here we have in Mt. 5$^{21-48}$ a series of contrasts between the old Law and the new. Each is in the form ' Ye have heard that it was said . . . But I say to you . . .' This form is most clearly displayed in the pronouncement on divorce (5$^{31 f.}$). Here the old rule is concisely stated in v. 31, and the new with similar brevity in v. 32. Passing from this to the cases of the *lex talionis* (5$^{38-42}$) and love of neighbour (5$^{43-48}$), we find that, while the old is still shortly stated, the new is considerably expanded, and that the extra matter is similar to matter given by Luke in the Q version of the Sermon. Thus we read (5$^{38, \; 39a}$):

You have heard that it was said: An eye for an eye and a tooth for a tooth. But I tell *you* not to resist the evil (person or act).

[1] It may be no more than a coincidence, at any rate an interesting one, that the *Didache* in its general outline is very near to this scheme. I, The substance of the Christian life (1^{1}–10^{6}), divided into two parts, (a) morality (1^{1}–6^{2}), (b) piety (7^{1}–10^{6}); II, the Christian Mission and its workers (11^{1}–13^{7}); III, Church life and organisation (14^{1}–15^{4}) (cf. Mt. 18. Has the scheme been modified to meet new needs?); IV, Eschatology (16$^{1-9}$). In three out of four heads the *Didache* agrees with the scheme.

Then the exhortation continues: ' But whoever strikes *thee* on the right cheek . . .' This is parallel to Lk. 6[29 f.]: ' To him who strikes thee on the cheek . . .'   The change from ' you ' to ' thee ' is another sign that we are now dealing with a new source; and the conclusion is that the original antithesis ended with the word ' evil.'   In that case it is similar to the saying on divorce.   The same holds of Mt. 5[43-48], though not so obviously, because the overlapping with Q begins earlier.[1] Again, in 5[27-30] we have a saying (5[27 f.]), which is true to the type, followed by a further exhortation, which has a parallel in Mk. 9[43-48].   The conclusion of the whole matter is that the original kernel of the passage 5[21-48] was a series of six brief antithetical statements comprising verses 21–22a, 27–28, 31–32, 33–34a, 38–39a, 43–44a.

A similar group of sayings can be extracted from Mt. 6[1-18].   Here three acts of piety—almsgiving, prayer, and fasting—are described antithetically.   The antithesis is between ' the hypocrites ' and the believer.   The form is well marked: ' When thou doest alms do not . . . as the hypocrites do . . . and thy Father who sees in secret will reward thee.'   This series occupies Mt. 6[2-4, 5-6, 16-18].

Concerning the date and place of origin of M we cannot do more than make reasonable conjectures.   If the hypothesis of a group of antitheses in Mt. 5[21-48] is sound, we can fix a probable lower limit for the compilation of the Sermon on the Mount in its M form and perhaps for the whole M collection.   In Mt. 5[21-22a] we have the first antithesis proper.   What follows in 22b may be part of it also, or an expansion of it.   Then in 23 f. comes the exhortation beginning ' If then thou art offering thy gift on the altar . . .'   This presupposes that the Temple is still standing.   It is extremely unlikely that such a word would be incorporated in a collection of maxims for practical use after A.D. 70, when the Temple was destroyed. And probably we should go farther and say not later than about 65, since in the last few years before the Jewish war relations between Jewish Christians and Jews became increasingly strained.   Now on our theory 5[23 f.] has been inserted into an already existing document—the six antitheses.   If this insertion took place in the process of the compilation of what we now call M, it is evidence that the compilation took place not later than about A.D. 65.

At the same time there is some reason for thinking that the date cannot be much before 65.   In Mt. 5[17-20] we have a passage purporting to give the attitude of Jesus to the Jewish Law.   In this section *vv.* 18 f. are very significant.   ' For verily I say unto you, Till heaven and earth pass away, one jot or one tittle shall in no wise pass away from the law, till all things be accomplished ' (5[18]).   This verse has a parallel in Q (Lk. 16[17]): ' But it is easier for heaven and earth to pass away, than for one tittle of the law to fall.'   This Q version of the saying stands between two sayings which in effect contradict it: ' The law and the prophets (were) *until John*: from that time the gospel of the Kingdom of God is preached, and every man entereth violently into it ' (Lk. 16[16]); and ' Every one that putteth away his wife, and marrieth another, committeth adultery: and he that marrieth one that is put away from a husband committeth adultery ' (Lk. 16[18]).   Lk. 16[16] implies that since the appearance of John a new thing has come into the world to take the place of the Law.   Lk. 16[18] is a flat contradiction of the provision of the Law relating to

---

[1] On this see the Commentary below, p. 161.

divorce. The solution of this problem is, I venture to think, that the saying (Lk. 16[17]) was originally ironical: it was a comment, not on the eternity of the provisions of the Law, but on the obstinate conservatism of the Scribes. The Matthæan form of the saying shows no trace of this. Here the Law in all its details is represented as absolutely binding, at all events, till the end of the world. Coupled with this is the saying (5[19]): 'Whosoever therefore shall break one of these least commandments, and shall teach men so, shall be called least in the kingdom of heaven: but whosoever shall do and teach them, he shall be called great in the kingdom of heaven.' It may well be thought that we have here a reflection of the disputes which arose out of the Gentile mission (Acts 15) and of the deep suspicion with which Paul was regarded by the more extreme Jewish Christians (Acts 21[15-25]). These two verses (Mt. 5[18 f.]) will then point to a time after A.D. 50 as the time for the compilation of M, and probably nearer 60 than 50. If 5[19] be thought to refer to Paul, it may be doubted whether it would have been added after the news of his martyrdom was known in the East. For it might well be that his martyr's death would be regarded as atoning for his laxity in matters of the Law. In that case we should have a further small confirmation of the date 65 as the lower limit.

In the light of this discussion of the date of M it is not difficult to guess its place of origin. Its most striking characteristics all point in one direction, and far the most probable conjecture is that which connects M with the Jewish Christians of Judæa, with their headquarters at Jerusalem. Such sayings as Mt. 10[6] reflect the interests of a community which felt that its mission was to the circumcision (cf. Gal. 2[7 f.]). The extreme respect for the Law coupled with a violent antagonism to the lawyers is best understood in a community at once proud of its Jewish heritage and at loggerheads with the official guardians of that heritage. This can only be the churches of Judæa—or a section of them—in the years before the fall of Jerusalem.

The general character of the source agrees with these inferences from particular passages. The 'atmosphere' is more definitely Palestinian Jewish than in any other of the gospel documents. It is in M that we get reminiscences of Rabbinic terminology most widespread. Here also the sayings are often closely parallel to the sayings of the Rabbis. The whole passage Mt. 22[11-14], the Matthæan appendix to the parable of the Great Feast, is very similar to a parable preserved in the Talmud.[1]

But M is not merely Christianised Rabbinism. There are other and characteristic strains in its composition. It shows clear traces of the influence of the teaching of John the Baptist. The burden of John's teaching as given in Q is the impending judgement and the sharp division between the righteous and the wicked. This feature reappears with great force in many of the parables peculiar to M. (Mt. 13[24-30, 47-50], 22[11-14], 25[1-13, 31-46]). Characteristic teaching of the Baptist is put into the mouth of Jesus; and that this is no accident is shown by the fact that John's phrase 'offspring of vipers' (Mt. 3[7] = Lk. 3[7], Q) reappears in the mouth of Jesus in Mt. 12[34], 23[33] (M) and nowhere else in the New Testament. These facts are the more impressive if, as I think very probable, the M parable of the

---

[1] The Teaching of Jesus, p. 35, n. 3.

Wheat and Tares (13^{24-30}) is an adaptation of Mark's parable of the Seed growing secretly (Mk. 4^{26-29}); and if the parable of the Dragnet is an expansion of a genuine saying of Jesus preserved in Mt. 13^{47} and meaning that the Kingdom of God takes hold of all sorts of people.[1]   In this connexion it is worth remembering that the scene of John's activity was Judæa, and that his influence was exerted most fully on the population of Judæa and Jerusalem (Mk. 1^5).

Again, we may note in M the strong Church-interest, the feeling that Christians are a compact body of believers sharing a common body of doctrine, a common rule of life, a common discipline and organisation, and a common hope.   Of the teaching in M two-thirds is represented as addressed to the disciples, a quarter is polemical, and only a small fraction—less than one-tenth—is public preaching. The document reflects the situation of a community which is not only compact but also self-contained, we might almost say driven in upon itself, facing a rather hopeless task as a missionary body, and bitterly conscious of the strength of the opposition; yet holding on grimly to its rule of faith and life and hoping for its speedy vindication at the final consummation of the present evil age.

From what has been said it will be evident that M is a source to be treated with caution.   Doubtless it preserves much authentic teaching of Jesus; but there are good grounds for suspecting that there has been a considerable amount of adulteration from the Jewish side and from the teaching of John the Baptist. Each piece of teaching must be considered on its merits and in comparison with what is given in the earlier and more reliable source Q.

(c) The Matter peculiar to Lk.

The question how Lk. was put together is still under discussion, which centres round what is known as the Proto-Luke hypothesis.   This hypothesis was stated by Dr. Streeter in the *Hibbert Journal* for October 1921, and, more fully, in *The Four Gospels* (1924), ch. viii.   It rests on an analysis of the text of Lk. from which it appears that this Gospel falls into two main parts, one dependent on Mk., the other almost entirely independent.   This latter part consists, according to Streeter, of : 3^1–4^{30}, 5^{1-11}, 6^{14-16}, 6^{20}–8^3, 9^{51}–18^{14}, 19^{1-27}, 19^{37-44}, $21^{18,\ 34-36}$, 22^{14}–24^{53}. This part is an amalgam of Q and the matter peculiar to Lk., which includes both narratives and teaching.   The essence of the Proto-Luke theory is that this Q + L makes up a short gospel by itself and that it had a separate existence as Luke's first draft of his work, being subsequently expanded by the addition of the sections derived from Mk., and finally by the prefixing of the narratives of the birth and infancy.[2]   The alternative to this is to suppose that Mk. or some more primitive document, from which Mk. is descended, is the foundation document into which the Q and L material has been inserted.   However this question may be settled, the fact remains that in what is called Proto-Luke we have solid blocks of material made up, so far as one can see, of alternate layers of Q and L.

---

[1] R. Otto, *Reich Gottes und Menschensohn*, p. 47.
[2] For an elaboration and defence of the Proto-Luke theory see Vincent Taylor. *Behind the Third Gospel; The First Draft of St. Luke's Gospel; The Formation of the Gospel Tradition;* and *The Gospels: a Short Introduction.*

This stratified structure extends as far as 17^{37}, which is the end of the last section from Q.[1] Thereafter all the non-Marcan material seems to be derived from L.

What remains, when we take away from 'Proto-Luke' the sections derived from Q, is a mixture of narrative and teaching. The teaching from this source is as follows. Brackets indicate cases where it is doubtful whether the passage should be given to Q or L.

Lk. 3^{10-14}, 9^{51-56}, $10^{1,\ 4-7,\ 17-20,\ 25-42}$, $11^{(1-4),\ 5-8,\ 37-41,\ 53-54}$, $12^{(1),\ 13-21}$, $13^{1-9,\ (15),\ (31-33)}$, $14^{(5),\ 7-14,\ 28-33}$, 15^{1-32}, $16^{1-13,\ 14-15,\ 19-31}$, $17^{7-10,\ 18-41}$, 18^{1-14}, $19^{11-27,\ 39-44}$, $21^{12-15,\ 18-26,\ 28,\ 34-36}$, $22^{24-30,\ 31-33,\ 35-38}$, 23^{27-31}.

It will be observed that in ch. 21 somewhat more is allowed to L than Streeter assigns to Proto-Luke. On this point see the Commentary *ad loc*.

Surveying this material, one is struck by the fact that there is little or no sign of the topical arrangement which we found in Q and M. L begins with a fragment of the preaching of John (3^{10-14}), and this is followed a little later by $10^{1,\ 4-7,\ 17-20}$, which belongs to the Mission charge. But in both cases the probable explanation is that this L material stands where it does because it has been attracted to corresponding material in Q. Towards the end of the L teaching we have a series of parables and sayings (15^{11-32}, 16^{14-15}, 17^{20-21}, 18^{9-14}, and possibly also 16^{19-31}, and 19^{11-27}) with a considerable amount of common interest; but this group is broken up by other matter and does not form a compact whole. Its present position may reflect what is no doubt the historical truth that the opposition between Jesus and the Jewish religious authorities came to a head towards the end of the ministry. Still later in the collection comes a group of sayings roughly corresponding to the eschatological sections in Q and M; but with this striking difference that in L the reference is largely to the impending downfall of Jerusalem. This group includes 19^{39-44}, $21^{12-15,\ 18-26,\ 28,\ 34-36}$, 23^{27-31}, and possibly 22^{35-38}. One way of explaining this difference is to say that the matter in Lk. 21 is a rewriting by Luke of the corresponding matter in Mk. 13 in the light of the fall of Jerusalem in A.D. 70. But as it happens Luke has kept in 21^{25-28} a plain reference to the final consummation, which is closely connected with the other events; and Goguel makes the good point that 'Luke might have transmitted, but he cannot have created, an unfulfilled prophecy whereby the fall of Jerusalem and the final cataclysm were combined.'[2] Moreover, we have the evidence of Mk. $13^{1f.}$ and of L sections quite independent of Mk. 13 (Lk. 19^{41-44}, 23^{27-31}) that Jesus did prophesy the fall of Jerusalem—just as, eight centuries before, Amos had prophesied the fall of Samaria. And, lastly, such drastic rewriting of his sources is not in Luke's manner, especially where the words of Jesus are concerned. It may well be, therefore, that Luke found this prophecy of the fall of Jerusalem in his sources. This does not, of course, mean that the section as it stands is necessarily or even probably a faithful report of what Jesus may have said on this subject.

The unsystematic character of the L teaching compared with Q and M suggests that we are not here dealing with a more or less official compilation for

---

[1] Harnack assigned Lk. 19^{12-27}, 22^{28-30} to Q; Streeter also gives 19^{11-27} to Q; Bussmann, I think rightly, does not go beyond 17^{37}.

[2] *Harvard Theological Review*, xxvi. 28.

the instruction of Church members, but with oral tradition. This supposition gains some support from the fact that a large proportion of the matter is in the form of parables. There are fourteen in this source, several of them of considerable length. Now we are explicitly told that the parable was constantly used by Jesus in His public preaching. We are therefore entitled to assume that the parables would be the most widely known, as they would certainly be the most easily remembered utterances of Jesus. Further, many of them are of the sort that would have a special appeal to the common people who heard Him gladly, showing, as they do, the sympathy and friendliness of Jesus towards those whom a more rigid piety tended to despise.

At this point we may take account of another fact, the high proportion of polemical matter in L. Almost two-fifths of the whole is polemic, just over one-third is public preaching, and only about a quarter private instruction to the disciples. The polemic is different from that of the other sources in this respect, that in place of open attack we find the subtler method of rebuke by means of parables such as the Prodigal Son or the Pharisee and the Publican. This is the kind of thing that would not easily slip the memory of anyone, least of all those publicans and sinners who found a friend in Jesus.

If, then, the L material is derived from oral tradition, we must ask: when, where, and by whom? To these questions the most probable answer is: about A.D. 60, by Luke at Cæsarea during Paul's detention there. If we are right in thinking that Q is an earlier document connected with the Church at Antioch, it is quite possible that Luke had a copy of it by this time, and that he expanded it by addition of stories and sayings collected from Christians with whom he would certainly come into contact during his long stay at Cæsarea.

4. *THE FORM OF THE TEACHING*

The most important distinction to be made here is that between utterances which are an integral part of a story and those which are independent of any narrative setting, between *ad hoc* utterances and considered statements. It is to be expected *a priori* that in the teaching of Jesus we shall find both kinds and that in general the former kind of saying will occur most often in polemical contexts, where a quick and effective reply to criticism has to be made; the latter in more leisurely talk for the instruction of friends and disciples. It is not probable that highly elaborated poetical utterances like Lk. 17$^{26-30}$ on the Day of the Son of Man or Lk. 12$^{24-48}$ on the loving care of the Father were improvised on the spur of the moment; whereas the retort of Jesus in Mk. 2^{17} has all the appearance of spontaneity. The Gospels furnish a good number of these brief stories whose point is a saying of Jesus. Taylor[1] recognises some thirty-two such 'pronouncement-stories,' and it is noteworthy that nineteen of them are polemical. The distinction between these pronouncement-stories and sayings which do not have a narrative setting is not that the more circumstantial pronouncement-story is historically more reliable; for the difference in form is most probably the result of difference in the circumstances of their origin. The word of Jesus is in the one

[1] *The Formation of the Gospel Tradition*, pp. 63–84.

case repartee and in the other pure teaching. But the distinction is useful in exposition when we have to deal with short detached sayings like the three in Mk. 9⁴⁹ᶠ·, where a convincing interpretation becomes very difficult if not impossible. In such cases it may well be that our difficulties arise from the fact that we are dealing with pronouncements stripped of the narrative setting which would make them intelligible.

The material presented by Q, M, and L consists mainly of the second sort of teaching, deliberate religious and moral instruction which can be understood by itself without any narrative context; and within this class we are presented with all kinds of utterances, from the stark simplicity of the Golden Rule to the high elaboration of the parable of the Prodigal Son.

The simplest form of the teaching is provided by such sayings as Lk. 6³⁹, ' Can one blind man act as guide to another? Will not both fall into the ditch? '; Lk. 10⁷ᵇ, ' The labourer is worthy of his hire '; Lk. 10¹⁶, ' He who hearkens to you, hearkens to me, and he who rejects you, rejects me; and he who rejects me rejects Him that sent me.' It should be noted that the first of these sayings is called, in the text, a parable (*parabolē*). Now *parabolē* is the Greek equivalent of the Hebrew word *māshāl*, which commonly means what we should call a proverb, as well as what we understand by parable. That is to say, the Hebrew *māshāl* (Aramaic *mathlā*) covers both proverb and parable, a point which is very important when we come to consider the nature of parable.[1]

A special class of these brief sayings comprises the Beatitudes and Woes. Both are common in the Old Testament and later Jewish writings, the former especially in the Psalms and Wisdom literature, the latter in the prophetic books. It is important to remember that these exclamations are *not* blessings and curses. A great deal of nonsense is written and spoken about Jesus cursing the Pharisees. A blessing or a curse in the proper sense of the words implies a wish that good or evil may come upon the person blessed or cursed. The beatitude and the woe are highly emotional statements of fact, and not wishes at all; and it would be more accurate to say, ' Alas for you Pharisees . . .' than ' Woe unto you Pharisees . . .' as a translation of the words of Jesus in these passages. There are no beatitudes in Mk., but they are found in Q (Lk. 6²⁰⁻²², 7²³, 10²³, (11²⁸), 12⁽³⁷, ³⁸⁾, ⁴⁰), M (Mt. 5⁵, ⁷⁻¹⁰, 16¹⁷), and L (Lk. 14¹⁴, 23²⁹). Woes appear in Mk. (13¹⁷, 14²¹), Q (Lk. 6²⁴⁻²⁶, 10¹³, 11³⁹⁻⁵², 17¹), M (Mt. 23¹⁵⁻¹⁶), but none in L.

Very numerous and important are the precepts, both commands and prohibitions, covering various aspects of the Christian life: the disciple's relation to God, to his neighbour, to property, to the chances and changes of human existence. Usually these are stated simply and left to carry conviction by their own power of self-authentication to anyone who has a heart that will understand. Occasionally the way of Jesus is put in contrast with current rules or practice, notably in the collection of antitheses (Mt. 5²¹⁻⁴⁸) and in the directions concerning works of piety (Mt. 6¹⁻¹⁸) and ranks and titles (Mt. 23⁶⁻¹²).

Or the teaching may be given in the form of dialogue, and here we must distinguish between conversations with disciples, e.g. Lk. 9⁵¹⁻⁵⁶, with friendly disposed persons other than disciples, e.g. Lk. 11²⁷ᶠ·, and with opponents, e.g. Mk. 3²²⁻²⁶.

[1] See *The Teaching of Jesus*, pp. 57–81.

The special value of dialogue for the interpretation of the teaching is that by presenting the sayings of Jesus in their context it enables us to gather the original sense of the sayings with greater ease and certainty than might otherwise be the case. The uncertainty which sometimes attends the interpretation of the isolated saying is well illustrated by the Q passage Lk. 12⁵⁷⁻⁵⁹||Mt. 5²⁵f.: ' And why even of yourselves judge ye not what is right? For as thou art going with thine adversary before the magistrate, on the way give diligence to be quit of him; lest haply he hale thee unto the judge, and the judge shall deliver thee to the officer, and the officer shall cast thee into prison. I say unto thee, Thou shalt by no means come out thence, till thou have paid the very last mite.' The context of this saying in Lk., which is presumably its Q context, shows that it has to do with the coming judgement: and it is probably to be regarded as a parable —just as a wise citizen does his utmost to settle an action out of court, so the wise man will be well advised to escape what is coming by timely repentance. In the Sermon on the Mount, however, the context is changed and the eschatological parable has become an ordinary rule of everyday life: and if we had not the Lucan version, we should probably never suspect that it was anything else. Even with the hint given by the Q context the interpretation given here cannot be regarded as more than highly probable, because we cannot be absolutely certain that the Q context is the original context. If we knew with some certainty the circumstances in which the words were spoken, we should feel more confidence about the interpretation of them.

It is otherwise with the immediately following section in Lk. (13¹⁻⁵). There the other side of the conversation is indicated, and this furnishes the clue to what is the most likely interpretation of the saying of Jesus.[1]

A common form of the dialogue is that in which Jesus is asked a question and replies. Here again we have to distinguish the questioners. There is the disciple who brings his question to the Master because he wants instruction, e.g. Lk. 11¹⁻⁴. Or there is the friendly outsider who comes to see what Jesus has to say on some problem in which he is interested. Such a case is the question concerning the chief commandment, of which we have two independent versions (Mk. 12²⁸⁻³⁴ and Lk. 10²⁵⁻²⁸). Or again the questioners may be hostile to Jesus and their questions trap questions, e.g. Mk. 12¹³⁻¹⁷. In dealing with documents where large masses of teaching have been collected it is necessary to consider carefully in every case where the reply of Jesus really ends, and how far matter not originally part of the reply, but nevertheless bearing upon the subject under discussion, has been attracted to it. This seems to have happened in the Q version of the Beelzebul controversy (Lk. 11¹⁴⁻²⁶), where at least one saying (Lk. 11²⁴⁻²⁶), which has nothing to do with the original charge, has been tacked on to the reply of Jesus, because it has a bearing on the general subject of demon-possession.

Two important features of the teaching remain for consideration: our Lord's use of poetic form and His practice of teaching in parables.

It is now generally recognised that a large part of the teaching is, like the oracles of the Hebrew prophets, cast into poetic form. Such passages will be noticed in the Commentary, and here it will be necessary only to make a few

[1] See the Commentary, ad loc.

observations on the nature of Hebrew poetry.[1] The characteristic feature of this kind of poetry is what is known as ' parallelism ' or the rhyming of thoughts. In an English heroic couplet we look for a correspondence in the two lines first in the number of stressed syllables and then in the sound of the final syllables. In a pair of Latin hexameters we expect a certain amount of correspondence in the arrangement of long and short vowels. In a Hebrew couplet there is a certain correspondence of rhythm and, most important, a correspondence in thought. Bishop Lowth, the pioneer in this field, recognised three kinds of parallelism or correspondence in thought, to which he gave the names synonymous, antithetic, and synthetic. The first two kinds of parallelism are easily recognised and understood. For example, in Ps. 18[25 ff.].

> With the merciful thou wilt show thyself merciful;
> With the perfect man thou wilt show thyself perfect;
> With the pure thou wilt show thyself pure;
> And with the perverse thou wilt show thyself froward.
> For thou wilt save the afflicted people;
> But the haughty eyes thou wilt bring down.

Here the first two lines are in synonymous parallelism and the last two are antithetic. The middle lines show a mixture of both kinds. Considered as wholes, they are in synonymous parallelism; but if we take the separate terms, those are antithetic. Hebrew parallelism is not a cast-iron system, but is capable of immense variety in the application of the fundamental principles. The weak point in Lowth's classification is the ' synthetic.' Synthetic parallelism is really just a name to cover pairs of lines which are somehow connected but not by way of strict synonymous or antithetic parallelism. In this class we should probably recognise that there are some couplets which display *partial* synonymous or antithetic parallelism, and others where there is no parallelism at all in the strict sense but rather *continuation* of the thought of the first line in the second.[2] In other words, we must not expect to find Hebrew poetry constructed on a rigorous system of couplets each consisting of a pair of strictly parallel lines; rather we must look for infinite flexibility in the use of this form, strict parallelism alternating with partial, and with what may be called ' continuation.' To this we have an analogy in the English use of rhyme. Any four lines of verse may be rhymed in a variety of patterns: 1 with 2 and 3 with 4—heroic couplets; or 1 with 3 and 2 with 4; or 2 with 4, 1 and 3 being unrhymed; or 1 with 2 and 4, 3 being unrhymed, as in Fitzgerald's *Omar Khayyam* stanzas; or 1 with 4 and 2 with 3 as in Tennyson's *In Memoriam*. There is the same variety in the Hebrew use of parallelism as in the English use of rhyme.

Parallelism can be employed on a still larger scale. Just as in Spenser's *Prothalamion* we have the same scheme of rhymes repeated with but slight variation

---

[1] The best treatment of the subject in English is G. B. Gray's *The Forms of Hebrew Poetry*. For the application of the principles to the Gospels see, above all, *The Poetry of our Lord*, by C. F. Burney. Reference may also be made to *The Teaching of Jesus*, pp. 50–56.

[2] See Gray, *op. cit.*, pp. 49 ff.

in each of the ten stanzas of eighteen lines, and as in the choruses of Greek drama we have strophe and antistrophe answering line for line in metrical structure, so in Hebrew poetry it is possible to have whole strophes parallel to one another. This complex parallelism is to be seen in a tentative shape, and not yet fully carried out, in the Old Testament, for example in the series of oracles in the book of Amos (1^3–2^{16}). Perfect specimens are to be found in the poetry of Jesus.

With this much by way of explanation, we may give a few out of the many examples of poetic structure in the teaching, reserving fuller treatment of them till a later stage.

1. Simple synonymous parallelism:

> He causeth His sun to rise upon evil and good
> And raineth upon just and unjust. (Mt. 5^{45}.)

2. Simple antithetic parallelism:

> Every good tree bringeth forth good fruits,
> But the corrupt tree bringeth forth evil fruits. (Mt. 7^{17}.)

3. Slightly more elaborated, producing a parallelism between two short strophes of three lines each:

> Ask, and it shall be given you;
> Seek, and ye shall find;
> Knock, and it shall be opened to you.
>
> For every asker receiveth;
> And the seeker findeth;
> And to the knocker it shall be opened. (Lk. $11^{9f.}$ = Mt. $7^{7f.}$.)

4. Still more complex strophic parallelism:

> And as it happened in the days of Noah,
> So shall it be in the days of the Son of Man:
>> They ate, they drank,
>> They married, they gave in marriage,
> Till the day when Noah went into the ark
> And the Deluge came and destroyed them all.
>
> Likewise as it happened in the days of Lot:
>> They ate, they drank,
>> They bought, they sold,
>> They planted, they built.
> But in the day when Lot went forth from Sodom,
> Fire and brimstone rained from heaven and destroyed them all.
> Just so shall it be in the day when the Son of Man is revealed. (Lk. 17^{26-30}.)

Closely related to the use of poetic form in the teaching is the use of metaphor, simile, parable, and allegory. Both alike are products of the poet's mind; and just as in poetic form we find all degrees of elaboration, so in the use of pictorial imagery we find a similar variation from the simple metaphor ' You are the light of the world ' (Mt. 5¹⁴) to the complexity of the great parables.

The distinction between metaphor and simile is that in the simile the comparison is explicit, e.g. ' I send you forth *as* sheep in the midst of wolves; therefore be wise *as* serpents and harmless *as* doves ' (Mt. 10¹⁶). In the metaphor the compared object actually takes the place of the object to be illustrated, e.g. ' I came to cast fire upon the earth ' (Lk. 12⁴⁹), ' Strive to enter in by the narrow door ' (Lk. 13²⁴). It is clear that the metaphor presupposes the simile. The metaphor ' I came to cast fire upon the earth ' is only intelligible if ' fire ' stands for something else which may well be compared to fire.

The parable rests upon this basis and in its simplest forms it is obvious that it is nothing but an extended simile or metaphor. In the parables of the mustard seed and the leaven we have extended simile. ' To what is the kingdom of God like . . .? It is like a mustard seed . . .' Then the parable goes on to point out those characteristics in the mustard seed which make it a good illustration of the nature of the Kingdom. In the parable of the lamp (Lk. 11³³‖Mt. 5¹⁵) we have an extended metaphor. We are told certain things about the lamp, and it is left to our own common sense or insight to discover what the lamp stands for. A more highly elaborated example of the same sort is the parable of Dives and Lazarus (Lk. 16¹⁹⁻³¹). We are given the stories of the rich man and the poor beggar, but we are not told who or what they represent.

What is essential to the parable is that there should be a real analogy between what is narrated in the parable and that which the parable is intended to explain or illustrate. The mustard seed grows from small beginnings to something great, and so does the Kingdom. The kindled lamp must light the way into the house; then so—let us say—must the enlightened disciple guide others into the Kingdom of God. In the simpler parables there is one such point to be set before the hearers with the utmost possible clearness and convincing power. But there need not be only one. It is the mark of mastery in the construction of parables that the story told can be made to illustrate and illuminate the truth at several points. The parable of the Prodigal Son has one main point—the outgoing love of God. This is not the only one. The parable has several subsidiary points, and it is a more perfect parable for having them. For these subsidiary points do not destroy the unity of the parable: on the contrary, they serve to throw the central point into stronger relief.

The characteristic feature of the true parable is that this central point is always an appeal to the insight of the hearers. It demands a moral judgement on the behaviour of the characters in the story; and, on the basis of that judgement, it issues its challenge to faith and life. A human father, with all his faults and follies, will not mock his hungry children with stones for bread. Then if you believe in a heavenly Father at all, you must believe that in Him is all that is best in human fatherhood and more besides. Even an unscrupulous judge will give a righteous judgement for the sake of peace and quietness: and shall not the Judge of all the earth do right? The Good Samaritan is good? Then go and do likewise. You admire the business acumen of the Dishonest Steward? Then see whether you cannot apply your own wits with equal assiduity to better purposes. Where the

2

parable succeeds, it succeeds by inspiring faith and by stimulating conscience: where it fails, it fails because men cannot or will not see the point or, if they see it, will not respond.

This enables us to distinguish properly between parable and allegory. For the difference between the two is not one of form or construction, but one of inner meaning and purpose. This is clear from the etymology of the two words. Parable signifies essentially a comparison, a setting of two facts or sets of facts side by side, so that an analogy between them may be established. Allegory is essentially a mode of speech, the description of a fact or set of facts in terms appropriate to another fact or set of facts. Allegory had its beginnings among the Greeks at the time when the old tales about the Olympian gods were falling into discredit for the excellent reason that they ' ascribed to the gods all things that are a shame and a disgrace among mortals, stealings and adulteries and deceivings of one another.' [1]   One way of saving the old myths was to maintain that they were not to be taken literally, but as figurative accounts of something else. This is the allegorical method. It was employed, for example, by one Heraclitus, who undertook to show that the stories told by Homer about the doings of the gods in the Iliad were in reality picturesque descriptions of natural phenomena. Then all that the reader of Homer needs is a sort of dictionary which will tell him that when the poet mentions Apollo he really is speaking about the sun, that Apollo shooting arrows is a poetic way of describing the sun's rays, and so on. So interpreted the Iliad becomes the first example of ' Natural Science without tears.' Philo of Alexandria applied the same method to the Old Testament and found his own philosophy concealed in the patriarchal narratives. St. Paul found the secret of the Law and the Gospel adumbrated in the story of Hagar and Sarah. In all these cases we have old traditional material allegorically interpreted: the new meaning is read into the old story. The allegorist may, however, not find anything suitable at hand: he must then try to make a story of his own, which will embody the doctrine he wishes to impart. Then we get such masterpieces of allegory as the *Pilgrim's Progress* and the *Holy War*. Here again there is no obvious and inevitable connexion between the story told and the doctrine to be conveyed. The connexion is made by Bunyan himself, who furnishes the characters and scenes of his story with significant names. These names are at once an indication that the story is not to be taken at its face value, and the code by which its real meaning may be discovered. Now what is common to all these examples is the fact that the story is regarded as the means for conveying correct information or true doctrine about matters with which the story as such has no apparent connexion; and the other fact that the discovery of the true meaning depends on being able to translate the terms used in the story into the terms of the doctrine. The allegory is thus a conventional form by which information may be conveyed to the reader in an interesting and attractive way. This information may be anything from a system of natural science to a body of religious dogma. The point is that what is offered is information claiming to be true.

This discussion is necessary because it has been claimed that there are among the parables of Jesus some which are not parables at all, but allegories. It has

[1] Xenophanes of Colophon, fr. 11 (Diels).

further been suggested that only the true parables—not the allegories—should be regarded as genuine creations of Jesus.   If we are to make this distinction between parables and allegories, it is essential that we should make it on the right basis; and in the light of this discussion we must look at the purpose of the stories rather than at the outward form.   The ultimate difference between a parable and an allegory is that the parable is meant to create trust in God and love to man by an appeal to conscience and insight, while the allegory is meant to convey information, stimulating interest by an appeal to the imagination.   If this test be applied to the parables in the Synoptic Gospels, it will be found that they are for the most part genuine parables, and that in the few cases where we have an allegory, as, for example, in Matthew's parable of the Wheat and Tares, it is probably to be explained as a later allegorising of what was originally a parable.

5. THE MEANING AND PERMANENT VALUE OF THE TEACHING

' My yoke is easy and my burden is light.'   Easy and light are not the epithets that one would spontaneously apply to the teaching, particularly to its moral demands.   Indeed, the criticism most commonly levelled at it is that it is magnificent but impracticable, a beautiful dream which can never come true in such a world as this.   This criticism may mean anything or nothing.   If it means that the demands of Jesus are of such a kind that no Parliament would enact them and that no police force could enforce them, it is doubtless correct; but it may be questioned whether Jesus ever contemplated such a consummation.   Or again, it is suggested that while the teaching may have been all very well for simple first-century Palestine, it is not adequate to our complex twentieth-century civilisation. To which it may be replied that the supposed greater complexity of modern life is largely a myth.   Greater ease and rapidity of communication have made more obvious the complexity that has been there all the time.   The Egyptian grain harvest affected Rome and, through Rome, the whole Roman Empire as really in the first century as the American grain harvest affects the world in the twentieth. Only then it took somewhat longer for the results to appear than it does now. More than that, the matters with which Jesus was concerned are not affected by the alleged complexity of modern life.   What He thought and said about marriage and divorce has to do with realities that are not touched by the fact that the first-century Jewish husband could divorce his wife by writing out a document that would go comfortably on a half-sheet of notepaper, while the twentieth-century husband must go through a long, complicated, and expensive legal process.

It will simplify the discussion if we admit the truth at the outset: that the teaching of Jesus is difficult and unacceptable because it runs counter to those elements in human nature which the twentieth century has in common with the first—such things as laziness, greed, the love of pleasure, the instinct to hit back, and the like.   The teaching as a whole shows that Jesus was well aware of this and recognised that here and nowhere else lay the obstacle that had to be surmounted. The question is: how?

We may construe what Jesus said as the enunciation of a new Law, simpler and at the same time more searching and more exacting than the old.   The propounder of such a Law would, of course, be open to the practical objection that if people had found the old Law too difficult, they would be still more liable to fail under the new with its more drastic requirements. ' If thou hast run with the footmen, and they have wearied thee, then how canst thou contend with horses? ' Further, it may be objected to this legal interpretation that, in the last resort, Jesus reduces the whole Law to a pair of commandments, love towards God and love towards neighbour, and that love cannot be the subject of legislation; for it is of the very essence of love that it should be freely given, spontaneous, and not the laboured response to an external requirement.

Recognising this difficulty, we may try the opposite course and suggest that the teaching is not the promulgation of a new set of rules of piety and morality, but rather the inculcation of a certain temper and spirit which should govern man's attitude to God and neighbour. This interpretation is at once met by the practical objection that ' temper ' and ' spirit ' are vague terms; that the thing they stand for can easily degenerate into mere sentimentalism; and that the sentimentalist, in spite of his fine feelings, is often singularly ruthless and cruel in action. Moreover, the teaching does not confine itself to the spirit and temper of man, but goes on to specify definite kinds of action and to approve or condemn them.

The way out of this impasse is seen when we take account of the following facts:

(a) To the Jew the Law was not merely a set of rules of conduct such as might have been evolved by human wisdom considering the pros and cons of different lines of action and carefully working out the greatest happiness of the greatest number. It was a revelation of God's will and therefore of God Himself. Jesus stands in this tradition, and where He criticises or amends the existing Law it is in order to express more adequately what is for Him the will of God.

(b) Jesus is not concerned with the academic analysis of conduct into act, intention, motive, and so on. He is concerned with the whole character which expresses itself in life and action. The interest and importance of acts are that they reveal persons.

(c) Jesus is not the mere theorist in theology and ethics, but Himself the embodiment of His teaching. In the Gospels the life illuminates the teaching and the teaching the life, just because they are all of a piece.

This means that the teaching must be regarded in a new light. It has to do not with mere acts and motives but with the fundamental relation of man's will to God's. Repentance is not a striving to bring one's conduct into line with the Law or with the higher righteousness demanded by Jesus. Neither is it a painful scrutiny of one's motives with a view to substituting, let us say, unselfish for selfish motives. It is a return of the whole personality to God, a submission of the will to His will, the acceptance of His sovereignty. Now it is by this act of submission that the Kingdom of God is entered, and it is this decisive change that is presupposed in the detailed teaching of Jesus. The change itself is made possible by the new experience of God as Jesus reveals Him, that is, as the merciful loving Father who seeks and saves the lost. This tranforming experience bears fruit in life and conduct; and the examples of the higher righteousness given by Jesus in

His teaching are, so to speak, samples of this fruit.   The word 'fruit' is used advisedly, for there is a certain spontaneity and inevitableness about this new behaviour that cannot be attained by mechanical obedience to rules or by meticulous scrutiny of one's motives.

It should thus be apparent that the teaching of Jesus has to do not with the rightness of actions and motives or with the academic discussion of the *summum bonum*, but with the achievement of good living.   This means the identification of human wills with the will of God so that one's life becomes part and parcel of the purpose of God in the world.   Such life is as difficult and arduous as the composition of a Beethoven symphony is difficult, even for a Beethoven, and as spontaneous and inevitable.   We cannot legislate in advance for such life: it creates its own rules in the light of the unfolding purpose of God.   Nor can we judge it, for the only final criterion is the whole purpose of God, which is known to God alone.   Such life is inspired, creative, adventurous.   It is movement towards a goal: and for the purposes of that pilgrimage the teaching of Jesus is a compass rather than an ordnance map.   He who grasps it in its wholeness and simplicity is sure of his direction: he must pick his own steps.

At this point we may consider one other difficulty that may be raised concerning the teaching, this namely, that the whole teaching and the whole life of the early Church was dominated by the belief that the end of the existing world-order was close at hand.   Then it may be urged that in His teaching Jesus was not laying down rules for the permanent use of mankind, but only issuing a kind of emergency legislation to cover the short interval before the final consummation. The teaching is in fact an interim ethic.   Granting the point that Jesus and His first followers believed the end of the existing world-order to be imminent, we must still reject the conclusions drawn with regard to the teaching.

In the first place 'interim-ethic' for such teaching in such circumstances is a misnomer.   If, in the belief that the whole monetary system of the world is going to be abolished next week, someone advises me to withdraw all my money from the bank and distribute it in charity, he may be giving me the best advice in the circumstances; but to dignify his advice with the name of 'ethic' or even 'interim-ethic' is to make a virtue of necessity with a vengeance.

But further, and this is the vital point, if the object of the teaching is to give direction rather than directions, to point to the goal of all good living rather than to legislate for particular cases, then the important thing is not whether the goal is near or far away, but whether the direction is correct.   If the object of Jesus was so to guide His followers that their lives should fit into the great purpose of God, the question whether that purpose would be realised in ten years or ten thousand became a minor consideration.   Now we must maintain that this was precisely the object of Jesus.   Where Kant says: 'Act so that the maxims of your will may be in perfect harmony with a universal system of laws,' Jesus says: Live so that your will may be in perfect harmony with the purpose of God.   That is the purport of 'Thy will be done on earth as it is in heaven' or 'Be ye merciful, even as your Father is merciful.'   It means: live so that your life is a fulfilment, in part at least, of God's purpose.   Whether that purpose in its completeness is to have immediate or ultimate fulfilment is a secondary consideration.

The teaching in its inmost nature is thus bound up with faith, the conviction that the world has meaning which can be expressed in terms of the wise and loving purpose of God; that man's sin and misery can be explained in terms of his opposition to that purpose, and cured by a new submission of man's will to God's; and that by this submission man's life acquires new unity, new meaning, new direction, and new hope.

TEXT AND COMMENTARY

I.—The Document Q

A. JOHN THE BAPTIST AND JESUS

(*Note.*—*In this reconstruction the order of Lk. is followed. For the convenience of readers who may use the commentary with a synopsis before them, the numbers of the paragraphs in Huck's Synopsis (8th ed.) are added in brackets at the head of each section. References in the commentary are, unless otherwise stated, to the text of Lk.*)

1. *THE PREACHING OF JOHN THE BAPTIST* (2, 4)

MT. 3[7-12]

LK. 3[7-9, 16, 17]

3 7 But when he saw many of the Pharisees and Sadducees coming to his baptism, he said unto them, Ye offspring of vipers, who warned you to flee from the wrath to 8 come? Bring forth therefore fruit worthy of [1] repentance: and think not to say 9 within yourselves, We have Abraham to our father: for I say unto you, that God is able of these stones to raise up 10 children unto Abraham. And even now is the axe laid unto the root of the trees: every tree therefore that bringeth not forth good fruit is hewn 11 down, and cast into the fire. I indeed baptize you [2] with water unto repentance: but he that cometh after me is mightier than I, whose shoes I am not [3] worthy to bear: he shall baptize you [2] with the Holy 12 Ghost and *with* fire: whose fan is in his hand, and he will throughly cleanse his threshing-floor; and he will gather his wheat into the garner, but the chaff he will burn up with unquenchable fire.

[1] Or, *your repentance.*
[2] Or, *in.*
[3] Gr. *sufficient.*

3 7 He said therefore to the multitudes that went out to be baptized of him, Ye offspring of vipers, who warned you to flee 8 from the wrath to come? Bring forth therefore fruits worthy of [1] repentance, and begin not to say within yourselves, We have Abraham to our father: for I say unto you, that God is able of these stones 9 to raise up children unto Abraham. And even now is the axe also laid unto the root of the trees: every tree therefore that bringeth not forth good fruit is hewn down, and cast into the fire. 15 And as the people were in expectation, and all men reasoned in their hearts concerning John, whether haply he were the 16 Christ; John answered, saying unto them all, I indeed baptize you with water; but there cometh he that is mightier than I, the latchet of whose shoes I am not [2] worthy to unloose: he shall baptize you 17 [3] with the Holy Ghost and *with* fire: whose fan is in his hand, throughly to cleanse his threshing-floor, and to gather the wheat into his garner; but the chaff he will burn up with unquenchable fire.

[1] Or, *your repentance.*
[2] Gr. *sufficient.*
[3] Or, *in.*

There is another, probably independent, account of John's preaching in Mk. 1[7f.]. As is commonly the case in Q sections, the verbal agreement between Mt. and Lk. begins with the words of the preacher. ' Pharisees and Sadducees ' (Mt. 3[7]) is a favourite phrase with Matthew (cf. Mt. 16[1, 6, 11, 12]). From Mk. 11[27-33] we learn that ' the High priests, scribes, and elders ' had rejected the baptism of John, and the same is reported of ' the Pharisees and lawyers ' in Lk. 7[29f.]. These two passages suggest that John's converts were drawn from the common people; and, so far, Luke's introduction is preferable to Matthew's, though it may perhaps be doubted whether either stood in Q. Lk. 3[15] is another piece of narrative setting introduced by the evangelist. It has no parallel in Mt., and it breaks the unity of the address.

39

Traces of the original Aramaic are to be seen in ' *begin* not to say ' (Lk. 3[8], cf. 13[25]), a literal translation of a common Aramaic idiom (Mt. 3[8] has ' think not to say,' which represents a better Greek, but a less faithful rendering of the original); and in the saying about raising up children to Abraham from stones, where there is probably a play upon words, the Aramaic words for ' children ' and ' stones ' being almost identical. Probably also in the phrase ' bring forth fruits,' lit. ' make fruits.' A single Aramaic verb may also lie behind ' bear ' (Mt. 3[11]) and ' unloose ' (Lk. 3[16]).

7, 8, 9, 17. John addresses his audience as ' offspring of vipers ' in sharp contrast to their own thought of themselves as children of Abraham. The serpent is the type of evil cunning: and at a later date we find ' the old serpent ' as a description of Satan (Rev. 12[9]). Cf. John 8[44], ' Ye (Jews) are of your father the devil.' Here ' offspring of vipers ' may well have much the same force as ' children of Satan.' Signs of repentance from such people are so amazing that they must have learned somewhere of the coming judgement. Here we come to the main theme of John's preaching, the wrath to come. John thinks of it as an essential part of the rule of God. There is to be a settling of accounts, and at it strict justice will be the order of the day. Evildoers will by no means escape the penalty of their misdeeds. Repentance is necessary, and this repentance must be real; it must issue in amendment of life. The fact that the guilty are of the Chosen People will not avail them—as many thought—in the day of judgement. Here John takes up a position that is as old as Amos, ' You only have I known of all the families of the earth: therefore I will visit upon you all your iniquities ' (Am. 3[2]). There will be no most favoured nation in the day that is coming. And that day is imminent. Already the axe is resting on the tree root, ready to be raised for the first blow. As nothing can save the unfruitful tree from the fire, so nothing will save an unrepentant and unreformed Israel from the judgement. The judgement may also be pictured in terms of the threshing-floor. Here only what is good is preserved: all that is worthless is destroyed in the fire. There is no doubt as to what is meant by the fire. We may compare *Psalms of Solomon* 15[6 f.], [10-15]: ' Flaming fire and the wrath against the ungodly . . . when it goeth forth against the sinners from before the face of the Lord, to destroy all the substance of the sinners. . . . For the mark of destruction is upon their forehead, and the inheritance of the sinners is destruction and darkness: and their iniquities shall pursue them as far as hell beneath. . . . And the sinners shall perish in the day of the Lord's judgement for ever, when God visiteth the earth with His judgement to recompense the sinners unto everlasting. But they that fear the Lord shall find mercy therein: and shall live in the righteousness of their God ' (trans. Ryle and James).

16. This brings us to what is the crucial point in the interpretation of the passage—the two baptisms. The coming baptism is described by both Mt. and Lk. as a baptism ' with the Holy Ghost and with fire.' In Mk. (1[8]) and John (1[33]) it is baptism ' with the Holy Ghost.' In Acts 1[5] the risen Lord says to His followers: ' John baptized with water; you will soon be baptized with the Holy Ghost.' In Acts 11[16], Peter, explaining his dealings with Cornelius, says: ' I remembered the word of the Lord,' referring back to Acts 1[5]. From Acts itself it is clear how

this word of the Lord was understood, namely as a prophecy fulfilled at Pentecost, when a baptism with the Holy Spirit was symbolised by tongues of fire descending on the disciples' heads. Now in Acts 19$^{1-6}$ we meet with disciples of John who have not even heard of a baptism with the Holy Spirit. But this is very strange if John did in fact teach that his own baptism was only a preliminary to another and richer baptism with the Spirit. These conflicting data are explicable on the hypothesis that the experience of the early Church led them to interpret ' baptism with fire ' as baptism with the Holy Spirit, and that this interpretation has already affected the passages in Acts 1 and 2 and also the form of John's saying in Mk. 1^8. It is then open to us to say that in Mt. and Lk. we have the original form of the saying as recorded in Q plus the interpretation put upon it by the early Church. This original Q form, which is also the better tradition of John's saying, had no reference to the Spirit. It ran: ' He will baptize you with fire.' So long as the Holy Spirit is retained, John's words are a promise: my baptism is a prelude to a better. When the reference to the Spirit is dropped, the true nature of the saying is apparent. It falls into line with the rest of John's preaching. The baptism with fire is parallel to the other references to fire and to be understood in the same way. The sense of the saying is not that John's baptism is the preliminary to something better, but that it is the last chance of escaping something very much worse, namely the coming judgement.

The agent in this coming crisis is not God. The language of *v.* 16 is not the kind that John would have used of God. ' He that is mightier than I ' means the Messiah. Might is one of the attributes of the Messiah (Is. 9^6, *Ps. Sol.* 17^{44}). There is no indication that John thinks of the Messiah as a supernatural being. The description given here would be appropriate to a human Messiah endowed with supernatural power and authority and similar to the judge and ruler foretold in *Ps. Sol.* 17$^{23-31}$. To look after the footgear of such a Person, which is normally a slave's job, would be for John a high honour.

The preaching of John as a whole belongs to the same strain as the preaching of the greatest Old Testament prophets. Like them, he has his message of doom for a sinful nation. But he goes farther. His task is not merely to proclaim the coming wrath, but also (again in the words of Amos) to prepare Israel to meet her God, to show a way of repentance and amendment whereby some at least may be delivered before it is too late. In this setting the baptism of John can perhaps be most readily understood by reference to the Jewish baptism of proselytes. As the baptism of the proselyte was part of the ceremony of dedication by which a Gentile was incorporated into Israel, so John's baptism is an act of rededication by which Israelites, who through sin have lost their right to the name, may be incorporated afresh into the true Israel.

2. *THE TEMPTATIONS OF JESUS* (8)

MT. 4$^{1-11}$	LK. 4$^{1-13}$
4 1 Then was Jesus led up of the Spirit into the wilderness to be tempted of the devil. 2 And when he had fasted forty days and 3 forty nights, he afterward hungered. And	4 1 And Jesus, full of the Holy Spirit, returned from the Jordan, and was led [1] by the Spirit in the wilderness during forty 2 days, being tempted of the devil. And

the tempter came and said unto him, If thou art the Son of God, command that 4 these stones become [1] bread. But he answered and said, It is written, Man shall not live by bread alone, but by every word that proceedeth out of the mouth of 5 God. Then the devil taketh him into the 6 holy city; and he set him on the [2] pinnacle of the temple, and saith unto him, If thou art the Son of God, cast thyself down: for it is written,

> He shall give his angels charge concerning thee:
> And on their hands they shall bear thee up,
> Lest haply thou dash thy foot against a stone.

7 Jesus said unto him, Again it is written, Thou shalt not tempt the Lord thy God. 8 Again, the devil taketh him unto an exceeding high mountain, and sheweth him all the kingdoms of the world, and the 9 glory of them; and he said unto him, All these things will I give thee, if thou wilt 10 fall down and worship me. Then saith Jesus unto him, Get thee hence, Satan: for it is written, Thou shalt worship the Lord thy God, and him only shalt thou 11 serve. Then the devil leaveth him; and behold, angels came and ministered unto him.

[1] Gr. *loaves.*
[2] Gr. *wing.*

he did eat nothing in those days: and when they were completed, he hungered. 3 And the devil said unto him, If thou art the Son of God, command this stone that 4 it become [2] bread. And Jesus answered unto him, It is written, Man shall not live 5 by bread alone. And he led him up, and shewed him all the kingdoms of [3] the world 6 in a moment of time. And the devil said unto him, To thee will I give all this authority, and the glory of them: for it hath been delivered unto me; and to 7 whomsoever I will I give it. If thou therefore wilt worship before me, it shall all be 8 thine. And Jesus answered and said unto him, It is written, Thou shalt worship the Lord thy God, and him only shalt thou 9 serve. And he led him to Jerusalem, and set him on the [4] pinnacle of the temple, and said unto him, If thou art the Son of God, 10 cast thyself down from hence: for it is written,

> He shall give his angels charge concerning thee, to guard thee:

11 and,

> On their hands they shall bear thee up,
> Lest haply thou dash thy foot against a stone.

12 And Jesus answering said unto him, It is said, Thou shalt not tempt the Lord thy God.
13 And when the devil had completed every temptation, he departed from him [5] for a season.

[1] Or, *in.*
[2] Or, *a loaf.*
[3] Gr. *the inhabited earth.*
[4] Gr. *wing.*
[5] Or, *until.*

Mk. (1[21 f.]) records the fact that Jesus was tempted, but does not specify the nature of the temptations. In the narrative setting of the Q account there is little agreement between Mt. and Lk. apart from words which they have in common with Mk. They agree against Mk. in calling the adversary 'devil' rather than 'Satan,' and in introducing the name Jesus at the beginning of the story. This latter agreement does not amount to much, since Luke, by introducing the genealogy between the Baptism and the Temptations, makes a fresh start necessary. If the name Jesus did stand in Q at this point, it would be an indication that the Q account of the Temptations was a self-contained section. Mt. and Lk. also agree in describing Jesus' fast; but the wording of the two accounts is different except for the verb 'hungered.' The fast and the hunger are the necessary prelude to the first temptation.

The most striking difference between Mt. and Lk. is in the order of the temptations. Matthew's arrangement works up to a fine dramatic climax, so fine that it is difficult to imagine what could have induced Luke to alter it, if it had stood so in his source. It is probable that the order in Lk. is the original Q order.

1 f. *Narrative introduction.* Mk. ($1^{12f.}$) tells us that Jesus was in the wilderness —the home of evil spirits—for forty days and that during that period He was tempted by Satan. Mt. ($4^{1f.}$) says that He was led into the wilderness to be tempted, that the forty days were spent in fasting, and that then the temptations began. (Similarly, in the story of the Baptism Mt. converts Mk.'s statement that Jesus came and was baptised into a statement that He came to be baptised.) Lk. has a combination of the two versions. With Mk. he makes the temptation continue throughout the forty days. With Mt. he describes the fast, and then commences a new set of temptations at the end of the forty days. It does not seem possible to determine how much of this is Q matter; but there must have been some reference to the fast and the hunger in order to make the first temptation intelligible. For the fast cf. Ex. 34^{28}, Moses' fast on Mt. Sinai. Forty days is the Jewish conventional figure for a considerable time. Mt. has 'forty days and forty nights' as in Ex. 34^{28}.

3 f. *The first temptation.* This and the temptation on the Temple are introduced by the words 'If thou art the Son of God.' The fact that this formula is not used in the temptation where Jesus is offered the kingdoms of the world, is a clue to its meaning here; for it may be safely conjectured that the reason why the tempter does not use the formula in that case is that if Jesus is the Son of God, the things which Satan is about to offer are already His by right, the right of the Messiah. But the term Son of God for Messiah is curiously rare in Hebrew and Jewish literature. In the Old Testament angels are called 'sons of God' and the name Son of God is given to Israel as a whole and to the king of Israel. In the Septuagint and the Apocrypha and Pseudepigrapha the name is given to Israel, to the godly and upright in Israel, and to the Messiah. (This last probably only in 4 *Ezra.*) In the Rabbinical literature it is used for Israel and for the Davidic Messiah. Here again the cases where it is used of the Messiah are few, and Billerbeck points out that they only occur where a Messianic interpretation of an Old Testament text is unavoidable. It may be, as he suggests, that the Rabbis deliberately avoided the expression because of its use by Christians as a designation of Christ. In any case, it is difficult to see what else Son of God can mean in the present context.

The challenge to the Messiah to transform stone into bread may best be explained by reference to the current belief that the Messianic Age would be marked by a miraculous abundance of material goods. Satan says in effect: If you are the Messiah, produce one of the recognised signs of the Messiah's coming. Jesus replies by quoting from Dt. 8^3, 'Man shall not live by bread alone.' Mt. (4^4) has the addition 'but by every word that proceedeth out of the mouth of God,' which cannot have stood in Q, because it is a quotation from the Septuagint. The force of the quotation appears when we take in the immediately preceding words in Dt. : 'And He humbled thee, and suffered thee to hunger, and fed thee with manna, which thou knowest not, neither did thy fathers know; that He might make thee know that man doth not live by bread only but by every thing that proceedeth out of the mouth of the Lord doth man live.' It was God who fed the people miraculously in the wilderness with food of His own providing; and not even the Messiah can usurp God's place, Even the Messiah is only God's servant. It is not his to command, but only to obey.

5-8. *The second temptation.* The differences between Mt. and Lk. are here considerable. Luke's 'led him up' without specification of place, and the words 'in a moment of time' suggest a visionary experience. Mt. (4^8) makes the place of the temptation a very high mountain from whose summit the whole inhabited world is actually visible. Such a mountain is mentioned in the *Apocalypse of Baruch* 76^3, and another in *Enoch* 24 f. The summit of the latter is like a throne, and it is here that God will sit when He comes down to visit the earth with goodness (*Enoch* 25^3). This mountain would be a very suitable scene for Satan's offer. The wording of the offer is fuller in Lk. than in Mt. The words 'and the glory of them' are awkwardly placed in Lk. 4^6, for 'of them' clearly refers back to the kingdoms of the world and what Satan is offering is the authority. The words may be accidentally misplaced or they may have crept into the text of Lk. from Mt. The claim of the tempter that the sole right of disposing of the authority is his does not appear in Mt. In the Q passage Mt. 11^{27} = Lk. 10^{22} similar words are used by Jesus. Does Mt. suppress them here as false and blasphemous in the mouth of Satan? The speech of Satan in Lk. is subtle: (*a*) the unqualified promise 'I will give it to you': (*b*) the claim 'It is mine to do with as I please'; (*c*) the trap 'I will let you have it on very easy terms.' In Mt. we have only the bald statement of the offer and the condition. This offer is rejected, again in terms borrowed from the Old Testament (Dt. 6^{13}) and slightly adapted to the situation. The original runs: 'Thou shalt fear the Lord thy God; and Him shalt thou serve.' Here 'worship'— better 'do homage to'—is substituted for 'fear,' and 'only' is added after 'Him.' Satan has said: 'I will make you ruler of the world, if you will do homage to me.' Jesus replies 'Homage is to be done to God, who is the sole object of man's loyalty and obedience.' Even the Messiah is only God's servant.

9-12. *The third temptation.* This takes place in Jerusalem. 'The holy city' (Mt.) is a common Jewish designation of the capital. What is meant by 'the pinnacle of the temple' is uncertain. The Greek word here translated 'temple' means the whole complex of buildings within the sacred enclosure, including the temple proper. In this case the pinnacle may be what was known as the 'Royal colonnade' on the south side of the outer court. This cloister overlooked a deep ravine, and Josephus (*Ant.*, xv. 11, 5) says that to look down from the roof made one giddy. The Jewish tradition that the Messiah would appear on the roof of the Temple and there proclaim deliverance to the people has no real connexion with this temptation; for there is no hint that the Messiah was expected to prove his title by leaping from the roof. The tempter, twice repulsed with scripture texts, tries a text himself. This is quoted from Ps. 91$^{11f.}$, which is obviously intended to be understood messianically. The challenge is: God has made this promise to the Messiah: if you are the Messiah, let Him fulfil it. This challenge is met by Jesus with words taken from Dt. 6^{16}. There the full text runs: 'Ye shall not tempt the Lord your God, as ye tempted Him in Massah.' 'Tempt' is hardly the right word either in Dt. 6^{16} or here: it is really a case of 'putting

God to the test.' The reference to Massah is explained by Ex. 17[1-7], where it is related how the Israelites by their complaints forced God's hand when they should have trusted His promises. To test God's good faith is to show one's own lack of faith. Again, the Messiah is only God's servant. It is not for him to dictate to God, but only to trust and obey. If the way of obedience means leaping over a precipice—or going to the Cross—that is another matter; but to thrust oneself into peril, merely to provide God with the occasion for a miracle, is not faith but presumption.

13. *Narrative Conclusion.* Mt. and Lk. both tell of the departure of the tempter, though in different words. Mt. adds the detail of the ministry of angels to Jesus from Mk. 1[13]. Lk. says that the tempter left after he had tried every kind of temptation. This doubtless means both the three here described and the others alluded to in *v.* 2. Lk. adds that the respite from temptation was only for a time. He may be thinking of the Passion, Satan's final attack, using Judas as his tool (Lk. 22[3]); though the kind of temptation pictured in this section is present throughout the ministry.

Concerning the temptation narrative Origen said: ' Two kings are struggling together to reign—the king of sin, the devil, and the king of righteousness, Christ.' It would, of course, be easy to take a much simpler line and interpret all the temptations in a moral sense as appeals to such universal human characteristics as the physical appetites, the lust for power, and the thirst for admiration; but, when we look at the narrative as a whole, it is clear that such an interpretation is inadequate. The temptations are fully intelligible only when they are taken in connexion with Jesus' sense of His divinely appointed mission to Israel. It is, however, argued that the temptations cannot be Messianic, because the primitive Church found in the miracles of Jesus one of the principal proofs of His Messiahship. To this it may be replied that even for the early Church miracles did not prove Messiahship; for miracles are recorded of the Apostles, who made no Messianic claims, and, moreover, it was believed that even the Antichrist could and would perform miracles (Mk. 13[22], 2 Thess. 2[9]). Further, the supreme proof that Jesus was the ' son of God ' was found in a miracle wrought by God and not by Jesus, the Resurrection (Rom. 1[4]). But even if the ground alleged were sound, it would prove, not that the temptations are not Messianic, but, what is antecedently probable, that the early Church could not have invented them.

Again it is urged against these stories that similar tales are told of the Buddha, of Zarathustra, and of numerous Christian saints. This argument, so far as it means anything at all, would appear to mean:

All temptation stories told about great religious leaders of antiquity are legendary.

Mt. 4[1-11] = Lk. 4[1-13] is such a story.

Therefore it is legendary.

We may venture to doubt the major premiss.

The first and third temptations in Lk.'s order recur in the course of the ministry in the repeated demand for a sign (Mk. 8[11-13]; Mt. 12[38-42]||Lk. 11[29-32]; Lk. 12[54-56], 23[8]; Mk. 15[32], and parallels). That is, they correspond to something real in the experience of Jesus. The same is true of the second temptation. The whole history of the Jewish people from 200 B.C. to A.D. 130 is solid testimony to the fact that if Jesus had wished to raise a revolt against Gentile domination, He would have found a following without difficulty. The temptations as a whole picture the clash between what Jesus knew Himself called by God to do, and what popular expectation demanded. And here we may note that Jesus does not set forth the positive features of His own conception of His ministry. He rejects a number of proposals quite decisively, as much as to say: Whatever else God may have appointed me to do, it is not this or this. This fact suggests that the experience recorded in the stories belongs to the early part of His work.

Granted that the stories report a genuine experience of Jesus, He must Himself be the narrator of them. It may be conjectured that they were told to the disciples after He had been recognised by them as Messiah and began to inform them of what Messiahship had come to mean for Him. In that case the present position of the section becomes highly significant, following as it does close upon the Messianic prophecies of John the Baptist. For, as we have seen, John's preaching represents the Jewish messianic expectation in its purest and highest form, the picture of a king who will reign in absolute righteousness. Even this is not good enough, much less the vulgar hope of a potentate who would, with God's assistance, restore the vanished glories of the kingdom of David and Solomon. Here is the characteristic of the temptation stories which it is difficult to attribute to anyone except Jesus Himself, the violence with which He flings behind His back the common Jewish notion of messiahship, and says: ' This is not the will of God, but the wiles of the Devil.' [1]

3. THE PREACHING OF JESUS

(a) THE BEATITUDES AND WOES (73, 74)

MT. 5[1-3, 4, 6, 11, 12]

5 1 And seeing the multitudes, he went up into the mountain: and when he had sat
2 down, his disciples came unto him; and he opened his mouth and taught them, saying,
3 Blessed are the poor in spirit; for theirs is the kingdom of heaven.
4 Blessed are they that mourn; for they shall be comforted.
6 Blessed are they that hunger and thirst after righteousness; for they shall be filled.
11 Blessed are ye when men shall reproach you, and persecute you, and say all manner of evil against you falsely, for my sake.
12 Rejoice, and be exceeding glad : for great is your reward in heaven: for so persecuted they the prophets which were before you.

LK. 6[20-26]

6 20 And he lifted up his eyes on his disciples, and said, Blessed are ye poor : for yours is
21 the kingdom of God. Blessed are ye that hunger now : for ye shall be filled. Blessed are ye that weep now : for ye shall laugh.
22 Blessed are ye, when men shall hate you, and when they shall separate you *from their company*, and reproach you, and cast out your name as evil, for the Son of man's
23 sake. Rejoice in that day, and leap *for joy* : for behold, your reward is great in heaven : for in the same manner did their
24 fathers unto the prophets. But woe unto you that are rich! for ye have received
25 your consolation. Woe unto you, ye that are full now! for ye shall hunger. Woe *unto you*, ye that laugh now! for ye shall
26 mourn and weep. Woe *unto you*, when all men shall speak well of you! for in the same manner did their fathers to the false prophets.

[1] So Karl Holl, *Gesammelte Aufsätze*, ii. 16 f.

20. The sermon as given in Mt. is much longer than that in Lk. The explanation is that in Mt. material from another source or sources is combined with the sermon as given in Q. This Q form is probably preserved in Lk. 6^{20-49}. In both Mt. and Lk. the sermon is addressed to the disciples. Mt. $5^{1f.}$ suggests that it is the disciples alone, Jesus having gone away with them to the hills to avoid the crowds. Cf. 8^1 and 8^{18}. The Lucan context, on the other hand, suggests the presence of the crowd as well as of the disciples . Cf. 6^{12-19}.

Lk. gives four beatitudes followed by four corresponding woes. In Mt. 5^{3-12} there are nine beatitudes, of which four—given above—correspond to those in Lk., four (Mt. 5^{7-10}) may be assigned to M., and one—' Blessed are the meek . . . '— seems to be an adaptation of Ps. 37^{11}; it may, however, also belong to M. In Lk. beatitudes and woes are in the second person throughout; in Mt. all except the last ($5^{11f.}$) are in the third person. In utterances of this sort the third person is much the commonest in the Old Testament, though the second person is also found occasionally there and quite frequently in other Semitic literature. The second person is probably the original here. In Mt. the phrasing of the beatitudes has been given a more edifying turn than in Lk. Here also it is likely that the stark simplicity of Lk. is the original. This simpler form is strongly eschatological. It paints in vivid colours the contrast between things as they are and things as they will be in the good time that is coming.

The first beatitude states the contrast in general terms. The meaning of the word ' poor ' is given by such passages as Ps. 69^{29-36}. In the Judaism of the last two centuries B.C. the term was practically a synonym for *Ḥāsīd*, i.e. ' saintly ' or ' pious,' in the best sense. So, for example, *Ps. Sol.* 10^7 : ' The saints also shall give thanks in the assembly of the people : and God will have mercy on the poor in the (day of) gladness of Israel.' Here ' the saints ' and ' the poor ' stand in synonymous parallelism. Again in the Talmud they are treated as synonyms (*Ber.* 6^b). The use of the word ' poor ' in this way goes back to the days of the Seleucid rule in Palestine. Then it was the poor above all who remained faithful to their religion and the Law. The well-to-do upper classes in Jerusalem allowed themselves to be tainted with heathenism. Hence ' rich ' tends to mean ' worldly ' and ' irreligious,' and ' poor ' the opposite. In this specialised sense the word is used here. In Mt. the paraphrase ' poor in spirit ' is an attempt to make this fact clear. The Kingdom of God belongs to these simple devoted souls, because they belong to it, having accepted God's will as the only rule of their lives. As they submit themselves to the obligations of the Kingdom, so they become heirs of its privileges.

21. This is now drawn out in more detail. The contrast between the present and the future lot of the godly is that between a famine and a feast. In Jewish and Christian imagery the good time coming is likened to a great feast. Cf. Is. 49^{10-12} ; Ps. 107^{1-9} ; Mt. $8^{11f.}$‖Lk. 13^{28-30} ; Mt. 22^{1-10}‖Lk. 14^{15-24} ; Lk. 22^{30}. It is obvious that this imagery is not to be taken literally. Cf. Amos $8^{11ff.}$—' a famine in the land, not a famine of bread, nor a thirst for water, but of hearing the words of the Lord.' For the Rabbis the Law is bread and wine. So here in Mt. we have the paraphrase ' hunger and thirst after righteousness,' which gives something near the sense of the bare statement in Lk. The righteousness in question

is not just the conformity of human conduct to a divinely appointed standard. It is the fulfilment by man of God's will *and* the fulfilment by God of His own purposes of grace and mercy (cf. Dodd, *Romans*, p. 12). In that fulfilment those who are now dissatisfied with themselves and with life as it is, will find complete satisfaction.

This contrast between the present and the future is as sharp as the difference between weeping and laughter, sorrow and joy. In Mt. the strong words are softened down, unnecessarily. For the sentiment and wording cf. Ps. 137[1-4] and 126. There the exiles sit by the waters of Babylon and weep ; and when God turns again the captivity of Zion, their mouth is filled with laughter and their tongue with singing. Just so the saints are homesick for the Kingdom of God ; and their joy cannot be perfected till it comes. Cf. Phil. 3[20].

22. But the present hardship of the godly does not consist only in the fact that what they hope for lies still in the future : there is also the fact that they live in a world where they and the thing for which they stand must inevitably be hateful to many. Hence they must be prepared to face hostility, opposition, and persecution for the sake of the Kingdom. Mt. 5[10] may be regarded as the M version of this beatitude. Cf. also Jas. 2[7]; 1 Pet. 4[14, 16]; Mk. 13[9-13]. There are some important differences between Mt. and Lk. in this beatitude. Lk. mentions four kinds of persecution, Mt. only three; and the wording is not the same. Lk. supplies the subject ' men '; it is probably not part of the original text of Q. These opponents ' hate.' They exclude the objects of their hatred from their society, and ' reproach ' them. It has been suggested that the separation or exclusion here referred to is a form of synagogue discipline, but this is unlikely (Billerbeck iv. 331). Corresponding to these three activities we have in Mt. ' reproach ' and ' persecute.' If we take ' persecute ' in the sense of ' drive away ' (cf. Mt. 10[23], 23[34]), it will be roughly equivalent to ' separate ' or ' exclude ' in Lk. The fourth kind of persecution is slander. The Lucan phrase ' cast out your name as evil ' is best explained as an attempt to translate a phrase found both in Hebrew and Aramaic. Literally translated the phrase runs ' send out an evil name upon,' and it means ' issue an evil report about.' Mt. gives the sense of the phrase correctly in the words ' speak evil against you.' The words ' all manner of ' and ' falsely ' are added by the writer of the Gospel. The former is a well-known editorial device of his, and the latter is an example of his somewhat pedantic way of making sweeping statements more precise. These hardships are borne ' for the sake of the Son of Man ' (Lk.) or ' for my sake ' (Mt.). Here the original wording is probably preserved by Lk. Mt. alters ' Son of Man ' to the personal pronoun elsewhere (Mt. 16[21]), and may well have done so here. The Son of Man is the embodiment of all that the persecuted saints hold sacred. On the meaning of ' Son of Man ' see my *Teaching of Jesus*, pp. 211–234.

23. The experience of opposition and persecution is no occasion for discouragement or complaint, rather for rejoicing. For it is a proof that those who endure it stand in the succession of the great servants of God in past ages, who received like treatment in their day. Moreover, it is only for a time. The fulfilment of God's purpose is sure, and in that consummation God's servants will find their reward with joy. The difference between Lk.'s ' for in the same manner did

their fathers unto the prophets ' and Mt.'s ' for so persecuted they the prophets which were before you ' may be explained by a slight confusion of the original Aramaic. It is probable that Lk. has the sense correctly in this case. Cf. Mt. 23²⁹ᶠᶠ·‖Lk. 11⁴⁷ᶠᶠ·.

The fourth beatitude should almost certainly be assigned to a late date in the ministry. It differs in tone from the other three. We feel that we are no longer concerned with the saints and their destiny in general terms, but with the fate of a definite group of people in a particular situation. Here Jesus is speaking to His chosen helpers about the things that actually threaten Him and them. Now in the Mission Charge (Lk. 10¹⁻¹⁶) the tone is still hopeful. Opposition there will be ; but, on the whole the messengers may expect a friendly reception. For a parallel to the fourth beatitude we have to go to passages like Mk. 10³⁸⁻⁴⁰; Lk. 19⁴¹⁻⁴⁴ ; Mk. 13⁹⁻¹³, 8³⁴⁻³⁸ ; and a number of others, all of which fall after Peter's confession. (Cf. *The Teaching of Jesus*, pp. 205 f.)

24–26. After the beatitudes Lk. has a corresponding set of four woes. These have no parallel in Mt., and it can be urged against them (*a*) that they are hardly in place in an address to *disciples* (but cf. Jas. 4¹³–5⁶), and (*b*) that they necessitate a fresh start in *v.* 27. On these grounds it has been suspected that they did not stand in Q, but have been brought in by Luke from another source, or else are his own composition. There is no entirely satisfactory solution of the problem. It might, however, be conjectured that the earliest form of the section consisted of the first three beatitudes with the corresponding woes ; that the fourth beatitude— a genuine saying of Jesus—was added later; and that finally the fourth woe was produced to round off the whole.

24, 25. The rich in the first woe are the opposite of the poor in the first beatitude. That is, they are the worldly people who care for and trust in material goods, money and the things that money can buy; who serve Mammon rather than God. They have their satisfaction now in the way they choose, and that is all. They lack nothing except the things that really matter. They have unlimited pleasure, but not lasting joy. When the day of reckoning comes, the things that now satisfy and please them will have an end and they will have nothing to put in their place.

26. This verse is the counterpart to *vv.* 22 f. Here again we are aware of a change of tone. It is the disciples who are being warned to beware of popularity. A ready welcome for themselves and their message may well be the first sign that they are being unfaithful to Him who sent them, forgetting the Kingdom of God, and coming to terms with the world. If this is a genuine saying of Jesus, it also must belong to the later period of the ministry.

(*b*) THE LAW OF LOVE (75)

MT. 5⁴⁴, ³⁹, ⁴⁰, ⁴², 7¹²	LK. 6²⁷⁻³¹
5 44 But I say unto you, Love your enemies, and 39 pray for them that persecute ·you. But whosoever smiteth thee on thy right 40 cheek, turn to him the other also. And if any man would go to law with thee, and	6 27 But I say unto you which hear, Love your enemies, ǀdo good to them that hate 28 you, ‖bless them that curse you, ǀpray for 29 them that despitefully use you.‖To him that smiteth thee on the *one* cheek ǀoffer

take away thy coat, let him have thy cloke
42 also. Give to him that asketh thee, and
from him that would borrow of thee turn
not thou away.

7 12 All things therefore whatsoever ye would
that men should do unto you, even so do
ye also unto them: for this is the law and
the prophets.

also the other; ||and from him that taketh
away thy cloke |withhold not thy coat also.
30 ||Give to every one that asketh thee; ||and
of him that taketh away thy goods ask
31 them not again.||And as ye would that
men should do to you, |do ye also to them
likewise. ||

The Lucan form of this piece of teaching appears to be the original. In Mt. the precepts and examples have been broken up and rearranged to fit into the ethical Antitheses from M. (see below, p. 159); and the Golden Rule has been transferred to the end of a long section in the Sermon on the Mount. The Lucan version, on the other hand, is in strict poetic form, showing parallelism and—on retranslation into Aramaic—rhythm and rhyme. See C. F. Burney, *The Poetry of our Lord*, p. 169. In the text above the ends of lines and half-lines are marked || and | respectively.

27a. A fresh start is made with the words ' But I say unto you which hear.' Those who think that the woes are an insertion here explain the words as an attempt to restore the connexion which has been broken. But see below on Mt. 5⁴³⁻⁴⁸, p. 161.

27b, 28. A general exhortation carrying a stage farther the commandment ' Thou shalt love thy neighbour as thyself.' In Mk. 12²⁸⁻³⁴ Jesus puts love to neighbour as an obligation second only to love to God. In the parable of the Good Samaritan He tacitly declines to set any limit to the scope of the term ' neighbour.' Here He carries His attitude to its logical conclusion: ' neighbour ' includes everyone, even enemies. That this love is not mere sentiment is shown by the remaining injunctions. It involves active beneficence, unfailing courtesy, and a goodwill so genuine that it will stand the test of being brought into the presence of God in prayer. It does not involve countenancing anything that is false or cruel or unjust. And it leaves room for a prophetic indignation against things which are clearly contrary to the will of God, and for maintaining unflinchingly what one sees to be true and good. In these two verses we have the completest expression of the ideal personal relation between man and man. And it is put forward primarily as that and nothing else. At a very early date it comes to be claimed that it is also the best policy: ' Love those that hate you, and you will have no enemy ' (*Didache* 1³). This may be true—it is very optimistic—but it is not the reason assigned by Jesus. The kind of love of which He is here speaking would cease to be what it is if any ulterior motive, however excellent, entered into it. It must be the spontaneous self-manifestation of a human nature that has been touched by the love of God and must now reproduce that love in itself in all relations with other men and women. In setting up this absolute ideal Jesus neither quotes nor contradicts Jewish principles. He brings to sharp and decisive expression ideals which show themselves in Judaism at its best ; and He clears away much in Jewish teaching that was inconsistent with those ideals. He says in effect to the Judaism of His day : This and this alone is the will of the God of our fathers and our God. His originality lies in the way in which He goes to the very heart of the prophetic religion, and sets free a spirit which was in danger of being stifled by Rabbinic fundamentalism on the one hand, and, on the other, by the very natural resentment and hatred of the Gentile, engendered by centuries of foreign oppression. It is necessary to remember that this ideal was set up before Jews whose land at that very moment was occupied, and not for the first time, by a foreign army; that among the theologians the question whether the word ' neighbour ' in Lev. 19[18] could apply to a non-Jew was a matter for serious debate; that in the popular Apocalyptic literature there was little love wasted on the Gentile nations. It was in this context that Jesus gave to Judaism, and to the world, this unqualified and uncompromising statement of the true Israelite ideal.

29 f. The change from plural to singular indicates that we have here a separate saying. The sermon consists of such utterances on various occasions brought together and topically arranged to show the general character of the preaching of Jesus. The purport of the injunctions in vv. 29 f. is, in Paul's words (Rom. 12[21]), ' Be not overcome of evil, but overcome evil with good,' which is more than nonresistance. It is the requiting of active enmity with active love. Lk. has first two cases of personal violence. (a) The slap on the face. Mt. here is more precise—' the right cheek.' But with a right-handed assailant the first blow would normally be on the left cheek of the victim. What is probably meant is a buffet with the back of the hand, which, according to the Mishnah (Baba Kamma 8[6], Danby, p. 343), was a peculiarly insulting assault and punishable by a specially heavy fine. (b) Robbery of a garment. Here Mt. pictures a very different case— a legal action. The plaintiff claims the defendant's shirt. According to Jewish law the actual possessor is deemed to have the legal right to the article possessed, and the onus of proof is on the claimant. The injunction given by Jesus then means that the defendant is not to insist on possessor's right, but to surrender the shirt. He is to go farther than that. He is also to give the plaintiff what he has not claimed, and apparently could not claim (Ex. 22[25 f.], Dt. 24[12 f.]), the outer garment, a sort of blanket or plaid, which served as clothing by day and bedding by night. G. Kittel thinks that the Mt. version is original, and Lk. an adaptation for Gentile readers who would not understand the technicalities of Jewish law. In Lk. we have the picture of the footpad who snatches the outer garment, and is to be presented with the shirt as well. In either case the issue would be nudism, a sufficient indication that it is a certain spirit that is being commended to our notice —not a regulation to be slavishly carried out. But this fact does not entitle us to evade the demand, which is here put forward in an extreme case. What Jesus here says is seriously, even if not literally, meant ; and His followers have the task of manifesting the spirit of the injunction in the varied situations which arise in actual life.

In v. 30 two fresh cases are dealt with, the beggar and the borrower. The followers of Christ are to be sensitive to the plight of the poor and needy, and their sympathy is to be practical. Lk.'s ' everyone ' may be his own. It does not appear in Mt.; and, as it is a favourite word with that evangelist, it is unlikely that he would have left it out, had it stood in Q. The second half of the injunction is a little obscure. In Mt. 5[42] we have a command not to repulse a borrower. This looks like an attempt to interpret what is given in Lk. It may be that the meaning here is: When someone has borrowed your property, do not be constantly dunning him to let you have it back. In all these transactions delicacy and consideration of the feelings of the other man are essential. Cf. *Ecclus*. 20[15]: 'To-day he lendeth, to-morrow he will demand it back : hateful is such an one.'

31. All that has been said so far can be summed up in the Golden Rule, which is now given in its positive form. The change from singular to plural is to be noted. The Lucan form is more original than that in Mt. 7[12] (see above, pp. 18 f.). Mt. adds the comment : ' For this is the law and the prophets.' He does the same kind of thing in Mt. 20[40]||Mk. 12[31]. The Rule appears in the negative form in *Tobit* 4[15] : ' What thou hatest, do to no man.' Hillel, who belonged to the generation before Jesus, gave as the essence of the Jewish Law the precept : 'What is hateful to thee do not to anyone else,' adding ' this is the whole Law and the rest is commentary ; go and study.' This negative form also appears in some MSS. in Acts 15[29] and in the *Didache* (1[2]). In the *Letter of Aristeas* § 207 we have advice to a king in these terms: ' As thou desirest that evils should not befall thee, but to partake of all that is good, thou shouldst act in this spirit to thy subjects and to offenders, and shouldst very gently admonish such as are virtuous; for God draws all men (to Him) by gentleness ' (Thackeray's transl.). Here we approach the positive form. The question whether the positive form states a higher moral ideal than the negative is one of little moment. The Rule as Jesus gives it is a rule of thumb for the purpose of guiding those who already accept the fundamental principles of love to God and love to neighbour when they are puzzled about what to do for the best in particular cases. What is important is that for Jesus these two great principles and this rule supersede all other rules and regulations, and are a complete and sufficient equipment for the adventure of good living. (See further my *Teaching of Jesus*, pp. 302–308.)

Additional Note

In his *Rabbinic Literature and Gospel Teachings*, pp. 103 f., Dr. C. G. Montefiore says : ' I would not cavil with the view that Jesus is to be regarded as the first great Jewish teacher to frame such a sentence as: " Love your enemies, do good to them who hate you, bless them that curse you, and pray for them who ill-treat you " (Lk. 6[27, 28]). Yet how much more telling his injunction would have been if we had had *a single story* about his doing good to, and praying for, a single Rabbi or Pharisee! One grain of practice is worth a pound of theory. . . . But no such deed is ascribed to Jesus in the Gospels. Towards his enemies, towards those who did not believe in him, whether individuals, groups, or cities (Matt. 11[20-24]), only denunciation and bitter words! The injunctions are beautiful, but how much more beautiful would have been a *fulfilment* of those injunctions by Jesus himself.'

This criticism raises the whole question of Jesus' consistency, how far His life answers to His own demands. This question cannot be properly discussed or finally settled on historical grounds, because we have not the materials. But on the point raised by Dr. Montefiore the following observations may be made:

(1) The bulk of the material which has gone to make our Gospels was collected together at a time when the relation between the Jewish religious leaders and the

Church was one of hostility. The former recognised in the new faith a threat to all that they held dear, and they did their utmost to put down what was, from their point of view, a dangerous heresy. There was thus everything to induce collectors of traditions about Jesus to select those stories which showed Rabbis and priests in an unfavourable light, and to leave on one side tales which showed Jesus in a benevolent attitude towards the enemies of the Church. Indeed, it is not, I think, improbable that sayings of Jesus have been made sharper and more bitter in the process of tradition by reason of this bitterness between Synagogue and Church.

(2) Much of the denunciation in the Gospels comes under the heading of prophetic indignation. Much of it is directed, not so much against persons as against abuses in the system. In trying to find the personal attitude of Jesus to the Rabbi or Pharisee from the Gospels, we are in much the same position as if we had to discover from Hansard's reports of debates on matters of critical importance the personal relation of statesmen to one another.

(3) From what we are told in the Gospels it appears that Jesus found that the most urgent need was among another class of people than the Rabbis and Pharisees. He was known as the friend of publicans and sinners, doubtless because He gave them the first claim on His time and strength.

(4) While it is true that Jesus defended Himself with vigour when He was attacked, it must be admitted that many of His denunciations are the answer, and we must maintain the proper answer, to criticisms levelled from the Pharisaic point of view at His teaching and practice. Where a scribe came to Him in a friendly spirit and with a desire to find truth, he received friendly and generous treatment (Mk. 12[28-34]). If we have a story of how Jesus publicly rebuked one synagogue-ruler (Lk. 13[15-17]), we read also of the raising of the daughter of Jairus.

(5) If it is right to quote Mt. 11[20-24] as showing the indignation of Jesus at the refusal of the Galilean towns to receive His message, it is equally legitimate to quote Lk. 13[34] and Lk. 19[41 ff.] as evidence of the real feelings of Jesus in the face of opposition and enmity.

To sum up, I should say that, taking such evidence as we have, it suggests that the opportunities for the kind of thing that Dr. Montefiore desiderates were few, partly because Jesus gave Himself so much to the service of those who needed help more than the Rabbis and Pharisees, partly because when He did come into contact with the Rabbis and Pharisees, His first task was commonly to defend Himself against their criticisms. Secondly, even if there were stories of friendly contacts, their chance of survival in the formative period of the tradition would be small. And thirdly, we have evidence that behind the indignation of Jesus at the rejection of His message there is a deep disappointment and sorrow.

(c) IMPERFECT AND PERFECT LOVE (75)

MT. 5[46, 47, 44, 45, 48]	LK. 6[32-36]
5 46 For if ye love them that love you, what reward have ye? do not even the[1] publicans 47 the same? And if ye salute your brethren only, what do ye more *than others*? do not even the Gentiles the same?	6 32 And if ye love them that love you, |what thank have ye? |for even sinners love those 33 that love them.||And if ye do good to them that do good to you, | what thank have ye? 34 |for even sinners do the same.||And if ye

44 Love your enemies. . . .

45 that ye may be sons of your Father which is in heaven : for he maketh his sun to rise on the evil and the good, and sendeth rain
48 on the just and the unjust. Ye therefore shall be perfect, as your heavenly Father is perfect.

¹ That is, *collectors or renters of Roman taxes :* and so elsewhere.

lend to them of whom ye hope to receive, | what thank have ye? |even sinners lend to
35 sinners, to receive again as much.||But love your enemies, and do *them* good, and lend, ¹ never despairing ;||and your reward shall be great, |and ye shall be sons of the Most High: |for he is kind toward the un-
36 thankful and evil.||Be ye merciful, even as your Father is merciful.

¹ Some ancient authorities read *despairing of no man.*

In this passage the kind of love demanded by Jesus is further defined. First it is distinguished from the kind of human affection and benevolence which rests largely upon a more or less enlightened self-interest, and finds its proverbial expression in such sayings as ' Dog does not eat dog ' or ' Honour among thieves ' (32–34). Genuine love is purged of selfishness and considers only the need of its objects, not their attitude to the giver, nor their deserts. In this respect it is akin to God's love (35 f.). In Lk. the poetic structure is again visible. In Mt. the sayings have been rearranged and abbreviated, and other matter has been incorporated with them. It is quite possible that the amount of other matter in Mt. outweighs what has been taken from Q.

32–34. Three verses with a recurring refrain in the middle of each. The ordinary sort of relation established on the level of ' One good turn deserves another ' is all very well, but there is nothing in it to deserve the special approval of God. The word rendered ' thank ' in R.V. is the regular word in the LXX for the approbation and goodwill of a superior, especially the approval and favour of God. ' Sinners ' is a term of wide application in later Judaism. The opposites ' righteous ' and ' sinners ' are common in the Psalms and later literature. The ' righteous ' are those who know and keep the Law: ' sinners ' are those who either do not know it (e.g. the Gentiles, cf. Gal. 2¹⁵) or who, knowing it, cannot or will not obey its provisions. For ' sinners ' Mt. has ' publicans ' (5⁴⁶) and ' Gentiles ' (5⁴⁷). The word here translated ' Gentiles ' occurs three times in Mt., but not in Mk. or Lk.; and the collocation of ' publican ' and ' Gentile ' is found again in Mt. 18¹⁷.

35. The new standard of goodness must rise above the ' fifty-fifty ' level. Love must be given where none is given in return, benefits conferred where none are deserved, loans must be made when lending seems to be throwing good money after bad. The words ' never despairing ' do not mean ' never despairing of getting your money back.' They apply to all three injunctions and mean the same thing as Paul's ' Let us not be weary in well-doing ' (Gal. 6⁹), or ' Be ye stedfast, unmoveable, always abounding in the work of the Lord, forasmuch as ye know that your labour is not in vain in the Lord ' (1 Cor. 15⁵⁸). The way of Jesus may seem to be useless, even futile, when judged by immediate results; but it must be persevered with in the faith that it is God's way. Those who so persevere will have their reward in the approval of God, if not in the thanks of men. More than that, they will have that approval in its highest form; God will recognise them as His sons, for something of His own nature will be reflected in them. The name here used for God ' The Most High ' is, as a Divine proper

name, peculiar to Lk. ($1^{32, 35, 76}$, 6^{35}) and Acts (7^{48}). It is used as an adjective 'the most high God' in Mk. 5^7 = Lk. 8^{28}; Acts 16^{17}; Heb. 7^1. It is common in later Jewish writings—Ecclesiasticus (about 50 times), Daniel, *Enoch*, *Jubilees*, and 4 *Ezra* (68 times in chs. 3–14). It was a term admirably fitted to form a bridge between Judaism and the higher Greek religion, between the one Lord of Jewish monotheism and the First Principle of Greek thought. To the Jew it expressed the ideas of the supremacy and omnipotence of God. The corresponding verse in Mt. has 'your Father which is in heaven' a characteristic Matthæan and Jewish term. Of the two Lk. is the more likely to be original. On the verse as a whole cf. *Ecclus* 4^{10} (Hebrew).

'Be as a father to orphans, and in place of a husband to widows;
Then God will call thee "son," and will be gracious to thee, and deliver thee from the Pit.'

For 'Then God will call thee "son"' the Greek version has 'And thou shalt be as a son of the Most High.'

36. The motive and driving power for this way of living is now stated. It is the imitation of God. This way is right and good because it is God's way. He is kind to those who deserve no kindness. (Mt. 5^{45} expresses this in a different and probably independent form.) But it is not mere imitation of a Divine standard set up, so to speak, in heaven. It is the reproduction, in daily life and in relations with other men, of something which has come down to earth and touched our own lives. We are to copy this god-like way—and are able to do so—just because we have experienced its working ourselves. We love, because He first loved us (1 John 4^{19}). For 'merciful' (Lk.) Mt. has 'perfect.' In favour of the former is the fact that in the Old Testament the epithet 'merciful' is given to God, hardly ever to man; and the epithet 'perfect' to man, never to God. As God is the standard of comparison, we expect a recognised *Divine* attribute to be mentioned. On the Merciful as a name for God see Dalman, *Words of Jesus*, p. 204. On the imitation of God as a Jewish ideal see Abrahams, *Studies in Pharisaism and the Gospels*, ii. 138 ff.

(d) JUSTICE AND MERCY (76)

MT. $7^{1, 2}$	LK. $6^{37, 38}$
7 1 Judge not, that ye be not judged. 2 For with what judgement ye judge, ye shall be judged: and with what measure ye mete, it shall be measured unto you.	**6** 37 And judge not, and ye shall not be judged :| and condemn not, and ye shall not be condemned :|release, and ye shall 38 be released:|give, and it shall be given unto you;|good measure,|pressed down, shaken together,|running over,|shall they give into your bosom.|For with what measure ye mete| it shall be measured to you again.|

37, 38. On the rhythmical structure of Lk. $6^{37 f.}$ see Burney, *The Poetry of our Lord*, pp. 114 and 123. The parallel in Mt. is shorter; but the longer version in Lk. shows the poetic form and is probably the original. It also links up better with the thought of the preceding passage. The singling out of God's mercy as the attribute which is to be the model for human conduct leads naturally to the question how the misdeeds of others are to be treated. We are to return good for evil; but surely we are not to condone the evil. Even if we forgive the offence, we must surely condemn it. Jesus says it is not our business to sit in judgement on our neighbours. The whole business of judging persons is in God's hands, for He alone knows the secrets of men's hearts. This does not mean that we are not to use all the moral insight we possess in order to discover what is right and wrong; but that we are to confine ourselves to that field and refrain from passing judgement on persons. For our judgement is itself a factor in shaping their lives, and a harsh judgement may help a fellow-creature on the road to perdition. ' Give a dog a bad name—and hang him.' ' Release ' in this context may mean ' acquit ' or ' forgive.' The former sense is scarcely appropriate since man is not to sit in judgement at all, either to condemn or to acquit. For the sense ' forgive ' we may compare Mt. 18²⁷, where the verb is used of remitting a debt. And as debt is a common figure for sin, the transition from the idea of cancelling a debt to forgiving an offence is an easy one. And this brings us back to the positive demand to give. Not content with cancelling the debt, the merciful man makes a further gift to the debtor: so the merciful man not only forgives the wrong, he goes farther and shows kindness to the wrongdoer. And in so doing he finds favour with God. ' They ' is probably—as in the Rabbinic literature—a way of referring to God. ' Good measure, pressed down, shaken together, running over ' is a figure drawn from the corn-market where corn is being sold by measure. We are told that the corn-merchants in Egypt still use Arabic terms corresponding to those in Lk., when commending their wares to a prospective customer. They offer corn at so much a measure ' shaken, pressed together, overflowing.' [1] ' Bosom ' means the fold formed by a loose garment overhanging a girdle. This was often used as a pocket (Plummer). There is in the picture of the packed and overflowing measure the idea of a kindness on God's part that will go far beyond the kindness of man, so that even a little kindness on man's part meets with a lavish reward from God. For the measure that man uses with his fellows is the measure that God will use with him. (Another version of this saying, Mk. 4²⁴.)

These illustrations are drawn from the law-court and the market-place; but the thing they illustrate is not a legal or a commercial relation between God and man or between man and man. What underlies all that Jesus here says is a simple and fundamental spiritual law. ' Forgive and you will be forgiven: condemn and you will be condemned ' is not tit for tat, but the expression of the truth that nothing more surely shuts out a man from love than a censorious and unforgiving disposition. He who will not forgive closes his own heart against God's forgiveness. He who despises and hates his fellow-man closes his own heart against God's love.

[1] I am indebted for this information to Mr. G. Swan, Superintendent of the Egypt General Mission.

(e) A COLLECTION OF PARABLES (76–78)

MT. 15[14], 10[24, 25a]	LK. 6[39, 40]
15 14 Let them alone: they are blind guides. And if the blind guide the blind, both shall fall into a pit. **10** 24 A disciple is not above his [1] master, 25a nor a [2] servant above his lord. It is enough for the disciple that he be as his [1] master, and the [2] servant as his lord.	**6** 39 And he spake also a parable unto them, Can the blind guide the blind? shall they 40 not both fall into a pit? The disciple is not above his [1] master: but every one when he is perfected shall be as his [1] master.

[1] Or, *teacher*.
[2] Gr. *bondservant*.

[1] Or, *teacher*.

The section Lk. 6[39-49] consists of a series of parables all of which, except these first two, have parallels in Mt.'s Sermon on the Mount. The fact that Mt.'s parallels to Lk. 6[39 f.] are in a different context casts some doubt on the right of these verses to a place here, the more so as they come somewhat awkwardly between the exhortations about judging and the parable bearing on the same topic (Lk. 6[41 f.]). On the other hand, it may be said that Mt. 15[14] is an obvious insertion in the place where it stands. It is not even connected with the M material which immediately precedes it. And Mt. 10[24 f.] equally is part of an artificial construction made by the first evangelist; and, where it stands the point of the saying is that the disciple need not expect to fare any better than his master. It is possible that both Mt. 15[14] and 10[24 f.] belong to M rather than Q. The question whether Lk. 6[39 f.] should be regarded as Q or L will then depend on whether it can be shown to fit into its present context.

39, 40. The question form (Lk.) is probably the original rather than the assertion (Mt.). In Mt. the saying is made to refer to the Pharisees. Cf. Mt. 23[16] (M) where the Scribes and Pharisees are called ' blind guides.' This reference is not necessarily implied in the saying as it stands in Lk. It is perhaps better to make the connexion with what has gone before in this way: No man is free from sin, and therefore no man has the right to condemn another. But equally no man has the right to dictate to another what is his duty. For one sinner to judge another is a piece of presumption. For one sinner to legislate for another is to court disaster. The only person who is fit to guide others is one who has himself seen the light. The only true teacher is he who has first been taught of God. This prepares the way for the claim that where such a teacher appears he is to be heard with respect. One who is thus inspired is not on the same level as other men. He is not there to be argued with, but to reveal spiritual truth. Those who hear him are not superiors to whom he submits his opinions for approval, but pupils to whom he declares truth, which they reject at their peril. The most that the pupil can do is, by humbly receiving the truth, and applying it in faith to his own life, to come to see it as truth with something of the same clearness and certainty that the master sees it. This is, in fact, the justification for the authority with which Jesus teaches. He does not say, ' I will undertake to demonstrate,' but ' I tell you; and if you accept what I tell you in humility and trust, you will find for yourselves that it is true.' This verse is then the statement in general terms of a principle, which is presently to be more particularly applied in 6[46, 47-49].

(i) *The Mote and the Beam* (76)

MT. 7[3-5]	LK. 6[41, 42]
7 3 And why beholdest thou the mote that is in thy brother's eye, but considerest not 4 the beam that is in thine own eye? Or how wilt thou say to thy brother, Let me cast out the mote out of thine eye; and 5 lo, the beam is in thine own eye? Thou hypocrite, cast out first the beam out of thine own eye; and then shalt thou see clearly to cast out the mote out of thy brother's eye.	6 41 And why beholdest thou the mote that is in thy brother's eye, but considerest not 42 the beam that is in thine own eye? Or how canst thou say to thy brother, Brother, let me cast out the mote that is in thine eye, when thou thyself beholdest not the beam that is in thine own eye? Thou hypocrite, cast out first the beam out of thine own eye, and then shalt thou see clearly to cast out the mote that is in thy brother's eye.

This parable takes up the thoughts just enunciated. It is directed to those who, themselves sinners, presume to sit in judgement on and to correct their fellows. The agreement in language between Mt. and Lk. is close. The parable is frankly hyperbolical. One utter absurdity is exposed by another. Cf. Mk. 10[25] (Camel and eye of needle) and Mt. 23[24] (Gnat and camel). The mote and beam recur in another connexion in a saying of R. Tarphon (*c.* A.D. 100), who said: ' I should be surprised if there were anyone in this generation who would accept correction. If one says to a man, " Remove the spelk from your eye," he will reply, " Remove the beam from yours." ' The figure may belong to a Jewish proverbial saying, which has been used independently by Jesus and Tarphon, or it may be that the saying of Tarphon is a piece of anti-Christian polemic, with this parable in view. We know that Tarphon was a strong opponent of the Palestinian Christians. (See Schürer, ii. 444 f.)

41, 42. *The mote.* The Greek word means any small dry object, a splinter or chip of wood, small twig or the like. The parable starts from the fact that man is by nature quick to perceive and arraign wickedness in other people. The contemplation of human folly and sin, with the aid of a looking-glass, is a less congenial occupation; but very salutary. This truth is a commonplace both in Greek and Hebrew thought. ' It is better to condemn one's own faults than those of others' (Democritus (5th cent. B.C.) fr. 60). Having perceived the shortcomings of our neighbours, we now proceed to put them right. The blind will lead the blind. This zeal for the reformation of others coupled with a serene complacency about one's own life is stigmatised by Jesus as hypocrisy. If the desire for social reformation were really sincere, the reformation would begin at home. It is still the case that our natural inclination is to make ourselves happy and our neighbours virtuous: and the conjecture may be hazarded that the world would be a better and a happier place if we attempted instead to make ourselves better and our neighbours happier. The followers of Jesus certainly have the task of showing the right way to others; but to do that they must first find it themselves. And an essential preliminary to that is to discover where they themselves are at fault. ' First cast the beam out of thine own eye.' A reformed character is the most effective instrument for effecting the reformation of others.

(ii) *Character and Life* (77)

MT. 7[16-20]

7 16 By their fruits ye shall know them. Do *men* gather grapes of thorns, or figs of 17 thistles? Even so every good tree bringeth forth good fruit; but the corrupt tree 18 bringeth forth evil fruit. A good tree cannot bring forth evil fruit, neither can a corrupt tree bring forth good fruit. 19 Every tree that bringeth not forth good fruit is hewn down, and cast into the fire. 20 Therefore by their fruits ye shall know them.

MT. 12[33-35]

12 33 Either make the tree good, and its fruit good; or make the tree corrupt, and its fruit corrupt: for the tree is known by its 34 fruit. Ye offspring of vipers, how can ye, being evil, speak good things? for out of the abundance of the heart the mouth 35 speaketh. The good man out of his good treasure bringeth forth good things: and the evil man out of his evil treasure bringeth forth evil things.

LK. 6[43-45]

6 43 For there is no good tree|that bringeth forth corrupt fruit;||nor again a corrupt 44 tree|that bringeth forth good fruit.||For each tree is known by its own fruit.|| For of thorns men do not gather figs,| nor of a bramble bush gather they grapes.|| 45 The good man out of the good treasure of his heart bringeth forth that which is good; |and the evil *man* out of the evil *treasure* bringeth forth that which is evil:||for out of the abundance of the heart his mouth speaketh.||

The material here given by Lk. is split up and incorporated with other material in Mt. Lk. 6[43]||Mt. 7[18]; Lk. 6[44a]||Mt.12[33b], cf. Mt. 7[16a], [20]; Lk. 6[44b]||Mt.7[16b]; Lk. 6[45]||Mt. 12[35], [34b]. Mt. 7[16-20] is attached to a warning against false prophets (7[15]) and indicates how they may be distinguished from true. Mt. 12[33-35] is inserted into Jesus' defence against the charge of casting out demons by Beelzebul. It is curious that in both cases we find expressions borrowed from the preaching of John the Baptist: Mt. 7[19] = Mt. 3[10b], and in Mt. 12[34] ' Ye offspring of vipers ' from Mt. 3[7]. It is difficult to resist the conclusion that the Q material given here in Lk. has been freely adapted in Mt. to other purposes.

The passage as it stands in Lk. makes a good connexion with what precedes. The influence of a man on his fellows, for better or worse, depends on his life; and the quality of his life depends on his character.

43, 44. The word translated ' corrupt ' means properly ' rotten,' ' putrid,' ' rancid.' This cannot be the meaning here, for the fruit of even the worst trees is ripe before it is rotten. Moreover, the same adjective is used in Mt. 13[48] to describe freshly-caught fish, which would certainly not be rotten, though they might well be unfit for food. It seems therefore that we must understand ' corrupt ' to mean something like ' useless,' ' worthless.' This curious use of the Greek word (*sapros*) may be influenced by the fact that the Aramaic verb ' to be evil ' (*b'ēsh*) is etymologically identical with the Hebrew verb *bā'ash*, ' to stink.' Also the wild grapes in Isaiah's parable of the Vineyard (Is. 5[2], [4]) have a name in Hebrew, which means literally ' stinking things.' We may then perhaps think of the ' corrupt tree ' as a wild tree producing fruit—not rotten—but unsuitable for eating because it is harsh and bitter. The transition from this to the next verse is then easy and straightforward. If we cannot distinguish the crab tree from Cox's

Orange by inspection, we have only to try the fruit. The fig and the grape, two of
the most highly prized fruits of Palestine, are not gathered from thorn bushes and
brambles. So Luke. Mt. 7[16] has grapes from thorns and figs from thistles. It is
worth noting in favour of Mt. that the word translated ' thorn ' here is the word
used in the LXX for the ' wild grapes ' of Is. 5[2, 4]; and also that the fruit of the
thistle bears at least a faint resemblance to a fig. The plants mentioned are typical
weeds (Gen. 3[18], Hos. 10[8]), from which no useful produce can be expected.

45. The obvious application of the parable. From the good man a good influence will come. The words ' bringeth forth ' in Mt. and Lk. represent two
different Greek words, which are themselves alternative translations of a single
Aramaic word, which in this context can best be rendered by ' utters.' The
utterances of the man express his character, for speech is the outpouring of what is
in the heart. So the Rabbis use the expressions ' What is in the heart is in the
heart ' and ' What is in the heart is in the mouth ' for feelings repressed and feelings expressed respectively. The parable has a special application to the man who
admonishes and instructs others. If he is not a good man himself, his instruction
is worthless, as useless for its purpose as the produce of thorns and thistles for food.
If his own character is good, then his words will be the bread of life to others, who
receive them and live by them. But given such a teacher, will men act upon his
teaching? The experience of Jesus is given in the next verse.

MT. 7[21]	LK. 6[46]
7 21 Not every one that saith unto me, Lord, Lord, shall enter into the kingdom of heaven; but he that doeth the will of my Father which is in heaven.	6 46 . And why call ye me, Lord, Lord, and do not the things which I say?

The form in Mt. is fuller, but that in Lk. is probably the original. It is more
direct and personal, and it links up both with what precedes and what follows.
Mt. takes the saying as if it meant that true piety consists in producing good
actions, as a good tree produces good fruit. But the tree parable here is not the
same as the tree parable in the preaching of John the Baptist. As we have seen,
the point here is that good teaching can come only from one who is good at heart.
Now Jesus says to His contemporaries: ' You recognise my right to teach, and you
pay respect to me by calling me " Lord, Lord "; but you do not act on my teaching.' There are few sadder words in the New Testament than Lk. 6[46]: and all the
pathos has gone in the version given by Mt.

(iii) *Wise and Foolish Building* (78)

MT. 7[24-27]	LK. 6[47-49]
7 24 Every one therefore which heareth these words of mine, and doeth them,|shall be likened unto a wise man, which built 25 his house upon the rock:||and the rain descended,|and the floods came,|and the winds blew,| and beat upon that house;| and it fell not:| for it was founded upon 26 the rock.|| And every one that heareth these words of mine, and doeth them not,|	6 47 Every one that cometh unto me, and heareth my words, and doeth them, I will 48 shew you to whom he is like: he is like a man building a house, who digged and went deep, and laid a foundation upon the rock: and when a flood arose, the stream brake against that house, and could not shake it: [1] because it had been well 49 builded. But he that heareth, and doeth

shall be likened unto a foolish man, 27 which built his house upon the sand:||and the rain descended,|and the floods came,| and the winds blew,|and smote upon that house;|and it fell:|and great was the fall thereof.||

not, is like a man that built a house upon the earth without a foundation; against which the stream brake, and straightway it fell in; and the ruin of that house was great.

1 Many ancient authorities read *for it had been founded upon the rock;* as in Matt. vii. 25.

This section, which concludes the Sermon both in Mt. and Lk., contains a double parable. The two characters, the wise builder and the foolish, are described in turn and in parallel terms. This duplication is a common feature of the teaching of Jesus. Cf. Mk. $2^{21f.}$, 9^{43-48}; Lk. 12^{24-28} = Mt. 6^{26-30}; Lk. 13^{18-21} = Mt. 13^{31-33}; Lk. 10^{13-15} = Mt. 11^{21-23}; Lk. 4^{25-27}, 13^{2-5}, 14^{28-33}, 15^{4-10}; Mt. 13^{44-46}, 23^{16-21}. The parallelism of structure in the two parts of the parable is better preserved in Mt. than in Lk. In Lk. this feature has been sacrificed to the Greek style of the evangelist.

A similar parable is attributed to Elisha ben Abuya (*c.* A.D. 120). It is to the effect that a Jew, who has much knowledge of the Law and many good works, is like a man who lays stone foundations for his house and builds thereon with sun-dried brick. Though floods may come, the house is not affected because its foundations are sound. But the man who has much knowledge of the Law and no good works is like a man who lays foundations of sun-dried brick, and builds thereon with stone. If only a small flood comes, the house collapses because the foundations are not sound.

47–49. Lk.'s ' every one that cometh unto me ' is not strictly relevant to the parable, which is concerned only with hearing and doing. On the other hand, ' a man ' seems better than Mt.'s ' a wise man ' (*v.* 24) and ' a foolish man ' (*v.* 26). The issue shows plainly enough that one is wise and the other foolish; and Mt. is apt to paint the lily. Lk. appears to have elaborated the laying of the foundation. His builder takes great pains to get down to rock. But the point is not the amount of labour expended, but the choice of a suitable foundation. The simpler statement of Mt. is to be preferred, as is also Mt.'s dramatic description of the tempest. ' Because it had been well builded ' (Lk.) misses the point. We are to imagine both houses as equally well built. The only difference is that correctly given by Mt.: one was founded on rock and the other on sand. In his description of the second house and its fate Lk. is briefer. The fuller form in Mt. is more likely to be the original.

The point of the parable lies in the difference between the two foundations: the one sure and stedfast, the other shifting and unstable. All the other features in the two cases are identical. The rock is ' hearing and doing.' The teaching is heard, and accepted, and becomes a firm conviction issuing in action. Such solid conviction makes a stable foundation; it gives unity and consistency to life. The sand is ' hearing without doing.' The teaching is heard; but it is only one among many interests and motives, and there is no solid centre of conviction in the man's life. So in the day of stress and crisis the one man stands firm and the other goes under. What this crisis is we can only conjecture. It may mean one of those times of severe testing, which constantly recur in human history, when men's loyalty to their professed beliefs is tried to the uttermost. Or it may mean the final judgement (cf. 1 Cor. 3$^{13\,ff.}$). In favour of the former view are such sayings as Mt. 10$^{32\,f.}$ = Lk. 12$^{8\,f.}$ (Q); Mk. 13^{13}, etc.

We have already seen reason for thinking that the Temptations are placed in Q after the Messianic prophecy of John in order to bring out the difference between John's conception of the Messiah and that which Jesus held. When we consider the Sermon as a whole, we may well think that its position is also significant, and again by way of contrast with John's preaching. John's sermon begins with a denunciation of his hearers : ' Ye offspring of vipers, who warned you to flee from the wrath to come ? ' Jesus begins : ' Blessed are ye poor: for yours is the kingdom of God.' Thus at the outset the contrast is stated. For John the coming kingdom means primarily judgement; for Jesus it means primarily deliverance, salvation. For John the God, whose kingdom it is, is inflexible righteousness; for Jesus He is the Father whose nature is to be merciful (6$^{35\,f.}$). The demand of John is for repentance coupled with such reformation of conduct as will satisfy the Judge in the coming assize; the demand of Jesus is that men should show in their hearts and lives that merciful love that is characteristic of God. The most that John can hold out to his followers is escape from the coming wrath; Jesus speaks of the coming kingdom as a gift from God to man, a gift bringing satisfaction and joy to the sons of God.

It is thus quite wrong to say, as is sometimes said, that Jesus merely takes up and carries on the mission of John. His preaching has much in common with John's. There is the same insistence on moral issues in both, the same demand that men should turn from sin to righteousness, from the service of self and Mammon to the service of God, the same sense of the urgency of the message. These things are extremely important; but they are not so important as the points where Jesus differs from John and goes far beyond him. These positive and characteristic features are brought out plainly in the Sermon, and John's preaching, the Temptations, and Jesus' preaching are so placed at the beginning of Q that a reader cannot fail to see the contrast between the best that could be offered under the old order and the new thing that has come into the world with Christ.

4. *THE CENTURION OF CAPERNAUM* (79)

MT. 8$^{5-10,\ 13}$	LK. 7$^{1-10}$
8 5 And when he was entered into Capernaum, there came unto him a centurion, beseeching him, and saying, Lord, my [1] servant lieth in the house sick of the palsy, 7 grievously tormented. And he saith unto 8 him, I will come and heal him. And the centurion answered and said, Lord, I am not [2] worthy that thou shouldest come under my roof: but only say [3] the word, 9 and my [1] servant shall be healed. For I also am a man [4] under authority, having under myself soldiers: and I say to this one, Go, and he goeth; and to another, Come, and he cometh; and to my [5] servant,	7 1 After he had ended all his sayings in the ears of the people, he entered into Capernaum. 2 And a certain centurion's [1] servant, who was [2] dear unto him, was sick and at the 3 point of death. And when he heard concerning Jesus, he sent unto him elders of the Jews, asking him that he would-come 4 and save his [1] servant. And they, when they came to Jesus, besought him earnestly, saying, He is worthy that thou 5 shouldest do this for him: for he loveth our nation, and himself built us our synagogue. 6 And Jesus went with them. And when he

10 Do this, and he doeth it. And when Jesus heard it, he marvelled, and said to them that followed, Verily I say unto you, [6] I have not found so great faith, no, not 13 in Israel. . . . And Jesus said unto the centurion, Go thy way; as thou hast believed, so be it done unto thee. And the [1] servant was healed in that hour.

[1] Or, *boy*.
[2] Gr. *sufficient*.
[3] Gr. *with a word*.
[4] Some ancient authorities insert *set*: as in Luke vii. 8.
[5] Gr. *bondservant*.
[6] Many ancient authorities read *With no man in Israel have I found so great faith*.

was now not far from the house, the centurion sent friends to him, saying unto him, Lord, trouble not thyself: for I am not [3] worthy that thou shouldest come 7 under my roof: wherefore neither thought I myself worthy to come unto thee: but [4] say the word, and my [5] servant shall be 8 healed. For I also am a man set under authority, having under myself soldiers: and I say to this one, Go, and he goeth; and to another, Come, and he cometh; and to my [1] servant, Do this, and he doeth 9 it. And when Jesus heard these things, he marvelled at him, and turned and said unto the multitude that followed him, I say unto you, I have not found so great 10 faith, no, not in Israel. And they that were sent, returning to the house, found the [1] servant whole.

[1] Gr. *bondservant*.
[2] Or, *precious to him*. Or, *honourable with him*.
[3] Gr. *sufficient*.
[4] Gr. *say with a word*.
[5] Or, *boy*.

Cf. John 4[46-53].

This section raises a number of peculiar problems. (1) It is the only narrative in Q. (2) The agreement between Mt. and Lk. is confined to the dialogue. In the narrative setting the only verbal agreements are in the three words ' entered,' ' Capernaum,' and ' centurion.' (3) The dialogue is a complete and self-contained story apart from the narrative: and the point of it is the saying of Jesus, ' I have not found so great faith, no, not in Israel.' (4) This statement of Jesus implies a ministry that has already lasted some time. Such words are hardly appropriate at the beginning of His mission. (5) Immediately after this saying Mt. has another Q oracle (Mt. 8[11f.]) which has a parallel in Lk. 13[28f.]. These facts suggest some inferences which may now be given in descending order of probability. (1) It is almost certain that the dialogue alone belongs to Q. The narrative framework is supplied independently by Mt. and Lk. (2) The fact that in their narrative settings Mt. and Lk. agree on the place Capernaum suggests that, either in Q or in the tradition of the Palestinian Church, the incident was definitely located in that town. (3) It is possible that this fact is responsible for the present position of the whole story (dialogue + narrative) in Mt. and Lk. A story about a centurion at Capernaum must be placed in the Capernaum period of the ministry. (4) It is possible that the original unexpanded dialogue stood later in Q. (5) It may be conjectured that Mt. 8[11f.] is, for once, not conflation, but an indication of the original context of the dialogue. If this were so, we should have an excellent connexion between the first three sections of Q and what is now the fifth: John's question to Jesus and Jesus' testimony to John (Lk. 7[18-35]), where the difference between John and Jesus, which is implicit in the first three sections of Q, is made quite clear and definite.

1-5. Lk. begins by making the connexion between the conclusion of the Sermon and this incident. Mt. inserts the cleansing of the leper (Mk. 1[40-45]) between the departure from the mountain and the arrival in Capernaum. Mt. makes the centurion approach Jesus in person and state his trouble. Lk. begins with a narrative of the circumstances, describing the illness of the servant and the regard in which he was held by his master. The word used by Lk. means ' slave.' In Mt. 8⁶ the Greek word may mean ' servant ' or ' son,' much the same as the English word ' boy.' In John (4⁴⁶) the invalid is definitely the ' son ' of the petitioner. In Lk. 7⁷ the ' slave ' of v. 2 has become ' boy ' as in Mt.: and in v. 8 the centurion speaks of his ' slave ' as if the slave were another person than his ' boy.' Taking all these facts into consideration, the balance of probability is in favour of 'son' rather than 'slave.' For the phrase 'who was dear to him' (R.V.) offers two alternatives in the margin. The papyri provide numerous examples where the adjective is used to describe soldiers with long and distinguished service, and it has even been suggested that in Lk. 7² the epithet means ' honourable,' and originally belonged to the centurion. As the text stands it doubtless means that the centurion held his slave in high esteem. Lk. having understood ' boy ' in the sense ' slave ' rather than ' son ' produces a reason for the remarkable concern of the master, a concern which would be perfectly natural and would need no explanation, if it was a case of father and son. The centurion does not, as in Mt., come himself to Jesus, but sends first a deputation of Jewish elders with the request that Jesus will come and heal the slave. The elders here are the local magistrates, the leading citizens of the town. It may be noted that the participation of the Jewish elders is hardly consistent with the subsequent statement, ' I have not found such faith in Israel.' The elders come to Jesus and add their own pleas to the centurion's request. The reason for their friendly attitude to the heathen soldier is now given. He has shown a friendly disposition towards Jews and Judaism, and proved his goodwill by building the local synagogue. He is portrayed as one of a very numerous class in this period, Gentiles who were attracted by Jewish monotheism and by the high moral standard of Judaism. Such people were adherents of the synagogue without actually becoming proselytes to Judaism. There are inscriptions from Egypt showing that synagogues were occasionally built by non-Jews; and the Palestinian Talmud has a story of the presentation of a synagogue lamp by a Roman emperor. The ruins of a synagogue at Tell Hum, the probable site of Capernaum, belong to a later period.

6–10. Jesus accedes to the request of the elders and proceeds with them. Near the house they are met by a second deputation, this time composed of the centurion's friends. They are charged with a message from the centurion practically identical with what, in Mt., the centurion himself says to Jesus. The second deputation is an expression of the humility of the man, and this is made explicit in v. 7, which has no parallel in Mt. and is not to be regarded as original. The power of Jesus is such that it will be sufficient if He gives the command that the boy should recover. The word ' only ' in Mt. 8⁸ is editorial: cf. Mk. 2²⁶, Mt. 12⁴; Mk. 11¹³, Mt. 21¹⁹; Mk. 13³², Mt. 24³⁶. Lk.'s ' and my servant shall be healed ' is literally ' and let my boy be healed,' imperative followed by a jussive, a construction found in Hebrew. The words ' for I also am a man set under authority ' are difficult; for the centurion goes on at once to say that he has men under him to whom he gives orders, whereas the opening phrase means one who receives orders. Torrey (*The Four Gospels*, p. 292) tries to get over the difficulty by supposing that the word ' set ' is a misrendering of an Aramaic original, and that the true rendering would be something like ' exercising authority.' This is not convincing, because the word ' set ' occurs only in Lk. Another and perhaps more likely explanation is that there has been confusion of the two senses of the Aramaic preposition *tĕḥōth*. This word means both ' under ' and ' in place of.' What the centurion really said was, ' I am the representative of the government ' or ' the deputy of the commander-in-chief.' This makes sense with what follows and also makes clear the analogy between the centurion's position and that of Jesus. Both are representatives of the king, the centurion of Antipas (probably) and Jesus of God; and both have such authority as belongs to their respective offices. Jesus is deeply impressed by the centurion's saying and utters the comment, ' I have not found such faith, no, not in Israel.' It is now clear what the faith in question is: it is the recognition by the centurion of Jesus as the representative of God, endowed with Divine power and authority. With this comment the original Q section closes. Mt. adds another saying from Q (Mt. 8[11f.]), which *may* be part of the original context of the passage. Lk. goes on immediately to report the cure. He does not mention any command of Jesus that the cure should take place, unless the comment ' I have not found such faith ' is meant to effect the cure. All that happens is that the messengers have their conversation with Jesus, and, on their return, find the ' slave ' in good health. Mt. (8[13]) makes Jesus speak the word asked for: ' As thou hast believed, so be it done unto thee,' and the cure takes place forthwith.

The miracle has several features in common with the story of the Syro-Phœnician woman (Mk. 7[24-30]||Mt. 15[21-28]). In the one case we have mother and daughter, in the other father and son (probably). In both cases the petitioner is a Gentile; in both Jesus is persuaded to perform the miracle by an apt saying of the petitioner; in both the healing is performed in the absence of the patient (the only two cases of this sort in the Synoptic Gospels); and, curiously, in both the accounts differ widely in the narrative part and agree closely in the dialogue. It is possible, as Dibelius suggests, that the original form of the incident in Mk. 7[24-30] also contained little more than the conversation between Jesus and the woman.

A similar miracle is related of R. Hanina ben Dosa (*c.* A.D. 70). Here the son of Rabban Gamaliel was ill and the Rabban sent two scholars to Hanina to request his prayers. Hanina saw them coming, went up on to the roof of his house and prayed. When he came down he said to the messengers: ' Go, for the fever has left him. . . .' They took careful note of the time, and, on returning home, learned that that was the exact moment at which the fever had left the patient (b. *Berach*, 34b.). Cf. Mt. 8[13], ' in that hour,' and John 4[50-53].

The most probable conclusion of the whole matter would seem to be that the dialogue is the original kernel, which belonged to Q and probably stood later in the document. This original has been furnished with two different narrative settings, which appear in Mt. and Lk. These narrative settings agree in stating that the cure was effected; and this was probably implied in the original Q story. But the interest of the compiler of Q was not in the cure of the boy, but in the contrast between the faith of the Gentile and the unbelief of Israel. Now if the dialogue with the centurion is out of place here, we again get a good connexion between the Sermon of Jesus and the next Q section, which is John's enquiry from prison and the reply of Jesus. This will give one large block of Q material : (1) the preaching of John comprising exhortation to repentance and Messianic prophecy; (2) the temptations of Jesus in which the current Messianic idea is rejected; (3) the preaching of Jesus displaying a higher morality than John's; and (4) a final settlement of accounts between Jesus and John, in which it is made clear how great John was, and how much greater is the new thing that has come into the world with Jesus.

5. JOHN AND JESUS: THE FINAL RECKONING

(a) JOHN'S CHALLENGE TO JESUS (81)

MT. 11[2-6]

LK. 7[18-23]

11 2 Now when John heard in the prison the 3 works of the Christ, he sent by his disciples, and said unto him, Art thou he that 4 cometh, or look for another? And Jesus answered and said unto them, Go your way and tell John the things which 5 ye do hear and see: the blind receive their sight, and the lame walk, the lepers are cleansed, and the deaf hear, and the dead are raised up, and the poor have [1] good 6 tidings preached to them. And blessed is he, whosoever shall find none occasion of stumbling in me.

[1] Or, *the gospel.*

7 18 And the disciples of John told him of all 19 these things. And John calling unto him [1] two of his disciples sent them to the Lord, saying, Art thou he that cometh, or look 20 we for another? And when the men were come unto him, they said, John the Baptist hath sent us unto thee, saying, Art thou he 21 that cometh, or look we for another? In that hour he cured many of diseases and [2] plagues and evil spirits; and on many 22 that were blind he bestowed sight. And he answered and said unto them, Go your way, and tell John what things ye have seen and heard; the blind receive their sight|the lame walk,||the lepers are cleansed,|and the deaf hear,||the dead are raised up,|the poor have [3] good tidings 23 preached to them.||And blessed is he, whosoever shall find none occasion of stumbling in me.||

[1] Gr. *certain two.*
[2] Gr. *scourges.*
[3] Or, *the gospel.*

The narrative introduction is much longer than in Lk. than in Mt. As Mt. is apt to cut down redundant detail (cf. his treatment of Mk. 5[21-43], Mt. 9[18-26]), it is possible that Lk. 7[18-20] is original. The words ' in prison ' (Mt. 11[2]) may also belong to Q. Lk. could leave them out because he had already reported the imprisonment of John (3[19 f.]). Lk. 7[21] is an editorial insertion to provide the messengers with first-hand evidence. The answer in *vv.* 22 f. is poetry, which Lk. has treated as if it were prose.

18. ' All these things.' If *vv.* 18–20 belong to Q, and if our interpretation of Lk. 7[1-10] is correct, ' these things ' can only be the contents of the Sermon (6[20-49]). The contrast between that and the preaching of John is sufficiently violent to call forth the question: ' Art thou he that cometh? ' The coming one, according to John, was to execute judgement: Jesus comes preaching mercy and loving-kindness. This is the falsification of John's predictions.

19–23. The two disciples have a parallel in Mk. 6[7], 11[1], and in the

story of R. Hanina (above, p. 65). It may be doubted whether ' the Lord '
stood in Q. It is a favourite title of Jesus in Lk. ' He that cometh ' refers back
to John's own preaching (Lk. 3[16]||Mt. 3[11]). The implication of the question is
that John has already entertained the idea that Jesus may be the fulfilment of
his prophecy; but that what he now hears causes him to have serious doubts.
The kind of Messiah that John has in mind would not behave like this. The
messengers bring the question to Jesus, who at once, according to Lk., proves His
title by performing a series of miracles. This is just the sort of sign which Jesus
elsewhere refuses to give. In Mt. this section from Q is brought into the story
at a later stage when a sufficient number of miracles have already been related
in the ordinary course of the narrative. It is difficult to believe either that *v.* 21
stood in Q or that it corresponds to the facts. The real answer of Jesus is not a
sign, but a reiteration of what He stands for. It is cast in poetic form (cf. Burney,
The Poetry of our Lord, p. 117); and is expressed in terms reminiscent of the great
promises in Isaiah (cf. Is. 26[19], 29[18 f.], 35[5 f.], 61[1]). The point of this declaration
lies in the deliberate contrast between it and the preaching of John. John looked
for the destruction of the morally unfit. Jesus affirms that His business is not
the destruction of such people, but their restoration to moral health. ' They
that are whole need not the physician, but they that are sick.' Jesus thus in
effect answers John's question by saying: ' Yes—but not the kind that you
expected.' He adds to this words which mean: ' Do not be distressed if things
are not turning out in accordance with your plan.'

(*b*) JESUS' TESTIMONY TO JOHN (82)

MT. 11[7-11, 16-19]   LK. 7[24-35]

11 7 And as these went their way, Jesus
began to say unto the multitudes concerning John, What went ye out into the
wilderness to behold? a reed shaken with
8 the wind? But what went ye out for to
see? a man clothed in soft *raiment*? Behold,
they that wear soft *raiment* are in kings'
9 houses. 1 But wherefore went ye out? to
see a prophet? Yea, I say unto you,
10 and much more than a prophet. This is
he, of whom it is written,
Behold, I send my messenger before
thy face,
Who shall prepare thy way before
thee.
11 Verily I say unto you, Among them that
are born of women there hath not arisen
a greater than John the Baptist: yet he
that is 2 but little in the kingdom of
heaven is greater than he.
16 But whereunto shall I liken this generation? It is like unto children sitting
in the marketplaces, which call unto
17 their fellows, and say, We piped unto
you, and ye did not dance; we
18 wailed, and ye did not 3 mourn. For
John came neither eating nor drinking,

7 24   And when the messengers of John were
departed, he began to say unto the multitudes concerning John, What went ye out
into the wilderness to behold? a reed
25 shaken with the wind? But what went ye
out to see? a man clothed in soft raiment?
Behold, they which are gorgeously ap-
parelled, and live delicately, are in kings'
26 courts. But what went ye out to see? a
prophet? Yea, I say unto you, and much
27 more than a prophet. This is he of whom
it is written,
Behold, I send my messenger before
thy face,
Who shall prepare thy way before
thee.
28 I say unto you, Among them that are born
of women there is none greater than John:
yet he that is 1 but little in the kingdom of
29 God is greater than he. And all the
people when they heard, and the publicans, justified God, 2 being baptized with
30 the baptism of John. But the Pharisees
and the lawyers rejected for themselves the
counsel of God, 3 being not baptized of
31 him. Whereunto then shall I liken the
men of this generation, and to what are

19 and they say, He hath a [4] devil. The Son of man came eating and drinking, and they say, Behold, a gluttonous man, and a winebibber, a friend of publicans and sinners! And wisdom [5] is justified by her [6] works.

¹ Many ancient authorities read *But what went ye out to see? a prophet?*
² Gr. *lesser.*
³ Gr. *beat the breast.*
⁴ Gr. *demon.*
⁵ Or, *was.*
⁶ Many ancient authorities read *children*: as in Luke vii. 35.

32 they like? They are like unto children that sit in the marketplace, and call one to another; which say, We piped unto you, and ye did not dance; we wailed, and ye 33 did not weep. For John the Baptist is come eating no bread nor drinking wine; 34 and ye say, He hath a [4] devil. The Son of man is come eating and drinking; and ye say, Behold, a gluttonous man, and a winebibber, a friend of publicans and 35 sinners! And wisdom [5] is justified of all her children.

¹ Gr. *lesser.*
² Or, *having been.*
³ Or, *not having been.*
⁴ Gr. *demon.*
⁵ Or, *was.*

This section is marked by close verbal agreement between Mt. and Lk. It falls into two parts: (i) Lk. 7²⁴⁻²⁸, containing the testimony proper, and (ii) 7³¹⁻³⁵ grim comment on the reception given to John and Jesus. These two parts are separated in Lk. by a statement that John was accepted by the common people and rejected by the recognised exponents of piety and morality (7²⁹ᶠ·). In Mt. there is at this point a passage about John (Mt. 11¹²⁻¹⁵). The first half of it is perhaps Q; it has a parallel in Lk. (Mt. 11¹²ᶠ·‖Lk. 16¹⁶). The rest appears not to belong to this source. It is of course possible that Mt. 11¹²⁻¹⁵ comes from M. What is reasonably certain is that it did not stand in Q at this point. For Lk. 16¹⁶ stands in a group of disconnected oracles, and it is not credible that Lk. would have removed it from its place here, where it would fit admirably, to another place, where it has no proper context at all. It is much more likely that Mt. has provided the detached saying with an appropriate setting.

24–26. 'Were departed' (Lk.), 'went their way' (Mt.), is a very common translation variant. Jesus, having justified His own way to John, now proceeds to justify John to the people. The wilderness was the place of John's preaching (Mk. 1⁴). 'What did you go out into the wilderness to see? A reed shaken by the wind? Surely not.' The point of this first suggestion may be understood in the light of a Rabbinical saying (b. *Ta'anith* 20a): 'Man should strive to be tender like the reed and not hard like the cedar.' The meaning is that the reed gives to every wind that blows, the cedar does not. The question then means: 'Did you expect to find the Baptist a complaisant, easy-going person? Of course you did not. Indulgence was the last thing you would expect from him.' Then the reference to soft apparel becomes clear. (The wearers of it are in kings' courts; but John is in the king's prison.) Just as John had no mercy on others, so he had no mercy on himself. His austerity was austerity all round. He was neither self-indulgent nor indulgent to other people. He was a prophet of the same kind as Amos.

27. But John is more than a prophet. He is a prophet in the fullest sense, and something more. This is explained by the quotation from the Old Testament, which follows. Under the influence of statements, such as Mt. 11¹⁴, which identify John with Elijah, the text quoted here is usually taken to be from Mal. (3¹), where the return of Elijah is prophesied (4⁵ᶠ·). The quotation re-

appears in Mk. 1[2] in almost identical words. There it is combined with Is. 40[3]. The text of Malachi, however, differs considerably from the text quoted in Q:

Mal. 3[1]. Behold I send my messenger, and he shall prepare *the* way before *me*.

Lk. 7[27]. Behold I send my messenger *before thy face*, who shall prepare *thy* way before *thee*.

Ex. 23[20] (LXX). And behold I send my messenger before thy face, that he may guard thee in the way.

In Malachi, and in *Ecclesiasticus* (48[1-11]), the messenger (= Elijah) is the forerunner of God Himself, and there is no idea of a Messiah. In John's preaching John is the forerunner of the Messiah, and there is no suggestion that John identifies himself with Elijah. In the Pseudepigrapha the place of Elijah in the last days is taken by others, and he plays no distinctive part. In the popular expectation in the days of Jesus, as reflected in Mk. 8[28], 9[11-13], John 1[21], the return of Elijah was looked for; but Mk. 8[28] is clear evidence that John was not identified with Elijah. In Rabbinic speculation [1] there are three Elijah doctrines: (*a*) Elijah belongs to the tribe of Gad. He prepares the way for God and is the redeemer of Israel. This view is a development of that in *Ecclus.* 48. It does not have much influence on Rabbinic thought. (*b*) Elijah belongs to the tribe of Benjamin. He is the forerunner of the Messiah, and his principal task appears to be the announcement of the good news of the Messiah's coming. (*c*) Elijah belongs to the tribe of Levi. He is the High Priest of the Messianic age. He is thus a colleague of the Messiah rather than his forerunner. In the early Christian speculation both Elijah and Moses have a rôle in the last days. The belief in a return of Moses could be based on Dt. 18[15, 18], 34[10]. Moses appears with Elijah in the Transfiguration scene; and the two witnesses in Rev. 11[3-13] are probably Moses and Elijah (see Charles, *Revelation*, i. 281). 'The prophet' (John 6[14], 7[40]) is perhaps a reference to the second Moses promised in Dt. 18. Cf. also John 1[21], where the Baptist is asked, ' Art thou Elijah ? ' and ' Art thou the prophet '; and Mk. 8[28], ' one of the prophets.' In this maze of conflicting views it is difficult to arrive at any satisfactory conclusion. The identification of John with Elijah is stressed especially in Mt. It is denied absolutely in John, where the Baptist himself is made to reject the identification (John 1[21]). This is very strange if the identification was known to have been made by Jesus Himself. It is also very strange that Jesus should make a quotation which agrees word for word with the LXX version of Ex. 23[20] in its first part, and with nothing in the Old Testament in its second part. One solution, proposed by J. Weiss and accepted by Merx, is that *v.* 27 is an interpolation in Lk. For this there is a certain amount of textual evidence. Its removal still leaves an excellent connexion between *v.* 26 and *v.* 28. It would then be likely that it did not stand in Q. Its place in Mt., which is textually secure, could be explained by the supposition that it belonged to the collection of ' testimonies ' of which Mt. made use. Its presence in the MSS. of Lk. would be due to early assimilation to Mt. In favour of this hypothesis is the fact that the same text has found its way into Mk. 1[2], where it makes nonsense. The reason why the identification of John with Elijah

---

[1] See the account given by Billerbeck, *Kommentar*, iv. pp. 781–798.

was stressed, and that particularly in Mt., may be found in Justin's *Dialogue with Trypho* (§§ 8, 49, 110), where Justin has to meet the objection from the Jewish side that the true Messiah must be anointed and proclaimed as such by Elijah.

If, then, *v.* 27 does not belong to Q, what is meant by saying that John is a ' prophet—and more ' ? The natural interpretation appears when we look at John's work. For he did not only prophesy: he also acted. He announced the coming of ' the stronger one,' and he actively prepared a people for the approaching crisis. He is John the Baptist rather than John the prophet.

28. ' Verily ' in Mt. 11[11] is probably original, and perhaps also ' prophet ' in Lk. John is the greatest man that ever lived—outside the Kingdom of God. This saying implies that the kingdom is in some real sense a present reality, and bound up with Jesus and His followers. For we cannot suppose that the words are meant to exclude John from the coming Kingdom altogether. There is a distinction between the Kingdom as it is revealed in the present age in Jesus and those who follow Him, and the Kingdom as it is to be fully realised in the future. John does not belong to the former; but he has his share in the latter. The least in the Kingdom—in its present manifestation—is greater than John, not by what the least in the Kingdom does for God. John set up a record of devotion and self-sacrifice not easy to be equalled, much less surpassed. Where the least in the Kingdom has the advantage is in what God does for him here and now. The real parallel to John in the Old Testament is not Elijah but Moses. Just as Moses led the children of Israel to the borders of the Promised Land, but could not himself enter, so John led his followers up to the verge of the new order initiated by Jesus, but could not himself enter. He was the last and greatest of the heroes of faith, who looked for ' the city that hath foundations, whose builder and maker is God,' who died without receiving the promises.

29 f. These verses are not part of the testimony of Jesus to John, nor of Q. They may be from Lk.'s special source or they may be comment of his own. Cf. Mk. 11[27-33] and parallels, and Mt. 21[28-32]. For the collocation of Pharisees and lawyers see Lk. 11[37-52]. The curious expression ' justified God ' occurs frequently in the *Psalms of Solomon* (2[16], 3[5], 4[9], 8[7, 27, 31], 9[3]). It means that they acknowledged God to be in the right, when they confessed their sins and were baptized. The Pharisees and lawyers, who rejected John's baptism, tried to put themselves in the right against God. ' For themselves ': perhaps the Aramaic ethic dative, best left untranslated.

31 f., 33–35. The whole matter is rounded off with a parable, whose point is the unresponsiveness of men to any sort of high religious appeal. The way of John is too strait and the way of Jesus too lax for their taste. The parable of the children in the market-place, who will play neither weddings nor funerals, is perfectly simple and obvious. The ascetic discipline of John is rejected as madness. The same criticism was also passed on Jesus Himself (Mk. 3[22]), and, at a later date, on Mohammed (cf. Muir, *The Life of Mohammad* (1923), p. 48). It is a quick and easy way of dealing with such troublesome persons. ' The Son of Man ' here is obviously meant to refer to Jesus Himself. It is probable that the phrase here, both in Mt. and Lk., rests on a misunderstanding of an Aramaic idiom in which the phrase ' that son of man ' = ' that man ' is used as a periphrasis for the

first personal pronoun (see *The Teaching of Jesus*, pp. 217 f.). ' Glutton and wine-bibber ' need not be understood in the sense that the life of Jesus was a round of feasting. So far as the Gospels go, they do not suggest anything of the sort. Possibly the real offence was not the occasional feasts, but the failure to observe the fasts prescribed by Pharisaic piety (cf. Mk. 2[18 ff.]). ' Friend of publicans and sinners ' was true enough. But the quality of the friendship was determined by Jesus and not by the publicans and sinners. It raised them without lowering Him. Nevertheless there were doubtless many in that generation who were prepared to be convinced that a man is known by the company he keeps; and could not perceive that this very friendship lay at the heart of the Gospel (Mk. 2[15 ff.]). Yet in spite of indifference and opposition, both John and Jesus had found a response from the common people, who regarded John as a prophet (Mk. 11[32]) and heard Jesus gladly (Mk. 12[37]). They repented at the preaching of John (Lk. 7[29]; Mt. 21[31 f.]) and they accepted the friendship of Jesus. The wisdom of God was justified by results. As the text stands in Mt. and Lk., the results may be thought of as things accomplished, ' works ' (Mt.), or as the people who have been changed for the better, ' children ' (Lk.). It is, however, possible, as Lagarde suggested, that behind the two words lies a common Aramaic original. The point of the saying is not affected in any case; for it is simply that while the failure of both John and Jesus with one section of the community is a fact, it is also a fact that both John and Jesus found a response in another section, and that this response is itself a proof that the work of both was part of God's plan. The baptism of John *was* from heaven, and so is the good news, for which it paved the way and by which it is superseded.

With this testimony to John the first main section of Q comes to an end. In it the contrast is drawn, not between the Law and the Gospel, but between Prophecy and the Gospel. For John is not a scribe, but the greatest of the prophets. And, like most of the prophets, he is a lonely figure. He was admired, respected, reverenced, and feared. One wonders whether he was loved. He made every effort and every sacrifice in the service of his calling. He achieved much, yet somehow not enough. ' The least in the Kingdom of God is greater than he.' It is only on the background of the Gospel that we can see the magnificence of his failure. As against those who rejected him John was in the right. He was justified by those who repented at his call. But his message was not the Gospel, and in these Q passages the difference between John's prophetic message and the Gospel of Jesus is set forth. John's Messianic ideal is rejected; instead of the ruler and judge of his expectation there comes one who is first and foremost God's servant among men. John's message is ' Save yourselves from him that cometh.' He comes, and it appears that His business is to save men from themselves. With that something better than righteousness is given, and this is set out in the Sermon, with its insistence on the merciful love of God as the ground of man's hope and the norm of man's life. With the manifestation of this love in the world the Kingdom has in a real sense come and John's prediction is at once fulfilled and falsified.

B. JESUS AND HIS DISCIPLES

1. *CANDIDATES FOR DISCIPLESHIP* (138)

MT. 8[19-22]	LK. 9[57-62]
8 19 And there came [1] a scribe, and said unto him, [2] Master, I will follow thee whither-20 soever thou goest. And Jesus saith unto him, The foxes have holes, and the birds of the heaven *have* [3] nests; but the Son of 21 man hath not where to lay his head. And another of the disciples said unto him, Lord, suffer me first to go and bury my 22 father. But Jesus saith unto him, Follow me; and leave the dead to bury their own dead.	9 57 And as they went in the way, a certain man said unto him, I will follow thee 58 whithersoever thou goest. And Jesus said unto him, The foxes have holes, and the birds of the heaven *have* [1] nests; but the Son of man hath not where to lay his head. 59 And he said unto another, Follow me. But he said, Lord, suffer me first to go and 60 bury my father. But he said unto him, Leave the dead to bury their own dead; but go thou and publish abroad the king-61 dom of God. And another also said, I will follow thee, Lord; but first suffer me to bid farewell to them that are at my 62 house. But Jesus said unto him, No man, having put his hand to the plough, and looking back, is fit for the kingdom of God.

[1] Gr. *one scribe.*
[2] Or, *Teacher.*
[3] Gr. *lodging-places.*

[1] *Gr. lodging-places.*

The next five sections of Q all have to do with discipleship: its conditions, its duties, its privileges. The conditions are defined in this section by particular examples of would-be disciples who come to Jesus. Only two of Lk.'s three cases have parallels in Mt. It is therefore possible that Lk. 9[61f.] comes from L rather than from Q. Where Mt. and Lk. are parallel the agreement is close in the dialogue, but not in the narrative setting.

. 57, 58. The scene is the road with Jesus and others making a journey by land. In Mt. the interview takes place when Jesus is on the point of embarking on a boat. For Lk.'s ' a certain man ' Mt. has the more definite ' a scribe '; and this scribe addresses Jesus as ' Master.' The differences serve to show that most probably the dialogue is the whole of the original tradition. The would-be disciple anticipates a possible ' Follow me ' (cf. Mk. 1[17, 20], 2[14]) by himself offering to follow Jesus. The reply of Jesus is in effect: ' Count the cost.' It is metaphorically expressed, and opinions differ as to the meaning of the terms employed. The view that *v.* 58 is a popular proverb put into the mouth of Jesus may be dismissed. Proverbs, in order to survive, must contain some element of truth: and this proverb is required to say that man, in contrast to foxes and birds, has no home; which is plain nonsense. For man, of all the living creatures, has provided himself with the most elaborate and permanent lodgings. A second possibility is that ' Son of Man ' is here, as in Lk. 7[34], a periphrasis for ' I.' This is not, I think, likely. We require an interpretation which will give point to the strange conjunction of foxes and birds, as well as to the phrase ' Son of Man.' Now as an apocalyptic symbol the birds of the air stand for the Gentile nations, and the phrase is used again in this sense by Jesus in the parable of the Mustard Seed (see below, p. 123). In *Enoch* (89) ' foxes ' is a symbol for Ammonites, a people racially akin to, but politically enemies of Israel. Jesus Himself uses the epithet ' fox ' of Herod (Lk. 13[32]). Then the sense of the saying may be: everybody is at home in

Israel's land except the true Israel. The birds of the air—the Roman overlords, the foxes—the Edomite interlopers, have made their position secure. The true Israel is disinherited by them: and if you cast your lot with me and mine you join the ranks of the dispossessed, and you must be prepared to serve God under those conditions.

59, 60. Mt. and Lk. again differ over the setting of the saying. In Lk. Jesus gives His call, and the prospective disciple asks for a short postponement. In Mt. a disciple asks leave to go first and bury his father. The word ' first ' comes very awkwardly in Mt.'s account. Of the two, Lk.'s account is to be preferred. The duty of giving decent burial to the dead ranked high among the Jews in any case, and more especially in the case of near relatives. But the claims of the Kingdom of God take precedence of all others. Mt. gives the words ' Follow me ' in Jesus' reply to the request. They are more in place where Lk. has them. The saying ' Leave the dead to bury their own dead ' seems harsh, and it has been proposed to get over this by supposing a mistaken rendering of the Aramaic, and that what Jesus really said was something like ' Leave the dead to the burier of their dead ' (see Abrahams, *Studies in Pharisaism and the Gospels*, ii. 183 f.). The objection to this is that the son himself would be the natural and proper person to see to the burial of his father. Nor is it likely that there is a distinction in meaning between the dead who are to bury and those who are to be buried, the former being the spiritually dead, the latter the physically dead. The utterance is a paradoxical way of saying: ' That business must look after itself; you have more important work to do.' What the more important work is is explained by Lk. This extra clause, which has no parallel in Mt., probably does not belong to Q. The command is ' Follow me,' not—or at any rate not yet—' Go and preach.'

61 f. With this third case compare the call of Elisha (1 Kings 19^19-21). Elijah was less exacting than Jesus. The position is that the business of the Kingdom of God is urgent (Lk. 10²). The little parable about the plough would be obvious to an agricultural community. ' Fit for the Kingdom of God ' means here fit for its tasks, rather than worthy of its rewards.

In all three cases it is emphasised that the way of discipleship, or the service of the Kingdom, is not an easy thing. It offers no obvious advantages, and it makes extremely exacting demands. Those, therefore, who would attach themselves to Jesus must count the cost of their allegiance; they must be prepared to endure hardship; they must be willing to sacrifice their own feelings; they must give absolute priority to the work of the Kingdom, and give themselves to it with perfect singleness of purpose.

2. *THE MISSION CHARGE* (139)

The mission of the disciples is one of the best-attested facts in the life of Jesus. There is an account of the sending out of the Twelve in Mk. (6^6-13); it is clear from the agreements of Mt. and Lk. that Q contained a mission charge; the analysis of the long composite address in Mt. 9^37-10^42 shows that it contains material taken from Mk. and Q, and also from M, which must also have had a version of the mission charge. Lk. has two missions and two mission charges. The first of these (9^{1-6}) is derived from Mk. 6^{6-13}.   The second (10^{1-16}) contains matter which can certainly be assigned to Q, and other matter which we shall see reason to assign to L.   The mission charge is thus attested by all the sources.   For the purposes of analysis it will be convenient to consider the whole block, Lk. 10^{1-20}. The starting-point is the observation (Bussmann, *Synoptische Studien*, ii. 64) that the saying Lk. 22^{35} refers back to the mission charge.   Now 22^{35} stands in a context derived from Luke's special source.   The inference is that this source also contained an account of the mission charge.   If Lk. has preserved anything of the L charge we should expect to find it in 10^{1-20}.   We should not expect to find any Marcan material in this section, since that is already used fully in Lk. 9^{1-6}.   If, then, there is any reason to suppose that Lk. 10^{1-20} is composite, it will be a compound of Q + L.

Now in Lk. 22^{35} we read: ' When I sent you forth without purse, and wallet, and shoes, lacked ye anything? '; and here in 10^4 ' carry no purse, no wallet, no shoes.'   This exact correspondence in the two lists is very striking, the more so as the list in Mk. $6^{8\,f.}$ is different.   Moreover, the word here translated ' purse ' occurs only four times in the New Testament, all in Lk.   Next we observe that Lk. 10^8 is in part a repetition of *vv.* 6 f., and that *vv.* 8–12 form a unity by themselves.   The inference to be drawn from these facts, coupled with what we otherwise know of Lk.'s editorial methods, is that *vv.* 4–7 form an extract from L.   We need have no hesitation in assigning *vv.* 2 f. and 13–16 to Q; and probably *vv.* 8–12 are also from that source.   Lk. 10^1 may be either L or an editorial introduction by Lk., with the balance of probability decidedly in favour of the former alternative; for in 17–20 we have a reference back to *v.* 1, and, as 17–20 most probably comes from L, it seems likely that *v.* 1 does also.   There seems no good reason why Lk. should have invented the mission of the Seventy-two.   It is more probable that he found the Seventy-two in his source L and that the fact that seventy-two missioners were mentioned was an indication to him that this was a separate mission from that related in Mk.   This does not, of course, dispose of the question whether there was in fact more than one mission.   It still remains possible that the mission of the Seventy-two in L is a doublet of the mission of the Twelve in the other sources. The result of the analysis then is that we assign to Q *vv.* 2, 3, 8–12, 13–16, and to L *vv.* 1, 4–7, 17–20.   It may be added that the amount of agreement between Mt. and Lk. in the ground covered by Lk. 10^{4-7} is exceedingly small.

(a) The Commission

MT. $9^{37\,f.}$, 10^{16a}.	LK. $10^{2\,f.}$
9 37 Then saith he unto his disciples, The harvest truly is plenteous, but the **38** labourers are few. Pray ye therefore the Lord of the harvest, that he send forth labourers into his harvest. **10 16** Behold, I send you forth as sheep in the midst of wolves.	**10 2** And he said unto them, The harvest is plenteous, but the labourers are few: pray ye therefore the Lord of the harvest, that he send forth labourers into his harvest. 3 Go your ways: behold, I send you forth as lambs in the midst of wolves.

2. The introductory words in Mt. are more likely to represent Q than those in Lk.   Lk. has ' he said unto them,' because the audience has already been described in *v.* 1 (L).   The saying is the best explanation of the sayings in the preceding

section of Q. The seeming harshness of Jesus and His almost brutal thrusting into the background of natural feelings and obligations are due to the overwhelming urgency of His task. The King's business requires haste. He leaves no room for the kind of selfishness that takes shelter behind the plea that charity begins at home. Moreover, the demands which He makes are not His only : they are God's. The right to demand such sacrifices and the power to make them can come only from God. It is God who must send out the labourers to do God's work. And that the messengers chosen by Jesus are bidden to pray is an indication that the prayer is to be, in the first instance, one of self-dedication to God's will, cf. Is. 6[8].

3. The figure is abruptly changed. In the Apocalyptic literature (*Enoch* 90[6-17]) the lambs are a symbol for the *Ḥăsîdîm*, those in Israel who, in times of persecution and defection, had remained loyal to the Faith. ' Sheep ' in Mt. 10[16] is a translation variant (see the Greek versions of Lev. 3[7], 2 Sam. 6[13]). ' Go your ways ' is probably original, perhaps omitted by Mt. because in his composite discourse he has a great deal more to say, and the dismissal would be premature. The task of the disciples is not going to be easy. The kingdom to which they belong is one to which the kingdoms of the world are hostile, and they must not expect better treatment from the Herods and the Cæsars than the *Ḥăsîdîm* had from Antiochus.

(b) MISSIONARY METHODS

LK. 10[8-12].

Cf. Mt. 10[11a, 7, 8, 14, 15].
Cf. Mk. 6[10f].

MT. 10[15].

10 15 Verily I say unto you, It shall be more tolerable for the land of Sodom and Gomorrah in the day of judgement, than for that city.

10 8 And into whatsoever city ye enter, and they receive you, eat such things as are
9 set before you: and heal the sick that are therein. and say unto them, The kingdom
10 of God is come nigh unto you. But into whatsoever city ye shall enter, and they receive you not, go out into the streets
11 thereof and say, Even the dust from your city, that cleaveth to our feet, we do wipe off against you: howbeit know this, that
12 the kingdom of God is come nigh. I say unto you, It shall be more tolerable in that day for Sodom, than for that city.

8 f., 10 f., 12. Mt. at this point is an elaborate conflation of material borrowed from Mk., Q, and M, and parallels with Lk. are confined to single words and phrases, except for Mt. 10[15]. The directions fall into two parts. (i) Procedure where the reception is friendly: accept their hospitality in the spirit in which it is offered. This is not the time to raise questions about whether, for example, tithe has been given from the food offered, or whether it is ritually clean. There are more important things to do. Then also do for them what lies in your power— heal their sick. And, what is the *raison d'être* of the mission, proclaim the Kingdom as a present reality, which has come near and touched them in the person of its members, in their power to help and heal, and in the message itself. The whole of the dealings of the messengers with the people, to whom they come, are to be a manifestation of the Kingdom in its grace and saving power. (ii) Where the reception is unfriendly, no time is to be wasted. The disciples are to pass on to

more promising fields.   But before going away they will publicly and solemnly
disclaim all responsibility for the consequences of that city's refusal to hear their
message.   The significance of the ritual of wiping the feet before leaving the city
is that the city is reckoned as heathen, and its inhabitants as no part of the true
Israel, even though it is a city of Israel and its people Jews by birth.   Cf. the notes
on John's baptism (Lk. 3¹⁶, above, pp. 40 f.).   The Kingdom has come near to
them and they have rejected it.   Their blood will be upon their own heads in the
coming judgement, and the disciples are relieved from responsibility.   Cf. Ezek.
3¹⁶⁻²¹.   For ' that day ' Mt. 10¹⁵ has ' the day of judgement,' a phrase which does
not occur in Mk. or Lk.   It is probably an editorial explanation.   For ' Sodom '
(Lk.) Mt. has ' land of Sodom and Gomorrah,' which is doubtless an editorial
expansion to bring the saying into closer agreement with the Old Testament story.
In Rabbinical usage it is Sodom alone that is singled out as a type of obstinate
wickedness.   (See the passages collected by Billerbeck, *Komm.* i. 572 ff.)   Rabbinical belief excluded the people of Sodom and Gomorrah from any part in the life
to come.

The instructions given in this section are clearly coloured by the belief that
the final crisis is imminent.   This is why the missionaries are not to waste time.
They are few, and the ground to be covered is great, and the time is short.   It is
greatly to be feared that with the abandonment of the belief in the imminent end
of the world, the sense of the urgency of the preaching of the Kingdom has been
lost ; that, hypnotised by the idea of progress, we should forget that there is such
a thing as repentance.

(c) THE WOES ON THE GALILEAN CITIES

MT. 11²⁰⁻²⁴

LK. 10¹³⁻¹⁵

11 20 Then began he to upbraid the cities wherein most of his [1] mighty works were 21 done, because they repented not. Woe unto thee, Chorazin! woe unto thee, Bethsaida!‖for if the [1] mighty works had been done in Tyre and Sidon which were done in you,‖they would have repented 22 long ago in sackcloth and ashes.‖How-beit I say unto you, it shall be more toler-able for Tyre and Sidon in the day of 23 judgement, than for you.‖And thou, Capernaum, shalt thou be exalted unto heaven? thou shalt [2] go down unto Hades:‖for if the [1] mighty works had been done in Sodom which were done in thee,‖ it would have remained until 24 this day.‖Howbeit I say unto you, that it shall be more tolerable for the land of Sodom in the day of judgement, than for thee.‖	10 13 Woe unto thee, Chorazin! woe unto thee, Bethsaida! for if the [1] mighty works had been done in Tyre and Sidon, which were done in you, they would have re-pented long ago, sitting in sackcloth and 14 ashes. Howbeit it shall be more toler-able for Tyre and Sidon in the judge-15 ment, than for you. And thou, Caper-naum, shalt thou be exalted unto heaven? thou shalt be brought down unto Hades.

[1] Gr. *powers*.
[2] Many ancient authorities read *be brought down*.

[1] Gr. *powers*.

The woes on the Galilean towns are not strictly relevant to the work of the
disciples, and it is noteworthy that Mt. does not include them in his account of

the mission charge. In his arrangement they come between the testimony of Jesus to John (11^{7-19}) and the Doxology (11^{25-27}). In Lk. also the next Q section is the Doxology ($10^{21f.}$). It is therefore possible that the original order of Q was Lk. $10^{2f., 8-12, 16, 13-15, 21f.}$, and that v. 16 and vv. 13–15 have changed places in Lk.'s editing. The saying about the fate of recalcitrant cities in v. 12 would tend to attract vv. 13–15; and it may be urged that v. 16 would come more effectively after v. 12. than after v. 15. If that is so, then the introduction in Mt. 11^{20} may be from Q. The fuller form of the second oracle as given in Mt. $11^{23f.}$ deserves the preference over the shorter form in Lk. It preserves the strophic parallelism, which is so characteristic a feature of the teaching.

13, 14. 'Woe unto thee,' rather 'Alas for thee.' Chorazin is not mentioned elsewhere in the Bible, nor in Josephus. The solitary reference in the Talmud is textually uncertain. The place is identified with the present-day *Chirbet kerāze*, about 3 miles N. of *Tell hūm* (Capernaum). Bethsaida on the E. side of the Jordan, near its entry into the Sea of Galilee, christened Julias by Herod Philip in honour of the daughter of Augustus. It is identified with *et-tell*, about 5 miles from Capernaum. The mention of the mighty deeds done in these two places shows vividly what gaps there are in the story of the ministry. There is no account whatever in the Gospels, apart from this mention, of any visit of Jesus to Chorazin. Yet activity there must have been, and that of such a sort that it would have brought the heathen cities, Tyre and Sidon, to repentance. Sackcloth is mourners' garb. The ashes were either sprinkled on the head of the mourner (so apparently Mt.), or the mourner sat in them (so Lk.). Tyre and Sidon will be more leniently dealt with in the judgement, because they have not had the opportunity which Chorazin and Bethsaida have had and rejected.

15. Capernaum was a centre of the Galilean ministry of Jesus. It had had a better chance than most of accepting the message. The rhetorical question and its answer are reminiscent of the taunt-song against the king of Babylon (Is. 14^{13-15}):

'And thou saidst in thy heart, I will ascend into heaven,
I will exalt my throne above the stars of God;
And I will sit upon the mount of Assembly in the uttermost north:
I will ascend above the heights of the clouds; I will be like the Most High.
Yet thou shalt be brought down to Sheol, to the uttermost parts of the pit.'

Unbridled ambition and brazen self-confidence close the door to the messengers of God and open the way to destruction. Capernaum has stood firm, where even Sodom would have wavered in its wicked ways, and this will be in favour of Sodom in the day of judgement.

(d) CONCLUSION OF THE MISSION CHARGE

(MT. 10^{40})	LK. 10^{16}
10 40 He that receiveth you receiveth me, and he that receiveth me receiveth him that sent me.	10 16 He that heareth you heareth me; and he that rejecteth you rejecteth me; and he that rejecteth me rejecteth him that sent me.

Cf. Mk. 9^{37}. Whosoever shall receive one of such little children in my name, receiveth me : and whosoever receiveth me, receiveth not me, but him that sent me.

I am inclined to think—Mk. 9[36] notwithstanding—that these three are all forms of one and the same original saying. There are certain sayings about the treatment of children (see notes on Lk. 17[1], p. 138), and others about the treatment of disciples of Jesus; and there has been a certain amount of confusion in the tradition owing to the fact that Jesus spoke of His disciples as ' children.' It will be observed that these three sayings are all in the same poetic form, which Burney called climactic parallelism. Lk. 10[16] is to be assigned to Q. About Mt. 10[40] one may have doubts whether it should be labelled Q or M. It is possible that the original form of the saying was fuller than any of the three existing versions. Perhaps it ran:

> He that heareth you heareth me;
> [And he that heareth me heareth him that sent me:]
> And he that rejecteth you rejecteth me;
> And he that rejecteth me rejecteth him that sent me.

The conclusion that all three passages go back to a common original is further strengthened by the observation that the Aramaic verb *qabbēl* means both ' to receive ' and ' to hear ' in the sense of ' obey.' (Cf. Gen. 3[17], Heb. LXX, and Peshitta ' hear ': Targums ' receive '; similarly Gen. 21[12], 23[6, 8, 13]). Likewise ' rejecteth ' here may be the opposite of ' receive ' or ' hear,' that is, it may signify the rejection either of the persons or of their message. (It may be that in Mk. 6[11] we have side by side alternative renderings of the one Aramaic original in ' not receive you ' and ' nor hear you.')

The messengers are, in a sense, the Kingdom of God itself. The solidarity is impressive. The disciple represents in the fullest sense Jesus, and Jesus represents in the fullest sense the Kingdom of God. What they offer is God's offer and what they claim is God's claim. Cf. Mk. 8[38] where the true text is probably ' me and mine,' i.e. ' me and my disciples,' rather than ' me and my words ' [1]; and Mt. 25[31-46].

3. *THE PRIVILEGES OF DISCIPLESHIP*

(a) THE KNOWLEDGE OF GOD (141)

MT. 11[25-27]	LK. 10[21f.]
11 25 At that season Jesus answered and said, I [1] thank thee, O Father, Lord of heaven and earth, that thou didst hide these things from the wise and understanding, 26 and didst reveal them unto babes: yea, Father, [2] for so it was well-pleasing in 27 thy sight. All things have been delivered unto me of my Father: and no one knoweth the Son, save the Father ; neither doth any know the Father, save the Son, and he to whomsoever the Son willeth to reveal *him*.	10 21 In that same hour he rejoiced [1] in the Holy Spirit, and said, I [2] thank thee, O Father,|Lord of heaven and earth,|that thou didst hide these things from the wise| and understanding, and didst reveal them unto babes:|yea, Father;|[3] for so it 22 was well-pleasing in thy sight.|All things have been delivered unto me of my Father:|and no one knoweth who the Son is, save the Father;| and who the Father is, save the Son,|and he to whomsoever the Son willeth to reveal *him*.
[1] Or, *praise*. [2] Or, *that*.	[1] Or, *by*. [2] Or, *praise*. [3] Or, *that*.

[1] On the text of Mk. 8[38] see C. H. Turner in *Journal of Theol. Stud.*, xxix. 2 f. Mk. does not use the possessive adjective in the sense ' my,' but always the genitive of the pronoun.

The differences between Mt. and Lk. are very few. The most important is
' knoweth the Son (Father) ' (Mt.) and ' knoweth who the Son (Father) is ' (Lk.).
The phrase ' in the Holy Spirit ' is probably Lk.'s own. The clause about the
Father's knowledge of the Son is rejected by Harnack and Wellhausen as a very
early interpolation. Burney (*The Poetry of our Lord*, 133, 171 f.) found that in
Aramaic retranslation the passage ' forms a rhythmical poem which rhymes
regularly couplet by couplet.' To carry out the scheme he has to delete the
words ' and understanding,' and to add the words ' I give glory to thee ' after
' Yea,-Father.' The rhythm is three stresses to the line. The passage is full of
Semitic turns of phrase, and certainly Palestinian in origin. There is no good
reason for doubting its authenticity. (See *The Teaching of Jesus*, pp. 109–112.)

21. ' In that same hour ' corresponds exactly to the Rabbinic phrase *bĕ'ōthāh*
shā'āh. The phrase ' at that season ' in Mt. is one of Mt.'s editorial phrases
(cf. Mk. 2^{23} with Mt. 12^1, and Mk. 6^{14} with Mt. 14^1). ' Thank ' here signifies
glad acknowledgement of God's goodness and wisdom in ordering His revelation
as He ordered it. ' Father ' *Abba* without any qualification is Jesus'—not the
Jewish—way of speaking to God. (See note on Mt. 6^9, below, p. 168.) ' Lord
of heaven and earth ' is an alternative to the very common Jewish title for
God, ' Lord of the world.' What is meant by ' these things ' depends on how
we understand ' all things ' in *v.* 22, and on what we make of the following
clauses of that verse. What has been revealed so far in Q is the nature of the
Kingdom of God and His righteousness. In Palestine ' the wise ' means primarily
the learned in the Law. Actually the Rabbis preferred to call themselves ' disciples of the wise '; but that was due to their modesty. ' Understanding ': the
Greek word here is frequently used in the LXX to translate a Hebrew word
meaning ' intelligent,' ' discerning.' So far as it is possible to distinguish between
the two words, ' understanding ' seems to refer to a quality of mind, a capacity
which one has or has not; ' wise ' implies the natural gift plus something more
added as the result of exercise. The revelation here spoken of has passed by the
learned and the clever, and come to the babes, the simple and childlike, the
followers of Jesus drawn from the relatively uneducated and unsophisticated.
' For so it was well-pleasing in thy sight ' corresponds to a common Jewish phrase.

22. ' All things have been delivered unto me.' The verb ' deliver ' is that
commonly used of the handing down of knowledge from teacher to pupil (Mk. 7^{13};
Lk. 1^2; 1 Cor. $11^{2, 23}$). It can also be used of the handing over of power and
authority (Lk. 4^6). Here the whole context is in favour of the former sense.
The revelation, the complete revelation of God and His purpose, has been entrusted to Jesus. One immediate result is that He holds the revelation not as
' from God ' merely, but ' from my Father.' Another result is that He is conscious
of being God's chosen instrument for the disclosure of this revelation to others.
Nobody knows the Father as He knows Him, and all who are to come to a like
knowledge must learn of Jesus. The knowledge of God here spoken of is not
abstract theology, the learning of a set of propositions about the nature and
attributes of the Deity. It is knowledge of the Father, a new personal relation
between God and man, in which all that the Old Testament writers mean by
' knowledge of God ' finds full scope and expression. For in Old Testament

ways of speech ' knowledge of God ' stands for a religious activity of man, the joyful discovery and recognition of God and all that God means for man and his life. This is the knowledge that Jesus claims to possess and impart. And if this is right interpretation, it is clear that the text of Mt. ' knows the Father ' is to be preferred to Lk.'s ' knows who is the Father.' It is also probable that the clause about the Father knowing the Son is an interpolation. It is not relevant to the things that are being stated here. The whole passage is concerned with a glorious revelation of God, and the only significance of the Son in this connexion is that He is the first recipient of this revelation and the sole mediator of it to the rest of the world.

(b) The Joy of the Kingdom (142)

MT. $13^{16 f.}$	LK. $10^{23 f.}$
13 16 But blessed are your eyes, for they see; 17 and your ears, for they hear. For verily I say unto you, that many prophets and righteous men desired to see the things which ye see, and saw them not; and to hear the things which ye hear, and heard them not.	10 23 And turning to the disciples, he said privately, Blessed are the eyes which see 24 the things that ye see: for I say unto you, that many prophets and kings desired to see the things which ye see, and saw them not; and to hear the things which ye hear, and heard them not.

Mt. has taken this saying and inserted it in a new context, where the understanding of parables is under discussion. This has involved small changes in Mt. 13^{16}, which completely alter the sense. There can be no doubt that Lk. is here more faithful to Q. The alterations made by Mt. bring the saying into closer agreement with the text from Is. $6^{9 f.}$ quoted in Mt. $13^{14 f.}$

23, 24. Lk.'s introductory words would seem to belong to Q. They can scarcely be editorial, seeing that almost the same formula is used to introduce the immediately preceding verse. The formula ' Blessed are the eyes . . .' is just a striking way of saying ' Blessed are you.' Cf. Lk. 11^{27}, 23^{29}. The blessedness consists not in the fact that their eyes are open (as in Mt.), but in the fact that there is something to be seen by the open-eyed, the manifestation, namely, of the kingdom of God. This is where the disciples have the advantage over the prophets and the righteous kings of old. They also were looking for something; but they looked in vain, because it was not yet come. In this sense the least of the followers of Jesus is greater than the greatest of the prophets (Lk. 7^{28}). ' Prophets and kings ' (Lk.) is preferable to ' Prophets and righteous men ' (Mt.). The latter collocation is characteristic of Mt. Cf. Mt. 10^{41} (M), 23^{29}.

The point of the saying is that what for all former generations lay still in the future is now a present reality. What was for the best men of the past only an object of faith and hope is now matter of present experience. Anyone who has his eyes open can see the unmistakable signs that the Kingdom has drawn near: anyone who has ears to hear can hear the proclamation of the good news. With this beatitude compare and contrast another, which belongs to the middle of the first century B.C. (Ps. Sol. 17^{50}).

> Blessed are they that shall be born in those days,
> To behold the good things which God shall bring to pass in the gathering together of the tribes.

Lk. 10²³ᶠ· says that 'those days' have come; God is bringing the good things to pass, and all who now turn to Him will prove for themselves that it is so. This makes the transition to the next section of Q.

(c) FREE ACCESS TO GOD (148)

MT. 7⁷⁻¹¹	LK. 11⁹⁻¹³
7 7 Ask, and it shall be given you; seek, and ye shall find; knock, and it shall be 8 opened unto you: for every one that asketh receiveth; and he that seeketh findeth; and to him that knocketh it shall 9 be opened. Or what man is there of you, who, if his son shall ask him for a loaf, will 10 give him a stone; or if he shall ask for a 11 fish, will give him a serpent? If ye then, being evil, know how to give good gifts unto your children, how much more shall your Father which is in heaven give good things to them that ask him?	11 9 And I say unto you, Ask, and it shall be given you; seek, and ye shall find; knock, and it shall be opened unto you.‖ 10 For every one that asketh receiveth; and he that seeketh findeth; and to him that 11 knocketh it shall be opened.‖And of which of you that is a father shall his son ask ¹ a loaf, and he give him a stone? or a fish, and he for a fish give him a serpent? 12 Or if he shall ask an egg, will he give him 13 a scorpion?‖If ye then, being evil, know how to give good gifts unto your children, ‖how much more shall *your* heavenly Father give the Holy Spirit to them that ask him?‖
	¹ Some ancient authorities omit *a loaf, and he give him a stone? or.*

This passage, which shows close agreement between Mt. and Lk., is in poetic form (cf. Burney, *op. cit.*, pp. 67, 82, 114). The three short (two-stress) lines in *v.* 10 answer to the three lines in *v.* 9; and the triple form is carried into the short parable which follows (*vv.* 11 f.), though here there is serious doubt about the text. The clause about the loaf and the stone is omitted in Lk. by B 1241 Sahidic, MSS. of the Old Latin, Sinaitic Syriac, Armenian, Marcion, and Origen. Many scholars regard it as an assimilation of the text of Lk. to that of Mt. But the question whether it stood in Lk. is distinct from the question whether it stood in Q; and, leaving the text of Lk. on one side, we have three points in the parable. The first is attested by Mt. (and Lk.?), the second by Mt. and Lk., the third by Lk. alone. The evidence for the place of the first point in Q is at least as good as that for the third; and the fact that the poem is in a triple form favours a threefold parable. The only other important difference between Mt. and Lk. is in Lk. 11¹³, where Lk. has 'the Holy Spirit' and Mt. 'good things.' The latter is surely the original.

9, 10. The giver is God; and the opener is God. The parallelism requires us to suppose that the finding is also possible only by God's grace. The blessings of the new age are not the fruits of 'progress' or 'evolution': they are the result of an act of God in history, His response to human needs and longings. The repetition of the particular injunctions in the form of general truths is another way of saying that this is God's will; this is how God chooses to bestow His benefits. The gifts are not just what may be called spiritual gifts, but all things that the Father sees His children need (cf. Lk. 12²²⁻³⁴ Q). The thing to be sought is the Kingdom of God, which, being found, is the satisfaction of all needs (Lk. 12³¹). The door to be knocked at is the door which gives entrance into the Kingdom of God.

11 f., 13. The situations supposed in the parable are deliberately and frankly

absurd. Each question demands the answer, ' Of course not.' Then follows the conclusion: ' If you, bad as you are, know how to love your children, *a fortiori* God will know how to treat His children.' This is one of Jesus' favourite methods of instruction. He takes human nature at its best and then says: ' God is all that and far more.' The implication, which Jesus here leaves His hearers to draw for themselves, is that if you weak and sinful men are such that your children can bring their requests to you with confidence, how much more can you bring your requests to a Father who is perfect. R.V. in this verse has ' *your* heavenly Father,' which is a paraphrase. The Greek text of most MSS. is, literally translated, ' the Father from heaven ' where the words ' from heaven ' go with ' Father ' and not with ' give.' This text can hardly be right, and there is something to be said for Merx's idea that the insertion of the article before ' from heaven ' in the Greek MSS. is a Marcionite interpolation. In my opinion the true text of Lk. is ' How much more will the Father give from heaven a Holy Spirit to those who ask Him.' The text of Q was the same except that it had ' good things ' as in Mt., which Lk. altered to ' a Holy Spirit.' For the idea of good gifts from heaven, cf. James 1[17], ' Every good gift and every perfect boon is from above, coming down from the Father of lights.' It may be added that ' the Father,' which we take as the true text of Lk. and Q here, is true to Jesus' way of speaking about God, and to God.

The conclusion of the whole matter is that disciples may trust God absolutely for all their needs. This trust rests on a twofold basis: the knowledge that God is perfect love, and the knowledge that they are God's servants for whom He takes responsibility. Both these grounds for trust are intimately bound up with the disciples' relation to Jesus. It is through Him that they know the Father, and it is through Him that their call to the service of the Kingdom comes.

Looking back over this second main block of Q material, one feature of it is very striking. That is the order in which the material is presented. It begins by stressing the hardships and difficulties of discipleship, goes on to enlarge upon the tasks, and only at the end does it speak of the privileges and joys. Whatever else Q may be, it is a very honest document.

C. JESUS AND HIS OPPONENTS

1. *THE BEELZEBUL CONTROVERSY* (149)

(a) The Charge

MT. 12[22-24]	LK. 11[14-16]
12 22 Then was brought unto him [1] one possessed with a devil, blind and dumb: and he healed him, insomuch that the 23 dumb man spake and saw. And all the multitudes were amazed, and said, Is 24 this the son of David? But when the Pharisees heard it, they said, This man doth not cast out [2] devils, but [3] by Beelzebub the prince of the [2] devils.	11 14 And he was casting out a [1] devi! *which was* dumb. And it came to pass, when the [1] devil was gone out, the dumb man spake; and the multitudes marvelled. 15 But some of them said, [2] By Beelzebub the prince of the [3] devils casteth he out 16 [3] devils. And others, tempting *him*, sought of him a sign from heaven.
[1] Or, *a demoniac.* [2] Gr. *demons.* [3] Or, *in.*	[1] Gr. *demon.* [2] Or, *In.* [3] Gr. *demons.*

Cf. Mk. 3[20-22].

This is one of the rare occasions on which Mt. and Lk. show a certain amount of agreement about the narrative setting of a Q passage. They agree that the debate followed on an exorcism performed by Jesus, that the patient was dumb, that the cure was proved by the fact that he could afterwards speak, and that the crowds were astonished. Mt. adds that the man was blind and is then committed to the awkward statement that 'the dumb man spake and saw.' He also has the question of the crowd which is lacking in Lk. In Lk. those who make the accusation are not particularly specified: in Mt. they are the Pharisees: in Mk. 3²² they are scribes who have come down from Jerusalem. Mk. does not have the story of the exorcism at all. Instead, the charge is linked up with another story that the opinion was abroad that Jesus was insane. In Mk. 3²² these two points are kept distinct: the insult 'He's mad,' and the accusation 'He is in league with Beelzebul'; and the two charges are answered separately, the first in Mk. 3²⁸⁻³⁰ and the second in Mk. 3²³⁻²⁷. In Q the question of Jesus' sanity is not raised at this point, and consequently Mt. in 12³¹⁻³⁶ is answering a charge that has not, in his account, been made. Lk. in v. 16 has the statement that Jesus was also asked for a sign. This request is not dealt with until 11²⁹, an indication that it is not editorial. For Lk. would hardly have inserted here introductory matter to something which was not going to be treated until 13 verses later. Lk. has here been faithful to his source, even though it involved a certain awkwardness in the flow of the narrative. Mt., on the other hand, deserts Q here and makes a fresh start with an introduction of his own at Mt. 12³⁸.

14. The statement that the demon was dumb is more primitive than Mt.'s description (cf. Mk. 9¹⁷, ²⁵). The symptoms of the patient are transferred to the demon who is believed to cause them. When the demon goes out he carries his dumbness away with him.

15. The indefinite subject 'some of them' seems to be the original. The temptation to make the indefinite definite is stronger than that to make the definite indefinite. The terms of the charge are almost identical in all three gospels. That Jesus used black magic continued to be urged from the Jewish side for centuries after this first promulgation of the charge. (Cf. Justin, *Dial.* § 69; Klausner, *Jesus of Nazareth*, pp. 18–54). The name of the chief of the demons offers a complete set of problems of its own. There are three forms in the MSS.: Beelzebub, Beelzebul, and Beezebul. This last is the reading of the Vatican and Sinaitic MSS. and is accepted by W. Foerster as representing the Palestinian pronunciation of the name Beelzebul. The form Beelzebul is the most generally accepted. The name does not occur in Jewish literature, which is surprising. The meaning of the name is disputed (cf. Billerbeck, *Komm.*, i. 631–635). Jewish imagination showed a certain fertility in devising names for the arch-fiend. Thus we get Mastema in *Jubilees*, Sammael in Rabbinic literature, Asmodaeus in *Tobit*, Beliar in *Jubilees, Sibylline Oracles, Test. XII Patriarchs, Ascens. Isaiah*. 'By Beelzebul' is literally 'in Beelzebul,' i.e. 'in the power of' or 'empowered by,' analogous to the phrase 'in the Holy Spirit.'

16. The seekers after a sign did not regard the casting out of demons as convincing; for others besides Jesus could perform this feat (v. 19). They ask for something more startling by way of proof. Proof of what? His messiahship?

Or His right to speak and act as He did? The popular view (Mk. 8[28]) was that He was a prophet, and this is the view that is doubted by the Pharisee in Lk. 7[39]. Possibly some sign that He was a prophet was asked for, such as was related of Elijah (1 Kings 18[30-39]) or Isaiah (2 Kings 20[8-11]).

(b) THE REPLY OF JESUS

This is given by all three Synoptics. The disposition of the material is shown in the following table; which, for reasons which will appear, is carried beyond the limits of the reply proper.

MT. 12[25-37]		MK. 3[23-30]		LK. 11[17-23]	
25 f.	Divided kingdom, etc.	23–26.	Divided kingdom, etc.	17 f.	Divided kingdom.
27.	How do your sons do it?	—		19.	How do your sons do it?
28.	If I by the spirit of God . . .	—		20.	If I by the finger of God . . .
29.	The strong man bound.	27.	The strong man bound.	21 f.	The strong man bound.
30.	He who is not with me . . .	—		23.	He who is not with me . . .
31 f.	The unforgivable sin.	28–30.	The unforgivable sin.	—	
33.	Tree and fruits.	—		—	
34–37.	Character and speech.	—		—	
—		—		24–26.	Return of the ejected demon.
—		[31–35. Jesus' true relatives.]		27 f.	Compliment to Jesus' mother.
38.	Demand for a sign (cf. Lk. 11[16]).	—		—	
39 f.	The sign of Jonah.	—		29f.	The sign of Jonah.
41 f.	Men of Nineveh and Queen of Sheba.	—		31 f.	Queen of Sheba and men of Nineveh.
43–45.	Return of the ejected demon (cf. Lk. 11[24ff.]).	—		—	
46–50.	Jesus' true relatives.	31–35.	Jesus' relatives.	[8[19-21].	Jesus' true relatives.]

Lk. 11[17-26] is, I think, a Q collection of sayings on demons and demon-possession. Verses 17–23 are all more or less relevant to the charge made against Jesus, though actually the first piece (vv. 17 f.) is an effective and sufficient reply. V. 19 is also a counter to the charge. Verses 20 and 21 f. are relevant, but have more to do with the positive aspects of Jesus' activity against the demons and their head, than with the rebuttal of the accusation. The saying in v. 23 winds up the whole series of utterances, vv. 17–22, and was doubtless regarded by the compiler of Q as the close of Jesus' reply. Mk. has two elements in common with Q: vv. 23–26 and v. 27. This is all the Marcan reply to the charge; for vv. 28–30 deal with the statement that Jesus was mad. The implication is that the collocation of 'Divided kingdom' and 'Strong man bound' is older than Mk. or Q. There is enough agreement of Mt. and Lk. against Mk. in Mt. 12[25f.] and Lk. 11[17f.] to make it probable that this item stood in Q; and the Lucan version of the 'Strong man bound' is so completely different in wording from the Marcan that the two must be independent. Lk. vv. 21 f. may, of course, come from L. It is very remarkable that Mt. 12[29] shows no trace of agreement with Lk. 11[21f.] against Mk. 3[27] in a context where Mt. is borrowing freely from Q. If Lk. 11[21f.] is assigned to L, it raises a difficulty. For we have then to assume either that Lk.

by a happy accident hit on this exact point in Q for the insertion of the L passage, or that the arrangement of the material has been influenced by that of Mt. The latter supposition is as near to incredible as makes no matter; and the invocation of happy accidents is to be deprecated. We may therefore, though with some hesitation, assign Lk. 11²¹ᶠ· to Q, and assume that the two replies had got together at a stage in the tradition anterior to Mk. and Q.

An interesting point which emerges from the comparison of Mk. and Lk. (i.e. Q) is that 3³¹⁻³⁵ in Mk. and Lk. 11²⁷ᶠ· in Q occupy the same relative positions. Both come at the end of a series of sayings on demon-possession. Moreover, they have a common sentiment. ' Whosoever shall do the will of God, the same is my brother, and sister, and mother ' (Mk. 3³⁵): ' Blessed are they that hear the word of God and keep it.' This suggests the possibility that Mk. 3²⁰⁻³⁵ was already a closed section before it was incorporated in the Gospel; and that Lk. 11¹⁷⁻²⁸ is a similar complete section.

MT. 12²⁵⁻³⁰	LK. 11¹⁷⁻²³
12 25 And knowing their thoughts he said unto them, Every kingdom divided against itself is brought to desolation; and every city or house divided against 26 itself shall not stand: and if Satan casteth out Satan, he is divided against himself; 27 how then shall his kingdom stand? And if I ¹ by Beelzebub cast out ² devils, ¹ by whom do your sons cast them out? 28 therefore shall they be your judges. But if I ¹ by the Spirit of God cast out ² devils, then is the kingdom of God come upon 29 you. Or how can one enter into the house of the strong man, and spoil his goods, except he first bind the strong 30 man? and then he will spoil his house. He that is not with me is against me; and he that gathereth not with me scattereth.	11 17 But he, knowing their thoughts, said unto them, Every kingdom divided against itself is brought to desolation; ¹ and a house *divided* against a house 18 falleth. And if Satan also is divided against himself, how shall his kingdom stand? because ye say that I cast out 19 ² devils ³ by Beelzebub. And if I ³ by Beelzebub cast out ² devils, by whom do your sons cast them out? therefore shall 20 they be your judges. But if I by the finger of God cast out ² devils, then is the 21 kingdom of God come upon you. When the strong man fully armed guardeth his 22 own court his goods are in peace: but when a stronger than he shall come upon him, and overcome him, he taketh from him his whole armour wherein he 23 trusted, and divideth his spoils. He that is not with me is against me; and he that gathereth not with me scattereth.
¹ Or, *in.* ² Gr. *demons.*	¹ Or, *and house falleth upon house.* ² Gr. *demons.* ³ Or, *in.*

17 f. First refutation of the charge. Mk. calls it a parable. Mt. 12²⁵ᶠ· is a conflation of Mk. and Q. ' Knowing their thoughts ' belongs to Q. It does not imply thought-reading; for they had spoken their views (*v.* 15). Jesus saw what they meant: and it was something like this. The sending away of demons is nothing. It could be done by arrangement with their chief. To convince us you must do something which requires *Divine* power. (Cf. Ex. 7⁸–8¹⁹.) The statement that demons can be cast out in alliance with Satan is answered by the contention that Satan is not such a fool. He has his kingdom; and, like all kingdoms, its strength lies in its unity. Why should Satan raise civil war in his own realm? Lk. appears to have only the one picture. The kingdom in the throes of civil war is laid waste and the houses fall in ruins together (R.V. margin is the literal rendering of the Greek). Mk. and Mt. have the picture of the divided

kingdom and the divided household. There are three possibilities: (1) Supply
the word ' divided ' as in the R.V. text; (2) assume that R.V. mg. is correct,
that there was only one parable, as in Lk., and that the second parable in Mk.
and Mt. is a mistaken expansion of a detail in the first; (3) assume that there
were two parables and that Lk., by a misunderstanding, has reduced the second
to a detail of the first. We have no means of arriving at a sure decision; I prefer
(2). Happily the decision of this point does not affect the interpretation of the
passage as a whole.

19 f. A further objection, carrying the war into the enemies' camp. Jesus is
not the only one who casts out demons. There were also Jewish exorcists. Cf.
Josephus, *Ant*. VIII, ii. 5; Billerbeck, *Komm*., iv. 533 ff.; Acts 19[13] with Lake and
Cadbury's notes (*Beginnings of Christianity*, iv. 240). Will the critics of Jesus offer
the same explanation of the exorcisms performed by members of their own party?
(' Your sons ' = your adherents. So the adherents of Hillel are called the
' household of Hillel ' = ' school of Hillel '). Jesus does not stay to discuss this
point, but goes on to give the true significance of His own exorcisms. They are
a manifestation of the Kingdom of God. So far from being signs of an alliance
with Satan, they are signs of warfare against him. They are part of the struggle
between the Kingdom of God and the kingdom of Satan. ' Finger of God '
(Lk.) is the true Q text altered by Mt. to ' spirit of God.' See *The Teaching of
Jesus*, 82. For an interesting archæological illustration of this passage and of
Ex. 8[19], on which this saying ultimately depends, see Flinders Petrie in *Ancient
Egypt*, Sept. 1932, p. 69: ' A wood carving of a finger, springing from a falcon's
head. That head was the emblem of Ra and of Horus. . . . Such a symbol as
a finger for divine action was familiar in Egypt. . . . No doubt the wooden
finger . . . was used in ceremonial and magical acts by the priests.' The finger
of God is here a symbol for the might of the Kingdom of God revealed as saving
helpless men and women, and destroying the power of Satan. Jesus Himself is
the medium through which the power of the Kingdom becomes operative. ' He
does not " bring " the Kingdom—a notion entirely strange to Jesus Himself—
but the Kingdom brings Him with it ' (Otto, *Reich Gottes und Menschensohn*, 80).
In one other respect this saying is extremely important. Arbesmann (*Das Fasten
bei den Griechen u. Römern*, p. 20) describes the elaborate preparations necessary to
fit men for intercourse with the Deity, quoting Porphyry: ' that when they (the
evil demons) have departed the Parousia of the god may take place.' This is in
sharp contrast with our text, where the exit of the evil spirits is the *result* of the
Divine presence, not the *preparation* for it. This is the difference between the
Gospel and other religions.

21 f. Another picture of the war between the two opposing kingdoms. It is
based on Is. 49[24f.], an oracle describing Jehovah's deliverance of His people
from an enemy, who is described as ' the mighty one.' As retold here the strong
man is Satan, who claims sway over the world (Lk. 4[6]). His ' goods ' and his
' spoils ' (*v.* 22) are his human victims. His ' whole armour ' represents the
hosts of demons. The stronger one who comes upon him and defeats him is
Jesus Himself, as God's representative, armed with divine power. Cf. *Ps. Sol.* 5[4]
and the note of Ryle and James.

23. The concluding verse goes closely with *vv.* 21 f. The situation is one where no man can be neutral. It is war to the knife between the Kingdom of God and the kingdom of Satan. Jesus is God's chosen instrument for the waging of that war. He who takes his place by the side of Jesus, takes his place in the army of God. He who ignores the summons, is reckoned to the enemy. Cf. Lk. 9⁴⁹ f. for the other side of the picture. On gathering and scattering, cf. *Ps. Sol.* 17²⁸, 'And he (the Messiah) shall gather together a holy people, whom he shall lead in righteousness '; and 4¹³ ' He (the wicked) never ceaseth to scatter and bereave.' The Kingdom of God is the one constructive unifying redemptive power in a distracted world; and every man has to choose whether he will take sides with it or against it.

(c) A Saying on Demon-possession (150)

MT. 12⁴³⁻⁴⁵	LK. 11²⁴⁻²⁶
12 43 But the unclean spirit, when ¹ he is gone out of the man, passeth through waterless places, seeking rest, and findeth **44** it not. Then ¹ he saith, I will return into my house whence I came out, and when ¹ he is come, ¹ he findeth it empty, **45** swept, and garnished. Then goeth ¹he, and taketh with ² himself seven other spirits more evil than ² himself, and they enter in and dwell there: and the last state of that man becometh worse than the first. Even so shall it be also unto this evil generation.	**11 24** The unclean spirit when ¹ he is gone out of the man, passeth through waterless places, seeking rest; and finding none, ¹ he saith, I will turn back unto my house **25** whence I came out. And when he is come, ¹ he findeth it swept and garnished. **26** Then goeth ¹ he, and taketh *to him* seven other spirits more evil than ² himself; and they enter in and dwell there: and the last state of that man becometh worse than the first.
¹ Or, *it.*	¹ Or, *it.*
² Or, *itself.*	² Or, *itself.*

The charge of casting out demons by Beelzebul has been more than adequately dealt with in the foregoing verses. This piece stands here in Q because it deals with exorcism, and presumably it was convenient for purposes of instruction to have it along with kindred matter. Mt., who doubtless saw that it was not strictly relevant to the Beelzebul controversy, has removed it to a place after the speech against the sign-seekers; and his closing words ' Even so shall it be also unto this evil generation ' are modelled on phrases in the Q passage on sign-seeking, e.g. Lk. 11³⁰. The agreement between Mt. and Lk. is close.

24–26. ' Unclean spirit ' represents one of the Jewish synonyms for ' demon.' The whole description is in terms of Jewish beliefs about demons and demon-possession which Jesus shared with His contemporaries. The waterless places, i.e. the desert, are the natural home of demons. But the ejected demon is no longer content with a bedouin life. He wishes himself back in his old quarters enjoying a settled life. A visit of inspection shows that they have been cleaned and decorated. Mt. has the further detail that they are vacant. This ascertained the demon collects seven others, worse than himself, and together they take possession. It may be assumed that the demon does not bring the seven others out of sheer benevolence. The idea is rather that the eight of them will be better able to resist a second exorcism than one alone.

The meaning of the whole seems to be that exorcism by itself is not sufficient. The expulsion of the demon and the restoration of the victim to his normal condition leaves things exactly as they were before the demon first took possession. If the demon is to be kept out something more must be done than can be done by a mere exorcist. Now Jesus claims that His ejection of demons is not mere exorcism, but a manifestation of the Kingdom of God. It is the power of God that expels the demon. Then God must take possession of the vacant dwelling. The former house of the demon must become God's property, what Paul calls (1 Cor. 3^{16}) 'a temple of God,' the dwelling-place of the Holy Spirit. Cf. 2 Cor. 6^{16}; Eph. 2^{22}. In modern language the old obsessions, complexes, morbid fears and desires, and so on must be replaced by new loyalties and affections. The man whom God has delivered must give himself, body, soul, and spirit, to God and the service of His Kingdom.

2. *FLATTERY REBUKED* (151)

LK. 11$^{27f.}$

No parallel in Mt.
Cf. Mt. 12$^{46-50}$ = Mk. 3$^{31-35}$.

11 27 And it came to pass, as he said these things, a certain woman out of the multitude lifted up her voice, and said unto him, Blessed is the womb that bare thee, and the breasts which thou didst suck. 28 But he said, Yea rather, blessed are they that hear the word of God, and keep it.

27, 28. On the relation of this section to the foregoing see above, p. 85. The introductory words in *v*. 27 are editorial. The formula is characteristically Lucan. It connects this incident in time and place with the preceding controversy; but the probability is that we have here a separate incident, and that such connexion as there is is topical rather than real. The exclamation of the woman is a common form of compliment when one wishes to be specially complimentary. Cf. Gen. 49^{25}; Mishnah, *Aboth*, 2^8 (Danby, p. 448); other Rabbinic examples are given by Billerbeck (ii. 187 f.). In particular it is said of the Messiah that when he comes people will say ' Blessed is the womb from which he came forth ' (*Pesikta*, ed. Buber, 149*a*). The response of Jesus is curt. For ' yea rather ' ' Nay rather ' would be better. The force of the Greek is something like ' So *you* say: (but) I say.' For the thought cf. Mk. 3$^{34f.}$; Lk. 6^{46}||Mt. 7^{21}; Lk. 6^{47ff}·||Mt. 7$^{24-27}$; Rom. 2^{13}; John 13^{17}. Jesus was not deluded by people who made pious noises, and He brought them back to realities by the shortest possible route. A similar case is Lk. 14^{15} and the following parable of the Great Feast. (See below, pp. 128 ff.)

The incident has a certain connexion with what has gone before, in particular with *v*. 23. There Jesus makes His demand for decision for or against Him, which is the same thing as for or against the cause of God's Kingdom. Here He is offered fine words. But fine words are not an adequate response to His demands. Decision is not just saying ' Lord, Lord,' but doing what He says.

3. *AGAINST SIGN-SEEKERS* (152)

(a) The Sign of Jonah

Mt. 12³⁸⁻⁴⁰   Lk. 11²⁹ f.

12 38   Then certain of the scribes and Phari-   11 29   And when the multitudes were gather-
sees answered him, saying, [1] Master, we   ing together unto him, he began to say,
39 would see a sign from thee. But he   This generation is an evil generation: it
answered and said unto them, An evil   seeketh after a sign; and there shall no
and adulterous generation seeketh after   sign be given to it but the sign of Jonah.
a sign; and there shall no sign be given   30 For even as Jonah became a sign unto
to it but the sign of Jonah the prophet: the Ninevites, so shall also the Son of
40 for as Jonah was three days and three   man be to this generation.
nights in the belly of the [2] whale; so
shall the Son of man be three days and   Cf. Mk. 8¹¹⁻¹³||Mt. 16¹⁻⁴.
three nights in the heart of the earth.

[1] Or, *Teacher.*
[2] Gr. *sea-monster.*

In Mk. 8¹¹ᶠᶠ· the request for a sign comes from the Pharisees, whom Mt. (16¹)
turns into Pharisees and Sadducees. Here Mt. gives an introduction in which
certain of the scribes and Pharisees are the petitioners. The true Q introduction
is most probably to be found in Lk. 11¹⁶. Then Mt. 12³⁸ may be regarded as
editorial; and the narrative introduction in Lk. 11²⁹ comes under suspicion.

29, 30. The desire for a sign is a desire for something stupendous. This
demand for a convincing display of supernatural power is said by Paul to be the
characteristic feature of Judaism (1 Cor. 1²²). The construction in Lk. suggests
that this seeking after a sign is an indication of the wickedness of the generation.
In Mt. it seems rather that such an evil generation has no right to expect a sign.
Mt. describes the generation as 'evil and adulterous' (Lk. 'evil' alone) which
may be original. 'Adulterous' is used, as often in Old Testament prophecy, in
the sense of 'unfaithful to God,' 'apostate.' This meaning would be unfamiliar
to Gentile readers, and Lk. may have dropped the word for that reason. In Mk.
the request for a sign is met by a flat refusal. In Q a sign is offered—from ancient
history. Jonah was a sign to the Ninevites: so the Son of Man will be a sign to this
generation. How? This question arises for us on the assumption that Lk. 11³⁰ is
genuine Q and a genuine word of Jesus. One answer to the question is offered in
Mt. 12⁴⁰. The analogy between Jonah and the Son of Man is that Jonah pre-
figures the descent of Christ to Hades and His return from the abode of the dead.
Or so it seems. It is then possible to object that Mt. 12⁴⁰ is prophecy after the
event and represents not a word of Jesus, but a reflection of the Christian community on the word more accurately preserved in Lk. 11³⁰. In support of this it is
urged that the Ninevites knew nothing of Jonah's submarine adventures, and that
he appeared before them as a preacher of repentance in face of coming judgement.
The preaching of Jonah is the sign. This criticism of Mt. 12⁴⁰ is at first sight
plausible: it is, however, open to one very serious objection. Jonah was certainly
inside the great fish for three days and three nights (Jon. 1¹⁷). But the whole early
Christian tradition (Mt. included) is unanimous on the point that Jesus was buried
on a Friday afternoon and rose again on a Sunday morning. He was in the grave

for three days—if we count Friday and Sunday as days—and *two* nights. We are thus faced with a supposed prophecy after the event, which begins by falsifying the event—a somewhat strange phenomenon.[1] It may, however, be pointed out that in Mt. 4[13] Capernaum, which lay in the old tribal territory of Naphtali, is assigned to Zebulun and Naphtali in order to give point to the following quotation from Isaiah. It is possible that the author of Mt. 12[40] thought that his account was near enough to the facts. If then we dismiss Mt. 12[40] as early Christian explanation of Lk. 11[30] (= Q), we have to seek an interpretation of the latter passage. It is suggested by Bultmann [2] that the meaning is: as Jonah came from a distant land to the Ninevites, so will the Son of Man come from heaven to this generation. The sign asked for is the Son of Man himself, when he comes in judgement (cf. Mt. 24[30]). The objection to this view is that the analogy is not close. For Jonah came preaching repentance; the Son of Man comes to execute judgement. The sign of Jonah was of some use to the Ninevites: it gave them opportunity to repent. The sign of the Son of Man will be of no use to this generation; for when it comes, it will be too late to repent. Such a sign is hardly worthy of the name of sign. Another solution proposed is that the original saying of Jesus did not go beyond Lk. 11[29], and that both Lk. 11[30] and Mt. 12[40] are interpretative glosses. But even glosses have a meaning; and we should only be free to call Lk. 11[30] or 12[40] a gloss if the meaning were such that it could not reasonably be supposed to be the thought of Jesus. Yet another proposal is that ' Jonah ' in Lk. 11[29] and Mt. 12[39] was originally ' John ' (the Baptist). That the confusion of the two names was possible is shown by Mt. 16[17] compared with John 21[15]. The only sign to be given is, then, John the Baptist. In this case it would be impossible to regard Lk. 11[30] and Mt. 12[40] as anything but glosses on the corrupted text. Against this solution is the fact that it would deprive the ministry of Jesus of significance.

Before we can hope to solve the problem we must ask what those who asked for a sign wanted. The answer is that they wanted something that would authenticate Jesus to them, prove to them that He was indeed God's messenger to them. Then presumably the Ninevites might have put the same demand before Jonah; and if Jonah had produced some miracle to prove his bona fides, that would be Jonah's sign. But in the story of Jonah no such sign is either asked by the Ninevites or given by Jonah. Jonah himself was the only sign to the people. That can only mean that he and his message were such that of themselves they carried conviction to the Ninevites. People listening to Jonah recognised the voice of God. That, and only that, is what will be given to this generation. Once more God is speaking through the ' Son of Man.' For those who are not wilfully deaf to the message it is self-authenticating. The ' Son of Man ' is the sign in exactly the same way that Jonah was. Cf. Is. 8[18].

It remains to determine the meaning of ' Son of Man ' in this saying. If the interpretation just given is correct, ' Son of Man ' here is used, as in Lk. 7[34], in the sense ' a certain man ' i.e. ' I who speak.' Jesus Himself is the sign, the only sign, that will be given. The Q passage is then in real agreement with Mk. 8[11f.]. It

---

[1] G. Kittel, *Rabbinica*, pp. 36 f.
[2] *Geschichte der Synoptischen Tradition*,[2] p. 124.

refuses just as definitely as Mk. 8¹² the request for a supernatural vindication of Jesus. It is to be noted that Jesus as His own sign differs from Jonah in one respect. Jonah only preached. Jesus both preaches and acts. His ministry is the manifestation of the Kingdom of God; He Himself is the manifestation of the Kingdom. And in Him the Kingdom is self-authenticating. The progress of His ministry will be the proof of His mission from God.

This interpretation is confirmed by the following verses, in which Jesus contrasts the response of the Gentiles with the unresponsiveness of Israel. We may compare the case of the centurion of Capernaum and the woes on the towns of Galilee.

(b) Gentile Responsiveness and Israelite Obstinacy

MT. 12⁴¹f.	LK. 11³¹f.
12 41 The men of Nineveh shall stand up in the judgement with this generation, and shall condemn it: for they repented at the preaching of Jonah; and behold, ¹ a 42 greater than Jonah is here. The queen of the south shall rise up in the judgement with this generation, and shall condemn it: for she came from the ends of the earth to hear the wisdom of Solomon; and behold, ¹ a greater than Solomon is here.	11 31 The queen of the south shall rise up in the judgement with the men of this generation, and shall condemn them: for she came from the ends of the earth to hear the wisdom of Solomon; and behold, 32 ¹ a greater than Solomon is here. The men of Nineveh shall stand up in the judgement with this generation, and shall condemn it: for they repented at the preaching of Jonah; and behold, ¹ a greater than Jonah is here.
¹ Gr. *more than*.	¹ Gr. *more than*.

The two cases are stated in closely parallel terms. The difference in order between Mt. and Lk. is best explained on the supposition that Lk.'s order is that of Q, which Mt. has reversed in order to bring together the sayings about Jonah. The Lucan order is chronological. The two gospels are almost identical in the wording.

31. The queen of the south (1 Kings 10¹⁻¹³) is the queen of Sheba. She plays a great part in Arabic legend, where her name is given as Bilkîs. ' The South,' i.e. the Southern land, corresponds to the Arabic name of the territory, *Al-Yaman*, the modern Yemen, in S. Arabia. This heathen princess will be raised from the dead to appear at the final judgement along with the Jewish contemporaries of Jesus. Rabbinical eschatology distinguishes between those who are so bad that they are not raised at all, but are left in Gehenna, where they have been since death; and those who are raised for the judgement. The latter may be awarded bliss or torment in the judgement. See Mishnah, *Sanhedrin*, 10³ (Danby, 397 f.); Moore, *Judaism*, ii. 287–322, 377–395. Jesus says that in the coming judgement the fact that the queen of the South responded to such revelation as was available in her day will be damning evidence against those who fail to respond to the fuller revelation given by Himself. The phrase ' a greater than Solomon ' is literally translated in R.V. mg. The adjective is neuter in both verses here, and in Mt. 12⁶, where a similar expression occurs. In Mt. 11⁹ = Lk. 7²⁶ the adjective should be regarded as masculine. The neuter adjective here and in Mt. 12⁶ refers not to

Jesus personally, but to that which is manifested in Him, the Kingdom of God, which is a greater thing than the wisdom of Solomon or the preaching of Jonah.

In *v.* 31 Lk. has ' the men of this generation ' against Mt.'s ' this generation.' The latter is to be preferred. Lk. has a weakness for the Greek word here represented by ' men.' (Cf. Cadbury, *Style and Literary Method of Luke*, p. 189.) In *v.* 32 Lk. has refrained from inserting it, perhaps on account of ' the men of Nineveh.'

In both examples the effect on the Gentiles is produced, not by some violent breach of natural laws, but by the demonstration of spiritual power. The queen is fascinated by Solomon's God-given wisdom (1 Kings 3⁵⁻¹⁵); the Ninevites are convinced by Jonah's divinely inspired preaching. Now God is revealing Himself again to His own people in the ministry—preaching, teaching, healing—of Jesus; and the response is miserably inadequate. This concludes the speech against sign-seekers; but not all that Jesus has to say about signs. For the next section deals with the true sign, under the figure of light.

(c) THE TRUE ' SIGN FROM HEAVEN '—LIGHT (153)

MT. 5¹⁵, 6²²ᶠ.

LK. 11³³⁻³⁶

5 15 Neither do *men* light a lamp, and put it under the bushel, but on the stand; and it shineth unto all that are in the house.
6 22 The lamp of the body is the eye:||if therefore thine eye be single,||thy whole
23 body shall be full of light.||But if thine eye be evil,||thy whole body shall be full of darkness.||If therefore the light that is in thee be darkness,||how great is the darkness!||

11 33 No man, when he hath lighted a lamp, putteth it in a cellar, neither under the bushel, but on the stand, that they which
34 enter in may see the light. The lamp of thy body is thine eye:||when thine eye is single,||thy whole body also is full of light;||but when it is evil,||thy body also
35 is full of darkness.||Look therefore whether the light that is in thee be not
36 darkness. If therefore thy whole body be full of light, having no part dark, it shall be wholly full of light, as when the lamp with its bright shining doth give thee light.

Mt. by putting these sayings into the Sermon on the Mount (though Mt. 5¹⁵ may be from M) indicates his belief, which is no doubt correct, that they were originally addressed to the disciples. That they are in their proper place in Q in the Lucan order is obvious as soon as we see that they have to do with the one true sign. Just as the first sign of God's creative activity was the command ' Let there be light,' so the sign that God is at work for the salvation of men is the shining of the spiritual light in the lives of men.

33. There are two distinct sayings in this section, *v.* 33 and *vv.* 34–36. The former has a parallel in Mk. 4²¹ᶠ·: ' And he said unto them, Is the lamp brought to be put under the bushel, or under the bed (and) not to be put on the stand? For there is nothing hid, save that it should be manifested; neither was (anything) made secret, but that it should come to light.' Mk.'s question form of the saying may well be original. There are three Old Testament ideas involved in the verse. (i) The source and creator of light is God. (ii) The spirit of man is the lamp of the Lord (Prov. 20²⁷). (iii) The Servant of the Lord is a light to the Gentiles (Is. 42⁶). It is God who kindles the lamp (Ps. 18²⁸) in giving new spiritual power to a man.

And when this happens it cannot and ought not to be hidden. The transformed character is to be a beacon to those who are still in darkness to draw them to God. Cf. Mt. 5[14] ' Ye are the light of the world ' and 5[16] ' Even so let your light shine before men.' There is a small but significant point of difference between Lk. 11[33] and Mt. 5[15]. In Lk. the light is placed on the lamp-stand ' that they which enter in may see the light ': in Mt. to give light to those who are in the house. The latter contemplates a reformation within Judaism, the former conversions from outside. Mt. 5[15] is akin to the M version of the Mission Charge (Mt. 10[5f.]). Lk. 11[00] shows the wider interest characteristic of Q. Those who have the light, those who have been kindled by God, inherit the task of the Servant of Jehovah. They are to be a light to the Gentiles. On the whole saying cf. 2 Cor. 4[6].

34 f. The second saying is a distinct parable in poetic form. Burney (p. 131) maintains that the version given in Mt. is rhythmically superior to that in Lk. In describing the diseased eye Lk. has certainly sacrificed the parallelism to brevity. The conclusion (Mt. 6[23b]) seems to be better than Lk. 11[35]. For a retranslation into Aramaic see Burney loc. cit.

As this is a parable based on physical facts, the description of the facts must not be mixed up with other considerations. It is not relevant to the interpretation of the saying that ' a good eye ' is used in Jewish teaching as a synonym for a generous disposition and ' an evil eye ' for a covetous disposition. We are not here concerned with the business of the moralist, but with that of the oculist. The lamp of the body is the eye. The condition of the eye determines whether the whole man is a blind man or a seeing man. If the eye is ' single '—i.e. clear, sound, healthy— the man himself will be a seeing man. If the eye is ' evil '—i.e. diseased—the man himself will be blind. (For dark = blind cf. Ps. 69[23] and Targum Onkelos to Dt. 28[65].) ' Thy whole body ' is a literal rendering of an Aramaic expression which means ' you yourself' (Dalman, Gramm. [2], §17[12], p. 115). The saying then comes to this:

> The lamp of the body is the eye (or *Your* lamp is your eye).
> If your eye is healthy, you yourself will see:
> If your eye is diseased, you yourself will be blind.

The conclusion drawn from these facts is differently expressed in Mt. and Lk. In Lk. it is a caution: Beware lest the light that is in thee be darkness. In Mt. it is an exclamation: If the light that is in thee be darkness, what a darkness! We pass here from the parable to the moral. If what you imagine to be clear-sightedness is really blindness; if your supposed cleverness and penetration are really dullness and stupidity; if when you think you are facing the realities of your situation, you are really ignoring the vital facts—what then? Sure and certain disaster for yourself and all who are influenced by you. (I suspect that the force of this conclusion was enhanced in the original utterance by the fact that in Palestinian Aramaic the word ' light ' was used euphemistically for ' blindness.') Cf. Lk. 6[39] ' Can the blind lead the blind? Will not both of them fall into the pit? '

36. This verse has no parallel in Mt., and as it stands the only sense which it offers is a dull and obvious platitude. That is most probably why Mt. omits it. Lk., faithful to his source, has left it in even though he could make little or nothing

of it.   The verse is omitted by D, and also by 7 MSS of the old Latin version, and
the Curetonian Syriac, doubtless because of the difficulty of turning senseless
Greek into sensible Latin or Syriac.   In the Sinaitic Syriac and 2 old Latin MSS.
there appears a version differing from the Greek text.   This is an attempt to get
over the difficulty by emendation.   What appears to be the true solution is offered
by Torrey, who suggests (*The Four Gospels*, p. 309) that the Greek text, translated
in R.V. ' it shall be wholly full of light,' ' renders (incorrectly) *nahīr leh'wē kōllā*.
This last word, rendered correctly as the adjective in the first clause of the verse, is
here unquestionably *the noun*, " the whole, everything." The man who is full of
light lights the world about him.' Torrey accordingly translates *v*. 36: ' If however your whole body is lighted up, with no part dark, then all about you will be
light; just as the lamp lights you with its brightness.' This brilliant suggestion
clears up in the simplest way the worst difficulty of the Greek text.   It should be
added that here again, as in *v*. 34 ' your whole body ' means ' you yourself.' If
you yourself are illuminated, have an eye for spiritual things, you will be like a
lamp in the darkness to all around you.   This verse is then the Q equivalent of
Mt. 5^{14} ' you are the light of the world.' It is also the other side of the picture
drawn in *v*. 35.   The disciple who really sees the truth is the opposite of the blind
guide.

So then we have the true and only sign from heaven, the light of God's revelation.   This light shines in Jesus, and through Him in His followers.   Its shining
beacon is a guide to those who are in darkness.   If they follow the light, they too
will come to their desired haven.

4. *AGAINST PHARISAISM* (154)

Lk. 11$^{37-52}$ contains a series of woes, three addressed to the Pharisees and three
to the lawyers.   The whole series is preceded by an introductory narrative leading
up to a dispute between Jesus and a Pharisee on the subject of hand-washing.
The group of woes against the lawyers is furnished with a short introduction.   The
woes are followed by a short narrative describing the reactions of the scribes and
Pharisees.   Mk. (12$^{38-40}$) has a speech against the scribes.   This brief utterance
contains no woes, and is not directly addressed to the scribes.   The Pharisees are
not even mentioned.   The Marcan speech is a warning against the practices of the
scribes, and is apparently uttered in public teaching.   Mt. (23$^{1-36}$) presents a long
discourse, addressed to the crowds and Jesus' own disciples.   This discourse is,
like all the great speeches in Mt., a conflation.   It uses matter from Mk. 12$^{38-40}$;
it has other matter in common with Lk. 11$^{37-52}$, and therefore presumably from
Q; and it has sayings peculiar to Mt. and probably derived from M.   Mt. 23 has
seven woes, six of which are addressed to the scribes and Pharisees by name.   The
discourse is concluded with the lament over Jerusalem (23$^{37-39}$) from Q (cf. Lk.
13$^{34f.}$), and there is no account of its effect on the scribes and Pharisees.   Mt. goes
straight on to the eschatological discourse.

We now turn to the arrangement in detail, to see what can be surmised about
the composition of the discourses.   We begin with a table of contents in parallel
columns.

MT. 23		MK. 12		LK. 11	
2 f.	Moses' seat.			37 f.	Narrative introduction.
4.	Heavy burdens.			39–41.	External purity.
5.	Show of piety.			42.	I. Woe, Tithes.
6 f.	Pride of place.	38 f.	Scribal pride.	43.	II. Woe, Pride of place.
8–12.	Warning against pride.	40.	Scribal fraud	44.	III. Woe, Hidden tombs.
13.	I. Woe, Closing Kingdom.		and sham	45.	The lawyer's protest.
15.	II. Woe, Proselyte hunters.		piety.	46.	IV. Woe, Heavy burdens.
16–22.	III. Woe, Oaths and vows.			47 f.	V. Woe, Tombs of the
23 f.	IV. Woe, Tithes.				prophets.
25 f.	V. Woe, External purity.			49–51.	Blood of the prophets.
27 f.	VI. Woe, Whited sepulchres.			52.	VI. Woe, Key of know-
29–32.	VII. Woe, Tombs of the				ledge.
	prophets.			53 f.	Anger of scribes and
33.	Threat of judgement.				Pharisees.
34–36.	Blood of the righteous.				

The discrepancies in order between Mt. and Lk. are very striking, and equally striking is the wide divergence in language between the two Gospels in passages which they have in common. The following verses of Mt., which have no parallel in Mk. or Lk., may be provisionally assigned to M: *vv.* 2 f., 5, 7^b–12, 15–22, 24, 28, 32 f. From Mk. *vv.* 6, 7^a seem to be derived. The remaining verses have contacts with Lk., and if any part of Mt. 23 is derived from Q, it is here that we must look for it in the first instance. It may be noticed that the great bulk of the matter common to Mt. and Lk. comes from the woes. But taking the woes as a whole the correspondence in order between Mt. and Lk. is not striking. This may be shown by two tables. The first (A) is based on the Mt. order of woes; the second (B) on Lk. In either case the second column gives the number of the answering woe in the order of the other Gospel.

A.	Mt.	Lk.		B.	Lk.	Mt.
	I	VI			I	IV
	II	—			II	*vv.* 6 f. (not a woe)
	III	—			III	VI
	IV	I			IV	*v.* 4 (not a woe)
	V	*vv.* 39–41 (not a woe)			V	VII
	VI	III			VI	I
	VII	V				

The only coincidence in order here is that woes IV, VI, VII in Mt. correspond to I, III, V in Lk. If we now turn to the possible Q matter in Mt. we find what may be displayed in the following table.

Mt.	Lk.
v. 4	*v.* 46 (woe IV)
v. 13 (woe I)	*v.* 52 (woe VI)
v. 23 (woe IV)	*v.* 42 (woe I)
vv. 25 f. (woe V)	*vv.* 39–41
v. 27 (woe VI)	*v.* 44 (woe III)
vv. 29–31 (woe VII)	*vv.* 47 f. (woe V)
vv. 34–36	*vv.* 49–51

Mt. 23⁴ and Lk. 11⁴⁶ deal with the same subject. But Lk. 11⁴⁶ is a woe and Mt. 23⁴ is not. The agreements in wording are insignificant beside the differences. And 23⁴ comes in the middle of a section which seems to be solid M. For these reasons we may regard it as more probably M than Q. The same considerations apply to Mt. 23¹³. Mt. 23²³ is the first verse in the chapter than can be assigned with any real confidence to Q. There is identity of subject-matter and considerable agreement in wording with Lk. 11⁴². Mt. 23²⁵ f. is a woe: Lk. 11³⁹⁻⁴¹ is not. The subject-matter is the same; but the agreements in wording are not very numerous. In Mt. 23²⁷ and Lk. 11⁴⁴ the subject is the same; but the treatment of it is different and the verbal agreement is practically nil. Mt. 23²⁹⁻³¹ and Lk. 11⁴⁷ f. deal with the same point but again the measure of agreement in wording is small, though not negligible. The same is true of Mt. 23³⁴⁻³⁶ compared with Lk. 11⁴⁹⁻⁵¹. The result is that Mt. 23²³ is the only verse that can be given to Q with any sort of confidence.

The conclusion to which these facts seem to point is that in the main Mt. 23 is derived from M. In places—notably vv. 23, 25 f., 29–31, 34–36—the M material may well have been conflated with Q; but it remains likely that the backbone of the chapter is M. The coincidences in order between Mt. and Lk. will then be coincidences between M and Q and point to a stage in the tradition anterior to these two sources. At that stage, we may surmise, the woes concerning meticulous tithing, the whited sepulchres (or hidden tombs), and the tombs of the prophets, together with the saying about the blood of the prophets (or righteous men) were already fixed in that order.

The question remains whether the Lucan version of the speech is to be assigned to Q or L. So far we have assumed that it is Q, which is the general opinion. Streeter assigns Lk. 11⁹⁻⁵² to Q; Bussmann gives 11³⁴⁻12¹ to his source R, which for our purposes is the same as giving it to Q; Harnack recognised vv. 39, 41, 42, 44, 46–52 as belonging to Q. Bultmann thinks that Q contained originally seven woes, corresponding to vv. 43, 46, 52, 42, (39), 44, 47 in Lk. and vv. (4, 6), 13, 23, 25, 27, 29 in Mt.; and that Lk. has made a larger composition by setting them in a narrative frame (37–39a), by the little piece of dialogue (v. 45), and the narrative conclusion (53 f.). That is, the passage is Q with the editorial additions of Lk.

The crucial question is whether the division of the woes between Pharisees and lawyers in Lk. is original or the creation of Lk. himself. My own feeling is that Lk. found it and did not create it, though he may have written v. 45 to help the transition from the one set of woes to the other. In that case we have as the nucleus of the Q version of the speech six woes, three against Pharisees and three against lawyers. (Cf. the four beatitudes and four woes in Lk.'s version of the preaching of Jesus.) Lk. 11⁴⁹⁻⁵¹ was already firmly attached to the fifth woe in the source as Lk. had it. It is then possible to suppose that Lk. 11³⁷⁻⁴¹ is a separate section (from L?), which Lk. has used as the introduction to the six woes; and that 11⁵³ f. (with or without 12¹) is the conclusion of the story told in vv. 37–41. The coincidences in language between Lk. 11³⁹⁻⁴¹ and Mt. 23²⁵ f. would then be explained as due to the overlapping of M and L. To Q I should assign with considerable confidence vv. 42–44 and 46–52 of Lk.

(a) The Woes against Pharisees

LK. 11[42-44]

Cf. Mt. 23[23].

Cf. Mk. 12[38 f.]; Mt. 23[6 f.]; Lk. 20[46].

Cf. Mt. 23[27]

11 42 But woe unto you Pharisees! for ye tithe mint and rue and every herb, and pass over judgement and the love of God: but these ought ye to have done, 43 and not to leave the other undone. Woe unto you Pharisees! for ye love the chief seats in the synagogues, and the saluta-44 tions in the marketplaces. Woe unto you! for ye are as the tombs which appear not, and the men that walk over *them* know it not.

The first three woes are spoken to Pharisees. The Pharisees may be described as ' practising Jews ' using the word ' practising ' in somewhat the same sense as in the phrase ' practising Catholics.' Their origin can be traced back to the days when the Seleucid overlords of Palestine attempted to force Greek religion and culture upon the Jewish people, with some success. Those who, in that crisis, remained faithful to the religion of Israel—often at the cost of their lives—received the name *Ḥăsîdîm*, ' the saints ' or ' the godly.' Later, when their object had been attained by arms, and religious freedom was assured, they refused to join in the further military and political plans of the Maccabean leaders and received the nickname *Pěrûshîm* or ' Separatists.' This name they accepted and construed in their own way as meaning separateness from everything ungodly as judged by the Law of God. (See further, *The Teaching of Jesus*, pp. 184–188 and literature there cited.)[1] From the beginning their concern is essentially with the practice of religion. The interpretation of the Law and the working out of the theology and morals of Judaism they left to experts, the scribes. These belonged largely, though not entirely, to the Pharisaic party, and were its intellectual leaders. The scribes are thus a group within the much larger body of Pharisees. It was not necessary to be learned in order to be a Pharisee. The essence of the Pharisaic life was strict obedience to the Law as interpreted by the scribes. It is in accord with this definition that the woes against Pharisees are all concerned with the practice rather than with the interpretation of the Law. As the Greek text stands the sweeping denunciations are directed against the whole Pharisaic party. Whether this was the case in the original Aramaic is a question which cannot be answered. All that can be said is that ' Woe unto you Pharisees! for ye tithe . . . ' represents Aramaic which could equally well be rendered ' Woe unto you Pharisees who tithe . . .' (compare the beatitudes and woes, Lk. 6[20-26]). The reference could then be not to the whole body of Pharisees, but to those among them who were Pharisees only on the surface. That such people existed is confirmed by Jewish evidence (Billerbeck, iv. 336–339, gives the passages); and it is at least possible that Jesus had them in mind rather than the whole body of the Pharisees.

42. ' Woe unto you ' better ' Alas for you.' See Introduction, p. 29. The payment of tithe was an essential part of the religious obligation of the Jew, and

---

[1] I am not entirely satisfied with this explanation of the origin of the name ' Pharisee.' It is, I think, possible that the name originally meant ' Persianizers ' and referred to characteristic Pharisaic beliefs, which had close affinities with the religion of Zarathustra. But this theory must be reserved for fuller discussion elsewhere.

4

the question whether any given kind of farm or garden produce was subject to tithe was one for experts. The really important things in this connexion were of course the main crops; but scribal conscientiousness saw to it that rules were laid down for all kinds of produce. The question in this woe is whether the assertion is that the Pharisees observe these rules in the minutest detail or whether in their zeal to appear righteous they go beyond the rules and give tithe where none is required. In Lk. the specified kinds are mint and rue. There is no evidence that mint was subject to tithe, and definite evidence that rue was not subject (*Shebi'ith* 9[1], Danby, p. 49). And certainly not every kind of herb was subject to tithe. The Lucan version of the woe thus asserts that more is done, in the matter of trifles, than even the scribal interpretation of the Law requires. This suggests that it is only some of the Pharisees who are here accused. It is unlikely that all Pharisees would go to such lengths and equally unlikely that Jesus would make an accusation against the whole body, which any member of it could immediately disprove. Mt. 23[23] gives a different list: mint, dill, and cummin. Dill was liable to tithe (*Ma'aseroth* 4[5], Danby, p. 72) and so was cummin (*Demai* 2[1], Danby, p. 21). It is possible that Lk.'s rue and Mt.'s dill both go back to a single Aramaic original. The Aramaic names of these two plants could easily be confused in writing. As it stands Mt.'s text is not clear. It gives mint, which was not tithed, and dill and cummin, which were. This is explicable on the assumption that it is a conflation of M and Q. The M text perhaps contained dill and cummin and understood the saying as pillorying the meticulous observance of the tithe laws by the Pharisees. The mint is then an intrusion from the Q version, which asserts that some Pharisees in order to gain a reputation for piety pay tithe where no tithe is due. The Q version as given by Lk. seems to be on all grounds preferable. It may be paraphrased ' Alas for you hypocritical members of the Pharisaic party, who simulate piety by paying tithes where none are required.' That their piety is a sham is proved by the fact that along with their extreme conscientiousness in trifles goes a remarkable indifference in the really vital matters, ' judgement and the love of God.' ' Judgement ' is here, as often in the Old Testament, the quality which fits one to be a judge, i.e. a keen sense of right and wrong, an inward rectitude, an unshakeable determination to uphold what is right and true and good. The love of God is the essence of true religion. It is to be noted that in the Jewish account the Pharisee who is a Pharisee from the motive of love is set in contrast with six other sorts of Pharisee to their disadvantage. (Billerbeck, iv. 339.) Mt. has a different list of weightier matters of the law—'judgement and mercy and faith ' —again probably a conflation of M and Q.

' But these (judgement and the love of God) ought ye to have done, and not to leave the other (the tithing of mint, etc.) undone.' This sentence cannot belong to Q. For the tithing of mint, etc., was a thing that could very well be left undone, seeing that it was not required by the Law or by the scribal tradition. In Lk. it is omitted by Marcion and by the Codex Bezae; and it may be a very early interpolation from Mt. 23[23].

43. This occupation with the details of religion, the successful performance of the minor pieties, produces spiritual pride. Concentration on the central things would produce humility. This is true of Christianity as well as Judaism.

Those who are meticulous in the payment of their religious taxes expect others to show a proper appreciation of their exemplary piety. Having no inner assurance of God's approval, their need of human recognition is all the greater. The danger is that they will be satisfied with the latter and never even feel their need of the former. The charge of seeking this human recognition is made independently in Mk. 12³⁸ᶠ·, but not in the form of a woe. ' The chief seats in the synagogues,' cf. Mt. 23², ' Moses' seat ' and notes thereon (below, p. 228). ' Salutations '—we might almost say ' salaams.' The regular salutation was ' Peace upon thee ' and the principle laid down in the Palestinian Talmud (*Berachoth*, II. 4ᵇ. 24; Billerbeck, i. 382) is that a man must salute his superior in the knowledge of the Law. But in practice we find that distinguished Rabbis preferred to waive the right, and be themselves the first to make the salutation. We may suspect that in Pharisaism, as in other circles, those whose title to respect was shaky were foremost in insisting on their dignity. And again we may think that the indictment of Jesus is not directed against the whole body of Pharisees, but only against a section.

44. This woe appears in Mt. 23²⁷; but there the treatment is different. Mt.'s point is that the tomb which outwardly looks fine and clean is full of rottenness: so the Pharisee who is outwardly a model of piety and morality is a mass of corruption within. The Lucan form of the saying depends on the law in Num. 19¹⁶ that contact with a grave defiles a man for seven days. There are Pharisees like unmarked graves. Other people come in contact with them and are defiled thereby. The Lucan form appears to be the original. Whited sepulchres (Mt.) is not a good simile for hypocrites. For the point of the whitening is that it advertises the fact that the grave is what it is (see Abrahams, *Studies*, ii. 29–32), and warns the passer-by of the risk of defilement. The Lucan form asserts that there are Pharisees who have nothing about them to warn the unsuspecting that they are really bad men whose influence will be thoroughly evil.

These three woes are all concerned with character and conduct. There is in them no polemic against Pharisaism as a system. Nor, I think, does Jesus arraign the whole body of the scribes and Pharisees. The impression that He did so is given by Mt. If we read these woes in Lk.'s version, keeping out of our minds any ideas derived from Mt. 23, it seems that here we have a condemnation of bad Pharisees such as could be made, and was made, from the Pharisaic side. The Pharisaic ideal was a genuine religious ideal; and the men who gave themselves to it were mostly sincere and earnest. To maintain that all Pharisees were *ipso facto* hypocrites is as absurd as to claim that they were all saints. The truth is that some of them were men of eminent saintliness, many kept a worthy standard both in piety and morality, and some were complete frauds. It is to this last class that the woes really apply. Note that Jesus does *not* say: ' You ought to concentrate on the love of God and drop tithes ' or ' It is time that these marks of respect were done away with.' He is not here attacking the system, but those who abuse it for their own advantage. And those who loved the system and believed in it were always ready to do the same. The real Pharisee, the ' Pharisee from love ' would agree with Jesus, though certainly not with all the explanations of what Jesus is supposed to have meant.

(b) THE WOES AGAINST SCRIBES

46. Cf. Mt. 23⁴.

47 f. Cf. Mt. 23²⁹ ³¹.

49–51. Cf. Mt. 23³⁴⁻³⁶.

52. Cf. Mt. 23¹³.

11 45 And one of the lawyers answering saith unto him, [1] Master, in saying this thou
46 reproachest us also. And he said, Woe unto you lawyers also! for ye lade men with burdens grievous to be borne, and ye yourselves touch not the burdens with
47 one of your fingers. Woe unto you! for ye build the tombs of the prophets, and
48 your fathers killed them. So ye are witnesses and consent unto the works of your fathers: for they killed them, and ye
49 build *their tombs*. Therefore also said the wisdom of God, I will send unto them prophets and apostles; and *some* of them
50 they shall kill and persecute; that the blood of all the prophets, which was shed from the foundation of the world, may
51 be required of this generation; from the blood of Abel unto the blood of Zachariah, who perished between the altar and the [2] sanctuary: yea, I say unto you, it
52 shall be required of this generation. Woe unto you lawyers! for ye took away the key of knowledge: ye entered not in yourselves, and them that were entering in ye hindered.

[1] Or, *Teacher*.
[2] Gr. *house*.

45. The transition from the woes against Pharisees to the three woes against scribes is effected in *v.* 45. It may be doubted whether it stood in Q. If it is the editorial work of Lk., that is an indication that he found the two sets of woes distinguished in his source, and felt himself called upon to make a link between the two. The connexion is not particularly good since the foregoing woes do not touch the scribes as such, but only in so far as they belong to the Pharisaic party. Lk. uses the word 'lawyer' rather than scribe. 'Lawyer' would certainly convey the true sense better to a Gentile reader, to whom 'scribe' would suggest a clerk or secretary rather than an expert in Jewish religion and law. 'Reproachest' is too weak a translation; better 'insultest.'

46. The three woes against scribes deal with their attitude to the Law, the prophets, and the Kingdom of God. The first concerns their interpretation of the Law. It is important to realise what Jesus does *not* say. He does not say that the scribes make one law for themselves and another for the ordinary people. The most stringent interpreters among the Rabbis were commonly themselves most particular in their observance. For the Rabbis there was only one Divine Law, written in the Old Testament or handed down by oral tradition from Mt. Sinai; only one true interpretation of it; only one proper application of it in any given case. And that Law rightly interpreted and applied was absolutely binding on all Jews, scribes included. Moreover, as lawyers the scribes could not do otherwise than they did. They were neither inspired prophets nor higher critics. They were the guardians of what they believed to be a God-given rule of faith and morals, every syllable of which was divinely inspired. Their business was

merely to expound. The business of Israel, themselves included, was to obey. That this mass of legislation formed a burden which few were able to bear cannot be disputed. The result was that in the days of Jesus there was a sharp division between those who were bearing the burden with more or less success and those who failed, between the righteous and sinners.

Jesus does not suggest that the requirements should be relaxed in favour of the weaker brethren, that the heavy burdens should be borne exclusively by scribes and Pharisees, and a lighter one prepared for the publicans and sinners. His complaint is that the scribes will not lift a finger to help those who break down under the burden. The scribe, as such, expounds the Law; he may himself keep it; but he has nothing to say to the Israelite who fails to keep it, except 'You have sinned: you must repent and begin again.' This is the point of Jesus' accusation. It comes with all the greater force because He lavished so much love on the Law's failures, so much that He became known as ' the friend of publicans and sinners.' The Law is the expression of God's will. But ultimately God's will must be the working out of the Father's love for His children; and there is something wrong with an interpretation of the Law which results constantly in God's children being estranged from Him because they cannot keep the Law. There is something wrong with scribal labours which multiply the number of ways in which a man may offend God, but cannot help him to please God.

47 f. In the second woe the attitude of the scribes to prophecy is challenged. Put in a word the criticism is: The only prophet you honour is a dead prophet. In the parallel in Mt. 23[29] the characteristic Matthæan 'prophets and righteous men' appear. The reference to the building of tombs for the prophets may be bitter irony. Outwardly you seem to pay honour to the great prophets of the past; but your real object is to make permanent the work of your fathers. They killed the prophets: you make sure that they stay dead. It is possible that here Jesus is hitting at the absolute supremacy given by the scribes to the Law. If we may judge from the Scripture quotations ascribed to Him in the Gospels, He turned rather to the prophetic books and the psalter. Out of 94 quotations in the Synoptic Gospels, only 24 are from the Law; 46 are from the prophetic books; and 24 from the third division of the Hebrew canon, 23 of them from Psalms and Daniel. But in the scribal view the Law was supreme. Prophecy could confirm, but could not reform, it; and the book of Ezekiel was at one time in danger of exclusion from the Old Testament, because it was thought to be at variance with the Law. If the great prophetic figures of the past had thus to play second fiddle to the Law, what chance was there that the living voice of prophecy would receive a hearing? John the Baptist supplied the answer to that question. The whole attitude of the scribes to prophecy, past or present, is according to Jesus proof that they agree with those who killed the prophets.

49–51. The second woe is followed by a passage which has been a fruitful field for discussion and conjecture. (a) It is commonly held that these verses are a quotation from a Jewish apocryphal book; and that the quotation has been put into the mouth of Jesus in the process of tradition. The upholders of this theory are unable to verify the quotation, as the book in question cannot be produced. They think it must have been lost. The main reason for thinking that the verses are a quotation is the fact that in Lk. they open with the words 'Therefore also said the wisdom of God'; but, so far as the usage of the gospels is anything to go by (cf. Mt. 22²⁴; Mk. 7¹⁰, 12³⁶; John 1²³, 12³⁹, ⁴¹), this would imply that the wisdom of God wrote the supposed book, as Moses was believed to have written the Law, or David the Psalms, or Isaiah the book of Isaiah. A much better way of taking the Lucan introductory formula is to regard it as equivalent to 'God, in His wisdom, said.' It is a commonplace that Jewish thought tended to personify the attributes of God. In the Rabbinical literature the attributes of Justice (*middath had-dîn*) and Mercy (*middath hā-raḥămîm*) are constantly personified and represented as speaking. When we read in these writings that 'The attribute of Justice said,' we realise that this is a picturesque way of saying 'God, in His justice, said.' For the orthodox Jew the wisdom of God was an attribute of God. As revealed to men it was the Law, the Torah, which is also sometimes personified. But this personification is only a mode of speech. It makes for greater vividness; but it does not imply that God's justice, mercy, wisdom, and so on, are separate personal entities. (See Moore, *Judaism*, i. 414 ff.) (*b*) Along with the view that these verses are a quotation goes a further theory that Mt. 23³⁷⁻³⁹ is a continuation of the same quotation, which Lk. has transferred to another place (Lk. 13³⁴ᶠ·). This is very unlikely, for two reasons. First, it does not appear to be Lk.'s practice to break up his sources in this way. If Lk. 11⁵¹ marked the end of a block of Q material in Lk. and Lk. 13³⁴ the beginning of the next block of Q, there would be something to be said for the theory; but this is not the case. Secondly, a comparison of Mt. and Lk. in the passages in question is strongly against the theory. Mt. 23³⁴⁻³⁶ contains (in Greek) 72 words, Lk. 11⁴⁹⁻⁵¹ contains 58. The two versions of the saying agree in 22 words and partly agree in 7. Taking Lk.'s shorter version as standard the amount of agreement between Mt. and Lk. is under 50 per cent. Now Mt. 23³⁷⁻³⁹ contains 56 words and Lk. 13³⁴ᶠ· 53. There is agreement between the two in 45 words and partial agreement in 4. Again taking Lk. as the standard, the amount of agreement between Mt. and Lk. is near 90 per cent. It is difficult to believe that this wide divergence followed by almost word-for-word agreement could have taken place in the quotation of a single short passage of little more than a hundred words.

49, 50 f. All that has happened in the past and is happening in the present to the messengers of God is foreseen and provided for by God in His wisdom. He sends out His prophets and messengers knowing the fate that awaits them. For 'prophets and messengers' Mt. (23³⁴) has 'prophets, and wise men, and scribes,' generally regarded as more original than Lk. But see below, pp. 238 f. The 'apostles' of R.V. is better rendered 'messengers.' The term 'apostles' has a technical ecclesiastical sense, which ought not to be read into the text here. Jesus used the Aramaic equivalent of the word, and—as I think—gave it as a name to certain of His disciples; but He used it in a wide sense to designate anyone who had a mission from God to men. Cf. Lk. 13³⁴ = Mt. 23³⁷, 'Jerusalem, which killeth the prophets, and stoneth them that are sent unto her.' 'Messengers' is a wider term than 'prophets': and in this sense all prophets are messengers, though all messengers are not necessarily prophets. The fate of these representatives of God is death and persecution. It is described in greater detail in Mt. 23[34]. The result of this behaviour to the men of God is that the persecutors will have to answer for their misdeeds. The ' that ' which stands at the beginning of the verse represents the common Semitic idiom by which the result of an action is spoken of as if it were the purpose of the action. ' The blood of all the prophets ' is difficult, for the text goes on to give as examples two men who were not prophets. Abel in Jewish tradition is a type of righteousness; but I do not know that he is anywhere called a prophet. Zachariah, on the most probable interpretation, is the Zechariah whose death is described in 2 Chron. 24[20f.]; and he was not a prophet, but a priest. Mt. (23[35]) has ' all the righteous blood,' which fits better with what follows. The righteous blood is what is called in the Old Testament ' innocent blood,' i.e. blood unrighteously shed. That such blood clamours for vengeance is a common idea in the Old Testament (Gen. 4[10]; Jb. 16[18]; Is. 26[21]; Ezek. 24[7f.]; 2 Ki. 9[26]) and in Jewish thought (Billerbeck, i. 940 ff.). Compare and contrast Heb. 12[24]. It should be noted that the blood of Abel is represented as crying for vengeance (Gen. 4[10]); and that in the account of the death of Zechariah (1 Chron. 24[22]) the dying priest says, ' The Lord look upon it and require it ': also that in Jewish legend the blood of this Zechariah refused to soak into the ground until vengeance was exacted by Nebuzaradan (Billerbeck, *loc. cit.*) Cf. Robertson Smith, *Religion of the Semites*,[2] p. 417. n. 5. ' This generation ' will have to answer for all the crimes of its predecessors because it will not break with the past in the only possible way—by repentance and submission to the will of God.

52. The third woe against the scribes. The statement of the charge in Mt. 23[13] is different. There the scribes and Pharisees are accused of closing the Kingdom against those who wished to enter. This may refer to their opposition to John the Baptist and Jesus. But then it does not appear that their opposition prevented those who really wished to enter the Kingdom from doing so. It can hardly mean that they prevented Gentiles from being converted to Israel, for that is contradicted by *v.* 15. The Matthean form looks like an attempt to clarify the more difficult form of the saying in Lk. The ' knowledge ' here meant is the knowledge of God as revealed in the Old Testament. Of this revelation the scribes were the custodians, and the charge against them is that by their method of interpretation they have obscured the simple and central truths there given. The knowledge of God as Father and King and of His rule of love and mercy has been buried under an ever-increasing mass of traditions and precedents and pettifogging rules. Continually busied with the details of the Law they forgot the great principles of the prophetic religion; and the finished product of their expert labours was not so much a revelation of God as of their own ingenuity, calculated to make men despair of themselves rather than trust in God, to turn men away from the Kingdom rather than bring them into it.

Additional Note: The Death of Zachariah

In commenting on Lk. 11[51] we have assumed that the Zachariah there mentioned is the Zechariah whose fate is described in 2 Chron. 24[20ff.]. This view is by no means universally accepted; and, at one time or another, other identifications have been proposed. As the matter is of importance for the dating of the New Testament documents, the point must be discussed in detail. In Lk. the name is Zachariah simply: in Mt. 23³⁵ it is Zachariah the son of Barachiah. The following identifications have been made.

(1) Zacharias the father of John the Baptist. The story of his murder in the Temple appears in early Christian apocryphal literature. It is referred to by Epiphanius (*Haer.* xxvi. 12), quoting from a Gnostic work called ' The Birth of Mary ' (*Trans.* M. R. James, *Apocryphal New Testament*, p. 19). It is also found in the *Protevangelium*, xxiii f. (James, *op. cit.*, p. 48), in the Coptic conclusion of the *Apocalypse of Paul* (James, *op. cit.*, p. 554), and in the *Latin Infancy Gospels* (ed. James), pp. 90 ff. Another version of the story was known to Origen and Peter of Alexandria (H. Smith, *Ante-Nicene Exegesis of the Gospels*, iv. 75; v. 85–96). Origen identified this Zacharias with the Zachariah of Mt. 23³⁵ and Lk. 11⁵¹.

(2) Zechariah the prophet (*c.* 520 B.C.) son of Berechiah and grandson of Iddo (Zech. 1¹, ⁷), of priestly descent (Neh. 12⁴, ¹⁶), co-worker with the prophet Haggai (Ezra 5¹, 6¹⁴—in both places called Zechariah son of Iddo). Concerning the death of this prophet nothing is known. In late Jewish tradition he was confused with the Zechariah mentioned in 2 Chron. 24²⁰ ᶠᶠ·. The passages are: Targum on Lam. 2²⁰ and Josippon 80.

(3) Zechariah son of Jehoiada a priest, stoned ' in the court of the house of the Lord ' by the people at the command of Joash (2 Chron. 24²⁰ ᶠᶠ·). ' And when he died he said, The Lord look upon it and require it ' (24²²). According to Rabbinic tradition, his blood would not dry up, but remained till the time of the destruction of Solomon's Temple, when it was avenged by Nebuzaradan. Rabbinical passages in Billerbeck, i. 940 ff.

(4) Zechariah son of Baris, murdered in the Temple in A.D. 67 by two Zealots. The story is told by Josephus (*BJ* iv. 334–344). The name of his father is differently given in the MSS. of Josephus as Baris, Baruch, and Bariscaeus. Baris is the reading adopted by Niese and Thackeray. The latter says (note on *BJ*, iv. 335) that the reading Baruch is negligible. The identification of this Zechariah with the Zachariah of our text is as old as Chrysostom. It was also held by Grotius. For these it meant that the words of the text were a prediction made by Jesus and duly fulfilled in A.D. 67. The same identification is made by Wellhausen and Meyer; but for them it is prophecy after the event and proves that the saying is later than A.D. 67.

It may be assumed that our text is from Q. The first question then concerns the name of the victim. Is the Q text (*a*) Zechariah son of Barachiah (Mt.) or (*b*) Zachariah (Lk.)? If (*a*), then who is meant?

(i) There is no evidence that the prophet Zechariah was martyred; but there is evidence that in late Judaism there was a confusion between Zechariah the prophet and Zechariah the priest who was killed in the Temple. It is possible that this confusion was already made when Q was compiled or still earlier.

(ii) Zacharias the father of John hardly comes into account. The legend of his death looks like an attempt to make the facts fit the saying.

(iii) Zechariah the son of Baris might be meant, but:

(α) Baris or even Bariscaeus is not the same as Barachias.

(β) There is no suggestion that this man was a prophet: all that Josephus tells us is that he was a respectable law-abiding citizen of Jerusalem, who was the victim of the illegal violence of the Zealots.

(γ) The legend of the death of Zacharias the father of John is so far evidence against this identification. For there would be no need to invent a death for Zacharias the father of John, if there was already a murdered Zechariah provided by Josephus.

(δ) If Zechariah the son of Baris were meant, it would bring the date of Q down later than 67, which is on other grounds improbable.

If (*b*), then the words ' son of Barachiah ' are an editorial expansion in Mt.

(i) Mt. might have confused Zechariah the priest with Zechariah the prophet.

(ii) The legend of the death of Zechariah the father of John is not likely to have been in circulation when the Gospel of Mt. was compiled.

(iii) Assuming a date later than 67 for the compilation of Mt. it is just possible that Mt. knew of the fate of Zechariah son of Baris and supposed that this was the Zechariah referred to in Q, and that Jesus had prophesied his fate. As Chrysostom and Grotius were able to believe this, it is possible that Mt. believed it too.

But if Zechariah alone is the text of Q we have to ask whether it is a correct report of the words of Jesus; and if so, what *He* meant.

Here we have a further complication. It is argued that the Lucan form of the saying indicates that it is a quotation from a written source. This view is to be rejected for the reasons given above. If the words were a quotation from a Jewish prophetic-apocalyptic writing, that document would be earlier than Q, and the objection raised against Zechariah the son of Baris in iii(δ) becomes still stronger. If the words are a genuine utterance of Jesus, He can only have meant Zechariah the priest or have confused that Zechariah with Zechariah the prophet. In either case the incident referred to is that recorded in 2 Chron. 24.

(*c*) CONCLUSION OF THE SPEECH AGAINST PHARISAISM

Lk. 11[53f.] is the conclusion of Lk.'s narrative setting of the speech against Pharisaism. It is followed by a short self-contained anecdote (12[1]), giving another saying of Jesus again Pharisaism. Lk. 12[1] has an independent parallel in Mk. 8[14-21], which is probably the more original setting of the saying. It does not seem likely that Lk. 12[1] is derived from Q. More probably it is a fragment of Lk.'s separate tradition (L), inserted here in what seemed to him an appropriate context. Actually Lk. 11[53]–12[1] breaks the connexion between 11[52] and 12[2-3]. Lk. 12[2f.] I take to be the conclusion of the speech against Pharisaism. In 12[4] a new beginning is made with the words ' And I say unto you, my friends.'

MT. 10[26f.]	LK. 12[2-3]
10 26 Fear them not therefore: for there is nothing covered, that shall not be revealed; and hid, that shall not be known. 27 What I tell you in the darkness, speak ye in the light: and what ye hear in the ear, proclaim upon the housetops.	**12** 2 But there is nothing covered up, that shall not be revealed: and hid, that shall 3 not be known. Wherefore whatsoever ye have said in the darkness shall be heard in the light; and what ye have spoken in the ear in the inner chambers shall be proclaimed upon the housetops.

Cf. Mk. 4^{22}||Lk. 8^{17}

4 22 For there is nothing hid, save that it
       should be manifested; neither was *anything*
       made secret, but that it should come to
       light.

2. The sayings are in poetical form. Mk. 4^{22} appears in a context which
makes it refer most probably to the coming manifestation of the Kingdom in
power. In Mt. the sense is different: the saying prepares the way for an exhortation to the disciples to utter publicly the things that Jesus has confided privately
to them. This is inevitable, since Mt. has incorporated the section of Q represented by Lk. 12$^{2-9}$ in his Mission Charge to the Twelve. If our analysis of the
text is correct these verses in Lk.—and in Q—are really a warning to the opponents of Jesus that a time is coming when their doings will be exposed. Bultmann
argues that the saying was originally no prophetic word of encouragement, but
a popular warning against entrusting secrets to anyone, and so purely secular.
He maintains that in Q it is already interpreted as a promise, for only so could
it be used in the Christian tradition. Mt. carries the process farther in the same
direction. It may, however, be doubted whether the original form of the saying
is a proverb of worldly wisdom. It belongs rather to the order of things represented by Mt. 6$^{1-18}$. The things which are said and done in secret are not concealed from God; and in the Judgement all will be brought to light. There are
scribes and Pharisees who may well dread this coming exposure.

3. The original form of the saying is preserved by Lk. Mt. has adapted it to
its context in the Mission Charge. ' Wherefore ' would be better translated
' because.' Darkness is a figure for secrecy (cf. Sophocles, *Antigone*, 692), and
light for publicity. The words ' in the inner chambers ' do not appear in Mt.,
and are probably added by Lk. They spoil the parallelism, which is between
' spoken in the ear ' and ' proclaimed upon the housetops.' ' Spoken in the ear,'
i.e. whispered, stands for secret communications ; ' proclaimed upon the housetops ' means public announcement. (Cf. Billerbeck, i. 580.)

5. *DISCIPLES UNDER PERSECUTION* (155, 157)

In the preceding sections the nature of the opposition to Jesus and His message
has been exposed. The remainder of this portion of Q (Lk. 12$^{4-12, \ 22-34}$) is a
series of exhortations to the disciples concerning their behaviour in face of this
situation. The first part (12$^{4-12}$) deals with conduct when persecuted, and its
keynotes are loyalty and trust. Verses 4–9 have a parallel in Mt.'s Mission
Charge (10$^{28-33}$). Mt. here borrows from Q. Besides this there is an independent
parallel to *v.* 9 in Mk. 8^{38}||Lk. 9^{26}. Lk. 12^{10} has an independent parallel in
Mk. 3$^{28f.}$. Mt. 12$^{31f.}$ is a conflation of Mk. and Q. Lk. 12$^{11f.}$ has an independent parallel in Mk. 13^{11}, and what is probably another in Lk. 21$^{14f.}$ (L?). Mt.
10$^{19f.}$ is a conflation of Mk. and Q.

(a) FEARLESSNESS

MT. 10$^{28-31}$	LK. 12$^{4-7}$
10 28 And be not afraid of them which kill the body, but are not able to kill the soul: but rather fear him which is able to	12 4 And I say unto you my friends, Be not afraid of them which kill the body, and after that have no more that they can do.

29 destroy both soul and body in [1] hell. Are not two sparrows sold for a farthing? and not one of them shall fall on the ground 30 without your Father: but the very hairs 31 of your head are all numbered. Fear not therefore; ye are of more value than many sparrows.

[1] Gr. Gehenna.

5 But I will warn you whom ye shall fear: Fear him, which after he hath killed hath [1] power to cast into [2] hell; yea, I say unto 6 you, Fear him. Are not five sparrows sold for two farthings? and not one of them is 7 forgotten in the sight of God. But the very hairs of your head are all numbered. Fear not: ye are of more value than many sparrows.

[1] Or, authority.
[2] Gr. Gehenna.

4, 5. The beginning of a new section is marked by the words ' And I say unto you my friends,' dropped by Mt. because the whole passage is incorporated in the Mission Charge. This is the only place in the Synoptic Gospels where Jesus calls His disciples ' My friends.' Cf. John 15[14f.]. Mt. 10[28] ' but are not able to kill the soul ' looks like an attempt to make the words ' after that have no more that they can do ' more precise. As the text stands in Lk. it gives a perfectly good sense. The disciples are not to fear men; for man's extreme penalty is a mere nothing compared with the consequences of apostasy. Cf. 4 Macc., 13[14f.], ' Let us not fear him who thinketh he kills; for a great struggle and peril of the soul awaits in eternal torment those who transgress the ordinance of God.' What is to be dreaded is now stated. It is the condemnation of God. The Lucan form of the saying is the more original. Mt. 10[28b] is abbreviation. With Lk.'s ' cast into Gehenna ' compare Mk. 9[43, 45, 47]. The destruction of body and soul in Gehenna (Mt. 10[28]) is an alteration of the general statement to bring it into more exact agreement with Jewish belief. This belief is stated in Tos. Sanhedrin 13[3]: ' The wicked of Israel in their bodies, and the wicked of the nations of the world in their bodies go down to hell and are punished in it for twelve months. After twelve months their souls become extinct, and their bodies are burned up, and hell casts them out, and they turn to ashes, and the wind scatters them and strews them beneath the soles of the feet of the righteous ' (Moore, Judaism, ii. 387). The expression ' Yea, I say unto you ' (Lk.) is characteristic of Q. Cf. Lk. 7[26]||Mt.11[9]; Lk. 11[51]. It is omitted in Mt.'s abbreviated form of the saying. The R.V. translation ' hell ' stands for Gehenna, the Græcised form of the Hebrew Gehinnom. The idea of Gehenna as a place of punishment for the godless after the final Judgement first appears in the second century B.C. Originally it is a place of punishment for the godless Israelites only; but this restriction was soon dropped, and in the days of Jesus it was thought of as prepared for all sinners, who were to be sent to it after the Judgement. Soon after the middle of the first century A.D. Gehenna began to be conceived as the place where sinners would be punished in the period between death and the Judgement. In this passage Gehenna means the place of torment for those who are condemned in the final Judgement. (Cf. Billerbeck, iv. 1029 ff. and Abrahams, Studies, ii. 41-49.)

6, 7. If God the Judge is to be feared, God the King is to be trusted. No human persecution is to be allowed to corrupt the loyalty of the disciples to God or to diminish their trust in Him. The duty of trusting God is illustrated first by the case of sparrows sold for food. Mt. and Lk. differ here. Mt. has ' two for a farthing ': Lk. ' five for two farthings.' More correct equivalents in English money would be a halfpenny and a penny respectively. Lk. may be the more original: five is used in Jewish reckoning in much the same way as we use ' half a dozen.' At the end of the third century A.D. an edict of the Emperor Diocletian fixed the maximum price of ten sparrows at a sum equivalent to threepence-halfpenny. The sparrow's is the cheapest life in the market; but it is not outside God's care. A similar saying is ascribed to Rabbi Simeon ben Jochai (c. A.D. 150): ' No bird perishes without God—how much less a man!' ' Not one of them shall fall on the ground without your Father' (Mt.) is to be preferred to Lk.'s ' not one of them is forgotten in the sight of God.' For it makes clearer the connexion between the illustration of the sparrows and the reference to the hairs of the head, which is inserted between the illustration and the conclusion to be drawn from it. The force of the saying that the hairs of your head are all numbered is ' Not one hair of your head shall fall to the ground without your Father.' Cf. 1 Sam. 14^{15}. The sparrow cannot be killed apart from God's will; but you cannot suffer the smallest injury apart from God's will. God cares for the sparrow: he cares still more for you. ' Ye are of more value than many sparrows ' correctly translates the Greek; but the Greek is most probably a mistranslation of the Aramaic. The conclusion required is ' Ye are of much more value than sparrows.' The difference is qualitative, not quantitative. So Wellhausen.

(b) LOYALTY

MT. 10$^{32-33}$, 12^{32}

10 32 Every one therefore who shall confess [1] me before men, [2] him will I also confess before my Father which is in heaven.
33 But whosoever shall deny me before men, him will I also deny before my Father which is in heaven.
12 32 And whosoever shall speak a word against the Son of man, it shall be forgiven him; but whosoever shall speak against the Holy Spirit, it shall not be forgiven him, neither in this [3] world, nor in that which is to come.

Lk. 12$^{11f.}$. Cf. Mt. 10$^{19f.}$
[1] Gr. *in me.*
[2] Gr. *in him.*
[3] Or, *age.*

LK. 12$^{8-12}$

12 8 And I say unto you, Every one who shall confess [1] me before men, [2] him shall the Son of man also confess before the 9 angels of God: but he that denieth me in the presence of men shall be denied in the presence of the angels of God.
10 And every one who shall speak a word against the Son of man, it shall be forgiven him: but unto him that blasphemeth against the Holy Spirit it shall not 11 be forgiven. And when they bring you before the synagogues, and the rulers, and the authorities, be not anxious how or what ye shall answer, or what ye shall 12 say: for the Holy Spirit shall teach you in that very hour what ye ought to say.

[1] Gr. *in me.*
[2] Gr. *in him.*

8 f. The duty of loyalty to God does not remain an abstraction. Jesus Himself is the object of it. It is as if He said: ' He that is faithful to me is faithful to Him that sent me.' The Jewish martyrs of the Maccabean age showed their loyalty to God by their obedience to the Law: the disciples will show the same loyalty to God in their devotion to Jesus. In Him the Kingdom of God is manifested. There are only two alternatives, acknowledgement or denial: there is no middle position. The second half of the saying is reported independently in Mk. 8^{38}:

> 8 38 For whosoever shall be ashamed of me and of my words in this adulterous and sinful generation, the Son of man also shall be ashamed of him, when he cometh in the glory of his Father with the holy angels.

It is to be noted that Mk. here agrees with Lk. in distinguishing between Jesus and the Son of Man. The substitution of ' I ' for ' the Son of man ' in Mt. is editorial work. The original Q form of the saying is that of Lk. What, then, is the meaning of this distinction between Jesus and the Son of Man? It may be that Jesus in His earthly ministry is only Son of Man designate. The force of ' him shall the Son of man also confess ' will then be ' him will I also confess when I become Son of man '; and the text of Mt. will be a correct interpretation of the saying. It is, I think, more probable that the distinction is a real one, and that the ' Son of man ' here stands for the Remnant, the true Israel of which Jesus is the head. This view is fortified if we accept what is probably the true reading in Mk. 8³⁸ ' me and mine ' rather than ' me and my words.' The idea that the community—Christ plus those that are His—will confess or deny people at the final consummation may seem strange; but it seems also to be implied in Mt. 25³¹⁻⁴⁶ (M); Mt. 19²⁸ (M); Lk. 22³⁰ (L). Cf. also 1 Cor. 6²ᶠ·, and the discussion in my *Teaching of Jesus*, pp. 263–270. Moreover, the solidarity of Jesus and His followers is stressed in such sayings as Lk. 10¹⁶ (Q), ' He that heareth you heareth me; and he that rejecteth you rejecteth me.' So ' Whosoever shall be ashamed of me and mine ' (Mk. 8³⁸) is really equivalent to the Lucan ' he that denieth me ' (12⁹). In the final consummation the confessors and deniers on earth will be confessed or denied by the Son of Man, that is, by the true spiritual Israel speaking through Christ its King.

The R.V. mg. ' confess in me ' ' confess in him ' gives the literal translation of the Greek text, which is itself a literal rendering of the Aramaic idiom. For ' the angels of God ' (Lk.) Mt. has ' my Father which is in heaven.' The latter is a favourite Matthæan expression and probably editorial here. It has been suggested (Dalman, *Words of Jesus*, 209 f.) that ' the angels of God ' is a pious periphrasis for God. There is, however, no Jewish example of such a usage, and it would be very unlikely that Jesus spoke thus or that Luke made Him speak thus. More likely we should take the words in Lk. as they stand, and regard ' before the angels of God ' as another way of saying ' in heaven ' or ' in the presence of God.' Cf. Lk. 15⁷ and 15¹⁰.

10. This saying also has an independent parallel in Mk. 3²⁸ᶠᶠ·.

> 3 28 Verily I say unto you, All their sins shall be forgiven unto the sons of men, and their blasphemies wherewith soever 29 they shall blaspheme: but whosoever shall blaspheme against the Holy Spirit hath never forgiveness, but is guilty of an 30 eternal sin: because they said, He hath an unclean spirit.

In the Marcan context it is Jesus' reply to the charge that He was mad; and it is probable that this is the original. It is to be noted that in Mk. there is no word about blasphemy against the Son of Man; but there is a reference to the blasphemies of the sons of men, i.e. the blasphemies which men utter against one another. Such insults, it is said, are forgivable; it is only blasphemy against the

Holy Spirit that is unforgivable. Here we have the original form of the saying. In Q the saying is detached from its context, and the blasphemies of men have become blasphemies against the Son of Man. This makes an impossible situation. For it has just been said that he who denies Christ will be denied in the Judgement. Now it is said that he who speaks a word (= blasphemes) against the Son of Man will be forgiven. The difficulties disappear when it is recognised that ' the Son of Man ' in Lk. 12[10] should be ' a man.' The compiler who brought the saying into its present Q context in Aramaic may have been aware of this and understood it to mean that slanders against the disciples would put the slanderers in gravest peril, since the same Holy Spirit that worked in Jesus worked also in His followers. But if this was the case in the Aramaic Q, it has been obscured in the Greek.

Blasphemy against the Holy Spirit is not merely a matter of bad language. It is far more deadly than that. It is the extremest form of opposition to God. He who blasphemes against the Holy Spirit has identified himself so completely with the kingdom of evil that for him evil is good, ugliness beauty, and falsehood truth; and so the workings of the Holy Spirit appear to him as madness.

11 f. This saying is reported independently in Mk. 13[11] with a parallel, which may be independent (L?) in Lk. 21[14f.].

MK. 13[11]

> 13 11   And when they lead you to *judgement*,
> and deliver you up, be not anxious
> beforehand what ye shall speak: but
> whatsoever shall be given you in that
> hour, that speak ye: for it is not ye that
> speak, but the Holy Ghost.

Mt. 10[19f.] is a conflation of Mk. 13[11] and Lk. 12[11f.] (Q). In the persecution of the disciples the forms of law will be invoked. They will be prosecuted before Jewish courts (synagogues) and Gentile tribunals (the rulers and the authorities cf. Lk. 20[20]). In Rabbinic Hebrew the word ' authority ' (*rāshūth*) is similarly used of the Gentile government. When the disciples—many of them simple and unlearned men—find themselves in this position, their defence will be provided for them by Divine inspiration. Cf. Acts 4[8, 13]. In Lk. 12[12], Mk. 13[11] it is ' the Holy Spirit ' that inspires the defence: in Mt. 10[20] this has been changed to ' the Spirit of your Father ': in Lk. 20[15] it is Christ Himself who will supply what has to be said. ' The Holy Spirit ' is no doubt the original.

In all the campaign of defamation and persecution to which they will be exposed the disciples are to keep the faith, keep faith with God, and faith in God. Their first duty is to obey God at all costs; and their chief reliance is to be upon God, whom they serve and who will see them through. This is only possible if all worldly advantages and selfish ambitions are put in the background. You cannot serve God and mammon; and equally you cannot trust God and mammon. The concluding section of this part of Q sets forth this principle.

(c) FREEDOM FROM WORLDLY CARES

Lk. 12[22-31] begins with an exhortation not to be anxious about material things. The force of the exhortation in this context is obvious. Such anxiety is a hindrance to the single-minded service of God. The disciple is in danger of having business of his own to which he must attend before he can give himself to God's work. It also undermines trust in God. ' Trust in God and keep your powder dry ' very soon reduces itself to ' keep your powder dry ' or to ' God is on the side of the big battalions ' or to ' Heaven helps those who help themselves '—in more senses than one. Material things are not, however, despised or rejected. They are put in their place. ' Seek the Kingdom, and these things shall be added unto you.' Material things have a place in the Kingdom both among its benefits (12^{31}) and in its service ($12^{33f.}$). They can be used and enjoyed for the glory of God, but only by those who give first place to God.

MT. $6^{25\text{-}33}$	LK. $12^{22\text{-}31}$
6 25 Therefore I say unto you, Be not anxious for your life, what ye shall eat, or what ye shall drink; nor yet for your body, what ye shall put on. Is not the life more than the food, and the body than the 26 raiment? Behold the birds of the heaven, that they sow not, neither do they reap, nor gather into barns; and your heavenly Father feedeth them. Are not ye of 27 much more value than they? And which of you by being anxious can add one cubit 28 unto his ¹ stature? And why are ye anxious concerning raiment? Consider the lilies of the field, how they grow; they 29 toil not, neither do they spin: yet I say unto you, that even Solomon in all his glory was not arrayed like one of these. 30 But if God doth so clothe the grass of the field, which to-day is, and to-morrow is cast into the oven, *shall he* not much more 31 *clothe* you, O ye of little faith? Be not therefore anxious, saying, What shall we 32 eat? or, What shall we drink? or, Wherewithal shall we be clothed? For after all these things do the Gentiles seek; for your heavenly Father knoweth that ye have 33 need of all these things. But seek ye first his kingdom, and his righteousness; and all these things shall be added unto you. ¹ Or, *age*.	12 22 And he said unto his disciples, Therefore I say unto you, Be not anxious for *your* ¹ life, what ye shall eat; nor yet for your body, what ye shall put on.‖For 23 the ¹ life is more than the food, and the 24 body than the raiment.‖Consider the ravens, that they sow not, neither reap; ‖which have no store-chamber nor barn; and God feedeth them: of how much 25 more value are ye than the birds!‖And which of you by being anxious can add a 26 cubit unto his ² stature? If then ye are not able to do even that which is least, why are ye anxious concerning the rest? 27 Consider the lilies, how they grow; they toil not, neither do they spin; ‖yet I say unto you, Even Solomon in all his glory 28 was not arrayed like one of these.‖But if God doth so clothe the grass in the field, which to-day is, and to-morrow is cast into the oven; ‖how much more *shall he* 29 *clothe* you, O ye of little faith?‖And seek not ye what ye shall eat, and what ye shall drink, neither be ye of doubtful 30 mind. For all these things do the nations of the world seek after: but your Father knoweth that ye have need of 31 these things. Howbeit seek ye ³ his kingdom, and these things shall be added unto you. ¹ Or, *soul*. ² Or, *age*. ³ Many ancient authorities read *the kingdom of God*.

The whole of this Q section has been embodied by Mt. in his Sermon on the Mount. The verbal agreement between Mt. and Lk. is high.

22 f., 24, 27. ' And he said unto his disciples ' marks the beginning of a new section. Mt. has altered the introductory formula in the interests of his continuous discourse. Verses 22 f. state the theme of the paragraph. Jesus is not preaching asceticism. He does not suggest that there is any religious value in starvation or nakedness. What He demands is a sense of proportion and a true valuation of things. Food is not an end in itself, but only a means to an end, the maintenance of life. Similarly dress is necessary for the protection of the body. Life and health

are more important than food and clothing.   It is possible that there is here a tacit
criticism of the multitude of scribal regulations about permitted and forbidden
foods and articles of clothing—whether an egg laid on a Feast-day might be eaten
or not, and the like.   But the main point is the more general one that God has
given man life and that He may be trusted to give also what is necessary for the
maintenance of life.   This is enforced by two illustrations.   These two short pieces
are an excellent example of what I have called compound parallelism (*Teaching of
Jesus*, pp. 54 ff.).   The two illustrations as wholes answer to one another; and the
several parts of each are also in parallelism.   This can best be shown by setting the
two pieces out in lines.

> I.   Consider the ravens,   *(a)*
>   That they neither sow nor reap;   *(b1)*
>   They have no barn or storehouse;   *(b2)*
>   And God feeds them: *(d)*
>   How much better are you than the birds!   *(f)*
>
> II. Consider the lilies,   *(a)*
>   How they neither toil nor spin,   *(b)*
>   Yet I tell you that Solomon in all his glory
>   was not arrayed like one of these.   *(c)*
>   But if God so clothe the grass   *(d)*
>   Which to-day is in the field   *(e1)*
>   And to-morrow is cast into the oven;   *(e2)*
>   How much more you, O ye of little faith ?   *(f)*

In the first strophe the Lucan text is better than that in Mt.   ' Ravens ' (Lk.)
is generalised by Mt. to ' birds.'   Then when ' birds ' appears in the last line Mt.
has to alter it to ' them.'   The parallelism of lines 2 and 3 in Lk. is destroyed in
Mt.'s ' they sow not, neither do they reap, nor gather into barns ' which is more
logical but less poetical.   In the second strophe the words ' they grow ' are
omitted by some important authorities for the text of Lk.   They are probably an
intrusion from Mt.; and the true text of Q is as given in line 2.   It is closely
parallel in form to the corresponding line in strophe I.   The original text of Lk. is:
' How they neither spin nor weave '; that of Mt.: ' How they grow; they toil not,
neither do they spin.'   The form of the line in Lk. is preferable to that in Mt.; but
the verbs of Mt. are more likely to be original than those of Lk.   Lk.'s ' spin ' and
' weave ' is more logical; but the ' toil ' and ' spin ' of Mt. probably represents a
play upon words in Aramaic ('ămal and 'ăzal).   So the original Q form of the line
may be reconstructed: ' How they neither toil nor spin.'   The translation given in
strophe II, line 5 is preferable to that of R.V.

Jesus here appeals to the wild birds and the wild flowers, which owe nothing to
human care.   God gives them existence and life, and God provides for them.   If
He does that for the lower forms of life, He will do no less for man.   In the second
strophe by ' the lilies ' may be meant the purple anemone, which would be contrasted with the royal purple of Solomon (so Dalman).   It should be noted how
Jesus here makes use of an old motif (Job 8[12], 14[2]; Ps. 37[2], 90[5f.], 103[15f.]; Is. 37[27],

40[6-8]), in which the brief life of the plant is used as an illustration of the shortness of human life. To-day the wild plants are a brave show: to-morrow they will be withered and dried up, so much fuel for the oven. But Jesus gives the old motif an original and characteristic turn. For Him the moral of the tale is not ' These things pass, and so must we,' but ' God lavishes infinite pains on these things, brief though their span of life is: how much more will He care for His children.'

25 f. Between the two illustrations a further argument is introduced. The translation of *v.* 25 presents a difficulty; for the Greek word translated ' stature ' in R.V. commonly means ' age.' The question is whether the words mean ' Which of you by being anxious can increase his height? ' or ' Which of you by being anxious can prolong his life? ' Commentators are divided on this point. In the present context the former alternative is the more likely. The section is concerned with food and clothing; and for first-century Palestine food and clothing depended mainly on the growth of crops and the produce of the farm generally. These are the very things about which the small farmer is constantly worrying. Jesus says: if it were possible to stimulate growth by worrying, you ought to be able to do it in your own persons. If you cannot make yourself grow, how can you expect to make the corn grow by worrying? All growth depends on God. Verse 26 has no parallel in Mt.

29, 30. The version of the saying in Mt. (*v.* 31) appears to be the more original. Compare the saying of the first-century Rabbi Eleazar: ' Whoever has bread in his basket and asks, What shall I eat to-morrow, is none other than those of little faith ' (*Sotah*, 48*b*). The true attitude of man towards God in these matters is given in the Lord's Prayer. The constant anxiety about material things is characteristic of the Gentiles. One is reminded of the pagan fertility cults and other magical devices to secure material goods. Since the days of Hosea it had been a dogma in Israel that it is God alone who gives the corn and the wine and all the other produce of nature. The knowledge that these things come from the Father as His gifts to His children, that they come not capriciously but out of His perfect knowledge of man's needs and His perfect love for His children, this is the true antidote to anxiety and fear and to the superstition that follows in their train.

31. Life is more important than food; but there is something more important than life itself—the Kingdom of God. This comes first and disciples must place it first. They must pray ' Thy Kingdom come: Thy will be done ' *before* they say ' Give us our daily bread.' Jesus establishes a hierarchy of values; and at the head stands the Kingdom. His claim is that nothing else can be understood or valued aright until this is given its rightful place. Once men have done this, they will know the true value of their own lives and of all other things: and in that knowledge they will find deliverance from fear and anxiety. The Lucan form of the saying is the more original. ' And his righteousness ' and ' all ' in Mt. 6[33] are characteristic Matthæan touches.

(d) CONFIDENCE IN GOD

LK. 12[32]

12 32   Fear not, little flock; for it is your
        Father's good pleasure to give you the
        kingdom.

32. This verse has no parallel in Mt.   Compare Lk. 22²⁹ᶠ. (L); Mt. 21⁴³.   The little flock is a handful of lambs in the midst of wolves (10³); a seemingly hopeless position.   The search for the Kingdom seems to be a fool's errand.   But in the last resort success in this quest does not depend on human power or wisdom, but upon God.   It is God who gives the Kingdom, as He gives all else.   The Kingdom, as here conceived, is the Kingdom that is to be, the perfect condition of existence for God's children.

(e) INDEPENDENCE OF WORLDLY GOODS

LK. 12³³⁻³⁴

Cf. Mt. 6¹⁹⁻²¹ (M?)

12 33 Sell that ye have, and give alms;||make for yourselves purses which wax not old, ||a treasure in the heavens that faileth not.||where no thief draweth near, neither 34 moth destroyeth.||For where your treasure is, there will your heart be also.||

33, 34. Mt. 6¹⁹⁻²¹ is similar to these verses; but the differences are large.   It is possible, as Bussmann suggests (*Syn. Stud.*, ii. 82 f.) that Mt. is here drawing from his special source (M) and that Lk. 12³²⁻³⁴ is the Q version of the saying.   The voluntary poverty here recommended depends chiefly on the recognition that all the world's goods are of little value in comparison with the good things of the Kingdom.   Further, there is the conviction that the coming of the Kingdom with all its benefits is very near.   This conviction is dominant in the early Church, and certainly goes back to Jesus Himself.   The fact that the attempt was made in the earliest days of the Jerusalem community to put this precept into practice (Acts 2⁴⁴ᶠ., 4³²⁻³⁷) is strong evidence for the authenticity of the saying.   The motive for hoarding is gone, if that is at hand which will demonetise all existing wealth.   But that is not all.   The saying has to do with the belief, common in every age, that wealth is power, and the consequent temptation to trust mammon rather than God.   Jesus here asserts that in reality money is a very weak thing.   So far from being a protection it requires to be protected.   The millionaire spends one half of his life in acquiring his million and the other half in trying to keep it.   So material goods, which should serve man, become his master; and the thought, strength, and love that should be devoted to God and His Kingdom are given instead to mammon.

D. THE FUTURE

In the preceding sections the message and mission of Jesus have been set out in relation to the best that had been thought and achieved before Him (section A), in relation to those who hear His call (section B) and those who reject and oppose Him (section C).   The interest now turns more definitely to the future and the fulfilment of what has been prepared for by John and revealed in Jesus.   In this concluding section of Q there are four main divisions: (1) The present time a time of crisis in view of the approaching end.   (2) The peril of neglect and refusal of the message.   (3) The demands of discipleship in view of the end.   (4) The final consummation.   There is no sharp division between the present section and the preceding. The thought of the disciples under persecution and opposition leads naturally to the thought that this present state is but the prelude to another condition in which faithfulness will receive its reward.

The view which dominates the whole of this section is that the existing order is coming to an end, and that the end will come soon and suddenly. It will break into the normal order of human existence like a thunderbolt out of a clear sky. This is the earliest form of the Christian expectation, as appears from 1 Thess. 5¹⁻¹⁰. It is also the view of Lk. 21³⁴⁻³⁶ (L) and Mk. 13³²⁻³⁷. This view stands in sharp contrast to the programme outlined in Mk. 13⁵⁻³¹. There the end is led up to by a series of catastrophes. There can be little doubt that the teaching of Jesus is more accurately represented by Q and its allies than by Mk. 13⁵⁻³¹; and it seems probable that the solution of the contradiction is that Mk. 13⁵⁻³¹ is a document made up, in the main, of genuine sayings of Jesus, but so arranged that the total impression is wrong. Cf. *The Teaching of Jesus*, pp. 260 ff.

The first part of this eschatological section of Q may be divided up somewhat as follows. The present time is a time of crisis: (*a*) for the disciples (12³⁵⁻⁴⁸); (*b*) for Jesus Himself (12⁴⁹⁻⁵³); (*c*) for Israel (12⁵⁴⁻⁵⁹). This is so because (*d*) forces have been set in motion which lead inevitably to one result (13¹⁸⁻²¹). With the coming of Jesus something has happened which marks the end of the old order and the beginning of the new. Soon the change will be complete. The call to men and women is a call to repent while there is still time. To those who have already accepted the yoke of the Kingdom it is a call to be watchful and faithful in the time that remains. It is the old challenge that is set before the people: ' Choose you this day whom ye will serve.' But it comes with a new urgency because it is backed by a new revelation of the nature of God and of His Kingdom. In the light of that revelation to refuse the challenge is to take a terrible responsibility.

1. *THE TIME OF CRISIS*

(*a*) For the Disciples (158, 159)

LK. 12³⁵⁻³⁸

Cf. Mt. 25¹⁻¹³ (M).

12 35 Let your loins be girded about, and
36 your lamps burning; and be ye yourselves like unto men looking for their lord, when he shall return from the marriage feast; that, when he cometh and knocketh, they may straightway open unto him.
37 Blessed are those [1] servants, whom the lord when he cometh shall find watching: verily I say unto you, that he shall gird himself, and make them sit down to meat, and shall come and serve them.
38 And if he shall come in the second watch, and if in the third, and find *them* so, blessed are those *servants*.

[1] Gr. *bond-servants*.

35-38. Lk. 12³⁵⁻³⁸ has no parallel in Mt.; but Mt. 25¹⁻¹³ has several features in common with this passage. The girt loins signify readiness and the lighted lamp watchfulness. The time when the servants will be required is uncertain. ' Men ' (*v.* 36) means servants (Preuschen-Bauer, col. 108); and the ' looking for ' their master is a looking with eager expectancy, a waiting to welcome Him. For the disciples the consummation is the consummation of their *hopes*. The significance of the marriage feast may be left an open question for the moment. See below, p. 225. The point is that the master of the servants is absent and the exact time of his return is unknown to them. They will not even see him coming. The first intimation of his presence will be his knock at the door. Those who are prepared for his appearance will find that it spells the highest happiness for them. Hitherto they have given of their best to their master: now he will give to them service for service and benefit for benefit. We must compare Lk. 17$^{7-10}$. There the point is that the very thing that is here promised is the last thing that servants would dare to expect. So the point here is that the reward of watchfulness and faithfulness will be something beyond all expectation. The saying ends with a fresh emphasis on the uncertainty of the time of the Parousia. The reference to second and third watch implies the Jewish division of the night into three periods. Roman practice divided the night into four watches. The latter system appears in Mk. 13^{35}. The servants must be prepared to stay awake all night if necessary. So the disciples must continue watchful, even after their first expectations have been disappointed. ' Blessed are those servants ' is an exclamation: ' How happy are those servants! ' Compare Philip Doddridge's paraphrase of this passage in his hymn beginning

' Ye servants of the Lord,
Each in his office wait.'

MT. 24$^{43-44}$	LK. 12$^{39-40}$
24 43 ^{1} But know this, that if the master of the house had known in what watch the thief was coming, he would have watched, and would not have suffered 44 his house to be ^{2} broken through. Therefore be ye also ready: for in an hour that ye think not the Son of man cometh.	12 39 ^{1} But know this, that if the master of the house had known in what hour the thief was coming, he would have watched, and not have left his house to 40 be ^{2} broken through. Be ye also ready: for in an hour that ye think not the Son of man cometh.
^{1} Or, *But this ye know.* ^{2} Gr. *digged through.*	^{1} Or, *But this ye know.* ^{2} Gr. *digged through.*

A second parable stressing the unexpectedness of the end. The agreement between Mt. and Lk. is close. ' Hour ' (Lk. 12^{39}) should perhaps be preferred to ' watch ' (Mt. 24^{43}). Cf. Lk. 12^{40} = Mt. 24^{44}; Lk. 12^{46} = Mt. 24^{50}. Several early and important authorities omit the words ' have watched and ' in Lk. 12^{39}. This shorter text may be the original in Lk. and Q, and the added words an editorial gloss in Mt., which has crept into MSS. of Lk. ' Left ' (Lk.) and ' suffered ' (Mt.) are translation variants. Cf. the Greek versions of Dan. 4$^{12, 23}$.

39 f. This second parable makes the same point as the preceding. The figure here employed appears again in 1 Thess. 5$^{2ff.}$, ' The day of the Lord so cometh as a thief in the night.' Cf. 2 Pet. 3^{10}; Rev. 3^{3}, 16^{15}. ' Digged through ' (R.V. mg.) is a more literal rendering of the Greek than ' broken through.' Cf. Mt. 6^{19}; Job. 24^{16}. The expression depends on the fact that in Palestine the walls of houses were commonly made of clay. The practice of digging through the wall

rather than forcing the door of the house may have been due to superstitious motives. Cf. Trumbull, *The Threshold Covenant*, pp. 260 f. For those who are not prepared the coming of the Son of Man means disaster. This coming of the Son of Man, which Paul, using a term borrowed from the Old Testament, calls ' the day of the Lord,' stands for the Judgement, the final vindication of righteousness and the end of evil. It is the full manifestation of the Kingdom of God in power and glory; and this means, among other things, the vindication of all who have accepted the Kingdom and been faithful. The origin of the idea is in Dan. 7.

MT. 24[45-51]	LK. 12[41-46]
24 45 Who then is the faithful and wise [1] servant, whom his lord hath set over his household, to give them their food in due 46 season? Blessed is that [1] servant, whom his lord when he cometh shall find so 47 doing. Verily I say unto you, that he 48 will set him over all that he hath. But if that evil [1] servant shall say in his heart, 49 My lord tarrieth; and shall begin to beat his fellow-servants, and shall eat and 50 drink with the drunken; the lord of that [1] servant shall come in a day when he expecteth not, and in an hour when he knoweth not, and shall [2] cut him asunder, and appoint his portion with 51 the hypocrites: there shall be the weeping and gnashing of teeth.	12 41 And Peter said, Lord, speakest thou this parable unto us, or even unto all? 42 And the Lord said, Who then is [1] the faithful and wise steward, whom his lord shall set over his household, to give them their portion of food in due season? 43 Blessed is that [2] servant, whom his lord when he cometh shall find so doing. 44 Of a truth I say unto you, that he will set 45 him over all that he hath. But if that [2] servant say in his heart, My lord delayeth his coming; and shall begin to beat the menservants and the maid-servants, and to eat and drink, and to be 46 drunken; the lord of that [2] servant shall come in a day when he expecteth not, and in an hour when he knoweth not, and shall [3] cut him asunder, and appoint his portion with the unfaithful.
[1] Gr. *bondservant.* [2] Or, *severely scourge him.*	[1] Or, *the faithful steward, the wise* man *whom, etc.* [2] Gr. *bondservant.* [3] Or, *severely scourge him.*

The task of the disciples is not confined to watchfulness. They have positive duties to perform and those who stand nearest to Jesus have the heaviest responsibility. The work is the work of the Kingdom as already defined in the Mission Charge. And at the end this work will be examined. Cf. 1 Cor. 4[1-5]. The agreement between Mt. and Lk. is close.

41. This verse has no parallel in Mt., which is curious since Mt. is following Q from 24[43] to 24[51]. If the verse stood in Q, Mt. has omitted it. It is commonly regarded as the work of Lk. On the other hand, Mt. may have omitted it because it was difficult to understand what it meant. It certainly is difficult. When Peter asks whether ' this parable ' refers to ' us,' he presumably means the Twelve; and the most natural interpretation of ' this parable ' is the immediately preceding parable of the thief in the night. But it is impossible to see what special reference this parable could have to the Twelve rather than to anyone else. Possibly ' this parable ' means the whole passage Lk. 12[35-40], with the promise of *v.* 37 specially in view. Peter is then asking whether the privileges there mentioned are for the Twelve alone or for all disciples. If *v.* 41 is genuine, this seems to be the only suitable interpretation. There is now the further difficulty that *vv.* 42–46 do not give an answer to the question put in *v.* 41. We can only conclude that if Lk.

invented *v.* 41, he did so for some purpose which he succeeded in concealing from his readers. Editorial glosses are usually more transparent than this. Perhaps the truth is that the verse stood in Q and that Mt. omitted it because it was as obscure to him as it is to us

42–44. The reply of Jesus is another parable. The subject of the story is the servant who, in the absence of the master, is made responsible for the welfare of his fellow-servants. From the contrasting *v.* 45 it is clear that *v.* 42 is very much compressed. It begins by asking who is to be chief among the servants, and immediately goes on to explain this headship in terms not of rule, but of service. This is in entire agreement with the principle laid down in Mk. 10$^{42-45}$, 9^{35}; Mt. 23^{11}. Cf. John 21$^{15ff.}$. We might venture to paraphrase: ' If anyone deserves the name of wise and faithful steward, it is he, who being left in charge of his fellow-servants, devotes himself to their welfare.' This makes a good connexion with *v.* 43. Such a servant will have the approval of his master and will be amply rewarded—with larger duties and responsibilities. Compare the parable of the Talents. The good time that is coming at the end of the present age is not described in the teaching of Jesus, save in figurative terms. But there is here a definite hint that it is not passive enjoyment, but a larger and more satisfying activity that is promised; a more àbundant and fruitful life with fuller opportunities of service.

45. The other side of the picture. The servant who conceives his position as an opportunity to gratify the lust for power and authority and to satisfy his own selfish desires. Mt. (24^{48}) designates him as ' evil,' explaining the obvious. ' Say in his heart ' is the common Hebrew idiom for ' think.' ' Begin to beat ' is another Semitism. The use of ' begin ' as a kind of auxiliary verb with no special significance is a common Aramaic idiom.

46. The servant who acts in this way will have a rude awakening. The return of his master will be sudden and unexpected; and it will mean deposition and punishment for him. As the Greek text stands the punishment is death. There is no authority for the marginal alternative ' severely scourge.' The method of execution is the antique one of cutting the victim in two or hewing him in pieces. (Homer. *Od.* 18^{339}; 2 Sam. 12^{31}; Heb. 11^{37}, etc.) But it may be questioned whether the Greek text is reliable at this point. For (1) if the master has cut the servant in two, the appointing of his portion among the unfaithful is a superfluous anticlimax; and (2) *vv.* 47 f. in Lk. go on to describe the punishment for unsatisfactory servants in detail, and in the worst case it is only severe scourging. Perhaps we have here a mistranslation of the Aramaic. It may be pointed out that the Hebrew word for ' to cut in pieces ' is *nittach*, and that the corresponding Aramaic verb *nattach* means to ' take away,' ' separate.' The original sense here may therefore have been ' he will separate him [from the rest] '; cf. Mt. 25^{32}. ' Appoint his portion ' is a Jewish idiom. ' Unfaithful ' (Lk.) is preferable to ' hypocrites ' (Mt.): it stands in contrast to ' faithful ' in Lk. *v.* 42. Mt. (*v.* 51) adds ' there shall be the weeping and gnashing of teeth,' a favourite expression in that gospel; cf. Mt. 13$^{42, 50}$, 22^{13}, 25^{30}; and 8^{12} with the parallel in Lk. 13^{28}.

47 f. The nature of the punishment is now described in Lk. 12$^{47f.}$. These verses have no parallel in Mt. It may be conjectured that Matthew omitted them

because he realised the finality of ' cut him asunder.' Luke will have kept them, being, as usual, faithful to his source.

LK. 12⁴⁷⁻⁴⁸

12 47 And that [1] servant, which knew his lord's will, and made not ready, nor did according to his will, shall be beaten with 48 many *stripes*; but he that knew not, and
    [1] Gr. *bondservant*.

did things worthy of stripes, shall be beaten with few *stripes*. And to whomsoever much is given, of him shall much be required: and to whom they commit much, of him will they ask the more.

The punishment of unfaithful servants depends on whether the offence was wilful disobedience or mere stupidity and folly. The distinction is the same as that made in the Old Testament between sins of ignorance and sins committed ' with a high hand.' And ignorance in this connexion does not necessarily mean absolute ignorance: it can mean the peculiar human tendency to forget the rule at the critical moment. So the Rabbis in the Mishnah (*Sabbath* 7[1]): ' A great general rule have they laid down concerning the Sabbath: whosoever, forgetful of the principle of the Sabbath, committed many acts of work on many Sabbaths, is liable only to one sin-offering; but if, mindful of the principle of the Sabbath, he yet committed many acts of work on many Sabbaths, he is liable for every Sabbath [which he profaned] ' (Danby, p. 106). Similarly here: he who knowingly flouts the will of his master will have the severer punishment; he who is forgetful of it, the lighter. This is applicable especially to the disciples. They, more than anyone else, have been admitted to the confidence of Jesus. Accordingly, a greater faithfulness will be expected of them, than of the less intimate of the hearers and followers of Jesus. This principle is stated in general terms (*v.* 48[b]). With the whole passage (Lk. 12[41-48]) cf. 1 Cor. 4[1-5].

We may now see a connexion with *v.* 41. Peter asks whether the fine promises made in *v.* 37 are for the Twelve specially. The reply of Jesus is in effect: ' I make no promises to you: I give you tasks. Your reward depends on the spirit and manner in which you perform those tasks. He who would be great in the Kingdom of God must be the servant of all.'

(b) FOR JESUS HIMSELF (160)

MT. 10³⁴⁻³⁶   LK. 12⁴⁹⁻⁵³

10 34 Think not that I came to [1] send peace on the earth: I came not to [1] send peace, 35 but a sword. For I came to set a man at variance against his father, and the daughter against her mother, and the daughter in law against her mother in 36 law: and a man's foes *shall be* they of his own household.
    [1] Gr. *cast*.

12 49 I came to cast fire upon the earth;||and 50 what will I, if it is already kindled?||But I have a baptism to be baptized with;|| and how am I straitened till it be ac- 51 complished!||Think ye that I am come to give peace in the earth?||I tell you, Nay; 52 but rather division:||for there shall be from henceforth five in one house divided,||three against two, and two 53 against three.||They shall be divided, father against son, and son against father;||mother against daughter, and daughter against her mother;||mother in law against her daughter in law, and daughter in law against her mother in law.||

This section is in poetical form (cf. Burney, p. 90). The first two verses of Lk. are absent from Mt. Perhaps he dropped them as not strictly relevant in the context in which he was incorporating the rest of the Q passage. Verse 36 of Mt. does not appear in Lk.: it is the end of the prophetic oracle (Micah 7⁶), upon which the saying is based. Whether it stood in Q or has been supplied in Mt. from the Old Testament it is difficult to say. The latter seems the more probable alternative.

49 f. These two verses express in poignant terms the heavy burden which His mission lays upon Jesus. He, who above all others wishes to establish friendship and brotherly love among men, must create strife and division. For the Kingdom of God comes to cut across all the natural relations of men. Its absolute demands take precedence of all human claims, friendships, family affection. Jesus cannot speak smooth and comfortable words to His generation. And in these lines we see the desperate tension in the kindest of all hearts between His own tenderness and the hardness of His task. The nearest parallel to this tragedy is to be found in the ' Confessions ' of Jeremiah, where there is a similar struggle in the prophet's mind ' between fidelity to his prophetic commission and the natural feelings and impulses of his heart ' (Skinner, *Prophecy and Religion*, p. 210; see the whole chapter, XI). This tension is given expression in Jer. 20⁹ (Skinner's translation) :

> If I said, ' I will seek to forget Him,
>   And speak no more in His name,'
> 'Twas like glowing fire in my breast,
>   Shut up in my bones.
> I was weary with keeping it under;
>   I could not hold out.

We should probably translate Lk. 12⁴⁹ :

> I came to cast fire upon the earth;
> And how I wish that it was now kindled!

The natural shrinking from a terrible necessity, and the clear vision that the task must be carried out. Along with this goes the sense that the fulfilment of the mission means extreme suffering for Himself, and that not merely as something incidental. The ' baptism ' is an essential, the essential part of His work. He is hampered and handicapped until it is accomplished. For this use of ' baptism ' cf. Mk. 10³⁸. The idea can be traced back to the Old Testament (Ps. 42⁷, 69², ¹⁵); and there is perhaps an echo of it in the Pauline phrase ' baptized into His death.'

51, 52 f. The remainder of the section has a parallel in Mt. 10³⁴⁻³⁶. It dwells further on the point made in *v.* 49. The manifestation of the Kingdom means warfare to the bitter end against evil; and evil is so firmly entrenched in human life and human relations that much suffering and heartbreak are inevitable before it can be cast out. Those who think that the Messiah will come and transform the world by a wave of the magic wand are sadly mistaken. The coming of Jesus brings tension: it brings to sharpest issue the struggle between the Kingdom of

God and the forces of evil. It compels men to take sides; and members of the same family may be in opposite camps. This is expressed in terms borrowed from Micah 7⁶. Cf. *Jubilees* 23¹⁶, ¹⁹, ' and in that generation the sons will convict their fathers and their elders of sin and unrighteousness. . . . And they will strive one with another, the young with the old, and the old with the young.' Mishnah, *Soṭah* 9¹⁵, ' with the footprints of the Messiah presumption shall increase and dearth reach its height. . . . Children shall shame the elders and the elders shall rise up before the children, " for the son dishonoureth, etc." (Micah 7⁶). The face of this generation is as the face of a dog, and the son will not be put to shame by his father ' (Danby, p. 306). The division ' three against two and two against three ' is a division of old and young. The household consists of the father and mother on the one side and the son and his wife and the daughter on the other. It is the new generation against the old. Cf. Mk. 2²¹ᶠ·, 3³¹⁻³⁵; Lk. 9⁵⁹⁻⁶², 11²⁷ᶠ·, 14²⁶. The picture here drawn by Jesus of the results of His work is in startling contrast to the kind of expectation shown in the rôle assigned to Elijah in Malachi 4⁵ᶠ·. Here again Jesus reverses current expectations about the coming of the Kingdom.

(c) FOR ISRAEL (160, 161)

LK. 12⁵⁴⁻⁵⁶

12 54 And he said to the multitudes also, When ye see a cloud rising in the west, straightway ye say, There cometh a 55 shower; and so it cometh to pass. And when *ye see* a south wind blowing, ye say, There will be a ¹ scorching heat; and it 56 cometh to pass. Ye hypocrites, ye know how to ² interpret the face of the earth and the heaven; but how is it that ye know not how to ² interpret this time?

¹ Or, *hot wind.*
² Gr. *prove.*

54 f., 56. This passage has no parallel in Mt. The similar saying in Mt. 16³ᶠ· is an early interpolation in that Gospel. It is said that the Lucan form of the saying agrees with the facts in Palestine, where rain comes from the West (cf. 1 Kings 18⁴⁴), and wind from the East and South is accompanied by heat-waves. (Cf. G. A. Smith, *Historical Geography of the Holy Land* ²⁰, pp. 66 ff.) These things are important to the Palestinian farmer, and he makes it his business to understand the significance of the weather signs. This meteorological sensitiveness stands in sharp contrast to the religious insensitiveness of the people. Things are happening in their midst, under their noses, of far greater significance; and they cannot or will not see the meaning of them. They cannot or will not realise that this is for them a time of crisis, when decisions must be made which are of supreme importance. The work of Jesus is the sign of the time. From it they ought to infer that the Kingdom of God has come upon them and that the final consummation is near. But they refuse to know the things that belong to their peace. If they did, they would hasten to repent and seek entrance into the Kingdom while there is still time.

This parable is followed by what is now rightly regarded as another parable bearing upon the same point. In Mt. it has been incorporated in the Sermon on the Mount and transformed into a moral rule. The Q context shows clearly that it is originally an eschatological parable.

MT. 5²⁵⁻²⁶

LK. 12⁵⁷⁻⁵⁹

5 25 Agree with thine adversary quickly,
whiles thou art with him in the way; lest
haply the adversary deliver thee to the
judge, and the judge [1] deliver thee to the
26 officer, and thou be cast into prison. Verily
I say unto thee, Thou shalt by no means
come out thence, till thou have paid the
last farthing.

[1] Some ancient authorities omit *deliver thee*.

12 57 And why even of yourselves judge ye
58 not what is right? For as thou art going
with thine adversary before the magis-
trate, on the way give diligence to be
quit of him; lest haply he hale thee unto
the judge, and the judge shall deliver
thee to the [1] officer, and the [1] officer shall
59 cast thee into prison. I say unto thee,
Thou shalt by no means come out
thence, till thou have paid the very last
mite.

[1] Gr. *exactor*.

57, 58 f. Verse 57 effects the transition from the preceding parable to this
one. It pillories the moral and spiritual blindness of the people. They can see
what is to their advantage in any sphere except the most important of all. If
they would take stock of their lives they would see that there was only one decent,
honest course open to them—to come to God in the deepest humility, confessing
their moral and spiritual bankruptcy and casting themselves on His mercy while
there is still time. If they were in the same strait financially, they would know
what to do. The shrewd Galilean peasant would not go to court with a hopeless
case. He would use every persuasion, every artifice to come to terms before the
hearing, and so avoid the possibility of being imprisoned for the debt with no
prospect of release until all is paid. The ' mite ' is the smallest copper coin,
equivalent to about one-sixteenth of a penny. It corresponds to the Jewish coin
known as the *pĕruṭah*. Mt. has ' farthing,' the Roman *quadrans*, a coin equal to two
mites. In the Mishnah the *quadrans* is not mentioned, and in the New Testament
' mite ' is the regular word for a very small amount of money. The only other place
in the New Testament where ' farthing ' is used is Mk. 12⁴², where it is introduced
by the evangelist to explain the meaning of ' mite ' to his Gentile readers. It is
therefore probable that ' mite ' is the original reading of Q.

The moral of the parable is sufficiently obvious. Men are even now on their
way to the court, where they must give account of their lives. For the comparison
of a sinner to an insolvent debtor see Mt. 18²³⁻³⁵; Lk. 7⁴¹⁻⁴³. The only hope for
men is to come to terms by repentance while there is still time.

The reason why the present time is a time of crisis is now stated in a double
parable in which the Kingdom of God is likened sucessively to Mustard Seed and
Leaven. The obvious point in these two parables is the fact that a small beginning is made whose consequences are great and far-reaching. Not only so, but
once the beginning has been made, the result is inevitable. The Kingdom has
begun to come in the mission of Jesus; and now it must run its course to the final
consummation. This means that Jesus and His little group of followers represent
the vital factor in the whole situation, the sign of the times. To understand the
mission of Jesus, to come to terms with what He represents, is a life and death
matter for men.

MT. 13³¹⁻³³

LK. 13¹⁸⁻²¹ (164)

13 31 Another parable set he before them,
saying, The kingdom of heaven is like
unto a grain of mustard seed, which a

13 13 He said therefore, Unto what is the
kingdom of God like? and whereunto
19 shall I liken it? It is like unto a grain of

32 man took, and sowed in his field: which indeed is less than all seeds; but when it is grown, it is greater than the herbs, and becometh a tree, so that the birds of the heaven come and lodge in the branches thereof.

33 Another parable spake he unto them; The kingdom of heaven is like unto leaven, which a woman took, and hid in three [1] measures of meal, till it was all leavened.

[1] The word in the Greek denotes the Hebrew seah, a measure containing nearly a peck and a half.

mustard seed, which a man took, and cast into his own garden; and it grew, and became a tree; and the birds of the heaven lodged in the branches thereof.

20 And again he said, Whereunto shall I
21 liken the kingdom of God? It is like unto leaven, which a woman took and hid in three [1] measures of meal, till it was all leavened.

[1] See marginal note on Matt. xiii. 33.

MK. 4[30-32]

4 30 And he said, How shall we liken the kingdom of God? or in what parable shall
31 we set it forth? [1] It is like a grain of mustard seed, which, when it is sown upon the earth, though it be less than all the
32 seeds that are upon the earth, yet when it

is sown, groweth up, and becometh greater than all the herbs, and putteth out great branches; so that the birds of the heaven can lodge under the shadow thereof.

[1] Gr. As unto.

18, 19. The parable of the Mustard Seed is reported independently in Mk. 4[30-32]. The version of it in Mt. is a conflation of Mk. and Q. The introduction in question form (Mk. and Lk.) corresponds to Jewish ways of introducing parables, and is surely original. It has disappeared in Mt. The grain of mustard seed is a proverbial Jewish expression for a minute quantity. Cf. Mt. 17[30] = Lk. 17[6] (Q); *Niddah* 5[2] (Danby, p. 750); also *Koran* 21[48]. According to Jewish rule the mustard plant is sown in the field and not in the garden; and so Mt.'s ' field ' is probably the original. In Palestine the mustard plant attains a height of eight and twelve feet and birds come to it for the seeds (*Encyclopædia Biblica*, col 3244). The reference to the ' birds of the heaven ' is probably significant. Both in apocalyptic and Rabbinical literature ' the birds of heaven ' stand for the Gentile nations. (Cf. *The Teaching of Jesus*, p. 133, n. 1); and an interest in the Gentiles is character-istic of Q. It is possible that we have here in parable what is said openly in a later Q passage (Lk. 13[28-30]).

There are two points in the parable. The first and most important is that mentioned above, that a process has been started which *must* go on to its inevitable end. Whether it will take a short time or long does not enter into the calculation. It is the same as in the seed parable in Mk. 4[26-29]. There also, once the seed is sown, each subsequent stage till the harvest follows inevitably. The second point lies in the contrast between the small and seemingly insignificant beginnings and the final realisation. The preaching and healing mission of the Carpenter of Nazareth hardly seems to usher in the new age. Yet it does.

20 f. These two points again come to expression in the companion parable of the Leaven. Once the leaven has been put into the dough the leavening process goes on inevitably till the whole is leavened; and this although there is no com-parison between the mass of dough and the small quantity of leaven.

The passages considered so far are all heavy with the sense of terrible urgency. We see Jesus Himself tasting the full bitterness of the conflict between the claims of His mission and the natural instincts and affections of the human heart. We see the constant demand for loyalty, courage, watchfulness. We hear the summons to repent while there is yet time. Obedience to this call is costly, only less costly than disobedience. There are those who will not hear the call; and our document now turns to speak of their fate.

2. THE FATE OF THE UNREPENTANT
(a) THE CLOSED DOOR (165)

LK. 13[22-30]

Lk. 13[23 f.] Cf. Mt. 7[13 f.]

Lk. 13[25]. Cf. Mt. 25[10-12].

Lk. 13[26 f.] Cf. Mt. 7[22 f.]

Lk. 13[28-30]. Cf. Mt. 8[11 f.]

MT. 8[11-12]

8 11 And I say unto you, that many shall come from the east and the west, and shall [1] sit down with Abraham, and Isaac, and 12 Jacob, in the kingdom of heaven: but the sons of the kingdom shall be cast forth into the outer darkness: there shall be the weeping and gnashing of teeth.

[1] Gr. recline.

13 22 And he went on his way through cities and villages, teaching, and journeying on 23 unto Jerusalem. And one said unto him, Lord, are they few that be saved? 24 And he said unto them, Strive to enter in by the narrow door: for many, I say unto you, shall seek to enter in, and shall not 25 be [1] able. When once the master of the house is risen up, and hath shut to the door, and ye begin to stand without, and to knock at the door, saying, Lord, open to us; and he shall answer and say to 26 you, I know you not whence ye are; then shall ye begin to say, We did eat and drink in thy presence, and thou didst 27 teach in our streets; and he shall say, I tell you, I know not whence ye are; depart from me, all ye workers of iniquity. 28 There shall be the weeping and gnashing of teeth, when ye shall see Abraham, and Isaac, and Jacob, and all the prophets in the kingdom of God, and yourselves 29 cast forth without. And they shall come from the east and west, and from the north and south, and shall [2] sit down in 30 the kingdom of God. And behold, there are last which shall be first, and there are first which shall be last.

[1] Or, able, when once.
[2] Gr. recline.

The Matthæan parallels to this section are scattered about in Mt. With the exception of Mt. 8[11-12] they are probably all to be assigned to M. The first is hardly a parallel at all. For Mt. 7[13 f.] is concerned with *two* ways, one leading to life and the other to death; while Lk. 13[24 f.] is concerned with *one* door, and the question is which side of the door a man is on. Mt. 25[10-12] belongs to the parable of the Ten Virgins, which is derived from M. Mt. 7[22 f.] shows very little verbal agreement with Lk. 13[26 f.]; and what there is is confined to the quotation from Ps. 6[8]. Mt. 8[11 f.], which is inserted into Mt.'s account of the Centurion of Capernaum, may be derived from Q: it has considerable resemblance to Lk. 13[28-30].

22 f., 24. These verses provide the setting for the speech of Jesus which follows. Whether *v.* 22 belonged to Q may be doubted. On the other hand, *v.* 23 may well be part of Q. Cf. Lk. 9[57-62] for similar openings. The question put to Jesus was one often discussed in Judaism, both with reference to Israel and to the Gentile nations. A great variety of answers is given showing all degrees of optimism and pessimism. The most despairing is that of 4 Ezra 8[1-3]: 'This age the Most High

has made for many, but the age to come for few. . . . Many have been created, but few shall be saved.' The question and the answers given presuppose that salvation depends in some way on the favouritism rather than the love of God. But it is not a matter of saying light-heartedly, ' We have Abraham to our father ' or of abandoning all hope for mankind. The reply of Jesus begins by asserting that the way of salvation is a door which God opens and man enters. The entry cannot be made without God. The gate of heaven opens only from the inside. But also man has to make his own way in, once the door is opened. And this is not easy. The entrance is narrow, and it is a case of struggling through rather than strolling in. If men fail to enter, it is not that God is unwilling to admit them, but that they will not enter on the only terms on which entrance is possible.

25-27. Moreover, the door does not stand open indefinitely. A time is coming, and soon, when the door will be shut. Here again the eschatological motive is clear. The discourse moves in a sphere that is strange to us with our ideas of progress and evolution. The notion that the world may come to an end to-morrow or next week is repugnant to us in a way in which it was not repugnant to Palestinian Jews of the first century. They believed that such a thing could happen, and many were convinced that it would come to pass in their own day. This means that there is only a limited time for repentance. When that time is up, it will be too late. Those who often passed by the open door will knock in vain at a door now shut. The words ' I do not know you ' mean ' I do not acknowledge you ': cf. Is. 63^{16}; 2 Tim. 2^{19}; and the general principle laid down in Mk. 8^{38}; Mt. 10^{33}; Lk. 12^{9}. In Mt. 7^{23} the words are ' I never knew you,' a phrase which, in Rabbinical circles, seems to have meant ' I don't wish to have anything to do with you.' Cf. Billerbeck, iv. 293. In face of this chilly reception all that the late-comers can claim is superficial contact with Jesus. They have sat at the same table with Him or have heard Him preach. They say in effect, ' You are one of us.' To which the answer is, ' You are none of mine.' The words are clearly addressed in the first instance to the Jewish contemporaries of Jesus; but their application can be extended to a much wider circle now. The quotation which follows, ' Depart from me all ye workers of iniquity,' is from Ps. 6^{8}.

28 f. These verses describe in vivid contrast what is going on inside and outside the closed door. Inside is light and joy. The patriarchs and prophets—the godly of every generation in Israel's history—and men from every quarter of the world— such as are spoken of elsewhere in Q: repentant Gentiles—sit down to the Messianic banquet in the Kingdom of God. (Cf. Is. 49^{12}; Mal. 1^{11}.) Outside darkness and despair, made deeper by the realisation of what has been missed. It may be noted that there is no mention here of special punishment for the unrepentant. They suffer enough in the loss of what might have been theirs.

30. Thus the Kingdom of God turns things upside down. Most of all, it upsets the calculations of those who believe that they have a prescriptive right to the favour of God, the kind of assurance expressed often in the apocalyptic literature, e.g.:

' Thou didst choose the seed of Abraham before all the nations

' And didst set Thy name upon us, O Lord; and Thou wilt abide among us for ever ' (*Psa. Sol.* 9$^{171.}$). Cf. Rom. 9$^{41.}$ As Jesus sees it, all this counts for nothing. In the last issue the fate of a man depends not on whether he is of the seed of Abraham, but on his response to the manifestation of the Kingdom of God. Judged by that criterion, 'they are not all Israel, which are of Israel: neither, because they are Abraham's seed, are they all children' (Rom. 9[6f.]). Publicans and harlots go into the Kingdom of God before the high priests and elders of the people (Mt. 21[31]). Gentiles show faith and insight such as cannot be found in Israel. Privilege is at an end: and the only passports to the Kingdom are repentance and submission to God.

(b) Lament over Jerusalem (167)

MT. 23[37-39]	LK. 13[34-35]
23 37 O Jerusalem, Jerusalem, which killeth the prophets, and stoneth them that are sent unto her! how often would I have gathered thy children together, even as a hen gathereth her chickens under her 38 wings, and ye would not! Behold, your 39 house is left unto you [1] desolate. For I say unto you, Ye shall not see me henceforth, till ye shall say, Blessed *is* he that cometh in the name of the Lord.	13 34 O Jerusalem, Jerusalem, which killeth the prophets, and stoneth them that are sent unto her! how often would I have gathered thy children together, even as a hen *gathereth* her own brood under her 35 wings, and ye would not. Behold, your house is left unto you *desolate*: and I say unto you, Ye shall not see me, until ye shall say, Blessed *is* he that cometh in the name of the Lord.

[1] Some ancient authorities omit *desolate*.

The warning given in the preceding passage is followed by a passage of deep pathos. According to Burney (*Poetry of our Lord*, p. 146), it is in the poetical form known as *Kīnā*, i.e. the rhythm of the old Hebrew dirge or elegy. The nature of the poem can best be shown by giving Burney's translation and arrangement of the passage. Burney's rendering follows the text of Mt.

> Jerúsalem, Jerúsalem, that sláyeth the próphets,
>   and stóneth her méssengers,
> How mány tímes have I lónged
>   to gáther thy chíldren,
> Like a hén that gáthereth her chícks
>   beneáth her wíngs:
> Yet ye would not.
> Behóld there remaíneth to yoú
>   your hoúse a desolátion.

The remainder of the passage does not fall into this rhythmical scheme. Many scholars regard these verses as the continuation of Lk. 11[49-51] and as part of the extract from a lost Jewish book. On this theory the speaker here is the Wisdom of God. Reasons have been given above for rejecting this view. If Burney is right, we have a further reason for maintaining that these verses are independent of Lk. 11[49-51]; for there is no suggestion of *Kīnā* rhythm about that passage.

34. The repetition of the name in address is extremely common in Jewish literature. The reputation of Jerusalem as a place where prophets are murdered is difficult to understand. There is the case of the prophet Uriah (Jer. 26[20 ff.]) in the Old Testament; and there are other murders of prophets (1 Kings 18[4, 13], 19[10])

not connected with Jerusalem; also the attempted murder of Jeremiah. In Jewish legend there is the murder of Isaiah. Further, the Zechariah whose murder is recorded in 2 Chron. 24[20 ff.] came to be identified with Zechariah the prophet. We should perhaps make allowance for a certain amount of poetic licence here, and take Jerusalem as typical of Israel as a whole. The present participles of the Greek text may then be taken to mean something like ' ever ready to slay the prophets and stone her messengers.' On the stoning of messengers it may be noted that Josephus (*Ant.* ii. 327), paraphrasing Exod. 14[10-12], says that the Israelites wished to stone Moses.

The words ' How often would I . . .' have been taken to imply more activity in Jerusalem on the part of Jesus than is recorded in the Synoptics. There is nothing impossible in the suggestion that He had visited Jerusalem and worked there on other occasions than the final one. The Synoptic Gospels imply a ministry lasting a year at least; but the Synoptic narrative accounts for less than half of this period. And there are other indications in the Synoptics pointing, though not in a decisive way, to the possibility that Jesus was no stranger to the capital when He came up for the last time. At the same time this text cannot be pressed. It says, ' How often have I longed,' not ' How often have I tried.' And we cannot be certain that ' Jerusalem ' is to be taken literally. The figure of the bird gathering her brood under her wings is found in the Old Testament: Dt. 32[11]; Ps. 17[8], 36[7]; and the Jew who converts a Gentile is said to bring him under the wings of the *Shekhinah* (the presence of God). It is not necessary to seek for any mystical meaning here. The sense is the quite simple one of bringing men into the Kingdom of God, it being remembered that for all practical purposes entry into the Kingdom is equivalent to becoming a disciple of Jesus. This, the central purpose of the ministry, has been frustrated by the fact that the people would not have anything to do with it. They are wedded to things as they are. In particular they still believe in their own doctrine of the Kingdom of God, which means the vindication of themselves by the power of God, the establishment of Jerusalem as the capital of the world, and the Temple of Jerusalem as the central and only sanctuary of mankind.

35. The inevitable issue of this doctrine and of the policy based upon it is ruin. These grandiose dreams of world-dominion will surely end in destruction for Jerusalem and the Temple. Cf. Mk. 13[1 f.]. Against the interpretation of ' your house ' as the Temple it is urged that in Jewish speech the Temple is invariably God's house and no one else's. (Billerbeck, i. 944.) (Yet in Is. 64[11] we have the expression ' Our holy and beautiful house' with reference to the First Temple.) The meaning then assigned to the words ' your house ' is ' your commonwealth.' This is possible. On the other hand, the words may well be spoken in bitter irony ' *your* Temple—so much more yours than God's.' In any case, the Temple and the Jewish commonwealth stand and fall together. Much more difficult is the interpretation of the next sentence. The chief problem is what is meant by the words ' until ye shall say . . .' Is the time here thought of some future visit of Jesus to Jerusalem, or is it the final consummation? According to Mk. 11[9], when Jesus made His entry into Jerusalem ' they that went before, and they that followed, cried, Hosanna; blessed is he that cometh in the name of the Lord.'

Mt. evidently does not regard the triumphal entry as a fulfilment of the saying, since he places the saying after his report of the entry. M. Goguel suggests that the words are spoken by Jesus at the time of the Feast of Tabernacles. Jesus has gone up to Jerusalem and worked there without much response. The force of the saying then is ' I am leaving Jerusalem and you will not see me again until Passover.' But it seems a very high-falutin way of conveying a very prosaic piece of information. The words ' Blessed is he . . .' are a quotation from Ps. 118²⁶, a psalm which has connexions with the great pilgrim feasts of Judaism, but especially with the Feast of Tabernacles. (Thackeray, *The Septuagint and Jewish Worship*, pp. 74 ff.) Now in the Jewish liturgy the prophetic lesson appropriated to Tabernacles is Zech. 14, which begins with a prophecy of the desolation of Jerusalem (Zech. 14¹ᶠ·), followed by the promise that God will then appear to establish His Kingdom over the whole earth (Zech. 14⁹). That appearance will be a coming of God with all the saints (Zech. 14⁵). There is also a piece of Rabbinical evidence connecting Ps. 118 with the final deliverance of Israel (Billerbeck, i. 850). It seems probable, therefore, that the time referred to in this saying is the time of the final consummation. The preceding passages suggest that the meaning is: ' The time will come when you will be ready to say to me, "Blessed is he that cometh in the name of the Lord "; but then it will be too late.'

(c) THE GREAT FEAST (170)

MT. 22¹⁻¹⁰

22 1 And Jesus answered and spake again in
2 parables unto them, saying, The kingdom of heaven is likened unto a certain king, which made a marriage feast for his son,
3 and sent forth his ¹ servants to call them that were bidden to the marriage feast:
4 and they would not come. Again he sent forth other ¹ servants, saying, Tell them that are bidden, Behold, I have made ready my dinner: my oxen and my fatlings are killed, and all things are
5 ready: come to the marriage feast. But they made light of it, and went their ways, one to his own farm, another to his
6 merchandise: and the rest laid hold on his ¹ servants, and entreated them shame-
7 fully, and killed them. But the king was wroth; and he sent his armies, and destroyed those murderers, and burned
8 their city. Then saith he to his ¹ servants, The wedding is ready, but they that were bidden were not worthy.
9 Go ye therefore unto the partings of the highways, and as many as ye shall find,
10 bid to the marriage feast. And those ¹ servants went out into the highways, and gathered together all as many as they found, both bad and good: and the wedding was filled with guests.

¹ Gr. *bondservants*.

LK. 14¹⁵⁻²⁴

14 15 And when one of them that sat at meat with him heard these things, he said unto him, Blessed is he that shall eat bread in
16 the kingdom of God. But he said unto him, A certain man made a great supper;
17 and he bade many: and he sent forth his ¹ servant at supper time to say to them that were bidden, Come; for *all* things
18 are now ready. And they all with one *consent* began to make excuse. The first said unto him, I have bought a field, and I must needs go out and see it: I pray
19 thee have me excused. And another said, I have bought five yoke of oxen, and I go to prove them: I pray thee have me
20 excused. And another said, I have married a wife, and therefore I cannot
21 come. And the ¹ servant came, and told his lord these things. Then the master of the house being angry said to his ¹ servant, Go out quickly into the streets and lanes of the city, and bring in hither the poor and maimed and blind and lame.
22 And the ¹ servant said, Lord, what thou didst command is done, and yet there is
23 room. And the lord said unto the ¹ servant, Go out into the highways and hedges, and constrain *them* to come in,
24 that my house may be filled. For I say unto you, that none of those men which were bidden shall taste of my supper.

¹ Gr. *bondservant*.

This parable again has to do with those who reject the Kingdom of God. And again it is made clear that those who are excluded from the Kingdom exclude themselves. The invitation is issued by God; but God will not drag the recipients of the invitation into the feast against their will.

The superiority of the Lucan version of the parable is obvious. It is clear, consistent, and straightforward. In Mt., on the other hand, the story as told by Lk. has been severely cut down, and new features introduced, which make nonsense of it. The most glaring case is Mt. 22⁶ᶠ·. There we are suddenly introduced to a group of persons called ' the rest,' who behave like the wicked husbandmen in Mk. 12¹⁻¹². Their shameful treatment of the messengers causes the king to send a punitive expedition against them to destroy them and their city. The amazing thing is that the feast, which was ready before these things happened, is still ready, and apparently fit to eat, when all is over. It is plain that *vv.* 6 f. are an interruption of the story; and most scholars regard them as an interpolation, an *ex post facto* reference to the destruction of Jerusalem in A.D. 70. This explanation would serve if *vv.* 6 f. were the only peculiarity in the Matthæan version of the parable. But we note that *v.* 6 recalls Mk.'s parable of the wicked husbandmen, and that Mt. 22³ᶠ· tells of two summonses to the feast, a feature which again recalls Mk. 12¹⁻¹². The true solution of the problem may be that Mt. has here combined the Q parable of the great feast with another parable, now lost, which was originally a companion parable to Mk. 12¹⁻¹². For a fuller discussion see *The Teaching of Jesus*, pp. 83–86. Mt. further joins on yet another parable—or a fragment of a parable—from his special source (Mt. 22¹¹⁻¹⁴: see below, pp. 226 f.).

15. The introductory verse is peculiar to Lk. There is therefore no certainty that it stood in Q. It does, however, make an excellent introduction to what follows, probably too good to be invented. One of Jesus' fellow-guests at a meal gives utterance to a characteristic piece of apocalyptic piety. The comparison of the realised Kingdom of God to a banquet is well known both in Rabbinical teaching and in the Gospels. The exclamation is apt to the circumstances of its utterance and impeccable in its sentiment. The reply of Jesus does not challenge the sentiment, but the sincerity of the speaker. He says in effect: ' You talk beautifully about the Kingdom of God; but you do not mean a word of it. If you had the opportunity for which you profess to crave, you would unhesitatingly reject it.' This is the essential point of the parable.

16, 17, 18 ff., 21, 22 f. 'A certain man' is God, and the feast is the Kingdom of God, considered as a great blessing which God is prepared to bestow. The double invitation is in accordance with Jerusalem custom, according to the Rabbinical commentary (*midrash*) on Lam. 4². The invited guests are in the first instance the righteous Jews; and the first invitation is a reference to the promises in the Old Testament. The servant who comes to announce that the feast is ready is Jesus Himself. But the guests who had accepted the invitation in the first instance, now wish to withdraw their acceptance. Cf. Mt. 21³⁰. The Greek phrase translated ' with one consent ' is probably a literal rendering of an Aramaic expression meaning ' immediately,' ' at once.' (So Wellhausen, Torrey.) The different excuses are offered with varying degrees of politeness; but they all come to the same thing: ' we have other and more important business to attend

5

to.' The claims of Mammon take precedence of the claims of God; and treasure on earth is more valuable than treasure in heaven. The report of the servant angers the master, who despatches the servant on a new errand. He is to bring in other inhabitants of the city, the despised and neglected members of the community: ' the poor ' who have no wealth or status to recommend them, and ' the maimed ' who are unattractive through physical defects. The word here rendered ' maimed ' is used in Greek to cover physical defects of all kinds. Strictly speaking, the blind and lame are sub-classes of the class ' maimed.' (Cf. Plato, *Crito*, 53A.) The fact that these guests are to be found in the same city as the original guests, suggests that they represent Jews of another class. If the first guests are the righteous Jews, the religious aristocracy, men of the Pharisaic type, these may well be the religious lower classes, the publicans and sinners: Israelites like the Pharisees, but bad Israelites from the Pharisaic standpoint. Even after these have been brought in, there is still room for others; so a new command is issued. The servant is to go beyond the city boundaries out on to the main roads. This is doubtless meant to suggest a mission beyond the borders of Israel to the Gentiles. ' Constrain ' here does not mean ' compel.' It expresses rather an insistent hospitality. Cf. Gen. 19³. Here we have another example of that interest in the Gentile mission which is so characteristic of Q. The order of events corresponds to the Pauline dictum, ' To the Jew first, and also to the Greek ' (Rom. 1¹⁶, 2⁹ᶠ·). 'That my house may be filled': the purpose of God is wider than Israel. The necessary corollary to the prophetic doctrine of God's universal rule is here drawn. Cf. Heb. 11³⁹ᶠ· The whole parable might be regarded as a *midrash* on Is. 49⁶.

24. The closing word excludes from the feast those, and those only, who have already excluded themselves. The only people who do not enter are those who do not wish to enter.

The issue in this parable, as in the preceding passages, is set out with the utmost clearness. Jesus does not here teach either a mechanically operating predestination, which determines from all eternity who shall or shall not be brought into the Kingdom. Neither does He proclaim that man's entry into the Kingdom is purely his own affair. The two essential points in His teaching are that no man can enter the Kingdom without the invitation of God, and that no man can remain outside it but by his own deliberate choice. Man cannot save himself; but he can damn himself. And it is this latter fact that makes the preaching of Jesus so urgent. For He sees the deepest tragedy of human life, not in the many wrong and foolish things that men do, or the many good and wise things that they fail to accomplish, but in their rejection of God's greatest gift.

3. *DISCIPLESHIP IN A TIME OF CRISIS*

The discourse is now turned back to the conditions of discipleship in such a time of crisis. It is very easy to remain outside the Kingdom of God: not so easy to enter. It is true that salvation is free: but it is not cheap. God gives the Kingdom: but the accepting of God's gift means the rejection of many other things. The Kingdom of God offers the greatest gifts: but it demands exclusive loyalty and whole-hearted devotion. The great feast is a feast and not a distribution of free rations. Those who wish to enjoy it must come in. They cannot have portions sent out for them to enjoy, while they busy themselves with other things. Consequently the closing sections of Q are devoted mainly to a reiteration in uncompromising terms of the conditions of discipleship.

(a) THE ABSOLUTE CLAIMS OF THE KINGDOM (171)

MT. 10[37-38]

10 37 He that loveth father or mother more than me is not worthy of me: and he that loveth son or daughter more than me is 38 not worthy of me. And he that doth not take his cross and follow after me, is not worthy of me.

LK. 14[25-27]

14 25 Now there went with him great multitudes: and he turned, and said unto 26 them, If any man cometh unto me, and hateth not his own father, and mother, and wife, and children, and brethren, and sisters, yea, and his own life also, he 27 cannot be my disciple. Whosoever doth not bear his own cross, and come after me, cannot be my disciple.

25. This verse, which is probably editorial, effects the transition from the preceding parable to the following exhortations.

26 f. One of the most uncompromising statements of the claims of the Kingdom in the New Testament. There are considerable differences between Mt. and Lk. in the form of the statement; but there are also signs of an Aramaic original underlying the variants. These are (i) ' hateth not ' (Lk.) ' loveth more ' (Mt.). In the Old Testament (e.g. Gen. 29[31ff.]; Dt. 21[15ff.]) ' love ' and ' hate ' stand side by side in contexts where it is obvious that ' hate ' is not to be taken in the literal sense, but in the sense ' love less.' The same idiom appears in the Talmud (*Ta'anith* 7[h]), where it is said of handsome Rabbis that ' if they hated their beauty, they would be more learned ' than they are. That is, if they thought less of their personal appearance, they would be better scholars. So here Lk.'s version is a literal rendering of the original; but the meaning is not that a disciple's relatives are to be hated by him, but that they must take second place in his regard. The first place in his affections must be given to the Kingdom manifested in Jesus. For an Old Testament parallel to this exclusive loyalty see Dt. 33[8f.]; and for the other side of this tremendous demand Mk. 10[28ff.]. (ii) The phrases ' is not worthy of me ' (Mt.) and ' cannot be my disciple ' (Lk.) may go back to a common original in Aramaic. See *The Teaching of Jesus*, pp. 237–240. (iii) The words ' bear ' (Lk.) and ' take '(Mt.) are translation variants. Cf. the Greek versions of Num. 14[33f.]. Verse 27 has a parallel in Mk. 8[34].

8 34 And he called unto him the multitude with his disciples, and said unto them, If any man would come after me, let him deny himself, and take up his cross, and follow me.

The taking up of the cross is the voluntary acceptance of martyrdom at the hands of the Roman Empire. Crucifixion is the typical Roman punishment; and the implication of the words is that Jesus is aware of an irreconcilable hostility between the Kingdom for which He stands and the Empire represented by Pontius Pilate.

Discipleship means the risk of being reckoned undutiful sons, bad husbands, dangerous agitators; and he who becomes a disciple accepts these risks with his eyes open, and is prepared to accept all the consequences that may follow. And this is not just a matter of a single moment of decision in a burst of enthusiasm. It demands a dogged endurance, the maintenance of the first enthusiasm right through to the end. This is enforced in:

(b) THE PARABLE OF THE SALT (171)

MT. 5^{13}	LK. 14^{34-35}
5 13 Ye are the salt of the earth: but if the salt have lost its savour, wherewith shall it be salted? it is thenceforth good for nothing, but to be cast out and trodden under foot of men.	14 34 Salt therefore is good: but if even the salt have lost its savour, wherewith shall it be 35 seasoned? It is fit neither for the land nor for the dunghill: *men* cast it out. He that hath ears to hear, let him hear.

Cf. Mk. 9^{50}.

9 50 Salt is good: but if the salt have lost its
saltness, wherewith will ye season it?

34 f. The saying occurs independently in a small collection in Mk. It is possible that the form in Mt. is independent of the other two, and derived from M. The opening words of Mt. 5^{13} (cf. Mt. 5^{14}) are correct interpretation of the meaning of the saying for Christians. The disciples are like salt, with its many uses in the house and in the field. And like salt they are of use only so long as they retain their characteristic quality. A disciple who has lost his zeal and devotion is like salt that has become insipid. Such salt is completely useless. The agricultural use of salt is well known in Egypt and Palestine. 'Fit neither for the land nor for the dunghill' is difficult, for the use of salt on the land is as manure. A very attractive solution is that of Perles, that 'land' is a mistaken rendering of an Aramaic word which ought to be translated 'seasoning.' It is a further point in favour of this restoration that it gives a play upon the two Aramaic words *tabbālā* (seasoning) and *zabbālā* (manure). It is possible that the saying was originally not just an exhortation to the disciples, but primarily a warning to Israel. Israel ought to be the salt of mankind; but the savour has gone out of Judaism. Let the disciples, the new Israel, beware lest they go the same way. In favour of this interpretation is the fact that the Talmud preserves an anecdote concerning R. Joshua ben Chananiah (c. A.D. 90) in which he makes fun of this saying. He is asked: 'If the salt becomes savourless, with what will it be salted?' He replies: 'With the after-birth of a mule.' It is retorted that the mule (which is barren) cannot have an after-birth, to which his answer is: 'Neither can the salt become savourless.' The natural interpretation of this is that in the Rabbi's view Israel is a salt that does not become insipid, and therefore stands in no need of seasoning, least of all by Jesus or His followers. (Billerbeck, i. 236; cf. G. Kittel, *Probleme*, p. 123.) The casting out of the useless salt into the street, the common refuse-tip in the East, follows on the recognition of its utter worthlessness. The additional words in Mt. 'trodden under foot of men' indicate that the street is the destination of the salt. The rejection of men from the Kingdom of God is described in similar terms in an earlier passage in Q (Lk. 13^{28}||Mt. 8^{12}).

The upshot of the matter is that men must choose whom they will serve; and, having chosen, they must be prepared to abide by their choice. The whole matter can be put in a single word, which is given in the next Q verse :

(c) The Last Word on Discipleship (174)

MT. 6[24]	LK. 16[13]
6 24 No man can serve two masters: for either he will hate the one, and love the other; or else he will hold to one, and despise the other. Ye cannot serve God and mammon.	16 13 No [1] servant can serve two masters: for either he will hate the one, and love the other; or else he will hold to one, and despise the other. Ye cannot serve God and mammon. [1] Gr. *household-servant.*

The two versions of the saying are identical except that Lk. has the word for ' domestic servant,' which is absent in Mt. Similar expressions are found outside the New Testament: Plato, *Rep.* viii. 555C. ' It is impossible for the citizens of a state to honour wealth, and at the same time acquire a proper amount of temperance; because they cannot avoid neglecting either the one or the other.' Persius, *Sat.* v. 154 ff., to one torn between avarice and extravagance: 'You have two hooks pulling you different ways—are you for following this or that? You must needs obey your masters by turns and shirk them by turns, by a division of duty.' Philo, *frag.* II, 649: ' It is impossible for love of the world to coexist with the love of God.' [1] *Poimandres*, IV. 6 : ' It is not possible, my son, to attach yourself both to things mortal and to things divine.' For the disciple of Jesus the irreconcilable alternatives are God and mammon. Mammon is the Aramaic word *māmōn*. Its derivation is disputed, but its meaning certain: it is wealth of every kind. The service of God *and* mammon is impossible, because their demands on man are irreconcilable. God calls for the utmost of self-dedication and self-sacrifice: mammon for self-assertion and self-aggrandisement. The only way for disciples is complete devotion to God, and this is not possible unless they are prepared to sit loose to all the things that human selfishness counts as goods.

These sayings on the absolute claims of the Kingdom are now followed by a number of utterances bearing upon special problems which arise in the life of the disciple. What is his relation to the old order given in the Jewish scriptures? How is he to act when he feels himself wronged by a fellow-disciple? In what way is he to face the difficulties of his task as a disciple? The sayings do not appear to be arranged in any systematic way. Indeed it seems probable that we have here a small collection of sayings linked together by the fact that they answer questions which arise in the community of the disciples.

(d) The Old and the New (176)

MT. 11[12-13]	LK. 16[16]
11 12 And from the days of John the Baptist until now the kingdom of heaven suffereth violence, and men of violence 13 take it by force. For all the prophets and the law prophesied until John.	16 16 The law and the prophets *were* until John: from that time the gospel of the kingdom of God is preached, and every man entereth violently into it.

[1] Cf. Billerbeck, *Komm.* i. 435.

The differences between Mt. and Lk. are considerable and striking; and Mt. is generally held to preserve the saying in a more original, because more difficult, form than Lk. The Lucan form is then explained as an attempt to clarify the obscurity of the original saying. It is, however, probable that the principal alterations are due to Mt. Thus the order of the clauses in Lk. is to be preferred: Mt. has reversed this order on transferring the saying to another context. In Mt. 11[13] the word ' all ' is a typical Matthæan gloss; and the word ' prophesied ' is a clumsy attempt to fill up the gap in the original statement. In order to get in his favourite word ' all,' Mt. has reversed the natural order ' the law and the prophets.' On the other hand it is probable that Mt. has kept the original wording in the statement that the Kingdom of God ' suffereth violence, and men of violence take it by force.' The question now arises as to the meaning of this difficult saying. ' Suffereth violence ' represents the Greek *biazetai*, which may be either passive, as R.V. takes it, or middle. In the latter case the meaning will be ' exercises force,' ' shows its power,' or the like. ' Take it by force ': the Greek verb used here (*harpazousin*) may have this meaning; but it may equally well mean no more than ' snatch at,' ' seize.' The Greek word translated ' men of violence ' (*biastai*) is exceedingly rare, and the meaning to be assigned to it in this passage is uncertain. The sense which we give to ' men of violence ' depends on the sense in which we take *harpazousin*. If the verb is regarded as signifying hostile action, then the ' men of violence ' will be the enemies of the Kingdom—demonic or worldly powers. If we suppose the verb to mean ' snatch at ' in the sense of making every effort to obtain what is seen to be a supreme blessing, then the ' men of violence' will be ordinary men who are roused to make great efforts by the prospect of securing a place in the Kingdom. Such are the possibilities. The most satisfactory interpretation of the saying is that given by Otto (*Reich Gottes und Menschensohn*, pp. 84–88). It involves rendering the saying as follows:

' The Law and the prophets were until John:
From that time the Kingdom of God exercises its power and men of violence snatch at it.'

How does the Kingdom of God exercise its power? By overcoming those forces of evil which degrade and destroy man. ' If I by the finger of God cast out devils, then is the Kingdom of God come upon you ' (Lk. 11[20]‖Mt. 12[28]). ' And into whatsoever city ye enter . . . heal the sick that are therein, and say unto them, The Kingdom of God is come nigh unto you ' (Lk. 10[8f.]; cf. Mt. 10[7f.]). The Kingdom shows its power in the work of Jesus and His messengers. Otto explains ' men of violence ' as the kind of men described in Mk. 9[42-48]; Lk. 9[57-62], 13[23f.], 14[26]. They are men who will take every risk and make every sacrifice in order to have their share in the Kingdom. It then appears that Lk. has, on the whole, interpreted the saying rightly. ' The Kingdom of God is proclaimed as good news, and everyone presses into it ' is not far from what we take to be the original sense of the saying. It is further to be noticed that the saying contrasts two periods in history: the period of the Law and prophets and the period of the Kingdom of God. The former is one of promise, the latter of fulfilment; and the ministry of the Baptist is the dividing line between the two. It is involved in this idea that the new era in some sense supersedes the old: the Law and the prophets take second place to the fuller manifestation of the Kingdom of God in its saving power, as delivering us from evil; whereas they could only warn against evil. This idea of the supersession of the Law by the fuller revelation of God is developed by Paul; but it has its roots here in Q. In the light of this interpretation the immediately following verse in Lk. becomes perplexing.

MT. 5[18]	LK. 16[17]
5 18 For verily I say unto you, Till heaven and earth pass away, one jot or one tittle shall in no wise pass away from the law, till all things be accomplished.	16 17 But it is easier for heaven and earth to pass away, than for one tittle of the law to fall.

This verse seems, at first sight, to assert the absolute eternity of the Law in its minutest details. The form in Mt. does not go so far: it only maintains the Law in full force until the final consummation. The Jewish view was that the Law remains in full validity throughout the present age and the Messianic period. Whether it was expected to be in force in the world to come is a question much more difficult to answer. (See Moore, *Judaism*, i. 269 ff.) The text as given in Mt. conforms exactly to the Rabbinical doctrine of the perpetuity of the Law. But is this what Jesus meant to say? It is difficult to believe so, when in the preceding verse we have a saying which implies that the Law is already in some measure superseded; and when in the next verse we have a saying on divorce, which, as we shall see, is inconsistent with the Law; to say nothing of other passages in the Gospels where Jesus treats the letter of the Law in a very revolutionary way.

If now we look at the Lk. version of the saying, bearing in mind the possibility that Mt. 5[18] is a revision of it to bring it explicitly into line with Rabbinical doctrine, another possibility at once emerges: that the saying in its original form asserts not the perpetuity of the Law but the unbending conservatism of the scribes. This interpretation is fortified when we take into account the true meaning of the word 'tittle.' This has usually been regarded as meaning the serif which distinguishes certain letters of the Hebrew alphabet, as it distinguishes G from C in English. But this is not so. The 'tittle' most probably stands for certain scribal ornaments added to certain letters in the Hebrew Scriptures (Billerbeck, i. 248 f.). These were no part of the Law itself, but an addition to it. The fact that they were placed on the tops of the letters, and that another name for them was 'crowns,' may have some bearing on the use of the word 'fall' in Lk. The tittle then is part of that scribal tradition which Jesus so often criticised The saying thus comes to mean: It is easier for heaven and earth to pass away than for the scribes to give up the smallest bit of that tradition by which they make the Law of none effect. The saying in its original form is not sound Rabbinical dogma but bitter irony. Lk. has faithfully preserved it; and it is only because we constantly read the verse through Mt.'s Jewish-Christian spectacles that we are misled as to its true purport.

The way in which Jesus feels free to revise the Law is illustrated by the next verse in Lk. This has to do with divorce and remarriage, and we must take into account the parallels in Mt. 5[32] (M) and Mk. 10[11 f.].||Mt. 19[9].

Cf. Mt. 5³¹ᶠ· (M), Mk. 10¹¹ᶠ·‖Mt. 19⁹.

LK. 16¹⁸

16 18 Every one that putteth away his wife, and marrieth another, committeth adultery: and he that marrieth one that is put away from a husband committeth adultery.

Mt. 5³¹ᶠ· runs:

'It was said also, Whosoever shall put away his wife, let him give her a writing of divorcement : but I say unto you, That every one that putteth away his wife, saving for the cause of fornication, maketh her an adulteress: and whosoever shall marry her when she is put away committeth adultery.'

The other relevant passages are:

MT. 19⁹

19 9 And I say unto you, Whosoever shall put away his wife, [1] except for fornication, and shall marry another, committeth adultery: [2] and he that marrieth her when she is put away committeth adultery.

[1] Some ancient authorities read *saving for the cause of fornication, maketh her an adulteress*: as in ch. v. 32.
[2] The following words, to the end of the verse, are omitted by some ancient authorities.

MK. 10¹¹⁻¹²

10 11 And he saith unto them, Whosoever shall put away his wife, and marry another, committeth adultery against 12 her: and if she herself shall put away her husband, and marry another, she committeth adultery.

The discussion of these passages is usually undertaken with a view to finding from the words of Jesus some clear rule for the Church in dealing with the question of divorce and remarriage. But for critical purposes, especially in the present context, the primary question is not what rules Jesus lays down concerning divorce and remarriage, but how the formulations here given compare with Jewish legislation about the offence of adultery. And here the essential point is that in Jewish Law adultery is *always* intercourse between a married woman and a man other than her husband. (In construing the law formal betrothal is regarded as equivalent to marriage.) Hence while a woman can commit adultery against her husband, a man cannot commit adultery against his wife. He càn only commit adultery against another married man. In the light of this the following observations may be made.

(*a*) The principle that a man cannot commit adultery against his own wife is flatly contradicted in Mk. 10¹¹, where the words ' against her ' can only refer to the first wife.

(*b*) The dictum Mk. 10¹¹ is taken over by Mt. in the parallel 19⁹ with two alterations, both highly significant. (i) Mt. introduces the excepting clause ' except for fornication,' and so brings the rule into agreement with the interpretation of the Jewish Law favoured by the school of Shammai. (ii) He omits the words ' against her.' This does not remove the contradiction between the dictum of Jesus and the Jewish definition of adultery; but it makes it somewhat less obvious.

(*c*) Mk. 10¹² flatly contradicts Jewish Law, in which the wife could not divorce her husband. In certain cases (*not* including infidelity on his part) she could compel him to divorce her; but in Jewish Law it is not proper to speak of a wife divorcing her husband. It is true that in two early Aramaic Jewish documents from Elephantine (*Aramaic Papyri of the Fifth Century B.C.*, ed. Cowley, Nos. 9 and 15) divorce of the husband by the wife is a legal possibility; but the community in Elephantine was eccentric in other respects, and can hardly be cited as an example of orthodox Jewish practice. A possible explanation of Mk. 10¹² is that given by Burkitt (*Gospel History and its Transmission*, pp. 98–101), that the verse is a direct reference to Herodias (Mk. 6¹⁷ᶠᶠ). The weak point in this explanation is that there is no evidence that Herodias *divorced* her husband.

(*d*) Lk. 16¹⁸ agrees substantially in its first half with Mk. 10¹¹ save that it has nothing corresponding to ' against her ' in Mk. In its second half it proceeds ' and he who marries a woman divorced from her husband commits adultery.' It is possible that this is the correct rendering of an original Aramaic which has been misunderstood and mistranslated in Mk. 10¹². If that be so we are dealing with the case in which a husband divorces his wife and both remarry. The dictum of Jesus is that the husband commits adultery against his divorced wife. This is involved in Lk. 16¹⁸ᵃ, and explicit in Mk. 10¹¹. Further, in the case of the divorced wife who remarries, the man who marries her commits adultery against her first husband. So Lk. 16¹⁸ᵇ, which is to be preferred to Mk. 10¹².

(*e*) There remains the formulation in Mt. 5³¹ᶠ. Here we have the same exception as in Mt. 19⁹. It is differently phrased, but its purport is the same. It makes the condition of divorce the same as that laid down by the Rabbinical school of Shammai. This Matthæan form differs from all the others in this, that it does not deal with the situation created if the divorcing husband remarries. What it does say is that a man who divorces his wife makes her become an adulteress, presumably if she marries again; and that the man who marries a divorced woman commits adultery. That is, if a divorced woman remarries, she and her second husband are both guilty of adultery; and the first husband is morally responsible for this state of affairs. This is perfectly consistent with the Jewish doctrine of adultery. And it is an extension of what is implied in Lk. 16¹⁸ᵇ.

(*f*) The conclusion to be drawn is that the Q form of the saying (Lk. 16¹⁸) is the original. Mk. 10¹¹ᵃ gives the sense of Lk. 16¹⁸ᵃ and makes it more precise by the addition of the words ' against her.' Mk. 10¹² is a misunderstanding of the Aramaic underlying Lk. 16¹⁸ᵇ. Mt. 19⁹ is Mk. 10¹¹ modified in the direction of Shammaite legal doctrine by the addition of the excepting clause. Mt. 5³² is an expanded version of the part of the dictum represented by Lk. 16¹⁸ᵇ. It may be the M version of the saying. It contains the excepting clause (as in Mt. 19⁹), which here *may* belong to the original text of M.

(*g*) The characteristic and original feature in our Lord's teaching on this subject is stated in Q and underlined in Mk.:—that a husband can commit adultery against his wife. This means that in respect of marriage after divorce both parties are put on a footing of absolute equality. For either to marry again is adultery. This fact is a strong argument against the genuineness of the excepting clauses in Mt. For the privilege there accorded is granted to the husband only, and it is not likely that Jesus, after correcting the one-sidedness of the Jewish

Law, would stultify what He had just done, by according to the husband a privilege withheld from the wife.

The passages just considered give the opinion of Jesus on the Jewish Law of divorce and remarriage. His positive teaching on the nature of marriage is given in Mk. 10[2-9]. Cf. *The Teaching of Jesus*, pp. 292 f.

(e) STUMBLING-BLOCKS (178)

MT. 18[6-7]	LK. 17[1-2]
18 6 But whoso shall cause one of these little ones which believe on me to stumble, it is profitable for him that [1] a great millstone should be hanged about his neck, and *that* he should be sunk in the depth of the sea. 7 Woe unto the world because of occasions of stumbling! for it must needs be that the occasions come; but woe to that man through whom the occasion cometh!	17 1 And he said unto his disciples, It is impossible but that occasions of stumbling should come: but woe unto him, through 2 whom they come! It were well for him if a millstone were hanged about his neck, and he were thrown into the sea, rather than that he should cause one of these little ones to stumble.

[1] Gr. *a millstone turned by an ass.*

MK. 9[42]

9 42 And whosoever shall cause one of these little ones that believe [1] on me to stumble, it were better for him if [2] a great millstone were hanged about his neck, and he were cast into the sea.

[1] Many ancient authorities omit *on me.*
[2] Gr. *a millstone turned by an ass.*

Compare also Mk. 9[37]|| Mt. 18[5]||Lk. 9[48], Mt. 10[40]||Lk. 10[16], Mk. 9[41]||Mt. 10[42], Mk. 6[11]|| Mt. 10[14]||Lk. 9[5].

A comparison of these passages shows how complicated, not to say confused, these sayings have become in the course of tradition. We may attempt to disentangle them; but it must be emphasised that any results attained cannot be more than probable conjectures. The root of the confusion is that Jesus said certain things about little children and certain things about His own disciples in their missionary work; and that He was accustomed to address His disciples as ' children.' See, for example, Mk. 10[24] and compare Mt. 11[25] = Lk. 10[21]. Now the early Church was more interested in the original disciples than in children; and we should expect the tendency of the tradition to be to transfer sayings concerning ' children ' or ' little ones ' to the disciples. The result is that in every case we have to ask whether a saying about ' children ' or ' little ones ' is to be taken literally or understood of the disciples.

Mk. 9[33-42] is a passage in which this problem is at its most acute. In this passage there are three verses which we must consider: 37, 41, 42. Mk. 9[37] has already been discussed above (p. 78) on Lk. 10[16]. It may be suspected that Mk. 9[41f.] were originally sayings concerning children. There is a steady movement in the direction of turning ' little ones ' into ' disciples ':

Lk. 17[2] ' one of these little ones.'

Mk. 9[42] ' one of these little ones that believe.'

Mt. 18[6] ' one of these little ones that believe on me.'

With Mk. 9⁴¹ we can compare Mt. 10⁴²:

Mk. 9⁴¹ ' For whosoever shall give you a cup of water to drink . . .'

Mt. 10⁴² ' And whosoever shall give to drink unto one of these little ones a cup of cold water only . . .'

Mt. 10⁴² shows considerable agreement with Mk. 9⁴¹; but it contains elements which are perhaps to be attributed to M. In any case ' one of these little ones ' seems to me to be more original than ' you.' It may therefore be supposed that the original saying was to this effect:

He who shows the smallest kindness to a child will surely be rewarded (Mk. 9⁴¹‖ Mt. 10⁴²).

He who harms a little child will surely be severely punished (Mk. 9⁴²‖Lk. 17²).

Such harm is inevitable; but woe to him who is responsible for it (Mt. 18⁷‖Lk. 17¹). The first two sentences are in antithetic parallelism. This interpretation of the saying suggests that the order of verses in Mt. is the original. It may be added that the great rewards and punishments are more appropriate on this interpretation. The disciple can look after himself; but the child is weak and helpless: and we do, in fact, feel more strongly about the treatment of children than of adults.

(f) DIFFERENCES WITHIN THE FELLOWSHIP (179)

LK. 17³⁻⁴

Cf. Mt. 18¹⁵, ²¹, ²² (M).

17 3 Take heed to yourselves: if thy brother sin, rebuke him; and if he repent, forgive 4 him. And if he sin against thee seven times in the day, and seven times turn again to thee, saying, I repent; thou shalt forgive him.

The parallel passage in Mt. is much more elaborate than Lk. 17³⁻⁴. The whole of Mt. 18¹⁵⁻²² is probably to be assigned to M. Cf. Streeter, *The Four Gospels*, pp. 257 f., and see below, pp. 209 ff. The saying, as it stands in Lk. (= Q), does not go into the question of the jurisdiction of the fellowship in disputes between its members. The injunction supposes that all such cases may be decided in a spirit of brotherhood by the parties concerned. The fact that the parallel in Mt. prescribes a quasi-legal procedure in such cases is itself evidence that it is a later development.

3, 4. ' Take heed to yourselves ' is followed immediately by an address in the second person singular. This does not create any difficulty. ' Thy brother ' means ' the brother of any one of you.' Does ' take heed to yourselves ' mean ' each of you take heed to himself ' or ' take heed to one another '? In view of Lk. 21³⁴ we should probably take the former alternative. ' If thy brother sin ': we must supply ' against thee ' as in v. 4. ' Rebuke him.' The advice is by no means superfluous, for the natural tendency is either to harbour a secret grudge or to complain to some third party. The nature of the Christian fellowship requires a certain frankness in the dealings of its members with one another. Repentance on the part of the offender and forgiveness by the injured party together make an end of the matter. The duty of the injured party to forgive is Jewish as well as Christian doctrine. ' In the case of man as well as God the condition of forgiveness is repentance and confession—in that of man, reparation also. When the wrongdoer makes this amends, it is the duty of the injured party to forgive him: " When thou hast mercy upon thy fellow, thou hast One to have mercy on thee; but if thou hast not mercy upon thy fellow, thou hast none to have mercy on thee " (*Tanḥuma*) ' (Moore, *Judaism*, ii. 154). And this readiness to forgive is not limited. Seven times is not to be taken literally: it means that forgiving is to go on indefinitely, so long as there is a sign of genuine repentance. The spirit here inculcated is that which is celebrated by Paul in 1 Cor. 13[4, 5, 7].

(g) THE POWER OF FAITH (180)

MT. 17[20] (M)

17 20   And he saith unto them, Because of your little faith: for verily I say unto you, If ye have faith as a grain of mustard seed, ye shall say unto this mountain, Remove hence to yonder place; and it shall remove; and nothing shall be impossible unto you.

LK. 17[5-6]

17 5   And the apostles said unto the Lord, 6 Increase our faith. And the Lord said, If ye have faith as a grain of mustard seed, ye would say unto this sycamine tree, Be thou rooted up, and be thou planted in the sea; and it would have obeyed you.

Cf. Mk. 11[23]

11 23 Verily I say unto you, Whosoever shall say unto this mountain, Be thou taken up and cast into the sea; and shall not doubt in his heart, but shall believe that what he saith cometh to pass; he shall have it.

Here again we have a complicated and confused tradition. Mk. 11[23] occurs in the story of the withering of the barren fig tree. Mt. 17[20], which is generally held to be derived from Q, is inserted by Mt. in the story of the cure of the epileptic boy. There it takes the place of the original reply of Jesus (as given in Mk. 9[29]) to the disciples' question why they could not cast out the demon. Mk. 11[23] and Mt. 17[20] both have ' mountain ' against Lk.'s ' sycamine tree,' and in this they have support from 1 Cor. 13[2]. Now 1 Cor. 13[2] is in close agreement with Mt. 17[20]. Both speak of a faith that will transfer a mountain from one place to another, but not of casting a mountain into the sea. 1 Cor. is thus proof that the saying in a form similar to Mt. 17[20] was current before about A.D. 55. Lk. 17[6] is quite different. It speaks of uprooting a tree and planting it in the sea. Mk. 11[23] has features from both pictures. Like Mt. 17[20] it has the removal of the mountain; and, as in Lk., the destination of the removed object is the sea. There is a *prima facie* case for the hypothesis that originally there were two independent sayings on the power of faith, one preserved in Mt. 17[20] and the other in Lk. 17[6]; and that Mk. 11[23] is a mixture of the two in the process of tradition.

It is, however, commonly held that Lk.'s version of the saying is not original, that he has substituted the tree for the mountain of the original saying, and that his version of the saying is an echo of the story of the cursing of the fig tree, which he omits in his Gospel. This view is open to the following objections:

(1) The tree that was cursed in Mk. 11 is a fig tree, not a ' sycamine.'

(2) When Lk. means ' fig tree ' he uses the proper Greek word for it. Lk. 17[6] is the only place in the New Testament where the ' sycamine tree ' is mentioned.

(3) There is Rabbinical evidence that the ' sycamore ' (Heb. *shikmāh*) was very deep-rooted. A rule of the Mishnah (*Baba Bathra* 2[11], Danby, p. 368) required it to be planted 50 cubits from a neighbour's cistern as against 25 cubits for other trees. ' Sycamine ' in Greek properly means the mulberry tree; but the Hebrew *shikmāh* in the Old Testament is translated by ' sycamine ' in the Septuagint. ' Sycomore ' appears in Lk. 19[4]; but this is from a different source, L. The conclusion is that ' sycamine ' in 17[6] is a mistranslation *in Q* of the Aramaic *shikmā*, and that here, as elsewhere, Lk. has faithfully copied what was in his source.

We may therefore regard Lk. 17[6] as a saying from Q, similar in meaning to the other saying preserved in Mt. 17[20] (M), and independent of it. This Q saying is introduced by Lk. 17[5], a verse which is commonly regarded as Lk.'s own composition. Bussmann (*Synoptische Studien*, ii. 90) thinks that it is the connecting verse in Q between *vv.* 3 f. and *v.* 6. The disciples, faced by the demand for unlimited readiness to forgive wrongs, see that this needs a great amount of faith; and so ask that their faith may be increased. Jesus replies that it is not a matter of quantity of faith. The smallest quantity, provided that it is genuine, is capable of accomplishing the seemingly impossible. The grain of mustard seed is a common Jewish expression for a minute quantity. It should be noted that the idea of *planting* a tree in the sea is frankly absurd. It is a plain warning against taking the saying in a sense that was never intended. The saying is a paradox of the same kind as the camel passing through the eye of a needle. Neither the one nor the other is meant to be attempted in the literal sense. But by faith men can do things that seem to be as absurd and impossible as transplanting trees and making them grow in the sea. This word of Jesus does not invite Christians to become conjurers and magicians, but heroes like those whose exploits are celebrated in the eleventh chapter of Hebrews.

4. THE DAY OF THE SON OF MAN (184)

(a) Longings and False Alarms

MT. 24[26-27]

LK. 17[22-25]

24 26 If therefore they shall say unto you, Behold, he is in the wilderness; go not forth: Behold, he is in the inner cham-
27 bers; believe [1] *it* not. For as the lightning cometh forth from the east, and is seen even unto the west; so shall be the [2] coming of the Son of man.

[1] Or, them. [2] Gr. *presence*.

17 22 And he said unto the disciples, The days will come, when ye shall desire to see one of the days of the Son of man, and
23 ye shall not see it. And they shall say to you, Lo, there! Lo, here! go not away,
24 nor follow after *them*: for as the lightning, when it lighteneth out of the one part under the heaven, shineth unto the other part under heaven: so shall the Son of
25 man be [1] in his day. But first must he suffer many things and be rejected of this generation.

[1] Some ancient authorities omit *in his day*.

Cf. Mk. 13[21-23].

13 21 And then if any man shall say unto you, Lo, here is the Christ; or, Lo, there;
22 believe [1] *it* not: for there shall arise false Christs and false prophets, and shall shew signs and wonders, that they may lead

23 astray, if possible, the elect. But take ye heed: behold, I have told you all things beforehand.

[1] Or, him.

Mk. and Q combine in testifying that Jesus prophesied the coming of bogus prophets and bogus messiahs, who would appeal to the Jewish hope of deliverance, by Divine help, from the oppressions of their enemies. Such people will represent the Messianic ideal which Jesus Himself has utterly rejected. See above, pp. 45 f. His disciples must also reject it and have nothing to do with it. The promised deliverance is not of the earth earthly, but from heaven. It is not a human movement, but a Divine intervention.

22–24. The opening formula marks the change of audience from that in Lk. 17$^{20f.}$. The saying which follows has no parallel in Mt. or Mk. ' The days will come ' is a common formula in Old Testament prophecy. The difficulty of the saying lies in the words ' one of the days of the Son of Man.' For ' the day of the Son of Man ' in the Gospels, like ' the day of the Lord ' in the Old Testament, is a point of time and not a period. It is what divides the present age from the age to come. Strictly speaking, therefore, it is not proper to speak of ' the days of the Son of Man '; and though the words occur in 17^{26} they have there a different sense. See notes *ad loc.* A most ingenious and attractive explanation is offered by Torrey (*The Four Gospels*, p. 312). The present text depends on a misunderstanding of the Aramaic adverb *lachdā* meaning ' very much,' as the numeral ' one ' with the sign of the accusative. The true meaning is then ' you will greatly desire to see the day of the Son of Man.' The disciples will be longing for the Parousia, and this hope deferred will expose them more than others to the dangers arising from false prophets and false Messiahs. Lk.'s ' Lo there! Lo here! ' has the support of Mk. Mt. gives a more circumstantial picture: the Messiah is in the wilderness—the mobilisation place of rebellions—don't go to join him; he is in the inner chambers—the places of intrigues and plots—put no trust in all that. Whence Mt. obtained these additional details we cannot say. It is unlikely that they come from Q; for if they had stood there Lk. would not have altered them to what is a mere repetition of *v.* 21^{a}. ' Go not away, nor follow after ' is a command to observe strict neutrality. These manifestations should rouse neither fear nor hope. They have nothing to do with the true deliverance which is to come from God. This, when it comes, will come without any preliminary plottings and skirmishings. It will be like the lightning—from above, and lighting up the whole world from horizon to horizon. Mt. makes the lightning come forth from the east and be seen even unto the west, which is not true to fact. ' Shineth ' (Lk.) and ' is seen ' (Mt.) are translation variants. Cf. the Greek versions of Dan. 12^{3}.

25. This verse, which has no parallel in Mt., is commonly regarded as an insertion by Lk. (cf. 24$^{25-27}$) influenced perhaps by the three passages in Mk. where the Passion of the Son of Man is predicted (Mk. 8^{31}, 9^{31}, 10$^{33f.}$). It should be noted, however, that the predictions in Mk. have in view a condemnation and execution at the hands of the leaders and rulers of the people, whereas this verse speaks of the Son of Man suffering many things and being rejected by this generation. Further, 'suffer many things and be rejected' is very vague, if it is an *ex post facto* reference to the Crucifixion. An interpolator would surely have given something more precise, something which left the reader in no doubt that it was His own death on the Cross that Jesus was predicting. If, as I think, the verse is from Q and a genuine utterance of Jesus, we have to ask what is meant by the sufferings

and rejection of the Son of Man. On the view which I take of the meaning of the name ' Son of Man,' the answer is that it is the Remnant that must suffer and be rejected by this generation: and that means Jesus and His disciples. This idea of an inevitable period of suffering before the final vindication is not strange to Q. We may refer to Lk. 11^{47-51}, $12^{4-12, 49-53}$, $13^{34f.}$.

(b) THE ESCHATOLOGICAL POEM

MT. 24^{37-39}	LK. 17^{26-30}
24 37 And as *were* the days of Noah, so shall 38 be the [1] coming of the Son of man. For as in those days which were before the flood they were eating and drinking, marrying and giving in marriage, until the day that Noah entered into the ark, 39 and they knew not until the flood came, and took them all away; so shall be the [1] coming of the Son of man.	17 26 And as it came to pass in the days of Noah, even so shall it be also in the days 27 of the Son of man. They ate, they drank, they married, they were given in marriage, until the day that Noah entered into the ark, and the flood came, and 28 destroyed them all. Likewise even as it came to pass in the days of Lot; they ate, they drank, they bought, they sold, they 29 planted, they builded; but in the day that Lot went out from Sodom it rained fire and brimstone from heaven, and 30 destroyed them all: after the same manner shall it be in the day that the Son of man is revealed.

[1] Gr. *presence.*

The poetic form of the passage is preserved in Lk. In Mt. the whole of the second strophe is sacrificed in the interests of brevity. On the structure of the poem, see above, p. 32. The Matthæan version of the first strophe is a prosaic paraphrase of what is given in Lk. The most striking feature about the poem as a whole is the discrepancy between the view of the final consummation here and that in Mk. 13^{5-31}. In Mk. 13^{5-31} the end is the last member of a series of predicted events. There is a gradual crescendo of catastrophes until we come to the appearance of the Son of Man. In Q the picture is very different. The world is going about its ordinary affairs; everything is normal. ' When they are saying, Peace and safety, then sudden destruction cometh upon them.' There can be little doubt that the Q account is to be preferred to the Marcan. It appears in a poetic form which is specially characteristic of the genuine teaching of Jesus; and it is supported by I Thess. 5^{1-10}; Mk. 13^{32-37}; Lk. 21^{34-36} (L). Mk. 13^{5-31} is probably to be regarded as a catena containing genuine sayings of Jesus so arranged that they give an incorrect impression of His teaching on this subject. (Cf. *The Teaching of Jesus*, pp. 260 ff.)

26, 27. The first strophe, *vv.* 26–27 compares the day of the Son of Man to the Deluge. ' The days of Noah ' in this context must mean the period which came to an end with the Flood. Then ' the days of the Son of Man ' is a similar expression formed for the sake of parallelism, and meaning the period which will be terminated by the ' Day of the Son of Man,' that is, the Parousia. ' Days of the Son of Man ' is not the plural of ' Day of the Son of Man,' but a poetical way of describing the last days of the existing order. This is perceived in Mt.'s version, where the Q passage is rewritten in this sense, and the strange expression ' days of the Son of Man ' avoided. The emphasis in the description is not on the sinfulness of the people, but on the fact that they were living in complete disregard of what was coming, immersed in their daily occupations and pleasures, planning and arranging their lives with no thought beyond their immediate interests, self-sufficient and self-satisfied, until sudden calamity overwhelmed them and their civilisation (Gen. 6^{11ff}·, 7^{21ff}·).

28 f., 30. The second strophe, vv. 28–30. The inhabitants of Sodom are described in similar terms to the generation of the Flood. The sins of Sodom were notorious; but it is not their sins that are mentioned. It is their indifference to the seriousness of their situation that proves their undoing. Noah in the Old Testament story is no paragon of the virtues, much less Lot. But both realised that the catastrophe must come, and both took means to save themselves. The Christian message is not for those who think that they deserve a better fate than their neighbours, but for those who, in the midst of universal indifference and complacency, realise the desperateness of their situation, and ask, ' What must I do to be saved? ' The things that happened in the remote past have a real bearing on the present. The most dangerous of all theological errors is that which says, ' He's a good fellow, and 'twill all be well,' rashly assuming that our indifference and carelessness have their counterparts in heaven and that God's holy purpose must inevitably come to terms with our shallow optimism.

(c) CLOSING SAYINGS

LK. 17$^{31-32}$

17 31 In that day, he which shall be on the housetop, and his goods in the house, let him not go down to take them away: and let him that is in the field likewise
32 not return back. Remember Lot's wife.

Cf. Mk. 13$^{14-16}$.

13 14 But when ye see the abomination of desolation standing where he ought not (let him that readeth understand), then let them that are in Judæa flee unto the
15 mountains: and let him that is on the housetop not go down, nor enter in, to
16 take anything out of his house: and let him that is in the field not return back to take his cloke.

The saying Lk. 17$^{31f.}$ has no Q parallel in Mt.: it has an independent parallel in Mk. It can hardly be considered relevant to its present context. For the advice given in the two verses is appropriate in the case of war—the siege of Jerusalem, for example. Then there is at least a chance of escape. But in the day of the Son of Man it is idle to think of flight. There is no place to which one may escape. The verses in Lk. are therefore commonly explained as an insertion by Lk. On the other hand, it can be urged that Lk. was sufficiently intelligent to see that such an insertion would be inappropriate at this point; and that it is much more likely that he has kept the unsuitable verses because they were in his source. This means that they belong to Q. Then how did they come to take this place in Q? The answer lies in v. 32 with its reference to Lot's wife. The name of Lot provides the connexion with the preceding poem: and this connexion is not logical but mnemonic. The conjunction of vv. 28–30 and vv. 31 f. goes back to the time of oral tradition: it is probably older than Q.

Verses 31 f. have nothing to do with the Parousia. They belong to another circle of ideas. Jesus prophesied the fall of Jerusalem as the Old Testament prophets had prophesied the fall of Samaria and Jerusalem before Him (Mk. 13[11].; Lk. 13[34f].). The natural tendency was for these two things—the fall of Jerusalem and the end of the existing world order at the Parousia—to be confused in the tradition. This has happened in Mk. 13. It may be that we have the beginnings of this confusion in this Q passage.

The picture is one of precipitate flight in face of imminent peril. In such circumstances the refugees dare not take time to collect their belongings. They must go as they are, and consider themselves fortunate if they escape with their lives. The story of Lot's wife (Gen. 19[26]) serves to give point to the warning.

MT. 10[39]	LK. 17[33]
10 39 He that [1] findeth his [2] life shall lose it; and he that [3] loseth his [2] life for my sake shall find it.	17 33 Whosoever shall seek to gain his [1] life shall lose it: but whosoever shall lose *his* [1] *life* shall [2] preserve it.
[1] Or, *found*. [2] Or, *soul*. [3] Or, *lost*.	[1] Or, *soul*. [2] Gr. *save it alive*.

Cf. Mk. 8[35].

8 35   For whosoever would save his [1] life shall lose it; and whosoever shall lose his [1] life for my sake and the gospel's shall save it.

[1] Or, *soul*.

This verse, as is shown by the context in which it is preserved independently by Mk., and by the context into which it is inserted by Mt. (Mission Charge), has to do originally with the loyalty of disciples to their calling and task. To save one's life at the cost of treachery to Jesus and His mission is to lose it; and to sacrifice one's life in the service of the Kingdom of God is to save it. We may conjecture that the saying was well known in the primitive community, and that it was commonly understood in this sense. Lk., who has a doublet of the saying in the Marcan context (Lk. 9[24]), must also have known this original and presumably correct interpretation of the saying. The inference is that he has it here a second time because it stood here in Q. Why does it stand here in Q? The answer may perhaps be furnished by the thought of Lk. 17[31f]. There the disciples are told that in certain circumstances they must save their lives by flight. Verse 33 then comes in as a reminder that there are cases in which this course is not open. Wherever running away would involve disloyalty to Jesus and the Kingdom of God, it is better to stay and die.

MT. 24[40-41]	LK. 17[34-35]
24 40 Then shall two men be in the field; 41 one is taken, and one is left: two women *shall be* grinding at the mill; one is taken, and one is left.	17 34 I say unto you, In that night there shall be two men on one bed; the one shall be 35 taken, and the other shall be left. There shall be two women grinding together; the one shall be taken, and the other shall be left.[1]

[1] Some ancient authorities add ver. 36. *There shall be two men in the field; the one shall be taken, and the other shall be left.* |

The first problem here concerns the text of Lk. As appears from the R.V. mg., there are two forms of the saying. The shorter, *vv.* 34 and 35 only, is the reading of the majority of the most ancient Greek MSS. and the Egyptian versions: the longer, *vv.* 34–36, is supported by two uncial MSS. (D and U) and the Latin, Syriac, and Armenian versions. In modern critical editions of the text *v.* 36 is omitted and commonly explained as an intrusion from Mt. 24⁴⁰. If this be so, the interpolator did his job thoroughly. For he not only borrowed Mt. 24⁴⁰ here: he also rewrote it in the style of Lk. 17³⁴ᶠ.. It is more probable that *v.* 36 was omitted by some intelligent scribe or reviser, who saw the words ' in that night ' in *v.* 34, and reflected that agriculture is not a nocturnal pursuit. He did not know, or forgot, that in Palestine farming does involve night work for shepherds (cf. Lk. 2⁸) and for watchmen set to guard fields, gardens, and orchards against thieves. (Cf. Feldman, *Parables and Similes of the Rabbis*, pp. 132 f.) ' The field ' in Palestinian thought is not restricted to arable land: it can be used for any kind of agricultural land whether cultivated or not. If we accept *v.* 36 as genuine, we have a complete picture of a Palestinian household consisting of husband and wife, two maidservants, and two menservants. The number of the male servants is determined by the fact that one is to be taken and one left in each case. Two is the normal number of persons to work a hand-mill.

34. The words ' in that night ' suggest that the saying is a continuation of the line of thought represented by the early Pauline ' the day of the Lord so cometh as a thief in the night ' (1 Thess. 5²). It is not to be taken literally as a prophecy that the Parousia will occur at night. R.V. translates ' two men on one bed.' The word ' men ' has no equivalent in the Greek text: and the Revisers' rendering depends on the fact that the numeral ' two ' and the pronouns ' the one ' and ' the other ' are all masculine. But it could not be otherwise if, as is probable, husband and wife are meant. Two persons are together (male *and* female): one (male *or* female) will be taken, and the other (male *or* female) will be left. In each case the masculine gender is inevitable. We have then the household with its master and mistress. One is taken, that is, gathered into the number of those destined to a share in the new age that is now coming in.

35 f. Two maids are working at the hand-mill. The same happens in their case. Two men are working in the fields. The same happens to them. The day of the Son of Man cuts across all human relations: it has no regard for ties of blood or marriage, for economic or social distinctions. It has its own principle of division and on that principle it makes a clean cut, separating mankind into two classes.

MT. 24²⁸	LK. 17³⁷
24 28 Wheresoever the carcase is, there will the ¹ eagles be gathered together.	**17** 37 And they answering say unto him, Where, Lord? And he said unto them, Where the body *is*, thither will the ¹ eagles also be gathered together.
¹ Or, *vultures*.	¹ Or, *vultures*.

The question ' where? ' and the related question ' when? ' have always had a fascination for those who let their imaginations play upon the apocalyptic hope. Thus in Zech. 14⁴ the appearance of God for the deliverance of His people takes

place on the Mount of Olives. Jesus declines to give details of time and place.
' Of that day or that hour knoweth no one, not even the angels in heaven, neither
the Son, but the Father ' (Mk. 13^{32}) is the answer to the question ' When shall these
things be? ' (Mk. 13^4). And here the question ' Where, Lord? ' is met by a saying,
probably proverbial, which does not answer the question, but says something else.
R.V. mg. ' vultures ' is more accurate than the text ' eagles.' But ' vulture ' for
the Palestinian does not have the unpleasant associations which it has for us.
When the vulture is mentioned in the Old Testament it is usually thought of as a
noble bird: e.g. Exod. 19^4; Dt. 32^{11}; Is. 40^{31}. One characteristic of the vulture
is the almost incredible swiftness with which it discovers and makes its way to its
prey. This swiftness on the prey is mentioned in Job 9^{26} and Hab. 1^8. Cf. also
2 Sam. 1^{23}; Jer. 4^{13}; Lam. 4^{19}. The saying here draws attention to what has
already been emphasised—the swiftness and suddenness of the coming of the day
of the Son of Man. Jesus says in effect: ' The whole present order of things is
nearing its end. Civilisation as you know it is dying. The important thing is not
to know the answers to questions about the exact time and place of the end; but
to be prepared for it. It is useless to ask for signs of the end, when the first sign of
the passing of the present age will be the arrival of the new order.'

Mt. has inserted the saying in a context in his eschatological discourse (chaps.
24 f.) which makes the introductory question superfluous. In the saying itself the
words ' body ' (Lk.) and ' carcase ' (Mt.) are translation variants. See the Greek
versions of Num. 14^{33}.

EPILOGUE

We may pause here to ask what is the total impression made upon us by this
very early attempt at a systematic account of the teaching of Jesus. And we must
bear in mind that the work is not the preached Gospel of the primitive Church, but
a supplement to the Gospel (see above, p. 10). If our division of the book is
approximately correct, it represents Jesus to us under three main aspects.

First it shows His connexion with the past. John the Baptist is the last and
greatest representative of the prophetic order: and John's preaching is all within
the framework of the old Covenant. It has to do with what God requires of Israel
and with what God will do for Israel; with the demands and promises of God.
The focal points of John's preaching are his call to repentance and reformation of
life, and his Messianic predictions. Jesus starts from this point; but He goes far
beyond John. He rejects the Messianic ideal of John and puts in its place the ideal
of the Kingdom of God. What this means to Him is shown in the Temptation
story and in the Great Sermon. In its essence it is God overcoming evil with good,
the love of God triumphant. Those who submit to it find that it is deliverance
and new life; but a new life turned to the service of God's Kingdom by the imitation of God. So we come to a more perfect righteousness than that of John. It is
no longer the bringing of one's life into conformity with a given standard of
conduct, but the reproduction in human nature of the creative merciful love of
God.

Secondly, this determines the task of Jesus and His disciples in the present. It is a mission, in the first instance to Israel, and through Israel to the world. To this mission all other interests must be subservient. Jesus gives to God and demands from His followers unqualified trust and complete devotion. No earthly good may seduce them from their allegiance to the Kingdom; no opposition or persecution may daunt them. This is the main theme of the two middle sections of Q.

Thirdly, Q gives us the expectation of Jesus concerning the future. The essence of it is that the existing world-order based upon selfishness is the exact contrary to the Kingdom of God. The economic structure of society, the social organisations, the political methods of the nations—these things flatly contradict all that Jesus means by the Kingdom of God. Therefore they are doomed to perish. It is clear from the Synoptic Gospels that Jesus expected the end of the existing order and the establishment of the new to come quickly, suddenly, and completely. But it is also clear that He regarded the question of times and seasons as something which God kept in His own hands. For Jesus and His disciples the immediate and urgent business was the service of the Kingdom.

The Gospel is the record of how Jesus gave Himself to that business, and how it took Him to the Cross. There the world seemed to say 'No' to His call: and God to His hopes. Defeated and discredited, deserted by His friends, and forsaken by God, He died alone. And overcame sin and death. In His bitter humiliation, in His lonely agòny, He was the realisation of His own demands and the fulfilment of His own hopes. In the light of the Easter experience the men of the primitive Church knew it, and all who know and love Jesus Christ crucified know it too. To the Jews a stumbling-block, to the Greeks foolishness, to us Jesus Christ in His helplessness and humiliation is the very power and wisdom of God.

II.—Teaching Peculiar to Matthew

WE have already seen that the teaching matter peculiar to Mt. falls into large blocks, and that the arrangement of the blocks corresponds at four points with that of Q (see Introd., p. 22). In dealing with this material we shall follow the scheme shown in the Introduction, at the same time taking account of smaller fragments, which do not fit into it. In considering these smaller fragments it is necessary to ask the question whether they belong to Mt.'s special source and have been removed by Mt. from their original context to a more suitable place in the chronological scheme of his Gospel, or whether they are editorial additions, or again whether they are fragments of floating tradition not previously incorporated in a collection. The problem is posed by the first piece of special Matthæan matter.

A FRAGMENT ON THE BAPTISM OF JESUS (6)

MT. 3^{14-15}

3 14 But John would have hindered him, saying, I have need to be baptized of thee, 15 and comest thou to me? But Jesus answering said unto him, Suffer [1] *it* now: for thus it becometh us to fulfil all righteousness. Then he suffereth him.

[1] Or, me.

In the account of the baptism Mk. narrates the bare fact: Jesus came and was baptised. Mt. (3^{13}) emphasises that it was the purpose of Jesus: He came to be baptised. This alteration is necessary to prepare the way for Mt. $3^{14f.}$. The tendency of this passage is obvious. It emphasises the subordination of John to Jesus, identifying Jesus at once with ' the stronger one ' prophesied by John: and it attempts an answer to the question why Jesus undergoes a repentance baptism if He is without sin. That this was a problem in the early Church is shown by a fragment of the apocryphal Gospel according to the Hebrews preserved by Jerome (James, *Apocryphal New Testament*, p. 6). ' Behold the mother of the Lord and his brethren said unto him: John the Baptist baptizeth unto the remission of sins; let us go and be baptized of him. But he said unto them: wherein (what) have I sinned, that I should go and be baptized of him? unless peradventure this very thing that I have said is (a sin of) ignorance.' The dialogue Mt. $3^{14f.}$ can hardly be historical. The words ' I have need to be baptized of thee ' will not fit into John's conception of the Messianic baptism, which is a baptism of fire, i.e. judgement. See on Lk. 3^{16}, above, p. 40. The fragment is early Christian apologetic and doubtless originated in circles where it was necessary to maintain that John the Baptist was the forerunner of the Messiah Jesus and that Jesus Himself was sinless; that is, in Jewish-Christian circles. It is not necessary to suppose that Matthew composed these verses. More probably they are a fragment of Palestinian Christian oral tradition which Matthew incorporated in his account of the baptism. The ' fulfilling of all righteousness ' (*v*. 15) is explicable if the interpretation of John's baptism given above (p. 41) be accepted. Jesus recognises in John's effort to create a new Israel the purpose of God; and willingly enters into it. The baptism of John is from heaven (Mk. $11^{29f.}$). That is sufficient for Jesus.

The question is not whether Jesus has or has not sins to confess, but whether He is to obey the call of God which comes through the last and greatest of the prophets. We come now to the first large section of the M teaching.

A. THE PREACHING OF JESUS

This is the M parallel to the Q section A3 (above, pp. 46–62). A certain amount of similarity in structure between M and Q has been noticed above (Introd., p. 22). As in Q, the Sermon opens with a collection of beatitudes.

1. *THE BEATITUDES* (19)

MT. 5^{7-10}

5 7   Blessed are the merciful: for they shall obtain mercy.

8   Blessed are the pure in heart: for they shall see God.

9   Blessed are the peacemakers: for they shall be called sons of God.

10   Blessed are they that have been persecuted for righteousness' sake: for theirs is the kingdom of heaven.

7. This beatitude is characteristic of the teaching of Jesus. It is the theme of the parable in Mt. 18^{23-35} (M); and it has parallels in thought in the other sources: e.g. Lk. $17^{3f.}$ (Q); Mk. 11^{25}. In Jewish teaching about God's forgiveness the start is made from the consideration of the case of the offender; and the principle is that if I have injured my neighbour in any way I must first make reparation to him and seek his forgiveness, and then ask forgiveness of God. Jesus thinks rather of the injured party. He must be ready to forgive the offender. That is to say, for Jesus the essential requisite for receiving God's forgiveness is to have a forgiving spirit oneself. This thought is also to be found in Judaism, *Ecclus.* 28^{2-5}:

> ' Forgive thy neighbour the injury (done to thee),
> And then, when thou prayest, thy sins will be forgiven.
> Man cherisheth anger against another;
> And doth he seek healing from God?
> On a man like himself he hath no mercy;
> And doth he make supplication for his own sins?
> He, being flesh, nourisheth wrath;
> Who will make atonement for his sins? '

Similarly, the Jewish Patriarch Gamaliel II (c. A.D. 90) says: ' So long as thou art merciful, the Merciful (i.e. God) is merciful to thee ' (*Tos. B.Q.* 10^{30}). Other Jewish parallels, Billerbeck, i. 203 ff. Such difference as there is between Jesus and Judaism is a difference of emphasis. Jesus lays great stress on the fact that he who will not forgive is thereby unfitted to receive God's forgiveness. It is not a matter of outward words or acts. Nor is it as if God offered a *quid pro quo*: ' You forgive your neighbour and I will forgive you.' It is a matter of inward character and disposition. The Christian who has not learned how to overcome evil with good, has not learned the first thing about the nature of God: he does not know God as a Christian ought to know God. If he did, he would see his offending neighbour, as it were, through God's eyes, and forgive him.

8. Cf. Ps. 24$^{3f.}$:

> ' Who shall ascend into the hill of the Lord?
> And who shall stand in his holy place?
> He that hath clean hands and a pure heart;
> Who hath not lifted up his soul unto vanity,
> And hath not sworn deceitfully.'

' Pure in heart ' is not to be construed as absolutely sinless. The meaning of the expression may be gathered from the promise attached. To ' see God ' is in Palestinian speech another way of saying ' appear before God '; and this has special reference to attending the Temple worship, especially that of the great Festivals. The Jewish Law recognises various kinds of bodily defilement, which disqualify a person from joining in the Temple worship, that is, from ' seeing God ' in this sense. The purifications prescribed in the Law serve to remove this physical disqualification. From this it is a simple matter to take the step that is taken in Ps. 24 and to think of an inward cleansing as the qualification for communion with God. The difference between Jesus and the Rabbis is that while they admit the necessity for both outward (levitical) purity and inward cleanness of heart, Jesus throws all the emphasis on the latter. For Him *the* condition of having fellowship with God, here or hereafter, is a clean heart, a heart that loves goodness and hates evil.

9. The peacemakers are not those who merely practise the negative virtue of non-resistance to evil. They are the people who overcome evil with good, and establish peace where there is discord and strife, who make up quarrels and reconcile enemies. This positive virtue is inculcated in the Rabbinical literature. There is a famous saying of Hillel (*Aboth* 1^{12}): ' Be of the disciples of Aaron, loving peace and pursuing peace, loving mankind and bringing them nigh to the Law.' Further citations in Montefiore, *Rabb. Lit. and Gospel Teachings*, pp. 27 ff. To be called sons of God means to be so called by God Himself, acknowledged and adopted by Him. Hence to be called sons of God is to be sons of God. In the Old Testament and in Jewish belief the title belongs to Israel (Dt. 14^1; Hos. 1^{10}; *Ps. Sol.* 17^{30}). Rabbi Akiba (martyred A.D. 135) used to say: ' Beloved are Israel for they were called children of God; still greater was the love in that it was made known to them that they were called children of God, as it is written (Dt. 14^1), " Ye are the children of the Lord your God " ' (*Aboth* 3^{15}; Danby, p. 452). The title is specially appropriated to the godly in Israel (*Wisdom* 2$^{13, 18}$; other passages in Billerbeck, i. 219). The peacemakers are the true Israel and acknowledged by God as His children.

10. This may be regarded as the M version of the saying which closes the Q set of beatitudes, Lk. 6$^{22f.}$‖Mt. 5$^{11f.}$ (See above, p. 48). In the Q version it is persecution as followers of Christ that is thought of: here it is persecution ' for righteousness' sake.' Righteousness is a favourite word in Mt., where it occurs seven times (not in Mk; once in Lk., in a poetical passage, 1^{75}). It gives to the beatitude a characteristically Jewish-Christian flavour. For in Jewish speech the words ' righteous ' and ' righteousness ' always have a reference, open or implied, to obedience to the Law. (See *Teaching of Jesus*, pp. 324 f.) The persecuted for

righteousness' sake would thus include the Jewish martyrs as well as the Christian, as in Heb. 11; whereas the Q form has reference only to persecuted followers of Jesus. The reward of those who endure persecution is a share in the Kingdom of heaven. ' Heaven,' as regularly in Mt., is not the future state of the righteous, but a substitute for the Divine name. This substitution of ' Kingdom of heaven ' for ' Kingdom of God ' is another touch of Jewish-Christian piety. It corresponds to a common Jewish usage.

5. It is possible that Mt. 5[5]:

Blessed are the meek: for they shall inherit the earth

should be added to this group of beatitudes. It is open to some suspicion on two grounds: (a) Its place in the series is not clear. In some MSS. it precedes ' Blessed are they that mourn . . .,' and in others it follows. This uncertainty about the place of a verse is often a sign of interpolation. (b) The thought is not very original. The saying looks as if it had been manufactured out of Ps. 37[11], ' The meek shall inherit the land.' The ' meek ' in Mt. 5[5] are the same people who are called the ' poor ' in Lk. 6[20] (Q). The promise of inheriting the earth implies the expectation of a Messianic kingdom to be established on earth in the future. But it may be doubted whether Jesus contemplated the establishment of such a kingdom. The day of the Son of Man appears to be the day of the final judgement rather than the day when the Messianic kingdom is to be established on earth: and after that day the place of the godly seems to be in heaven. On the whole it seems best to treat Mt. 5[5] as a Jewish-Christian interpolation.

2. SALT AND LIGHT (20)
MT. 5[13-16]

5 13 Ye are the salt of the earth: but if the salt have lost its savour wherewith shall it be salted? It is thenceforth good for nothing, but to be cast out and trodden 14 under foot of men. Ye are the light of the world. A city set on a hill cannot be hid.

15 Neither do *men* light a lamp, and put it under the bushel, but on the stand; and it shineth unto all that are in the house. 16 Even so let your light shine before men, that they may see your good works, and glorify your Father which is in heaven.

The opening phrases, ' Ye are the salt of the earth ' and ' Ye are the light of the world,' suggest that both verses 13 and 14 are from one source. And since *v.* 14 has no parallel in Lk. we may perhaps assign both verses to M. Again, *v.* 16, which has no parallel in Lk., and is therefore presumably M, presupposes *v.* 15. Verse 15 has a parallel in Lk.; but the parallel is only partial. It may well be that the whole passage *vv.* 13–16 is to be assigned to M.

13. See Lk. 14[34f.] (Q), above, p. 132.

14. The disciples of Jesus are the light of the world. So, in Is. 42[6], 49[6], is the Servant of the Lord. In the Rabbinical literature the title ' light of the world ' is given to God, Adam, Israel, the Law and the Temple, Jerusalem. In Rom. 2[19] the Jews are represented as thinking of themselves as ' a light of them that are in darkness,' and in Phil. 2[15] Christians are described as ' lights in the world.' In John 8[12] it is Jesus Himself who is the light of the world. The sense in which the saying is to be taken is given in *vv.* 15[f.].

The saying about the city seems to be irrelevant to the present context. It has a parallel in the Oxyrhynchus fragment I, 7.   (Grenfell and Hunt, *New Sayings of Jesus* (1904), p. 38): ' Jesus saith, A city built upon the top of a high hill and stablished, can neither fall nor be hid.'   It is probable that the saying is originally a piece of worldly wisdom.   There are two ways of obtaining safety.   One is to take up a commanding situation; the other is to hide oneself.   It is not possible to do both.   In its present position the saying appears to be meant to convey the same meaning as ' Ye are the light of the world.'   All eyes are upon the disciples, who must show to the best advantage.

15. See on Lk. 11³³ (Q), above, p. 92.

16. The disciples are to shine by their behaviour, which must be astonishingly good.   So good that men will see the disciples as living examples of God's power and grace, and praise Him, who can so transform human lives.

3. *THE NEW LAW* (21-27)

The kernel of this passage is a series of six brief antithetical statements, in which the provisions of the old Law are contrasted with the higher righteousness demanded by Jesus.   This original nucleus has been expanded by the addition of relevant material from various sources.   See above, Introd., pp. 23 f.

(a) INTRODUCTION. THE ATTITUDE OF JESUS TO THE LAW (21)

MT. 5¹⁷⁻²⁰

5 17 Think not that I came to destroy the law or the prophets: I came not to destroy, 18 but to fulfil. For verily I say unto you, Till heaven and earth pass away, one jot or one tittle shall in no wise pass away from the law, till all things be ac-19 complished. Whosoever therefore shall break one of these least commandments, and shall teach men so, shall be called least in the kingdom of heaven: but whosoever shall do and teach them, he shall be 20 called great in the kingdom of heaven. For I say unto you, that except your righteousness shall exceed *the righteousness* of the scribes and Pharisees, ye shall in no wise enter into the kingdom of heaven.

The plain purpose of this preamble is to prevent misunderstanding of the provisions which follow.   There was no point on which devout Palestinian Jews were more sensitive than on any attempt to tamper with the Law, which was for them something given directly by God Himself, and therefore perfect and irreformable.   Conservative Palestinian Christians were not only themselves sympathetic towards this high doctrine of the Law, but also under the necessity of defining the Jewish-Christian attitude to their national heritage.   They had to live in the midst of an orthodox—at times fanatically orthodox—Jewish community: and, more than that, they had to carry on the Christian mission among these very people (Gal. 2⁹).   For them it was essential that the positive teaching of Jesus should not appear to be an overthrowng of all that was most sacred to the devout Jew. The differences between the teaching of Jesus and orthodox Jewish doctrine must be shown to be due not to heresy on the part of Jesus but to His deeper and fuller understanding of the Law.   His pronouncements, so far from upsetting the Law, bring out its true meaning and purpose.   In this way, it might be hoped, the new wine would settle down in the old wine-skins.

17. The formula ' Think not that I came to . . . I came not to . . . but to . . .' recurs (Mt. 10³⁴).   There is no reason why Jesus should not have uttered this

saying. It is best understood in the light of Mk. 7⁶⁻¹³ and the Q sayings against the scribes (Lk. 11⁴⁵⁻⁵², above, pp. 100–103). Jesus accuses the scribes of stultifying the Law by their interpretation of it, and claims that His way brings to light the true meaning, the will and purpose of God in framing it. Cf. the treatment of marriage and divorce (Mk. 10¹⁻¹²). As against scribal interpretation of the Law and priestly conduct of the Temple worship (Mk. 11¹⁵⁻¹⁹), Jesus says: ' It is not I who make the Law of none effect, but you.' Something of this sort may well have been the original meaning of this saying: in its present context it makes Jesus sound too sympathetic towards orthodox Judaism.

18. This saying has a parallel in Q (Lk. 16¹⁷, see above, p. 135). In its present form and context the saying is an affirmation of the permanent validity of the Law in its minutest details. But such an affirmation by Jesus is hardly thinkable in view of such a passage as Mk. 10¹⁻¹². It is most probable that the Q form is the original, and that the meaning was as suggested in the notes on Lk. 16¹⁷. The words ' Till heaven and earth pass away ' maintain the Law in full force until the final consummation. Whether the whole Law would be necessary in the sinless and perfect life of the world to come is another question. ' One jot or one tittle ': on ' tittle ' see notes on Lk. 16¹⁷. The ' jot ' is the Hebrew letter ' *yod*,' the smallest consonant in the Hebrew alphabet. ' Till all things be accomplished ' is probably to be understood in the light of ' Till heaven and earth pass away.' The Law is given to man in the present world and is a complete revelation of God's will for man in his present situation. In the next world, after God's purpose in this has been completed, the situation may well be different; and man may no longer require the kind of revelation of God's will that was necessary for him in this world.

19. ' Break ' in this verse should be translated ' relax.' The Greek verb is used elsewhere in M as the equivalent of the Hebrew verb *hittir*. The person in view here is one who permits less than the Law requires either by allowing what it forbids or by exempting men from some of its positive requirements. In the phrase ' one of these least commandments ' the word ' these ' is literal translation of the Greek, which is in its turn literal translation of a common Aramaic idiom. The idiomatic rendering would be ' one of the least commandments.' The relaxing of the Law begins first in the practice of the man himself and then is taught by him as the true way for others. It has already been suggested above (Introd., p. 25) that it is St. Paul who is thought of in this verse. Such a man will be called—i.e. he will be—least in the Kingdom. Aramaic has no special form for the superlative of adjectives. So far as an Aramaic original is concerned ' little ' would be the same as ' least '; but no doubt ' least ' gives the accepted sense of the original in the circles where the saying was at home. The opposite to this character, the Jewish Christian who maintains the Law in its full stringency, demanding from others (and practising himself) strict obedience to the dietary laws, circumcision of Gentile converts to Christianity, and the like—such a man will be great in the Kingdom. We have in this verse the convictions of people like those who appear in Gal. 2¹²ᶠ·; Acts 15⁵. These sentiments are put into the mouth of Jesus: it is in the last degree unlikely that He thought or said such a thing.

20. The righteousness required for entrance into the Kingdom is that which is about to be explained in the antitheses which follow. The scribes and Pharisees, it is implied, have their interpretation of the meaning of the Law; and it is the wrong one. The right interpretation, which will be the true fulfilment of the Law, will penetrate below the surface and bring to light the fundamental principles, the spirit of the Law. A righteousness based on those first principles and not on mechanical obedience to precept and tradition is the condition of entry into the Kingdom. So the compiler seems to understand the saying.

(b) MURDER (22)

MT. 5[21-24]

5 21 Ye have heard that it was said to them of old time, Thou shalt not kill; and whosoever shall kill shall be in danger of the 22 judgement: but I say unto you, that every one who is angry with his brother [1] shall be in danger of the judgement; and whosoever shall say to his brother, [2] Raca, shall be in danger of the council; and whosoever shall say, [3] Thou fool, shall be 23 in danger [4] of the [5] hell of fire. If therefore thou art offering thy gift at the altar, and there rememberest that thy brother 24 hath aught against thee, leave there thy gift before the altar, and go thy way, first be reconciled to thy brother, and then come and offer thy gift.

[1] Many ancient authorities insert *without cause.*
[2] An expression of contempt.
[3] Or, *Moreh,* a Hebrew expression of condemnation.
[4] Gr. *unto* or *into.*
[5] Gr. *Gehenna of fire.*

To this passage Mt. adds *vv.* 25–26 derived from Q. See above, p. 122.

21, 22. ' Ye have heard '—often, in the reading of the Law in the Synagogue. Those ' of old time ' are the generation who were alive when the Law was given from Sinai. ' Thou shalt not kill ' (Exod. 20[13]; Dt. 5[17]) the sixth commandment of the Decalogue. The following clause: ' and whosoever . . . judgement ' is likewise based on the written Law. Cf. Exod. 21[12]; Lev. 24[17]; Dt. 17[8-13]. ' In danger of the judgement ' clearly means liable to trial and punishment as prescribed in the Law. All that is given in *v.* 21 is thus a concise and simple statement of the law concerning murder, as it stands in the Old Testament. Now comes the comment of Jesus. In its original form it probably did not go beyond the word ' judgement.' What follows is, then, to be regarded as later expansion of the saying. The point of the antithesis lies in the contrast between the outward act, of which an earthly court can take cognisance, and the inward disposition, which may or may not produce the act; but which is known to God and judged by Him. The judgement in the second case must be the judgement of God: no earthly tribunal can deal with the crime of hatred. The marginal note 1 of R.V. draws attention to an important variant in the text. The authorities against the words ' without a cause ' are weighty; and those which insert the words are also early and important. In favour of the latter is the fact that qualifying additions of this sort are quite in Mt.'s manner. It is probable that the addition is part of the true text of Mt.; and not part of the original saying, but a gloss inserted by the Evangelist himself. The insistence on the inward disposition can be paralleled from Judaism and from Gentile thought. A saying attributed to R. Eliezer (*c.* A.D. 90) runs: ' He who hates his neighbour, lo he belongs to the shedders of blood ' i.e. he is classed with the murderers.   The early Greek philosopher Democritus says: 'An enemy is not one who wrongs (us), but one who would like (to do so) ' (Fr. 89).

The meaning of the terms of abuse in the second half of the verse is still disputed.   Raca is not a Greek word.   It is perhaps best explained as a transliteration of the Aramaic *rêkā*, meaning ' empty,' and so ' empty-headed,' ' stupid,' ' blockhead.'   *Mōre* can be taken as Greek.   It then means, as in R.V., ' fool.' But this will hardly do, if the saying is seriously meant.   There is no point in threatening a man with the Sanhedrin for saying ' blockhead ' and with hell-fire for saying ' fool.'   It is therefore probable that *Mōre* represents the Rabbinic word *mōrā* with a shade of meaning contributed by the Hebrew word *Mōreh*.   This last means more than merely ' stupid ': it means ' stubborn,' ' rebellious,' and so ' obstinately wicked.'   The distinction between the two words will then be that *Raca* suggests a defect of intelligence, while *Mōre* makes the much more serious charge of moral defect.   The ' council ' is the Sanhedrin, the supreme court in the Jewish legal system.   On Gehenna see notes on Lk. 12[5], above, p. 107.   It may be doubted whether *v.* 22[b] is a genuine saying of Jesus.

23 f.   These verses do not belong to the original antithesis.   They are brought in at this point as being more or less relevant to the subject.   The duty of establishing peace takes precedence even of the Temple worship.   The Jewish rule in such cases, where a man has begun to carry out one religious obligation and remembers another, which he ought to carry out, is that the more important obligation takes precedence of the less important (Billerbeck, i. 284).   This saying to a Jew would mean that reconciliation was more important than sacrifice. Further, it is sound Jewish doctrine that a man must seek forgiveness from his neighbour whom he has wronged before he asks God's forgiveness for doing the wrong.   ' For transgressions that are between man and God the Day of Atonement effects atonement, but for transgressions that are between a man and his fellow the Day of Atonement effects atonement only if he has appeased his fellow ' (*Yoma* 8[9], Danby, p. 172).   (Cf. Hos. 6[6].)   Mt. 5[23f.] has nothing to do with Mk. 11[25-(26)]; see Mt. 6[14f.], below, p. 171.

(c) ADULTERY (23)

MT. 5[27-30]	Cf. MK. 9[43-48]
5 27 Ye have heard that it was said, Thou 28 shalt not commit adultery: but I say unto you, that every one that looketh on a woman to lust after her hath committed adultery with her already in his heart. 29 And if thy right eye cause thee to stumble, pluck it out, and cast it from thee: for it is profitable for thee that one of thy members should perish, and not thy whole body 30 be cast into [1] hell. And if thy right hand causeth thee to stumble, cut it off, and cast it from thee: for it is profitable for thee that one of thy members should perish, and not thy whole body go into [1] hell.	9 43 And if thy hand cause thee to stumble, cut it off: it is good for thee to enter into life maimed, rather than having thy two hands to go into [1] hell, into the unquench- 45 able fire.[2] And if thy foot cause thee to stumble, cut it off: it is good for thee to enter into life halt, rather than having 47 thy two feet to be cast into [1] hell. And if thine eye cause thee to stumble, cast it out: it is good for thee to enter into the kingdom of God with one eye, rather than having two eyes to be cast into [1] hell; 48 where their worm dieth not, and the fire is not quenched.
[1] Gr. *Gehenna*.	[1] Gr. *Gehenna*. [2] Ver. 44 and 46 (which are identical with ver. 48) are omitted by the best ancient authorities.

The original antithesis is given in *vv.* 27 f. The two verses which follow are additional relevant matter, of which we have an independent version in Mk. As the Marcan passage is reproduced in Mt. 18[8 f.], we may regard Mt. 5[29 f.] as the M version of the saying.

27. The Law as given to Israel (Exod. 20[14]; Dt. 5[17]), the seventh commandment of the Decalogue. For the Jewish definition of adultery, see on Lk. 16[18], above, p. 136.

28. The comment of Jesus. As in the case of murder, He distinguishes between the act and the inward disposition that produces the act. The lustful look is not actionable as adultery is; but it shows just as clearly the kind of character that is within. And the character is that of an adulterer in God's sight, even though there has been no adulterous act for which the man might be made to answer to an earthly court. The same line is taken by the Rabbis. Thus we have the Rabbinic dictum ' He who looks at a woman with desire is as one who has criminal intercourse with her ' (*Kalla*, § 1). For other sayings to the same effect see Montefiore, *Rabb. Lit. and Gospel Teachings*, pp. 41 ff.; Abrahams, *Studies*, ii. 205 f.

29 f. These verses are linked to the preceding by the offending eye. In Mk. the eye is dealt with last. It may be that Mt. has reversed the order to make a better connexion. But there is no real connexion. What is given in these verses is very strongly worded advice to tame the natural desires and passions at all costs. The point is the same as in 1 Cor. 9[27]: ' I buffet my body, and bring it into bondage: lest by any means, after that I have preached to others, I myself should be rejected.'

(d) DIVORCE (24)
MT. 5[31-32]

5 31 It was said also, Whosoever shall put away his wife, let him give her a writing of 32 divorcement: but I say unto you, that every one that putteth away his wife, saving for the cause of fornication, maketh her an adulteress: and whosoever shall marry her when she is put away committeth adultery.

Here we have an antithesis in something like its original form, without any accretions of teaching from elsewhere. There are parallels to the saying in Mk. 10[11 f.] and Q (Lk. 16[18]).

31. The reference is to Dt. 24[1]. In Jewish law marriage was a partnership which could be dissolved by the husband himself without having recourse to the courts. The divorce was effected by serving on the wife a document, properly drawn up and attested, declaring that she was no longer his wife. The rules governing the preparation and delivery of such ' writings of divorcement ' are codified in the Mishnah tractate *Gittin* (Danby, pp. 307-321). The form of the document is given in Lightfoot's *Horæ Hebraicæ* (ed. Gandell, Oxford, 1859) ii. 124, and in Billerbeck, i. 311 f.

32. Jesus forbids divorce. His reasons are given in Mk. 10[6-9] and are founded, not on the Mosaic regulations for divorce, but on the purpose of God in instituting marriage. The excepting clause ' saving for the cause of fornication ' is an interpolation, as is the similar excepting clause in Mt. 19[9]. The question on what grounds a man might divorce his wife was debated in Jesus' day by the

schools of Hillel and Shammai. The Matthæan form of the saying brings Jesus into agreement with the school of Shammai. But Jesus agreed with neither school. His attitude to the whole question is quite different from theirs. (See notes on Lk. 16[18], above, pp. 136 ff., and *Teaching of Jesus*, pp. 292 f.)

(e) VOWS AND OATHS (25)

MT. 5[33-37]

5 33 Again, ye have heard that it was said to them of old time, Thou shalt not forswear thyself, but shalt perform unto the Lord 34 thine oaths: but I say unto you, Swear not at all; neither by the heaven, for it is the 35 throne of God; nor by the earth, for it is the footstool of his feet; nor [1] by Jerusalem, for it is the city of the great King. 36 Neither shalt thou swear by thy head, for thou canst not make one hair white or 37 black. [2] But let your speech be, Yea, yea; Nay, nay: and whatsoever is more than these is of [3]the evil *one*.

[1] Or, *toward*.
[2] Some ancient authorities read *But your speech shall be.*
[3] Or, *evil*: as in ver. 39; vi. 13.

Parallels: Mt. 23[16-22]; James 5[12]. It is to be noted that in both cases the parallel is with the latter part of this section, beginning ' Swear not at all.' The difficulty in these verses lies in the fact that *v.* 33, as it stands, has to do with vows, while *vv.* 34–37 have to do with oaths. There are two possibilities: (*a*) *V.* 33 really is about vows. The natural conclusion will then be that the original antithesis ended with the words ' Swear not at all '; and the sense will be: The Law says, Do not break your vows, but perform what you have promised: but I say, Make no vows at all. (*b*) The antithesis is not concerned with vows at all, but with speaking the truth. In that case the words in *v.* 33 ' but shalt perform unto the Lord thine oaths ' are an intrusion. The sense of the passage would be: The Law forbids perjury: but I say, Do not take oaths at all, etc. This second alternative is to be preferred for the following reasons : (i) All the other antitheses are concerned with my duty to my neighbour. It is therefore probable that this one will be concerned with the social duty of truthfulness, rather than with vows, which are a concern between God and man. (ii) The second interpretation enables us to take the principal verbs in their most natural and obvious sense. (iii) It has the support of James 5[12].

33. As the result of the preceding discussion, we reject the clause ' but shalt perform . . . oaths ' as a mistaken attempt to explain ' thou shalt not forswear thyself.' The prohibition of perjury goes back to Lev. 19[12]: 'And ye shall not swear by my name falsely, so that thou profane the name of thy God.' Cf. Exod. 20[7]; Dt. 5[11]: the third commandment of the Decalogue. The Law does not forbid oaths; but it does forbid perjury, which is regarded as a profanation of the name of God.

34, 35, 36. The comment of Jesus forbids the use of oaths altogether. And this prohibition covers not only such ancient and solemn forms of oath as ' As the Lord liveth,' or that recorded in Mt. 26[63]. It forbids also those milder forms, which, since they did not involve an explicit mention of God, might be thought not to involve profanation of the Name. The argument of *vv.* 34–36 is that these apparently harmless oaths do involve a reference to God. Heaven is His throne, earth His footstool, Jerusalem His city—' the great King ' = God—man himself and every part of him is God's handiwork. It is God who ordains the black hair of youth and the white of old age.

37. What is required is something that cannot be supplied by oaths, however solemn—a disposition to speak the truth. Given that inward honesty all oaths become superfluous. Indeed, the plain Yes or No of an honest man is more reliable than the word of a liar, even though that word be supported by the most solemn oath. For ' Let your speech be, Yea, yea; Nay, nay ' James (5¹²) has ' let your yea be yea, and your nay, nay.' The form in Mt can be explained as mistranslation due to following an Aramaic original word by word. There can be little doubt that James 5¹² here gives the correct rendering. This is confirmed by the fact that in Jewish teaching the doubled yes or no is regarded as a form of oath.

There is ample evidence that the fortifying of statements by oaths of various kinds was a common Jewish practice, and also that the Rabbis disliked and condemned idle swearing. There are also Rabbinic parallels to the saying ' Let your yea be yea, and your nay, nay.' R. Huna said, ' The yea of the righteous is a yea; their no is a no.' (For this and other examples, cf. Montefiore, *op. cit.*, pp. 48 ff.) But the Rabbis never prohibited entirely the taking of oaths.

(f) RETRIBUTION (26)

MT. 5³⁸⁻⁴²

5 38 Ye have heard that it was said, An eye 39 for an eye, and a tooth for a tooth: but I say unto you, Resist not ¹ him that is evil: but whosoever smiteth thee on thy right 40 cheek, turn to him the other also. And if any man would go to law with thee, and take away thy coat, let him have thy cloke

41 also. And whosoever shall ² compel thee to go one mile, go with him twain. 42 Give to him that asketh thee, and from him that would borrow of thee turn not thou away.

¹ Or, *evil*.   ² Gr. *impress*.

This passage is composite. The original antithesis is contained in *vv*. 38, 39ᵃ. Verses 39ᵇ, 40, 42 have a parallel in Lk. 6³⁰ᶠ·, and are probably from Q. *V*. 41 is a saying of the same kind as those which precede it, and may be assigned to M.

38. The *lex talionis*: Exod. 21²²⁻²⁵; Lev. 24¹⁹ᶠ·; Dt. 19²¹. The law governing cases of injury to the person. What is prescribed is equivalence of injury and punishment. It is important to remember than when this rule is first instituted, it is a great advance; for it puts an end to the vendetta, the interminable blood-feud, as well as to the system of repaying injuries with interest. Cf. Gen. 4²³ᶠ·.

39. The comment of Jesus cancels this rule by which injury to the person is punished by the infliction of an exactly similar injury on the aggressor. In its place He lays down the principle ' Resist not him that is evil ' (R.V.) or ' Resist not evil ' (R.V. mg.). The Greek words may mean ' the evil person ' or ' the evil thing.' Which is originally meant must be determined, if at all, on other grounds. In favour of the former view is the fact that the Greek word translated ' resist ' commonly means to fight against. It is not ' passive resistance ' but active hostility that is implied in the word; and hostility of this sort is more naturally thought of as directed against persons. Further, it is part of the Christian life to resist evil and overcome it with good. The Christian warfare, according to Paul, is not against men but against the forces of evil. The saying

may then be taken to mean that the violence of the wrongdoer is not to be met by violence, either by way of revenge or by way of getting one's own blow in first. This conclusion must not, however, be taken in isolation. It forms part of the whole collection of antitheses; and it is to be understood in the light of the other members of the series. This means that it is not just an amendment of the existing law on humanitarian grounds. It is a demand for such a change in the character and disposition of the disciples that they will rather endure than inflict injury, and go on enduring injury rather than inflict it. Cf. 1 Cor. 6⁷, 13⁴⁻⁷. Further, we must take into account those passages in which Jesus speaks of the persecution of His followers, and invites them to rejoice when they are persecuted. This implies a radical alteration of their estimate of the dreadfulness of physical suffering, just as His sayings on wealth involve a radical change in the estimation of worldly goods. The attitude to those who wrong and injure us, required in the principle of Jesus, is thus only possible if we have come to the point at which we learn, so to speak, to despise suffering. But this point is only reached when we care so much for the Kingdom of God that we care very little about pleasure and pain; and that implies a radical change of character and disposition.

39ᵇ, 40, 42. On these verses see above, pp. 49–52.

41. The word translated ' compel ' is properly a technical term meaning to impress a person or his draught animals for the public service. The practice can be traced back to the institution, under the Persian empire, of a system of state couriers for the purpose of rapid communication between the central government and its subordinates. Speed was achieved by working the couriers in relays: and for the efficient working of the system it was essential that a courier should be able to requisition a horse if necessary. Under the Roman empire the same word is used for the requisition of similar services from civilians by the army (Dittenberger, *O.G.I.S.*, 665²¹, ²⁴). Cf. Epictetus, IV. i. 79. ' If there is a requisition and a soldier seizes it (your ass), let it go. Do not resist or complain, otherwise you will be first beaten, and lose the ass after all.' The same word is used for the requisitioning of personal service in Mk. 15²¹, where the Roman troops in charge of the Crucifixion impress Simon to carry the cross. It is therefore natural to suppose that Mt. 5⁴¹ is concerned with the situation which would arise if a Jewish civilian is impressed as a baggage-carrier by a Roman soldier of the army of occupation. If the victim is a follower of Jesus, he will give double what is demanded. The first mile renders to Cæsar the things that are Cæsar's; the second mile, by meeting oppression with kindness, renders to God the things that are God's.

(g) LOVE OF NEIGHBOUR (27)

MT. 5⁴³⁻⁴⁸

43 Ye have heard that it was said, Thou shalt love thy neighbour, and hate thine 44 enemy: but I say unto you, Love your enemies, and pray for them that persecute 45 you; that ye may be sons of your Father which is in heaven: for he maketh his sun to rise on the evil and the good, and sendeth rain on the just and the unjust. 46 For if ye love them that love you, what reward have ye? do not even the[1] publicans 47 the same? And if ye salute your brethren only, what do ye more *than others*? do not 48 even the Gentiles the same? Ye therefore shall be perfect, as your heavenly Father is perfect.

[1] That is, *collectors or renters of Roman taxes*: and so elsewhere.

In this section we have again a parallel in Lk.; and it begins unusually early, with *v.* 44. Lk. 6²⁷ begins ' But I say unto you which hear, Love your enemies . . .' But in what follows, while there is a good deal of agreement between Mt. and Lk. in thoughts, there is surprisingly little either in the order in which they are presented or in the wording. It may, therefore, be the case that Mt. and Lk. are independent in this passage, and that Mt. draws on M, and Lk. on Q. Further, the opening words of Lk. 6²⁷ suggest that in Q a fragment of this antithesis has been preserved. There would be nothing surprising in this; for the fragment in question gives one of the most striking and characteristic of the teachings of Jesus.

43 f. The existing law. ' Thou shalt love thy neighbour ' from Lev. 19¹⁸. It is perfectly clear what Lev. 19¹⁸ means by ' neighbour,' namely fellow-Israelite. The Rabbis gave to ' neighbour ' the widest possible meaning by including under the term not only born Israelites but also converts to Judaism from the Gentile nations. There was nothing in Lev. 19¹⁸ to indicate to a Jew in the days of Jesus that he ought to love Pontius Pilate. Indeed there was a great deal in the Penta- teuch to justify an opposite attitude. And the Pentateuch was regarded as in the fullest sense inspired. There would have been nothing surprising if any Jew had inferred from Lev. 19¹⁸ that his duty was to love his fellow-Jews and hate his Roman enemies. But Jewish literature is ransacked in vain for evidence that such a conclusion is explicitly drawn. ' Thou shalt love thy neighbour and hate thine enemy ' cannot be found. Now if we look at the other antitheses in this section, we find that the first member of the antithesis usually contains a bare statement of the existing rule: ' Thou shalt not commit adultery,' or ' an eye for an eye and a tooth for a tooth.' In Mt. 5³³ we have in addition to ' Thou shalt not forswear thyself ' the further clause ' but shalt perform unto the Lord thine oaths '; and it is precisely this additional clause that makes nonsense of the passage. The infer- ence is that the words ' and hate thine enemy ' are an interpolation. The moment they are removed the true force of the antithesis springs to light. It is not a matter of loving some and hating others. The antithesis in its stark simplicity is:

> The Law says, Thou shalt love thy neighbour.
> I say, Love your enemies.

Whether the original antithesis went on to give the rest of *v.* 44, or even the fuller version in Lk. 6²⁷ᶠ· it is not possible to say. It is not probable that it had more than this, because the characteristic feature of these sayings is their pointed epigrammatic brevity. That the true meaning of the saying is ' Love your enemies as well as your friends ' and not ' Love your enemies rather than hate them ' is shown by the examples which follow.

45. First, an appeal to God's way. In the order of nature He grants sunshine and rain to friend and foe alike.

46 f. Second, a demonstration that the ' higher righteousness ' required of a disciple requires something more than the sort of kindness and affection to be found among publicans and Gentiles, to say nothing of scribes and Pharisees.

48. Third, by a statement of the goal of all disciples, to be like God.

For further comment on these verses see notes on Lk. 6²⁷⁻²⁶, above, pp. 49–55.

6

On the basis of the preceding discussion we may conjecture that the original, unexpanded form of the antitheses was somewhat as follows:

Introduction   17 Think not that I came to destroy the Law or the prophets: I came not to destroy but to fulfil.

       20 For I say unto you, that except your righteousness shall exceed that of the scribes and Pharisees, ye shall in no wise enter into the Kingdom of heaven.

I   21 Ye have heard that it was said to them of old time, Thou shalt not kill; and whosoever shall kill shall be in danger of the judgement:

     22 But I say unto you, that every one who is angry with his brother shall be in danger of the judgement.

II   27 Ye have heard that it was said, Thou shalt not commit adultery:

     28 But I say unto you, that everyone that looketh on a woman to lust after her hath committed adultery with her already in his heart.

III   31 And it was said also, Whosoever shall put away his wife, let him give her a writing of divorcement:

     32 But I say unto you, that everyone that putteth away his wife maketh her an adulteress: and whosoever shall marry her when she is put away committeth adultery.

IV   33 Again, ye have heard that it was said to them of old time, Thou shalt not forswear thyself:

     34 But I say unto you, Swear not at all.

V   38 Ye have heard that it was said, An eye for an eye, and a tooth for a tooth:

     39 But I say unto you, Resist not him that is evil.

VI   43 Ye have heard that it was said, Thou shalt love thy neighbour:

     44 But I say unto you, Love your enemies (and pray for them that persecute you).

(Conclusion   48 Ye shall be perfect, as your heavenly Father is perfect.)

The main question arising out of this passage may be put thus: What is the precise difference between the righteousness of scribes and Pharisees, and the higher righteousness here demanded and exemplified? It is common ground that the Law is not to be destroyed but fulfilled. We do the scribes and Pharisees a monstrous injustice if we imagine that they did not conscientiously strive to carry out what was for them a divinely appointed rule of life. Indeed if any criticism is to be made, it is that they were too conscientious; that in their zeal for the minutest details of Law and tradition they were apt to lose sight of the larger moral purposes which the Law as a whole was meant to serve; that they made the Law an end in itself and forgot that the Law was made for man and not man for the Law. For the Pharisee fulfilment of the Law means obedience to everything that the Law commands; and since man can only obey the rules that he knows, perfect obedience involves study of the Law. These things, painstaking study and meticulous obedience, are fundamental in the position of the scribes and Pharisees. More than that: there is abundant evidence in the Rabbinical literature that Pharisaism included more than an elaborate casuistry issuing in a mechanical fulfilment of legal precepts. The adulterous eye is condemned in the Talmud as well as in the Sermon on the Mount; and Pharisaic legalism was adorned by what has been well named Pharisaic delicacy. It could hardly be otherwise with men who consecrated their lives to the study of the Old Testament prophecy and piety as well as its laws. The difference between the righteousness of the scribes and Pharisees and the righteousness here demanded by Jesus is not correctly stated by saying off-hand that the one is external and the other inward; that the one is concerned merely with the letter of the Law, the other with its spirit.

It becomes possible to see where the difference lies when we realise that neither the Law nor the moral requirement of the Sermon on the Mount is an ethical system in our sense. Both are fundamentally eschatological; that is to say, both are concerned primarily with the judgement of God, and not with the formulation of an ethical ideal, or the planning of a better social order, or with any of the things that interest the Western mind. To both the subscription may be added: This do and thou shalt live. The difference between Jesus and the scribes is that whereas they maintain that the issue of the judgement depends on a man's record, on what he has done or omitted to do, Jesus insists that the final test is the character of the man himself. It remains true, of course, that actions reveal character. ' By their fruits ye shall know them.' But actions do not fully reveal the whole nature and disposition of man, which can be known only to God Himself. Hence the injunction: Judge not, that ye be not judged.

The more abundant righteousness called for in the Sermon is thus not to be attained by having a larger total of good deeds and a smaller total of bad deeds than the scribes and Pharisees. Rather it requires a radical transformation of character and disposition. And it is surely significant in this connexion that when the ' Pharisee of the Pharisees ' really got into difficulties with the Law, it was with the one commandment in the Decalogue that does not have to do with overt acts (Rom. 7[7-12]). The things here demanded in the six antitheses are not put forward as the outline of a new and more rigorous interpretation of the Law, still less as the skeleton constitution for yet another Utopia, but as samples of the kind of fruit that will be produced in lives transformed by the Grace of God.

4. THE NEW PIETY (28–31)

The antitheses were occupied with the relations of man and man. The sections which follow deal with the relation of man to God, with what we might call religious exercises. There are three heads: almsgiving, prayer, and fasting. The passage extends over the first 18 verses of Chap. 6; and seems to have consisted originally of an introduction (v. 1), and three short sections: vv. 2–4, 5–6, 16–18. The middle section has been expanded by the addition of vv. 7–8 on wrong ways of praying, 9–13, the Lord's Prayer, and 14–15 on prayer for forgiveness. The three original sayings are antithetical in form. The antithesis is between those who engage in these exercises for show and those who do so from more worthy motives. There is a corresponding contrast in the manner of the exercise in the two cases, and also in the response of God. The form of the sayings is:

> Be not like the hypocrites with their ostentatious piety. They have their reward.
>
> You (the truly pious) will be unostentatious in your piety. And God will reward you.

The group of sayings is startling in what it includes and in what it omits. Almsgiving occurs to us as a good deed rather than an act of worship. Yet here it stands at the head of the religious exercises. The omission of any reference to the Temple and its worship is equally striking. These two things taken together remind us of the text quoted elsewhere by Jesus: ' I desire mercy and not sacrifice ' (Hos. 6^6).

(a) ALMSGIVING (28)

MT. 6^{1-4}

6 1 Take heed that ye do not your righteousness before men, to be seen of them: else ye have no reward with your Father which is in heaven.
2 When therefore thou doest alms, sound not a trumpet before thee, as the hypocrites do in the synagogues and in the streets, that they may have glory of men. Verily I say unto you, They have received their reward.
3 But when thou doest alms, let not thy left hand know what thy right hand doeth:
4 that thine alms may be in secret: and thy Father which seeth in secret shall recompense thee.

1. This verse forms the introduction to what follows. If that is so, ' righteousness ' must be a comprehensive term for the three activities which follow: almsgiving, prayer, and fasting. The Aramaic equivalent means both ' righteousness ' or ' piety ' and ' beneficence,' ' charity.' But the latter meanings are excluded in this verse by the fact that in v. 2, where almsgiving is specifically mentioned, another word is used. We must therefore understand by ' righteousness ' something like ' religious obligation ' or ' work of piety.' Such works of piety are to be done without ostentation, if they are to earn the approval of God. The superficial inconsistency between this verse and 5^{16} disappears when we take note of the motive in the two cases. In 5^{16} disciples are to let their light (their good deeds) shine before men for the glory of God: here it is a case of performing works of piety for self-glorification. The Rabbis speak in similar terms. R. Zadok (1st century A.D.) says: ' Make them (the words of the Law) not a crown wherewith to magnify thyself or a spade wherewith to dig. And thus used Hillel to say: He that makes worldly use of the crown shall perish. Thus thou mayest learn that he that makes profit out of the words of the Law removes his life from the world ' (*Aboth* 4^5, Danby, p. 453).

2. On private and public charity in Judaism see Moore, *Judaism*, ii. 162–179. There is abundant evidence both of the importance of almsgiving in Jewish religious life, and of the Pharisaic demand that the giving of charity should be as unostentatious as possible. The Rabbis recognised that alms could be given in

such a way that they served merely to gratify the vanity of the giver and to humiliate the recipient. On this point they are in complete agreement with Jesus. It follows that unless Jesus was being gratuitously unjust to the Pharisees, He cannot have equated ' hypocrites ' and Pharisees in this connexion. The hypocrites of this saying are not any party or class in Judaism. They are such people as answer to the description which follows, whether they be Pharisees or Sadducees or rank and file Jews or Gentiles or—for that matter—Christians. The sounding of the trumpet is to be taken as a metaphor, meaning that the hypocrites take steps to give the fullest publicity to their benefactions in order to obtain the greatest possible kudos. They spend their money not to relieve distress but to buy public admiration. They get what they pay for. The Greek verb translated ' they have received ' is found in business documents, where it is used of the settlement of accounts. The hypocrite's charity is a business transaction. He gives so much money; and, in return, he gets so much public admiration. The transaction is closed: he is paid in full.

3. The almsgiving of disciples is to be a strictly private affair. The relation of the right hand to the left is used by the Arabs as a type of the closest fellowship. So the verse may be taken to mean: do not let your nearest friend know about your charitable gifts. There are again abundant parallels in the Rabbinical literature. ' There were two chambers in the Temple: one the Chamber of Secrets and the other the Chamber of Utensils. Into the Chamber of Secrets the devout used to put their gifts in secret and the poor of good family received support therefrom in secret ' (*Shekalim* 5⁶, Danby, p. 158).

4. This charity, which is unknown to men, is known to God. ' Thy Father which seeth in secret ' is probably a misunderstanding of a Semitic idiom: the sense is: ' Thy Father which seeth that which is secret '—the secret almsgiving—' will reward thee.' Cf. Rom. 2¹⁶; 1 Cor. 4⁵, 14²⁵. This does not mean that a business transaction with God is substituted for a business transaction with men. It is not a case of saying ' private charity, which buys God's favour, is a better bargain than public charity, which only buys human admiration.' It means that secret almsgiving is the kind of which God approves, and that because the giver seeks nothing for himself. His sole motive is to relieve the distress of his neighbour. Just because the motive is unselfish, the deed wins the approval of God; but if the motive is to secure that approval, it ceases to be unselfish. True charity will receive the approval of God; but charity done to earn approval—even God's approval—is not true charity.

(b) PRAYER (29)

MT. 6⁵⁻⁶

6 5 And when ye pray, ye shall not be as the hypocrites : for they love to stand and pray in the synagogues and in the corners of the streets, that they may be seen of men. Verily I say unto you, They have received 6 their reward. But thou, when thou prayest, enter into thine inner chamber, and having shut thy door, pray to thy Father which is in secret, and thy Father which seeth in secret shall recompense thee.

5. In addition to the public services of Temple and Synagogue there were a number of private acts of worship which were obligatory on the individual Jew.

Concerning these there is a good deal of material in the Mishnah Tractate *Berakoth* (Danby, pp. 2–10). See also Moore, *Judaism*, ii. 212–238; Abrahams, *Studies in Pharisaism*, ii. 72–93. These regular times of prayer could be a wholesome spiritual discipline for the devout: they could also be an opportunity to the hypocrite to make parade of his sham piety. Here again we are not to make the equation hypocrites = Pharisees. Doubtless there were hypocrites among the Pharisees; but the Pharisees had no monopoly in the matter. And there were a great many Pharisees who were obviously and genuinely sincere in their piety. For the Pharisee as for Jesus the important thing in prayer is the direction of the soul towards God. For the ' hypocrite ' it is the admiration of his piety by men. He loves to be ' alone with God,' surrounded by a crowd of admirers. He gets what he works for.

6. In contrast to this sham piety the prayer of the disciples is to be a genuine communion with God. The ' inner chamber ' is not meant literally: it is, as in Lk. 12³; Mt. 24²⁶, a figure for complete privacy, whether in a closed room or out on the hillside. Everything is to be shut out that would distract the soul: the whole man is to be turned towards God. Such prayer is approved by God. ' Thy Father which is in secret ': it is doubtful whether the words ' which is ' belong to the true text. The analogy of *v.* 4 would suggest that it is the praying that is in secret rather than God; and this is supported by some ancient authorities for the text of Mt. Probably we should render: ' pray in secret to thy Father, and thy Father who seeth that which is secret shall recompense thee.' Cf. notes on *v.* 4. The saying does not disparage public worship or discourage disciples from joining in the service of the Synagogue with their neighbours. Jesus Himself used both Temple and Synagogue; and His first followers did the same without any apparent sense that they were disobeying any precept of their Master. What Jesus insists on here is that private devotions should be private. The reward of true prayer is not specified. It is sufficient that such prayer has the approval of God: how that approval is expressed is a secondary consideration.

The original saying on prayer ends here. It is followed by a brief saying in which a fresh contrast is set up with heathen forms of prayer. This saying (*vv.* 7–8) then forms a kind of introduction to Mt.'s version of the Lord's Prayer.

MT. 6⁷⁻⁸

6 7 And in praying use not vain repetitions, as the Gentiles do: for they think that they shall be heard for their much speaking. 8 Be not therefore like unto them: for ¹ your Father knoweth what things ye have need of, before ye ask him.

¹ Some ancient authorities read *God your Father*.

7. The Greek word translated ' use vain repetitions ' is exceedingly rare. Its etymology is disputed; but its meaning seems to be ' chatter ' or ' gabble.' It is not the length of time spent in praying or persistency in prayer that is criticised. Jesus Himself gave long periods to prayer; and he explicitly recommends persistent prayer, for example in the parable of the Importunate Widow. In the prayers of Gentiles the point where there is ' much speaking ' is in the address to the god or gods. In a polytheistic religion it is necessary to invoke the right deity, and in order to make sure it is advisable to call upon all who may be concerned.

Again, even if one knows the right god or goddess, it is equally important that the correct epithet should be employed in conjunction with the name. If the right deity is not invoked in the proper terms, the prayer may be ineffective. The difficulty is commonly met by the heaping up of names and epithets in prayer; and it may be this verbosity that is criticised in the saying.

8. In contrast to the Gentile the disciple of Jesus has to deal with one God, who is his Father. And there is no need to ransack the dictionary for the appropriate password; for this God already knows what the petitioner needs. The one word that serves for name and epithet in one is the name Father.

So far the exposition has largely been by negatives: how not to pray. Now Mt. gives the positive side: a concrete example of how to pray.

(i) The Lord's Prayer (30)

MT. 6⁹⁻¹³

6   9 After this manner therefore pray ye: Our Father which art in heaven, Hallowed
10 be thy name. Thy kingdom come. Thy will be done, as in heaven, so on earth.
11, 12 Give us this day ¹ our daily bread. And forgive us our debts, as we also have for-
13 given our debtors. And bring not us into temptation, but deliver us from ² the evil one.³

¹ Gr. our bread for the coming day.
² Or, evil.
³ Many authorities, some ancient, but with variations, add For thine is the kingdom, and the power, and the glory, for ever. Amen.

Another version of this prayer appears in Lk. 11²⁻⁴, which is probably to be assigned to L. In Lk.'s account the prayer was given by Jesus to His disciples in response to a request from them that He would teach them to pray as John the Baptist taught his disciples. The form in Mt. early became the form for liturgical use in the Church. In the *Didache* 8²ᶠ· we read: ' And do not pray as the hypocrites, but as the Lord commanded in His Gospel, pray thus.' Then follows the Lord's Prayer almost exactly as in Mt., with the doxology ' for thine is the power and the glory for ever,' and the injunction: ' Pray thus three times a day.' The prayer has very much in common with Jewish piety. Numerous parallels are given by Montefiore (*Rabb. Lit. and Gospel Teachings*, pp. 125 ff.) and Abrahams (*Studies*, ii. 94–108). The amount of agreement may be estimated by comparing the following made-up parallel, which is constructed entirely from materials drawn from Jewish sources (cf. Abrahams, *op. cit.*, pp. 98 f.):

' Our Father, who art in Heaven. Hallowed be Thine exalted Name in the world which Thou didst create according to Thy will. May Thy Kingdom and Thy lordship come speedily, and be acknowledged by all the world, that Thy Name may be praised in all eternity. May Thy will be done in Heaven, and also on earth give tranquillity of spirit to those that fear thee, yet in all things do what seemeth good to Thee. Let us enjoy the bread daily apportioned to us. Forgive us, our Father, for we have sinned; forgive also all who have done us injury; even as we also forgive all. And lead us not into temptation, but keep us far from all evil. For thine is the greatness and the power and the dominion, the victory and the majesty, yea all in Heaven and on earth. Thine is the Kingdom, and Thou art lord of all beings for ever. Amen.'

The originality of the Lord's Prayer lies in the composition as a whole, in the choice of just these petitions and no others, in the arrangement of them, in its brevity and completeness. It may be said that the teaching of Jesus on the fatherhood of God is summarised in the Lord's Prayer. 'This prayer is in fact a complete statement of what God's children should desire and ask of their Father in heaven: and since what we ask of God is the surest indication of the kind of God we believe in, this prayer may justly be taken as a sketch of what, in the thought of Jesus, the Father is.'

'The prayer falls into two main divisions, the first concerned with what may be called world issues, the second with the affairs of individuals. Both alike are conceived as being in the hands of the Father: the same God who orders the course of history with sovereign power also ministers to the daily needs, material and spiritual, of His individual children' (*Teaching of Jesus*, p. 113).

9. 'After this manner' is not to be pressed so as to exclude the use of the prayer itself. The disciples are to use the original and also to make other prayers of their own in the same spirit. 'Ye' is emphatic: the disciples in contrast to Gentiles. For 'Our Father which art in heaven' Lk. has simply 'Father.' Mt.'s phrase is an adaptation of the original 'Father' to conform to Jewish liturgical usage. The originality of Lk. is shown by the recorded prayer of Jesus Himself (Mk. 14[36]) and the testimony of Paul (Rom. 8[15]; Gal. 4[6]). The word which Jesus used in speaking to God, and which He taught His disciples to use, is the Aramaic word *abba*. The importance of this fact is well brought out by G. Kittel (*Die Religionsgeschichte und das Urchristentum*, pp. 92–95). In Aramaic the place of the possessive adjectives ' my,' ' thy,' etc., is taken by suffixes attached to the noun. So 'father' is *abba*; but ' my father ' is *abī*, ' our father ' is *abīnū*, and so on. Kittel maintains that the Jewish usage is that in speaking of an earthly father the suffixes are used of anybody's father except one's own. That is, one says ' thy father ' or 'their father,' but not ' my father.' For ' my father ' one says ' father ' simply, i.e. *abba*. But this way of speaking of one's earthly father does not hold when speaking of the Father in heaven. Jewish piety felt it unfitting to speak of God or to God in the same familiar and intimate way in which one spoke of or to one's earthly father. Therefore when ' my Father ' means God the form with the suffix, *abī*, takes the place of the simple *abba*. Jesus abolished this distinction. He used *abba* of God and taught His followers to do the same. This is an indication of the depth and intensity of His realisation of the Fatherhood of God, a realisation in which He would have His disciples share.

' Hallowed be thy name.' For Hebrew thought the name is not a mere word. It is in a sense the person so named. To know God's name is in a real sense to know God. When God acts ' for His name's sake ' it is practically equivalent to saying that He acts for His own sake. To hallow (make holy) the name of God is to regard Him as God, to give Him the worship and obedience that are due to Him. When God hallows His name it is by acting so that men are led to acknowledge Him as God and reverence Him accordingly. ' And as it is God's supreme end that all mankind shall ultimately own and serve Him as the true God, so it is the chief end of Israel . . . to hallow His name by living so that men shall see and say that the God of Israel is the true God. That is the meaning of . . .

the hallowing of the Name, as the supreme principle and motive of moral conduct in Judaism' (Moore, *Judaism*, ii. 103). In this petition 'may Thy name be hallowed' seems to mean both that God should hallow His name by His mighty acts and that men should hallow it by their acknowledgement of Him as the one true God, and by living in accordance with His will. So when the disciples live in such a way that men see their good works and glorify God (Mt. 5¹⁶), they hallow the name of God.

10. Above all God hallows His name by bringing in His Kingdom. So the petition: 'Thy Kingdom come' is intimately connected with 'Hallowed be thy name.' The coming of the Kingdom here asked is certainly the final consummation, the 'coming of the Kingdom of God in power' (Mk. 9¹). Cf. Mk. 8³⁸, 13³²; Lk. 12³², 22²⁹. In the fullest sense the Kingdom is still future and an object of hope rather than experience. The petition is that the hope may be fulfilled. In the primitive Church this hope is bound up with the expectation of the return of the risen Lord: and the early Christian equivalent of 'thy kingdom come' is '*marana tha*—Come our Lord.'

The rest of this verse: 'Thy will be done, as in heaven, so on earth' does not appear in the Lucan version of the prayer. The petition certainly has an eschatological sense: the time when the Kingdom has come will be a time when God's will will be supreme on earth as in heaven. But it need not be an exclusively eschatological petition. There is a sense in which the Kingdom comes whenever and wherever God's will is acknowledged and obeyed on earth. And the prayer, if it is to be sincerely prayed, must have a reference to him who prays it. Thy will be done—and done by me. Cf. Mk. 14³⁶, which is the best commentary on the petition.

11. 'Give us this day our daily bread.' 'Daily' in this verse is a guess. The Greek word so rendered does not occur in Greek literature outside the Lord's Prayer. But it does appear in a papyrus account-book from the Fayum. The text of this document was published by Flinders Petrie in 1889 in the volume *Hawara, Biamu and Arsinoe*. The original now appears to be lost. The interpretation of this text is helped by a Latin wall-inscription at Pompeii (*CIL* IV, Suppl. 4000 g). It appears that our Greek word may be the equivalent of the Latin *diaria*, the daily rations issued to slaves, soldiers, and workmen, etc. The Greek word can then be connected etymologically with another word signifying 'the coming (day),' i.e. to-morrow. This reflects the social environment of the Gospels. The bread issued to-day is for consumption to-morrow, so that everyone has his food in his house overnight. This is the state of affairs reflected in the parable Lk. 11⁵ᶠᶠ. and perhaps in Lk 12⁴²: cf. also James 2⁵. This puts the petition in a new light. The disciples are God's servants, and what they ask is a sufficient provision from day to day to enable them to perform the tasks which God appoints them to do: enough to-day to face to-morrow's duties. (Further details: F. Stiebitz in *Philologische Wochenschrift*, 16 July 1927, cols. 889–892 ; Deissmann in *Reinhold-Seeberg-Festschrift* (1929), i. 299–306).

12. 'Forgive us our debts.' For 'debts' the Lucan version (11⁴) has 'sins.' This is a translation variant. The one Aramaic word *hōbā* means 'debt,' 'sin,' and 'punishment for sin.' The use of 'debt' as a metaphor for 'sin' is common

in the teaching (Mt. 18²³⁻³⁵; Lk. 7⁴¹⁻⁴³). In this petition we have the characteristic doctrine of Jesus that God's forgiveness can only come to those who themselves show a forgiving spirit. For the Jewish view see on Mt. 5²³ᶠ·, above, p. 155. We have an anticipation of this petition in *Ecclus.* 28².

> ' Forgive thy neighbour the injury (done to thee),
>   And then, when thou prayest, thy sins will be forgiven.'

There are also Rabbinical parallels (Billerbeck, i. 424 ff.). But generally the Jewish insistence is on the duty of the offender to seek forgiveness of the injured party; that of Jesus on the duty of the injured party to offer forgiveness. Jesus would not, we may presume, have condemned the Jewish doctrine: nor would the Pharisees perhaps have condemned that of Jesus. It is a matter of emphasis; and it is the characteristic teaching of Jesus that is emphasised in this petition.

13. 'And bring us not into temptation.' The word ' temptation ' is ambiguous. It may mean ' trial ' in the sense of suffering, persecution, martyrdom; or it may stand for the seductions of sin. It is likely enough that the former meaning is uppermost. Cf. 1 *Macc.* 2⁴⁹⁻⁶⁴. Similarly *Ecclus.* 2¹ᶠ·.

> ' My son, when thou comest to serve the Lord,
>   Prepare thy soul for temptation.
>   Set thy heart aright and endure fimly,
>   And be not fearful in time of calamity.'

We may further compare Rom. 5³⁻⁵ with James 1²ᶠ·.

ROM.	JAMES
Let us also rejoice in our tribulations: knowing that tribulation worketh patience; and patience probation; and probation hope.	Count it all joy, my brethren, when ye fall into manifold temptations; knowing that the proof of your faith worketh patience.

For Judaism in the last two centuries B.C. as for the Church in the first three centuries A.D. temptation means above all religious persecution, persecution for righteousness' sake, for the Law or the Gospel. And in the last resort this is a moral temptation, as much as the temptations to theft or adultery. For persecution is the incentive to apostasy, the worst sin known to Judaism or the early Church. What this petition asks, therefore, is that disciples may not be exposed to trials so severe that their loyalty to God may be undermined. ' But deliver us from the evil (one).' Grammatically ' the evil ' may be neuter, ' the evil state or condition,' or masculine, ' the evil one.' ' The evil (one) ' is characteristically Matthæan. Cf. Mk. 4¹⁵ where Mk.'s ' Satan ' is turned by Lk. (8¹²) into ' the Devil,' and by Mt. (19¹⁹) into ' the evil one.' Further, the preposition used with the verb ' deliver ' suggests deliverance from a personal adversary rather than out of an evil condition. Finally, while the lot of the disciple may be evil in the present evil age (Gal. 1⁴), it is evil, and the age is evil, only because the present age is dominated by Satan. The petition asks not for deliverance from distress or suffering, but for deliverance from the arch-enemy of God and man. That such a being existed and was the head of a kingdom hostile to the Kingdom of God was an unquestioned belief in Judaism and in the early Church.

The doxology: ' For thine is the kingdom . . .' is omitted by three of the most important MSS. It appears to have been unknown to the early Fathers, Tertullian, Cyprian, and Origen. It is not in Lk.'s version of the prayer. Moreover, the text of the doxology is uncertain. The chief variants are:

For thine is the power for ever and ever (k).

For thine is the kingdom and the glory for ever and ever. Amen. (Old Syriac Cur.)

For thine is the power and the glory for ever. (*Didache* 8², Sahidic.)

The probability is that the doxology is no part of the original prayer, but came to be added when the prayer was used liturgically in the various churches. The current form may be the resultant of different local practices. It has some points in common with 1 Chron. 29¹¹ᶠ.

(ii) *A saying on Forgiveness*

MT. 6¹⁴⁻¹⁵

6 14 For if ye forgive men their trespasses, your heavenly Father will also forgive you.
15 But if ye forgive not men their trespasses, neither will your Father forgive your trespasses.

The first part of this saying has a parallel in Mk. 11²⁵:

And whensoever ye stand praying, forgive, if ye have aught against anyone; that your Father also which is in heaven may forgive you your trespasses.

Mk. 11²⁶, which is the equivalent of Mt. 6¹⁵, is rejected by modern editors on textual grounds.

The saying makes more explicit what is already contained in the petition for forgiveness in the Lord's Prayer. The form in Mk. looks more original. There there is exhortation to cultivate a forgiving spirit as the condition of receiving God's forgiveness. The disciples are almost to help God to forgive them. Here the thought is in process of being legalised. If you do this, God will do that. It is *quid pro quo*.

(c) FASTING (31)

MT. 6¹⁶⁻¹⁸

6 16 Moreover when ye fast, be not, as the hypocrites, of a sad countenance: for they disfigure their faces, that they may be seen of men to fast. Verily I say unto you, 17 They have received their reward. But thou, when thou fastest, anoint thy head, 18 and wash thy face; that thou be not seen of men to fast, but of thy Father which is in secret: and thy Father, which seeth in secret, shall recompense thee.

The third antithesis on religious exercises. Fasting was a regular feature in the Jewish religious calendar. In addition to the solemn fasts of the Day of Atonement, New Year, and the anniversaries of great calamities in Jewish history, there were special public fasts proclaimed from time to time, for example in time of prolonged drought. On all these see Moore, *Judaism*, ii. 55–69. In addition to these public fasts there were those which were undertaken by individuals as a means of religious and moral self-discipline. Such regular private fasts were observed by the Pharisees (cf. Lk. 18^{12}; Mk. 2^{18}) and the disciples of John the Baptist (Mk. 2^{18}). Among the Pharisees Monday and Thursday were the customary days for keeping private fasts. These private fasts offered an opportunity to those who wished to gain a reputation for exemplary piety. They could not only fast but also let all the world know that they were fasting. See further, Moore, ii. 257–266; Abrahams, *Studies*, i. 121–128.

16 ff. The verse has to do with the voluntary private fasts. The disfiguring of the face is achieved by not washing or anointing and by strewing ashes on the head. These outward signs advertise the fact that a fast is taking place. The ensuing popular admiration is the only reward for the exercise. The disciples may fast; but their fast is to be private. There is to be no external sign of the fast: rather they are to appear as they normally do, or even as if prepared for a feast. The Father who sees what is in secret will approve and reward.

How easily this high doctrine could be corrupted appears from the precept in the *Didache* 8^1: 'Let not your fasts be with the hypocrites, for they fast on Mondays and Thursdays, but do you fast on Wednesdays and Fridays.'

This concludes the section of the Sermon dealing with religious exercises. The next section (6$^{19-34}$) has to do with the proper attitude of the disciple towards worldly possessions. The greater part of it appears to be drawn from Q; but there are a few verses which may be from M.

5. *WORLDLY WEALTH AND WORLDLY CARES* (32–35)

(a) EARTHLY AND HEAVENLY TREASURE (32)

MT. 6$^{19-21}$

6 19 Lay not up for yourselves treasures upon the earth,| where moth and rust doth consume,|and where thieves [1] break through 20 and steal:||but lay up for yourselves treasures in heaven,|where neither moth nor rust doth consume,|and where thieves 21 do not [1] break through nor steal:||for where thy treasure is, there will thy heart be also.||

[1] Gr. *dig through.*

On the poetic form of these verses see Burney, p. 115, n. 2. According to him the rhythm in Mt. is different from that in the Lucan parallel (Lk. 12$^{33f.}$). If this is so, it is a further argument in favour of the view that Mt. here draws on M and Lk. on Q. Like the two preceding sections on the New Law and the New Piety this piece is cast in antithetic form. The wrong way is stated in *v.* 19, a short strophe of three three-beat lines: the right way in *v.* 20, which is similarly constructed. The whole is rounded off by the general truth in *v.* 21, which is a four-beat line. The agreement in wording between Mt. 6$^{19-20}$ and Lk. 12^{33} is exceedingly small. On the other hand *v.* 21 in Mt. agrees closely with Lk. 12^{34}. It is possible, therefore, that only *vv.* 19–20 are from M and that *v.* 21 is from Q.

19. What lies behind the saying is the thought that the accumulation and hoarding up of worldly goods is due to the desire for security, the desire to be rid of anxiety about the future. Then it is argued: so far from removing anxiety, the possession of such goods is a source of anxiety. For they themselves are liable to

loss and decay. They deteriorate by the agency of ' moth and rust.' ' Rust '
(lit. ' eating ') signifies any kind of corrosion or decay. It would include the
damage done by moth, and need not exclude other sorts of damage due to natural
causes. Besides this natural deterioration there is the constant danger of theft.

20. In contrast to earthly possessions is the treasure in heaven. This heavenly
wealth is a permanent possession exempt from the ravages of time, and beyond the
reach of thieves. Mt. does not specify what it is or how it is obtained. According
to the Q version of the saying, it is obtained by giving earthly goods in charity.
He that giveth to the poor lendeth to the Lord. Perhaps the same holds good in
this form of the saying, though it is not explicitly stated.

21. On this verse and vv. 19 f., see notes on Lk. 12³³ᶠ·, above, p. 114.

Mt. 6²²⁻²³ (Q). See on Lk. 11³⁴⁻³⁶, above, p. 93.

Mt. 6²⁴ (Q). See on Lk. 16¹³, above, p. 133.

Mt. 6²⁵⁻³³ (Q). See on Lk. 12²²⁻³¹, above, p. 111.

(b) ANXIETY (35)

MT. 6³⁴

6 34   Be not therefore anxious for the morrow:
for the morrow will be anxious for itself.
Sufficient unto the day is the evil thereof.

This verse comes at the end of the passage on worldly wealth and worldly cares,
which consists chiefly of extracts from Q. The verse itself has no parallel in Lk.,
and is probably not from Q. The question is whether it is a genuine saying of
Jesus derived from M or a bit of secular proverbial wisdom, which had got mixed
up with sayings of Jesus in the oral tradition of Palestinian Christians. It looks as
if the verse contained two proverbial sayings.

The first, ' Be not anxious for the morrow: for the morrow will be anxious for
itself ' begins by giving the complement to Prov. 27¹: ' Boast not thyself of to-
morrow; for thou knowest not what a day may bring forth ' (cf. James 4¹³⁻¹⁷).
There there is a warning against undue confidence about the future; here against
undue anxiety. There it is said that the morrow may falsify one's hopes; and here
one might expect something that would suggest that the morrow may prove one's
fears to be liars. Instead we have the cryptic statement that ' the morrow will be
anxious for itself.' It is possible that ' itself' is a mistranslation of the Aramaic
dīleh, meaning ' its own affairs '; but not very likely. The meaning appears to be
that it is foolish to worry about to-morrow, because to-morrow will bring its own
worries. That is, the morrow will bring its troubles ; but quite probably they will
not be the troubles about which we are gratuitously anxious to-day. This gives
added force to the following sentence, which says, in effect, ' why worry about
to-morrow? there's real trouble enough to-day, without bringing in to-morrow's
possible troubles.' There is a very similar saying in Ber. 9b.

The saying, as a whole, breathes that pessimism which commonly goes with
Oriental fatalism. The attempt to square it with Jesus' faith in the fatherly
providence of God may be regarded as wasted labour.

6. *THE RIGHT ATTITUDE TO ONE'S NEIGHBOUR* (36–39)

Practically the whole of this section is drawn from Q.

Mt. 7[1-5] (Q).   See on Lk. 6[37f.], [41f.], above, pp. 55 f., 58.

Mt. 7[7-11] (Q).   See on Lk. 11[9-13], above, p. 81.

Mt. 7[12] (Q).   See on Lk. 6[31], above, p. 52.

The only verse in this section which has no parallel in Lk. is Mt. 7[6].

MT. 7[6]

> 7 6 Give not that which is holy unto the dogs,
> |neither cast your pearls before the swine,|
> lest haply they trample them under their
> feet,|and turn and rend you.|

On the poetical form—four three-beat lines with rhyme—see Burney, pp. 131 f., 169; and on the saying itself Abrahams, *Studies*, ii. 195 f.

The dog is reckoned, in Rabbinical literature, among the wild beasts; the pig is an unclean animal.   In *Enoch* 89[42] the enemies of Israel are figured as dogs, foxes, and wild boars: and dogs = Philistines, wild boars = Edomites.   Rabbinical thought makes the further equation Edom = Rome.   But if there is a tendency in Judaism to speak of Gentile nations as ' dogs ' or ' swine,' it is not merely because they are Gentiles, but because they are the enemies of Israel, the deniers of Israel's religion, and so the enemies of Israel's God.   If we were to interpret the saying from a strictly Jewish point of view, we should take it to mean: Do not reveal the holy things of our religion to the Gentiles; for, so far from reverencing them, they will only be roused to a more intense hatred and oppression of Israel.   And this would truly represent the temper of some Jews, but not of all.   For there is abundant evidence of strong missionary activity among the Gentiles in this period. The truth seems to be that there were differing attitudes within Judaism; and that we cannot make generalisations about the Jewish attitude to Gentiles.   Some Jews adopted a narrow and exclusive attitude and tended to hate and despise the Gentile.   Their views often come to expression in the Apocalyptic literature. Others entertained more generous sentiments, as can be shown from many passages in the Rabbinical literature.   Something similar happened in the early Church, where we find a narrow, conservative, and exclusive party in Palestine, and a more generous, strongly missionary party with its headquarters at Antioch.   The tension between these two parties, between Paul and those who called themselves followers of James, is evident in the letter to the Galatians.   Mt. 7[6] looks very like a bit of apocalyptic Jewish exclusiveness, adopted by extreme Jewish Christians, and incorporated among the sayings of Jesus.   Later the Gentile Church turned the saying to face the opposite way, interpreting the holy thing as the Eucharist, and the dogs and swine as Jews, heretics, and unbaptised persons.   (Cf. Juster, *Les Juifs dans l'Empire Romain*, i. 320 f.)   An early stage in this process is reflected in the *Didache* 9[5]:

> But let none eat or drink of your Eucharist except those who have been baptised in the Lord's Name.   For concerning this also did the Lord say, ' Give not that which is holy to the dogs.'

7. *THE MOTIVE OF CHRISTIAN BEHAVIOUR: THE JUDGEMENT* (40–43)

(a) THE TWO WAYS (40)

MT. 7[13-14]

7 13 Enter ye in by the narrow gate: ||for wide [1] is the gate,|and broad is the way,|that leadeth to destruction,|and many be they 14 that enter in thereby.||[2] For narrow is the gate,|and straitened the way,|that leadeth unto life,|and few be they that find it.||

[1] Some ancient authorities omit *is the gate.*

[2] Many ancient authorities read *How narrow is the gate, &c.*

This saying is very different from Lk. 13[23f.] (Q). See above, p. 124. The structure is antithetical, as is so much of the M material in the Sermon. The figure of the two ways is found in the Old Testament (Jer. 21[8]; Ps. 1[6]; Prov. 14[12]), in Jewish literature (*Ecclus.* 21[10]; 4 *Ezra* 7[1-9]; the Jewish tract incorporated in the *Didache*, cf. 1[1f.], 5[1]; the Rabbinical writings—Billerbeck i. 460 ff.), and in classical writings (Hesiod, *Works and Days*, 287–292; Cebes, *Tabula* 15; Maximus of Tyre, *Diss.* 39[3]; Virgil, *Æn.* 6[540-543], etc.). It is possible that M has preserved a saying of Jesus cast in this commonplace form. More probably it is the M version of the Q saying (Lk. 13[23f.]). The point of Lk. 13[23f.] is the urgency of the Gospel message in view of the Judgement: go in at the door while it is still open. It may be conjectured that the saying has been moralised in the same way as Lk. 12[57-59], an eschatological parable which reappears in Mt. 5[25f.] as a moral rule. In favour of this view is the fact that what Mt. has in common with Lk. is the injunction to enter in by the narrow gate.

13. The thought of this verse is the commonplace that vice is more attractive than virtue, and that the line of least resistance is commonly the way to disaster. The ' destruction ' to which this way leads is something more than physical death. It is either complete annihilation or eternal punishment. The former seems more likely: it is complete death as opposed to eternal life; death with no hope of life as opposed to life with no fear of death.

14. The narrow way, the way of self-denial and self-sacrifice, is unattractive, and only firm determination and constant effort will keep a man on it; but at the end of it is life, eternal life, the life of the world to come.

The whole saying takes a very gloomy view of human life and destiny. In this respect it comes near to the spirit of 4 *Ezra*.

(b) FALSE PROPHETS AND THEIR FATE (41)

This passage appears to be a combination of Q and M material. It begins (*v.* 15) with a warning about false prophets who are like wolves disguised in sheepskins. Then it is said that they will be known by their fruits (*v.* 16[a]). This leads up to the Q passage on the tree and its fruits (16[b]–18||Lk. 6[43f.]), which is followed by a saying of John the Baptist (*v.* 19 = Mt. 3[10b]), and the repetition of *v.* 16[a]. The only fresh matter in this passage is *v.* 15.

7 15 Beware of false prophets, which come to you in sheep's clothing, but inwardly are ravening wolves.

False prophets are prophesied in Mk. 13²²ᶠ·: ' There shall arise false Christs and false prophets, and shall shew signs and wonders, that they may lead astray, if possible, the elect.   But take ye heed: behold I have told you all things beforehand.'   Also, independently of Mk., in Mt. 24¹¹: ' And many false prophets shall arise, and shall lead many astray.'   ' False prophet ' does not here mean one who prophesies what is false, though that is involved; but rather bogus prophet, one who pretends to be a prophet and is not.   The figure of the wolf disguised as a sheep goes with the thought of the disciples as the flock and Jesus as their shepherd. Cf. Lk. 10³‖Mt. 10¹⁶ (Q), above, p. 75.

Mt. 7¹⁶ᵃ. ' By their fruits ye shall know them ' effects the transition from v. 15 to the Q passage.

Mt. 7¹⁶ᵇ⁻¹⁸ (Q).   See on Lk. 6⁴³⁻⁴⁴, above, p. 59..

Mt. 7¹⁹ is a repetition of Mt. 3¹⁰ (Preaching of John the Baptist, Q)   See on Lk. 3⁹, above, p. 332; and Introduction, p. 25.

Mt. 7²⁰ repeats 16ᵃ.   Cf. Lk. 6⁴⁴ᵃ, above, p. 59.

(c) FALSE DISCIPLES AND THEIR FATE (42)

This section (Mt. 7²¹⁻²³) contains two sayings.   The first (v. 21) is commonly assigned to Q, the second (vv. 22 f.) to M; but it is quite possible that both are from M.   Mt. 7²¹ has a parallel in Lk. 6⁴⁶; but the verbal agreement between the two is confined to the words ' Lord, Lord ' and the verb ' do.'   Verbal agreement between Mt. 7²²ᶠ· and Lk. 13²⁶ᶠ· is confined to the words which they quote in common from Ps. 6⁹.

> **7 21**   Not every one that saith unto me,
> Lord, Lord, shall enter into the kingdom of
> heaven; but he that doeth the will of my
> Father which is in heaven.

This saying is given by Lk. (6⁴⁶) in what is undoubtedly the more original form.   The Matthæan version has been moralised.   Entry into the Kingdom is obtained by doing God's will, that is, by ' works of the Law,' even if we grant that it is by works of the new Law rather than the old.   Salvation depends on conduct, not on Christology.   This is in direct (conscious?) contrast to such a passage as Rom. 10⁹: ' If thou shalt confess with thy mouth Jesus as Lord . . . . thou shalt be saved.'   We may well think that the saying has been shaped by the controversy between Jewish and Pauline Christianity, the same controversy that appears in the Epistle of James.   The original saying has been given an anti-Pauline turn in Mt.'s version.   See further notes on Lk. 6⁴⁶, above, p. 60.

MT. 7²²⁻²³

> **7 22**   Many will say to me in that day, Lord, Lord, did we not prophesy by thy name, and by thy name cast out [1] devils, and by 23 thy name do many [2] might·· works?   And
>
> then will I profess unto them, I never knew you: depart from me, ye that work iniquity.
>
> [1] Gr. demons.   [2] Gr. powers.

This saying has likewise been modified by controversy.   The more original form is preserved by Lk. (13²⁶ᶠ·).   There the complaint is against unbelieving Jews who rejected the opportunity afforded them by the presence and work of

Jesus. Here it is against Christian false teachers. Moreover, the saying, as it stands in Mt., is in striking contrast to Mk. 9[38-41]. There is also a significant point of difference from Lk. in the quotation of Ps. 6[9]. Lk. has 'workers of unrighteousness' (adikia): Mt. has ' ye that work lawlessness' (anomia), in agreement with the LXX. ' Ye that work lawlessness' means ' ye whose acts are contrary to the Law'; and the Law in this connexion is the will of God as revealed to Moses and interpreted by Jesus, the new Law already expounded in Mt.'s Sermon. There is a distinct anti-Pauline bias in the M form of the saying. The M emphasis on conduct persists. We may compare the curious saying given in 2 Clem. 4[5] and in a marginal note in the cursive MS. 1424.

2 CLEM.	1424 mg.
If ye be gathered together with me in my bosom, and do not my commandments, I will cast you out, and will say to you, Depart from me, I know not whence ye are, ye workers of lawlessness (anomias).	The Jewish has here: If ye be in my bosom and do not the will of my Father which is in heaven, out of my bosom will I cast you away.

22. ' In that day' is the day of judgement (Is. 2[11, 17]; Zech. 14[6]). ' By thy name': R.V. suggests that ' the name' was used by these persons as a kind of charm or incantation, as in Acts 19[13]: ' But certain also of the strolling Jews, exorcists, took upon them to name over them which had the evil spirits the name of the Lord Jesus, saying, I adjure you by Jesus whom Paul preacheth.' But equally it may mean simply ' in thy name,' that is, claiming to act on behalf of and with the authority of Jesus. The latter interpretation fits all three activities: the former fits exorcism and the doing of miracles, but not prophesying. The early Church soon discovered that not all who called themselves prophets were the genuine article. The Didache (11[7 10]) lays down rules for distinguishing true prophets from impostors.

That demons could be exorcised and mighty works done in the name of the Lord was firmly believed in the primitive Church (cf. Acts 19[13]; James 5[14f.]; Irenæus, Haer. (ed. Harvey), II. iv. 6).

23. It is not denied that the prophecies, exorcisms, and mighty works have taken place. Only they do not prove that those who performed them are true disciples. The test by which the Lord recognises those that are His is the test of obedience to the will of God (v. 21). Cf. Didache 11[8]: ' But not every one who speaks in a spirit is a prophet, except he have the behaviour of the Lord. From his behaviour, then, the false prophet and the true prophet shall be known.' The rejection of the pretended disciples, ' I never knew you,' corresponds to the mildest form of ban as pronounced by the Rabbis (Billerbeck, iv. 293). As used by a Rabbi it meant something like ' I do not wish to have anything to do with you.' The words ' Depart from me . . . iniquity' are from Ps. 6[9].

(d) CLOSING PARABLE (43)

Mt. 7[24-27], the parable of the wise and foolish builders, is taken from Q (see notes on Lk. 6[47-49], above, p. 61).

The outstanding feature of the M teaching in the Sermon is its intense religious and moral earnestness. The Christians who made this collection had inherited the quality that is distinctive of Pharisaism at its best. And they had retained it when they embraced Christianity. They still revere the Law; but it is the Law as interpreted by Jesus and not as interpreted by the scribes. They have their forms of piety; but these are for use and not for display. Their religion is a secret communion of the soul with God, a dedication of themselves to unobtrusive service and quiet self-discipline. They sit loose to all worldly possessions and seek to be rich towards God. They are timid and conservative, distrusting any revolutionary departure from the ways that have been consecrated by the Jewish saints of former generations. The administration of the Gentile churches by a Paul is calculated to fill them with fear and dismay. Their task is to be the nucleus of a new and reformed Israel. And in carrying out that task they are blessed: blessed as they fulfil the Law of God in the way of mercy taught by Jesus, blessed as they attain purity of heart by prayer and fasting and self-giving, blessed as they live at peace with their people and make peace among them, blessed even when they have to endure persecution for the sake of the new righteousness taught and shown by Jesus. They are the scribes who have been made disciples unto the Kingdom of heaven and bring out of their treasures things new and old.

The antithetical character of the teaching is strongly marked throughout. The new interpretation of the Law is set in contrast to the old. The new piety is opposed to the sham religiosity of the hypocrites. The true wealth is contrasted with worldly gear. The way of life and the way of destruction are set side by side. The true disciple is set over against false prophets and Christians who have nothing of Christ save His name.

In all this it is made clear that what matters is character and conduct. Salvation comes to those who turn with a single mind to worship and obey God, walking in the way that has been opened up by Jesus.

Mt. adds his own comment on the Sermon as a whole (7[28 f.]).

8. *THE EVANGELIST'S POSTSCRIPT TO THE SERMON* (44)

MT. 7[28-29]

> 7 28 And it came to pass, when Jesus ended
> these words, the multitudes were aston-
> 29 ished at his teaching: for he taught them
> as *one* having authority, and not as their
> scribes.

28 f. The first half of verse 28 is a regularly recurring editorial formula in Mt. (cf. 11[1], 13[53], 19[1], 26[1]). It marks the close of the great discourses, which Mt. builds up in his Gospel. The remainder of the passage, from ' the multitudes ' to ' scribes ' is borrowed from Mk. 1[22]. The authority of Jesus is not to be misunderstood. It does not mean that He was dogmatic in His pronouncements and that the scribes by contrast were wavering and undecided. The scribes were very dogmatic: they were the guardians of an infallible tradition. The difference between Jesus and the scribes was that He spoke with the assurance of first-hand knowledge, with no appeal to tradition or precedent. His attitude was: ' I know

that this is true; and if you look at it candidly and sincerely, you will see for yourselves that it is true.' His ' Verily I say unto you ' and His ' He that hath ears to hear, let him hear ' go together. His teaching is the fruit of His insight; and His appeal is to the insight of His hearers.

B. THE MISSION CHARGE (58)

This is the M parallel to the Q section B2, above, pp. 73–78. Mt.'s account of the sending out of the disciples extends from 9³⁵ to 11¹, and is made up of materials derived from Mk., Q, and M. The analysis of the account into its components is exceedingly difficult in places owing to Mt.'s practice of conflating his sources. Nevertheless, a good deal of the structure can be made out with a fair degree of certainty.

The account begins with a narrative introduction (9³⁵–10⁵ᵃ). This tells of Jesus' own activity as He went about the country preaching and healing (9³⁵). This verse is based on Mk. 6⁶. Seeing the condition of the people He was sorry for them (9³⁶ from Mk. 6³⁴). Then follows the saying about the harvest and the labourers (9³⁷⁻³⁸||Lk. 10²: from Q; see above, p. 74). In 10¹ the summoning and commissioning of the Twelve is described in general terms. Here Mt. is dependent on Mk. 6⁷ and 3¹⁴ᶠ·. A list of the Twelve follows (10²⁻⁴). This list does not agree exactly with any of the lists in the New Testament. (See the excursus by Lake in *Beginnings of Christianity*, v. 37–46). After this narrative introduction comes the mission charge proper.

1. *THE SCOPE AND METHOD OF THE MISSION*

MT. 10⁵⁻⁸

10 5 These twelve Jesus sent forth, and charged them, saying,
  Go not into *any* way of the Gentiles, and enter not into any city of the Samaritans:
6 but go rather to the lost sheep of the house
7 of Israel. And as ye go, preach, saying,

8 The kingdom of heaven is at hand. Heal the sick, raise the dead, cleanse the lepers, cast out [1] devils: freely ye received, freely give.

[1] Gr. *demons*.

5. The verse begins with what is perhaps an editorial link to join the following teaching with what has gone before. The charge begins with a command which restricts the activities of the Twelve to Israel, excluding the Gentiles and the half-Jewish population of Samaria. ' A way of the Gentiles ' is probably a road leading to a Gentile city (cf. *Abodah Zarah* 1⁴, Danby, p. 437). The reference in that case will be to the Hellenistic cities of Palestine, for example the Decapolis. In these cities the Greek religion was dominant. Among the Samaritans the religion of Israel was held with reservations. Only the Pentateuch was accepted as canonical by them; and they had their own Temple on Mt. Garizim with their own priesthood and ritual. To orthodox Jews they were schismatic. Moreover, they were not regarded as pure-blooded Israelites (2 Kings. 17²⁴ᶠᶠ·). The Jewish attitude to them is expressed in *Ecclus.* 50²⁵ᶠᶠ:

  ' For two nations doth my soul feel abhorrence,
    (Yea), and (for) a third, which is not a people;

> The inhabitants of Seir and Philistia,
> And that foolish nation that dwelleth in Sichem.'

See, further, Moore, *Judaism*, i. 23–27; Billerbeck, i, 538–560.

6. Cf. Mt. 15²⁴, where Jesus says to the Canaanitish woman, ' I was not sent but unto the lost sheep of the house of Israel.' (This verse has no parallel in Mk.) These two sayings can scarcely be reconciled with Mt. 28¹⁹. The ministry of Jesus was in fact a ministry to the Jews; and we find that the leaders of the Palestinian community in the early days of the Church felt that their duty was to work among their own people (Gal. 2⁶⁻¹⁰). The conjecture may be hazarded that, with the number of missionaries available, the field of operations had to be restricted: and that whatever we may imagine Jesus' ultimate aim to have been, the obvious place to begin was with His own people. The danger in later times was that what had been a special arrangement to meet a definite situation should be turned into a dogma of general application.

7, 8. The content of the Mission preaching: The Kingdom is at hand. This is not merely an announcement about the future. The Kingdom is the future breaking into the present, and manifesting itself in the things which the disciples are to do in addition to their preaching. This combination of preaching and beneficent activity is their task as it is the task of their Master. The whole work is to be done without payment. This principle, it may be noted, governs the missionary work of Paul, who supported himself by manual labour in his evangelistic career.

MT. 10⁹⁻¹⁶

10 9 Get you no gold, nor silver nor brass 10 in your ¹ purses; no wallet for *your* journey, neither two coats, nor shoes, nor staff: for the labourer is worthy of his 11 food. And into whatsoever city or village ye shall enter, search out who in it is worthy; and there abide till ye go 12 forth. And as ye enter into the house, 13 salute it. And if the house be worthy, let your peace come upon it: but if it be not worthy, let your peace return to you.

14 And whosoever shall not receive you, nor hear your words, as ye go forth out of that house or that city, shake off the dust 15 of your feet. Verily I say unto you, It shall be more tolerable for the land of Sodom and Gomorrah in the day of judgement, than for that city. 16 Behold, I send you forth as sheep in the midst of wolves: be ye therefore wise as serpents, and ² harmless as doves.

¹ Gr. *girdles*.   ² Or, *simple*.

This passage is a conflation containing material from Mk., Q, and M. Verses 9–13 seem to consist of Mk. and M material; verses 14–16 of material from all three sources.

9 f. Equipment. There is considerable variation between the accounts given in our sources.

(1) Things prohibited:

MT. 10⁹ f.	MK. 6⁸ f.	LK. 9³· (‖MK.)	LK. 10⁴ (L?), cf. 22³⁵
Money (gold, silver, or copper)	Money (copper)	Money (silver)	Purse
Wallet	Wallet	Wallet	Wallet
Second shirt	Second shirt	Second shirt	—
Sandals	—	—	Sandals
Staff	—	Staff	—
—	Bread	Bread	—

(2) Things allowed:

MT. 10^9 f.	MK. 6^8 f.	LK. 9^3 (||MK.)	LK. 10^4 (L?), cf. 22^{35}
—	Staff	—	—
—	Sandals	—	—

Mk. is alone in permitting the staff and sandals, and in forbidding bread (for Lk. is here dependent on Mk.). In the list of prohibited things as given in Mt. and corroborated by the other accounts come money and the wallet (for carrying provisions). The natural inference is that the missionaries are to be like an invading army, and live on the country. They are to rely on the friendly hospitality of the people. (See further, notes on Lk. 22^{35}, below, p. 341.) The prohibition of staff and sandals is strange. One would have thought them most necessary on an undertaking of this sort. In the Mishnah (*Berakoth* 9^5, Danby, p. 10) it is ordained that a man ' may not enter the Temple Mount with his staff or his sandal or his wallet.' This is on account of the holiness of the place. It is possible that the mission of the disciples is meant to be regarded as a specially sacred undertaking, and that they are to set out upon it as if they were setting out to worship in the Temple. The saying ' the labourer is worthy of his food ' appears in Lk. 10^7 (L?) with ' hire ' for ' food.' Cf. *Didache* 13^1: ' Every true prophet who wishes to settle among you is worthy of his food. In 1 Tim. 5^{18} the Lucan form is quoted, apparently as scripture. St. Paul seems to have known the saying, for he writes, ' Even so did the Lord ordain that they which proclaim the gospel should live of the gospel ' (1 Cor. 9^{14}).

11–14. These verses describe the procedure to be adopted on arrival at a town or village. Verses 11 and 14 are based largely on Mk. 6^{10} f.; 12 & 13 appear to belong to M. These two verses have a parallel in Lk. 10^6 f. (L); but the verbal agreement is very small, and it seems probable that neither version is derived from Q. The Q account of the procedure to be adopted seems to me to be in Lk. 10^{8-12}.

11. Mt. is alone in giving the first step, that of finding in a strange town someone ' worthy,' i.e. esteemed and respected by his fellow-citizens. Having found a suitable lodging they are to stick to it for the period of their stay. Here Mt. is in agreement with Mk. (6^{10}) and L (Lk. 10^7).

12 f. On coming to the house a greeting is to be uttered. The form of words is given in Lk. 10^5 as ' Peace to this house.' The Aramaic *shĕlām* means both ' greeting ' and ' peace.' It is the same thing as the Mohammedan *salaam*. This greeting is here thought of as no mere formality, but as a real benediction. If the household are really deserving people the greeting will take effect on them, they will have some good of it. Otherwise the benefit will accrue to the disciples themselves. There is here a feeling for the power of the spoken word in blessing or cursing. Once the word is uttered it is irrevocable. (Cf. Crawley, *Oath, Curse, and Blessing.*)

14. This verse is borrowed from Mk. 6^{11} with alterations necessitated by the insertion of Mt. 10^{12} f. Mk. has ' whatever place does not receive you '; but Mt., having gone on to speak of greeting households, alters this to ' whoever does not receive you.'; and is then committed to saying that the disciples are to leave that house or city. The verse seems to say: ' If anyone does not receive you, leave the place.' This can hardly be original. The Marcan version: ' If any place does not

receive you, leave it' is more likely to be correct. On the significance of the wiping of the feet before leaving, see notes on Lk. 10$^{10\,f.}$, above, p. 76. It may be added that the Mishnah (*Berakoth* 9^5) cited above on *vv.* 9 f. goes on to prohibit a man from entering the Temple mount ' with the dust on his feet.' This suggests that the disciples are to rid themselves of the dust of the unresponsive town before resuming their sacred mission.

15. From Q. See notes on Lk. 10^{12}, above, p. 75.

16. The first half of the verse is from Q. See notes on Lk. 10^3, above, p. 76. The injunction ' be ye wise as serpents and harmless as doves ' is peculiar to Mt. and may be assigned to M. Paul may have had it in mind when he wrote Rom. 16^{19}. The wisdom of the serpent was proverbial. Cf. Gen. 3^1. The Greek word translated ' harmless ' means originally ' undamaged.' Then it comes to have the positive sense ' unblemished,' ' pure.' The disciples are to be clever enough to see through the frauds and shams of the world, but not so clever as to try such devices themselves. The same contrast between serpents and doves occurs in a saying of R. Jehuda b. Simon (*c.* A.D. 320). It is to the effect that Israel in relation to God is like a dove; in relation to the Gentiles like a serpent.

2. *THE MISSIONARIES UNDER PERSECUTION* (59)

Mt. 10$^{17-22}$ is drawn from Mk. 13$^{9-13}$. See notes, *ad. loc.*

MT. 10$^{23-25}$

10 23 But when they persecute you in this city, flee into the next: for verily I say unto you, Ye shall not have gone through the cities of Israel, till the Son of man be come.
24 A disciple is not above his ^{1} master,
25 nor a ^{2} servant above his lord. It is enough for the disciple that he be as his ^{1} master, and the ^{2} servant as his lord. If they have called the master of the house ^{3} Beelzebub, how much more *shall they call* them of his household!

^{1} Or, *teacher*.
^{2} Gr. *bondservant*.
^{3} Gr. *Beelzebul*: and so elsewhere.

23. These rather pessimistic verses are hardly in harmony with the other accounts of the sending out of the Twelve. It is assumed in the other sources that the missioners may expect a friendly reception. Their message may be rejected; but there is a difference between rejecting a message and persecuting those who bring it. See *Teaching of Jesus*, pp. 221 f. The motive for haste is the imminence of the coming of the Son of Man. But nowhere in the Gospels is there any suggestion on the part of Jesus that the coming of the Son of Man is to take place so quickly as this. The most that is said in Mk. is that the Kingdom will come with power within the lifetime of some of the contemporaries of Jesus (Mk. 9^1). And it is emphasised that the time of this great event is known only to God (Mk. 13$^{32\,f.}$). Now there is evidence in these three verses of Mt. that the evangelist is bringing together material that properly belongs elsewhere in the story. The idea that the disciples will be persecuted rather than hospitably received (*v.* 23) belongs to a later stage in the ministry (cf. Lk. 22$^{35ff.}$.) Again in *v.* 25 there is a reference to calling the master of the house Beelzebul; and in Mt. the Beelzebul incident does not come in until Chap. 12. The conclusion seems to be that *v.* 23 is out of place in this context. It reflects the experience and the expectations of the primitive Palestinian Church.

24 f. There is a partial parallel in Lk. 6⁴⁰ (Q). But there the point is different. See notes, above, p. 57. Here the force of the saying is that the disciple need not hope to fare any better than his master. That is, the disciples must expect to be treated very much as Jesus has been treated. It can hardly be doubted that the Q form is the original, and that the M version is the result of reading the Q form in the light of later events in the ministry and in the experience of the Jerusalem church. The shorter version of the saying in Lk., which refers only to the teacher-disciple relation, is probably to be preferred. The additional figure of servant and master may well come from the Jewish proverb ' It is enough for the servant to be like his master ' (Billerbeck, i. 577 f.). Verse 25ᵇ is clearly out of place in this context in Mt. There is nothing against it as a genuine saying of Jesus; but it belongs to a time when opposition has become definite and strong.

Mt. 10²⁶⁻³³ derived from Q. See notes on Lk. 12²⁻⁹, above, pp. 105–109.

Mt. 10³⁴⁻³⁶ from Q. See notes on Lk. 12⁵¹⁻⁵³, above, pp. 120 f.

Mt. 10³⁷⁻³⁸ from Q. See notes on Lk. 14²⁶⁻²⁷, above, pp. 131 f.

Mt. 10³⁹ from Q. See notes on Lk. 17³³, above, p. 145.

3. CONCLUSION OF THE MISSION CHARGE (63)

MT. 10⁴⁰–11¹

10 40 He that receiveth you receiveth me, and he that receiveth me receiveth him 41 that sent me. He that receiveth a prophet in the name of a prophet shall receive a prophet's reward; and he that receiveth a righteous man in the name of a righteous man shall receive a righteous 42 man's reward. And whosoever shall give to drink unto one of these little ones a cup of cold water only, in the name of a disciple, verily I say unto you, he shall in no wise lose his reward. 11 1 And it came to pass, when Jesus had made an end of commanding his twelve disciples, he departed thence to teach and preach in their cities.

40. This verse has a parallel in Lk. 10¹⁶, and it may belong to Q. But it is also possible that it is the M version of a saying that has not been completely preserved in any of our sources. See notes on Lk. 10¹⁶, above, pp. 77 f. The Matthæan version emphasises the positive side and says nothing about the rejection of the divine message. The compiler of M seems to have wished to end the Mission Charge on an optimistic note.

41. Peculiar to Mt. The collocation of prophets and righteous men occurs again in Mt. 13¹⁷, where Lk. (10²⁴) has ' prophets and kings.' To receive a prophet ' in the name of a prophet ' is to receive a prophet as such, recognising him as God's messenger. Similarly, to receive a righteous man in the name of a righteous man is to receive him as one who shows the divinely appointed way in his life. In the one case it is the acceptance of the will of God proclaimed; in the other the acceptance of the will of God exemplified. Such treatment of the servants of the Kingdom is reckoned as service of the King Himself. (Cf. Mt. 25³⁴⁻⁴⁰.)

42. There is a parallel to this verse in Mk. 9⁴¹:

9 41 For whosoever shall give you a cup of water to drink in my name, that ye are Christ's, verily I say unto you, he shall in no wise lose his reward.

On the original form of the saying see notes on Lk. 17¹ᶠ·, above, pp. 138 f. There it is argued that Jesus meant ' little children ' literally in these sayings (Lk. 17²; Mk. 9⁴¹ᶠ·; Mt. 10⁴²). The tendency of the tradition was to turn ' children ' into ' disciples'; and that has clearly happened here. Whatever may have been the meaning of Jesus, the meaning of Mt. is that kindness shown to a disciple *qua* disciple will surely be rewarded. For the disciple represents the Kingdom of God and service done to a representative of the Kingdom is reckoned as service done to the King. Compare the Rabbinical saying (*Gen. Rabbah* on Gen. 23¹⁸) : ' Whoever gives a piece of bread to a righteous man, it is as though he had fulfilled the whole Law.'

Ed. Meyer in his work on the origin and beginnings of Christianity (i. 143 n. 1) saw in Mt. 10⁴⁰⁻⁴² a reflection of the organisation of the Christian community into the Twelve or the Apostles (*v.* 40), the Christian Prophets, the members of outstanding piety and mature faith (the ' righteous ') (*v.* 41), and the rank and file members (the ' little ones ') (*v.* 42). It is unlikely that such a clear-cut division was present to the mind of the compiler of M or to the Evangelist. It is more probable that we have here collected together a number of sayings considered relevant to the business of the Christian mission. They are linked together not by the supposed organisation of the community, but by the catchwords ' receive ' and ' reward.'

11¹. The discourse is rounded off with the characteristic formula of the Evangelist. See on Mt. 7²⁸ᶠ·, above, p. 178. The verse is editorial. It is noteworthy that Mt. has nothing further to say about the progress of the Mission. Contrast Mk. 6¹²ᶠ·; Lk. 10¹⁷⁻²⁰. For Mt. the discourse is the important thing; and its importance is in its bearing on the work of the Church in the Evangelist's own day Its precepts are not confined in their application to the original Mission of the Twelve but are valid for all time.·

The portions of the Mission Charge which may be assigned to M reflect the aims and aspirations of the Palestinian community. Their task is the evangelisation of ' the circumcision.' Their business is not with Samaritans or Gentiles but with the lost sheep of the house of Israel. The method is simple: start with the ' worthy,' the best characters that Judaism produces; and work outwards. The results are in God's hands. By some people the messengers will be hated and persecuted; by some they will be welcomed and helped. God will deal with all that in due time. The task of the disciples is not that of bringing in the Kingdom. That is God's work. Their business is to prepare Israel for the coming of the Son of Man; and that coming cannot be long delayed.

C. VARIOUS SAYINGS

1. *JOHN THE BAPTIST AND ELIJAH* (65)

Mt. 11¹⁴⁻¹⁵

11 14 And if ye are willing to receive ¹*it*,
15 this is Elijah, which is to come. He that
hath ears ² to hear, let him hear.

¹ Or, him.
² Some ancient authorities omit *to hear*.

These two verses come in the Matthæan account of Jesus' testimony to John the Baptist (Mt. 11[7-19]), derived mainly from Q. It is possible that *vv*. 14[f.] are from M—they have no parallel in Lk.—but more likely that they are an editorial comment, whether of the compiler of M or of the Evangelist. In favour of the view that the insertion is due to Mt. is the fact that a similar editorial comment occurs in Mt. 17[13], where there is nothing corresponding in Mk. (9[9-13]). The fact is that the identification of John with Elijah is peculiarly at home in Mt.; and it may be conjectured that the identification was made by Jewish Christians who had to meet the objection from the Jewish side that the true Messiah would be anointed and proclaimed by the returned Elijah, that this had not happened in the case of Jesus, and that therefore Jesus was not the true Messiah. The obvious way of countering this argument was to say that Elijah had indeed come and prepared the way for Jesus—in the person of the Baptist. That Jesus Himself anticipated and met the objection, or indeed that He cared very much about fulfilling the current Jewish Messianic expectations, is most unlikely. See further Billerbeck, iv. 779-798; and the notes on Lk. 7[24-35], above, pp. 67-71.

2. *THE GOSPEL INVITATION* (68)

MT. 11[28-30]

11 28 Come unto me, all ye that labour and are heavy laden, and I will give you rest.
29 Take my yoke upon you, and learn of me; for I am meek and lowly in heart:
and ye shall find rest unto your souls.
30 For my yoke is easy, and my burden is light.

This invitation follows in Mt. immediately on the Q passage, Mt. 11[25-27]||Lk. 10[21-22], above, pp. 78 ff. For an attempt to show that Mt. 11[25-30] is a single piece consisting of three strophes, and that the whole passage stood in Q, see Norden, *Agnostos Theos*, pp. 277-308. But the absence of these verses from Lk. is a fatal objection to the theory that they stood in Q. It is hardly credible that Lk. would have omitted a saying so entirely after his own heart, if it had stood in his source. It must therefore be assigned to M. But even if it be assigned to M, its genuineness may be disputed. The view is quite widely held that the saying is a quotation from a Jewish wisdom book, and that it has been put into the mouth of Jesus. In support of this view many parallels from Jewish wisdom literature can be quoted, in which the Divine Wisdom personified speaks: Prov. 1[20-33], 8[1-36]; *Ecclus.* 24[19-22], 51[23-27]. In this last passage personified Wisdom says:

23 Turn in unto me, ye unlearned,
And lodge in my house of instruction.
24 How long will ye lack these things?
And (how long) shall your soul be so athirst?

Then the author himself testifies:

25 I open my mouth and speak of her,
Acquire Wisdom for yourselves without money.
26 Bring your necks under her yoke,
And her burden let your soul bear;

> She is nigh unto them that seek her,
> And he that is intent (upon her) findeth her.
> 27 Behold with your eyes that I laboured but (little) therein,
> And abundance of peace have I found.

But under all this poetical eloquence it is plain enough what the author is really commending: it is the study of the Law. ' He that taketh hold of the Law findeth her ' (i.e. Wisdom) 15¹, cf. 34⁸, 21¹¹; Moore, *Judaism*, i. 263 ff. In fact, the identification of Wisdom and the Law is a commonplace in Judaism. It can then be argued that in Mt. 11²⁸⁻³⁰ it is not Jesus who speaks but Wisdom, and that therefore the passage is a quotation similar to the passages quoted above. It is true that the book from which the supposed quotation is taken is otherwise quite unknown; but this difficulty is not felt. Otto (*op. cit.*, pp. 137 ff.) admits that the words are a quotation; but holds that the quotation was made by Jesus Himself, speaking as the representative of the divine Wisdom, *in persona Sapientiæ*. But it does not seem necessary to assume that the words are a quotation. If the author of *Ecclesiasticus* could think of such words, so might Jesus. Further, it is not necessary to suppose that there is any reference to Wisdom in the text as it stands. The verbal similarities to *Ecclus.* 51²³ᶠᶠ· may suggest, but they do not necessitate, such a reference. It is surely more natural to suppose that Jesus is here speaking as the representative, not of the divine Wisdom, but of the Kingdom of God. This may be best seen if we begin with *vv.* 29 f.

29 f. ' Take my yoke upon you and learn of me.' *Ecclus.* 51²⁶ says: ' Bring your necks under her yoke.' It is clear that what is meant there is the yoke of the Law; for the ' house of instruction ' in *v.* 23 is nothing else but the *Beth ha-Midrash*, the school of the Law. The injunction of Ben Sirach can then be compared with the saying of R. Nehunya b. Ha-Kanah (*c.* A.D. 70): ' He that takes upon himself the yoke of the Law, from him shall be taken away the yoke of the kingdom (i.e. the oppression of worldly powers) and the yoke of worldly care ' (*Aboth* 3⁵; Danby, p. 450). Devotion to the Law of God sets a man free from the cares and troubles of the world. The Law in this sense is the written Law plus the interpretation given in the ' house of instruction.' Jesus says, Take my yoke upon you; and His yoke is not the same thing as the yoke of the Law. It is the yoke of the Kingdom. There is thus a contrast between the word of Jesus and the word of Ben Sirach as well as a similarity: and the contrast is more important than the similarity. To take upon oneself the yoke of the Kingdom is to accept the sovereignty of God and to give oneself to His service. And what that means is something to be learnt from Jesus, who is meek and lowly in heart. This learning is not merely receiving instruction, even such instruction as is conveyed in the Sermon on the Mount: it is learning from the example of Jesus Himself how to serve God and man in love. (See *The Teaching of Jesus*, pp. 237–240.) In this way of discipleship men find rest to their souls, which is substantially what Ben Sirach claims to have got from the Law: ' abundance of peace have I found ' (51²⁷). It thus appears that Jesus claims to do for men what the Law claimed to do; but in a different way. In comparison with the yoke of the Law the yoke of the Kingdom is easy and light. Cf. Lk. 11⁴⁶. In comparison with

the way of the scribes the way of Jesus is simple: and His claim is that whereas the scribes load men with grievous burdens, His way gives rest to the weary and heavy-laden (*v.* 28). ' Come unto me ' then means ' Become my disciples,' and that means in practice ' Enter the Kingdom of God.' ' Take my yoke upon you ' means in effect ' Take the yoke of the Kingdom upon you,' and that means ' Enter the Kingdom of God.' There is thus no necessity to regard these verses as other than a genuine saying of Jesus.

3. *THE SABBATH* (69, 70)

MT. 12⁵⁻⁷

12 5 Or have ye not read in the law, how that on the sabbath day the priests in the temple profane the sabbath, and are guilt-
6 less? But I say unto you, that ¹ one

7 greater than the temple is here. But if e had known what this meaneth, I desire mercy, and not sacrifice, ye would not have condemned the guiltless.

¹ Gr. *a greater thing.*

These verses are inserted by Mt. into the Marcan account of the controversy provoked by the disciples' plucking and eating corn on the Sabbath. This plucking of corn was allowed by the Law (Dt. 23²⁵). But to do it on the Sabbath was not allowed. Plucking corn was a kind of harvesting, and harvesting was work, and work was forbidden. We may call this pettifogging if we please—and then go and ask what difference English law makes between the theft of a penny and the theft of a hundred pounds. Theft is theft whether the amount be small or great: and work is work whether it be done in a few minutes or many hours. So the Rabbis could justly argue. The act of the disciples was a serious matter from the point of view of strict Judaism. It meant a new attitude towards the Sabbath, an attitude which is bluntly stated in Mk. 2²⁷. The behaviour of the disciples is defended by Jesus first by the case of David and the shewbread. To this Mt. adds the present passage.

5. ' Have ye not read in the law? ' The Law nowhere commands the violation of the Sabbath in so many words. But it contains rules for the Temple service, which cannot be carried out unless the priests work on the Sabbath. The general principle for the interpretation of the Law is that positive commandments for which a definite time is prescribed take precedence of the Sabbath law if the two happen to clash. Hence the rule of the scribes that ' The Temple service takes precedence of the Sabbath,' i.e. the priests are allowed to work on the Sabbath in order to carry out the ritual.

6. Jesus claims that something more important than the Temple and its ritual has come into the world. That something is the Kingdom of God. He does not break through the traditions of the scribes merely in order to be different, but in obedience to a higher obligation, the claims of the Kingdom.

The fact that these verses appear in the matter peculiar to Matthew is a strong argument in favour of the genuineness of the saying. The conservative Jewish Christians who gathered this material together were not the people to invent sayings of this kind.

7. If this verse goes with the preceding, it is an indication that the whole passage (*vv.* 5–7) originally had a narrative setting of its own other than that into

which it is now incorporated.   There were doubtless other occasions on which the behaviour of Jesus and His disciples was condemned as a breach of the Sabbath. The text ' I desire mercy, and not sacrifice ' is from Hosea 6[6], and as quoted it agrees with the Hebrew against LXX and Targum.   Mt. inserts it again (9[13]) in the Marcan narrative 2[13-17].   The same text was used by the Rabbis, who interpreted ' mercy ' in the sense of acts of loving-kindness (Billerbeck, i. 500). ' The guiltless ' in the present context will be the disciples.   But as the whole passage probably had a context of its own originally, we cannot say what the original reference of the word was.

MT. 12[11-12]

12 11   And he said unto them, What man shall there be of you, that shall have one sheep, and if this fall into a pit on the sabbath day, will he not lay hold on it, 12 and lift it out? How much then is a man of more value than a sheep? Wherefore it is lawful to do good on the sabbath day.

Another saying which Mt. has inserted into a Marcan context, the story of the healing of a man with a withered hand in the synagogue on the Sabbath (Mk. 3[1-6]).   Mt. omits Mk. 3[3]: ' And he saith unto the man that had his hand withered, Stand forth,' and puts this saying in its place.   His interest is in the Sabbath question rather than in the details of the story.   The argument in *vv*. 11, 12*a* is presumed by Mt. to settle the question, and consequently the first half of Jesus' question in Mk. 3[4] becomes the conclusion of the argument in Mt. 12[12b]. The same argument is used again in the story of the healing of a dropsical man on the Sabbath (Lk. 14[1-6], which is to be assigned to L).   It is reasonable to suppose that the Lucan story gives the argument in its original narrative setting. In that case we may suppose that in the M compilation the argument alone was found, without any accompanying narrative (as in the case of Mt. 12[5-7]), and that the evangelist inserted it in what he considered to be a suitable context. The alternative to this would be that in the case both of Mt. 12[5-7] and 12[11f.] the sayings had narrative settings in M, and that Mt., in the interest of brevity, suppressed these and incorporated the teaching in other suitable narratives.

The argument is introduced into the story of a healing on the Sabbath.   The scribal answer to the question: ' Is it lawful to heal on the Sabbath? ' would have been: ' If the life of the patient is in danger, Yes; if not, No ' (Billerbeck, i. 623). They would have said that the man with the withered hand could safely wait till the Sabbath was past for his cure.   Cf. Lk. 13[14].

11. On the point raised in this verse it is not possible to say with certainty what the scribes would have said in our Lord's day.   Opinions were still divided in the Rabbinical schools at a much later time.   Some said that if an animal fell into a pit on the Sabbath, it was lawful to bring food to it there.   Others held that it was further permissible to place mattresses and cushions under it, so that it might get out by its own exertions.   In the so-called ' *Fragments of a Zadokite Work* ' 13[23] (Charles's edition) the rule is laid down: ' And if it (an animal) falls into a pit or ditch, he shall not raise it on the Sabbath.'   But the regulations of this document do not represent normative Judaism.   In view of the uncertainty in the Talmudic period it would be rash to assume that there was any fixed rule

in the time of Jesus. Further, the form of the question suggests that Jesus is not appealing to rule but to the actual practice of His hearers. Compare the form of question in Mt. 7⁹‖Lk. 11¹¹; Lk. 11⁵. The question is addressed to men as men; and ordinary humanity is expected to supply the answer.

12a. The conclusion is drawn from the expected answer by the favourite Rabbinical argument known as ' light and heavy,' the equivalent of our *a fortiori*. If so much may be done for one of the lower animals, how much more ought to be done for a man. Here the argument ends. The following words ' Wherefore . . . day ' are no part of the saying, but borrowed from Mk. 3⁴.

Additional Note : *Jesus and the Sabbath Laws*

Anyone who forms his views about the Jewish Sabbath from a study of the Rabbinical regulations alone will probably come to the conclusion that it is an elaborate bondage. Such a conclusion would be quite mistaken. It can be easily corrected by reading such a book as Mr. Loewe's *Mediæval Hebrew Minstrelsy*, where the joy of the devout Jew in the Sabbath finds poetical expression in many songs. Much that seems to the outsider to be an intolerable burden is custom that has been sanctified by long usage. In the first century A.D. the observance of the Sabbath had become the hall-mark of Judaism. It was something by which every Jew, without distinction of age or sex, was shown to belong to the Chosen People. And this observance had been maintained at no small cost. See the magnificent story told in 1 *Macc.* 2²⁹⁻³⁸, or that related by Josephus (*Contra Apionem*, i. 209–211). The faithful Jew would keep the Sabbath even at the price of his life.

The keeping of the Sabbath was a direct commandment in the Decalogue; but it was a commandment in general terms. The great mass of detailed rules came not from the written Law, but from tradition. The Mishnah says (*Hagigah* 1⁸; Danby, p. 212): ' The rules about the Sabbath . . . are as mountains hanging by a hair, for [teaching of] Scripture [thereon] is scanty and the rules many.' Here we have a plain hint that much of the Sabbatarian practice of Judaism was ancient custom hallowed by long observance.

Jesus cannot have been unaware of the great price which had been paid by His people for the right to keep the Sabbath. He cannot have been insensitive to the sacred associations of the observance in Jewish homes and in every department of Jewish life. Why then does He deal so drastically with the thing that was so sacred to His people, a thing which He had doubtless been taught in childhood to regard as sacred?

The answer to this question is given in principle in Mt. 12⁵ᶠ. The requirements of the Temple worship override the Sabbath laws: and the Kingdom of God is a greater thing than the Temple worship. It is the tremendous importance and urgency of the service of the Kingdom that justifies for Jesus the way which He takes. In this connexion the prohibition of staff, sandals, and wallet in the Mission Charge may be very significant. These things were forbidden in Jewish law to one going up to the Temple: they are forbidden again by Jesus to men setting out on an undertaking more important than the Temple service. The service of the Kingdom overrides the Sabbath laws. It is a work that can and must be done even on the Sabbath. It is a task that goes on all seven days of the week.

At this point we may ask whether this has not a bearing on the incident related in Mk. 2²³⁻²⁸. Surely what is described in *v.* 23 is not just a quiet Sabbath afternoon stroll. Should we not rather think of Jesus and His disciples really journeying from one place to another on the missionary work of the Kingdom? Should we not think of the plucking of the corn, not as an idle pastime, but as something done to satisfy real hunger?

Further light is thrown on the problem by the incident told in Lk. 13¹⁰⁻¹⁷. There the affliction of the woman, who is healed on the Sabbath, is described as possession by a ' spirit of infirmity ' and it is subsequently said by Jesus that she has been ' bound by Satan ' for eighteen years. This brings out plainly the fact that the work of the Kingdom in the mind of Jesus, and indeed throughout the New Testament, is a warfare against the power of Satan. Every healing is a blow struck against the supreme enemy of the Kingdom of God. ' If I by the finger of God cast out demons, then has the Kingdom of God come upon you.' But Satan does not keep the Sabbath. Evil works seven days a week. And the warfare against Satan must go on on the Sabbath as well as on the other six days.

We therefore conclude that Jesus did not break through the Sabbath rules lightly or unadvisedly, but because ' the King's business required haste '; because the service of the Kingdom of God and the warfare against the kingdom of Satan must go on day in and day out; because the business on which God had sent Him was the most important business in the world.

4. *CHARACTER AND WORD* (86)

Mt. inserts into Mk.'s account of the Beelzebul controversy (Mk. 3²⁰⁻³⁰) passages drawn from Q, and at the end he adds a section (Mt. 12³³⁻³⁷) which seems to consist of Q and M material. Verses 33, 35, and 34ᵇ, have a parallel in Lk. 6¹³⁻¹⁵ and a doublet in Mt. 7¹⁶⁻²⁰. See above, pp. 59 f. Verses 34ᵃ, 36, and 37 are peculiar to Mt.

MT. 12³⁴ᵃ

12 34a Ye offspring of vipers, how can ye, being evil, speak good things?

' Offspring of vipers ' appears in the account of the Baptist's preaching (Q). Mt. makes Jesus also use the expression; but he is alone in doing so. The expression occurs again Mt. 23³³. The sentence may be an editorial composition to make the transition from *v.* 33 to *v.* 34ᵇ, or it may come from M. It reflects the peculiar feature of M—and Mt.—a fierce dislike of the scribes and Pharisees, which, curiously, goes with a tremendous veneration of the Law. Whether the saying is a genuine utterance of Jesus may be doubted.

MT. 12³⁶⁻³⁷

12 36 And I say unto you, that every idle word that men shall speak, they shall give account thereof in the day of judgement.

37 For by thy words thou shalt be justified, and by thy words thou shalt be condemned.

36. The Greek word translated ' idle ' means originally ' unemployed '; then ' lazy,' ' idle.' Here it means something like ' purposeless.' The ' idle ' word is distinguished from the deliberate, purposeful utterance. The statement of *v.* 36 is now a commonplace in psychology. The whole technique of psycho-analysis is built upon the principle that the ' idle ' word reveals character more truly and completely than the deliberate, considered statement. The things that a man says when he is ' off his guard,' when he does not stop to think, are commonly the things that also ' give him away.' The idle word reveals character, and character determines destiny.

37. The change of person from plural to singular suggests that the statement of *v.* 36 is being reinforced by the quotation of some proverbial saying. Such sayings are common in the East. ' If there goes forth good from the mouth of (men, it is well), and if a curse shall go forth (from) their mouth, the gods will curse them' (*Words of Ahikar* 123 f., Cowley, *Aramaic Papyri*, p. 224). There is Rabbinical evidence (Billerbeck, i. 639 f.) for the Jewish belief that the record of a man as kept in heaven included his words, even his harmless utterances, as well as his acts.

D. PARABLES OF MISSIONARY WORK

Mt. 13 is a composite structure containing materials drawn from Mk., Q, and M. The framework is supplied by Mk. 4^{1-34}; and the Q and M passages are inserted into this or appended to it.

Mt. 13^{1-9} = Mk. 4^{1-9}. The Parable of the Sower.

Mt. 13^{10-15} is based on Mk. 4^{10-12}, the discussion on the purpose of parabolic teaching. But Mt. makes two additions. At 13^{12} he inserts the saying which in Mk. does not come until 4^{25}. And he adds *vv.* 14 f. (= Is. $6^{9f.}$) from his collection of *Testimonia*.

Mt. 13^{16-17} are from Q. See on Lk. $10^{23f.}$, above, pp. 80 f.

Mt. 13^{18-23} = Mk. 4^{13-20}. Interpretation of the Parable of the Sower.

Mt. omits Mk. 4^{21-25} at this point. He has a parallel to Mk. 4^{21} in Mt. 5^{15}; to Mk. 4^{22} in Mt. 10^{26}; to Mk. 4^{24} in Mt. 7^2; and Mk. 4^{25} has already been inserted at Mt. 13^{12}.

Mt. 13^{24-30}, the Parable of the Wheat and Tares, takes the place of Mk. 4^{26-29}, the Parable of the Seed growing inevitably.

Mt. 13^{31-32}, the Parable of the Mustard Seed is a conflation of Mk. (4^{30-32}) and Q (Lk. $13^{18f.}$). See above, pp. 122 f.

Mt. 13^{33}, the Parable of the Leaven, from Q (Lk. $13^{20f.}$). See above, pp. 123 f.

Mt. 13^{34} from Mk. $4^{33f.}$.

Mt. 13^{35} (= Ps. 78^2) again probably from a collection of Testimonia. Cf. *vv.* $14^f.$

Mt. 13^{36-43}. Interpretation of the Parable of the Wheat and Tares.

Mt. 13^{44-46}. Parables of the Treasure and the Pearl.

Mt. 13^{47-50}. Parable of the Net.

Mt. 13^{51-53}. Conclusion of the Parabolic Discourse.

The passages which may be assigned to M are *vv.* 24-30, 36-43, 44, 45 f., 47-50, 51 f.

1. *THE PARABLE OF THE WHEAT AND TARES* (96)

In chapter 13 Mt. is following Mk. closely.   Except for two short passages he reproduces the whole of Mk. 4.   The two passages are Mk. 4^{21-25}, for which he has parallels elsewhere; and Mk. 4^{26-29}.   In place of Mt. 4^{26-29} he gives this parable; and a comparison of the language in detail strongly suggests that Mt. 13^{24-30} is an expansion of Mk. 4^{26-29}.   (Cf. *The Teaching of Jesus*, p. 222.)   The reason for this procedure can only be conjectured.   Mk. 4^{26-29} is one of the most cryptic of all the parables.   Even now there is no small difference of opinion as to its meaning.   Lk. omits it altogether.   It may be suggested that the reason for Lk.'s omission and Mt.'s remodelling is the same—the obscurity of the parable.   It is hardly possible to determine whether the Evangelist himself produced the new version of Mk. 4^{26-29} or whether the work had already been done.   There is a little evidence in favour of the former alternative.   In Mk. 4^{31} the mustard seed is sown ' on the ground.'   In Mt. 13^{31} this is altered to ' in his field '; and this may safely be regarded as Mt.'s editorial revision.   Now in Mk. 4^{26} we have again ' on the ground,' and in Mt. 13^{24} ' in his field.'   It is natural to assume that this change is the work of the same hand as the change in Mt. 13^{31}, and that possibly the same hand that made this change made all the rest.   But that is no more than a guess.

<table>
<tr><td>

MT. 13^{24-30}

13 24   Another parable set he before them, saying, The kingdom of heaven is likened unto a man that sowed good seed in his
25 field: but while men slept, his enemy came and sowed [1] tares also among the
26 wheat, and went away.   But when the blade sprang up, and brought forth fruit,
27 then appeared the tares also.   And the [2] servants of the householder came and said unto him, Sir, didst thou not sow good seed in thy field? whence then hath
28 it tares?   And he said unto them, [3] An enemy hath done this.   And the [2] servants say unto him, Wilt thou then that
29 we go and gather them up?   But he saith, Nay; lest haply while ye gather up the tares, ye root up the wheat with them.
30 Let both grow together until the harvest: and in the time of the harvest I will say to the reapers, Gather up first the tares, and bind them in bundles to burn them: but gather the wheat into my barn.

[1] Or, *darnel*.
[2] Gr. *bondservants*.
[3] Gr. *A man* that is *an enemy*.

</td><td>

MK. 4^{26-29}

4 26   And he said, So is the kingdom of God, as if a man should cast seed upon the
27 earth; and should sleep and rise night and day, and the seed should spring up and
28 grow, he knoweth not how.   The earth [1] beareth fruit of herself; first the blade, then the ear, then the full corn in the ear.
29 But when the fruit [2] is ripe, straightway he [3] putteth forth the sickle, because the harvest is come.

[1] Or, *yieldeth*.
[2] Or, *alloweth*.
[3] Or, *sendeth forth*.

</td></tr>
</table>

24. The introductory formula reappears in Mt. 13^{31}, and, with change of verb, in 13^{33}.   The three M parables in this chapter have no special introduction (Mt. $13^{44, 45, 47}$).   The rest of the verse is the same as Mk. *v.* 26 except that in view of what is to follow Mt. specifies ' good ' seed.

25. ' But while men slept,' cf. *v.* 27 of Mk.   The sowing of the weeds takes place at night.   ' Tares ' (Gr. *zizania*); the Greek name is of Semitic origin. (Accadian *zizānu*.)   The plant is now generally identified with the ' darnel '

(R.V. mg.), *Lolium temulentum,* which grows to a height of about two feet and closely resembles wheat.   It produces grain similar to that of wheat in size, but of a dark colour.   It appears in Rabbinical literature under the name *zūn,* Aram. *zūnā.*

26. This verse again is an adaptation of *v.* 28 in Mk. ' Appeared ' means presumably that the darnel was recognisable as such.   As it was sown at about the same time as the wheat, this cannot well be its first appearance above ground. Perhaps the darnel would now be distinguishable by the darker colour of the grain.

27, 28, 29. The Matthæan parable now goes its own way.   It is not clear why the servants should be surprised at the appearance of darnel among the wheat, unless it was present in great quantity, which is not stated.   The surprising thing would be a field that did not have some weeds.   It is also not clear how the farmer knows that this is the work of an enemy.   'An enemy,' R.V. mg. ' a man that is an enemy,' lit. ' an enemy a man ': probably a Semitism (Dalman, *Gramm.*[2], p. 122). The proposal of the servants to weed the cornfield at this stage is so absurd that it would hardly have been made in real life.   It is required not because such things are done in farming, but for the sake of the interpretation which is to follow.   We are dealing here not with parable but with allegory.   The master gives the obvious reply to an absurd question.

30. The wheat and darnel will be sorted out at the harvest, when the wheat will be preserved and the darnel burned.   The reapers are not identical with the farm-workers, but apparently special workers employed for the harvest.   But again this does not square with real life.   The farmer may employ extra men in harvest time; but his regular workers also do their share.   This distinction between ' servants ' and ' reapers ' does not arise naturally out of the story.   It is imported for the purposes of the interpretation: that is, it is allegory and not parable.   The binding of the darnel into bundles corresponds to the binding of the wheat into sheaves.   This verse is a clear reminiscence of the preaching of John the Baptist.

It is now clear what Mt. 13[24-30] is.   It is an allegory constructed out of material supplied by Mk.'s parable (4[26-29]) combined with the eschatological teaching of the Baptist.   The story, as it stands, is an allegory composed for the sake of the explanation which is to follow.   It is not to be regarded as a genuine parable of Jesus.

THE INTERPRETATION OF THE PARABLE (100)

MT. 13[36-43]

13 36 Then he left the multitudes, and went into the house: and his disciples came unto him, saying, Explain unto us the 37 parable of the tares of the field.   And he answered and said, He that soweth the 38 good seed is the Son of man; and the field is the world; and the good seed, these are the sons of the kingdom; and the tares are the sons of the evil *one*; 39 and the enemy that sowed them is the devil: and the harvest is [1] the end of the 40 world; and the reapers are angels.   As therefore the tares are gathered up and burned with fire; so shall it be in [1] the 41 end of the world.   The Son of man shall send forth his angels, and they shall gather out of his kingdom all things that cause stumbling, and them that do 42 iniquity, and shall cast them into the furnace of fire: there shall be the weeping 43 and gnashing of teeth.   Then shall the righteous shine forth as the sun in the kingdom of their Father.   He that hath ears, let him hear.

[1] Or, *the consummation of the age.*

The explanation of the parable follows the original story point by point. The correspondence is so exact that the suspicion is confirmed that the story has been made to fit the explanation. See the discussion on allegory (Introd., pp. 34 f.). This didactic device is found often in the Jewish Apocalypses. Compare, for example, Dan. 7. And similar detailed interpretations of passages of the Old Testament occur in the Rabbinical commentaries, the Midrash, especially in the homiletic parts. The explanation has as little claim to be considered authentic teaching of Jesus as the parable.

36. The explanation is given privately to the disciples. In the Marcan narrative the withdrawal of Jesus and His followers from the multitude takes place at an earlier stage, after the parable of the Sower. Mt. postpones it to this point, with the result that the following parables of the Treasure, Pearl, and Net, are represented as spoken to the disciples alone.

37. Mt. identifies Jesus with the Son of Man. He does the same elsewhere: cf. Mt. 16¹³ with Mk. 8²⁷. This identification was undoubtedly made by the early Church; but did Jesus Himself make it? Cf. Mk. 8³⁸. Do the Son of Man sayings in the Synoptics amount to the claim: I am that Son of Man who is spoken of in the *Similitudes of Enoch*? Or is Son of Man in the teaching a symbol, the name for an ideal which Jesus realised in His life and death? If we take, as I think we must, the latter view, then ' He that soweth the good seed is the Son of Man ' is primitive Church dogma, and not teaching of Jesus.

38, 39. ' The field is the world.' This does not agree with the facts. The field of the activity of Jesus was Palestine. It does not agree with the M programme of the Mission (Mt. 10⁵ᶠ.), where the field is Israel in the narrowest sense of the word. It does agree with Mt. 28¹⁸⁻²⁰, that is, it is early Christian dogma. The good seed is not, as we might expect, on the analogy of the parable of the Sower, the teaching. It stands for ' the sons of the Kingdom.' These are the people who are qualified to enter the Kingdom, the true disciples. The expression is found only in Mt. It does not occur in the Rabbinical literature. In Mt. 8¹² the parallel in Lk. is ' you '; and there it is clear that ' sons of the Kingdom ' means Jews, those who by birth were deemed to have a right to a place in the Kingdom. Here the sons of the Kingdom are qualified by discipleship rather than by birth. And their qualification stands good. Cf. Dalman, *Words of Jesus*, pp. 115 f.; Abrahams, *Studies*, ii. 187 f. The ' sons of the evil one ': the phrase is the equivalent of John the Baptist's ' offspring of vipers.' Cf. also John 8⁴⁴, ' Ye are of your father the devil,' and 1 John 3¹⁰, ' the children of the devil.' The ' sons of the evil one ' are those who belong to the kingdom of Satan. He plants them in the world and they grow according to his plan. The harvest is the ' end of the world ' or the ' consummation of the age ' (R.V. mg.). Analogous expressions in Apocalyptic and Rabbinical literature suggest that the meaning is the end of the existing world-order. This does not, for the Hebrew mind, necessarily carry with it the abolition of the material world. It may mean a transformation of it. It is essentially the end of a period of history, that period in which Satan still has some power, a period which can consequently be described as ' the present evil age.' It will come to an end when Satan is finally overthrown, and God alone reigns in the world. The expression is peculiar to Mt. in the Gospels (Mt. 13³⁹, ⁴⁰, ⁴⁹, 24³, 28²⁰). The participation of angels in the Judgement is little mentioned in the Rabbinical literature.   It appears more commonly in the Apocalypses.   E.g. *Enoch* 53[3-5]: ' I saw all the angels of punishment abiding (there) and preparing all the instruments of Satan.   And I asked the angel of peace who went with me: " For whom are they preparing these instruments? "   And he said unto me: " They prepare these for the kings and the mighty of this earth, that they may thereby be destroyed." ' Cf. *Enoch* 54[6], 55[3], 56[1ff.], 62[11], 63[1], 100[4f.]; *Ass. Mosis* 10[2].

40, 41.   Verses 40–43 are the point of the whole matter   The parable itself and all the foregoing exposition of it only prepare the way for this.   The problem is the problem of a mixed community; a Church which contains genuine Christians and others, a Church which contains strict observers of the Jewish Law, and others who are lax; a Church which knows the ascetic rigour of James the Just and the scandals of Corinth.   And in these verses the Evangelist gives his solution of the problem.   The false brethren will be separated from the true at the Judgement. The Son of Man, the returning Christ, will depute His angels to make the separation.   ' The things that offend ' is literally ' the scandals.'   The corresponding Hebrew word means originally something which causes one to stumble, a stone in the path or the like.   Then it gains a moral significance and becomes something which causes one to sin.   Then since occasions to sin may be persons as well as things, it can be used of a person who tempts one to sin.   It is so used in Mt. 16[23], ' He turned and said unto Peter, Get thee behind me, Satan: thou art a stumbling-block unto me.'   In this last sense we should interpret the present passage.   It is not things but persons here, those who by their teaching or example cause others to go wrong.   Cf. Rom. 14[13-23]; 1 Cor. 8[9].   These, the worst offenders, are mentioned first.   Then come those who ' do lawlessness.'   See on Mt. 7[23], above, p. 177.

42, 43.   The ' furnace of fire ' occurs again in 13[50] and nowhere else in the Gospels.   Cf. Rev. 1[15], 9[2]; IV *Ezra* 7[36]:

' And then shall the pit of torment appear,
   and over against it the place of refreshment;
The furnace of Gehenna shall be made manifest,
   and over against it the Paradise of delight.'   (Box's translation.)

The Rabbis also described Hell as a furnace of fire.   (Billerbeck i. 673.)   ' There shall be weeping and gnashing of teeth.'   Cf. *Enoch* 108[3]: ' Their names shall be blotted out of the book of life and out of the holy books . . . and they shall cry and make lamentation in a place that is a chaotic wilderness, and in the fire shall they burn.'   The gnashing of teeth expresses the utter despair of the victims. This refrain is characteristic of Mt.   Cf. 8[12], 13[50], 22[13], 24[51], 25[30].   The happy lot of the righteous stands out by comparison with the fate of the wicked.   Cf. Dan. 12[2f.]: ' And many of them that sleep in the dust of the earth shall awake, some to everlasting life, and some to shame and everlasting contempt.   And they that be wise shall shine as the brightness of the firmament.'   The righteous will be clothed with a supernatural glory.   Cf. Mt. 17[2]; *Enoch* 39[7], 104[2]: ' But now ye shall shine as the lights of heaven, ye shall shine and ye shall be seen, and the portals of heaven shall be opened to you.'   The closing word, ' He that hath ears, let him hear,' goes back to Ezek. 3[27], where God says to the prophet: 'But when I speak with thee, I will open thy mouth, and thou shalt say unto them, Thus saith the Lord God: He that heareth, let him hear; and he that forbeareth, let him forbear: for they are a rebellious house.' It emphasises the Divine authority of the prophetic message and the personal responsibility of the hearer for what he makes of it. As used by Jesus the force of the saying is the same. He means: ' What I say to you is God's truth. If you will face it honestly, you will see that it is. The responsibility lies with you.' The Evangelist has used this word of Jesus to give force and impressiveness to his interpretation. ' Let every Church member look to himself and see how this parable fits his own case.'

This allegory and its interpretation we may regard as probably the free composition of the Evangelist himself. We now come to three genuine M parables. The first two form a pair and may be considered together.

2.　THE HIDDEN TREASURE AND THE VALUABLE PEARL (101)

MT. 13[44-46]

13 44　The kingdom of heaven is like unto a treasure hidden in the field; which a man found, and hid; and [1] in his joy he goeth and selleth all that he hath, and buyeth that field.

45　Again, the kingdom of heaven is like unto a man that is a merchant seeking 46 goodly pearls: and having found one pearl of great price, he went and sold all that he had, and bought it.

[1] Or, *for joy thereof.*

These two parables have a direct bearing on the missionary work of the disciples. The thesis of both of them is that once a man sees the Kingdom of God as it really is, he will spare no effort and consider no sacrifice too great to attain to it. The object of all the preaching of the Kingdom is therefore to convince men that the Kingdom is the most precious thing conceivable, so precious that in comparison with it all other goods lose their value. It is wealth which demonetises all other currencies.

44. The treasure hidden in the field: cf. Mt. 25[18, 25]. The treasure is obviously not hidden by the present owner. The parable is not concerned with the question how the finder comes to discover the treasure, or who put it there originally. Still less does the question of the morality of the finder's behaviour arise. The point of the parable is that the finder realises that he has stumbled upon something of great value, and immediately sets about securing it for himself. If you will show such energy and determination in order to secure worldly wealth, how much more you should strive to secure the treasure of all treasures. There are Rabbinical parallels to the story (Billerbeck i. 674). The legal question as to the right of the buyer to the treasure would be governed by the rule laid down in the Mishnah (*Baba Bathra* 4[8 f.], Danby, p. 371).

45 f. The point of the second parable is the same as that of the first. Here the merchant's procedure is not open to criticism. The fact also that he is seeking for pearls of fine quality, while the hero of the former parable stumbles on the treasure by chance, is probably not to be unduly stressed. The point is that having found the pearl of pearls, he deems it good business to sell everything he

has in order to obtain it.   The fact that he would presumably have to sell it again in order to live is also not relevant to the parable.

It is one of the curiosities of New Testament interpretation that the pearl in this parable came to be identified, not with the Kingdom, but with Christ Himself. (Cf. H. Usener in the *Festschrift* for Weizsäcker, pp. 203–213).

3. *THE PARABLE OF THE NET* (102)

Mt. 13¹⁷ ⁵⁰

13 47   Again, the kingdom of heaven is like unto a ¹ net, that was cast into the sea, and gathered ∗ of every kind: which, 48 when it was filled, they drew up on the beach; and they sat down, and gathered the good into vessels, but the bad they 49 cast away.   So shall it be in ² the end of the world: the angels shall come forth, and sever the wicked from among the 50 righteous, and shall cast them into the furnace of fire: there shall be the weeping and gnashing of teeth.

¹ Gr. *drag-net.*
² Or, *the consummation of the age.*

In its present form this parable is a companion piece to the parable of the Wheat and Tares; but it may be doubted whether the present form is the original. The interpretation (*vv.* 49 f.) does not fit the parable.   In the parable it is the fishermen themselves who sort the fish.   That is, the missionary disciples of Jesus. But in the interpretation it is the angels who undertake this task.   Further, in the parable the fishing presumably represents missionary work (cf. Mk. 1¹⁷); but it is very curious missionary work which wins people only in order to reject them immediately they are won.   As it stands, the parable does not make sense; and the interpretation does not arise out of the parable, but is an irrelevancy tacked on to it.   These difficulties are met by the hypothesis of Otto (*op. cit.*, pp. 99 102) that the genuine parable of Jesus is contained in *v.* 47 and that the rest is later expansion.

47. On this view the original parable has nothing to do with good and bad Christians.   It has to do with the fact that just as a net collects fish of many different species, so the preaching of the Kingdom brings in men of many different sorts and conditions, men from all levels of society and of all degrees of culture, and so on.   The point then is clear that the thing which God offers to men in the proclamation of the Kingdom is offered to all men, high and low, rich and poor, wise and simple, Pharisee and publican.   And it is also implicit that all alike need that which is offered.   This simple truth is completely obscured by the additional verses.

48. The net is emptied and its contents sorted by the fishermen.   Following the figure used in *v.* 47, this can only mean that the missionaries sit in judgement on their converts, thus usurping the task which Jesus elsewhere reserves for God or God's representative.   Contrast Mt. 7¹.   This, the plain meaning of the parable, is corrected in *v.* 49 by the introduction of the angels.   But this correction is at the expense of the parable.   The bad fish are rejected and the good retained. This also is very curious.   For the object of the preaching is to save sinners (cf. Mk. 2¹⁷); and there seems little point in throwing them out as soon as they are caught.   But it is clear from *v.* 49 that the explanation is not in terms of missionary activity, but in terms of an existing Church which is a mixed body

already containing true Christians and false. The evangelist is occupied with the same problem as in the parable of the Tares; and he offers the same solution. Cf. 13⁴¹⁻⁴³. Verses 48–50 appear for what they are, a clumsy attempt to foist on to *v.* 47 a view identical with that expressed in the parable of the Tares. Verse 47 is a genuine parable of Jesus: the rest is Matthæan embroidery.

4. *CONCLUSION OF THE PARABOLIC DISCOURSE* (103)

MT. 13⁵¹⁻⁵³

13 51   Have ye understood all these things? 52 They say unto him, Yea. And he said unto them, Therefore every scribe who hath been made a disciple to the kingdom of heaven is like unto a man that is a householder, which bringeth forth out of his treasure things new and old. 53 And it came to pass, when Jesus had finished these parables, he departed thence.

51. This verse may be regarded as an editorial transition to the following saying. It refers to the whole collection of parables in chapter 13; and it is exceedingly unlikely that they were all delivered on one occasion, or indeed that they where all delivered by Jesus. The question and the answer of the disciples both belong to the artificial situation which Mt. has himself created in this chapter.

52. It is difficult to see what is the force of ' therefore ' in this saying. Presumably it means that because the disciples understand the teaching just given in the parables, they are to be regarded as scribes who have been made disciples to the Kingdom of heaven. But the disciples, so far as we know, were not scribes, but fishermen and the like. Cf. Acts 4¹³. The meaning of the saying itself is not obscure. The scribe, as scribe, knows the Law; as a disciple of the Kingdom he knows the Gospel. From the point of view of the Palestinian Jewish Christian, he knows all that is worth knowing. He has at command the best both of Judaism and Christianity. We find a similar idea among the Rabbis. R. Akiba is compared to a full treasury. Rab Chisda (late 3rd cent. A.D.) explained ' new and old ' (Song of Songs 7¹³) thus: the ' old ' is the written Law; the ' new ' is the words of the scribes. It may be that something similar is meant by old and new in this saying. The old will be the Law of Moses; the new will be the new interpretation given by Jesus. A concrete example of such a combination would be the Gospel of Mt. itself, or the composite work in the *Didache* produced by incorporating sayings of Jesus into the Jewish document of the ' Two Ways.' What, however, is not clear is how this saying is to be reconciled with such sayings as are given in Mk. 2²¹ᶠ·, or with the collection of antitheses in Mt.'s Sermon, where Jesus puts his ' I say unto you ' in contrast to prescriptions from the written Law. It is beyond doubt that the sharpest and most obvious conflict in the ministry of Jesus was that between His teaching and the scribal interpretation of the written Law. Mt., more than any other Gospel, emphasises this fact. But Mt. also attempts, here and elsewhere, to suggest that the conflict goes no deeper than that; that it is a dispute about the exegesis of the Law, and that the Law itself is not in question. Both Jesus and the scribes knew better than that. They knew that the teaching of Jesus was revolutionary; that if it was accepted, the Law as well as the scribal interpretation would be

put on a new footing. The bitter hostility of the scribes to Jesus is not mere professional jealousy. It is based on the recognition that the logical issue of Jesus' teaching is the end of the Law. They saw clearly from the Jewish side what Paul later saw with equal clearness from the Christian side. Jewish Christianity did its best to hold a mediating position; but it was an impossible task. This saying expresses perfectly the Jewish-Christian ideal: it may well be doubted whether it represents the convictions of Jesus Himself.

53. The closing formula of the Evangelist. See on 7²⁸ᶠ·, above, p. 178.

E. VARIOUS SAYINGS

Between the close of the parabolic discourse and the beginning of the discourse on the Church (chap. 18) we have a series of sayings and comments inserted in Marcan contexts. The passages to be considered under this head are Mt. 15¹²ᶠ·, ²²ᵇ⁻²⁵, 16²ᵇ⁻³, 17⁻¹⁹, 17²⁰.

1. A SAYING ON WEEDS (115)

MT. 15¹²⁻¹³

15 12 Then came the disciples, and said unto him, Knowest thou that the Pharisees were ¹ offended, when they heard this 13 saying? But he answered and said,

Every ² plant which my heavenly Father planted not, shall be rooted up.

¹ Gr. *caused to stumble.*
² Gr. *planting.*

The verses 12–14 are inserted by Mt. into the Marcan record of the dispute about the washing of hands. Verse 14ᵇ is derived from Q. See on Lk. 6³⁹, above, p. 57. Verse 14ᵃ is the Evangelist's transition from v. 13 to v. 14ᵇ. Verses 12 f. have no parallel.

12. The short narrative introduction is necessary to prepare the way for the saying which follows. It is to be regarded as the work of the Evangelist.

13. In the present context the weeds can only be the Pharisees who took offence at the preceding saying. In the Rabbinical literature Israel and especially the pious Israelites are thought of as a planting of God. The idea goes back to Is. 60²¹: 'Thy people also shall be all righteous, they shall inherit the land for ever; the branch of my planting, the work of my hands, that I may be glorified.' In the Mishnah (*Sanh.* 10¹, Danby, p. 397) this text is quoted as proof of the proposition that 'All Israelites have a share in the world to come.' The doctrine that righteous Israelites are the planting of God is found in the *Psalms of Solomon* (1st cent. B.C.) 14²ᶠ·: 'The saints of the Lord shall live therein for ever: the garden of the Lord, even the trees of life, such are his saints. The planting of them is rooted for ever: they shall not be plucked out all the days of the heaven: for the portion and the inheritance of God is Israel.' The saying in Mt. is most naturally regarded as a warning against the thoughtless optimism of those who accepted such congenial doctrine as that expressed in the above passages. The saying could be applied in many ways. Mt. here applies it to the Pharisees. He could have used it with equal effect in the situation implied by the parable of the Tares. It is one of those general statements that are capable of many

applications. It may be a genuine saying of Jesus; but we have no guarantee that its present application in Mt. is the original application.

2. JESUS AND THE GENTILE WORLD (116)

MT. 15[22-25]

15 22 And behold, a Canaanitish woman came out from those borders, and cried, saying, Have mercy on me, O Lord, thou son of David; my daughter is grievously 23 vexed with a [1] devil. But he answered her not a word. And his disciples came and besought him, saying, Send her

24 away; for she crieth after us. But he answered and said, I was not sent but unto the lost sheep of the house of Israel. 25 But she came and worshipped him, saying, Lord, help me.

[1] Gr. demon.

This passage occurs in the Mt. parallel to Mk.'s account of the Syro-Phœnician woman (Mt. 15[21-28]||Mk. 7[24-30]). The whole passage in Mt. is remarkable for its small amount of agreement with Mk. except in the dialogue, Mt. 15[26-27]||Mk. 7[27-28]. The Matthæan and Marcan accounts of this incident are in this respect surprisingly like the Matthæan and Lucan accounts of Jesus' dealings with the Centurion of Capernaum (above, pp. 62-66). It is even suggested by Dibelius that this story was originally delivered simply as a dialogue between Jesus and the woman; and that there may have been a common source of Mt. and Mk., which contained only the conversation and left the cure to be understood. Whatever the explanation, the divergence between Mt. and Mk. in the narrative setting of the conversation is very striking and demands explanation. It may, of course, be that Mt.'s special source contained an account of the incident, and that Mt. has conflated that account with Mk. In that case it would be reasonable to suppose that some part at least of vv. 22-25 comes from M.

22. ' Canaanitish ' occurs only here in the N.T. It reflects the old distinction between the Israelites and the previous occupants of the Holy Land. Mk. describes the woman as a ' Greek, a Syrophœnician by race,' where ' Greek ' probably refers to her religion. ' Came out from those borders ' can hardly be right, since in v. 21 Jesus has already entered the territory. Perhaps we should take the words ' from those borders ' with woman and render: ' a Canaanitish woman from those borders (i.e. belonging to that part of the country) came out.' Alternatively it could be argued that the discrepancy points to a change of source in Mt. The Marcan narrative represents Jesus as going into the territory of Tyre and Sidon, and Mt. follows it in v. 21. But perhaps the M account of the incident did not allow Jesus to enter this heathen land. Perhaps it represented the heathen woman as leaving her own country and coming over the frontier to lay her petition before Jesus. This would be consonant with the M version of the Mission Charge (Mt. 10[5f.]); and it would imply that the M insertion begins at v. 22.

The titles used by the woman, ' O Lord ' and ' Son of David,' both suggest that Jesus is the Jewish Messiah. ' Son of David ' is the title of the expected Messianic king in Ps. Sol. 17[23]. ' Lord ' is the natural title by which to address such a personage. With the combination we may compare the commonly occurring ' My lord the King ' in address to kings in the Old Testament.   On these titles see Dalman, *Words of Jesus*, pp. 316–331.

23, 24, 25. The silence of Jesus is doubtless meant to be a tacit refusal of the request.   The implication of ' she crieth after us ' is that Jesus and the disciples are walking on and paying no heed to the woman.   The disciples find the woman's pursuit annoying and ask Jesus to get rid of her.   Jesus answers in terms similar to those of the Mission Charge ($10^{5f.}$): ' Go not into any way of the Gentiles, and enter not into any city of the Samaritans: but go rather to the lost sheep of the house of Israel.'   While this piece of dialogue is taking place the woman comes forward, throws herself on the ground before Jesus and begs for His help. The subsequent dialogue follows the account in Mk.

The authenticity of this saying in its present context is open to doubt.   It is quite possible that Jesus believed and said that His task lay among His own people, at any rate in the first instance.   It is also possible that such a saying, like the similar injunction in the Mission Charge, was restricted in its application to the circumstances of the moment.   See the notes on $10^{5f.}$, above, pp. 179 f. But that Jesus meant to lay this proposition down as a dogma and never looked beyond the borders of Israel is very unlikely.   The generalisation of the saying is more probably the work of the Jewish-Christian community.

[THE SIGNS OF THE TIMES] (119)

[MT. 16^{2-3}]

16 2 But he answered and said unto them, [1] When it is evening, ye say, *It will be* fair 3 weather: for the heaven is red.   And in the morning, *It will be* foul weather to-day; for the heaven in red and lowring.   Ye know how to discern the face of the heaven; but ye cannot *discern* the signs of the times.

[1] The following words, to the end of ver. 3, are omitted by some of the most ancient and other important authorities.

This passage from the words ' When it is evening ' onwards is generally regarded as an interpolation, though a very early one, in the text of Mt.   There is the strongest textual evidence against the passage.   Cf. Streeter, *The Four Gospels*, pp. 241 f.   Further, there is another saying on weather-signs in Lk. 12^{54-56} (Q), above, p. 121.   The Lucan saying agrees with the observed facts about the weather of Palestine.   The saying in Mt. agrees with English weather-saws; but how far it holds of Palestinian weather is not clear.   Rabbinical sayings about the weather-signs (Billerbeck, i. 727 f.) are concerned, as in Lk., with cloud and wind, not with the appearance of the sky at dawn and sunset.

3.   *THE PLACE OF PETER IN THE CHURCH* (122)

MT. 16^{17-19}

16 17 And Jesus answered and said unto him, Blessed art thou, Simon Bar-Jonah: for flesh and blood hath not revealed it unto thee, but my Father which is in 18 heaven.   And I also say unto thee, that thou art [1] Peter, and upon this [2] rock I will build my church; and the gates of 19 Hades shall not prevail against it.   I will give unto thee the keys of the kingdom of heaven: and whatsoever thou shalt bind on earth shall be bound in heaven: and whatsoever thou shalt loose on earth shall be loosed in heaven.

[1] Gr. *Petros*.
[2] Gr. *petra*.

Few passages in the New Testament have given rise to so much discussion as these three verses. The saying, particularly *vv.* 18 f., is one of the main proof-texts for the Roman Catholic doctrine of the Papacy. The critical questions raised by the passage come under two main heads: (*a*) Is it a part of the genuine text of Mt. ? (*b*) If it is, is it a genuine saying of Jesus ?

(*a*) It has been held that the passage, or at least part of it, is interpolated in Mt. The textual evidence for this view is of the slenderest. The strongest point against the passage is the fact that it is not mentioned by the Fathers of the second century. But this argument from silence loses much of its weight when we reflect that the matters with which these men were concerned were, for the most part, matters in which the assertion of the primacy of Peter would not be specially relevant. The primacy of Peter would not be a very useful weapon against Gnosticism, for example. There does not seem to be any good reason against regarding these verses as a genuine part of the Gospel.

(*b*) But if they are genuine Mt., are they a genuine saying of Jesus ? They stand alone. Mk. knows nothing of this strong commendation of Peter. Indeed, the Marcan account, taken by itself, would not suggest that Peter's declaration was received with any great enthusiasm by Jesus. And, in any case, the absence of the saying from the Marcan account is very difficult to explain. The principal arguments against the genuineness of the saying are as follows:

(i) The word ' church ' occurs only here and Mt. 18¹⁷ in the Gospels. Both passages are suspect. This suspicion does not rest merely on the fact that the word occurs only twice. There are many words in the Gospels which occur only once or twice, and are none the less reliable for that. The difficulty is that this word occurs in Mt. here in a saying which has no parallel in Mk., though Mk. records the incident. It occurs again (Mt. 18¹⁷) in a passage which has a parallel in Q (Lk. 17³ᶠ·), and again the Q parallel knows nothing about the peculiar Matthæan details. (See above, p. 139.) Further, the author of Lk.–Acts knows the word ' church ' and the thing signified by the word very well. He uses the word more than a score of times in Acts, but never in his Gospel, either in speech or narrative. Finally, the word as used in Mt. seems to reflect the conditions of a later time. In Mt. 18¹⁷ it can hardly mean anything but the local community: here it clearly means the whole Church. (Hort, *Christian Ecclesia*, pp. 9 ff.) But this state of affairs—a great Church, whose constituent members are smaller communities—belongs to the period of Acts. In the Gospels we have a body of disciples with Jesus at their head expecting the coming of the Kingdom of God.

(ii) The second argument arises out of the first. Jesus and His followers expect the coming of the Kingdom. Therefore, it is contended, Jesus cannot have founded a Church in the ordinary sense of the word, an institution which was to continue for centuries, and do the work that had been done by Temple and Synagogue in Judaism. To this it is replied that ' church ' in the New Testament is really the Christian equivalent of the Old Testament ķāhāl, and means not a new religious organisation but the new Israel. The followers of Jesus are the true spiritual Israel, the chosen people of God. At this point we can bring in a Jewish parable from the old homiletic Midrash, *Yelammedenu.* It is about a king who planned the building of a palace: ' He dug in several places seeking proper ground for a foundation; at last he struck rock beneath, and said, Here I will build, so he laid the foundations and built.   Just so when God sought to create the world, He examined the generation of Enoch and the generation of the Flood, and said, How can I create the world when these wicked people will rise up and provoke me to anger?   When He saw Abraham who was to arise, he said, Now I have found a rock (*petra*) on which to build and establish the world.   For this reason He calls Abraham a rock (Is. 51[11.]).'   (Moore, *Judaism*, i. 538).   On this analogy it can be contended that Peter is the foundation of the New Israel   But this does not carry with it the doctrine of the primacy of Peter.   It is one thing to be the foundation and quite another to be the ruler of the New Israel.   And it may be added that if the phrase Kingdom of God means anything, it means that God is sole ruler of the New Israel.

(iii) It is urged against the saying that if it were genuine, Peter must have enjoyed an authoritative position as ruler of the primitive Church, and that the earliest documents show that no such absolute status was accorded to him.   In Acts 11[2ff.] he has to justify his dealings with the centurion at Joppa; and at Antioch Paul ' resisted him to the face, because he stood condemned ' (Gal. 2[11]). There is no satisfactory answer to this objection.

(iv) It is argued that the description ' rock ' is unsuitable to the somewhat unstable character of Peter.   It might be suggested that ' live wire ' would be a more apt description than ' rock.'   To this it is replied that it is not the character of Peter that is the foundation.   It is rather Peter as the recipient of Divine revelation and as proclaiming this revelation, that is the foundation.   But again this will scarcely carry with it the primacy of Peter.   For it can hardly be asserted that the reception of such revelations and the proclamation of them when received is in the New Testament the peculiar prerogative of Peter.

(v) It may be added that the idea of one of the Twelve being given a position of primacy is not consistent with other sayings of Jesus.   Jesus commonly thinks and speaks in terms of the coming Kingdom; and there there is no primacy of any apostle.   In Mt. 19[28] (M)||Lk. 22[30] (L) there are twelve thrones, apparently of equal importance.   In Mk. 10[35-45] the request of the sons of Zebedee for the leading places is rejected, not on the ground that the primacy belongs already to Peter, but on the ground that it is not in the power of Jesus to confer such rank.   The M parable of the Labourers in the Vineyard (Mt. 20[1-16]) goes even farther in this direction.   It suggests that even the Twelve must not look for special reward or recognition in the end of the day.

For these reasons we should not regard the saying as a genuine utterance of Jesus.   It is, however, of Palestinian origin; and it is possible at least to surmise how and when it became current.   In 1 Cor. we get evidence of the existence of a Petrine party, whose influence was felt even in Corinth.   There is nothing to show that Peter himself had worked there, and so gathered followers like Paul and Apollos.   The Petrine party in Corinth seems to stand for claims made on behalf of Peter to have some kind of oversight of the Gentile churches.   Against all such claims Paul defends his own position as father in Christ of the Corinthian community (1 Cor. 4[15]).   Moreover, in this epistle he identifies Christ Himself with the rock (*petra*), by a piece of Rabbinical exegesis (10[4]).   And in this epistle he insists on the fact that there is not and cannot be any foundation of the Church but Christ Himself. ' Other foundation can no man lay than that which is laid, which is Jesus Christ ' (3[11]). In view of these facts we may conjecture that the kind of claim for Peter which we have in Mt. 16[18 f.] was being pressed in the fifties of the first century, and that Paul is resisting it in Corinth when he writes 1 Cor. It may also be conjectured that the challenge implied in the claim was directed against Paul himself. He was always suspect to the Palestinian Church; and it is possible that the elevation of Peter was meant to act as some kind of check upon Paul.

17. The first verse is in form a beatitude. Peter is given his full name Simon Bar-Jonah. *Bar* is the Aramaic word for ' son.' In John 21[15ff.] Peter is addressed as Simon son of John. The Semitic form of John is Jochanan. It is possible that Jonah is an abbreviation of Jochanan. There is no clear proof of this (Dalman, *Gram.*[2] 179, n. 5); but Jona appears as a variant in MSS. of the Septuagint, where the Hebrew has Jochanan. The exact form of the name of Peter's father must remain doubtful. ' Flesh and blood ' is a characteristic Rabbinical phrase. It stresses humanity as opposed to divinity. The revelation is from heaven and not of men. As the saying stands, this revelation can only be the fact that Jesus is ' the Messiah, the Son of the living God.' Now it appears to be common ground in the early Church that it is the Resurrection which manifests this fact (Acts 2[36]; Rom. 1[4]). Peter's confession may therefore be regarded as an inspired utterance, prophetic in character. This is significant in view of the fact that Peter, who is the first to assert the Messiahship of Jesus, is also the first witness of the Resurrection (Lk. 24[34]; 1 Cor. 15[5]). These facts gave to Peter a special distinction; and the beatitude of this verse may well express the feelings of his Jewish fellow-Christians. In view of the silence of Mk. it must be considered doubtful whether it represents the response of Jesus to his Confession.

18. The play upon the name Petros and the word *petra* (' rock ') indicates an earlier play on the Græcised Aramaic nickname Kephas, which is the same thing as the Aramaic noun *kêphā* meaning ' rock.' Cf. John 1[43]. The Aramaic name is undoubtedly the original. Paul calls Peter Kephas regularly in Gal. and 1 Cor. (' Peter ' only Gal. 2[7 f.]). The nickname was given to Peter by Jesus Himself, but whether in jest or earnest we cannot say. The similar nickname ' Sons of thunder ' bestowed on James and John seems to be playful rather than serious, a gentle rebuke to their hasty temper. The possibility cannot be excluded that Jesus called Peter ' Rock ' as a similar mild rebuke to Peter's instability. What, then, is the rock upon which the Church is to be built? The obvious intention of the verse is that we should understand Peter himself to be the rock. Other interpretations have been suggested: the rock is Peter's Confession, or the fact of the Messiahship just acknowledged by Peter, or other things even more fanciful. But they all have to be forced upon the text. They depend on bringing in another ' rock ' and ignoring the ' rock ' that is already there in the words, ' Thou art Kêphā,' ' Thou art the Rock.' On this rock, on Peter himself, the Church is to be built. This figurative use of the verb ' build ' is specially characteristic of Jeremiah in the Old Testament. With him it has the sense of establishing and maintaining, and the object of the verb is Israel. Here and in 1 Cor. 2[10-17] the same figure is employed and the object of the verb is the Church. But Paul is quite clear that the founda-

tion is Christ, not Peter. There is, however, a sense in which it might be said that the Church was built on Peter; and that depends on the fact that Peter is the first witness to the Resurrection. In this sense he is the first member of the Church, the first witness to the fact that Jesus has been made both Lord and Christ, and declared to be the Son of God with power by the resurrection of the dead. This would explain why the gates of Hades cannot prevail against it. It is the Church of a Messiah who has already triumphed over death. The expression ' the gates of Hades ' comes from Is. 38[10], where the words ' In the noontide of my days I shall go into the gates of Sheol ' are a poetical way of saying ' I shall die prematurely.' Cf. *Wisdom* 16[13]; III *Macc.* 5[51]; *Ps. Sol.* 16[2]. Hades is the Greek equivalent of the Hebrew Sheol, the abode of the dead. To say that the gates of Hades will not prevail against the Church is the same thing as to say that death will not have any power over it. As ' death hath no more dominion over ' Christ (Rom. 6[9]), so it will have no more dominion over the Church. The whole verse thus seems to belong to the post-Resurrection period, and to express the convictions founded upon the Resurrection appearances of which Peter is the first witness.

19. Cf. Is. 22[22], a prophecy concerning Eliakim the son of Hilkiah: ' And the key of the house of David will I lay upon his shoulder; and he shall open, and none shall shut; and he shall shut and none shall open.' Here the key is ' the symbol of unlimited authority over the royal household ' (Skinner, *ad loc.*). The meaning must be similar in Mt. Peter is to be God's vice-gerent in all the affairs of the Kingdom on earth. This means that he is the ruler of the Church. The kind of power which he is to exercise is further defined as binding and loosing. ' Bind ' and ' loose ' are Rabbinical technical terms meaning ' forbid ' and ' permit ' respectively. The authority of Peter is an authority to declare what is right and wrong for the Christian community. His decisions will be confirmed by God. That is, Peter is to have the same powers in the Church as were enjoyed by the scribes in Judaism. The grant of exclusive power to Peter is inconsistent with Mt. 18[18], where the same powers are given to the whole body of disciples. Of the two Mt. 16[19] is less likely to be original.

The question remains whether we should regard these verses as part of Mt.'s special source M. We have already seen that they are not an interpolation into the text of Mt. It is also very unlikely that they are a free composition of Mt. himself; for we have seen reason to think that the doctrine expressed in them was current in Jewish-Christian circles in the fifties of the first century. It may therefore be presumed that they were a part of the Jewish-Christian tradition which Mt. incorporated in his gospel. That is, they probably belong to M.

4. FAITH THAT REMOVES MOUNTAINS (126)

MT. 17[20]

Here again we have a verse inserted into a context where Mt. is following Mk. Mt. 17[14-21] is an abbreviation of Mk. 9[14-29], the story of the healing of the epileptic boy. At the end the disciples ask Jesus privately why they were not able to effect the cure. The reply of Jesus in Mk. (9[29]) is: ' This kind can come out by nothing, save by prayer.' In Mt. the answer to the same question is given (17[20]) as follows:

17 20 And he saith unto them, Because of your little faith: for verily I say unto you, If ye have faith as a grain of mustard seed, ye shall say unto this mountain, Remove hence to yonder place; and it shall remove; and nothing shall be impossible unto you.

Following on this many MSS. add: ' But this kind goeth not out save by prayer and fasting.' But this addition is absent from the best authorities for the text of Mt. and is rejected by modern editors. Mt. 17²⁰ has parallels in Lk. 17⁶ (Q); Mk. 11²³||Mt. 21²¹. For a discussion of the various forms of the saying see above, pp. 140 f.

To ' remove mountains ' is a Jewish proverbial expression for doing the seemingly impossible. In the Rabbinical literature the title ' Uprooter of mountains ' is given to some scholars who have a gift for solving apparently insoluble problems in the exegesis of the Old Testament. The saying as given here agrees with 1 Cor. 13². It may therefore be regarded as early and assigned to M.

Why has Mt. substituted it here for the answer given in Mk.? No certain answer can be given to this question; but it may be noted that elsewhere Mt. writes in such a way as to suggest that he regards faith as the one essential for the performance of miracles. In 14³¹ it is implied that the only thing that prevents Peter from walking on the water is lack of faith; and in 16⁸ the suggestion is that if the disciples had faith they would not be worrying about a shortage of bread, presumably because faith could produce a supply miraculously.

F. THE NATURE OF THE CHRISTIAN FELLOWSHIP

In chapter 18 Mt. gives a discourse about the Church and the duties of its members towards one another. For the first part of the composition (vv. 1–9) he is dependent chiefly on Mk.: the remainder (vv. 10–35) is a solid block of M material. The Marcan basis of Mt. 18¹⁻⁹ is Mk. 9³³⁻³⁷, ⁴²⁻⁴⁸. Bultmann thinks that behind the Marcan section 9³³⁻⁵⁰ lies a short didactic piece of tradition bearing on the duties of members of the Fellowship to one another and the like. This comprised vv. 35, 37, 41–50; and Mk. has turned it into a scene from the life of Jesus by prefixing the narrative verses 33 f. This is also the view of Dibelius (*Formgeschichte*², p. 260), though he leaves it an open question whether the narrative setting comes from Mk. or was already created in the process of tradition. This is not an impossible theory; but it may be noted that the real difficulty in Mk. 9³³⁻³⁷ is created by v. 36. It has already been suggested above (p. 78), in discussing Lk. 10¹⁶, that Mk. 9³⁷ really has to do with disciples and not with children. That is, it is part of the answer to the question, Who is greatest among the disciples? and it says that all are on the same footing, because all are representatives of the one Master and of the one God. Mk. 9³⁶ is a mistaken attempt to provide a narrative preparation for the phrase ' one of such little children ' in v. 37. The introduced child now takes the centre of the stage with results that can be clearly seen in Mt. and Lk. In Lk. the saying Mk. 9³⁵ᵇ is transferred to the end of the story. In Mt. more drastic alterations are made. For Mt. apparently sees, what we see, that the saying in Mk. 9³⁷ is not really adequate to the situation created by Mk. 9³⁶. He therefore introduces at this point the more appropriate saying from Mk. 10¹⁵ and rewrites it to fit the existing situation.   The result is Mt. 18³ᶠ·:

MT. 18²⁻⁴

18 2 And he called to him a little child, and set 3 him in the midst of them, and said, Verily I say unto you, Except ye turn, and become as little children, ye shall in no wise 4 enter into the kingdom of heaven.   Who-soever therefore shall humble himself as this little child, the same is the ¹ greatest in the kingdom of heaven.

¹ Gr. *greater*.

This is not M material but a free adaptation of Mk. 10¹⁵; and it may be noticed that when Mt. comes to the story of the blessing of the children in Mk. (10¹³⁻¹⁶) = Mt. 19¹³⁻¹⁵, he omits *v.* 15 of Mk., presumably because he has already made use of it in this context.   Verse 3 is Mt.'s interpretation of Mk. 10¹⁵: ' Whosoever shall not receive the kingdom of God as a little child, he shall in no wise enter therein.'   Mt. understands this to mean that the disciples must become like little children.   In what respect they are to resemble children is stated in *v.* 4.   It is humility.   There is no parallel in Rabbinical literature to the idea that the child is the type of humility, which is not surprising; for the natural child is not humble.   But humility is the virtue required in the disciples and Mt. accordingly finds it in the child.   He may have been helped by the saying given in Mt. 23¹²; Lk. 14¹¹, 18¹⁴, where it is taught that he who exalts himself will be humbled, and he who humbles himself will be exalted.

The first nine verses of Mt. 18 can now be allocated as follows:

1*a* Editorial; 1*b* from Mk. 9³⁴; the whole verse an editorial rewriting of Mk. 9³³ᶠ· so as to save the face of the disciples.

2 from Mk. 9³⁶.   3 f. a free rewriting of Mk. 10¹⁵.   5 from Mk. 9³⁷. 6 from Mk. 9⁴².   7 from Q; see on Lk. 17¹ᶠ·, above, pp. 138 f.   8 f. from Mk. 9⁴³, ⁴⁷ᶠ·.   The rest of chapter 18 may be assigned to M.

1.   THE CHURCH AND THE OUTSIDER (133)

MT. 18¹⁰, ¹²⁻¹⁴

18 10 See that ye despise not one of these little ones; for I say unto you, that in heaven their angels do always behold the face of 12 my Father which is in heaven.¹   How think ye? if any man have a hundred sheep, and one of them be gone astray, doth he not leave the ninety and nine, and go unto the mountains, and seek that 13 which goeth astray?   And if so be that he find it, verily I say unto you, he rejoiceth over it more than over the ninety and nine which have not gone 14 astray.   Even so it is not ² the will of ³ your Father which is in heaven, that one of these little ones should perish.

¹ Many authorities, some ancient, insert ver. 11, *For the Son of man came to save that which was lost.*   See Luke xix. 10.
² Gr. *a thing willed before your Father*.
³ Some ancient authorities read *my*.

For Mt. this passage is clearly a unity, for *v.* 14 refers back to *v.* 10.   That being so, Mt. can hardly have understood the ' little ones ' of *vv.* 10 and 14 to be children; for in *vv.* 3 f. it is necessary to become like a little child in order to enter the Kingdom, and in this section the ' little ones ' are compared to lost sheep.   It is therefore probable that Mt. understood ' the little ones ' of *v.* 10 in some other sense than ' children.'   Now Lk. has a parallel to Mt. 18¹²ᶠ· in

Lk. 15$^{4-7}$, which I assign to L. The context in which Lk.'s three parables are there set is instructive. All three parables are spoken to scribes and Pharisees who were shocked by Jesus' friendly reception of disreputable characters. Such men and women, publicans and sinners, attached themselves to Jesus, and some of them were doubtless disciples of His. As such He could call them ' little ones.' If, then, we assume the genuineness of the saying, it is possible that it was spoken in the first instance to scribes and Pharisees, who made the criticism that Jesus was collecting the dregs of society about Himself. Later this saying becomes a warning to the Church not to adopt the censorious attitude which Jesus had condemned in the scribes and Pharisees.

10. Cf. Lk. 18^9: ' Certain which trusted in themselves that they were righteous, and set all others at nought.' The ' little ones ' are repentant sinners who are drawn into the circle of the disciples of Jesus. The belief that men are under the care of angels is found in Judaism. Cf. Ps. 91^{11}: ' He shall give his angels charge over thee, to keep thee in all thy ways'; *Tobit* 5$^{6, 22}$; Rabbinical passages, Billerbeck, i. 781 ff.; iii. 437 ff. The statement that these angels always ' behold the face ' of God is not to be taken literally. As in 2 Kings 25^{19} the phrase ' behold the face of ' means ' have direct access to.' These angels can at any time report to God concerning their charges.

11. This verse is omitted by the leading authorities for the text and rejected by modern editors.

12 f. Cf. Lk. 15$^{3-6}$. The parable of the Lost Sheep clearly has to do with sinners and not with children. The numbers ' a hundred,' ' one,' and ' ninety-nine ' are often used by the Rabbis: examples in Billerbeck, i. 784 f. ' Doth he not leave the ninety and nine and go unto the mountains . . .? ': another possible rendering of the Greek is ' Doth he not leave the ninety and nine upon the mountains, and go . . .? ' The hill-country is thought of as the grazing-place for the flock. Lk. has ' Doth he not leave the ninety and nine in the wilderness, and go . . .? ' The account of the shepherd's doings on finding the lost sheep is much fuller in Lk. than in Mt. This may be due to Mt.'s habit of abbreviating, or it may be that the details have been lost in the process of tradition.

14. The Matthæan conclusion differs widely in wording from the corresponding verse (7) in Lk. R.V. mg.: ' a thing willed before your Father ' is a more literal rendering than R.V. text. It corresponds to a common Hebrew and Aramaic formula, which reflects the Jewish fear of anthropopathism in speaking about God. Lk. has ' there shall be joy in heaven.' It may be noted that the Hebrew and Aramaic words underlying R.V. mg. ' a thing willed ' (*rāsōn* and *ra'wā*) mean both ' decision ' and ' pleasure.' The same ambiguity is in them as in the English word ' pleasure.' ' Pleasure ' does not mean quite the same thing in ' It gives me great pleasure ' and in ' His Majesty's pleasure.' In Lk. the underlying Aramaic is taken in the sense ' God is pleased '—though it is more cautiously expressed than that. In Mt. the other sense is taken: ' God wills.' These are not mere translation variants: there is a difference of interpretation, which is an indication that the saying has come down to us through two different lines of tradition. The authorities for the text of Mt. are divided between ' your Father ' and my Father,' with a slight preponderance in favour of ' my.' If the word

Father occurred at all in the original form of the saying, it is probable that Jesus would say neither ' your Father in heaven ' nor ' my Father in heaven ' but simply ' the Father ' (*abba*). More probably, however, He said none of these. The passage, as appears from the Lucan parallel, is originally polemical; and it is more likely that Jesus said ' Heaven ' (= God, as often in Jewish speech) as in Lk., and that this has been expanded in M to ' my (your) Father in heaven.'

It would be rash to infer from *v.* 14 that the teaching of Jesus is that none of the ' little ones ' will perish. God's good purpose is that they should be saved, but human freedom is a fact, and Jesus elsewhere recognises the fact that man can reject the salvation of God and so perish. The Lucan form of the saying is different and perhaps more original.

2. *LIFE WITHIN THE CHURCH* (134 f.)

MT. 18[15-20]

18 15 And if thy brother sin [1] against thee, go, shew him his fault between thee and him alone: if he hear thee, thou hast 16 gained thy brother. But if he hear *thee* not, take with thee one or two more, that at the mouth of two witnesses or three 17 every word may be established. And if he refuse to hear them, tell it unto the [2] church: and if he refuse to hear the [2] church also, let him be unto thee as the 18 Gentile and the publican. Verily I say unto you, What things soever ye shall bind on earth shall be bound in heaven:

and what things soever ye shall loose on 19 earth shall be loosed in heaven. Again I say unto you, that if two of you shall agree on earth as touching anything that they shall ask, it shall be done for them 20 of my Father which is in heaven. For where two or three are gathered together in my name, there am I in the midst of them.

[1] Some ancient authorities omit *against thee*.

[2] Or, *congregation*.

There is a parallel to *v.* 15 in Lk. 17[3] (Q), and another to *vv.* 21 f. in Lk. 17[4] (Q). The verbal differences between Mt. and Lk. are great; and the most natural interpretation of the evidence is that the two passages come through different lines of tradition. Lk. 17[3f.] is from Q. Mt. 18[15-22] gives us the same original saying that is preserved in Lk. 17[3f.], but changed and enlarged by the addition of other matter in the process of the M tradition.

15. See notes on Lk. 17[3] (Q), above, pp. 139 f. In the Q form the saying has to do with wrongs committed by one member of the community against another. This is made clear in Lk. 17[4]. It can be argued that in Mt. the saying has been developed into a rule for dealing with any kind of sin in the community. It has become a rule of Church discipline. This interpretation involves deleting the words ' against thee ' as an assimilation to Lk. 17[4]. The words are rejected by Hort and Tischendorf. The procedure in dealing with a wrongdoer then falls into three stages. The person who knows of the offence is to reprove the offender. If that fails, he is to reprove him before witnesses. If this produces no effect the offence is to be published to the Church. These three stages all have in view the bringing of the offender to repentance. If they all fail, he is to be considered as no longer a member of the Church. The first step rests on the injunction in Lev. 19[17]: ' Thou shalt not hate thy brother in thine heart: thou shalt surely rebuke thy neighbour, and not bear sin because of him.' There are many Rabbinic sayings on the duty both of giving and accepting reproof. R.

Tarphon claimed that disaster overtook the Jews in A.D. 70 because they did not know how to give or accept reproof rightly. ' Thou hast gained thy brother'—as such. For if the measures to be taken all fail, he is lost as a brother; he ceases to be a member of the community. In Jewish usage ' brother ' stands for co-religionist, fellow-member of the Jewish community as a religious group. It is distinguished from ' neighbour,' which means fellow-member of the Jewish people as a nation (Billerbeck, i. 276). A similar usage is found in pagan religious communities (Deissmann, *Bible Studies*, pp. 87 f.; Lake and Cadbury, *Beginnings of Christianity*, v. 92, 378 f.). The Christian use of the term ' brother ' depends on the knowledge of God as Father; but the term was already there to be filled with its Christian meaning.

16, 17. The second stage is preparatory to the third. If the offender will not hear friendly reproof the official discipline must be put in motion. Here, according to Mt., it is necessary to take account of the Law as laid down in Dt. 19[15]: ' One witness shall not rise up against a man for any iniquity, or for any sin, in any sin that he sinneth: at the mouth of two witnesses, or at the mouth of three witnesses, shall a matter be established.' This principle is accepted here. No Church member is to be condemned by the Church on the evidence of one witness. By taking one or two members with him the person concerned ensures that if the offender has to be brought before the Church, there will be adequate evidence against him. Even at this stage it is still possible for the offender to avoid the next stage by mending his ways. But if he remains obstinate, there is no course open but to lay the matter before the Church. The Church here is clearly a body of no great size. If M is the Jerusalem tradition, ' the Church ' may be the Jerusalem Church. It is in any case the local community. If the Church cannot obtain satisfaction, there is nothing for it but to regard the offender as no longer a brother. ' Gentile ' stands in contrast to Israelite; and the Church regards itself as the true Israel. It is also practically synonymous with ' sinner ': cf. Gal. 2[15]. The use of the word ' Gentile ' in this connexion is evidence that we are dealing with Jewish-Christian tradition. A Gentile-Christian community would have been strongly tempted to change the word. (Cf. Streeter, *The Four Gospels*, p. 258.) The same collocation of publican and Gentile occurs in Mt. 5[46f.], which is probably from M (see above, p. 161).

18. Cf. Mt. 16[19]. The authority there given to Peter alone is here given to the Church. In the present context it may be argued, with Billerbeck (i. 738 ff., 792 ff.), that the binding and loosing have to do with the proceedings just described. If the Church puts the offender under a ban, or if it releases him from the ban, its verdict stands good before God. Josephus uses the verbs ' bind ' and ' loose ' in this way in his *Jewish War*, i. 111: ' They (the Pharisees) became at length the real administrators of the state, at liberty to banish and to recall, to loose and to bind, whom they would.' There ' loose ' and ' bind ' are used of persons so that ' bind ' is practically equivalent to ' banish ' and ' loose ' to ' recall.' So here ' bind ' may be equivalent to ' expel from the community ' and ' loose ' to ' restore to fellowship ' (cf. 1 Cor. 5[1-5]). But it is also probable that *v.* 18 did not always stand in this context. And the fact that it is things, and not persons, that are to be bound and loosed is an indication that originally the

saying had reference to the definition of right and wrong, and not to the discipline of Church members.

19, 20. ' Again I say unto you ' introduces a fresh saying, only loosely connected with what has gone before. As the corporate decision is valid in God's sight, so corporate prayer is powerful with Him. Two is the smallest number that can constitute a brotherhood or community. And in this matter two is much more than twice one. The underlying thought is that where two—or more—Christians are in perfect agreement, the thing that brings them into agreement is the thing that is greater than themselves, the thing that makes them one, the Kingdom of God. It is only real Christian agreement that is covered by this saying—not compromise or conspiracy. It is only agreement about things that can honestly be asked for in prayer. The selfish desires of A plus the selfish desires of B do not constitute an agreement in the sense in which the word ' agree ' is used here. What does constitute an agreement is shown by *v.* 20. It is the kind of thing that Christians can come to when they meet together in the name of Christ, and with His presence in their midst. The speaker is the risen and glorified Christ whose spiritual presence is a reality in the community of His followers (cf. Mt. 28[20]). There is a similar Jewish saying in *Aboth* 3[a]: ' R. Hananiah b. Teradion (died *c.* A.D. 135) said: If two sit together and words of the Law [are spoken] between them the Divine Presence rests between them, as it is written (Mal. 3[16]), Then they that feared the Lord spake one with another: and the Lord hearkened, and heard, and a book of remembrance was written before him, for them that feared the Lord, and that thought upon his name.' Cf. *Aboth* 3[6] (Danby, p. 450). Verse 20 appears in a rather different form in some old authorities (D, Syr. sin., with support from g, Sahidic, and Clement of Alexandria): ' For there are not two or three gathered together in my name, with whom I am not in the midst of them.' This is regarded as the more primitive form of the saying by Wellhausen and Klostermann; and this view may be right. The reading of the text may well be an attempt to produce a smoother version of the saying, which in its D form seems to show traces of its Aramaic origin.

MT. 18[21-22] (135)

18 21 Then came Peter, and said to him, Lord, how oft shall my brother sin against me, and I forgive him? until 22 seven times? Jesus saith unto him, I say not unto thee, Until seven times; but, Until [1] seventy times seven.

[1] Or, *seventy times and seven.*

A dialogue on forgiveness of wrongs done by one member of the community to another member. There is a parallel in Lk. 17[4] (Q), see above, pp 139 f. According to Jerome there was yet another version in the apocryphal Gospel used by the Nazarenes. It is as follows: ' If thy brother (saith he) have sinned by a word and made thee amends, seven times in a day receive thou him. Simon his disciple said unto him: Seven times in a day? The Lord answered and said unto him: Yea, I say unto thee, unto seventy times seven times. For in the prophets also, after they were anointed by the Holy Spirit, the word of sin was found.' (James, *Apocryphal N.T.*, p. 6.) Here ' the word of sin ' is a Semitism, meaning ' somewhat of sin.' This form of the saying has been regarded as the original; but it may equally be a compound of Mt. and Lk.

The form of the saying in Mt. differs from Lk. principally in that there is here no mention of the repentance of the offender. Possibly it is taken for granted in the Mt. version. Whether the question and answer form is true historical reminiscence or a creation of the Evangelist it is not possible to determine.

21 f. It is Jewish teaching that the offender must repent, apologise, and make reparation for the wrong done. It is then the duty of the injured party to forgive him. The finest statement of the doctrine is in the *Testaments of the XII Patriarchs*, Gad 6[3-7]: 'Love ye one another from the heart; and if a man sin against thee, speak peaceably to him, and in thy soul hold not guile; and if he repent and confess, forgive him. . . . But if he be shameless and persisteth in his wrong-doing, even so forgive him from the heart, and leave to God the avenging.' ' Seven times ' is a round number. Cf. Gen. 4[15]; Lev. 26[21]; Prov. 24[16]. The taking of vengeance seven-fold represents the stage of desert justice anterior to the *lex talionis*—an eye for an eye, a life for a life. In this verse and the following we have a reminiscence of this old law of vengeance. In Gen. 4[24] the song of Lamech runs:

> If Cain shall be avenged seven-fold,
> Truly Lamech seventy and seven-fold.

The blood-feud is to be carried on without mercy and without limit. The reply of Jesus in *v.* 22 says: Just as in those old days there was no limit to hatred and vengeance, so among Christians there is to be no limit to mercy and forgiveness. At what period the 77-fold vengeance of Lamech $(70 + 7)$ became $70 \times 7 = 490$-fold is not clear; but it already appears in the *Testament of Benjamin*, chap. 7, and may be regarded as pre-Christian. It is possible that R.V. mg. is right in translating the Greek ' seventy times and seven '; but no good parallel is quoted for such a construction of the Greek, and the early versions are in favour of 70×7.

3. THE PARABLE OF THE UNMERCIFUL STEWARD (136)

MT. 18[23-35]

18 23 Therefore is the kingdom of heaven likened unto a certain king, which would make a reckoning with his [1] servants. 24 And when he had begun to reckon, one was brought unto him, which owed him 25 ten thousand [2] talents. But forasmuch as he had not *wherewith* to pay, his lord commanded him to be sold, and his wife, and children, and all that he had, and 26 payment to be made. The [3] servant therefore fell down and worshipped him, saying, Lord, have patience with me, 27 and I will pay thee all. And the lord of that [3] servant, being moved with compassion, released him, and forgave him 28 the [4] debt. But that [3] servant went out, and found one of his fellow-servants, which owed him a hundred [5] pence: and he laid hold on him, and took *him* by the 29 throat, saying, Pay what thou owest. So his fellow-servant fell down and besought him, saying, Have patience with me, and 30 I will pay thee. And he would not: but went and cast him into prison, till he 31 should pay that which was due. So when his fellow-servants saw what was done, they were exceeding sorry, and came and told unto their lord all that 32 was done. Then his lord called him unto him, and saith to him, Thou wicked [3] servant, I forgave thee all that debt, 33 because thou besoughtest me: shouldest not thou also have had mercy on thy fellow-servant, even as I had mercy on 34 thee? And his lord was wroth, and delivered him to the tormentors, till he 35 should pay all that was due. So shall also my heavenly Father do unto you, if ye forgive not every one his brother from your hearts.

[1] Gr. *bondservants*.
[2] This talent was probably worth about £240.
[3] Gr. *bondservant*.
[4] Gr. *loan*.
[5] The word in the Greek denotes a coin worth about eight pence halfpenny.

The parable is introduced here, as the introductory ' therefore ' shows, in order to illustrate the point made in *vv.* 21 f. This it does not quite do. For the point of *v.* 22 is not merely that one should be ready to forgive, but that one should be ready to forgive again and again. The point of the parable is just that one must be ready to forgive; and there is nothing in the parable about repeated forgiveness. It may therefore be assumed that the connexion of the parable with the saying is one which has been made in the tradition or by Mt. himself. The parable itself emphasises a characteristic feature in the teaching of Jesus—that only a forgiving spirit can receive forgiveness, that a mean and revengeful disposition shuts out God's forgiveness, that the wrath of God is kindled against the hard and relentless more than against the weak and foolish.

23, 24, 25, 26 f. ' A certain king,' lit. ' a man a King,' i.e. a human king in contrast to the divine King. The servants are probably not slaves or domestic servants but government officials. The term would cover court officials or ministers of state, and provincial governors, as well as people in lower positions. These persons are all to present their accounts to be audited. One shows a deficiency of ten thousand talents, a colossal sum equivalent to about two million pounds. The exaggeration may well be deliberate in order to heighten the contrast with the hundred pence of *v.* 28. Otherwise it might be conjectured that the numerical signs for 10 and 10,000 have been confused, and that originally the debt amounted to 10 talents, about £2,000. If the debt amounted to two millions, the sale of the debtor and his family would not suffice for ' payment to be made.' For the enslavement of children through the insolvency of the father cf. 2 Kings 4[1]; Neh. 5[5]; Is. 50[1]. In Jewish law the wife is not sold into slavery; but if the husband is so sold, the wife may accompany him into bondage. The debtor asks for time to pay. The king goes far beyond this request by cancelling the whole debt. The word translated ' debt ' means literally ' loan ' (R.V. mg.). This may perhaps mean that the debtor had been working with capital lent for that purpose by his master; cf. 25[14 ff.] His deficiency could then be regarded as embezzlement. See on *v.* 30.

28, 29, 30. In sharp contrast to the generosity of the king is the subsequent behaviour of the steward. The fellow-servant is presumably a ' colleague ' in the royal service as in Ezra 4[9, 17, 23], etc. The amount of the debt is trifling in comparison with that which the king has just cancelled. A hundred ' pence ' would hardly amount to £4. The drastic method of debt-collecting adopted here may be illustrated from the Mishnah (*Baba Bathra* 10[8], Danby, p. 382): ' If a man seized a debtor by the throat in the street . . .' The debtor asks for time to pay in much the same terms as were employed by his creditor a short time before. But his entreaties are in vain. He is not sold into slavery but imprisoned till the debt be paid. On imprisonment for debt, see Deissmann, *Light from the Ancient East*, p. 267. In Jewish law an Israelite could sell himself into slavery if he could not make a living as a free man, or he could be sold by order of the Court if he was convicted of theft and had not property sufficient to replace what he had stolen. But he could not be sold if he had stolen less than his own value in the slave-market (Billerbeck, iv. 698 ff.). Presumably, therefore, it was not in the power of the creditor here to sell his debtor. No doubt it is to be understood that the imprisonment of the debtor follows on legal action by the creditor; cf. Mt. 5²⁵ᶠ·.

31, 32 f., 34. The other servants are ' exceeding sorry.' The same expression occurs in Mt. 17²³, and in the LXX Neh. 5⁶; Jonah 4⁴, ⁹, where the Greek verb translates a Hebrew verb meaning ' to burn with anger.' It is therefore probable that the servants were not so much distressed at the fate of the debtor as indignant at the disgraceful behaviour of the creditor. Consequently they do not raise a subscription to pay the debt but go and reveal what has happened to the king. The king shares their opinion and takes immediate action against the unmerciful steward. ' Thou wicked servant ': cf. Mt. 25²⁶; Lk. 19²². The king had set an example of mercy which the steward ought to have followed. Without this example his conduct might have been understood: with it, it is inexcusable. So in the last resort the command that Christians are to be merciful rests upon the fact that God is merciful, and not upon considerations of expediency such as that mercy is the best policy (Lk. 6³⁶). The behaviour of the king sets the standard for his subjects. The king is angry at the hard-heartedness of the steward as he was not angry about the original debt. He hands the steward over to the ' tormentors ' (basanistæ); cf. Ecclus. 30³⁵ (33²⁷): ' Yoke and thong bow down the neck, And for an evil servant (there are) stocks and chastisements (basanoi).' The punishment is to continue till the original debt is wiped out. Doubtless the thought here is of punishment after death. If so, the idea of torment is present, but not the idea of eternal torment. Cf. Lk. 12⁵⁷⁻⁵⁹ (Q).

35. The moral of the tale. Even the saved are not safe; and a harsh and unforgiving disposition in a Christian puts him back to where he was before he became a Christian. The forgiveness demanded is ' from your hearts ' (cf. Is. 59¹³; Test. Gad 6⁷, quoted on 18²¹ᶠ· above). That is, it is not to be a mere form of words, but a genuine expression of sincere feeling; not forgiveness because forgiveness is a duty, but forgiveness as the natural self-expression of a merciful and forgiving disposition.

The discourse closes with the customary Matthæan formula.

MT. 19¹

19 1 And it came to pass when Jesus had finished these words, he departed from Galilee, and came into the borders of Judæa beyond Jordan.

G. SERVICE AND REWARD

This section consists of three pieces, Mt. 19¹⁰⁻¹², 19²⁸, and 20¹⁻¹⁶. The first is appended to the Marcan pericope on divorce (Mk. 10²⁻¹²‖Mt. 19¹⁻⁹); the second is inserted into the Marcan context (Mt. 19¹⁶⁻³⁰‖Mk. 10¹⁷⁻³¹); the third is inserted between two Marcan sections (Mk. 10¹⁷⁻³¹‖Mt. 19¹⁶⁻³⁰ and Mk. 10³²⁻³⁴‖Mt. 20 ¹⁷⁻¹⁹).

1. MARRIAGE AND CELIBACY (187)

MT. 19¹⁰⁻¹²

19 10 The disciples say unto him, If the case of the man is so with his wife, it is not 11 expedient to marry. But he said unto them, All men cannot receive this saying, 12 but they to whom it is given. For there are eunuchs, which were so born from their mother's womb: and there are eunuchs, which were made eunuchs by men: and there are eunuchs, which made themselves eunuchs for the kingdom of heaven's sake. He that is able to receive it, let him receive it.

10, 11, 12. This passage is added at the end of the section in which Jesus has stated the true ideal of marriage as a Divine ordinance and deprived the husband of the power to divorce his wife. (See notes on Lk. 16[18] (Q), above, pp. 136 ff.) The upshot of this teaching is to strip the husband of all the onesided privileges which were his under the Jewish law. That being so, it is possible to explain *v.* 10, though not in any sense that is creditable to the disciples. For if *v.* 10 refers back to the foregoing teaching, it can only mean that the disciples say to Jesus: ' If that is your idea of marriage, we prefer to remain unmarried '; and it is somewhat hard on the disciples to have to suppose that they were not only spiritually blind but also insolent. There remain two possibilities. Either *v.* 10 is the composition of Mt. for the purpose of making the transition from the sayings on marriage to that on celibacy. In that case ' this saying ' in *v.* 11 must point forward to *v.* 12. Or, what is perhaps more probable, we have in *vv.* 10–12 the conclusion of a passage, and what preceded *v.* 10 is lost. Comparison of this passage with 1 Cor. 6[12]–7[40] would suggest that it may have been a saying pointing out the possibility of a clash between the claims of matrimony and the claims of the Kingdom. (Cf. Lk. 9[59-62]||Mt. 8[21f.]; Lk. 14[26f.]||Mt. 10[37f.].) The reply of the disciples would then be the perfectly sensible one that such a clash of loyalties, with its possibilities of acute suffering, can be avoided by not marrying at all. ' This saying,' in *v.* 11, will then refer to the disciples' suggestion. Jesus says in effect: Celibacy all round would solve the problem; but celibacy all round is not practicable. The suggestion is well enough for those who can accept it; but there are many who cannot embrace a celibate life—a fact which Paul recognises in 1 Cor. 7. There are, however, those for whom the celibate life is the natural and inevitable thing. There are those for whom marriage in the full sense is an impossibility for physical reasons: either because they are ' eunuchs from their mother's womb,' i.e. sexually impotent from birth; or because they have been ' made eunuchs by men,' i.e. rendered sexually impotent by a surgical operation. This distinction is recognised in the Rabbinical treatment of the subject (Billerbeck, i. 805 f.) There is yet a third class—those who have ' made themselves eunuchs for the kingdom of heaven's sake.' Does this mean that they have voluntarily submitted to an operation whereby they become sexually impotent, or does it mean simply that they have voluntarily embraced a life of celibacy? The following considerations favour the latter alternative. (1) The whole sentiment of Judaism was against castration. The eunuch was disqualified for membership of the community (Deut. 23[1]). A Jew simply would not understand how this operation could serve the ends of the Kingdom of God. (2) The word ' eunuch ' and the abstract noun derived from it appear in early Christian literature with the sense, unknown to classical or Hellenistic Greek, of ' celibate ' and ' celibacy ' respectively. The classic example is Clement of Alexandria's definition (*Paed.* III, 4, 26): ' The true eunuch is not he who cannot but he who will not indulge himself.' (3) There is no evidence that Jesus had any sympathy with asceticism for asceticism's sake. He requires—and makes—the greatest sacrifices for the sake of the Kingdom. If the Kingdom requires the sacrifice of the happiness of marriage, the sacrifice is to be made. Self-mutilation cannot add anything to the fullness of such sacrifice. (4) The literal sense is as inappropriate here as it is in Mk. 9[43-48] and

Mt. 5²⁹ᶠ· (see notes, above, p. 157). (5) Jesus, John the Baptist, Paul, and probably some of the Twelve were unmarried; others of the Twelve sacrificed their home-life for the sake of the Kingdom. But that was all. There is no word of any becoming eunuchs in the literal sense of the word. The conclusion is that the three classes of eunuchs in this verse fall into two. The first class comprehends those who cannot marry; the second those who can but do not, who sacrifice their happiness, but not their manhood, for the sake of the Kingdom of God.

There is an excellent account of the early exegesis of this difficult passage by Bauer in the Heinrici *Festschrift*, pp. 234–244.

2. THE REWARD OF THE TWELVE (189)

MT. 19²⁸

19 28 And Jesus said unto them, Verily I say unto you, that ye which have followed me, in the regeneration when the Son of man shall sit on the throne of his glory, ye also shall sit upon twelve thrones, judging the twelve tribes of Israel.

28. This saying is introduced into the Marcan context between the question of Peter (Mk. 10²⁸∥Mt.19²⁷) and the answer of Jesus (Mk. 10²⁹∥Mt.19²⁹). It has a parallel in Lk. 22²⁸⁻³⁰; but verbal agreement between the two is confined to the closing words of the saying. It is therefore most probable that Mt. 19²⁸ belongs to M and Lk. 22²⁸⁻³⁰ to L. Cf. Streeter, *The Four Gospels*, p. 288. We may also compare the promise in Rev. 3²¹: He that overcometh, I will give to him to sit down with me in my throne, as I also overcame, and sat down with my Father in his throne '; cf. 20⁴; 2 Tim. 2¹¹ᶠ·.

' Ye which have followed me,' as the reference to twelve thrones shows, must be the twelve close companions of Jesus as distinct from the general body of those who heard and responded to His preaching. The original answer to Peter's question as given in Mk. 10²⁹ᶠ· contains no such restriction to the Twelve. The ' regeneration ' (*palingenesia*) is a technical term in Stoic philosophy, where it signifies the beginning of a new cycle in the cosmic process. But not new in the strict sense, for each new cycle is just a repetition of the old. ' Stoicism held that the whole universe, which had come into being by condensation out of the Divine Fire, would one day be resolved again into the Divine Fire, but that then, after a period, another universe, just like the present one, would be formed, run a precisely similar course, and be reabsorbed into the Fire, and so on, world after world for ever' (E. Bevan, *Christianity*, p. 11). The Jewish expectation was different. They also expected the end of the existing order and the beginning of a new one. But the new order would be really new and not a mere repetition of what had gone before. It would really be the second volume of the history of the world and not a reprint of volume one. So ' regeneration ' or *palingenesia* in a Jewish or Jewish-Christian context means a new era that is really new, a new creation. Jewish views as to how this would happen differed considerably (Billerbeck, iii. 840 ff.). For some it meant a radical transformation of the existing world; for others it meant that the present world would revert to the condition described in Gen. 1², and that out of this formless mass God would create a new world;

for others again it meant that the existing world would be completely abolished and that God would create a new world absolutely *de novo*. The important thing is that it will be a new era that is new.

In this new age the Son of Man will ' sit on the throne of his glory.' The expression occurs again in Mt. 25³¹. The ' throne of glory ' is properly God's throne. In the Rabbinical view it is one of the things which were created before the world; and its place is in the seventh heaven. The notion that anyone except God could sit on this throne is foreign to Jewish thought, with one exception— the so-called *Similitudes of Enoch*. So *Enoch* 45³: ' On that day Mine Elect One shall sit on the throne of glory and shall try their works, and their places of rest shall be innumerable.' Cf. 51³: ' And the Elect One shall in those days sit on My throne '; 55⁴, 61⁸, 62²⁻⁵, 69²⁷. The Lucan version of the saying has nothing of this, but: ' I appoint unto you a kingdom, even as my Father appointed unto me.'

' Ye also shall sit upon twelve thrones.' Bultmann and others regard this promise as put into the mouth of the Risen Lord by the primitive Christian community. But it is hard to see how the primitive Church could have invented a saying which promises a throne, amongst others, to Judas Iscariot. The saying surely belongs to a much earlier period, before the treachery of Judas was suspected, much less known. ' Judging ' may be taken in the literal sense, in which case the saying means that the Twelve are to be assessors at the Last Judgement (cf. Mt. 25³¹ff.; 1 Cor. 6³). Or the word may be taken in the wider sense, common in the Old Testament, of ' ruling,' ' administering ' (cf. 1 Sam. 8⁵; *Ps. Sol.* 17²⁸: ' And he (the Messiah) shall gather together a holy people, whom he shall lead in righteousness; and shall judge (= rule) the tribes of the people that hath been sanctified by the Lord his God.'). The former sense seems, on the whole, to be intended here; and the latter sense in the Lucan version of the saying. This suggests that there was doubt in the early Church as to the correct interpretation of what was meant by sitting on twelve thrones judging the twelve tribes of Israel. It is also uncertain what is meant by the twelve tribes of Israel: whether the words are to be taken literally as meaning the Jewish people, or metaphorically for the spiritual Israel, the Church. (Rev. 7⁴⁻⁸; Rom. 2²⁹; Gal. 3²⁹, 6¹⁶; Phil. 3³; 1 Pet. 1¹; James 1¹; Hermas, *Sim.* 9¹⁷.)

In the Rabbinical literature we find the idea that the righteous Israelites are to assist in the final Judgement (Billerbeck, iv. 1103 f.). This view is based on the text Dan. 7⁹ ' I beheld till thrones were placed, and one that was ancient of days did sit.' The plural ' thrones ' is taken as meaning that God will have assessors at the Judgement. This interpretation may perhaps underlie the Septuagint version of Dan. 7²², where it is said that God ' gave the judgement (*krisin*) to the saints of the Most High ' (cf. *Wisdom* 3⁸). It is possible that some such meaning as this is the original meaning of this saying, in which case it would be in substantial agreement with the description of the Judgement in Mt. 25³¹ff.. But the saying is obscure and certainty is probably unattainable.

3   *THE PARABLE OF THE LABOURERS IN THE VINEYARD* (190)

MT. 20$^{1-16}$

20 1   For the kingdom of heaven is like unto a man that is a householder, which went out early in the morning to hire labourers 2 into his vineyard. And when he had agreed with the labourers for a ¹ penny a day, he sent them into his vineyard. 3 And he went out about the third hour, and saw others standing in the market- 4 place idle; and to them he said, Go ye also into the vineyard, and whatsoever is right I will give you. And they went 5 their way. Again he went out about the sixth and the ninth hour, and did like- 6 wise. And about the eleventh *hour* he went out, and found others standing; and he saith unto them, Why stand ye here all 7 the day idle? They say unto him, Because no man hath hired us. He saith unto them, Go ye also into the vineyard. 8 And when even was come, the lord of the vineyard saith unto his steward, Call the labourers, and pay them their hire, beginning from the last unto the first.

9 And when they came that *were hired* about the eleventh hour, they received every 10 man a ¹ penny. And when the first came, they supposed that they would receive more; and they likewise received 11 every man a ¹ penny. And when they received it, they murmured against the 12 householder, saying, These last have spent *but* one hour, and thou hast made them equal unto us, which have borne the burden of the day and the ² scorching 13 heat. But he answered and said to one of them, Friend, I do thee no wrong: didst not thou agree with me for a 14 ¹ penny? Take up that which is thine, and go thy way; it is my will to give unto 15 this last, even as unto thee. Is it not lawful for me to do what I will with mine own? or is thine eye evil, because 16 I am good? So the last shall be first, and the first last.

¹ See marginal note on ch. xviii. 28.
² Or, *hot wind*.

In its present context this parable stands in sharp contrast to what has gone before. The promise of special pre-eminence to the Twelve is balanced by a strong affirmation of equality of reward in the Kingdom. The Twelve who have laboured with Jesus from the beginning of His Ministry will receive neither more nor less than any other disciple: and they may not expect or claim more. But if the parable be taken by itself, without reference to the context in which Mt. has placed it, other possible interpretations present themselves. For example, it may be regarded as an answer to the criticism that Jesus opened the Kingdom to the publicans and harlots. Cf. Mt. 21³¹: ' Verily I say unto you that the publicans and harlots go into the Kingdom of God before you.' Or, again, it may be taken as a sketch of the whole history of Israel (cf. Mk. 12¹⁻¹²). The sense will then be that the disciples of Jesus will receive the same reward as the patriarchs and prophets (cf. Lk. 13²⁸⁻³⁰ (Q), above, pp. 125 ff.). In any case, the essential point of the parable is that the rewards of the Kingdom are not measured by man's desert but by God's grace. At the same time, the parable cannot be made to support the thoroughgoing Pauline and Lutheran doctrine of salvation by grace alone. There is not a shadow of suggestion that those who have worked in the vineyard all day have not earned their wages. All that is asserted is that it is God's good pleasure to pay full wages to those who have earned less than full wages. The parable does not attack the idea of merit in general, but only the notion that some people, be they the ' Fathers ' or the Pharisees or the Apostles, have special merits which require special reward from God, and that others who have less to commend them ought to receive less from God. Indeed, the parable has nothing to do with the question of salvation by grace or works. It is concerned entirely with the question whether

there are distinctions within the Kingdom; and what it says is that the love of
God is such that He makes no such distinctions, but gives to all alike.

1 f. According to Jewish law a working day lasts from sunrise till the appearance of the stars at evening. A 'penny' is the Roman *denarius* equivalent to
about 8½*d*. But the purchasing power of money was greater then than now. A
good ox could be bought for 100 denars, a young bullock for 20, a ram for 8,
and a lamb for 4 (Mishnah, *Menachoth* 13⁸ ; Danby, p. 512). One denar per day
was considered a good wage. The great Hillel did manual labour for half that
sum; and R. Meir, who was an accomplished scribe, earned 2 denars a day as a
writer of documents.

If we may think of the parable as covering the whole history of Israel, we may
take these earliest workers to be the Fathers. Then perhaps the express stipula-
tion of the payment may be a reference to the Covenant between God and
Israel.

3 f., 5. The third hour is about 9 a.m. The market-place appears as the
resort of the unemployed. No scale of wages is agreed in the case of the men
hired on this occasion. They are promised a fair remuneration. The procedure
is repeated at the sixth hour (about noon) and the ninth hour (about 3 p.m.).
Is it fanciful to see in these successive excursions a reference to the summonses
issued to Israel from time to time through the prophets?

6 f. The last stage, about the eleventh hour (about 5 p.m.). On the interpretation suggested, the eleventh hour is the period of John the Baptist and Jesus
Himself. There are still many who have not found their places in the vineyard
—the publicans and harlots for whom there seemed to be no place there (?).
They also are taken in and given work to do.

8. The day comes to an end. It is the end of the present age. The time of
labour is ended and the time of reward has come. According to the Law
(Lev. 19¹³, Dt. 24¹⁴ᶠ·) the labourer was entitled to have his wages at the end of
the day's work. In this parable the actual payment is done not by the householder
himself, but by his steward. We may compare the description of the Judgement
in Mt. 25³¹ᶠᶠ·, where the verdicts and sentences are given not by God, but by the
Son of Man (see below, p. 249). The payment begins with the last employed.
It is possible that there was a view that those who survived till the Parousia
would have some sort of advantage over those who did not. Paul is at pains to
contradict such a view in 1 Thess. 5¹⁵ᶠ·.

9–12. Those who have worked for an hour receive a full day's pay.
Those who have worked for longer periods up to the full day receive the same,
though only those who have worked twelve hours are explicitly mentioned. They
feel that they are unjustly treated. If payment is at the rate of one denar for an
hour's work, surely they should get twelve denars. Alternatively they should get
what they bargained for, and the last-comers should get a twelfth of the amount.
It is not right that those who have put in so little work should be made equal
to those who have laboured so abundantly under the most trying conditions.
The 'scorching heat' is the midday heat: the 'hot wind' of the mg. is not in
place here. The objection of the labourers is based on human ideas of justice
between man and man.

13–15. The reply of the householder is based not upon these considerations, but upon his own generosity. So far as justice goes there is no ground for complaint. Those who worked all day received the full day's pay. What they call justice is really envy and covetousness. The 'evil eye' is a common Rabbinical name for a mean and envious disposition, as the 'good eye' is for a generous and unselfish character. If the master chooses to be generous he can be, for he has already been just. In giving extra to the late-comers he deprives the others of nothing to which they are entitled. They have their just payment: let them take it and go.

16. So human estimates are reversed. This closing comment does not fit the parable. For the essence of the parable is not that the last become first and the first last, but that such terms as first and last cease to have any meaning. This verse is probably a comment by the Evangelist. Cf. 19³⁰.

With all explanations made that can be made this parable leaves one with the sense that if we consider the services rendered by the various sets of workmen, the policy of the householder is neither strict justice nor sound economics. To this it can only be replied that it is fortunate for most of us that God does not deal with us on the basis of strict justice and sound economics. In the last resort the rewards of such poor service as men can give to the Kingdom are not an exact *quid pro quo*. They are an expression of God's love towards His servants; and God's love cannot be portioned out in quantities nicely adjusted to the merits of individuals. There is such a thing as the twelfth part of a denar. It was called a *pondion*. But there is no such thing as a twelfth part of the love of God.

On Jewish views of service and reward see Moore, *Judaism*, ii. 89–111; Montefiore, *Rabbinic Literature and Gospel Teachings*, pp. 285–299; Billerbeck, iv. 484–500.

H. THE REFUSERS

Cf. the Q passages collected under D2, above, pp. 124–130. The passages to be considered under this head are two parables: the Two Sons (21²⁸⁻³²), and the Marriage Feast (22¹⁻¹⁴). The former is peculiar to Mt.; the latter has a parallel in Lk. 14¹⁶⁻²⁴, which is assigned to Q. In addition to these there is a saying connected with the cleansing of the Temple (21¹⁴⁻¹⁶), which may be considered in this connexion; and a pair of comments, probably the Evangelist's own work (21⁴³, 22⁴⁰).

1. *THE OFFENCE OF ENTHUSIASM* (198)

MT. 21¹⁴⁻¹⁶

21 14 And the blind and the lame came to him 15 in the temple: and he healed them. But when the chief priests and the scribes saw the wonderful things that he did, and the children that were crying in the temple and saying, Hosanna to the son of David; they were moved with indigna- 16 tion, and said unto him, Hearest thou what these are saying? And Jesus saith unto them, Yea: did ye never read, Out of the mouth of babes and sucklings thou hast perfected praise?

With this passage we must compare Lk. 19[39f.] (L) where the enthusiasm of the crowd accompanying Jesus towards Jerusalem likewise comes under criticism:

LK. 19[39-40]

19 39   And some of the Pharisees from the multitude said unto him, Master, rebuke
40 thy disciples. And he answered and said, I tell you that, if these shall hold their peace, the stones will cry out.

The differences are considerable. In Lk. the incident takes place before the triumphal entry; in Mt. it comes after the cleansing of the Temple. In Mt. it is children who are full of enthusiasm; in Lk. the disciples. And the reply of Jesus in Mt. is quite different from that in Lk.

14, 15. The statement of this verse at once creates difficulties. For according to an ancient maxim the blind and the lame were excluded from the Temple. ' The blind and the lame shall not come into the house ' (2 Sam. 5[8], R.V. mg.). How this maxim was understood is made plain by the Septuagint rendering: ' The blind and the lame shall not enter into the house of the Lord.' This rule is confirmed in the Mishnah (*Hagigah* 1[1]; Danby, p. 211): ' All are subject to the command to *appear* [*before the Lord* (at the three great feasts)]; excepting a deaf-mute, an imbecile, a child, one of doubtful sex, one of double sex, women, slaves that have not been freed, a man that is lame or blind or sick or aged, and one that cannot go up [to Jerusalem] on his feet.' Cf. Acts 3[2, 8]. Further, Mk. records no healings in Jerusalem. This verse must consequently be regarded as untrustworthy. (See further, Dalman, *Sacred Sites and Ways*, pp. 288 ff.) The high priests and scribes take umbrage at the miracles and the shouting of the children. In Lk. it is ' some of the Pharisees ' who object to the clamour of the disciples. It is to be noted that when the priests and scribes complain to Jesus, they say nothing about the miracles, but complain only about the shouting. This is a further indication that the reference to the healings is an insertion into the story.

16. ' Hearest thou what these are saying? ' The implication is that Jesus ought to stop them. Their cries are seditious and revolutionary, calculated to lead to a breach of the peace. Besides, such behaviour in the Temple is far from reverent. If Jesus allows it to go on He must take responsibility for it. The answer of Jesus is ' Yes '—I do hear it and approve of it. This is fortified by an appeal to Scripture, Ps. 8[2]. This quotation agrees with the LXX ' Out of the mouth of babes and sucklings thou hast prepared praise for thyself,' against the Hebrew: ' Out of the mouth of babes and sucklings thou hast established strength.' This fact tells strongly against the authenticity of the saying, and suggests that the scripture quotation has ousted the original reply as given in Lk. 19[40]. The meaning of the quotation in this context is that the shouts of the children are by a kind of divine inspiration. Flesh and blood has not revealed to them that they should cry ' Hosanna to the son of David,' but the Father in heaven. Cf. Mt. 16[17]. See further on Lk. 19[39f.], below, pp. 318 f.

2. THE PARABLE OF THE TWO SONS (203)

MT. 21 [28-32]

21 28 But what think ye? A man had two sons; and he came to the first, and said, 29 [1] Son, go work to-day in the vineyard. And he answered and said, I will not: but afterward he repented himself, and 30 went. And he came to the second, and said likewise. And he answered and 31 said, I *go*, sir: and went not. Whether of the twain did the will of his father? They say, The first. Jesus saith unto them, Verily I say unto you, that the publicans and the harlots go into the 32 kingdom of God before you. For John came unto you in the way of righteousness, and ye believed him not: but the publicans and the harlots believed him: and ye, when ye saw it, did not even repent yourselves afterward, that ye might believe him.

[1] Gr. *Child*.

The passage falls into two parts: the parable proper and its meaning (28–31), and an explanation (32). The connexion between the two parts is artificial, for the explanation does not fit the parable. The religious authorities said 'No' to the call of John, and did not repent subsequently: the publicans and harlots said 'Yes,' and acted accordingly. Verse 32 has nothing to do with *vv.* 28–31, which form an independent and self-contained piece to be considered by itself.

Verses 28–31 present a very complicated textual problem, for they have come down to us in no fewer than three forms, each form supported by important manuscripts or versions. The three forms are as follows:

I. The first son says 'No' and repents: the second son says 'Yes' and does nothing. Who did the will of his father? The first.

II. The first son says 'No' and repents: the second son says 'Yes' and does nothing. Who did the will of his father? The second.

III. The first son says 'Yes' and does nothing: the second son says 'No' and repents. Who did the will of his father? The second.

I is the form adopted by Tischendorf and R.V. II is defended by Merx and Wellhausen. III is the text adopted by Westcott and Hort. There is no certain solution of the purely textual problem; but for the purposes of understanding the story the variations can be reduced to two: I and III against II. For I and III say the same thing in different words. They agree that it is the son who says 'No' and repents that does the father's will. Their version makes the priests and scribes condemn themselves. In II, on the other hand, the answer given is contrary to expectation. The son who says 'Yes' and does nothing is the one who does the father's will! Those who defend this text say that the priests and scribes see the point of the parable and deliberately give the wrong answer in order to avoid the inevitable application to themselves. The difficulty about this explanation is that Jesus goes on to make application as if they had given the right answer. This can only be met by arguing that the reply of Jesus is not the application of the parable but an outburst of indignation. The question whether the priests and scribes condemned themselves or not, which is the only question of interpretation, must remain an unsolved problem.

28–30. The words 'But what think ye?' link the parable on to the preceding section in Mt., in which the challenge to the authority of Jesus is met by the question about John's baptism: was it a divine institution or a human device

(Mt. 21²³⁻²⁷∥Mk. 11²⁷⁻³³)? The opening of the parable is similar to Lk. 15¹¹. The first son answers brusquely that he will not go. Afterwards he is sorry and goes. The father makes the same request to the other son. It has been argued against text III that the request to the second son is not necessary, if the first son has consented to go. But it would be a very small vineyard that had room only for one labourer. The second son answers very politely—in contrast to his brother— and does nothing further. The politeness is probably significant. The Greek word translated ' sir ' is the same that is translated ' Lord ' in Lk. 6⁴⁶: ' And why call ye me, Lord, Lord, and do not the things which I say? ' Cf. Mt. 7²¹.

31. The question is now put, and only one answer is possible to the question as put. For the question is who *did* the will of the father. The R.V. text (I) makes the priests and scribes give the correct answer. The reply of Jesus identifies the two sons. The son who first said ' No ' and then repented stands for the ' publicans and harlots,' the typical representatives of the immoral and irreligious section of the community. The other son is the type of the priests and scribes, or of that section of them that maintained the outward appearance of piety without any real devotion to the will of God. There are several points of contact here with Mt. 7²¹.

MT. 7²¹	MT. 21³⁰ f.
7 21 Not every one that saith unto me, *Lord, Lord,* shall *enter into the kingdom* of heaven; but he that *doeth the will of* my *Father* which is in heaven.	21 30 f. I go, *Sir.* Publicans and harlots *go into the kingdom* of God before you. Whether of the twain *did the will* of his *father?*

32. A separate saying which Mt. has made into a comment on the parable Actually it is a saying about John the Baptist with a parallel in Lk. 7²⁹ f.:

> 7 29 And all the people when they heard, and the publicans, justified God, being baptized with the baptism of John. But the Pharisees and the lawyers rejected for themselves the counsel of God, being not baptized of him.

' John came unto you in the way of righteousness ' means ' he came with the way,' i.e. he brought it and showed it to you. The way of righteousness is the demand for repentance and reformation which John preached. In Lk. it is called ' the counsel of God.' But John's message found no response among the religious leaders. His converts were drawn from the publicans and harlots (Mt.) or ' the people and the publicans ' (Lk.) And even the testimony of the amended lives of the outcasts was not enough to convince the priests and scribes that John was sent from God and had a message for them.

An Editorial Addition

MT. 21⁴³, [⁴⁴]

21 43 Therefore say I unto you, The kingdom of God shall be taken away from you, and shall be given to a nation bringing 44 forth the fruits thereof. ¹ And he that	falleth on this stone shall be broken to pieces: but on whomsoever it shall fall, it will scatter him as dust.
	¹ Some ancient authorities omit ver. 44.

43. This verse is probably to be regarded as an editorial comment of Mt., making the application of the parable of the Wicked Husbandmen. It has no parallel in Mk. or Lk., and it does not fit the parable itself. For the parable threatens the wicked husbandmen with destruction, not merely with dispossession. Further, *v.* 43 clashes with *v.* 45. After the very pointed explanation of the parable given in *v.* 43, it seems superfluous to say that the priests and Pharisees perceived that the parable was directed at them. The ' nation ' that is to succeed to the Kingdom is probably the Church, the new Israel.

44. This verse is generally regarded as an early interpolation into Mt. from Lk. 20[18]. It is omitted by several early authorities for the text; and it is out of place here. It ought to stand before *v.* 43. See on Lk. 20[18], below, p. 322.

3. THE PARABLE OF THE MARRIAGE FEAST (205)

MT. 22[1-14]

22 1 And Jesus answered and spake again 2 in parables unto them, saying, The kingdom of heaven is likened unto a certain king, which made a marriage feast for 3 his son, and sent forth his [2] servants to call them that are bidden to the marriage 4 feast: and they would not come. Again he sent forth other [2] servants, saying, Tell them that are bidden, Behold, I have made ready my dinner: my oxen and my fatlings are killed, and all things are 5 ready: come to the marriage feast. But they made light of it, and went their ways, one to his own farm, another to his 6 merchandise: and the rest laid hold on his [1] servants, and entreated them shame- 7 fully, and killed them. But the king was wroth; and he sent his armies, and destroyed those murderers, and burned their 8 city. Then saith he to his [1] servants, The wedding is ready, but they that were 9 bidden were not worthy. Go ye therefore unto the partings of the highways, and as many as ye shall find, bid to the 10 marriage feast. And those [1] servants went out into the highways, and gathered together all as many as they found, both bad and good: and the wedding was 11 filled with guests. But when the king came in to behold the guests, he saw there a man which had not on a wedding- 12 garment: and he saith unto him, Friend, how camest thou in hither not having a 13 wedding-garment? And he was speechless. Then the king said to the [2] servants, Bind him hand and foot, and cast him out into the outer darkness; there shall be 14 the weeping and gnashing of teeth. For many are called, but few chosen.

[1] Gr. *bondservants.*   [2] Or, *ministers.*

The first part of the parable (*vv.* 1–10) corresponds to Lk. 14[15-24] (see above, pp. 128 ff.). Verses 11–14 are peculiar to Mt. They are best explained as part of another parable which Mt. has appended to *vv.* 1–10. But when we consider *vv.* 1–10, it is quite impossible to make a consistent story of it. The most glaring example is in *vv.* 4 and 8. In *v.* 4 the feast is ready, and in *v.* 8 it is still ready, although in the meantime armies have been mobilised, a punitive expedition sent against the city, murderers executed, and the city burned. On the other hand *vv.* 1–10 have definite points of contact with Lk. 14[15-24]. These coincidences may be stated as follows: A man makes a feast. He sends for the guests, who will not come because they have other business to attend to. He cancels the original invitations and sends his servants to collect other guests from the streets. This is done and the feast takes place. The Matthæan story is shorter than the Lucan by the omission of the various excuses made by the first set of guests, and by giving only one expedition of the servants to collect new guests. The foundation of the Mt. parable is thus an abbreviated version of what is given in Lk.

The extra material in Mt. may now be considered. The feast is a marriage feast given by a king for his son. Servants are twice sent out to invite the guests. The first set are sent, it seems, to invite the guests before the feast is actually prepared. The second set go out when the feast is ready (as in Lk.); but the words of their message are peculiar to Mt. The servants are maltreated and killed. The king is angry and punishes the murderers.

Two explanations of this extra material are possible: interpolation or conflation. Against interpolation is the fact that when the supposed interpolations are put together they make the outline of a parable similar to Mk.'s parable of the Wicked Husbandmen (Mk. 12¹⁻¹²). It is therefore more probable that we have to do with the conflation of the original Q parable of the Great Feast with another parable of the same kind as Mk. 12¹⁻¹². Cf. *The Teaching of Jesus*, pp. 83–86.

1. The words ' He spake in parables unto them ' are characteristic of Mk. ' In parables,' Mk. 3²³, 4², ¹¹, 12¹.

2. The marriage feast for the king's son is a figure for the Messianic age with all its joys. Cf. Moore, *Judaism*, ii. 363 ff.; Rev. 19⁹; 4 *Ezra* 2³⁸⁻⁴¹.

3 f. The twofold invitation is peculiar to Mt. We are told that it is still the custom in the East to issue a preliminary invitation to the guests, followed by a second when the feast is ready. If the detail may be pressed the first invitation will correspond to the mission of the great prophets, the second to that of Jesus and the Apostles. The invited guests are then the recalcitrant Jews. They reject both invitations. The plural ' servants ' in both cases, as against Lk.'s ' servant ' will correspond to the prophets and Apostles (both plural). For the terms of the message in v. 4 cf. Prov. 9¹⁻⁶. ' All things are ready ': R. Akiba used to say, ' All is made ready for the banquet ' in the world to come (*Aboth* 3¹⁶ ; Danby, p. 452). Cf. Rev. 19¹⁷.

5. This verse appears to summarise what is given in Lk. 14¹⁸f..

6. Who are ' the rest '? The abrupt introduction of these persons suggests that we have here a change of sources. It may be surmised that the original parable told how the guests set upon the servants. But Mt. following the Q parable in v. 5 has already described the behaviour of the guests in that story. In the Q story the guests merely decline to come: in the M story they maltreat the messengers. Mt. adopts the simplest expedient. In the new composite parable some of the guests simply decline and ' the rest ' maltreat the servants and kill them. Cf. Mt. 23²⁹⁻³⁶, 5¹⁰⁻¹².

7. This verse is commonly taken to be an interpolation by the Evangelist, a prophecy after the event, referring to the downfall of Jerusalem in A.D. 70; but the statement is in quite general terms and is in agreement with such passages as Lk. 13³⁴f. (Q); Mk. 12⁹, etc. The explanation that it is the continuation of v. 6, from another parable, is to be preferred.

8 f. Mt. now returns to the parable of the Feast as told in Q. These verses give in an abbreviated form what is told by Lk. in 14²¹⁻²⁴. ' They that were bidden were not worthy ' corresponds to Lk. 14²⁴: ' For I say unto you, that none of those men which were bidden shall taste of my supper.' ' The partings of the highways ' (Lat. *exitus uiarum*) may be the places where the main roads of the city issue into the country round about, or street-junctions within the city. As the city has already

been burned in *v.* 7, perhaps Mt. means us to understand that the servants are to collect the refugees as they escape from the catastrophe, the Jews who avoid the fate of their recalcitrant brethren and become Christians. Cf. Acts 2⁴⁰.

10. The wedding can now take place. The hall for the banquet is filled with guests. Here Lk.'s parable comes to an end; but Mt. has still more to add. There is to be a further sifting of the guests (11–14), and the way is prepared for this additional matter by the statement that the guests comprise 'both bad and good.' Cf. the parables of the Wheat and Tares (Mt. 13²⁴⁻³⁰) and the Net (13⁴⁷⁻⁵⁰).

11–14. The conclusion of Mt.'s parable is very similar to a parable of R. Johanan ben Zakkai on the necessity of timely repentance. The Jewish parable is as follows (*Shabb.* 153ᵃ): ' Like a king who invited his servants to a feast, and did not specify a time for them. The astute ones among them adorned themselves and sat at the gate of the palace. They said, " There is no lack in the palace " (consequently the feast may begin at any time). The foolish ones among them went to their work. They said, " There is no feast without preparation " (consequently it will not occur immediately). Suddenly the king asked for his servants. The astute ones among them came into his presence as they were, adorned; and the foolish ones came into his presence as they were, dirty. The king was pleased with the astute ones and angry with the foolish ones. He said, " Let these who adorned themselves for the feast sit down and eat and drink. Let those who did not adorn themselves for the feast stand and look on." ' The moral is that men should live in this world in such a way that they may always be ready for the next.

11. The king comes in to ' behold ' the guests. The Greek verb probably means no more than ' look in on ' in the sense ' visit.' Cf. Rom. 15²⁴. He finds a man without a wedding-garment. The question may be asked: how could people just brought in at a moment's notice be expected to be dressed for the feast? This difficulty is sometimes met by the supposition that wedding-garments were issued to hastily invited guests as they entered the feast. But the complaint against the offender in *v.* 12 is not that he refused a wedding-garment but that he came in without one. Nor is this the only inconsistency. In *v.* 10 we are told that both good and evil persons were brought into the feast. But here we have only one guest who is to be expelled from the company. Why only one? It cannot be for the sake of the dialogue, for the offender when questioned has nothing to say. One is tempted to surmise that the one man of the parable is meant for some one person—a Judas, or (if party feeling ran high enough) a Paul? As early as Irenæus the wedding-garment is understood to signify works of righteousness.

12. The guest when taxed with his discourtesy is ' speechless.' The Greek verb here is a strong one used elsewhere of ' muzzling ' an animal.

13. The king turns to the servants (the Greek word used here is different from that in *vv.* 1–10) ·and commands them to bind the offender hand and foot and cast him into the outer darkness. An early form of the text (D, old Latin, old Syriac, Irenæus) reads : ' Take him up by the hands and feet, etc.' The binding hand and foot would be in place if the ' outer darkness ' is another name for Hell. If, however, the offender is merely to be excluded from the feast, the latter reading might be preferred. The ' outer darkness ' is a phrase peculiar to Mt. (8¹², 22¹³, 25³⁰). In Jewish literature ' darkness ' appears to stand for

Gehenna. Cf. *Enoch* 103$^{5-8}$: ' Woe to you, ye sinners, when ye have died. . . . Into darkness and chains and a burning flame where there is grievous judgement shall your spirits enter.' Also *Ps. Sol.* 14^6, 15^{11}; *Orac. Sib.* 4^{43}; Rabbinical parallels in Billerbeck, iv. 1076 ff. It is probable that Mt.'s ' outer darkness ' means the same, and that the binding is part of the picture. ' There there shall be weeping and gnashing of teeth ' is a characteristic refrain in Mt. (8^{12}, 13$^{42, 50}$, 22^{13}, 24^{51}, 25^{30}). It occurs once in Lk. (13^{28} Q); see notes above, p. 125. Whether we are meant to think of this refrain as the remark of the king or of Jesus or of Mt. is not clear.

14. This verse does not fit with what has just preceded. For in *vv.* 11-14 many are called, and all but one are chosen. Nor does it fit with *vv.* 1-10; for there many are called and none are chosen. It can be made to fit the whole composition, *vv.* 1-14, since out of all who are invited at various times only a part sit down to the banquet in the end. This shows that the verse is a comment added by the Evangelist who put the separate parables together. Whether it is a genuine saying of Jesus or not cannot be surely determined. It agrees with a good deal of His other teaching to this extent at least, that He has occasion to lament the fact that there are only too many who are called and will not hear the call. There are Jewish parallels to the saying in 4 *Ezra* 8^3: ' Many have been created, but few shall be saved '; 9^{15}: ' There are more who perish than shall be saved.' Cf. *Apoc. Baruch* (Syr.) 44^{15}.

Editorial Comment (208)

MT. 22^{40}

In the section 22$^{34-40}$ Mt. is following the corresponding section in Mk. 12$^{28-34}$, the question about the greatest commandment. He records the answer of Jesus that the first commandment of all is to love God, and the second to love one's neighbour. After giving this answer Mk. continues (12^{31b}): ' There is none other commandment greater than these.' He then goes on to tell of further conversation between Jesus and the enquirer (12$^{32ff.}$). Mt. drops *vv.* 32-34 entirely, and for Mk. 12^{31b} substitutes a conclusion of his own:

22 40 On these two commandments hangeth the whole law, and the prophets.

The Marcan conclusion asserts that no other commandment can take precedence of these two. That is, these two stand in a class by themselves. Mt.'s conclusion says something different, that these two commandments are the fundamental principles upon which all other commandments in Scripture are based. Mt. thus tacitly excludes the possibility of a clash between the two great commandments and the rest, whereas Mk. reckons with such a possibility and declares how it is to be decided. The Marcan version is the more original of the two: the Matthæan alteration is dictated by Jewish-Christian reverence for the Law.

I. THE SPEECH AGAINST PHARISAISM (210)

On the Q version of this speech (Lk. 11$^{37-52}$) see above, pp. 94-105. There it is argued that the greater part of the material in Mt. 23 is derived from M, though something has been added from both Mk. and Q. The last verses of the chapter (37–39) are undoubtedly from Q; and *v.* 23 is also probably from this source. There has been conflation of M and Q in other verses. Again, *vv.* 6–7 appear to be borrowed from Mk. 12³⁸ ᶠ·. But the backbone of the chapter is M. The chapter may be divided as follows: (1) Denunciation of the pride and hypocrisy of scribes and Pharisees (1–7). (2) Warning to the disciples not to be like them (8–12). (3) Seven woes against the scribes and Pharisees (13–36). Prophecy concerning Jerusalem (37–39).

1. *DENUNCIATION OF SCRIBES AND PHARISEES*

MT. 23¹⁻⁷

23 1 Then spake Jesus to the multitudes and 2 to his disciples, saying, The scribes and the 3 Pharisees sit on Moses' seat: all things therefore whatsoever they bid you, *these* do and observe: but do not ye after their 4 works; for they say, and do not. Yea, they bind heavy burdens ¹ and grievous to be borne, and lay them on men's shoulders; but they themselves will not 5 move them with their finger. But all their works they do for to be seen of men: for they make broad their phylacteries, and 6 enlarge the borders *of their garments*, and love the chief place at feasts, and the chief 7 seats in the synagogues, and the salutations in the marketplaces, and to be called of men, Rabbi.

¹ Many ancient authorities omit *and grievous to be borne.*

1. The opening part of the speech is addressed to the general public and the disciples. It is not spoken to the scribes and Pharisees but at them. Only at *v.* 13 does direct address to the religious leaders begin. Mk. 12³⁸ has: ' And in his teaching he said,' again speaking not to the scribes and Pharisees but to the general public. Mt.'s addition of the disciples is important. The rules laid down are to hold for the Church.

2. ' The scribes and Pharisees sit on Moses' seat.' This has hitherto been explained as a figure of speech, meaning that the scribes and Pharisees are the constituted authorities for determining the Law, just as Moses was in his day. They are the guardians of the tradition handed down from the days of Moses. Cf. *Aboth* 1¹⁻¹², where the chain of tradition is traced from Moses to Hillel and Shammai (Danby, pp. 446 f.). Recent archæological work in Palestine shows that the ' Seat of Moses ' was no mere figure of speech, but a part of the furniture of the Synagogue. " The first ' Seat of Moses ' was unearthed at Hammath-by-Tiberias, and was followed by another at Chorazin. We know that whereas the congregation sat on the stone benches that are still found along the side walls of many of the ancient synagogues, or else on mats on the floor, ' the elders' sat ' with their faces to the people and their backs to the Holy (i.e. to Jerusalem).' It was evidently for the most distinguished among ' the elders ' that the stone chair found *near the south wall* of the Hammath synagogue was reserved. This was no doubt ' the Seat of Moses ' " (E. L. Sukenik, *Ancient Synagogues in Palestine and Greece,* pp. 58 f., where a most interesting account of these seats (with illustrations) is given). The Seat of Moses is thus the visible tangible sign of the authority which the scribes and Pharisees enjoyed.

3. This authority is here recognised as binding upon the disciples, who might well feel embarrassed by the number of authorities established in M—Peter

(16[19]), the Church or the Twelve (18[18]), and now the scribes and Pharisees. It is hardly possible to believe that if Jesus said to the scribes and Pharisees: ' Ye leave the commandment of God, and hold fast the tradition of men ' and ' Ye reject the commandment of God that ye may keep your tradition ' (Mk. 7[8 f.]), He could also have set up the scribes and Pharisees as authorities for His disciples. ' Do not after their works,' i.e. do not be like them. ' They say and do not ' appears to be a proverbial expression in Aramaic (*Ber. Rabba* on Gen. 21[1], ed. Theodor, p. 555). The importance of ' doing ' the Law is stressed also by the Rabbis. Simeon, the son of Gamaliel, says: ' Not the expounding [of the Law] is the chief thing but the doing [of it] ' (*Aboth* 1[17], Danby, p. 447). R. Eleazar b. Azariah (*c.* 50–120) used to say: ' He whose wisdom is more abundant than his works, to what is he like? To a tree whose branches are abundant but whose roots are few; and the wind comes and uproots it and overturns it. . . . But he whose works are more abundant than his wisdom, to what is he like? To a tree whose branches are few but whose roots are many; so that even if all the winds in the world come and blow against it, it cannot be stirred from its place ' (*Aboth* 3[18], Danby, p. 452). The question continued to be a live issue in Judaism. ' R. Tarphon and the Elders were once sitting in an upper chamber in the house of Nitzah in Lydda; the following question was propounded before them: Which is the greater, study or practice? R. Tarphon answered and said: " Practice is the greater." R. Akiba answered and said: " Study is the greater." All [the others] answered and said: " Study is the greater, because study induces prac-tice " ' (*Kidd.* 40b). In the case of Akiba that was certainly true; and in many other cases besides. But there is clear evidence in the Rabbinical literature itself that study did not always induce practice. Neither in Judaism nor in any other religion is theological learning a guarantee of sanctity. And there was always the danger in Judaism—and not in Judaism only—that men would be so en-grossed in the *minutiæ* of the Law that they would have no time for the central principles which were its true *raison d'être*.

4. In Q (Lk. 11[46], above, p. 100) this verse appears as the first woe against the scribes. The Greek word translated ' grievous to be borne ' is omitted by many ancient authorities for the text of Mt. It may be an intrusion from Lk. 11[46]. The collocation ' heavy ' and ' hard to bear ' occurs in Prov. 27[3]. ' Move ' here probably = ' remove ' (cf. Rev. 2[5], 6[14]). See notes on Lk. 11[46] (above, p. 100) and Lk. 16[17] (above, p. 135). The charge against the scribes is that they are doctrinaire and conservative to the last degree. Precedents are more important to them than people.

5–7. These verses contain further charges, introduced by the statement that the scribes and Pharisees do all their works for show. Their ostentation is then described in terms which have a parallel in Mk. 12[38-40].

MK. 12[38-40]

12 38 And in his teaching he said, Beware of the scribes, which desire to walk in long robes, and *to have* salutations in the 39 marketplaces, and chief seats in the synagogues, and chief places at feasts: 40 they which devour widows' houses, and for a pretence make long prayers; these shall receive greater condemnation.

The common matter in the two accounts may be seen by a comparison in parallel columns.

MT.	MK.
(a) They make broad their phylacteries.	(1) They desire to walk in long robes.
(b) They enlarge the borders (of their garments).	(2) And (to have) salutations in the marketplaces.
(c) They love the chief place at feasts.	(3) And chief seats in the synagogues.
(d) And the chief seats in the synagogues.	(4) And chief places at feasts.
(e) And the salutations in the marketplaces.	(5) Who devour widows' houses.
(f) And to be called of men, Rabbi.	(6) And for a pretence make long prayers.

In these two lists there are obvious correspondences: (c), (d), (e) = (4), (3), (2). There are equally obvious differences: (f) has no parallel in Mk., and (5) has no parallel in Mt. The remaining cases are (a) and (b) in Mt. and (1) and (6) in Mk. It has been suggested that (a) and (6) really correspond (cf. Burney, *Aramaic Origin of the Fourth Gospel*, p. 10 n.; Abrahams, *Studies* ii. 203 ff.). This depends on the fact that the Late Hebrew and Aramaic name for phylacteries (*tephillin*) also means, in Hebrew, prayers. There is a similar ambiguity in the Aramaic word for ' broaden.' So it is argued that the Aramaic which means ' they make broad their phylacteries ' could be also translated ' they make long their prayers.' It is most probable that the version in Mt. gives the original sense of the saying. What, then, is meant by broadening the phylacteries? The phylactery consisted of: (a) a small leather box containing certain texts of the Old Testament written on parchment; (b) a leather strap to which this box was attached. Two phylacteries were worn, one on the head, the other on the left arm. (Full description in Billerbeck, iv. 250–276.) If ' make broad ' is to be taken in the literal sense it must mean broadening the strap. But not very much could be done in this way. Alternatively the enlarging of the phylacteries might be understood to mean increasing, not the phylacteries themselves, but the wearing of them. The time to wear phylacteries, in the Rabbinical ideal, is all day and every day except Sabbaths and Festivals. But exceptions were allowed in certain cases. What was regarded as absolutely essential was that the pious Jew should wear them at the time of his morning and evening devotions; and it is significant that the *Letter of Aristeas* (§ 158) and Josephus (*Ant.* iv. 212 f.) mention them in the same context as these daily devotions. Along with this goes the fact (Billerbeck, iv. 264) that the Rabbis found the general mass of the people unwilling to rise to their demands in the matter of wearing phylacteries. This suggests that originally the time for wearing them may have been the times of morning and evening prayer, and that it was the Rabbis who extended the wearing to all day. In that case it may be this extension that is criticised in our text.

There remain two counts in the indictment: (b) ' They enlarge the borders (of their garments) ' and (1) ' They desire to walk in long robes.' Again it is possible that these two are equivalent. The ' borders ' (*kraspeda*) are usually taken to be the tassels (*ṣiṣiōth*) ordained in the Law (Num. 15[38 ff.]; Dt. 22[12]). These tassels were to be fixed at the four corners of the rectangular shawl used as an outer garment (Billerbeck, iv. 277–292). As no maximum length was prescribed for these decorations, those who wished to make a display of piety might make the tassels as long as they pleased. The 'long robe' in Mk. (*stolē*) is the Jewish *tallīth*, the outer garment of all classes of the community. The scribe was distinguished from ordinary people by the voluminousness of his *tallīth*, and the way he wore it. Properly the time to wear this garment was at prayer, and in the performance of certain other duties of the scribes (Billerbeck, ii. 31 ff.). The Marcan passage complains that the scribe *walks about* in his *tallīth*. The Matthæan version says that he 'enlarges the borders.' This may mean that he lengthens the tassels; but it is much more naturally understood of the enlargement of the garment itself. The common root of Mt. and Mk. might then be a saying against those ostentatiously pious who loved to parade their voluminous prayer-shawls.

If these suggestions are correct, (*a*) and (*b*) and (1) and (6) belong together. They are a protest against the Rabbinic tendency to make the wearing of the phylacteries and the prayer-shawl a constant practice outside the set times for prayer; a protest against the idea that a man becomes specially devout by perpetually wearing the uniform of devotion. It is suggested that this going about continually dressed as if for prayer is a kind of hypocrisy.

It may be further concluded that (*a*) and (*b*) in Mt. have come by a line of tradition independent of Mk. That is, they are assigned to M. The next three items in Mt.—(*c*), (*d*), (*e*)—may be derived from Mk.

' The chief places at feasts ' were given, according to later Rabbinical rule, to the oldest guests. Precedence was by age. But the earlier practice gave precedence to the most learned. That precedence in banquets was highly esteemed is shown by Lk. 14[7-11]. On the ' chief seats in the synagogues ' see notes on *v.* 2, above, p. 228. ' Salutations in the marketplaces ': see notes on Lk. 11[43], above, p. 99. ' To be called of men, Rabbi ' may be regarded as a doublet of ' Salutations in the marketplaces.' It is the M equivalent of the Marcan phrase. Mt. has kept both the Marcan and M forms because the latter is necessary as the introduction to what follows in *v.* 8. ' Rabbi ' is an honorific form of address equivalent to ' Sir.' The nearest parallel in English usage is the custom of addressing judges of the High Court, when on the bench, as ' My Lord,' although they are not usually peers. Later the word becomes the regular title of the Palestinian teachers of the Law.

2. *WARNING TO THE DISCIPLES*

MT. 23[8-12]

23 8 But be not ye called Rabbi: for one is your teacher, and all ye are brethren. 9 And call no man your father on the earth: for one is your Father, [1] which is 10 in heaven. Neither be ye called masters: for one is your master, *even* the Christ. 11 But he that is [2] greatest among you shall 12 be your [3] servant. And whosoever shall exalt himself shall be humbled; and whosoever shall humble himself shall be exalted.

[1] Gr. *the heavenly.*
[2] Gr. *greater.*
[3] Or, *minister.*

8. There is no room in the community of the disciples for the distinctions used in Judaism. The use of the passive rather than the active voice of the verb is

significant. What is forbidden is not the desire to show respect to a brother, but the desire to have it shown to oneself by the brethren. Such titles are a danger because they can so easily produce spiritual pride. That is the practical consideration. There is further—and this is the vital matter—a fundamental objection in principle. The community knows no human authorities: God is the teacher. The idea goes back to the Old Testament and in particular to the prophetic literature and the Psalms. It appears in the terms of the New Covenant: ' I will put my law in their inward parts, and in their heart will I write it; and I will be their God, and they shall be my people: and they shall teach no more every man his neighbour, and every man his brother, saying, Know the Lord: for they shall all know me, from the least of them unto the greatest of them, saith the Lord ' (Jer. 31³³f·). ' And all thy children shall be disciples of Jehovah ' (Is. 54¹³).

9. ' Father ' (abba) as an honorific title belongs pre-eminently to the three patriarchs, Abraham, Isaac, and Jacob. Certain specially distinguished Rabbis are also called ' Fathers of the world,' e.g. Hillel and Shammai (Eduyoth 1⁴, Danby, p. 422). Further, the title Abba is prefixed to the names of a considerable number of first- and second-century Rabbis (Billerbeck, i. 919). And we have the principle in Sifre Dt. § 34: ' As the disciples are called ' Sons,' so the teacher (Rab) is called ' Father ' (Ab).' It is not certain how the saying is to be translated. Besides the R.V. rendering, the following is possible: ' Call no one of your number " Father " on earth.' ' Abba ' is the name for God, and is to be kept for Him. It is not to be given to members of the community. The words ' which is in heaven ' (R.V. mg. ' the heavenly ') are an unnecessary explanation by the Evangelist, who has also added the words ' on the earth ' to complete the picture. The original form of the saying was, I think: ' Call no one of your number " Father ": for one is your Father,' corresponding in form to v. 8. It is possible that the words ' And all ye are brethren,' at the end of v. 8, should stand at the end of v. 9; but the weight of MS. authority is against this change.

10. ' Masters ': the Greek word (kathēgētēs) occurs only here in the New Testament. It means in the first instance ' guide ' and then ' teacher ' ' instructor.' In Modern Greek it means ' professor.' Its meaning in the present context may be elucidated by the fact that Josephus and Philo respectively use the cognate words exēgētēs and hyphēgētēs when speaking of the Rabbis as interpreters of the Law. What Mt. means to say may therefore be that Christ is the sole interpreter of the will of God to men. And Jesus certainly appears in that capacity in Mt.'s Sermon on the Mount, particularly in Mt. 5¹⁷⁻⁴⁸ and 6¹⁻¹⁸. Many modern scholars reject v. 10 as a doublet of v. 8. It may be an attempt of Mt. or his source to find a place for Christ as an authority in the Church, seeing that vv. 8 f. refer to God alone. On the other hand, the Gospels are full of the authority with which Jesus taught, and there can be no doubt that He did claim the right to make known the will of God. It is therefore possible that v. 10 is a genuine saying of Jesus, except for the words ' the Christ,' which may be regarded as an explanatory comment.

11 f. These two verses have parallels elsewhere in the Gospels. They are brought in here as warnings against pride and rivalry within the community. With v. 11 cf. Mk. 9³⁵‖Lk. 9⁴⁸; Mk. 10⁴³f·‖Mt. 20²⁶f·; Lk. 22²⁶ (L?). In all these

cases the saying is the answer of Jesus to manifestations of personal ambition among His disciples. With *v.* 12 cf. Mt. 18⁴ (above, p. 207) Lk. 14¹¹, 18¹⁴ (below, pp. 279, 312). The saying, which is doubtless a genuine saying of Jesus, has excellent parallels in the Rabbinical literature: ' God will exalt him who humbles himself, God will humble him who exalts himself ' (*Erubin* 13ᵇ). Further examples in Montefiore (*op. cit.*, pp. 328 f.).

3. *THE WOES AGAINST SCRIBES AND PHARISEES*

(i) MT. 23¹³

23 13 But woe unto you, scribes and Pharisees, hypocrites! because ye shut the kingdom of heaven [1] against men: for ye enter not in yourselves, neither suffer ye them that are entering in to enter.[2]

[1] Gr. *before.*

[2] Some authorities insert here, or after ver. 12, ver. 14, *Woe unto you, scribes and Pharisees, hypocrites! for ye devour widows' houses, even while for a pretence ye make long prayers: therefore ye shall receive greater condemnation.* See Mark xii. 40; Luke xx. 47.

This corresponds to the third Q woe against the lawyers (Lk. 11⁵², above, p. 103). In spite of the difference of wording, the sense in both versions of the woe is the same. See the notes on Lk. 11⁵².

Some MSS. insert either before *v.* 13 or after it an additional woe based on Mk. 12⁴⁰. The uncertainty in the placing of this extra verse is a sign that it is an interpolation. It is omitted by the leading authorities for the text, and rejected by modern editors.

(ii) MT. 23¹⁵

23 15 Woe unto you, scribes and Pharisees, hypocrites! for ye compass sea and land to make one proselyte; and when he is

become so, ye make him twofold more a son of [1] hell than yourselves.

[1] Gr. *Gehenna.*

The outstanding characteristics of Judaism, in contrast to contemporary pagan religion, were its strong monotheism and its high ethical standard. Social and political factors made it impossible for these things to be hid from the Gentile nations. The Jews were scattered all over the civilised world of those days; and wherever they were present in sufficient numbers they founded a synagogue. These synagogues of the Dispersion became the centres of strong Jewish propaganda, and inevitably attracted to themselves thoughtful Gentiles, who had become disgusted with the old myths and felt that if a God was to be adored, he must first be respected and reverenced. The synagogues drew those who were perplexed and disquieted by the moral laxity of the age. In Judaism they found a God who was Himself holy, who also demanded holiness of His votaries; who was righteous, and required righteousness; who was merciful, and demanded mercy. The result was that the synagogues of the Dispersion gathered round themselves a fringe of earnest and thoughtful Gentiles who came to be known as the ' God-fearing ' (Gr. *Sebomenoi*; Lat. *Metuentes*). These people were not proselytes in the full sense. They were not members of the synagogue, but adherents, who worshipped the God of the Jews and tried to live up to the moral standards of Judaism. Full membership of the Jewish community required further steps to be taken. (1) The convert must be further instructed in the Jewish Law, and must accept it in its entirety. (2) A male convert must be circumcised. (3) All converts must submit to the proselyte bath. (4) The proselyte must offer sacrifice in the Temple at Jerusalem. Only a certain proportion of the God-fearers were prepared to take these final steps, and only those who did so were proselytes in the true sense of the word. The proselyte was thus a full Jew, and differed from other Jews in this only, that he was a Jew by conversion and not by birth. See Moore, *Judaism* i. 323–353; Juster, *Les Juifs dans l'Empire Romain* i. 253–290; Lake, *Beginnings of Christianity*, v. 74–96. Parkes, *The Conflict of the Church and the Synagogue*, pp. 23–26. The scribes and Pharisees make all efforts to obtain converts to Judaism.

' A son of Gehenna ' should naturally mean one who is destined for Genenna as ' son of the world to come ' means one who is destined for heaven. It may be supposed that, as is often the case, the converts tended to be even more zealous than their teachers, more Pharisaic than the Pharisees.

(iii) MT. 23[16-22]

23 16   Woe unto you, ye blind guides, which say, Whosoever shall swear by the [1] temple, it is nothing; but whosoever shall swear by the gold of the [1] temple, he
17 is [2] a debtor. Ye fools and blind: for whether is greater, the gold, or the [1] temple that hath sanctified the gold?
18 And, Whosoever shall swear by the altar, it is nothing; but whosoever shall swear by the gift that is upon it, he is [2] a debtor.
19 Ye blind: for whether is greater, the gift,
or the altar that sanctifieth the gift?
20 He therefore that sweareth by the altar, sweareth by it, and by all things thereon.
21 And he that sweareth by the [1] temple, sweareth by it, and by him that dwelleth
22 therein. And he that sweareth by the heaven, sweareth by the throne of God, and by him that sitteth thereon.

    [1] Or, *sanctuary*: as in ver. 35.
    [2] Or, *bound* by his oath.

This woe is peculiar to Mt. The passage falls into two parts (*vv.* 16–19 and 20–22). The first part is criticism of the distinctions made between oaths; the second a positive assertion that all the forms of oath used are, in the last resort, swearing by God. This latter part has points in common with Mt. 5[33-37].

16. ' Blind guides ': cf. Mt. 15[14], where the Pharisees are described as ' blind guides of the blind,' and Lk. 6[39], with notes, above, p. 57. The ' blind guides ' here take the place of the ' scribes and Pharisees ' of the other woes. It is possible that this passage was not a woe at all originally, but a piece of criticism which has been turned into a woe by Mt. or his source.

' Whosoever shall swear.' The Mishnah (*Nedarim* 1[3], Danby, p. 264) contradicts the statement in this verse. But the contradiction is only in appearance; for the Mishna is dealing with vows, and this passage is concerned with oaths. The vow and the oath are two quite distinct things, and are carefully distinguished in Jewish writings. The Greek verb translated ' swear ' in Mt. is used in the LXX to translate the Hebrew verb *shāba'*, ' to swear,' but *never* to translate the Hebrew *nādar*, ' to take a vow.' There does not appear to be any Rabbinical testimony either to confirm or to contradict the statements in Mt. 23[16, 18] concerning the validity of the various forms of oath there described. The gold of the temple might mean either the contents of the temple treasury or the golden utensils and decorations of the temple; probably the latter. The phrase ' it is nothing ' and ' he is a debtor ' signify ' the oath is not binding ' and ' the oath is binding ' respectively.

17. An oath 'by gold' is not binding: an oath 'by the gold of the temple' is. It is obvious that it is the temple that differentiates this gold from all other gold. The important thing is not that it is gold but that it is *temple* gold. That is, the temple matters more than the gold.

18 f. A similar case to that in *vv.* 16 f. There is nothing sacrosanct about a lamb or a bullock in itself. It acquires a certain sacredness by being laid upon the altar. So in the Mishnah (*Zebahim* 9¹, Danby, p. 481): 'The Altar makes holy whatsoever is prescribed as its due.' This again means that the altar is more important than the offering.

20. This verse goes with 21 f. The object of the two latter verses is to show that the mere fact that the name of God is not mentioned in taking an oath counts for nothing. The substitution of something else for the Divine name is an evasion, for all the time it is God who is thought of, though it is only something connected with God that is mentioned. That being so, it may be suspected that there is something wrong with *v.* 20. What we should expect is: ' He therefore that sweareth by the altar, sweareth by it, and by Him to whom offering is made thereon ' or something else to the same effect. There is no point in the verse as it stands; for it has just been argued in *vv.* 18 f. that the things offered on the altar have no significance apart from the altar. It may be conjectured that the original form of the saying had something like ' sweareth by it, and by Him that is above it,' i.e. by God.

21 f. The significance of the temple in an oath is that it is thought of as the temple of God, the place where God dwells. Similarly, heaven is significant as the throne of God. The temple as God's house and heaven as His throne are Old Testament ideas. See further the notes on Mt. 5³³⁻³⁷, above, pp. 158 f.

(iv) MT. 23²³⁻²⁴

23 23 Woe unto you, scribes and Pharisees, hypocrites! for ye tithe mint and ¹anise and cummin, and have left undone the weightier matters of the law, judgement, and mercy, and faith: but these ye ought to have done, and not to have left the 24 other undone. Ye blind guides, which strain out the gnat, and swallow the camel.

¹ Or, *dill.*

23. This verse has a parallel in Lk. 11⁴² (Q). On the relation of the two versions of the woe see above, pp. 97 f. In Mt.'s list of things tithed the mint probably comes from Q, and the dill and cummin from M. Mint was not liable to tithe; dill and cummin were. In that case the M form of the woe is a protest against the meticulous fulfilment of legal trifles, and the neglect of vital matters. The ' weightier matters ' are the more important matters. R. Judah the Patriarch said: ' Be heedful of a light precept as of a weighty one, for thou knowest not the recompense of reward of each precept ' (*Aboth* 2¹, Danby, p. 447). The three essentials, judgement, mercy, and faith, are reminiscent of the classical statement of prophetic religion in Mic. 6⁸: ' He hath showed thee, O man, what is good; and what doth the Lord require of thee, but to do justly, and to love mercy, and to walk humbly with thy God? ' Humble walking with God is just what in Judaism is meant by ' faith,' a combination of trustful obedience to God's commandments and humble confidence in His good promises. Such faith is the religious root of

the right relation to one's neighbour described as judgement and mercy. Faith puts man in the right relation to God; judgement and mercy put him in the right relation to his neighbour. And the exercise of judgement and mercy is, in a sense, an imitation of God; for the two great attributes of God in Jewish thought are the attributes of justice (*middath ha-dīn*) and the attribute of mercy (*middath hā-rachǎmīm*).

These, the weightier matters of the Law, you ought to have done, and not to have left the other, the lighter matters, undone. The tithing of dill and cummin was obligatory; but justice, mercy, and faith take precedence. The sentence appears in Lk. 11⁴² (Q), but is probably an interpolation there. (See notes, above, p. 98.) Here it is more in place; but it may be doubted whether it is a genuine word of Jesus. It is rather an editorial attempt to let the polemic of Jesus have its full effect against the scribes and Pharisees, and at the same time save the Law and the tradition from attack. Jesus must not appear to be antinomian, however strongly he may attack the lawyers.

24. ' Blind guides,' as in *v.* 16. The straining out of gnats refers to the practice of straining wine through a cloth or fine wicker basket (Mishnah, *Shabbath* 20ª, Danby, p. 117). It appears from the Talmud (*Chullin* 67ª) that an insect called by the Jews *Yabchush* was thus removed from the wine, and there is evidence that it was believed that this creature was generated in the dregs of wine and in the mass of pressed grapes in the wine-press (Bochart, *Opera*, iii. 562 ff.). The ground for filtering the wine so carefully is Lev. 11⁴¹: ' And every creeping thing that creepeth upon the earth is an abomination; it shall not be eaten.' But the camel also is an unclean beast (Lev. 11⁴). The saying then pillories the elaborate precautions taken in minor matters and the carelessness about big things. Like other sayings in the Gospels it is frankly hyperbolical.

Mt. 23²³ᶠ. differs from Lk. 11⁴² (Q) in this, that the latter is a charge against some hypocritical Pharisees that they do things not required by the Law in order to gain a reputation for great piety; while the charge in Mt. is that hypocritical scribes and Pharisees devote themselves to the minutiæ of the Law and neglect the more important matters.

(v) MT. 23²⁵⁻²⁶

23 25 Woe unto you, scribes and Pharisees, hypocrites! for ye cleanse the outside of the cup and of the platter, but within they are full from extortion and excess.

26 Thou blind Pharisee, cleanse first the inside of the cup and of the platter, that the outside thereof may become clean also.

This woe has a parallel in Lk. 11³⁹⁻⁴¹ (L) where it is not a woe but a criticism of the Pharisees. The version in Mt. is the simpler of the two: it confines itself strictly to the question of the ritual cleanness of vessels. This vast and complicated subject is treated in the Mishnah tractate *Kelim*. In chapter 25 of this tractate (Danby, pp. 640 ff.) the distinction between the outside and the inside of utensils is made. The chief question in this woe is whether the whole is to be taken literally, or whether the cup and the platter are used figuratively of the scribes and Pharisees themselves. The latter view seems to be preferable (*a*) in view of the following woe in Mt. *vv.* 27 f.; and (*b*) in view of the context of the Lucan parallel (Lk. 11³⁷⁻⁴¹).

25. The scribes and Pharisees are very particular about ritual purity, not only of vessels but also of their own persons. But just as a ritually clean vessel may be full of poison, so a ritually clean person may be full of ' extortion and excess.' The word translated ' excess ' means properly ' incontinence.'

26. Any effective cleansing must begin from within. Cf. Mk. 7¹⁸⁻²³. The figure of the cup is maintained as in the previous verse. The words ' and of the platter ' are omitted in this verse by important early authorities. It is probable that they are an interpolation to bring *v.* 26 into agreement with *v.* 25. See further on Lk. 11³⁹ᶠᶠ·, below, p. 269.

(vi) MT. 23²⁷⁻²⁸

23 27 Woe unto you, scribes and Pharisees, hypocrites! for ye are like unto whited sepulchres, which outwardly appear beautiful, but inwardly are full of dead 28 men's bones, and of all uncleanness. Even so ye also outwardly appear righteous unto men, but inwardly ye are full of hypocrisy and iniquity.

27. This woe has a parallel in Lk. 11⁴⁴ (Q). See above, p. 99. The whitewashing of sepulchres took place in the spring. The date appointed in the Mishnah (*Shekalim* 1¹, Danby, p. 152) is 15th Adar (Adar approximately = March). The object of this was to guard the people, especially the priests, against accidental defilement by contact with the tombs. The coat of whitewash thus acted as a warning to passers-by to keep their distance. This was its real purpose; and it is merely incidental that it gave a smart appearance to the tombs. ' Dead men's bones and all uncleanness ': the words ' all uncleanness ' doubtless emphasise the fact that the uncleanness of a corpse was reckoned the most pervasive and contagious of all kinds of uncleanness (Mishnah, *Kelim* 1⁴, Danby, pp. 604 f.).

28. The application of the comparison. The scribes and Pharisees make a brave display of piety and goodness; but behind this imposing façade there is nothing but hypocrisy and iniquity. But the comparison breaks down at the vital point. For in this verse the outward appearance of righteousness is assumed in order to *conceal* the evil condition within; whereas the whitewashing of the tombs *advertises* the fact that they are full of corruption. The simplest solution of the contradiction is to suppose that the word ' whited ' in *v.* 27 should be deleted as a piece of mistaken antiquarianism, supplied by Mt. or some other early authority; and that the original reference has nothing to do with the whitewashing of tombs, but rather with the fact that the sepulchres of famous or wealthy persons were often elaborately built and carved. Thus, for example, Josephus, speaking of the sepulchres of the Patriarchs at Hebron (*Jewish War*, iv. 532), says, ' Their tombs are shown in this little town to this day, of really fine marble and of exquisite workmanship.' The contrast between the outward attractiveness and the inward corruption would then be complete, and the parallel perfect.

The Lucan woe is quite different, and probably independent. It does not seem probable that the two woes can be traced back to a common root; nor is there any means of saying with absolute certainty which is the more original. The Lucan form has the merit of brevity and simplicity; and the Matthæan may be an attempt to elaborate it.

(vii) MT. 23²⁹⁻³⁶

23 29 Woe unto you, scribes and Pharisees, hypocrites! for ye build the sepulchres of the prophets, and garnish the tombs of 30 the righteous, and say, If we had been in the days of our fathers, we should not have been partakers with them in the 31 blood of the prophets. Wherefore ye witness to yourselves, that ye are sons of 32 them that slew the prophets. Fill ye up 33 then the measure of your fathers. Ye serpents, ye offspring of vipers, how shall 34 ye escape the judgement of ¹hell? There-fore, behold, I send unto you prophets, and wise men, and scribes: some of them shall ye kill and crucify; and some of them shall ye scourge in your synagogues, 35 and persecute from city to city: that upon you may come all the righteous blood shed on the earth, from the blood of Abel the righteous unto the blood of Zachariah son of Barachiah, whom ye slew between the sanctuary and the altar. 36 Verily I say unto you, All these things shall come upon this generation.

¹ Gr. *Gehenna*.

This section, except for *vv.* 32–33, has a parallel in Lk. 11⁴⁷⁻⁵¹; see above, pp. 101 ff.

29. The words 'and garnish the tombs of the righteous' do not appear in Lk. The conjunction of prophets and righteous men is characteristic of Mt.: cf. 10⁴¹, 13¹⁷. The insertion of the words here may be prompted by the fact that neither of the examples given in *v.* 35 was a prophet. It may be noted that Mt. has 'Abel the righteous' where Lk. has only 'Abel.'

30 f. They perceive and condemn the wickedness of their ancestors; and they recognise the outstanding merits of those whom their ancestors persecuted. They are quick to champion causes that no longer need championship, to stand up in defence of reputations that are already assured. But the prophets suffered because they challenged the accepted beliefs and standards of their day. Their heresies are now orthodoxy. And scribes and Pharisees are as tenacious in defence of this new orthodoxy as their ancestors were in defence of what was orthodoxy in their day. The prophets are canonised; but woe betide anyone who ventures farther along the way that they marked out. The very spirit that leads scribes and Pharisees to build the tombs of the old prophets will make them dig the graves of new prophets.

32 f. No parallel in Lk. 'Fill ye up then the measure of your fathers' is to be regarded as bitter irony, if the imperative is the true reading. The injunction means most probably: continue and bring to completion the evil work which your ancestors began. Destroy the messengers of God in your generation, as they did in theirs. When you have made your contribution the cup of Israel's iniquity will be full, and the judgement will come. How can you hope to escape it? These verses make the introduction to what follows. It is unlikely that they are a genuine utterance of Jesus. Verse 33 is an imitation of the saying of John the Baptist (Mk. 3⁷‖Lk. 3⁷, Q). The verses may have stood in M or they may be Mt.'s editorial work effecting the transition from *v.* 31 to *v.* 34.

34. Mt. does not have the reference to the wisdom of God (Lk. 11⁴⁹). The oracle, *vv.* 34–36, thus appears not as a decree of God in His wisdom but as a decree of Jesus. The word 'therefore' is probably to be regarded as looking forward to *v.* 35: 'It is for this reason that I send . . . namely, in order that upon you may come all the righteous blood. . . .' The sending of prophets to a people who will not receive them has its parallel in the Old Testament: e.g.

Jer. 7²⁵ᶠ·, ' Since the day that your fathers came forth out of the land of Egypt unto this day, I have sent unto you all my servants the prophets, daily rising up early and sending them: yet they hearkened not unto me, nor inclined their ear, but made their neck stiff: they did worse than their fathers.' Cf. Jer. 25⁴ᶠᶠ·. The order prophets, wise men, scribes is a little puzzling. Rabbinical Judaism would almost certainly have given the order: prophets, scribes, wise men. In the Mishnah the title ' scribes ' is used for the authorities of earlier times. The ' sages ' or ' wise men ' are the contemporary authorities. On the other hand, in the New Testament the contemporary Jewish authorities are called ' scribes.' If then the text here has a purely backward reference, there is no difficulty about the prophets. They are the men whose teachings appear in the second division of the Hebrew canon. The most natural interpretation of ' wise men ' will be that they were teachers such as those who appear in Proverbs or *Ecclesiasticus*. And the ' scribes ' will be such men as Ezra, ' the men of the Great Synagogue,' and others enumerated in *Aboth* 1. But it is possible that the reference is not entirely to the past, but that it has some bearing on contemporary conditions. In that case the term ' prophets ' would be extended to include such a man as John the Baptist. ' Wise men ' would have the meaning of teachers of wisdom such as is found in Proverbs, etc. ' Scribes ' might then be taken in another meaning: not as referring to the great legal authorities of the past but to religious teachers in the present. This use of the term is found in a saying of R. Eliezer ben Hyrcanus (*Sotah* 9¹⁵, Danby, p. 306), where the scribes are teachers of religion and of lower rank than the Sages. It might then be conjectured that Mt. has in mind the order of *didaskaloi* or teachers in the Church. The scribes are the teachers in the Jewish-Christian community. Cf. Mt. 13⁵²: ' Therefore every scribe who hath been made a disciple to the kingdom of heaven is like unto a man that is a householder, which bringeth forth out of his treasure things new and old.' In favour of this latter interpretation is the fact that the context of the verse is a woe against scribes and Pharisees. It is therefore not likely that ' scribes ' and ' wise men ' in the ordinary Jewish sense of Rabbis will be represented as the chosen messengers of God. The easiest interpretation is that the envoys are prophets, teachers of wisdom, and Jewish-Christian teachers. And in that case it is clear that the text of Mt. is less original than that of Lk. See on Lk. 11⁴⁹, above, pp. 102 f.

The fate of God's envoys is described in much greater detail here than in Lk. This detail supports the interpretation just given and strengthens the suspicion that Mt. is expanding the shorter Lucan version in the light of the experience of the early Church. At the same time it is to be remembered that Jesus elsewhere spoke of the certainty of persecution for His disciples, and claimed that disciples must be ready to take up the cross. Yet ' kill and crucify ' is awkward, the more so as crucifixion was not a Jewish but a Roman form of execution. Jews could only get disciples crucified by denouncing them to the Roman authorities on some charge punishable in that way under Roman Law. Cf. Mk. 13⁹: ' Before governors and kings shall ye stand for my sake, for a testimony unto them.' The scourging in synagogues is a regular Jewish punishment, prescribed in Deut. 25²ᶠ·. There the number of stripes is fixed at forty. In actual practice the maximum number inflicted was thirty-nine for any one offence. St. Paul relates that he suffered this punishment five times (2 Cor. 11²⁴). The regulations governing the punishment by scourging are given in the Mishnah tractate *Makkoth*, Danby, pp. 401–408. On the persecution from city to city see Mt. 10²³, above, p. 182.

35 f. See on Lk. 11⁵⁰ᶠ·, above, pp. 102 f. 'That upon you may come all the righteous blood.' Cf. Mt. 27²⁵. The meaning is that the judgement for all these murders will come upon this generation. On Zachariah son of Barachiah see above, pp. 103 ff.

37–39. These verses are from Q ; see above, pp. 126 ff.

J. ESCHATOLOGY

The eschatological matter peculiar to Mt. consists of (1) two brief insertions in Marcan contexts (Mt. 24¹⁰⁻¹² and 24³⁰ᵃ), and (2) a long appendix to the Marcan eschatological chapter (13), containing the parable of the Ten Virgins (25¹⁻¹³), the parable of the Talents (25¹⁴⁻³⁰ and the picture of the Last Judgement (25³¹⁻⁴⁶).

1. *THE INSERTIONS IN MARCAN CONTEXTS*
(a) MT. 24¹⁰⁻¹² (215)

24 10 And then shall many stumble, and shall deliver up one another, and shall 11 hate one another. And many false prophets shall arise, and shall lead many 12 astray. And because iniquity shall be multiplied, the love of the many shall wax cold.

This passage is inserted in Mt.'s version of what has come to be known as the 'Little Apocalypse.' It has already been argued that the Little Apocalypse does not represent the genuine teaching of Jesus, which is given rather in Lk. 17²⁶⁻³⁰, above, pp. 143 f. It may be further suggested that two factors have contributed to shape the expectations of the early Church as we find them set down in Mk. 13⁵⁻³¹. One is the necessity of accounting for the delay of the Parousia. And here the simplest expedient is to assert that the forces of evil must make one more final effort before the Kingdom of God is manifested in power. We find this explanation in use as early as 2 Thess. 2¹⁻¹². (I am inclined to regard 2 Thess. as a genuine epistle of Paul and prior in date to 1 Thess.) The other factor is the belief, widespread in Jewish Apocalypses, that the final consummation would be preceded by a period of trouble and distress, the so-called 'Woes of the Messiah,' the birth-pangs of the New Age. This Jewish belief goes back to Dan. 12¹: 'And at that time shall Michael stand up, the great prince which standeth for the children of thy people: and there shall be a time of trouble, such as never was since there was a nation even to that same time: and at that time thy people shall be delivered, every one that shall be found written in the book.' Further evidence in Billerbeck, iv. 977–986.

The feature of the Matthæan addition (24¹⁰⁻¹²) is that it adds a prophecy of strife and apostasy within the Church to the predictions of woe given in Mk. 13. It is very unlikely that it is genuine teaching of Jesus.

10. Many will stumble, that is, they will take offence (cf. Mt. 11⁶‖Lk. 7²³) when their expectations are not immediately realised. They will be disillusioned and ' fed up.' The community will be divided by mutual suspicions and hatreds. This latter feature seems to be an adaptation of the genuine saying of Jesus preserved in Q (Lk. 12⁵¹⁻⁵³), where the reference is to divisions in Judaism caused by the mission of Jesus and not, as here, to divisions in the community caused by the delay of the Second Coming. Cf. Mk. 13¹², where the point is the same as in Lk. 12⁵¹ff..

11. This verse may be the M version of Mk. 13¹¹f.; Lk. 17²³ (Q); cf. Rev. 19²⁰. *Apoc. Baruch* 48³⁰⁻³⁷. Josephus (*Jewish War*, vi. 283–287) tells of a multitude of false prophets who arose during the siege of Jerusalem, ' suborned by the tyrants to delude the people '; and in particular of the destruction of six thousand refugees who had been misled by a false prophet.

12. In 4 *Ezra* 5¹f. the signs of the end are thus described: ' Behold the days come when the inhabitants of earth shall be seized with great panic, and the way of truth shall be hidden, and the land of faith be barren. And iniquity (*iniustitia*) shall be increased above that which thou thyself now seest or that thou hast heard of long ago.' Cf. *Enoch* 91⁷. Similarly in the Mishnah *Sotah* 9¹⁵ (Danby, p. 306): ' With the footprints of the Messiah presumption shall increase and dearth reach its height . . . and the empire shall fall into heresy and there shall be none to utter reproof. The council-chamber shall be given to fornication. . . . The wisdom of the Scribes shall become insipid and they that shun sin shall be deemed contemptible, and truth shall nowhere be found.' Such passages as these sufficiently explain the multiplying of iniquity or increase of lawlessness in this verse. We may, however, wonder whether there is not a further reference here to the controversy between Jewish and Gentile Christianity on the matter of the observance of the Law. The love which grows cold in these circumstances is doubtless brother love of Christians towards one another, as in Rev. 2⁴.

(b) MT. 24³⁰ᵃ (219)

24 30 And then shall appear the sign of the Son of man in heaven: and then shall all the tribes of the earth mourn, and they	shall see the Son of man coming on the clouds of heaven with power and great glory.

In *v.* 29 Mt. is following Mk. 13²⁴f.. In *v.* 30 the words ' and then ' are derived from Mk. 13²⁶. The following words ' shall appear . . . mourn ' have no parallel in Mk. With ' they shall see the Son of man . . .' Mt. resumes his transcription of Mk.

There are striking similarities between Mt. 24³⁰ and Rev. 1⁷: ' Behold, he cometh with the clouds; and every eye shall see him, and they which pierced him; and all the tribes of the earth shall mourn over him.' In both texts we have the combination of two Old Testament passages: Dan. 7¹³ and Zech. 12¹⁰, ¹². In both the reference is eschatological. Whether Rev. 1⁷ is dependent on Mt. 24³⁰, or both on a common source, it would be difficult to say. ' The sign of the Son of Man ' may be the Son of Man Himself or, what is perhaps more probable, some supernatural appearance which heralds His coming. There is a great variety of opinions in early Christian literature on the nature of the sign. (See

Bousset, *The Antichrist Legend*, pp. 232 ff.) A very early belief was that the Cross had been taken up to heaven at the time of the Ascension, and that it was the sign that would appear in the sky at the time of the Parousia. Cf. *Gospel of Peter* x. 39 (James, *Apocryphal New Testament*, p. 92); *Epistle of the Apostles* xvi. (*op. cit.*, p. 490).

'All the tribes of the earth shall mourn.' The meaning is that the nations of the world which have not accepted the Gospel will now be without hope. The original sense of the passage in Zech. 12$^{10-12}$ is that the Jews will mourn as a sign of repentance for past misdeeds. But that original sense has been abandoned; and the text of Mt., as it stands, shows the standpoint of Jewish Apocalyptic with its prophecies of woe for the Gentile nations.

The insertion is not to be regarded as a word of Jesus but as a piece of half-Christianised Jewish apocalyptic, inserted by Mt. at this point.

2. *THE ESCHATOLOGICAL PARABLES*

(a) THE TEN VIRGINS (227)

MT. 25$^{1-13}$

25 1 Then shall the kingdom of heaven be likened unto ten virgins, which took their [1] lamps, and went forth to meet the 2 bridegroom. And five of them were 3 foolish, and five were wise. For the foolish, when they took their [1] lamps, 4 took no oil with them: but the wise took oil in their vessels with their [1] lamps. 5 Now while the bridegroom tarried, they 6 all slumbered and slept. But at midnight there is a cry, Behold, the bridegroom! Come ye forth to meet him. 7 Then all those virgins arose, and 8 trimmed their [1] lamps. And the foolish said unto the wise, Give us of your oil;

9 for our [1] lamps are going out. But the wise answered, saying, Peradventure there will not be enough for us and you: go ye rather to them that sell, and buy for 10 yourselves. And while they went away to buy, the bridegroom came; and they that were ready went in with him to the marriage feast: and the door was shut. 11 Afterward come also the other virgins, 12 saying, Lord, Lord, open to us. But he answered and said, Verily I say unto you, 13 I know you not. Watch therefore, for ye know not the day nor the hour.

[1] Or, *torches*.

This parable is a curiously involved mixture of ideas drawn from various sources. The first part seems to present a parallel to the Q parable of the servants who wait for their master's return from the marriage (Lk. 12$^{35-38}$). The closing verses (10–12) seem to be derived from another parable in Q (Lk. 13$^{23-27}$). The division of the virgins into two classes, the one destined for bliss and the other for exclusion from the good time that is coming, reflects that characteristic Matthæan dichotomy found in other parables peculiar to Mt., and going back eventually to the preaching of John the Baptist. Along with this goes another idea, that of Christ as the heavenly bridegroom. This idea of the marriage of Christ and the Church is the New Testament equivalent of the Old Testament idea of God as the bridegroom of Israel (cf. Hos. 2^{16}; Is. 54^{6}; Ezek. 16$^{7 f.}$). In the New Testament cf. 2 Cor. 11^{2}; Eph. 5$^{25, 32}$; Rev. 19^{7}.

1, 2, 3 f. The procedure which seems to be implied in the parable is that the bride awaits the coming of the bridegroom at her own home. The virgins are her friends who are to meet the bridegroom when he comes with his friends, and then join in escorting the couple back to the bridegroom's home, where the wedding-feast will take place.   And here comes the first difficulty.   For the bride is not mentioned at all in the parable.   By all the New Testament analogies the bride is the Church; but it is quite plain that the ten virgins represent the Church, and the Church as a mixed community containing good and bad members.   There is no room for the bride in the story because her place has been taken by the brides-maids.   What is meant by the lamps and the oil is not clear.   All have lamps and all the lamps have oil.   The only fault of the foolish is that they have no reserve supply of oil.   This means that they cannot keep their lamps going right through to the end.   This would suggest that the moral of the lamps is perseverance in faith.   ' He that endureth to the end, the same shall be saved ' (Mk. 13¹³||Mt. 24¹³).

5, 6 f., 8, 9, 10, 11 f.   The bridegroom tarries—the second Coming of Christ is delayed.   Meanwhile all, wise and foolish alike, slumber and sleep.   This is in strange contrast to the moral of the parable (v. 13): ' Watch therefore, for ye know not the day nor the hour.'   At midnight the coming of the bridegroom is announced and all prepare to meet him.   The lamps have apparently been burn-ing all the time, for the wicks now require to be trimmed, and the oil in them is exhausted or nearly so.   The foolish appeal to the wise for oil from their reserve stock.   But the wise have no oil to spare, and advise the foolish to go and buy; though one would not expect that shops would be open at midnight.   There is, however, no suggestion that the foolish virgins were unsuccessful in their quest for oil even at that late hour.   But while they are on this errand the bridegroom comes, the party go in to the feast, and the door is shut.   Those who were ready are inside; those who were not ready are outside.   The qualification for entrance is readiness in all respects and at all times.   This is confirmed when the foolish virgins arrive, having now provided themselves with the extra supply of oil.   Their request for admission to the feast is refused point-blank.   Admission, therefore, does not depend on having lamp or oil, but on having lamp and oil at the precise moment when these things are required.   It may then be argued that the original and essential point of the story is that the ten maidens have one task and one only, to be ready with lamps burning brightly when the bridegroom appears.   Those who fulfil that task enter the feast; those who fail are shut out.   What is meant by keeping the lamp burning brightly may be understood by reference to another M saying, Mt. 5¹⁶: ' Even so let your light shine before men, that they may see your good works, and glorify your Father which is in heaven.'

13. The moral of the story.   If it is the moral of the story, it is clear that ' Watch ' must be taken in another sense than ' keep awake ': for (a) the maidens do not keep awake (v. 5), and (b) the point of the story is the necessity of being ready in all respects when the bridgroom arrives.

Additional Note on the text of Mt. 25¹

The commentary above assumes that the true text of the parable is substantially as given in R.V.   There is, however, one important variant in v. 1; and in order to avoid complicating further what is already complicated enough, the bearing of it may be considered separately.   In v. 1 the virgins go forth ' to meet the bridegroom.' A considerable number of early and important authorities have ' to meet the bridegroom and the bride.' The genuineness of this reading is defended by Prof. Burkitt (*Encyclopædia Biblica*, col. 4991; *Journ. Theol. Stud.*, xxx (1929), pp. 267–270).

If this is the true text, the ten virgins will not be bridesmaids waiting in the neighbourhood of the bride's home, but ' neighbours' children, fellow-townsmen of the bridegroom but not his particular friends,' and ' their plan is to light up the approach to the bridegroom's house as a welcome, in return for which they would hope to have some share in the rather promiscuous hospitality of an oriental festivity ' (Burkitt, p. 269). The religious interpretation of this is then that the bridal party stands for the Son of Man and all His angels, and the ten girls stand for the disciples. This is the interpretation offered by Dr. Burkitt in his more recent exposition. In the earlier discussion of the parable in the *Encyclopædia Biblica* he suggested that the virgins were maidservants left in the bridegroom's house to keep watch while he went to bring the bride; and they stand for the Church.

The difficulty about Prof. Burkitt's latest interpretation is the fact that the disciples have to be equated with people who stand in no very close relation to the bridegroom or to the wedding-feast. Elsewhere Jesus speaks of the disciples as the sons of the bridechamber (Mk. 2^{19}), which seems more like what we should expect. If one had to choose between the two views put forward, one would incline to prefer the earlier.

Further, if the virgins represent disciples, they represent in some sense the Church. What then does the bride stand for? The answer is that bride, bridegroom, and the whole bridal retinue together stand for the Son of Man and His angels. But the New Testament usage is that the bridegroom is Christ and the bride the Church. This suggests a possible third interpretation, which is put forward with all reserve and as no more than a conjecture.

Jewish thought was at home with the idea of Israel as the bride of God. And Israel did not mean only the Jews of any one generation. It was Israel as a historical entity, a living unity through the ages. The early Church claimed to be the continuation of this true Israel; and this claim would be most cogent on the part of the Jewish-Christian branch of the Church. It is then possible to suggest that the bride in the parable is the true Israel, by which is meant the Israel of the patriarchs and prophets and Jewish Christians. The ten virgins stand for the Gentile converts. The wise among them are those who accept the Jewish-Christian standard of conformity to the Law. The foolish are those who do not. In support of this it may be urged that both lamp and oil are used as figures for the Law. Ps. 119^{105}; Prov. 6^{23}: ' The commandment is a lamp; and the law is light.' *Apoc. Baruch* 59^{2}; 4 *Ezra* 14$^{20 f.}$. For the comparison of the Law with oil cf. Feldman, *Parables and Similes of the Rabbis*, pp. 164 f.; Billerbeck, ii. 357: ' As oil is light for the world, so also are the words of the Law light for the world ' (*Dt. Rabba* 7).

It must, however, be emphasised again that all this is conjecture. One is left at the end with the suspicion that the parable as presented in Mt. is the working up of something originally much simpler, in the same way that Mt.'s parable of the Wheat and Tares is the working up of Mk.'s parable of the Seed growing secretly.

What this original, and probably genuine, parable was like we have now no means of determining; but we may guess that its point was the necessity of being fully prepared for the coming of the day of the Son of Man.

(b) THE TALENTS (228)

MT. 25[14-30]

25 14 For *it is* as *when* a man, going into another country, called his own [1] servants, and delivered unto them his goods.
15 And unto one he gave five talents, to another two, to another one; to each according to his several ability; and he
16 went on his journey. Straightway he that received the five talents went and traded with them, and made other five
17 talents. In like manner he also that
18 *received* the two gained other two. But he that received the one went away and digged in the earth, and hid his lord's
19 money. Now after a long time the lord of those [1] servants cometh, and maketh a
20 reckoning with them. And he that received the five talents came and brought other five talents, saying, Lord, thou deliveredst unto me five talents: lo, I
21 have gained other five talents. His lord said unto him, Well done, good and faithful [2] servant: thou hast been faithful over a few things, I will set thee over many things: enter thou into the joy of
22 thy lord. And he also that *received* the two talents came and said, Lord, thou deliveredst unto me two talents: lo, I
23 have gained other two talents. His lord said unto him, Well done, good and

faithful [2] servant; thou hast been faithful over a few things, I will set thee over many things: enter thou into the joy of
24 thy lord. And he also that had received the one talent came and said, Lord, I knew thee that thou art a hard man, reaping where thou didst not sow, and gathering where thou didst not scatter:
25 and I was afraid, and went away and hid thy talent in the earth: lo, thou hast
26 thine own. But his lord answered and said unto him, Thou wicked and slothful [2] servant, thou knewest that I reap where I sowed not, and gather where I did not
27 scatter; thou oughtest therefore to have put my money to the bankers, and at my coming I should have received back mine
28 own with interest. Take ye away therefore the talent from him, and give it unto him
29 that hath the ten talents. For unto every one that hath shall be given, and he shall have abundance: but from him that hath not, even that which he hath
30 shall be taken away. And cast ye out the unprofitable [2] servant into the outer darkness: there shall be the weeping and gnashing of teeth.

[1] Gr. *bondservants.*
[2] Gr. *bondservant.*

This parable has a parallel in Lk.'s parable of the Pounds (Lk. 19[12-27]) which is to be assigned to L. This means that the main outline of the story was already fixed before the M and L traditions took shape; and makes it probable that the parable, in its original form, goes back to Jesus Himself. The story itself is told with considerable detail in both versions; but much of the detail is artistic amplification, given to make the story, as a story, more vivid and lifelike. It is therefore the more important in all this wealth of detail to try to perceive what is the central and essential point. This does not lie in any of the details, as for example the significance of the talents, or of their distribution, but in the principle of Jewish Law assumed throughout the parable though nowhere expressly stated; the slave belongs to his master, and all that the slave produces or earns belongs to his master. For the legal texts see Billerbeck, i. 970 f. Translated into religious terms this means the absolute claim of God upon man. Man himself, all that he has, and all that he can produce, all belong to God. The purpose of man's existence is to serve God, and apart from such service his life is meaningless and worthless. The reward of such service is opportunity for further and larger service; and the worst punishment for failure to serve is just to be deprived of the opportunity to serve at all.

14. The master going into another country may be taken to represent God. In that case the other country is heaven. The servants—better rendered here ' bondservants ' (R.V. mg.) or ' slaves,' and so throughout the parable—are men, who are made responsible for the conduct of God's business on earth. The immediate application is of course to Israel and, within Israel, especially to the disciples of Jesus. The goods may be anything in the world, the whole raw material of man's work conceived as a service offered to God.

15. The talents have no special significance. They are introduced simply as a means of expressing the varied opportunities of the slaves in terms of a common denominator—money. The modern use of the word ' talent ' in the sense of a special kind of ability does not enter in at all. All that is implied is that in the distribution of ' the goods ' one slave receives goods to the value of five talents £1,000–1,200; another gets over £400 worth; another over £200 worth. The distribution is governed by the abilities of the servants. The most capable is given the largest responsibility; and it is assumed that no slave is allotted a task beyond his powers. The master now leaves the slaves to get on with the work. So far as the work is concerned they are as good as free. Possibly the master could have got more abundant results by staying and directing all the operations; but that, it would seem, is not his purpose. So doubtless the world might be better managed if there were more interference from heaven. But if the end in view is that men should become God's children rather than His puppets, it may be that non-interference is necessary.

16 f., 18. The first two slaves go to work and succeed in doubling what has been entrusted to them. The actual doubling is doubling of goods. As in the description of the distribution, so here the value of the work done and the results produced are reduced to the same common denominator—money. The third slave—it might equally have been one of the other two—makes no use of his opportunities. For the burying of valuables as a way of keeping them in safety cf. Mt. 13⁴⁴, above, p. 196.

19. In due course the master comes to see how the slaves have managed his property. The same situation occurs in Mt. 18²³ᶠᶠ· and the same expression, ' make a reckoning,' is used. In Mt. 18 the reference is clearly not to the final Judgement and here such a reference is only necessitated by v. 30, which is probably not part of the original parable. It is worth noting that in Jewish literature we have the idea of an annual Judgement, which takes place on the Jewish New Year's Day. So in the Mishnah (Rosh ha-Shanah 1², Danby, p. 188): ' On New Year's Day all that come into the world pass before him (God) like legions of soldiers, for it is written, He that fashioneth the hearts of them all, that considereth all their works (Ps. 33¹⁵).' Cf. Abrahams, Festival Studies, pp. 19–24; Companion to the Daily Prayer Book, pp. cxcvi–cxcix; Authorised Daily Prayer Book (ed. Singer), pp. 249–252; Billerbeck, iii. 230 f. At this time the doings of each man are reviewed and a verdict passed on them. The ensuing period from New Year's Day until the Day of Atonement is allowed for repentance; and on the Day of Atonement the sentence, whatever it may be, is pronounced.

20–23. The first two servants report in much the same terms (vv. 20, 22) and are commended in much the same terms (vv. 21, 23). The reward of faithful service is first the approval of the master, and second the opportunity for more abundant and more responsible service. So Ben Azzai says: ' The reward of a duty [done] is a duty [to be done] ' (*Aboth* 4², Danby, p. 453). Cf. the passage quoted by Montefiore (*op. cit.*, p. 332): ' God does not give greatness to a man till He has proved him in a small matter: only then He promotes him to a great post. Two were proved and found faithful, and God promoted them to greatness. He tested David with the sheep . . . and God said, Thou wast found faithful with the sheep, I will give thee *my* sheep that thou shouldst feed them. And so with Moses, who fed his father-in-law's sheep. To him God said the same.' The words ' enter thou into the joy of thy lord ' have nothing corresponding in Lk. They give a definitely eschatological cast to the scene. But this is not necessarily original. It may be that the fuller service is service in the world to come; but this is not necessarily implied in the story as a whole.

24 f. The third slave has now to justify himself if he can. The obvious course is to complain about the conditions of his service and to blacken the character of the master. He is a hard man, who enriches himself by the labours of other people. He reaps where he has not sown and gathers where he has not scattered. This latter clause should probably be translated ' garnering where thou hast not winnowed.' The Greek word translated ' scatter ' in R.V. probably represents the Aramaic verb *děrā*, which means both to scatter and to winnow. The fear of the slave is to be understood as the fear of losing what had been entrusted to him in any enterprise which he might undertake. His argument appears to be: If I make a profit the master gets it; if I make a loss he will come upon me to make it good. Therefore the best course is to do nothing. ' Lo, thou hast thine own'—no more and no less.

26. The master makes no attempt to rebut the charge. As between master and slave the statement of the case is correct. That *is* the situation. The slave works and the master takes the results of his labours. The good and faithful slave accepts the situation and does his best in it. The slave who refuses to do his best is a bad slave. He ought to have been a good and faithful slave and trusted that the master would be kind and generous. It is to be noted that the master does not accept the designation ' hard man.' The point of this verse in religious terms is that it is insolence and presumption on man's part to question the terms on which God has created him and given him a place in the world. It is not man's business to sit in judgement upon God. It is his business to do his best in the situation in which he finds himself. It is his business to live and work and die for the glory of God. That is his privilege: and his highest reward is to be allowed to go on doing it. The well-known prayer of Ignatius Loyola is very much to the point here.

27. The law concerning deposits with bankers is given in the Mishnah (*Baba Metziah* 3¹¹, Danby, p. 352): ' If a man left money in the keeping of a money-changer and it was sealed up, he (the money-changer) may not make use of it and, therefore, if it was lost he is not answerable for it; if the money was loose he may make use of it and, therefore, if it was lost he is answerable for it.' That is, if the bank is used merely as a safe-deposit, it is so used at one's own risk. But if the money is put into the bank on a deposit account, the banker can use it for

his business, is bound to restore it in full, and will pay some interest for the use of it. Therefore in depositing the money at a bank the slave would not be risking the capital, and he would be ensuring some increase for his master.

28 f. The punishment for neglected opportunity is deprivation of opportunity. But God's work goes on; and the task which one man refuses is given to another who will do it. Verse 29 states the general principle. It is so briefly stated as to be cryptic. It may be expanded thus: To him who has added something of his own to what I entrusted to him, more of mine shall be entrusted and he shall have abundance. But from him who has added nothing of his own to what I entrusted to him, shall be taken away what I entrusted to him.

30. With this statement the parable reaches what ought to be its conclusion; and this is the last verse which has a parallel in Lk. Mt., however, has another verse describing further punishment for the slave. The verse is largely made up of phrases which are favourites with Mt.: ' cast into the outer darkness ' (Mt. 8[12], 22[13], 25[30], and nowhere else in the New Testament) ; ' there shall be the weeping and gnashing of teeth ' (Mt. 8[12], 13[42, 50], 22[13], 24[51], 25[30]; elsewhere only Lk. 13[28]).

Eusebius in his *Theophany* discusses this verse with reference to an apocryphal gospel (the Gospel according to the Hebrews or the Gospel according to the Nazarenes), which he believed to be the Hebrew original of Mt. The passage is given in James, *Apocryphal New Testament*, p. 3. He informs us that in this gospel there were three servants, ' one who devoured his master's substance with harlots and flute-girls, another who multiplied it by trading, and another who hid the talent.' The second was accepted, the third only rebuked, and the first was shut up in prison. Eusebius then goes on to conjecture that *v.* 30 in Mt. may refer to the servant who ' ate and drank with the drunken,' apparently referring back to Mt. 24[49]. It is more probable that the parable in the apocryphal gospel is an attempt to deal with *v.* 30 in Mt. That is, it was soon perceived that *v.* 30 did not really belong to the case of the man who buried his talent. He had been dealt with in *vv.* 28 f. The ' unprofitable servant ' must be yet another, and so the servant who wastes his capital in debauchery is invented. The apocryphal gospel is thus evidence that at an early date the separateness of *v.* 30 from *vv.* 28 f. was felt. But the true explanation of that separateness is most probably that it is an editorial addition by Mt. and no part of the original parable.

(c) THE LAST JUDGEMENT (229)

MT. 25[31-46]

25 31 But when the Son of man shall come in his glory, and all the angels with him, then shall he sit on the throne of his 32 glory: and before him shall be gathered all the nations: and he shall separate them one from another, as the shepherd 33 separateth the sheep from the [1] goats: and he shall set the sheep on his right hand, 34 but the [1] goats on the left. Then shall the King say unto them on his right hand, Come, ye blessed of my Father, inherit the kingdom prepared for you from the 35 foundation of the world: for I was an hungred, and ye gave me meat: I was thirsty, and ye gave me drink: I was a stranger, and ye took me in; naked, and 36 ye clothed me: I was sick, and ye visited me: I was in prison, and ye came unto 37 me. Then shall the righteous answer him, saying, Lord, when saw we thee an hungred, and fed thee? or athirst, and 38 gave thee drink? And when saw we thee a stranger, and took thee in? or 39 naked, and clothed thee? And when saw we thee sick, or in prison, and came 40 unto thee? And the King shall answer

and say unto them, Verily I say unto you, Inasmuch as ye did it unto one of these my brethren, *even* these least, ye did it 41 unto me. Then shall he say also unto them on the left hand, [2] Depart from me, ye cursed, into the eternal fire which is prepared for the devil and his angels: 42 for I was an hungred, and ye gave me no meat: I was thirsty, and ye gave me no 43 drink: I was a stranger, and ye took me not in; naked, and ye clothed me not; sick, and in prison, and ye visited me not.

44 Then shall they also answer, saying, Lord, when saw we thee an hungred, or athirst, or a stranger, or naked, or sick, or in prison, and did not minister unto 45 thee? Then shall he answer them, saying, Verily I say unto you, Inasmuch as ye did it not unto one of these least, 46 ye did it not unto me. And these shall go away into eternal punishment: but the righteous into eternal life.

[1] Gr. *kids.*
[2] Or, *Depart from me under a curse.*

This word-picture of the Last Judgement has no parallel in the other Gospels. Whether or not it belongs as a whole and in all its details to the authentic teaching of Jesus, it certainly contains features of such startling originality that it is difficult to credit them to anyone but the Master Himself. The frame of the picture is the conventional Jewish Apocalyptic expectation; but many details of the picture would seem to be the creation of Jesus Himself. On the Jewish expectations see Moore, *Judaism,* ii. 279–395; Billerbeck, iv. 1199–1212. In Jewish accounts the Judge is always God, except in the one case (*Enoch* 61[6]-63[12]) where the Messiah (the Elect One) performs this office; and even here there are clear indications (62[10-14]) that the Lord of Spirits (= God) has a decisive part in the proceedings, to say nothing of Messel's contention that the Elect One in this passage is a figure for Israel, and not for the Messiah. Mt.'s account of the Judgement differs from the usual Jewish view in this important respect that here the judge is not God but the Son of Man. In this respect it has some affinity with the passage in *Enoch* (61[6]-63[12]).

The principal characters in the drama are as follows: (1) the Son of Man accompanied by the angels, (2) all the Gentiles, (3) the King, (4) the King's Father, (5) the King's brethren. The identification of these characters is not easy in every case. It is, however, clear that the King's Father is God. It follows that God is not the Judge in this scene. It is then clear that the King is meant for Jesus Himself. Who, then, are the King's brethren? The obvious course is to suppose that they are the disciples of Jesus. This leads to an important conclusion: the King is not alone in the judgement, but is the representative and spokesman of a body of persons (' my brethren ') distinct from the other parties present. They are clearly not identical with those who are to be condemned; but neither are they identical with the righteous. For they have been the objects of neglect by the one party and of kindness and help by the other. We have thus three distinct parties: the King's brethren, and the two classes of Gentiles, those who helped (sheep) and those who did not help (goats). We must accordingly picture the scene thus: in the centre the King and his brethren; on the right hand of this party the good Gentiles; on the left hand the wicked Gentiles. What, then, is signified by the Son of Man? It would seem that there are two possibilities. Either the Son of Man is the same as the King, in which case ' Son of Man ' has the meaning commonly assigned to it in *Enoch*; or ' Son of Man ' stands for the body comprising the King and his brethren, in which case ' Son of Man ' approximates in meaning to ' Son of Man ' in Dan. 7[13], and the interpretation proposed by Messel for ' Son of Man ' in *Enoch*. The latter is, in my opinion, the correct interpretation.

It may be noted that there is a similar threefold division of mankind in the eschatology of Mohammed (*Koran*, Sura 56): ' When the inevitable day of judgement shall suddenly come . . . it will abase some and exalt others . . . Ye shall be separated into three distinct classes: the companions of the right hand; (how happy shall the companions of the right hand be!) and the companions of the left hand; (how miserable shall the companions of the left hand be!) and those who have preceded others in the faith, shall precede them to paradise.' But none of the three classes acts in a judicial capacity.

For further instances of the idea of the Judgement being carried out by a corporate body see notes on Mt. 19^{28}, above, pp. 216 f.

31. The coming of the Son of Man is spoken of in the Synoptic Gospels in Mk. 8^{38} and ‖s; 13^{26} and ‖s; 14^{62} and ‖s; in Q: Lk. 12^{40}‖Mt. 24^{44}; in M: Mt. 10^{23}, 25^{31}; in L: Lk. 18^{8}. Cf. also Lk. 17$^{24, 26, 30}$ (Q). The angels are often pictured in Jewish literature as in attendance upon God at the Judgement, and as assisting in the execution of it; but there is, according to Billerbeck, no mention in early Jewish literature of angels accompanying the Messiah (Billerbeck, i. 973 f.). ' The throne of his glory ' = His glorious throne. The throne of glory is one of the things which, according to Jewish belief, were created before the world. In Jewish thought it is essentially the throne of God. The only place in Jewish literature where anyone but God is said to sit on it is the *Similitudes of Enoch* (*Enoch* 37–71). There the Elect One sits on the throne or is set thereon by God (*Enoch* 45^{3}, 51^{3}, 55^{4}, 61^{8}, 62$^{2, 3, 5}$, 69$^{27, 29}$).

32 f. ' All the nations ': the usage of Mt. elsewhere would suggest that ' all the Gentiles ' is the rendering here. If it be asked where Israel comes into this scheme, it may be suggested that the true Israel is covered by the concept ' Son of Man,' interpreted as ' the people of the Saints of the Most High.' The Jews who have rejected the Kingdom as preached to them by Jesus and His disciples are reckoned among the Gentiles. See notes on Lk. 10$^{10\,ff.}$, above, pp. 75 f. The assembling of the people for judgement is done by the angels. Cf. Mt. 13^{41}. The separation takes place forthwith: the characters and records of the persons concerned are already known. It is judgement, not trial, for which the court is assembled. The right hand is the place of honour; and, in this connexion, the left hand the place of rejection. The same convention appears in the myth of Er (Plato, *Republic* x. p. 614). In the state after death Er saw judges ' who, after passing sentence, commanded the just to take the road to the right upwards through the heaven . . .; while the unjust were ordered to take the road downwards to the left.' Cf. Virgil, *Æn.* vi. 540 ff.

34. The King speaks. He is the spokesman of Himself and His brethren; and He speaks in the name of His Father. He is clearly to be identified as Christ, the spokesman and representative of the ' Son of Man,' the people of the Saints of the Most High. The favourable judgement which He has to deliver on those on the right hand is essentially the judgement of God, ' Come ye blessed *of my Father.*' ' Inherit ' means ' enter into the possession and enjoyment of.' That the Kingdom is ' prepared ' for them from the foundation of the world may mean

either that it was provided for in God's plan, though not actually created, or that it was actually created in the beginning and has been waiting for its inheritors till now. Cf. Dan 7²⁷; Lk. 12³²; 1 Cor. 2⁹. According to Jewish ideas, some things were created before the world. Various lists are given and the distinction is made between real creation and planning (Billerbeck, i. 981 ff.; ii. 334 f.). Other things were created in advance at the close of the sixth day of Creation (*Aboth* 5⁶, Danby, p. 456).

35. The ground for the favourable decision. It is a striking feature of this and the following verses that those on the right are not commended for abstinence from the cruder sins, nor are those on the left condemned for indulgence in them. Again, it is not that one group have been kind-hearted and the other callous. Honesty, chastity, kindness, and the like are very important things and their importance is duly stressed in the teaching of Jesus elsewhere. But here the vital question is not whether a man has lived a moral life or whether he has been decently kind to other people. It is how he stood towards the Kingdom of God: was he on the side of the Kingdom or against it?

35 f. Consequently in these verses the emphasis is on ' I ' and ' me,' and not on the verbs. The good deeds done were deeds done to help the cause of God. They were an acknowledgement of God's sovereignty as manifested in His representative Jesus Christ.

37–39. The righteous are not aware of having done any kindnesses to Jesus. They helped this or that good man in his need; but it was other people that they helped, not Him who speaks.

40. The answer of the King brings out clearly the solidarity of Christ and His brethren. He and His brethren are many, but together they are one—the Son of Man. Help given to one is help given to all, and above all to their Head. The same principle is laid down in Mk. 9⁴¹; Lk. 10¹⁶‖Mt. 10⁴⁰ (Q), see notes above, pp. 77 f ; Mt. 10⁴¹ᶠ· (M), see above, pp. 183 f. The fact that the phrase ' in my name ' is not used here probably signifies nothing. It is assumed that the help has been given to the disciples of Jesus, when they were engaged on their apostolic task, when they arrived in a strange town, hungry and thirsty, or when they were worn out and ill through toil and travel, when they were imprisoned for preaching the Gospel—why else should the brethren of Christ be in prison? Cf. 1 Pet. 4¹⁴⁻¹⁶· The deeds of the righteous are not just casual acts of benevolence. They are acts by which the Mission of Jesus and His followers was helped, and helped at some cost to the doers, even at some risk.

' One of these my brethren even these least ' is a literal rendering of the Greek, which is probably a literal rendering of a misunderstood Aramaic idiom. Translate ' one of the least of my brethren ' and cf. Mt. 5¹⁹, above, p. 154.

41. The King now turns to the other group. The principle of judgement in their case is the same as in the case of the righteous. The question is whether a man is for or against the Kingdom of God. And there is no such thing as neutrality. ' He that is not with me is against me; and he that gathereth not with me scattereth ' (Lk. 11²³‖Mt. 12³⁰ Q, above, p. 87). The Kingdom comes with definite claims upon every man. To ignore them is to reject them; and to reject them is to side with the enemy. Those on the left hand have chosen Satan

—by doing nothing—and to Satan they go.   Their own choice puts them outside the pale of God's blessing; and to be outside is to be under the curse.   The dreadful imagery of the eternal fire made ready for the Devil and his angels is doubtless appalling.   Once it was terrifying to the ungodly.   It is no longer terrifying because it is no longer believed by most people.   But it corresponds to a spiritual reality, to the fact that God having given us freedom, has given us freedom to reject Him, to be rebels against His will, to cut ourselves off from our true life.

42–45.   These verses present the other side of the case stated in *vv.* 35–40. In *v.* 44 the statement is abbreviated.

46.   The conclusion of the matter.   The destiny of both parties is unalterably fixed for ever.   Before the righteous is everlasting bliss; for the others there is no prospect but endless torment.   This is the conventional apocalyptic view.   Cf. Dan 12². The same remarks apply to this verse as are made on *v.* 41.

III.—Teaching Peculiar to Luke

AS there do not seem to be any signs of a special arrangement of the L material, the sections which follow are numbered consecutively as they occur in Lk.'s order. Where two or more consecutive passages are connected in subject-matter they are brought under the same number.

1. *TEACHING OF JOHN THE BAPTIST* (3)

LK. 3$^{10-14}$

3 10 And the multitudes asked him, saying, 11 What then must we do? And he answered and said unto them, He that hath two coats, let him impart to him that hath none; and he that hath food, let him do 12 likewise. And there came also [1] publicans to be baptized, and they said unto him, 13 [2] Master, what must we do? And he said unto them, Extort no more than that 14 which is appointed you. And [3] soldiers also asked him, saying, And we, what must we do? And he said unto them, Do violence to no man, neither [4] exact *anything* wrongfully; and be content with your wages.

[1] See marginal note on Matt. v. 46.
[2] Or, *Teacher*.
[3] Gr. *soldiers on service*.
[4] Or, *accuse* any one.

This passage shows the real weakness of John's preaching. He is at his most powerful in exposing and denouncing the wickedness of his age. His mission is to prepare the way for one mightier than himself. Consequently, when he is asked for positive constructive teaching, he has nothing new to offer. That people should treat one another kindly, that publicans should abstain from extortion and soldiers from bullying, was doubtless useful advice, but not an epoch-making moral discovery. John's ethical teaching here is the real ' interim ethic '—do your best in the circumstances till the Messianic age comes. Then things will be put on a proper footing.

10. The fiery preaching of coming judgement has its effect and the common people respond (cf. Lk. 7^{29}). 'What must we do'—to be saved? Some MSS. add these words. They are a gloss, but a gloss that gives the correct sense. The call is ' Bring forth fruits worthy of repentance ' (3^8). Then what will be considered worthy fruits?

11. John's answer in general terms is positive, even if not far-reaching. His demand for practical kindness to one's neighbour prepares the way for the more radical demand made by Jesus. For ' coats ' read ' shirts.' Those who have more than the bare sufficiency for physical needs are to share with those who have not even a bare sufficiency; the poor are to help the destitute. Did the people who listened readily to John consist mainly of those to whom a spare change of under-clothing meant comparative prosperity?

12. The publicans here are the collectors of customs as distinct from taxes. In Judæa at this time the taxes would be collected by Roman officials acting for the Procurator. The customs, however, were still farmed out. That is, the right to collect them was sold by the Roman authorities to the highest bidder, who then collected them through subordinate agents of his own. Any surplus remaining, after paying the sum offered to the Government and the cost of collection, went into the pocket of the contractor (publican). Such a system invited the collectors

to practise fraud and oppression in the exercise of their office, and fraud and oppression certainly took place. The result was that in Palestine and elsewhere the collectors of customs were despised and hated. In Judæa they were specially disliked for a further reason. The customs were collected for the Roman Emperor, and that by Jews. The publican thus appeared in the eyes of his patriotic fellow-countrymen as one who had sold his country for private gain. To the average Jew ' publican ' was synonymous with ' traitor and scoundrel,' and such collocations as 'publicans and sinners' or 'publicans and harlots' are taken as a matter of course.

For such people the day, whose approach John proclaimed, would be a day of reckoning; and it is not surprising that some, at any rate, of them were moved to repentance. They address John as 'Master' (Rabbi) and ask his advice. Are they to give up their occupation? Or are they to carry out their task in a new way?

13. John's reply is again interim ethic. Doubtless in the time that is coming Roman taxes and customs will be abolished. Meanwhile they are inevitable, and all that can be demanded is that those who collect the customs should be honest, and not use their position to enrich themselves at the expense of their neighbours. They are not to charge more than the amounts prescribed by law or custom. For an attempt to regulate the charges made by customs-collectors see the bilingual Palmyrene inscription of A.D. 137 in Bevan's *Commentary on Daniel*, pp. 214–219.

14. The question is put by soldiers. What kind of soldiers they were—Roman troops or mercenaries from the army of Herod Antipas—is not stated. It is unlikely that they were Roman in the strict sense, since ' the garrison of Judæa under the procurators was regularly composed of Syrian auxiliary cohorts ' (*Beginnings of Christianity*, v. 439). Such troops had not only to perform their proper military tasks. They were also largely employed in police duties. Here again there was large scope for violent and unscrupulous men to misuse their power.

15. John's reply does not suggest that they should give up their occupation. He tells them to abstain from oppressing the civil population, from extorting money from them by threats of violence or by blackmail. They have their wages: let them be content. This also is interim ethic—making the best of a bad job until the heaven-sent ' Stronger One ' comes, who will put all things right. John's positive teaching serves to mitigate the worst evils of an evil system; but it does not and cannot transform the system. It could relieve the sickness of society; but it was not the radical cure.

2. *OLD AND NEW WINE* (54)

LK. 5[39]

5 39   And no man having drunk old *wine* desireth new: for he saith, The old is [1]good.
       [1] Many ancient authorities read *better*.

This saying is appended by Lk. to the parable of the Wine-skins (Lk. 5[37f.]), which he has taken from Mk. (2[22]). The fact that wines improve with age was a commonplace in ancient literature. Here it is used to illustrate the power of tradition, established belief and custom in religion. The old ways are congenial; and those who are schooled in them will have nothing to do with new movements.

They do not necessarily condemn the new: they just do not want to have anything to do with it.

The reading ' better ' is to be rejected: and the adjective (*chrēstos*) would be better rendered by ' mellow ' or ' fit for use.' Old and new wines alike may be good or bad. Their quality does not depend on their age. But even a good new wine requires time to make it fit for use. What our connoisseur says in effect is: ' No wine is fit to drink till it is old.' Hence no religious belief or practice which has not the sanctity of age is worth following. Jesus here says that a great obstacle to the reception of new revelation is the *pietas* of religious people. Just so Horace finds an obstacle to the progress of literature in the veneration of the classics, and uses the same illustration (*Epistles* II, i. 34 f.).

Cf. *Aboth* 4[20] (Danby, p. 455), ' R. Jose b. Judah of Kefar ha-Babli said: He that learns from the young, to what is he like? To one that eats unripe grapes and drinks wine from his winepress. And he that learns from the aged, to what is he like? To one that eats ripe grapes and drinks old wine. Rabbi said: Look not on the jar but on what is in it; there may be a new jar that is full of old wine and an old one in which is not even new wine.'

3. *SAMARITAN UNFRIENDLINESS* (137)

LK. 9[51-56]

9 51 And it came to pass, when the days [1] were well-nigh come that he should be received up, he stedfastly set his face to go 52 to Jerusalem, and sent messengers before his face: and they went, and entered into a village of the Samaritans, to make ready 53 for him. And they did not receive him, because his face was *as though he were going* 54 to Jerusalem. And when his disciples James and John saw *this*, they said, Lord, wilt thou that we bid fire to come down 55 from heaven, and consume them [2]? But 56 he turned, and rebuked them.[3] And they went to another village.

[1] Gr. *were being fulfilled.*
[2] Many ancient authorities add *even as Elijah did.*
[3] Some ancient authorities add *and said, Ye know not what manner of spirit ye are of.* Some, but fewer, add also *For the Son of man came not to destroy men's lives, but to save* them.

This passage would be more important for our present purpose if the marginal readings were genuine. As they are commonly rejected as later interpolations into the text of Lk., we have no teaching in the proper sense of the word beyond the fact that Jesus sternly rejects the suggestion of James and John

The paragraph is the opening of a long section of Lk. (9[51]–19[48]) purporting to describe the journey of Jesus from Galilee to Jerusalem. The greater part of the section (9[51]–18[14]) is independent of Mk. The incident described in Mk. 9[33-37] (Lk. 9[46-48]) takes place in Capernaum. The next note of place is Mk. 10[1], however it is to be understood . (Cf. Burkitt, *Gospel History and its Transmission*, p. 96 n.) At Mk. 10[13] (Lk. 18[15]) Lk. rejoins Mk. Mk. 10[46] (Lk. 18[35]) brings Jesus to Jericho. In the result Mk. gives two fixed points for the journey: Capernaum (9[33]) and Jericho (10[46]). The only intermediate point is Mk. 10[1], and there is no certainty how that is to be interpreted; and therefore no certainty what route was followed by Jesus. The Lucan itinerary is equally difficult to follow. It is thus summarised by Burkitt (*Beginnings of Christianity*, ii. 486): ' Jesus now sets His face to go to Jerusalem, and is consequently not received at a Samaritan village (9[51 ff.]). The seventy-two are sent out and return (10[1, 17]). On the way Jesus is received by

Martha and Mary at a certain village (10³⁸). A number of incidents follow, several of which involve the presence of crowds (11¹⁴, ²⁷, ²⁹, 12¹, ¹³, ⁵⁴, 14²⁵), Pharisees (11³⁷, ⁵³, 13³¹, 14¹, 15², 16¹⁴), and a synagogue (13¹⁰), all on the way to Jerusalem (13²²). Presently Jesus is " journeying through the midst of Samaria and Galilee " (17¹¹), and so arrives at Jericho (18³⁵), from whence He goes up to Jerusalem (19²⁸)'. What is to be made of these details is a still unsolved problem; but it is most unlikely that they mark stages in a journey through Samaria from Galilee to Judæa. Whatever else Lk. 9⁵¹–18¹⁴ may be, it does not appear to be a chronicle.

51, 52. Lk. recognises that the close of the Galilean ministry is a turning-point in the life of Jesus. From now on events march inevitably towards His being ' received up,' i.e. most probably the Ascension. (Cf. Ryle and James on *Ps. Sol.* 4²⁰; Charles on *Apoc. Baruch* 46⁷; 2 Kings 2¹¹; Mk. 16¹⁹; Acts 1²; 1 Tim. 3¹⁶.) Jesus determines to go to Jerusalem. The route chosen is through Samaria. That this way was taken by Galilean pilgrims to Jerusalem is shown by Josephus (*Ant.* XX, vi. 1). In the *Life* (§ 269) Josephus says that this was the quickest route, the journey from Galilee to Jerusalem being possible in three days.

53. The Samaritans refuse hospitality to Jews going up to Jerusalem to the rival sanctuary. The refusal of hospitality was a serious matter. In the Palestinian Talmud a place is mentioned which has the name *Kefar Bīsh* (= evil village), and the name is explained as having been given because the inhabitants would not give hospitality to travellers.

54. James and John wish to take summary vengeance for this affront. Cf. 2 Kings 1⁹ff.. Their proposal is in keeping with their nickname ' Sons of Thunder.' We may wonder whether this was not the occasion on which the name was conferred. The addition ' even as Elijah did ' (R.V. mg.) is probably to be regarded as an interpretative gloss, establishing the parallel with 2 Kings 1⁹ff..

55 f. The shortest text, usually regarded as the original, is that given in R.V. (text). The two additions in R.V. mg. are usually rejected as interpolations, probably of Marcionite origin. The second may be an adaptation of the saying in Lk. 19¹⁰ (cf. John 3¹⁷). The first is a little better attested, and might conceivably be the original text of Lk.; but the weight of evidence is against both passages. Both, however, give correctly enough the sense of the rebuke. Evil is not overcome with evil but with good.

It is not clear whether the other village, to which Jesus and the disciples go, is another Samaritan village or not.

4. *THE MISSION OF THE DISCIPLES* (139)

LK. 10¹, ⁴⁻⁷

10 1 Now after these things the Lord appointed seventy[1] others, and sent them two and two before his face into every city and place, whither he himself was about to come.
4 Carry no purse, no wallet, no shoes: 5 and salute no man on the way. And into whatsoever house ye shall[2] enter, first say, 6 Peace *be* to this house. And if a son of peace be there, your peace shall rest upon him: but if not, it shall turn to you again. 7 And in that same house remain, eating and drinking such things as they give: for the labourer is worthy of his hire. Go not from house to house.

[1] Many ancient authorities add *and two*: and so in ver. 17.
[2] Or, *enter first, say.*
[3] Or, *it.*

1. For the reasons for regarding these verses as belonging to L see above, pp. 73–78. The doubt as to the exact number of missionaries goes back to a very early date, for seventy-two is given by the Sahidic and Old Syriac versions, while seventy is the reading of Irenæus. There can be little doubt that seventy-two is the correct reading. The mission is a mission to Israel and the number is determined, as is the number of the Apostles, by the thought of the twelve tribes. Later the number is reduced to seventy in accordance with the idea that there are seventy nations in the world. The smaller number reflects the interests of the Gentile mission. But the errand on which these disciples were sent out was certainly no Gentile mission. Lk. represents it as designed to prepare the way for the arrival of Jesus Himself; but if preparations were going on simultaneously in thirty-six different places, it is difficult to see how one person could overtake the work. Moreover, Jesus does not appear to follow up the preparations. In Lk. 10¹⁷ the seventy-two return to Him: He does not follow them. Further, Lk. 22³⁵ff· definitely seems to refer back to Lk. 10⁴; and in Lk. 22³⁵ff· it is the Twelve who are addressed. This last point suggests very strongly that the mission of the seventy-two is a doublet of the mission of the Twelve. How the number seventy-two came into existence in the tradition is an unsolved problem.

4–6. See on Mt. 10⁹f·, above, p. 180. The injunction to abstain from greetings by the way is illustrated by the injunction of Elisha to Gehazi (2 Kings 4²⁹): ' Gird up thy loins, and take my staff in thine hand, and go thy way: if thou meet any man, salute him not; and if any salute thee, answer him not again: and lay my staff upon the face of the child.' In this case the matter is one of life and death: no greetings are to be exchanged on the way because the business is urgent. So in the charge to the disciples their mission is a sacred one, and it is very urgent. There is no time to waste in wayside pleasantries. The greetings withheld on the journey are to be offered on reaching the destination. Cf. Mt. 10¹² and notes, above, p. 181. The greeting is no mere formula, as an exchange of compliments on the road might be. It is a manifestation of the Kingdom of God in word, the first intimation of the new grace and power that have come into the world, an announcement that ' the Kingdom of God is come nigh unto you.' This gives the meaning of ' a son of peace.' In Hebrew and Aramaic idiom ' son of ' may mean either ' possessor of ' or ' worthy of.' So ' son of peace ' may mean either a peaceable person or one worthy of peace. Since the peace in question here is the peace of God's Kingdom, the second meaning must be chosen. If there is anyone in the house worthy to receive this gift of God, he will receive it. Otherwise it will return to the messengers.

7. Where hospitality is received there the messengers are to stay. They are to accept the food and shelter of the household as a right. The labourer deserves his hire: and they who give up everything for the sake of bringing the good news to others are entitled to a subsistence while they do it. But they are also to be content with what is available. They are not to be seeking for better quarters and ampler rations. The labourer is worthy of his hire; but his hire is not the object of his labour.

On vv. 8–16, which I assign to Q, see above, pp. 75–78.

9

5. *THE RETURN OF THE MISSIONARIES* (140)

LK. 10[17-20]

10 17 And the seventy returned with joy, saying, Lord, even the [1] devils are subject 18 unto us in thy name. And he said unto them, I beheld Satan fallen as lightning 19 from heaven. Behold, I have given you authority to tread upon serpents and scorpions, and over all the power of the enemy: and nothing shall in any wise 20 hurt you. Howbeit in this rejoice not, that the spirits are subject unto you; but rejoice that your names are written in heaven.

[1] Gr. *demons.*

17. Here, as in *v.* 1, the true reading is probably ' seventy-two.' The mission is clearly understood to have been successful, at any rate from the point of view of the missionaries. The thing that pleases them is the fact that they have been able to perform exorcisms in the name of Jesus. For the use of the name of Jesus for this purpose cf. Lk. 9[49 f.]; Acts 19[13]. The power to overcome the demons is a cause for rejoicing because it is a sign of the presence of the Kingdom of God. See Lk. 11[20 ff.] (Q), above, p. 86. The same divine power which is manifested in the Master is now manifested in the disciples.

18, 20. This is confirmed by the reply of Jesus. The overcoming of the demons is the overthrow of their chief. The words of Jesus describe a visionary experience in which He watched Satan fall (Moulton, *Prolegomena*, p. 134) like lightning from heaven. There are two views about Satan in Judaism. According to one he had already been cast down from heaven in the beginning of time (Charles, *Revelation*, i. 323). According to the other, which has the support of the Old Testament passages Job. 1[6 f.]; Zech. 3[1 ff.], and perhaps also *Enoch* 40[7], he has at least access to heaven. The final overthrow of Satan was an integral part of the Jewish expectation of the good time coming, though there were different opinions as to who would be the agent: God Himself or the angels or the Messiah (Billerbeck, ii. 167 f.). It is significant that Jesus describes Himself as a spectator of Satan's downfall. The most natural inference is that He regards it as an act of God. This is a strong argument for the genuineness of the saying. Later Christology would not have assigned such a passive rôle to the Messiah. The fall of Satan is the beginning of the end of his kingdom. Something is achieved through the mission of Jesus and the disciples; and that which is thus begun must go on to its inevitable end in the complete subjection of the forces of evil and the full manifestation of the sovereignty of God. For the figure cf. Is. 14[12] and Rev. 12[8 f.]. The natural sequel to *v.* 18 is *v.* 20; and *v.* 19 may be regarded as an intrusion here.

While it is legitimate to rejoice over the subjection of the forces of evil, it must be remembered that this is only a means to an end. The warfare of the Kingdom is to make way for the peace of the Kingdom. The destruction of evil is part and parcel of the salvation of man. So the true reason for joy is that salvation is being achieved. 'There is more joy in heaven . . .' The 'spirits' here = the demons. In Jewish speech ' spirit,' without further qualification, regularly signifies ' evil spirit.' The figure employed to describe the salvation of the disciples is that their names are inscribed in the burgess-roll of the Kingdom. Heavenly books appear in Jewish literature and are distinguishable into four kinds: (1) the Book of Life or of the Living (Ps. 69[29], 87[4-6]; Exod. 32[32]; Dan. 12[1];

Phil. 4³; Heb. 12²³; Rev. 3⁵, 13⁸, 17⁸) containing the names of those who are members of God's Chosen People, and so destined for life, whether a life of prosperity in the Holy Land, or the life of the world to come; (2) the book containing the record of each man's deeds (Mal. 3¹⁶; Is. 65⁶; Rev. 20¹²); (3) the book containing the earthly destiny of men; (4) the book containing the Divine plan for the history of the world and the destiny of Israel and the nations. (See Billerbeck, ii. 169–176). It is the first of these books that is thought of here. That the disciples have their names inscribed in it means that they are destined for the bliss of the coming Kingdom.

19. This verse, which breaks the connexion between *vv.* 18 and 20 resembles slightly the words ascribed to the Risen Christ in the spurious ending of Mk. (16¹⁷f.). Cf. also Ps. 91¹³ :

Thou shalt tread upon the lion and the adder:
The young lion and the serpent shalt thou trample under feet,

and Dt. 8¹⁵. The serpents and scorpions may be thought of as semi-demonic creatures. The serpent in the story of the Fall is identified with Satan. Cf. notes on Lk. 3⁷, above, p. 40. The 'enemy' is Satan; and the promise of the verse is that nothing that Satan can do will be able to harm the disciples.

Lk. 10²¹⁻²⁴ (Q), above, pp. 78–81.

6. *THE WAY OF LIFE* (143)

LK. 10²⁵⁻²⁸

10 25 And behold, a certain lawyer stood up and tempted him, saying, ¹ Master, what 26 shall I do to inherit eternal life? And he said unto him, What is written in the 27 law? how readest thou? And he answering said, Thou shalt love the Lord thy God ² with all thy heart, and with all thy soul, and with all thy strength, and with all thy mind; and thy neighbour as 28 thyself. And he said unto him, Thou hast answered right: this do, and thou shalt live.

¹ Or, *Teacher.*
² Gr. *from.*

This piece of dialogue is generally regarded as the Lucan (L) parallel to Mk. 12²⁸⁻³¹,⁽³⁴⁾. Actually the only point of resemblance is the fact that the two great commandments are conjoined in both accounts. In Mk. the question put to Jesus is, so to speak, an academic one and one that seems to have been debated a good deal among the scribes, since the answers of distinguished Rabbis have come down to us. In Lk. it is a very practical question; cf. Mk. 10¹⁷. In Mk. Jesus gives the answer to the question: in Lk. it is given by the lawyer himself. In Mk. the comment of Jesus on the answer is: ' There is none other commandment greater than these.' Here it is: ' This do, and thou shalt live.' We are justified in assuming that the Lucan story is independent of Mk. Are they then different versions of the same incident? It might be argued that Lk. thought so, seeing that he omits the Marcan account from his Gospel. But if Lk. was interested chiefly in the point about the commandments, he may well have omitted the Marcan narrative on the ground that the essential point was already made in his own story, without staying to consider whether the two stories were different accounts of one and the same encounter. Further, the considerations which show the independence of the two accounts also suggest that they are accounts of two separate incidents.   For the chief connecting link, the conjunction of the great commandments, is precisely the sort of thing that could appear over and over again.   If a modern teacher of religion thought of such a thing as that, he would print it and it would make its way into the minds of the million.   But in the first century A.D. in Palestine the only way of publishing great thoughts was to go on repeating them in talk or sermons.

It is thus quite possible, even probable, that when Jesus gave His famous answer to the scribe's question in the Marcan story, it was not the first time that He had expressed the whole duty of man by putting together those two texts.   It must be emphasised that cases of this sort are not on all fours with the duplication of the miracles of feeding the multitude or with the two cleansings of the Temple.   Great teachers constantly repeat themselves.

We may therefore entertain the hypothesis that the lawyer in the Lucan story gives the reply (v. 27) which he already knows to represent the opinion of Jesus, and that he does so in order to raise the further question: Who is my neighbour? That is to say, the Lucan story begins in earnest where the Marcan leaves off; and Lk. 10$^{25-28}$ is really just introduction to what follows.   It states what is common ground between Jesus and the lawyer, what Jesus teaches and what the lawyer is prepared to accept in principle, though he requires further definition in detail.

25. Lk. uses the word ' lawyer ' rather than ' scribe,' because the latter would be easily misunderstood by Gentile readers of his Gospel.   The Greek word translated ' tempting ' does not necessarily have a hostile connotation.   It may mean no more than ' questioning,' but questioning with the idea of testing the qualifications of the person questioned.   The question itself contains no trap.   It is the supreme religious question, and so the supreme test of a religious teacher. By their answers to just this question all religions are judged.

26. The questioner is referred to the Law, of which he is an accredited expositor, for the answer to his question.   It is not expected that he will recite all its manifold commands and prohibitions, only that he should know the fundamental ends which these provisions are intended to secure.

27. The lawyer gives the answer which Jesus Himself gives in Mk. 12$^{28-31}$. This is not impossible or even improbable.   It has already been suggested that Jesus may have been teaching this doctrine before, and that it was well known that this was the way in which He construed the Law.   And, apart from that, there is the fact that in pre-Christian Jewish teaching the twin ideals of love to God and love to neighbour had been brought together in the *Testaments of the XII Patriarchs*.   E.g. *Iss. Issachar* 5$^{1f.}$

> Keep, therefore, my children, the law of God,
> And get singleness, and walk in guilelessness,
> Not playing the busybody with the business of your neighbour.
> But love the Lord and your neighbour,
> Have compassion on the poor and weak.

Cf. *Iss.* 7^6; *Test. Dan.* 5^3: 'Love the Lord through all your life, and one another with a true heart.'   The texts from the Old Testament here brought together are

Dt. 6⁵ and Lev. 19¹⁸. Philo, in his own way, makes the same conjunction when he describes the chief of the virtues as piety and philanthropy. (Cf. Drummond, *Philo Judæus*, ii. 315 f.). See further my *Teaching of Jesus*, pp. 302 ff.

28. The reply of Jesus gives complete approval to this solution of the problem. He says in effect: ' That is my answer to the question. It only remains to translate correct theory into regular practice, and you will find that it is the way of life for you.' There is nothing hypothetical about the sentence. Jesus says: ' This is the way to life, the life of the coming age; take it and you will find that it is so.' The moment this theory is put into practice, the question arises as to the scope of its application. This question is raised by the lawyer and answered by Jesus in

The Parable of the Good Samaritan (144)

LK. 10²⁹⁻³⁷

10 29 But he, desiring to justify himself, said unto Jesus, And who is my neighbour?
30 Jesus made answer and said, A certain man was going down from Jerusalem to Jericho; and he fell among robbers, which both stripped him and beat him, and
31 departed, leaving him half dead. And by chance a certain priest was going down that way: and when he saw him, he
32 passed by on the other side. And in like manner a Levite also, when he came to the place, and saw him, passed by on the
33 other side. But a certain Samaritan, as he journeyed, came where he was: and when he saw him, he was moved with

34 compassion, and came to him, and bound up his wounds, pouring on *them* oil and wine; and he set him on his own beast, and brought him to an inn, and took
35 care of him. And on the morrow he took out two ¹ pence, and gave them to the host, and said, Take care of him; and whatsoever thou spendest more, I, when I come back again, will repay thee.
36 Which of these three, thinkest thou, proved neighbour unto him that fell
37 among the robbers? And he said, He that shewed mercy on him. And Jesus said unto him, Go, and do thou likewise.

¹ See marginal note on Matt. xviii. 28.

29. The point of the lawyer's objection is that it is precisely when one begins to put such a rule as this into practice that difficulties arise. And they turn on the construction of the word ' neighbour.' ' Love God '—that goes without saying. Love one's family, or one's fellow-worshippers in the Synagogue, or one's colleagues in the Rabbinical school—that also is understood. But where does one draw the line between neighbour and not-neighbour, that is, between those who are entitled to this consideration from me and those who are not. All ancient civilisations drew the line somewhere, whether between Greek and Barbarian, Roman citizen and foreigner, freeman and slave, or Jew and Gentile. The context of Lev. 19¹⁸ shows plainly enough that ' neighbour ' there means fellow-Israelite. The concept might be enlarged by reckoning as neighbours those who, though not of Jewish race, embraced the Jewish faith; or it might be narrowed by excluding those who, though of Jewish blood, rejected or neglected the faith of their fathers. But at any rate the word ' neighbour ' ought to be definable; and it is for Jesus' definition that the lawyer asks.

It is often made a criticism of the parable of the Good Samaritan that it is no answer to the question posed. But this is a shallow criticism. Certainly no definition of ' neighbour ' emerges from the parable: and for a very good reason. The question is unanswerable, and ought not to be asked. For love does not begin by defining its objects: it discovers them. And failure in the observance of the great commandment comes not from lack of precise information about the application of it, but from lack of love. The point of the parable is that if a man has love in his heart, it will tell him who his neighbour is; and this is the only possible answer to the lawyer's question.

30. With the parable itself cf. 2 Chron. 28⁵⁻¹⁵. It has been suggested that this story is not fiction but fact, that Jesus Himself was the ' certain man ' who fell among thieves. In support of this hypothesis it could be urged that in Aramaic ' that man,' which is practically equivalent to ' a certain man,' is used as a polite periphrasis for the personal pronoun. But the theory cannot be proved, and should not be regarded as more than a possibility.

The road from Jerusalem to Jericho (about 17 miles) passes through country which is ' desert and rocky ' (Josephus, *War*, iv. 474), and suited by nature for the operations of brigands. Jerome reports that raiding bands of Arabs were active on the road in his day. The Greek word translated ' both ' in R.V. has rather the force of ' as you might expect,' or ' as their way is.' The evil work was thoroughly done, and when it was finished the victim was left without goods, without power to help himself or to follow his attackers, with very little between him and death.

31 f. Priest and Levite represented the national aristocracy of that period. It was to them that one might have looked for the manifestation of Judaism at its best. They above all others should have shown how to fulfil the commandment given in Lev. 19¹⁸. Their callousness stands in sharp contrast to the ideal of which they were the official guardians. It is possible that they were on their way home after serving in the Temple.

33. The Samaritan—a layman and, from the Jewish standpoint, a schismatic— shows a better spirit than the official exponents of Jewish piety. He would appear to be a travelling trader. Some difficulty has been felt at the idea of a Samaritan appearing on business in Judæa, especially as relations between Jews and Samaritans were bad at this time; and it has been supposed that originally the parable told not of a good Samaritan, but of a good ' Israelite.' In this case ' Israelite ' would mean a Jewish layman in contrast to the Priest and the Levite. This is not very likely; and if we have to deal with the difficulty of the Samaritan being on the road from Jerusalem to Jericho, it is simpler to suppose that originally the third to arrive on the scene was an '*am hā-āres*, i.e. a Jew who did not attend with proper strictness to the details of the legal system, a Jew who was not a ' practising ' Jew. Such a conjecture would make the change to ' Samaritan ' easily conceivable. But we should probably retain ' Samaritan ' in spite of the unlikelihood of finding a Samaritan travelling from Jerusalem to Jericho. The parable is fiction, not history. See notes on *v.* 36. In any case the point is that mercy and kindness were displayed by the last person from whom one would have looked for these qualities.

34, 35. The Samaritan renders first aid to the victim. Oil and wine, either separately or mixed, were recognised as healing agents both in Palestine (Mishnah, *Shabbath*, 19²; Danby, p. 116) and among the Greeks. Having made his man comfortable, the Samaritan brings him to an ' inn,' or rather caravanserai, where shelter and protection could be obtained for the night. More than that, on the following day, when he must continue his journey, the Samaritan pays in advance for such further care as his penniless protégé may require. The ' two pence ' are two *denarii*, silver coins worth about 8½*d*., but with much greater purchasing power. In the Mishnah four denars is the price of a lamb fit for sacrifice (*Menahoth* 13[8]; Danby, p. 512); and in Mt. 20[2] one denar is the day's wage for a working man. The good Samaritan further promises that on his return journey he will pay any further debt that may have been incurred.

36. Having told the story Jesus asks the lawyer for his opinion. The question is not whether the victim of the robbers was neighbour in a legal sense to any or all of those who encountered him, but whether any of them showed a neighbourly spirit towards him. The principle underlying the question is that while mere neighbourhood does not create love, love does create neighbourliness. Supposing, as we may, that the man who fell among thieves was a Jew, he was in fact ' neighbour ' in the technical Jewish sense to the Priest and the Levite; and he was not ' neighbour ' to the Samaritan. Yet his lawful ' neighbours ' were of no use to him in his extremity, and it was a man who was not his lawful ' neighbour ' who helped him. Love created neighbourliness. Hence the conclusion implicit in the whole parable: it is wrong to construe Lev. 19[18] in terms of ' neighbour '; you must construe it in terms of ' love.' For it is ' love ' that is fundamental, not neighbourhood.

37. The lawyer gives the only possible answer to Jesus' question, and this is met by the command: Go, and do thou likewise. This is the final answer to the lawyer's original question (*v.* 25): What shall I do to inherit eternal life?

7. *MARTHA AND MARY* (145)

LK. 10[38-42]

10 38 Now as they went on their way, he entered into a certain village: and a certain woman named Martha received 39 him into her house. And she had a sister called Mary, which also sat at the Lord's 40 feet, and heard his word. But Martha was [1] cumbered about much serving; and she came up to him, and said, Lord, dost thou not care that my sister did leave me to serve alone? bid her therefore that 41 she help me. But the Lord answered and said unto her, [2] Martha, Martha, thou art anxious and troubled about 42 many things: [3] but one thing is needful: for Mary hath chosen the good part, which shall not be taken away from her.

[1] Gr. *distracted.*
[2] A few ancient authorities read *Martha, Martha, thou art troubled; Mary hath chosen, &c.*
[3] Many ancient authorities read *but few things are needful, or one.*

Beside the teaching on the way to eternal life Lk. places this incident, whose purport is to show that that way is the supreme interest of men. The parable of the Good Samaritan shows the one way to the goal; the story of Martha and Mary insists that there is only one goal worth seeking.

38-40. The setting of the incident is vague. Presumably Lk.'s source did not give further particulars; and the two sisters do not appear elsewhere in the Synoptics. In the fourth gospel (11[1]) their home was in Bethany. Both Martha and Mary are Jewish names. Martha appears here as the head of the household: there is no mention of a brother Lazarus, as in John. She is the industrious capable housewife. Her sister Mary is more concerned to ' attend upon the Lord without distraction ' (1 Cor. 7[35]). To sit at the feet of a person is to be his pupil.

Cf. Acts 22[3], Paul brought up ' at the feet of Gamaliel '; *Aboth* 1[4] (Danby, p. 446):
' Let thy house be a meeting-house for the Sages and sit amid the dust of their
feet and drink in their words with thirst.' Martha, up to the eyes in work,
regards her sister's interest in theology with disapproval. Time enough to listen
when the household work is finished. (Though we may suspect that Martha was
one of those whose work is never finished.) She appeals to Jesus to send his new
disciple about her proper business.

41 f. The sense of Jesus' reply is clear enough in the main; but the exact form
of it is uncertain. As it has come down to us in MSS. and versions there are four
main forms:

    I. Martha, Martha, Mary hath chosen the good part, etc.
    II. Martha, Martha, thou art anxious and troubled about many things:
but one thing is needful: for Mary hath chosen the good part, etc.
    III. Martha, Martha, thou art anxious and troubled about many things:
but few things are needful: for Mary hath chosen the good part, etc.
    IV. Martha, Martha, thou art anxious and troubled about many things:
but few things are needful, or one: for Mary hath chosen the good part, etc.

Of these readings IV may be dismissed as a conflation of II and III. It is,
however, in that case evidence for the antiquity of III. Some ancestor of the
authorities, which have IV, had the reading III. Someone inserted in the margin
of his copy the words ' or one,' which then found their way into the text. I do
not consider it necessary to decide between ' but one thing is needful ' and ' but
few things are needful '; because I regard them as variant forms of an original
gloss on the text. They probably correspond to early variations in the interpretation of the story. Such interpretations were already current in the time of
Origen. For example, Martha is the type of Jewish Christianity, Mary of
Gentile Christianity: or Martha is the type of the practical life, Mary of the
contemplative: or again the ' many things ' stand for the numerous commandments of the Law while the ' few things ' are the Gospel commandments of love.
If, however, we ask what the two clauses could mean in the original context, it
would seem that ' few things ' can only be in contrast to ' many things.' Martha
is making great preparations; but something much simpler would be quite
adequate. On the other hand ' one thing ' can only anticipate ' the good part ':
the one thing needful is the good part which Mary has chosen.

    It seems most likely to me that the original answer ran: Martha, Martha, **thou
art anxious and troubled about many things: but Mary hath chosen the good
part**, etc. Some such reading appears to lie behind the quotation of this text by
Clement of Alexandria (ed. Stählin, iii. 166).

    The contrast between Martha and Mary does not lie where the patristic
commentators found it. It is something much simpler and more primitive. The
good thing which Mary has chosen is not the contemplative life, or the ethic of
the Sermon on the Mount, but the Kingdom of God. The true parallel in thought
to this saying is Lk. 12[29-31]||Mt. 6[31-33] (Q), above, p. 113. The contrast is between
Martha, immersed in the business of her little corner of the workaday world, and
Mary, who is of the kind that leave all to follow Christ. It could be urged, and

Martha makes the point, that in leaving all Mary has mostly left her duties in the house. A similar criticism could, however, have been made by Peter's wife or the father of James and John; and it can be said that the progress of the Gospel in the world would not have been what it was if there had not been those who heard a call that cancelled all other obligations. As the story stands Mary belongs to those who take the Kingdom of God by storm, who put their hands to the plough and do not look back, who leave the dead to bury their dead.

8. *THE LORD'S PRAYER* (146)

LK. 11[1-4]

11 1 And it came to pass, as he was praying in a certain place, that when he ceased, one of his disciples said unto him, Lord, teach us to pray, even as John also taught 2 his disciples. And he said unto them, When ye pray, say, [1] Father, Hallowed be 3 thy name. Thy kingdom come.[2] Give us day by day [3] our daily bread. And 4 forgive us our sins; for we ourselves also forgive every one that is indebted to us.

And bring us not into temptation.[4]

[1] Many ancient authorities read *Our Father, which art in heaven.* See Matt. vi. 9.

[2] Many ancient authorities add *Thy will be done, as in heaven, so on earth.* See Matt. vi. 10.

[3] Gr. *our bread for the coming day.*

[4] Many ancient authorities add *but deliver us from the evil* one (or, *from evil*). See Matt. vi. 13.

The Lord's Prayer, in the form familiar to us through liturgical use, appears in Mt. 6[9-13] (above, pp. 167–171). The Lucan version, which we assign to L, is shorter and differs from Mt. in several particulars. The true text of the Lucan form is not easy to establish, because the tendency in the copying of MSS. has been to conform it to the Matthæan, which was the version in the liturgical use.

1. The Prayer is here provided with a narrative setting. In Mt. it is incorporated into a collection of teachings on the general subject of prayer as a part of religious observance. Here the origin of the Lord's Prayer is described. It is given in response to a request from one of the disciples; and the disciple is led to make his request through observing that John's disciples had forms of prayer prescribed by their master. Three early Christian practices seem thus to be derived from imitation of John's discipline: baptism, common prayer, and regular fasts.

2. 'Father' is undoubtedly the true text of Lk. The marginal reading is an instance of the tendency to conform MSS. to the text of Mt. 'Father' is almost certainly the original form of the address, see above, p. 168. The two following petitions agree with Mt. But there is a remarkable variant reading: 'Thy holy Spirit come upon us and cleanse us.' In the version of Lk. published by the second-century heretic Marcion this petition takes the place of 'Hallowed be thy name'; and in two cursive MSS. as well as in the writings of Gregory of Nyssa, and Maximus Confessor it takes the place of 'Thy kingdom come.' By some scholars it is regarded as the original text of Lk., though not necessarily the original language of the Prayer. The strongest argument in favour of this reading is the fact that in 11[13] Lk. speaks of God giving the Holy Spirit to those who ask Him, where Mt. in the parallel passage (7[11]) speaks of God giving 'good things.' Mt.'s 'good things' is almost certainly the true representation of the Q text. If Lk.

is responsible for ' Holy Spirit ' in 11¹³, it is the more likely that he is responsible for the clause asking for the Holy Spirit here, for the two things hang together. But even if the petition is inserted by Lk. himself, it is unlikely that it is part of the original Prayer. More probably it may be regarded as an old petition, used in connexion with the baptism of converts, which found its way into the Lord's Prayer. Or it may be that both the petition here and ' Holy Spirit ' in 11¹³ are due to Marcionite revision. The addition in R.V. mg. ' Thy will be done, etc.,' is not genuine text of Lk., but assimilation to Mt.

3. See notes on Mt. 6¹¹, above, p. 169. The Lucan form of the petition is less original than the Matthæan. The request in Mt. asks for enough to-day to provide for to-morrow. In Lk. this is generalised into the request that every day we may have enough for the next day.

4. See notes on Mt. 6¹², above, p. 169. The L form of the petition is less concrete and definite than the Matthæan. In Mt. the prayer says ' we have forgiven '; and the thought is that definite known cases of offence have been disposed of in this way. Cf. Mt. 5²³ᶠ·, above, p. 156. In Lk. it is rather a regular practice that is stated in general terms—and statements in general terms are dangerous in prayer. Mt.'s form is to be preferred.

5. See notes on Mt. 6¹³, above, p. 170. The Lucan form omits the last petition for deliverance from the evil. The reading given in R.V. mg. is again a case of assimilation to the text of Mt.

The differences between the forms of the Prayer in Mt. and Lk. can be considered under two heads.

First, there are the differences in wording in the parts where Mt. and Lk. coincide; and here it must be said that in the main Mt.'s wording is to be preferred. The one case in which Lk. clearly deserves the preference is ' Father ' for ' Our Father which art in heaven.'

Secondly, there is the fact that the genuine text of Lk. gives a shorter version of the prayer than Mt. Here it is important to remember that the tendency of liturgical forms is to grow rather than to shrink through use. There is thus some antecedent probability that the shorter form is the more original. This is strengthened if we regard the petition ' Thy will be done, etc.,' as exposition of the immediately preceding ' Thy kingdom come,' and take the petition ' but deliver us from the evil (one) ' as commentary on ' Lead us not into temptation.'

We cannot do more than guess at the original form of the Prayer; but a tentative reconstruction on the basis of the evidence of Mt. and Lk. would be somewhat as follows:

> Father, Hallowed be thy name.
>> Thy Kingdom come.
>> Give us this day our bread for the coming day.
> And forgive us our sins, as we also have forgiven those who have wronged us.
>> And bring us not into temptation.

9. *THE PARABLE OF THE IMPORTUNATE FRIEND* (147)

LK. 11^{5-8}

11 5 And he said unto them, Which of you shall have a friend, and shall go unto him at midnight, and say to him, Friend, lend 6 me three loaves; for a friend of mine is come to me from a journey, and I have 7 nothing to set before him; and he from within shall answer and say, Trouble me not: the door is now shut, and my children are with me in bed; I cannot rise and give 8 thee? I say unto you, Though he will not rise and give him, because he is his friend, yet because of his importunity he will arise and give him [1] as many as he needeth.

[1] Or, *whatsoever things*.

Mt. follows the Lord's Prayer with a caution that God's forgiveness is conditional on a forgiving spirit in man; Lk. with a discourse (11^{5-13}, L + Q) on God's readiness to give to those who ask Him. The first part of the discourse is the present parable, which is peculiar to Lk. The second part is from Q, and has been treated above, pp. 81 f. This parable has a companion in the parable of the Importunate Widow (Lk. 18^{1-8}), which is also peculiar to this Gospel (below, p. 305). That parable may be regarded as comment on the petition 'Thy kingdom come'; this as comment on 'Give us this day our bread for the coming day.' The one looks forward to the final fulfilment of God's plan; the other has in mind the needs of God's servants while they wait and work for it. There is a certain superficial inconsistency between what is taught in this parable and the principle laid down in Mt. $6^{7f.}$ (M), particularly the words 'Your Father knoweth what things ye have need of before ye ask him.' But the inconsistency is more apparent than real. Certainly, if we think of God's providence as a piece of supernatural machinery, which distributes with infallible accuracy what every man ought to have, it may seem superfluous to express our desires in prayer. But the teaching of Jesus is that we are not dealing with a mere combination of omniscience and omnipotence, but with a Father who cares for us as persons; and that therefore our desires are His concern as much as our needs. If we are dealing with a government department, there may be nothing for it but to apply on the printed form and sign on the dotted line; but if we are dealing with a father, we may exercise more freedom of speech. Prayer is the means of establishing agreement between God's will and man's desires: and it may well be that the best of all ways of educating our desires is to express them to God in prayer. It may be that it is only by telling God frankly what we want that we can learn what we truly need.

5 f. The situation described is a simple one. There is the arrival late at night of an unexpected guest and the discovery that the contents of the larder are inadequate to the claims of hospitality. The only thing to be done is to knock up a friend and borrow what is needed. This the householder proceeds to do as politely as possible. Note the 'Friend' in the request: it is absent from the reply. Also the explanation offered for disturbing the friend at that time of night.

7. There is an absence of cordiality in the reply from within. It is a nuisance to be roused from one's sleep, a nuisance to have to unlock the door, a nuisance to have the children disturbed. The conclusion of the matter is 'I cannot arise and give thee.' Here, as so often, 'I cannot' camouflages 'I will not.'

8. But the hero of the parable will not take No for an answer, and it soon appears that the only way for his friend to continue his night's rest is to come down and supply what is required.

The conclusion is not explicitly drawn; but it is sufficiently obvious. If a human friend, who is a prey to moods and tempers, can be persuaded even against his inclination to get up and oblige you, how much more will God your Father and your perfect friend be ready to supply all your needs. The disciple who has this confidence will be able to open his heart freely before God. He will also be able to accept whatever God sends him. He will know how to say: 'I have learned in whatsoever state I am, therein to be content. I know how to be abased, and I know also how to abound: in everything and in all things have I learned the secret both to be filled and to be hungry, both to abound and to be in want. I can do all things in him that strengtheneth me' (Phil. 4$^{11\text{-}13}$).

10. *OUTWARD AND INWARD PURITY* (154)

LK. 11$^{37\text{-}41,\ 53,\ 54}$, 12^{1}

11 37 Now as he spake, a Pharisee asketh him to ^{1} dine with him: and he went in, 38 and sat down to meat. And when the Pharisee saw it, he marvelled that he had 39 not first washed before ^{1} dinner. And the Lord said unto him, Now do ye Pharisees cleanse the outside of the cup and of the platter; but your inward part 40 is full of extortion and wickedness. Ye foolish ones, did not he that made the 41 outside make the inside also? Howbeit give for alms those things which ^{2} are within; and behold, all things are clean unto you.

53 And when he was come out from thence, the scribes and the Pharisees began to ^{3} press upon *him* vehemently, and to provoke him to speak of ^{4} many

54 things; laying wait for him, to catch something out of his mouth.

12 1 In the mean time, when ^{5} the many thousands of the multitude were gathered together, insomuch that they trode one upon another, he began to ^{6} say unto his disciples first of all, Beware ye of the leaven of the Pharisees, which is hypocrisy.

^{1} Gr. *breakfast.*
^{2} Or, *ye can.*
^{3} Or, *set themselves vehemently against* him.
^{4} Or, *more.*
^{5} Gr. *the myriads of.*
^{6} Or, *say unto his disciples, First of all beware ye.*

On the composition of the whole passage 11^{37}–12^{1}, see above, pp. 94 ff. The conclusion there reached is that our present passage 11$^{37\text{-}41}$, 11^{53}–12^{1}, is the L framework into which Lk. has inserted the Q woes against scribes and Pharisees. This passage makes a complete and self-contained story whose subject is the same as that in Mk. 7$^{1\text{-}23}$, though the situation and the treatment of the topic are different. The central point (*vv.* 39–41) has a parallel in Mt.'s woes against scribes and Pharisees (Mt. 23$^{25f.}$, above, p. 236). But it is more likely that the woe has been extracted out of the story than that the story has been constructed round the woe.

37 f. The scene of the incident is a Pharisee's house, to which Jesus has been invited for a meal. The nature of the meal is uncertain. The ordinary Jewish practice was to have two meals per day (three on the Sabbath). These were taken in the morning and evening. But among that class of the community to which this Pharisee may well have belonged, the morning meal was not taken until about midday; and the practice was to take a little food, not a full meal, earlier in the

morning. It seems most probable that the meal in this case was a midday meal. Jesus shocked his host by sitting down to the meal without first washing. This ' washing ' consisted in pouring water over the hands; and it was customary before and after the meal (Billerbeck, i. 695–704). We are not told how the Pharisee expressed his surprise, whether in speech or merely by a raising of the eyebrows; but we are clearly to understand that there was some indication. This indication, whatever it was, provoked the reply of Jesus.

39 ff. The M version of this saying seems in the main to give it more correctly. There the figure is maintained throughout. Here the Lucan version wavers between parable and interpretation. It is probable, I think, that Jesus spoke throughout in terms of pots and pans, and left His hearers to make the obvious application of the parable. The vessel may be perfectly clean; but that is no advantage if its contents are putrid.

There is nothing in Mt. corresponding to *v.* 40 in Lk.; and the verse as it stands is exceedingly difficult to interpret. If we take the R.V. translation, we must understand the verse: ' " Did not God, who made the material universe, make men's souls also? " It is folly to be scrupulous about keeping material objects clean, while the soul is polluted with wickedness ' (Plummer). But perhaps we ought to translate differently: ' He, who has dealt with the outside, has not thereby dealt with the inside.' This involves taking the verb ' make ' not in the sense of ' create ' but in the sense in which it is used when we speak of ' making a bed ' i.e. putting it in order, making it fit for use.

Lk. *v.* 41 has a parallel in Mt. 23²⁶. But whereas Lk. has ' Give for alms those things which are within,' Mt. has ' Cleanse first the inside of the cup.' It is probable that Lk.'s ' give alms ' is a mistaken rendering of an Aramaic original correctly translated by Mt. Then the verse may be taken to say: ' Purify the inside (the heart), and then all is pure for you.' The meaning seems to be that the heart is what counts. If the heart is pure the whole man is pure. Defilement is cut off at the source. ' All things are clean unto you ' I take to mean ' The whole —outside and inside, the complete man—is clean, so far as you are concerned.' This agrees in substance with Mt. who says ' cleanse the inside, and you also cleanse the outside.' It is also in agreement with the teaching of Mk. 7¹⁸⁻²³. In this verse we have the application of the parable quite clearly in the mind of the speaker. For cleansing the inside of a vessel does not automatically cleanse the outside. But it can be said that if a man's heart is pure, he is pure.

We may compare the saying of Raba (died A.D. 352): ' A scholar (Rabbi) whose inward (thoughts) do not correspond to his outward (profession) is no scholar ' (Billerbeck, ii. 188).

53 ff. These verses describe the effect of this attack upon the hearers. They began to make a dead set against Jesus and to ' heckle ' him about all kinds of subjects. Every question was a trap by which they hoped to elicit a reply which might be turned against Him. Lk. seems to picture this contest as drawing a large crowd of the general public, all anxious to hear the dispute and jostling one another in their eagerness to get to the front. In the midst of the uproar Jesus turns to His disciples, who have not hitherto been mentioned, and says to His disciples first of all, ' Beware of the leaven of the Pharisees, which is hypocrisy.'

It is clear that Lk. must introduce the disciples at this point, because of the Q passage (12^{2-12}) which he is about to link on to this saying, and which is clearly addressed to disciples.   It is therefore possible that in his source the words of *v.* 1 were addressed to the assembled crowd.   This would explain the ' first of all.' The words, Lk. will have us understand, are meant to be heard by the crowd—as, presumably, in his source—but they are primarily for the disciples, to whom what immediately follows is addressed.   If this is the correct explanation it becomes unnecessary to repunctuate the verse and translate, with some scholars, ' He began to say to His disciples: Before all beware of the leaven, etc.'

On the above interpretation 12^1 forms a dramatic climax to the whole incident. It may be noted that we have a point of contact with Mk.'s account of a similar dispute, with this difference that the charge of hypocrisy comes at the end of Lk.'s story, whereas in Mk. it is the first item in Jesus' reply (Mk. $7^{6ff.}$).

On the ' leaven ' of the Pharisees cf. Mk. 8^{15}: Take heed, beware of the leaven of the Pharisees and the leaven of Herod.   This obscure saying was already a problem in the early days.   Mt. in the parallel (Mt. 16^6) changes Mk.'s text to ' leaven of the Pharisees and Sadducees ' and later interprets this (16^{12}) as the ' teaching of the Pharisees and Sadducees.'   Here the leaven is hypocrisy.   It is possible that the words ' which is hypocrisy ' are an explanatory comment either of Lk. or his source.   In the Rabbinical literature ' leaven ' is used figuratively of the evil disposition in man (Billerbeck, i. 728 f.).

In spite of the skill with which Lk. has presented the story, it remains more than possible that 12^1 was originally a separate fragment, which has nothing to do with what precedes or follows.

11. *THE PERIL OF COVETOUSNESS* (156)

LK. 12^{13-21}

12 13   And one out of the multitude said unto him, [1] Master, bid my brother divide the
14 inheritance with me.   But he said unto him, Man, who made me a judge or a
15 divider over you?   And he said unto them, Take heed, and keep yourselves from all covetousness: [2] for a man's life consisteth not in the abundance of the
16 things which he possesseth.   And he spake a parable unto them, saying, The ground of a certain rich man brought
17 forth plentifully: and he reasoned within himself, saying, What shall I do, because I have not where to bestow my fruits?
18 And he said, This will I do: I will pull down my barns, and build greater; and

there will I bestow all my corn and my
19 goods.   And I will say to my [3] soul, [3] Soul, thou hast much goods laid up for many years; take thine ease, eat, drink,
20 be merry.   But God said unto him, Thou foolish one, this night [4] is thy [3] soul required of thee; and the things which thou hast prepared, whose shall they be?
21 So is he that layeth up treasure for himself, and is not rich toward God.

   [1] Or, *Teacher.*
   [2] Gr. *for not in a man's abundance consisteth his life, from the things which he possesseth.*
   [3] Or, *life.*
   [4] Gr. *they require thy soul.*

For Lk. this incident seems to be the continuation of what has gone before. Lk. 12^{2-12} form the continuation of the saying in 12^1; and the crowd *v.* 13 is the same as that in *v.* 1.   But it is unlikely that the connexion is anything more than a literary device.   The passage *vv.* 13–21 is a self-contained unit, which Lk. has skilfully inserted between two Q passages.   It falls into two parts (*a*) a piece of dialogue between Jesus and a dissatisfied heir, leading up to (*b*) the parable of the Rich Fool. The first part has been supposed, for no very good reason, to be an artificial introduction to the parable. The connexion is good; and the most likely view is that the bit of dialogue, which is not in itself of vital importance, has been preserved by the fact that it was attached to the parable from the beginning.

13 f. The unknown person who appeals to Jesus is described by Lk. as 'one out of the multitude.' This description serves to link the incident to what has gone before. No doubt it replaces a still more indefinite phrase, such as, ' a certain man.' There is nothing odd in the man's bringing a question of this sort to Jesus. In Judaism the one Law covered everything. There was no sharp division between the secular and the sacred, between civil and ecclesiastical matters. The same authorities decided matters of religious belief and practice and matters of civil and criminal justice. The dictum ' This is a court of law, not a court of morals ' would have had no meaning to a Jewish scribe in the first century. A ' teacher ' (Rabbi) was the very person to decide both religious and, what we should call, legal questions. The rules of inheritance are given in the Mishnah (*Baba Bathra* 8–9, Danby, pp. 376–980). We are not told what the issue was in this particular case; and the details are irrelevant, since the reply of Jesus to the request makes it clear that he would refuse to adjudicate in any case. He refuses to be interested in the ' facts of the case,' because there is one outstanding fact which makes all the rest insignificant; the fact that two men, worshippers of the same God, members of the one Chosen People and of the same family, are separated and antagonised over the possession of a piece of property. What is needed is not a just settlement of the dispute by some third party, but that the parties themselves and all the multitude should feel the shame and disgrace of such a dispute. Cf. I Cor. 6[7 ff.]. If the brothers realise that, they will settle the matter amicably between themselves. Our Lord's curt refusal to have anything to do with the case is put in words reminiscent of Exod. 2[14].

15. The whole wretched business is in flat contradiction to the fundamental rule of life given in Lev. 19[18]: Thou shalt love thy neighbour as thyself. And the active cause of the trouble is just plain greed. What is needed is not the decision of this or any other case, but the elimination of that which makes the dispute. ' All covetousness ' means self-seeking in all its manifold shapes, both in the crude desire for material things and in the subtler forms which it can also take with those whose tastes are more refined. There is a twofold reason for avoiding it. First, it causes disunion and strife, as in the case which has given rise to this piece of teaching. And secondly, it leads nowhere. He who hopes to achieve fullness of life by increasing his possessions finds in the end that he has laboured for that which satisfieth not. It is true that a certain minimum of material goods is necessary for life; but it is not true that greater abundance of goods means greater abundance of life. Cf. Eccles. 2[1-11]; Ps. 49; Job 31[24 f.].

16, 17 f. This general principle is now driven home by the story of the Rich Fool (*vv*. 16–21). The parable has some affinity with the passage in *Ecclus.* 11[18 f.]:

> There is that waxeth rich from self-denial,
> And this is his allotted reward:

> What time he saith: ' I have found rest,
> And now I will enjoy my goods '—
> He knoweth not what lot shall befall;
> He shall leave (them) to others and die.

In the story as told by Jesus we are introduced to the hero when his ambitions are on the point of being realised. He already has abundance of material goods. The only problem remaining is that of storage. This is simply solved by demolishing the existing storehouses and building larger. Translated into modern terms— here is a man who has made a large fortune in business, and now wishes to retire. He realises his capital and invests all in trustee securities.

19. Having made all the necessary provision for the future the rich man will be able, he thinks, to spend the remainder of his days in enjoyment. Cf. Eccles. 8[15]: ' A man hath no better thing under the sun, than to eat, and to drink, and to be merry.' Tobit 7[10]; Euripides, Alc., 788 f.

20. But the rich man's plans for the future are destined not to be carried out. In the midst of his scheming he hears the summons that cannot be ignored. The R.V. mg. gives the literal rendering of the Greek. This impersonal 3rd person plural has the effect of a passive. It is, of course, God who requires the man's soul. The sting of the words lies, however, not in the announcement that the man must die, but in the following question, which shows clearly the real poverty of his life. He is lonely and friendless in the midst of his wealth.

For a perfect modern parallel to the story see Jung, *Collected Papers on Analytical Psychology*, pp. 399 ff.

21. This verse supplies the comment on the story. Whether it comes from Jesus Himself or from some early Christian or from Lk. is doubtful. It can be connected with the closing words of *v.* 20 by the consideration that if the rich man had employed his riches in an unselfish way, he would have had both friends on earth and treasure in heaven.

12. *THE URGENCY OF THE GOSPEL* (162)

LK. 13[1-9]

13 1 Now there were some present at that very season which told him of the Galilæans, whose blood Pilate had mingled with 2 their sacrifices. And he answered and said unto them, Think ye that these Galilæans were sinners above all the Galilæans, because they have suffered 3 these things? I tell you, Nay: but, except ye repent, ye shall all in like manner 4 perish. Or those eighteen, upon whom the tower in Siloam fell, and killed them, think ye that they were [1] offenders above 5 all the men that dwell in Jerusalem? I tell you, Nay: but, except ye repent, ye shall all likewise perish.

6 And he spake this parable; A certain man had a fig tree planted in his vineyard; and he came seeking fruit thereon, and 7 found none. And he said unto the vinedresser, Behold, these three years I come seeking fruit on this fig tree, and find none: cut it down; why doth it also cumber 8 the ground? And he answering saith unto him, Lord, let it alone this year also, till I shall dig about it, and dung it: 9 and if it bear fruit thenceforth, *well*; but if not, thou shalt cut it down.

[1] Gr. *debtors*.

This passage consists of two portions, both occupied with the same matter, the urgent necessity for timely repentance. The Gospel is good news, but only for those who will listen to it. It opens up a way of salvation for those who will leave the way of destruction. It is at once a warning and a promise: and in this passage, as in the immediately preceding Q section (12^{57-59}, above, p. 122), it is the warning note that is stressed.

1. The passage opens with a precise note of time; but the words ' at that very season ' do not really tell us anything. If Lk. himself inserted them in order to link this bit of L material to the preceding bit of Q, it can only be said that he did not show very much skill. The alternative is to suppose that the words were in the anecdote as it came to him, and that they refer to some context now lost. The Greek verb translated ' there were present ' can also mean ' there arrived,' and this rendering is to be preferred. The story which these persons told is not elsewhere recorded. The scene of the incident must be Jerusalem, for only there could sacrifice be offered. Galileans have come up to the Temple and are either slaughtering or assisting at the slaughtering of the victims when they are massacred by the Romans. There are evidences outside the New Testament of Pilate's brutality (e.g. Josephus, *Antiquities*, xviii. 60 ff., 85 ff.; *War*, ii. 175 ff.), but nothing that tallies with this story. The question at once arises whether this tale of Pilate's outburst is fact or fiction; and this goes with the further question why the story was brought to Jesus. Two answers may be given to this latter question. Either the story was told in the hope that it would rouse Jesus to lead a revolt against Rome, or in the hope that in His indignation He would say something about Pilate which might be used in evidence against Him on a charge of sedition. In the latter case the story did not even need to be true so long as it achieved its object. Those who came and told it would be, of course, enemies of Jesus. In the former case the tellers of the tale would presumably be ardent patriots. Their story would be the better of being true; but even if false, it would have served its purpose if it raised a revolt. For once started on a revolt there could be no going back. It is thus possible that the story was fiction from the beginning.

2 f. Whatever the motive may have been, the expected response did not materialise. Jesus was not to be drawn into criticism of the Roman governor or revolt against the Empire. Instead, He carries the whole matter out of the political into the religious sphere. Here it becomes another example of the kind of problem that created the book of Job. The easy solution would be to say, as Job's friends said, that the fate of the Galileans overtook them in the providence of God, and that it was doubtless a just punishment for some iniquity of which they were guilty. Jesus rejects this theory. If suffering were a punishment for sin, there would be a great deal more suffering than there is. While rejecting the retribution theory, Jesus does not put forward any alternative at this point. He leaves the ' problem of suffering ' and treats this story and another, which He brings forward Himself, as parables. And the point of the parables is the urgency of the Gospel.

Here are people going about their business in the Temple or the street, and suddenly death comes upon them. It is like the world in the days of Noah or Sodom and Gomorrah in the days of Lot. The fate of these people is a reminder not of their sins—they were neither better nor worse than many others—but of the urgency of the Gospel. Had they only known what was astir, been warned that Pilate was in a black mood or that the building was dangerous, they might have saved their lives. But there was nobody to warn them, and they perished. So this generation, says Jesus in effect, is walking—politically and religiously—straight for disaster. But the warning has been given, first by John the Baptist and now by Jesus. It is a warning to change direction before it is too late. ' Unless ye repent ye shall all likewise perish.'

4 f. The accident described in this verse is not mentioned elsewhere, which is not surprising, since it was an accident and not an ' incident.' It had no significance for the secular historian. The spring and reservoir of Siloam lay near the junction of the south and east walls of the city. The tower which collapsed may well have been some part of these ancient fortifications, and it is perhaps possible that the collapse was caused by the building operations carried out by Pilate to improve the water-supply of Jerusalem (Josephus, *Ant.* xviii. 60; *War*, ii. 175).

6. The lesson derived from the two incidents is further enforced by a parable. The parable is often regarded as having some relation to the incident of the fig tree narrated in Mk. 11$^{12-14, 20-25}$ and Mt. 20$^{18-22}$, but not in Lk. Actually the two stories have nothing in common except the fact that the fig tree produces no fruit. They are so different that it is extremely unlikely that either could have arisen from the other. All that can be said with any confidence is that Lk. may have omitted the Marcan incident from his Gospel because he already had this story of a barren fig tree and did not wish to duplicate it. Various attempts have been made to interpret the details of the parable; for example: the vineyard = Israel; the fig tree = Jerusalem; the vinedresser = Jesus; the three years = the ministry of Jesus (so Zahn); or the vineyard = Israel and the fig tree represents the individual (Jew) (so Wellhausen). But the point of the parable does not lie in details. It is meant to teach one lesson only, the need for timely repentance; and there is no profit in turning it into an allegory, nor any sort of certainty in the proposed identifications. Others can be devised which have as much or as little probability. For example, in the Rabbinical literature the Law is compared to a fig tree and the righteous to figs (Feldman, *Parables and Similes of the Rabbis*, pp. 155 ff.). But it would, I think, be a mistake to argue that this parable is concerned with the failure of the Law to produce righteous men and that therefore the Law is to be abolished.

A parallel to the parable has been found in the *Story of Ahikar*, 8^{35} (Syriac) (Charles, *Apoc. and Pseud.*, ii. 775). A comparison of the different versions, however, suggests that the Syriac version of *Ahikar* may have been influenced by reminiscences of the New Testament.

It was the custom in Palestine to plant fruit trees of all kinds in vineyards. According to Krauss (Billerbeck, i. 873) there were no vineyards, in the strict sense of the word, in Palestine, but only orchards in which all kinds of fruit trees stood together. A Rabbinical parable speaks of such a garden containing a row of fig trees, a row of vines, a row of pomegranate-trees, and a row of apple trees.

7 f. In spite of its favourable situation the tree produces no fruit; and this is not just an accident. This is the third fruitless year. The owner of the garden accordingly instructs the vinedresser to cut it down. (Cf. Lk. 3^9 = Mt. 3^{10}, Q.) It not only occupies space which might be used to better advantage. It is just a

glorified weed that exhausts the goodness of the land and yields nothing in return. The vinedresser will not, however, abandon hope of the tree, and pleads for another chance for it.   He will loosen the earth round its roots and manure it.   If it produces fruit in the following year, well and good.   (The leaving of the apodosis to be understood, as here, is a common idiom in the Semitic languages.) If there is still no result, then the tree can go.

The central point in the parable is the need for repentance.   Jesus says to His hearers: ' *You* are in the same position as that fig tree.'   The subsidiary point is the fact that God is both just and merciful.   The conversation between the owner of the vineyard and his workman is reminiscent of Rabbinical passages in which the attributes of God debate, the attribute of justice with the attribute of mercy.   If God dealt with Israel by strict justice, Israel would perish.   But He does not.   He gives another chance.   And if it is madness to fly in the face of His justice, it is desperate wickedness to flout His mercy.

13. *SABBATH OBSERVANCE* (163)

LK. 13[15-16]

This saying, from the story of the healing by Jesus of a crippled woman on the Sabbath, may be treated here as being allied to such sayings as Mt. 12[11f.] (above, pp. 188 f.) and Lk. 14[5] (below, p. 277).   It is Jesus' reply to the protest that the healing might easily have been postponed till the Sabbath was over.

13 10 And he was teaching in one of the 11 synagogues on the sabbath day.   And behold, a woman which had a spirit of infirmity eighteen years; and she was bowed together, and could in no wise lift 12 herself up.   And when Jesus saw her, he called her, and said to her, Woman, thou 13 art loosed from thine infirmity.   And he laid his hands upon her: and immediately she was made straight, and glorified 14 God.   And the ruler of the synagogue, being moved with indignation because Jesus had healed on the sabbath, answered and said to the multitude, There are six days in which men ought to work: in them therefore come and be healed, and not on the day of the sabbath. 15 But the Lord answered him, and said, Ye hypocrites, doth not each one of you on the sabbath loose his ox or his ass from the [1] stall, and lead him away to water- 16 ing?   And ought not this woman, being a daughter of Abraham, whom Satan had bound, lo, these eighteen years, to have been loosed from this bond on the 17 day of the sabbath?   And as he said these things, all his adversaries were put to shame: and all the multitude rejoiced for all the glorious things that were done by him.

[1] Gr. *manger*.

It is understood that cattle must be watered even on the Sabbath.   The rules for their management on the Sabbath are given in the Mishnah (*Shabbath* 5[1-4], Danby, pp. 103 f.).   The tying and loosing of knots were among the 39 kinds of ' work ' forbidden on the Sabbath (*Shabbath* 7[2], Danby, p. 106); but certain knots and fastenings were exempted from the general prohibition (*Shabbath* 15[1f.], Danby, p. 113).   Further rules for watering cattle on the Sabbath in *Erubin* 2[1-4], Danby, pp. 122 f.

On the point of the argument here, see the additional note on ' Jesus and the Sabbath Laws,' above, p. 190.

14. *THE HOSTILITY OF HEROD* (166)

LK. 13[31-33]

13 31 In that very hour there came certain Pharisees, saying to him, Get thee out, and go hence: for Herod would fain kill 32 thee. And he said unto them, Go and say to that fox, Behold, I cast out [1] devils and perform cures to-day and to-morrow, and the third *day* I am per-33 fected. Howbeit I must go on my way to-day and to-morrow and the *day* following: for it cannot be that a prophet perish out of Jerusalem.

[1] Gr. *demons.*

31. Here as in Lk. 13[1-5] we are left to speculate on the motives of those who brought the message to Jesus. It may be that these Pharisees were friendly disposed and wished to give warning of a real danger which threatened Jesus, and so save Him from the fate which had overtaken John the Baptist. There is evidence in Mk. 6[14ff.] that Herod had his eye on Jesus, and it may well have been a hostile eye. On the other hand there is the possibility that the warning was inspired by Herod himself or by his officers, and was a device to get Jesus out of Herod's territory without resorting to open expulsion. (Cf. Amos 7[10-17].) Unfortunately the available evidence is too scanty to allow us to do more than state possibilities.

The story itself implies that Jesus is still in the territory of Herod, that is, either in Galilee or Peræa. In that case the question remains open whether we ought not to think of the incident as taking place in such a set of circumstances as we have described in Mk. 8, prior to the departure of Jesus to Cæsarea Philippi.

32 f. The answer of Jesus is defiant. It characterises Herod in one uncomplimentary word, and then goes on to say in effect: ' I will go when I am ready; and when I go it will be for another reason than fear of Herod.' This stiff and uncompromising reply, together with the fact that the messengers are told to convey it to Herod, may incline us to think that Jesus regarded these Pharisees as semi-official emissaries of the Tetrarch rather than sympathisers with Himself.

' Fox ' in Jewish usage has a double sense. It typifies low cunning as opposed to straightforward dealing, and it is used in contrast to ' lion ' to describe an insignificant third-rate person as opposed to a person of real power and greatness. To call Herod ' that fox ' is as much as to say he is neither a great man nor a straight man; he has neither majesty nor honour.

The message goes on to say that the work which Jesus is doing for the souls and bodies of men will continue. It is not political agitation but a task of another kind to which God has sent Him; and He will continue with it, though only for a short time longer. ' To-day and to-morrow ' seems to be used in the general sense of ' a short time.' The Greek verb rendered ' I am perfected ' would be better translated by ' I am finished,' which has the same ambiguity as the original. It may mean ' my life is at an end ' or ' my work here is at an end.' If the former meaning is the correct one, we should have here a prophecy of the Passion. The same Greek verb is used later of Christian martyrdom. If the latter sense is the original, as seems more probable, the message means: ' I shall continue my work here for a little while longer and then finish with it.' The mission will be carried to its end; but that will not be long now.

There is some difficulty in the following statement that the period just described is to be spent in going away (from Herod's territory); and it is possible that ' to-day and to-morrow and the day following ' is a mistaken repetition from the preceding verse.   On the other hand it is to be remembered that the mission of Jesus is essentially a travelling mission.   There is thus no fundamental inconsistency in saying ' I shall continue my work in Galilee for some time yet ' and ' In the next few days (or weeks) I shall be moving out of Galilee.'   All that it amounts to is that Jesus will work His way towards Judæa and not flee thither.   ' While I am finishing my work here I shall be making my way out of Herod's territory.'   The reason for the move is not fear of Herod but what is expressed in the strange statement, ' It cannot be that a prophet perish out of Jerusalem.'   The Greek words translated ' it cannot be ' can also bear the meaning ' it is not appropriate '; and in view of the case of John the Baptist, whom Jesus regarded as a prophet and who certainly perished out of Jerusalem, we should prefer the meaning ' it is not appropriate.'   There is, then, a bitter irony in the words.   Herod must not be greedy: for Jerusalem has first claim on the blood of God's messengers.

15. SABBATH OBSERVANCE (168)

LK. 14[5]

There is a parallel to this saying in Mt. 12[11], where Mt. has inserted it into a Marcan narrative context, the story of the healing of the man with the withered hand (Mk. 3[1-6]).   Here the saying appears in a context of its own.   The person healed is suffering from dropsy; and Jesus performs the cure first and gives His reasons afterwards.   (Cf. Lk. 13[10-17].)

14 1   And it came to pass, when he went into the house of one of the rulers of the Pharisees on a sabbath to eat bread, that they 2 were watching him. And behold, there was before him a certain man which had 3 the dropsy. And Jesus answering spake unto the lawyers and Pharisees, saying, Is it lawful to heal on the sabbath, or not? 4 But they held their peace, And he took him, and healed him, and let him go. 5 And he said unto them, Which of you shall have [1] an ass or an ox fallen into a well, and will not straightway draw him 6 up on a sabbath day? And they could not answer again unto these things.

[1] Many ancient authorities read *a son*. See ch. xiii. 15.

The chief difficulty in the saying is textual.   The marginal reading ' son ' is adopted by Tischendorf and Westcott and Hort.   The evidence of MSS. and versions is remarkably divided; and, as Hort rightly urged (*Notes on Select Readings*), ' there is no intrinsic difficulty in either reading.'   A child might fall into a well as easily as an ass.   There are, however, considerations which seem to favour the reading ' ass.'   First the fact that the speech of Jesus is greatly coloured by the Old Testament and the fact that ox and ass often occur together there.   Secondly, the analogy of Lk. 13[15].   Thirdly, the general sense of the argument.   The most natural way of understanding it is that Jesus means to say: ' And how much more valuable is a man than an ox or an ass! '   (Cf. Mt. 12[12].)   This conclusion is not possible if we substitute ' son ' for ' ass.'   Not one of these arguments is decisive.   For the general purport of the argument see notes on Mt. 12[11f.], above, pp. 188 f.

16. *TABLE MANNERS* (169)

LK. 14[7-11]

14 7 And he spake a parable unto those which were bidden, when he marked how they chose out the chief seats; saying unto 8 them, When thou art bidden of any man to a marriage feast, [1] sit not down in the chief seat; lest haply a more honourable 9 man than thou be bidden of him, and he that bade thee and him shall come and say to thee, Give this man place; and then thou shalt begin with shame to take the 10 lowest place. But when thou art bidden, go and sit down in the lowest place; that when he that hath bidden thee cometh, he may say to thee, Friend, go up higher: then shalt thou have glory in the presence 11 of all that sit at meat with thee. For every one that exalteth himself shall be humbled; and he that humbleth himself shall be exalted.

[1] Gr. *recline not*.

This passage along with *vv.* 12–14 provides rules for the receiving and giving of hospitality. There can be little doubt that *vv.* 12–14 are just what they seem to be—precepts concerning the using of material goods in a charitable way. But there is some reason for thinking that originally *vv.* 7–11 were a parable of the Kingdom. It may be noted that in *v.* 7 what follows is described as ' a parable.' Then we find that advice similar to that given in *vv.* 8–11 is given in the Rabbinical literature as a rule of etiquette. R. Akiba reports as teaching of R. Simeon ben Azzai (*c.* A.D. 110): ' Stay two or three seats below thy place ' (i.e. the place to which thou art entitled), ' and sit until they say to thee, " Go (farther) up." Do not begin by going up because (in that case) they may say to thee, " Go (farther) down." It is better that they should say to thee " Go up, go up " than that they should say to thee " Go down, go down " ' (*Leviticus Rabbah* 1). Moreover, if we take this passage as a parable, it has obvious affinities with other teaching, e.g. the Parable of the Labourers in the Vineyard (Mt. 20[1-16]), and Jesus' treatment of the request of the Sons of Zebedee (Mk. 10[35-45]).

It is therefore probable that Jesus has here taken a Jewish rule of etiquette and used it as a parable of the Kingdom. Greatness in the Kingdom, whether in its present manifestation or in its final consummation, is determined not by our opinion of our deserts but by God's judgement. And we know from other sayings how God will determine the question of precedence. He will be greatest who is servant of all. One thing is certain. Greatness in the Kingdom will not be attained by standing on one's dignity.

7, 8 f. It is possible that this introductory verse is the expansion of a simpler formula, with a view to bringing the parable into the context provided by *v.* 1. Insistence on precedence was not peculiar to Jewish dinner parties. Theophrastus (*Characters* 21[2]) gives as one of the traits of the vain man that when he is invited out to dinner he does his utmost to secure the place of honour beside his host. The precise disposition of the places in a Jewish feast can hardly be determined with certainty (Billerbeck, iv. 618 ff.). In the time of Jesus the order of precedence seems to have been determined by the rank or distinction of the guests. Later (about A.D. 300) the rule came to be that precedence went with age. This parable certainly reflects the former rule since it supposes that the guest who has chosen the place of honour may have to vacate it in favour of a more distinguished guest. The displaced person must then go to the humblest place, presumably because all the other seats have, in the meantime, been occupied.

10. The wise course is to take the humblest place. If the host desires to give you honour, he will bring you to a more distinguished position. Then you will have honour, the real kind of honour which is conferred by others and not arrogated to yourself.

An independent version of the parable is given by some ancient MSS. after Mt. 20²⁸. The fact that it was interpolated just there is itself evidence that the parable was rightly understood in the early days of the Church. (See Streeter, *The Four Gospels*, pp. 241 f.) Yet another version is to be found in a papyrus fragment from Oxyrhynchus (Grenfell and Hunt, *New Sayings of Jesus*, p. 18; James, *Apocr. N.T.*, p. 26).

With the Jewish rule of etiquette we may compare Prov. 25⁶ᶠ·:

> Put not thyself forward in the presence of the king,
> And stand not in the place of great men:
> For better is it that it be said unto thee, Come up hither;
> Than that thou shouldest be put lower in the presence of the prince,
> Whom thine eyes have seen.

Also *Ecclus.* 3¹⁷⁻²⁰.

11. The whole is rounded off by a general statement, which seems to have been a favourite saying either with Jesus or His reporters. Cf. Mt. 18⁴, 23¹²; Lk. 18¹⁴. Pride and self-assertion in ordinary human society may be bad manners and bad policy. In the Kingdom of God such things are a contradiction of the fundamental principle of God's rule. There inevitably ' pride goeth before destruction, and a haughty spirit before a fall ': there there is only one kind of dignity, the kind that attaches itself to those who seek it not, but are content to serve God and man in love and humility.

17. *RULES OF HOSPITALITY* (169)

LK. 14¹²⁻¹⁴

14 12 And he said to him also that had bidden him, When thou makest a dinner or a supper, call not thy friends, nor thy brethren, nor thy kinsmen, nor rich neighbours; lest haply they also bid thee again, and a recompense be made thee.

13 But when thou makest a feast, bid the poor, the maimed, the lame, the blind: 14 and thou shalt be blessed; because they have not *wherewith* to recompense thee: for thou shalt be recompensed in the resurrection of the just.

In this section there does not appear to be any parabolic intention. The rules given are meant to be taken simply as they stand, and acted upon in the plain and natural sense. At the same time the plain and natural sense is not an injunction to rob Peter to pay Paul. Nor does Jesus say that hospitality to the poor is a better investment than hospitality to the rich. He opposes two kinds of hospitality. The one sort exists to gratify the desire for a ' good time,' the other to satisfy urgent need. The one sort resolves itself into a fair exchange; the other must always be a free gift. The kind of hospitality for which Jesus asks is the latter kind. It will include in its scope the poor, the maimed, the lame, the blind; and it will not exclude friends or brethren or kinsmen or even rich neighbours. But it will always be hospitality that is given, not hospitality that is exchanged.

12. Dinner and supper are the midday and evening meals; see on Lk. 11$^{37f.}$, above, p. 268. ' Brethren ' may perhaps mean the nearest relatives, the inner group in the wider circle of ' kinsmen.'

13 f. The guests to be invited to a feast are those who cannot return the hospitality; and the fact that they cannot is the best of all reasons for inviting them. Their inability to return the kindness is the measure of their need of it. In the mind of Jesus this principle goes far wider than food and drink. It lies behind His whole dealing with the morally bankrupt as well as with the economically depressed classes. For the besetting danger of the religious people of that day, as of every period, was that they tended to exchange hospitality in spiritual things, to enjoy the society of those who shared their beliefs and maintained with them the same standards of piety and morality. Their piety did not go out to the spiritually poor and maimed and lame and blind, as did that of ' the Friend of publicans and sinners.' So there is a sense in which this saying is also a parable; but that is only because with Jesus life is all of a piece, and it is the same spirit that prompts Him to give His food to the hungry and His love to the weaklings and failures.

The promise of reward for this kind of life is there as fact. You do not live in this way for the sake of the reward. If you do, you are not living in this way but in the old selfish way. Yet it is impossible to achieve, even for a moment, a pure unselfish kindness without knowing a blessedness that comes in no other way, a foretaste of something to be made perfect at the resurrection of the just.

With the injunction to invite the poor to the feast we may compare the saying of Jose ben Jochanan (c. 140 B.C.): ' Let thy house be opened wide and let the needy be members of thy household ' (Aboth 1^5, Danby, p. 446).

18. ON COUNTING THE COST (171)

LK. 14$^{28-33}$

14 28 For which of you, desiring to build a tower, doth not first sit down and count the cost, whether he have *wherewith* to 29 complete it? Lest haply, when he hath laid a foundation, and is not able to finish, all that behold begin to mock him, 30 saying, This man began to build, and 31 was not able to finish. Or what king, as he goeth to encounter another king in war, will not sit down first and take counsel whether he is able with ten thousand to meet him that cometh 32 against him with twenty thousand? Or else, while the other is yet a great way off, he sendeth an ambassage, and asketh 23 conditions of peace. So therefore whosoever he be of you that renounceth not all that he hath, he cannot be my disciple.

These verses are attached by Lk. to the Q passage Lk. 14$^{25-27}$ (see above, pp. 131 f.). They furnish a good example of a favourite teaching method of Jesus, that of the twin parables. The burden of them is to warn men against rash and unconsidered professions of discipleship. To become a disciple is much the same as joining the army in time of war. He who has not determined to venture all, even life itself, has no final defence against ignominious failure.

Epictetus issues a similar warning to those who think they can embrace his philosophy without much trouble to themselves. (Discourses, iii. 15): ' In every affair consider what precedes and follows, and then undertake it. Otherwise you will begin with spirit; but not having thought of the consequences, when some of them appear you will shamefully desist. . . . Consider first, man, what the matter is, and what your own nature is able to bear. . . . Do you think that you can act as you do, and be a philosopher? . . . You must watch, you must labour, you must get the better of certain appetites, must quit your acquaintance, be despised by your servant, be laughed at by those you meet; come off worse than others in everything, in magistracies, in honours, in courts of judicature. When you have considered all these things round, approach, if you please; if, by parting with them, you have a mind to purchase apathy, freedom, tranquillity. If not, do not come hither.'

28 ff. The first parable concerns the ordinary business of life. The ' tower ' might be a piece of fortification; but in that case it would be the work of a ruler; and rulers have generally contrived to find the money for such undertakings. More probably the Greek word translated ' tower ' means here a farm-building of some kind. The wise man will make a careful estimate of the cost of building before he begins, and not expose himself to ridicule by becoming the possessor of something which he can neither abandon nor complete.

31 f. In the second case we have high policy instead of private finance. When a king has a dispute with a neighbouring ruler, he does not at once resort to war to settle it. He first carefully considers what chance he has of success; and if his forces are hopelessly outnumbered by those of the enemy, he does his utmost to secure a peaceful settlement of the matter. It has been suggested (Thackeray, *Journal of Theol. Studies*, xiv. 389 f.) that Jesus had in mind the incident (2 Sam. 8⁹f.) of the submission of Toi, king of Hamath, to David.

33. The farmer will certainly consider the cost of the building; and if he finds that he can afford it, he will not hesitate to spend all that may be necessary. The king will weigh carefully his chances of success in battle against a bigger army; and if he believes that he has a reasonable chance, he will fling all his forces and all his resources into the conflict. The object of these parables is not to scare possible disciples away, but to enlist men and women who are ready to stake all with enthusiasm on an issue which they have first considered in cold blood. Discipleship does not rest on a momentary burst of feeling, an enthusiasm that may wane as quickly as it blazed up. It is for those who have considered the worth of the enterprise of Jesus, and who are prepared to pay the price of sharing in it. The verb translated ' renounce ' means to say farewell to a person and to renounce or give up a thing. Later it becomes a technical term in the monastic life. There is not in the teaching of Jesus any idea that worldly goods are to be regarded as evil, and rejected as hindrances to the ' spiritual life.' The true analogy to the kind of sacrifice here demanded is that which a man makes when he enters upon any great enterprise in which he must risk the loss of everything, his life included. The pioneers in the therapeutic employment of X-rays are the kind of people who answer most nearly to the description here.

19. *GOD AND THE SINNER—THREE PARABLES*
(*a*) The Lost Sheep and the Lost Coin (172)
LK. 15$^{1-10}$

15 1 Now all the publicans and sinners were drawing near unto him for to hear him. 2 And both the Pharisees and the scribes murmured, saying, This man receiveth sinners, and eateth with them. 3 And he spake unto them this parable, 4 saying, What man of you, having a hundred sheep, and having lost one of them, doth not leave the ninety and nine in the wilderness, and go after that which 5 is lost, until he find it? And when he hath found it, he layeth it on his shoul- 6 ders, rejoicing. And when he cometh home, he calleth together his friends and his neighbours, saying unto them, Rejoice with me, for I have found my sheep 7 which was lost. I say unto you, that even so there shall be joy in heaven over one sinner that repenteth, *more* than over ninety and nine righteous persons, which need no repentance. 8 Or what woman having ten [1] pieces of silver, if she lose one piece, doth not light a lamp, and sweep the house, and seek 9 diligently until she find it? And when she hath found it, she calleth together her friends and neighbours, saying, Rejoice with me, for I have found the piece which 10 I had lost. Even so, I say unto you, there is joy in the presence of the angels of God over one sinner that repenteth.

[1] Gr. *drachma*, a coin worth about eight pence.

The L material in chapters 15–19 might be called in a special sense the Gospel of the Outcast. There is in this section a great concentration of teaching, chiefly in the form of parables, whose purpose is primarily to demonstrate God's care for those whom men despise and condemn. This appears very clearly in the three parables which together make up chap. 15, in the parables of the Poor Widow (18$^{1-8}$) and the Pharisee and the Publican (18$^{9-14}$), and in the story of Zacchæus (19$^{1-10}$). This Divine love for the unloved and unlovable is, indirectly, the condemnation of the harsh and censorious attitude taken towards these unfortunates by more righteous folk. That the righteous fail from lack of kindness and human sympathy, and spoil themselves by pride, is one of the lessons of such passages as Lk. 16$^{1-8,}$ $^{14f.,}$ $^{19-31}$, 18$^{9-14}$. Again it is taught that even from the most unpromising people there can be a genuine response to kindness and understanding (17$^{11-19}$, 19$^{1-10}$). In Lk.'s arrangement this mass of material leads up to the account of Passion Week: it is as though the whole of Lk. from chap. 15 onwards were written to illustrate the Pauline text, ' God commendeth his own love toward us, in that, while we were yet sinners, Christ died for us.'

This ' Gospel of the Outcast ' begins with the three parables of chap. 15; and the root of the matter is that it is God Himself who wills that the outcasts should be gathered in. The attitude of Jesus to publicans and sinners is not a mere humanitarian enthusiasm on His part: it is the manifestation of the will and purpose of God. The scribes and Pharisees cannot accept that without qualification. They are represented as criticising Jesus because He is too free and easy with disreputable people. He, in His turn, criticises them for being too stiff and censorious. On the one side is the conviction, born of long and possibly sad experience, that ' evil communications corrupt good manners,' that it is not easy to touch pitch and not be defiled, that the will of God is that His chosen ones should separate themselves from everything that is evil. On the other side is the equally firm conviction that God wills the restoration of the outcast, and that God's way of restoration is the way of merciful love going out to seek and save the lost.

The first two parables in chap. 15 form a pair. Doubtless Lk. found them together in his source; and most probably they stood together in the tradition because they were so given by Jesus in the first instance. The practice of teaching by means of twin parables is one frequently adopted by Jesus, and several examples have already been noted. In both parables the main point is the same: the endless trouble that men will take to recover lost property, and their deep satisfaction when they succeed. The inference is that the publicans and sinners really belong to God, despite all appearances to the contrary, and that God really wants them back and will take trouble to win them back to Himself.

The parable of the Lost Sheep (vv. 4–7) has a parallel in Mt. 18$^{12-14}$ (above, pp. 207 ff.); and consequently Lk. 15$^{4-7}$ is by many scholars assigned to Q. It is more likely that we have here a case of the overlapping of sources, and that the Matthæan version belongs to M and the Lucan to L.

1–3. The narrative setting of the parables is very similar to that of another incident, in Mk. 2$^{13-17}$, especially vv. 15 f. (On this see my article, ' The Christology of the New Testament,' in the Congregational Quarterly, April, 1935, pp. 158 f.). It has been suggested that these introductory verses are Lk.'s own composition, which is possible; or that they are really the introduction to the parable of the Prodigal Son (note the singular ' this parable '), and that Lk. has inserted vv. 4–10 between the introduction and its proper sequel. The third possibility is that Lk. found the introduction and the three parables in his source as they stand. In view of the special characteristics of the section 15^1–19^{10} indicated above, one is inclined to think that a certain amount of gathering together of material had already taken place before Lk. set to work, and that this whole chapter was taken over by him substantially as we now have it.

The eagerness of the irreligious and immoral to listen to the most exacting of all teachers of religion and morality is very striking. They realised that He cared for them and believed in them enough to make His enormous demands upon them— and to bring His own perfect gift of understanding and sympathy. The scribes and Pharisees doubted the wisdom and propriety of such familiar friendship with publicans and sinners. (They are not the only religious people who have entertained such scruples.) Billerbeck quotes an old Rabbinical rule from Mekhilta on Exod. 18^1, 'Let not a man associate with the wicked, not even to bring him nigh to the Law.' This, no doubt, represents the strictest attitude, the attitude taken by the sharpest critics of Jesus. Whether every Pharisee would have maintained this rule in full strictness is another question. Jesus' reply to those who did criticise Him is given in the parables.

4–7. For these verses, cf. notes on Mt. 18$^{12-14}$, above, pp. 207 ff. The ' wilderness ' is not the sandy desert but open uncultivated pasture land where flocks and herds may be taken to graze. (Cf. Enc. Bibl., col. 1076, and 1 Sam. 17^{28}). So in Mk. 6^{35} the place where the five thousand are assembled is ' desert,' but in v. 39 the multitude are directed to sit down on the ' green grass.' In the Lucan version of the parable stress is laid on the persistent seeking by the shepherd ' until he find ' the lost sheep, and his joy at finding it is described much more fully than in Mt. For the picture of the shepherd carrying the exhausted animal on his shoulders, cf. Is. 40^{11}, 49^{22}; and the charming story from the Rabbinical commentary on Exodus, translated by Montefiore (*Rabb. Lit. and Gospel Teachings*, p. 259). The description of the shepherd summoning his friends and neighbours to share in his joy has no parallel in Mt. It is the kind of detail that Mt. readily omits. The conclusion drawn in Lk. (*v.* 7) differs entirely in wording from that in Mt. 18[14]. The purport of Lk.'s conclusion is that it pleases God—in both senses of the word ' please '—that sinners should repent: in Mt. it pleases God in the sense that it is God's will. ' Joy in heaven ' and ' joy in the presence of the angels of God ' are probably just cautious ways of saying that God is glad. Rabbinical teaching lays great stress also on the value of repentance; and there is ample evidence that the repentant sinner was generously treated. Philo teaches that God holds penitence in as high esteem as guiltlessness; and R. Abahu (end of third century A.D.) argues that God gives a higher place to repentant sinners than to the completely righteous. (Cf. Moore, *Judaism*, iii. 157 ff.) But the characteristic feature of these two parables is not so much the joy over the repentant sinner as the Divine love that goes out to seek the sinner before he repents.

8–10. The companion parable runs on parallel lines to the first. The essential point is the unwearied search for what is lost and the joy when it is found. The ' piece of silver ' is the *drachma*, a coin approximately equal in value to the silver *denarius*. See note on 10[35], above, p. 263. The total amount suggests that we are to think of the savings of a poor woman rather than of housekeeping money. The lighting of a lamp is natural in the circumstances. Palestinian houses nineteen centuries ago were not too well provided with windows. A Rabbinical parable (Billerbeck, ii. 212) has a similar picture of a man lighting many lamps to search the house for a lost coin. The thorough and careful search goes on till the missing coin is found. Then there is rejoicing with friends and neighbours. The same conclusion is drawn from this parable as from the preceding, though in somewhat shorter form. If man will take such trouble to recover his lost property, how much more trouble will God take to secure the return of His wandering children: and if this is God's way, then the way of Jesus with publicans and sinners is amply justified.

The attitude of God to sinners is now further displayed in the third parable.

(b) THE TWO SONS (173)

LK. 15[11-32]

15 11 And he said, A certain man had two 12 sons: and the younger of them said to his father, Father, give me the portion of [1] *thy* substance that falleth to me. And 13 he divided unto them his living. And not many days after the younger son gathered all together, and took his journey into a far country; and there he wasted his substance with riotous living. 14 And when he had spent all, there arose a mighty famine in that country; and he 15 began to be in want. And he went and joined himself to one of the citizens of that country; and he sent him into his 16 fields to feed swine. And he would fain have been filled with [2] the husks that the swine did eat: and no man gave unto 17 him. But when he came to himself he said, How many hired servants of my father's have bread enough and to spare, 18 and I perish here with hunger! I will arise and go to my father, and will say unto him, Father, I have sinned against 19 heaven, and in thy sight: I am no more worthy to be called thy son: make me as 20 one of thy hired servants. And he arose, and came to his father. But while he was yet afar off, his father saw him,

and was moved with compassion, and ran, and fell on his neck, and [3] kissed
21 him. And the son said unto him, Father, I have sinned against heaven, and in thy sight: I am no more worthy to
22 be called thy son[4]. But the father said to his [5] servants, Bring forth quickly the best robe, and put it on him; and put a ring on his hand, and shoes on his feet:
23 and bring the fatted calf, *and* kill it, and
24 let us eat, and make merry: for this my son was dead, and is alive again; he was lost, and is found. And they began to
25 be merry. Now his elder son was in the field: and as he came and drew nigh to the house, he heard music and dancing.
26 And he called to him one of the servants, and inquired what these things might be.
27 And he said unto him, Thy brother is come; and thy father hath killed the fatted calf, because he hath received him
28 safe and sound. But he was angry, and would not go in: and his father came out,
29 and intreated him. But he answered and said to his father, Lo, these many years do I serve thee, and I never transgressed a commandment of thine: and *yet* thou never gavest me a kid, that I
30 might make merry with my friends: but when this thy son came, which hath devoured thy living with harlots, thou
31 killedst for him the fatted calf. And he said unto him, [6] Son, thou art ever with
32 me, and all that is mine is thine. But it was meet to make merry and be glad: for this thy brother was dead, and is alive *again*; and *was* lost, and is found.

[1] Gr. *the*.
[2] Gr. *the pods of the carob tree*.
[3] Gr. *kissed him much*.
[4] Some ancient authorities add *make me as one of thy hired servants*. See ver. 19.
[5] Gr. *bondservants*.
[6] Gr. *Child*.

The attempt has been made to divide this parable into two at *v.* 24. The reasons in favour of this procedure are: (1) that in the two preceding parables nothing is said about the attitude of the ninety-nine sheep towards the stray, or about that of the nine pieces of silver towards the lost piece; and so it is an irrelevance to be told about the attitude of the elder brother: (2) that in *v.* 12 the father divides his property between the two sons, whereas in *vv.* 29–31 the father still seems to be himself in possession of the elder brother's share; and the elder brother is working for him on the land. With regard to the first it may be replied that the parables of the Lost Sheep and the Lost Coin are parables and not fables; and therefore we do not expect to hear about the feelings of the sheep or the coins. Further, there was no reason why Jesus having made two parables on this model should be compelled to make every other on the same pattern. To the second argument it may be replied that the inconsistency, if it be an inconsistency (see notes on *vv.* 11 f.), is not between *vv.* 11–24[a] and 24[b]–32; for the father is already giving orders to the elder brother's servants and disposing of his goods—in fact, acting as head of the household—in *vv.* 22 f. More than that, the younger son in the far country says, ' How many hired servants of my father's '—not ' my elder brother's.' If we are to cut the parable in two for inconsistency, the cut would have to be made at the end of *v.* 16, which is hardly a suitable place. There is, in fact, no good reason for supposing that the story is anything but a perfect unity.

The parable is distinguished from the other two by the fact that it makes two main points. The first, which it has in common with the others, is the care and patience of God towards the sinner and the joy with which the repentant sinner is received. The second is the rebuke to the harsh and censorious attitude taken up by the righteous towards sinners. The strength of this rebuke lies less in any formal charge brought against the elder brother than in the contrast between his attitude and that of the father.

Apart from these critical questions there is a further, and much more difficult, theological problem raised by the parable. This lies in the fact that there does not seem to be any place in it for the doctrine that God's forgiveness of sinners is made possible by the sacrificial death of Jesus. On this point it may be said first that the Christian doctrine of the Atonement is not based on this parable alone, but on the whole set of facts presented in the life and teaching of Jesus and in the experience of Christians. Secondly, this one parable does not offer, and was not meant by Jesus to offer, a complete compendium of theology. Its primary business is to justify the attitude of Jesus to sinners by showing that His way is the fulfilment of God's will concerning them, and that the way of the scribes and Pharisees is the wrong way. If the carrying out of the purpose of God leads, as in fact it did, to the Cross, then it becomes the business of Christians to include the Cross in the purpose of God and to think out, as best they can, how the death of Christ is involved in God's purpose of saving sinners. Christian theologians have in the past made this attempt, and various explanations have been offered. It is not our business here to discuss the question whether any one of these theories is completely satisfying. All that we have to do is to recognise that Jesus in this parable lays down the fundamental principle of God's relation to sinful men: that God loves the sinner while he is still a sinner, *before* he repents; and that somehow it is this Divine love that makes the sinner's repentance possible. This is the true point of the parable.

It is a fact of history and of Christian experience that this love of God becomes fully effective in the Cross; but this fact does not touch the basic principle laid down in the parable. It has to be explained in the light of that principle; and all that can be said is that any doctrine of the Atonement that explains the death of Jesus in such a way as to weaken the principle here laid down by Jesus Himself has no chance of ultimate survival.

11 f. The simplest explanation of the story is that the father represents God, the elder brother those scribes and Pharisees who criticised Jesus, and the younger brother the publicans and sinners whom Jesus befriended. Probably we should not attempt to go farther than this in the interpretation of the details. The Greek phrase rendered by ' the portion . . . that falleth to me ' is common in the papyri. It can be used either of privileges to which one is entitled or of obligations which one is bound to meet. A corresponding Aramaic phrase is found in the Elephantine Papyri (ed. Cowley, No. 28). On the Jewish law of inheritance see the Mishnah, *Baba Bathra* 8 f., Danby, pp. 376 ff. The owner of property could dispose of it either by will or by gift during his lifetime. If by will, his testamentary dispositions had to conform to the Law as laid down in Dt. 21[15-17] and Num. 27[8-11]. (Cf. *Encycl. Bibl.*, cols. 2728 f.) If by gift, he could dispose of the property without regard to the Old Testament provisions, which covered bequests only and not gifts. If such a gift is made, it does not normally take full effect until the death of the donor. In the meantime the property is settled. It remains in the possession of the donor; but he has no power to dispose of it. All that he can do is to lease it for the indeterminate period which will end at his death, when the property will automatically revert to the person to whom he assigned it by gift. That is, he can only sell his own life-interest in the property. Likewise the beneficiary under the gift cannot

dispose of the property immediately; for it is still subject to the donor's life-interest. If he sells it, the purchaser can only take possession at the death of the donor. This is the normal procedure, and it is illustrated by the relation between the father and the elder son.   Throughout the story the father still has complete use and enjoyment of what has been assigned to the elder son; yet he can say to him ' All that I have is thine.'

In the case of the younger brother it is necessary to suppose that a further step has been taken.   The younger son does not merely desire that the shares of his brother and himself should be determined by a deed of gift, which would normally become effective at the death of the father.   He wants immediate possession of his share.   This requires that the father not only makes an assignment of the property to the two sons, but also grants to the younger son the immediate possession of his share.   This he could do; but once it was done the younger son had, of course, no further right in the estate.   What remained was irrevocably assigned to his brother.   That parents could and actually did hand over their property to their heirs is shown by the fact that Ben Sirach advises against the practice (*Ecclus.* 33$^{19-23}$) :

> To son or wife, to brother or friend,
>   Give no power over thyself while thou livest;
> And give not thy goods to another
>   So as to have to ask for them again. . . .
> For it is better that thy children ask of thee
>   Than that thou shouldst look to the hand of thy sons. . . .
> When the days of thy life are ended,
>   In the day of death, distribute thine inheritance.

We must therefore understand the words ' he divided unto them his living ' as meaning that he executed a kind of deed of gift securing to either son his share of the inheritance, and then as a further act gave the younger son the immediate and absolute possession of what he would ordinarily have inherited in due course. The elder son having made no request, his share remains in the possession of the father, who has the use and enjoyment of it but not the right to dispose of it in any way that would infringe the elder son's sole right to inherit it.   If that is the situation, there is no inconsistency between the two parts of the parable.

13–16. The younger son lost no time in setting about the enjoyment of his new freedom.   He collected all together and, putting as large a distance as possible between himself and the paternal eye, he proceeded to lay out his money to what seemed to him the best advantage.   The Greek adverb translated ' with riotous living ' may mean that he spent his money ' extravagantly,' or that he spent it on dissolute pleasures, or both.   The elder brother (*v.* 30) evidently took the third view.   However that may be, it was not long until the funds were exhausted; and to crown his misfortunes the land of his adoption was visited by a serious famine, which doubtless provided the friends of his affluence with a good excuse for not helping him in the day of adversity.   He was thus reduced to working for his living, and that at what was in Jewish estimation one of the most loathsome and degrading of all tasks.   (Cf. the proverb preserved in the Talmud (*Baba*

Kamma 82^b): ' Cursed is the man who rears swine, and cursed is the man who teaches his son Greek philosophy.') But even this work would hardly produce a living: and the prodigal was reduced to such straits that he would gladly have shared the diet of the swine. R.V. ' He would fain have been filled: A.V. ' He would fain have filled his belly,' which is more vigorous and probably original. R.V. follows a large group of MSS. which here bowdlerise. The ' husks ' are the seed-pods of the carob tree (*Ceratonia siliqua*), also called the locust tree. The tree still grows in Palestine and the Mediterranean lands, and the pods are used as fodder for animals. Their use for human food is a mark of deep poverty. Hence the Rabbinical saying : ' When the Israelites are reduced to eating carob-pods, then they repent.'

17. The restoration of the prodigal begins when he first realises the wretchedness of his condition, when he sees himself as he really is. Contrast Rev. 3^{17}. The expression ' he came to himself,' i.e. came to his senses, is found in Greek, Latin, and Hebrew. The son in poverty in the far country contrasts his own condition with that of the humblest members of his father's household at home. The Palestinian Rabbis had a saying: ' When a son (abroad) goes barefoot (through poverty), then he remembers the comfort of his father's house.'

18 f. But the prodigal does not stop at vain regrets for what he has lost. With the realisation of his folly goes the resolve to make an end of it in the only way open to him, by returning to his father's house and submitting to the father's discipline. This involves confession that he has behaved disgracefully, admission that he has by his behaviour forfeited all his rights as a son, and so becoming humble enough to accept orders where formerly he had demanded gifts. It may be noted that he does not say, ' I really ought to arise and go,' but ' I will arise and go.' The Greek words translated ' I have sinned against heaven ' may mean either ' I have sinned heaven-high,' i.e. I have heaped transgression upon transgression till the sum of my sins is monstrous (cf. Ezra 9^6); or ' I have sinned against God,' heaven being the common Jewish periphrasis for God. (Cf. English ' Heaven forbid! ' = ' God forbid! ') The latter interpretation is preferable. ' In thy sight ' is just a verbal variation for ' against thee.' (Cf. 1 Sam. 7^6, 20^1.) The confession to the father means simply ' I have sinned against God and against thee.' Strict justice would disown him as a son; but perhaps mercy will accept him as a servant.

20. The resolve is followed by action, and the action by a response from the father far beyond anything the son had dared to expect. The eyes of the father are towards the far country, and he sees the son while the son is still a long way off. He knows only one emotion, pity for his son in his wretched condition. He runs to meet him, embraces him and kisses him. (Cf. Gen. 33^4; Acts 20^{37}.) The Greek word used for ' kissed ' signifies no mere formal salutation: he 'kissed him tenderly.'

21 ff. These demonstrations of love and compassion do not turn the son from the resolve which he had taken before he set out for home. If anything, they make him realise more keenly the wrong that he has done. So he begins his confession. But no sooner has he declared that he is unworthy of the name of son, than the father breaks in with orders to the servants which show plainly that he is still a son in his father's eyes. The father's love is stronger than the son's sense of un-

worthiness. ' In the rabbinical literature the paternal-filial relation between God and man is a common theme. R. Akiba . . . " Beloved (of God) are the Israelites, in that they are called sons of God; still more beloved in that it is made known to them that they are called sons of God " (Dt. 14¹). R. Judah (ben Ila'i) thought that the name sons was given them only when they behaved themselves like sons; but R. Meir refuted him by quoting passages in which they were called foolish sons (Jer. 4²²), untrustworthy sons (Dt. 32²⁰), breed of evil-doers, vicious sons (Is. 1⁴)—but sons notwithstanding Instead of its being said to them, Ye are not my people, they shall be called sons of the Living God (Hos. 1¹⁰). The relation is not annulled by sin ' (Moore, *Judaism*, ii. 203). The criticism that might be made of scribes and Pharisees was that, in their dealings with the publicans and sinners, they failed to rise to the height of their own best thoughts about God.

The R.V. marginal addition to *v.* 21, ' make me as one of thy hired servants,' although supported by some of the leading MSS., is almost certainly an interpolation from *v.* 19.

22–24. The returned prodigal instead of being treated às a servant, which was all he dared hope for, is received as a guest of honour. The ' best robe ' is literally the ' first robe,' i.e. first in quality and value. ' Put a ring,' literally ' give a ring.' The Greek reflects the Semitic idiom whereby the verb ' to give ' is used in the sense of ' to place.' The same usage appears in Lk. 12⁵¹, above, p. 119. The articles ordered by the father are more than mere necessities: the prodigal is to have the best of everything. He is not put on a plain wholesome diet suitable to his situation, but made chief guest at a banquet in honour of his return. Joy that he has come back outweighs all else. The father may have thought of his son as lost or dead; but he has never ceased to think of him as his son. Cf. the note on *vv.* 21 ff., above. The son may have forgotten the father, but the father has never disowned the son.

25. With this verse the elder son comes into the centre of the stage. As depicted for us, he stands in sharp contrast both to his brother and his father. His sympathies are as narrow as his ideals are high. He is incapable alike of the reckless selfishness of his brother and the reckless unselfishness of his father. It is perhaps a hint as to his nature that the mere fact that there is any gaiety in the house is a phenomenon calling for an explanation. The Greek word translated ' music ' may mean the sound of a number of instruments playing together or voices singing together; or it may be, as in Dan 3⁵, the name of one musical instrument somewhat like the bagpipes.

26 f., 28, 29 f. In reply to the enquiry of the elder son a servant explains the reason for the merrymaking. His answer contains no criticism of the younger son. It gives the true answer; but leaves the elder brother to find out the full details for himself. But it conveys enough information to rouse the anger of the elder brother, who refuses to join in the rejoicings. What is the use of trying to do one's duty if wastrels and scapegraces are to receive more consideration than upright and conscientious folk? So the father comes out and begs him to come in. It is to be noted that the father has to go out to both sons. The Greek tenses are significant: the father came out and was entreating him to come in, when he broke in on the entreaties with his accusations of unjust treatment. His years of faithful and

conscientious service have received no reward, while his brother's career of dissipation and debauchery has been celebrated with a great feast. The impression remains, however, that the chief reason why he never got so much as a kid to make merry with his friends was that he would not have known how to make merry if he had got it. His real annoyance is not for what he has not had, but for what his brother has got. Further, it would seem that any deprivation which the elder brother suffered merely meant that the capital which he must ultimately inherit grew so much the larger. It is the veal that sticks in his gullet, not the goat's-flesh. His references to his brother are in harsh and brutal terms. He disowns him as a brother and refers to him as ' this son of yours '—an expression of contempt, which is met in v. 32 by the rebuke, ' this brother of yours.' He paints the life of the prodigal in the worst possible colours. He says ' thy living ' although the father had actually made over the money in question to the son. He is the only authority for the harlots, and he does not say whence he had this piece of information. We feel that he is not trying to be just, much less generous, to the repentant sinner.

31 f. The father's reply is the last word; and it is a word that expresses his love for both his sons. ' Son ' is almost too stiff a rendering of the Greek. ' My dear boy ' would be nearer to the spirit of the word. The assurance ' all that is mine is thine ' is no doubt meant to tell the elder brother that the return of the prodigal does not affect his rights in any degree. He will inherit his whole share of the estate when the time comes. But no rights of the elder brother can prevent the father from rejoicing that the prodigal has returned; and the elder brother *ought* to share in the joy of his father. It would cost him nothing but a little kindness.

So the upshot of the matter is that the way of the father with the prodigal is God's way with sinful men and Jesus' way with publicans and sinners; and the last word of Jesus to the scribes and Pharisees who criticised Him is: ' It ought to be your way too.'

20. *THE CLEVER RASCAL* (174)

LK. 16¹⁻⁹

16 1 And he said also unto the disciples, There was a certain rich man, which had a steward; and the same was accused unto 2 him that he was wasting his goods. And he called him, and said unto him, What is this that I hear of thee? render the account of thy stewardship; for thou canst be no 3 longer steward. And the steward said within himself, What shall I do, seeing that my lord taketh away the stewardship 4 from me? I have not strength to dig; to beg I am ashamed. I am resolved what to do, that, when I am put out of the stewardship, they may receive me into 5 their houses. And calling to him each one of his lord's debtors, he said to the first, How much owest thou unto my lord? 6 And he said, A hundred ¹ measures of oil. And he said unto him, Take thy ² bond, and sit down quickly and write fifty. 7 Then he said to another, And how much owest thou? And he said, A hundred ³ measures of wheat. He saith unto him, 8 Take thy ² bond, and write fourscore. And his lord commended ⁴ the unrighteous steward because he had done wisely: for the sons of this ⁵ world are for their own generation wiser than the sons of the light. 9 And I say unto you, Make to yourselves friends ⁶ by means of the mammon of unrighteousness; that, when it shall fail, they may receive you into the eternal tabernacles.

¹ Gr. *baths*, the bath being a Hebrew measure. See Ezek. xlv. 10, 11, 14.
² Gr. *writings*.
³ Gr. *cors*, the cor being a Hebrew measure. See Ezek. xlv. 14.
⁴ Gr. *the steward of unrighteousness*.
⁵ Or, *age*.
⁶ Gr. *out of*.

This parable has always presented difficulties for the interpreter: and like most of such difficulties they arise from trying to press the details of the story instead of seeking for the main point. The parable becomes comparatively simple as soon as we realise that it is part of the L collection of material which we have called the Gospel of the Outcast. We are, in fact, still concerned with the great questions: what is God's way with sinners? and what ought to be the way of religious men with sinners? It is the latter question that is uppermost in this story, so that it may almost be regarded as an appendix to the parable of the Prodigal Son. In that parable the criticism of the elder brother is that he fails to show the gracious and pitiful spirit of his father: or, in other words, that the religious Jews fail to rise to the height of their own faith in God in their dealings with the immoral and the irreligious. Here the criticism of the scribes and Pharisees is that their attitude to the publicans and sinners is not even good policy, much less good religion. If they would show kindness and friendship to the outcasts, it would turn out for the good of themselves as well as of the publicans and sinners.

1. This interpretation is not affected by the fact that Lk. represents the parable as addressed to the disciples; for it is no article of the Christian faith that members of the Church are immune from the worst kind of Pharisaism, or that Christians are never in danger of becoming censorious, intolerant, and self-righteous. And, in any case, the Pharisees are thought of as still present. Cf. v. 14.

We have to resist the temptation to make exegetical equations. The rich man does not represent God, nor does the steward represent a disciple or a Pharisee. The point of the parable lies in v. 8; and it does not depend on anything but the story itself. The Greek word translated ' steward ' is used in the New Testament in three different senses: (a) of an overseer or head-servant responsible for the welfare and discipline of the rest of the household staff, as in Lk. 12⁴², above, p. 117; (b) of a bailiff or estate-manager, as here; (c) of a civic official like our city-treasurer, as in Rom. 16²³. In the present case it is reported to the master that the steward is squandering the property entrusted to him. We are not told whether or not the charge is true; but in view of the subsequent behaviour of the steward we may well think that it was not unfounded. ' Wasting his goods,' cf. Lk. 15¹³.

2 f., 4, 5 ff. The master takes immediate action. He orders the steward to hand over his accounts, and dismisses him from his post. The steward is evidently an employee and not a slave. If he were a slave his future would not be in doubt: he would be reduced to some menial post, not discharged. As it is, he is left wondering how he is to make a living. He is too soft for manual labour and too proud to beg. He must therefore live by his wits; and his plan is to show such kindness to his master's debtors that, when he is out of his present position, they will be under an obligation to entertain him. The fact that he will be robbing his master in carrying out the plan does not weigh with him. Having decided, he proceeds at once to action. Each debtor is interviewed; and we are given samples of the proceedings in two cases. Both debtors would seem to be persons who have purchased goods from the estate and have not yet paid for them. The steward holds their receipts for the goods, and now hands them back to be altered to the advantage of the debtors. In the first case the debt is in respect of 100 *baths* of oil. The *bath* is a Hebrew measure, and 100 *baths* may be computed to be = about

868 gallons. The bill is altered to 50 *baths*: that is, the debtor is presented with 434 gallons at the master's expense. The second debt is in respect of 100 *cors* of wheat = about 1,083 bushels. From the Mishnah (*Baba Metzia* 5[1], Danby, p. 355) it would appear that the price of wheat was 25 to 30 denars a *cor*; so that in reducing the debt from 100 to 80 *cors* the steward was making this debtor a present of 500 to 600 denars. In both cases the steward invites the debtor to do the falsifying of the accounts for himself.

8. 'His lord': the Greek text has simply 'the lord,' and it is still debated whether 'the lord' means the steward's master or Jesus Himself. Those who take the latter view point to a somewhat similar case in Lk. 18[6 ff.], where the commentator on the behaviour of the unjust judge is certainly Jesus Himself. In view of the beginning of *v.* 9, 'And I say unto you,' there can be little doubt that Lk. thought that 'the lord' in *v.* 8 meant the steward's master; and this probably means that that was the way in which the words were taken by the compiler of the source on which he is here dependent. And it may be urged that if we take 'the lord' as meaning Jesus the story ends rather abruptly. If we take 'the lord' to mean the master in the story, it is necessary to suppose that the steward's plan miscarried, and that somehow his master got to know what he was doing. If that were so, the master would be better able to pass judgement on the fraud considered merely from the point of view of its ingenuity, seeing that he had probably secured himself against pecuniary loss. On the other hand, if it is Jesus who is subject in *v.* 8, these suppositions are unnecessary: we do not need to know whether or not the scheme succeeded. We may, if we like, assume that it did. The difficulty, then, is that Jesus praised the dishonest steward; but this difficulty is largely imaginary. First the word 'praise' does not necessarily signify moral approval of the steward's plan. The ethical judgement on the plan is given in the description of its author as 'the unrighteous steward'; and the ground of the praise is given in the clause 'because he had done wisely.' It is the astuteness of the plan that is praised: and there is all the difference in the world between 'I applaud the dishonest steward because he acted cleverly' and 'I applaud the clever steward because he acted dishonestly.' Whether it is the employer or Jesus that speaks, we must take the purport of the speech to be: 'This is a fraud; but it is a most ingenious fraud. The steward is a rascal; but he is a wonderfully clever rascal.' The steward's cleverness is not an isolated phenomenon: it is part of the way of the world. The worldlings show far more *savoir faire* than the religious in dealing with their contemporaries. For even their roguery is often designed to procure them friends, while the pious only too often estrange those who might be friendly to them. The expressions 'sons of this world' (cf. 20[34]) and 'sons of light' (John 12[36]; 1 Thess. 5[5]; Eph. 5[8]) have no exact parallels in the Rabbinical literature; but the meaning of them is plain enough. With 'sons of light' we may compare 'every spirit of light' (*Enoch* 61[12]), a phrase which, according to Charles, 'embraces good spirits, human and angelic'; also 'the spirits of the good who belong to the generation of light' (*Enoch* 108[11]).

9. It may be doubted whether this verse belongs to the parable. The point of the parable is that if a bad man will take infinite trouble to get friends for his own selfish interests, the good man will surely take some trouble to make friends in a

better way and for better ends. The point of this saying is rather that by disposing of worldly wealth in the proper way, one will have treasure in heaven. The true parallel to this verse is in such sayings as Mt. $6^{19 ff.}$; Mk. 10^{21}; Lk. $12^{33 f.}$. The 'mammon of unrighteousness' is an expression that has no exact parallel in the Old Testament or other Jewish literature. In the Targums we find the phrase 'mammon of falsehood' and once (Targum on Hab. 2^9) 'mammon of wickedness.' Other passages which have a bearing on this verse are: Enoch 63^{10} where 'the mighty and the kings who possess the earth' (63^1) say: ' Our souls are full of un-righteous gain, but it does not prevent us from descending from the midst thereof into the † burden † of Sheol'; Ecclus. 5^8: ' Trust not in unrighteous gains, for they shall profit (thee) nothing in the day of wrath.' The one idea that seems to cling to all these phrases, including perhaps ' the mammon of unrighteousness,' is that of ill-gotten gain, whether acquired by force or fraud. It is ' dirty money,' and doubtless all money gets dirty at some stage in its history, if we could trace it out. But there is another and more radical sense in which, for Jesus, mammon is unrighteous: it is a rival to God for the service and love of man. ' Ye cannot serve God and mammon.' The only effective way to deal with it is to force it into the service of God by converting it from selfish to unselfish uses. In this way it can be made to procure one ' friends.' It is probable that the word ' friends ' signifies God Himself. Use the mammon of unrighteousness in such a way that you gain the friendship of God. Then in the day when earthly possessions are no longer of any use ' they ' will receive you into the eternal tabernacles. ' They ' in this context most probably means God. In the Rabbinical writings it is a common way of avoiding the mention of the divine name to use the verb in the 3rd person plural, just as in this verse.

Thus what is counselled in this saying is something that will produce the opposite result to that indicated in Enoch 63^{10} or in the fate of Dives (Lk. 16^{19-31}); and we may leave the question open whether this verse would not stand more appropriately as the moral of the parable of Dives and Lazarus.

21. SAYINGS ABOUT WEALTH (174)

LK. 16^{10-12}

16 10 He that is faithful in a very little is faithful also in much: and he that is unrighteous in a very little is unrighteous 11 also in much. If therefore ye have not been faithful in the unrighteous mammon, who will commit to your trust the 12 true *riches*? And if ye have not been faithful in that which is another's, who will give you that which is [1] your own?

[1] Some ancient authorities read *our own.*

10. This verse is unconnected with what precedes in *v.* 9 and with what follows in *vv.* 11 f. It could stand appropriately as a reflection on the promotion of the good servants in the parable of the Pounds (Lk. 19^{16-19}). In the Midrash, *Exodus Rabbah* (on Exod. 3^1), the principle is laid down that God ' does not give a big thing to a man until He has tested him in a small matter; and afterwards He promotes him to a great thing. This is illustrated by the cases of David and Moses. David was found satisfactory as a shepherd. ' The Holy One, blessed is He, said to him, " Thou hast been found faithful in the matter of the sheep: come

and be shepherd to my flock " (i.e. Israel).' Similarly, Moses was a good shepherd of his father-in-law's flock, and God took him to be shepherd of Israel. We may also compare the parable related by R. Simeon ben Eleazar (*Mekhilta* on Exod. 20²): A king appointed two overseers. One he put in charge of the store of straw, the other he put in charge of the treasury of silver and gold. He who was set over the straw turned out untrustworthy, and (at the same time) grumbled because he had not been set over the treasury of silver and gold. He who had been put in charge of the silver and gold said to him: ' Thou fool, thou hast been false in the matter of the straw; how much more in the matter of the silver and gold.' The point of this parable is that since the Gentile nations have failed to observe the simple moral rules (the so-called Noachide commandments: Moore, *Judaism*, i. 274 f.) given to them by God, it would be futile to give them the fuller code of the Jewish Law. In both Rabbinical parallels the contrast is between small and large opportunities of serving God: and it may be supposed that something of the same kind is intended in the saying of Jesus.

11. It may then be suggested that it is the same thought that is present in *v.* 11 The ' unrighteous mammon ' is just a way of speaking about worldly goods. These afford an opportunity for faithful service of God, if they are used in the right way. And all men are tested in this very way. If we cannot use the means and opportunities, which we now have, aright, what guarantee is there that we shall be any more satisfactory with larger opportunities and better means? It is perhaps worth considering whether this saying may not have at least an oblique reference to the kind of ambition among the disciples, of which we have record in Mk. 9³³⁻³⁷, 10³⁵⁻⁴⁵; Lk. 22²⁴⁻²⁷. It would then be a hint that greatness in the Kingdom is measured by service in the world as it is. The question: ' Who will commit to your trust the true riches? ' is another way of saying: ' Will God commit to your trust the true riches? '

12. If this world's wealth is called ' the unrighteous mammon,' and if the true riches is the ' treasure in heaven,' then we may think of the former as foreign wealth considered from the point of view of a citizen of the Kingdom, and of the goods of the Kingdom as the true wealth of its citizens. If the citizens of the Kingdom are not faithful in their use of the foreign currency—this world's goods —can God give them their own currency—the treasure of heaven? The Greek words translated ' that which is another's ' can equally mean ' that which is foreign.' There are three different MS. readings in this verse. For ' that which is your own ' some MSS. have ' that which is our own,' and a few ' that which is mine.' The interpretation given of the saying is not affected by these variants. If we read ' our ' it means that Jesus includes Himself with those to whom He is speaking: He too belongs to the Kingdom and its wealth is His. The reading ' mine ' would imply that the disciples do not participate in the treasure of the Kingdom except as being admitted to share with Jesus in what is primarily His heritage. In any case the contrast between the treasure of the Kingdom and the ' foreign ' currency of the world remains.

On *v.* 13, which is assigned to Q, see above, p. 133.

22. PRIDE CONDEMNED (175)

LK. 16¹⁴⁻¹⁵

16 14 And the Pharisees, who were lovers of money, heard all these things; and they 15 scoffed at him. And he said unto them, Ye are they that justify yourselves in the sight of men; but God knoweth your hearts: for that which is exalted among men is an abomination in the sight of God.

In these verses we have an isolated saying of Jesus condemning pride. As such it is suitably included in the collection of teachings which we have called the Gospel of the Outcast. The connexion with what goes before is, however, artificial. Lk. or the compiler of his special source has attempted to make a historical connexion where there is only a topical. The link between these verses and what precedes is provided by the words ' who were lovers of money.' This clause betrays itself as editorial by the fact that (1) what is condemned in the saying is not love of money but pride; and (2) the Pharisees were not in fact specially lovers of money. That charge would have fitted the Sadducees or the publicans very much better. The Pharisees certainly did not despise worldly possessions; but it was not they who held the great vested interests but the Sadducees; and it was not they who sold their country and their own souls for gain but the publicans.

Further, we may suspect that ' the Pharisees ' is not original either. What precedes this saying in L is a series of sayings in which the contrast is drawn between worldly wealth and ' treasure in heaven.' The people who would be likely to scoff at such teaching were certainly not the Pharisees but the Sadducees who did not believe in any future life worthy of the name. To the Sadducees, and probably to them alone in Judaism, the words ' treasure in heaven ' meant nothing at all. A further small point in favour of the view that this saying is addressed to the Sadducees is the fact that in that case we should have a play on their name in the saying itself. For the name Sadducee is connected with the root *sdk* = ' be righteous '; and this very root is used to translate ' justify yourselves ' in the Palestinian Aramaic version of these verses. That some such play upon the name is intended is suggested by the curious phrasing of *v.* 15: ' Ye are they that justify yourselves,' which may mean: ' You are the people who, by taking the name " Sadducee," make public claim to be the party of righteousness.' But God looks deeper than party labels, and knows that the name does not correspond to any real righteousness within. It is rather the expression of an overweening pride, which is utterly detestable in God's sight. The last clause of *v.* 15 may be paraphrased: ' human pride is idolatry in God's sight.' In Jewish thought the word ' abomination ' is practically a synonym for ' idol ' and ' idolatry.' Cf. 1 Kings 11⁵, ' Milcom the abomination of the Ammonites,' i.e. Milcom the national deity of the Ammonites; Dan. 11³¹, ' They shall set up the abomination that maketh desolate,' with reference to the introduction of heathen worship into the Temple at Jerusalem.

There is an excellent parallel to this in the *Mekhilta* on Exod. 20¹⁸ (not Exod. 20²¹ as in Moore, *Judaism*, ii. 275, and elsewhere). ' All who are lofty of heart (i.e. proud) are called " abomination," as it is said (Prov. 16⁵) " Every one who is lofty of heart is an abomination to the Lord "; idolatry is called " abomination," as it is said (Deut. 7²⁶) " and thou shalt not bring an abomination (i.e. an idol) into thine house." As idolatry pollutes the land and causes the Presence of God to withdraw from it, so also does pride.' Here in Rabbinical Judaism we have the clear recognition that human pride is as near being idolatry as makes no matter; and this passage confirms our interpretation of the saying of Jesus. Pride is idolatry in God's sight.

Now it is well known that the Sadducees were the aristocratic party in the Jewish commonwealth, holding the first place in riches and dignity. Josephus tells us that the Sadducean doctrines attracted none but the rich (*Antiq.*, XIII, x. 6) and those of the greatest dignity (*Antiq.*, XVII, i. 4). The insatiable love of wealth and the pride and insolence of the Sadducees are frequently alluded to in the *Psalms of Solomon* (see the Introduction to Ryle and James' edition, p. xlviii). So on all points we are justified in regarding this saying as probably directed against the Sadducees.

On *vv.* 16–18 (Q), see above, pp. 133–138.

23. *PARABLE OF DIVES AND LAZARUS* (177)

LK. 16[19-31]

16 19 Now there was a certain rich man, and he was clothed in purple and fine linen, 20 [1] faring sumptuously every day: and a certain beggar named Lazarus was laid 21 at his gate, full of sores, and desiring to be fed with the *crumbs* that fell from the rich man's table; yea, even the dogs came 22 and licked his sores. And it came to pass, that the beggar died, and that he was carried away by the angels into Abraham's bosom: and the rich man also 23 died, and was buried. And in Hades he lifted up his eyes, being in torments, and seeth Abraham afar off, and Lazarus in 24 his bosom. And he cried and said, Father Abraham, have mercy on me, and send Lazarus, that he may dip the tip of his finger in water, and cool my tongue; 25 for I am in anguish in this flame. But Abraham said, [2] Son, remember that thou in thy lifetime receivedst thy good things, and Lazarus in like manner evil things: but now here he is comforted,

26 and thou art in anguish. And [3] beside all this, between us and you there is a great gulf fixed, that they which would pass from hence to you may not be able, and that none may cross over from thence 27 to us. And he said, I pray thee therefore, father, that thou wouldest sent him to 28 my father's house; for I have five brethren; that he may testify unto them, lest they also come into this place of 29 torment. But Abraham saith, They have Moses and the prophets; let them hear 30 them. And he said, Nay, father Abraham: but if one go to them from the dead, 31 they will repent. And he said unto him, If they hear not Moses and the prophets, neither will they be persuaded, if one rise from the dead.

[1] Or, *living in mirth and splendour every day.*
[2] Gr. *Child.*
[3] Or, *in all these things.*

If the interpretation of *vv.* 14 f. given above is correct, we must ask whether this parable, which immediately follows it in L, may not also be intended as a warning to the same party. There are several considerations in favour of this view. (1) The description of the rich man in *v.* 19. He is wealthy; and the Sadducean party was the party of the wealthy. He wears purple, the colour associated with royal or quasi-royal dignity, and fine linen or lawn, the most luxurious fabric of the ancient world. The Sadducees were the aristocratic party in Judaism. He lived in luxury: so did the Sadducees. Anyone, in the days of Jesus, hearing this description would think at once of the priestly aristocrats of Jerusalem. (2) The dramatic contrast between the end of *v.* 22 and the continuation of the story in *v.* 23. The Sadducees did not believe in any real life after death. A man, in their view, achieved his full life in this world. If he lived on earth in felicity, died in peace, and was honourably buried, he had gained all that was to be gained: he had nothing further to hope for or to fear. This rich man obtains all that a Sadducee could expect; but the end of the Sadducean programme turns out not to be the end of the whole story. There is an unexpected continuation, which is described in v. 23. (3) The rich man, who has been sadly disillusioned by the turn of events, wishes (vv. 27–31) to warn his five brothers lest they come to the same unhappy end as himself. They are living as he lived in the belief that the grave is the end of all things. But if someone returned from the other side and told them the truth, they would realise that they must change their belief and their way of life. The reply of Abraham (v. 29) is significant. The brethren of the rich man are referred to the canonical Scriptures for proof of the life after death. *And those Scriptures were the only authority recognised by the Sadducees*, who rejected the additional doctrines of the Pharisees. And here it is to be noted that when Jesus undertakes to refute the Sadducean doctrine that there is no life beyond the grave, He appeals to the one authority which they recognised (Mk. 12²⁶ᶠ·).

In view of these considerations it may be concluded that the original hearers of this parable would have recognised in the story the description of a typical Sadducee.

There are numerous parallels to the story of the rich man and the poor man, and their changed fortunes in the next world. The fullest collection is that of Gressmann in the *Abhandlungen* of the Prussian Academy (Phil.-hist. Kl., 1918, No. 7). The most interesting of these parallels is the Egyptian story of a rich man and a poor man, who are buried on the same day. In the under-world their conditions are reversed, and the change is explained as due to the fact that the poor man had been virtuous on earth, while the rich man had not. They now receive the appropriate rewards. The moral is that he who is good on earth receives good in the under world, and he who is evil on earth receives evil in the under-world. The Jewish version of the tale occurs in several forms, of which the oldest appears to be that given in the Palestinian Talmud (*Hagigah*, II, 77d). It is as follows: ' Two godly men lived in Ashkelon. They ate together, drank together, and studied in the Law together. One of them died and kindness was not shown to him (i.e. nobody attended his funeral). The son of Ma'yan, a taxgatherer, died and the whole city stopped work to show him kindness. The (surviving) pious man began to complain; he said: " Alas that no (evil) comes upon the haters of Israel " (i.e. the wicked in Israel). In a dream he saw a vision; and one said to him: " Do not despise the children of your Lord (i.e. the Israelites). The one (the pious) had committed one sin and departed (this life) in it (i.e. his mean funeral cancelled it); and the other (the wealthy publican) had performed one good deed and departed (this life) in it " (i.e. his splendid funeral cancelled it). . . . After some days that godly man saw the godly one his (former) companion walking in gardens and parks beside springs of water (in Paradise). And he saw the son of Ma'yan, the publican, stretching out his tongue on the edge of a river; he was seeking to reach the water, and he could not.'

In both the Egyptian version and the Jewish the point of the story is that in the next world men are rewarded or punished according to their behaviour in this.   The similarities between these stories and the Lucan parable are sufficient to suggest the possibility that some such tale was current in Palestine in the days of Jesus, and was taken over by Him and adapted to His own purposes.   Whether, as Gressmann thought, the story originated in Egypt and travelled thence to Palestine, there to be adapted by the Rabbis and also by Jesus, is another question. But, granting that Jesus has taken over and adapted a current tale to His own purposes, we still have to ask what is the purpose that He has in view.   What is the point of the story as *He* tells it?

His version differs from the parallels in two respects.   It has a prologue and an epilogue.   The prologue gives the life-histories of the two men; and, very significantly, brings them into relation to one another.   It is not that one was very rich and the other very poor, but that the rich man had the opportunity to help the poor man and would not take it.   The epilogue (*vv.* 27–31) makes it clear why he would not help.   He had believed all his life that he had only one life to live; and therefore he had spent it entirely in seeking his own satisfaction, and wasted no time on thought for others.   The prologue and the epilogue are the parts of the parable that matter: and what they have to say is that the heartless conduct of the rich man is connected with his wrong beliefs.   His selfish life goes with his bad religion.   Translated into the terms of Jesus' own day: the Sadducees hold unworthy beliefs about God and man, and so their whole attitude to their fellow-men is wrong.   The difference between the Pharisees and Sadducees in this matter is that whereas the Pharisee is in danger of despising and rejecting those who are ignorant and degraded, the Sadducee is entirely wrapped up in himself and shows a callous indifference to the lot of all who are unfortunate, good, bad, and indifferent alike.

19. The rich man has all the appurtenances of his station in life.   His outer garment is dyed with the costly purple associated with royalty.   His underclothing is of the finest linen, the most delicate and expensive fabric known to the ancient world, and regarded by the Rabbis as a mark of luxury.   On ' fine linen ' (*byssus*, Heb. *būṣ*), see *Encyc. Bib.*, col. 2800.   The life of the rich man was one continual round of lavish entertainment.   In some authorities for the text his name is given.   The Sahidic version calls him Nineue.   In Ps. Cyprian, *De Pascha Computus*, his name is Finæus, in Priscillian it is Phinees, and in a marginal note to the versified Bible of Peter of Riga it is Amonofis.   It is unlikely that these names are anything but a later embellishment of the story.

20 f. The existence of Lazarus is in violent contrast to the life of the rich man. He was lying ill at the gates of the rich man's house.   The verb translated ' was laid ' is used of persons or animals prostrated by wounds or sickness.   Cf. Mt. 8[6], [14].   There is no reason to suppose that Lazarus had been carried there to beg alms.   His body was covered with ulcers, and he was in such poverty that he would gladly have eaten the bits that fell from the rich man's table.   In this his lot was similar to that of the Prodigal in the far country (cf. 15[16]).   It is possible that the word translated ' beggar ' represents the Aramaic *miskēnā*, which was used as a euphemism for ' leper.'   Cf. Littmann in *Z.N.T.W.* xxxiv (1935), p. 31.   He was so weak that he could not even drive away the vagrant dogs that nosed round him

and licked his sores, adding to his troubles, not relieving them. The name Lazarus is the Græcised form of the Hebrew name Eleāzār, shortened in Palestinian usage to Lazār, and meaning ' (he whom) God helps.' He certainly had no help from man. The utter wretchedness of Lazarus is illustrated by the Rabbinical saying (Beṣa 32[b]): 'There are three whose life is no life: he who depends on the table of another (for his food), he who is ruled by his wife, and he whose body is burdened with sufferings.'

22. The reversal of Lazarus' fortunes begins with his death His soul is carried away to Paradise by the angels. In the Rabbinical literature the idea that the souls of the righteous are conducted by angels is first expressed by R. Meir (c. A.D. 150); but it is found at an earlier date in the Testaments of the XII Patriarchs, Asher 6[4-6]: ' For the latter ends of men do show their righteousness (or unrighteousness), when they meet the angels of the Lord and of Satan. For when the soul departs troubled, it is tormented by the evil spirit which also it served in lusts and evil works. But if he is peaceful with joy he meeteth the angel of peace, and he leadeth him into eternal life.' The words ' into Abraham's bosom ' can be paralleled from the Rabbinical literature. The two clear cases of the use given by Billerbeck (ii. 226) both refer to martyrs, who after their sufferings are in Abraham's bosom. The phrase may be interpreted in two ways. It may stand for the place next to Abraham in the heavenly banquet. (Cf. the similar expression in John 13[23].) Or it may be, more generally, a way of describing close and intimate fellowship. (Cf. John 1[18] and the notes in Bernard's Commentary where similar expressions are adduced from Greek and Latin literature.) Both here and in the Rabbinical passages cited by Billerbeck the latter interpretation is the more suitable. It is to be noted that the destiny of Lazarus, as also of the rich man, is settled at death. There is no suggestion of an intermediate state pending a final judgement. Reward and punishment begin forthwith. There is, it seems, no ground in old Jewish belief for the notion either that ' Abraham's bosom ' was a part of Hades set apart for the righteous, or that Paradise was located in Hades or Sheol (Billerbeck, ii. 226 f.).

The fate of the rich man is now described. He died and was buried. That, according to the belief of the Sadducees, should have been the end of the story. If a man lived prosperously and happily, died in peace, and was honourably buried, he had had all that a man could ever expect. Their creed is stated in a polemical passage in Enoch 103[5-8] (transl. Charles):

' Woe to you sinners (i.e. Sadducees), when ye have died,
    If ye die in the wealth of your sins,
    And those who are like you say regarding you:
    " Blessed are the sinners: they have seen all their days.
    And now they have died in prosperity and in wealth,
    And have not seen tribulation or murder in their life;
    And they have died in honour,
    And judgement has not been executed on them during their life." '

Here the statement of the Sadducean creed ends. –It is followed by a contradiction from the Pharisaic point of view:

' Know ye that their souls will be made to descend into Sheol
And they will be wretched in their great tribulation.
And into darkness and chains and a burning flame where there is grievous judge-
    ment shall your spirits enter;
And the great judgement shall be for all the generations of the world.   Woe to
    you, for ye shall have no peace.'

23. So it turns out that the belief of Dives was mistaken.   There is something
after death, and for the rich man it is punishment.   It is important to observe just
what the nature of the disillusionment is.   The rich man, after his death, goes to
the very place where, according to Sadducean belief, he would expect to go; but
the place turns out to be quite different from the Sadducean picture of it.   Hades
is the regular equivalent in the LXX of the Hebrew Sheol; and in the earliest
Israelite belief Sheol is the under-world, the shadowy abode of the dead, to which
all men without distinction must come.   There they remain as ghostly relics of
their former selves.   They still exist, but their existence is not worth calling life.
There is nothing to hope for there and nothing to fear.   It is just the dumping-
ground for worn-out human beings.   After the Exile this view of Sheol or Hades is
modified.   The belief in a resurrection begins to set limits to the period during
which the dead remain in Sheol.   The belief in retribution after death comes in at
a later period and makes a distinction between the righteous and the wicked in
Sheol.   The belief in the immortality of the soul leads to the notion that the
righteous go direct to Paradise after death.   These factors work in various ways in
modifying Jewish eschatology as held by the Pharisees; but they do not touch at all
the beliefs of the Sadducees, who remain faithful to the old original idea of Sheol.
What the rich man in the parable discovers with horror and amazement is that
Hades is not what he believed it was, and what his brothers still believe it to be; but
something more like the Pharisaic picture as given for example in *Enoch* 22.   That
is, Hades is something very like Gehenna.

24, 25 f.   In his torments the rich man looks about for some help or relief, and
perceives Abraham far away and Lazarus with him in Paradise.   To them he
appeals for mercy.   He calls Abraham ' Father,' an indication that he himself is a
Jew.   The request for water recalls the Rabbinical parallel given above.   There
springs of water are part of the landscape of Paradise (cf. *Enoch* 22[9]), and thirst that
cannot be appeased is one of the torments of the damned (cf. 4 *Ezra* 8[59]).   The rich
man recognises Lazarus and knows his name.   It was not through ignorance that
Lazarus lay untended at his gate.   Abraham addresses the rich man as ' Child '
(cf. 15[31]).   His reply is that the request ought not to be granted, and in any case
cannot.   The fates of the persons concerned are determined by God and it is not
for Abraham or Lazarus to meddle in these matters.   The same inscrutable decree
that gave one abundance and the other misery on earth now reverses the lots.
Had the rich man shown mercy in his lifetime he might have had mercy now.   But
in any case there is no way from the one state to the other; an impassable gulf lies
between Paradise and Hades.

27 f.   The rich man now thinks of his brothers, who are living as he had lived,
believing what he had believed, and so dooming themselves to join him in torment.

He asks that Lazarus may be sent to them to testify to them. Of what? Of the only thing to which one returned from the dead could bear witness; the fact that there is a life beyond the grave, and the nature of it as retribution. The five brothers are in danger of punishment after death precisely because they do not believe in it. If an eye-witness were to go and tell them what had happened to Dives, they would be convinced, and amend their lives in order to avoid a like fate. The creed of the five brothers is the Sadducean creed.

29, 30. The reply of Abraham is that the Law and the prophetic books the one authority recognised by the Sadducees—contain the belief which the brethren reject. (See above, p. 297.) Lazarus could not tell them the truth any more plainly than it is already told by Moses and the prophets. Dives persists that his brothers really would be impressed if someone returned from the dead to testify. But the last word is that those who reject God's revelation will not be convinced in this way.

The difficulty, felt by many, of believing that the description of the torments of the rich man in the parable can truly represent the mind of Jesus, is at least mitigated if we can suppose that the central portion of the parable is a popular tale which Jesus has adopted, and that the really characteristic and important matter is that which He has added to it by way of prologue and epilogue. We may then contend that the purpose of Jesus in this parable is not to give information about the next world. Rather the point is that there *is* a future life, and that the heartless selfishness of the Sadducees arises from the fact that they deny this truth. ' Let us eat and drink for to-morrow we die ' means a low view of human life; and a low view of human life issues in callous indifference to the miseries of others. There is a striking parallel to this in the *Koran* (Surah 107[1-3]):

Seest thou not him who disbelieves in the Judgement;
He it is who repels the orphan,
And does not encourage the feeding of the poor.

If this interpretation of the purport of the parable is correct, we may reckon it also as a part of the ' Gospel of the Outcast,' teaching that God requires of man not only a merciful and understanding attitude towards the morally frail (as against the Pharisees), but also generous and gracious help for all the victims of poverty, sickness, or any other ill that may come upon man. The Sadducee could boast that he was not narrow-minded and strait-laced like his brethren the Pharisees. But he could not clear himself of the charge that he, who had the most abundant means and the best opportunities for showing a generous spirit, was remarkable only for hardness of heart.

24. *ON SERVING GOD* (181)

LK. 17[7-10]

17 7 But who is there of you, having a [1] servant plowing or keeping sheep, that will say unto him, when he is come in 8 from the field, Come straightway and sit down to meat; and will not rather say unto him, Make ready wherewith I may sup, and gird thyself, and serve me, till I have eaten and drunken; and afterward 9 shalt thou eat and drink? Doth he thank the [1] servant because he did the 10 things that were commanded? Even so ye also, when ye shall have done all the things that are commanded you, say, We are unprofitable [2] servants; we have done that which it was our duty to do. [1] Gr. *bondservant*. [2] Gr. *bondservants*.

The opening verses of chapter 17 are derived from Q (see above, pp 138–141). They are all clearly addressed to disciples; and this L passage, which is appended to them, may be taken to be spoken to the disciples also. The important question is whether it can be fairly included in the block of material which we have called the ' Gospel of the Outcast.' It can be argued that it would be in place in any context concerning the service of God, no matter what the nature of the service might happen to be. On the other hand we have clear indications in the teaching as to what Jesus conceived the service of God or the service of the Kingdom, in the special sense, to be. The business of a disciple as servant of God, in the full sense of the word, is to be the organ whereby the merciful love of God is manifested to men. The work *par excellence* of the disciple is to do what the Pharisee and the Sadducee fail to do. The Son of Man is come to seek and to save the lost; and the task of the disciple is that task. And there is no point at which he is entitled to say, ' I have done enough,' no point at which performance overtakes duty to God or the needs of men. The most devoted and tireless of the Apostles knew this; see 1 Cor. 9^{16ff}. See notes on Mt. 25^{14-30}, above, pp. 245–248.

7 f., 9. The endless claims of God's work are illustrated by the parable of the master and the slave. The slave has done a day's work, or what might fairly be deemed a day's work, on the farm. But on his return to the house he is not met with an invitation to sit down to a meal. Fresh tasks await him. He must prepare and serve food to his master; and when the master is satisfied, then he may attend to his own wants. Even when he has done all this he has not put his master under any obligation to him. He has not given anything that the master was not already entitled to demand.

10. The conclusion to be drawn from this example will then be something like this: if a mere man is entitled to make such far-reaching demands on the services of his servant, and that merely for his own profit and comfort, how much more is God entitled to require the utmost from His servants in the manifestation and extension of His Kingdom among men. So the conclusion might be drawn from God's side. Actually it is stated in terms of the disciple's obligation rather than of God's demands. So put it becomes: When you have done all that you can do, you have done no more than God is entitled to expect from you, and not enough to put God in your debt.

The difficulty in this verse lies in the word ' unprofitable.' The only other place in the New Testament where it occurs is Mt. 25^{30} in reference to a servant who had done nothing at all. That passage cannot help us here, where the servants have done all that they are commanded. The word is omitted by the better of the two MSS. of the Old Syriac version; and some scholars, on the strength of this omission, reject the word here and then take the sense to be, ' we are but servants; we have done only what we were bound to do.' It is urged that the emphasis is on the fact of being servants; not on a distinction between good and bad servants. But the point is that the servants *are* good, as good as they can be. And at their best they have not put God in their debt; they have only earned the right to be retained as servants; they have earned their keep. Or, in Pauline terms: ' If I preach the gospel, I have nothing to glory of; for necessity is laid upon me; for woe is unto me, if I preach not the gospel ' (1 Cor. 9^{16}). The same thought is found in a saying of Rabban Johanan b. Zakkai (died *c.* A.D. 80): ' If thou hast wrought much in the Law claim not merit for thyself, for to this end wast thou created.' ' Unprofitable ' here is much the same as ' having nothing to glory of,' or ' not claiming merit.'

25. THE COMING OF THE KINGDOM (183)

LK. 17[20-21]

17 20 And being asked by the Pharisees, when the kingdom of God cometh, he answered them and said, The kingdom of God cometh not with observation:	21 neither shall they say, Lo, here! or, There! for lo, the kingdom of God is [1] within you. [1] Or, *in the midst of you.*

This short passage presents serious difficulties. The first problem to be solved is that of deciding between ' within you ' (R.V. text) and ' in the midst of you ' (R.V. mg.). The difference of interpretation implied in the two renderings is of old standing, as may be seen from the following typical patristic quotations. For the sense ' within,' Origen on Joshua, *Hom.* xiii. 1. ' After the Lord Jesus has destroyed the king of sin from the city of our soul, our soul may become the city of God, and God may reign in it, and it may be said to us, " Behold the Kingdom of God is within you." ' For ' in the midst of you,' Ephraim Syrus, *Commentary on the Diatessaron* (Moesinger 211): ' " Behold the Kingdom is within your heart " which He (Jesus) said concerning Himself, who was standing in their midst.' This interpretation of Ephraim's is supported by the Old Syriac version and the Syriac Vulgate, both of which translate the Greek of Lk. in the same sense as R.V. mg. It must, however, be admitted that this rendering of the Greek word *entos* is not the obvious or natural one. Liddell and Scott do not recognise it. The natural way to translate *entos* is by ' within ' or ' in ': and this is confirmed by the fact that when Lk. means ' among ' he writes *en mesō* (22[27]).

But the matter does not end with this admission. For if the saying is authentic, *entos* is the translation of some Aramaic preposition; and both in Hebrew and Aramaic the corresponding prepositions are ambiguous in a way that *entos* is not. The ambiguity may be illustrated by a Rabbinical discussion which is recorded as having taken place in the middle of the second century A.D. on the meaning of the text in Exod. 17[7], ' Is the Lord among us (*bĕkirbĕnū*) or not? ' One Rabbi explains thus : The Israelites in asking this question meant to say, ' If He (God) provides us with food, like a king who dwells in a city (i.e. in the midst of his people), so that the city lacks for nothing, then we will serve Him; if not, we will rebel against Him.' The majority of the Rabbis, however, gave a different interpretation. The question meant: ' If we think our thoughts and He knows what we think (i.e. if He is literally within us and knows the secrets of each individual), then we will serve Him; if not, we will rebel against Him ' (*Pesikta* 28[a]). Here is exactly the same difference of interpretation as that between R.V. text and R.V. mg.; and here the difference of views is grounded in a real ambiguity in the meaning of the Hebrew word. The conclusion is that even if it be admitted that ' within ' is the natural and proper translation of *entos*, *entos* itself is only one of the possible translations of the probable original Aramaic, which would equally well be translated by *en mesō*, ' among.' (Cf. Field's *Hexapla* on Exod. 34⁹.)

We are thus driven back upon other considerations; and there are two which seem to be decisive in favour of the sense ' among ' rather than ' within.' First it is the Pharisees who are addressed, and it is not likely that Jesus would say that the Kingdom of God was ' within ' them. Such a statement would lay Him open to the obvious retort: ' Why then are you in open opposition to us? ' Secondly, the Kingdom of God is not here under discussion as a state of mind or a disposition in men. It is thought of as something which is to come. It is a fact of history, not of psychology. Moreover, Jesus speaks elsewhere of men entering the Kingdom, not of the Kingdom entering men. The Kingdom is a state of affairs, not a state of mind. This state of affairs can come to pass in God's providence, and men may find their place in it. The whole weight of the teaching of Jesus elsewhere seems to be in favour of saying, ' Lo, the Kingdom of God is among you.'

There remains yet another problem: how are we to interpret 'Lo, the Kingdom of God is among you '? Is it (1) a description of the present state of affairs, or (2) a prophecy about the future? This question is still in debate.

The form of the Pharisees' question shows that they are thinking of the Kingdom as something still future. They believe that it will come; and they ask ' when? ' That is, they ask the question which so many of the Apocalypses ask and attempt to answer. The answer of Jesus may mean that it is idle to ask *when* the Kingdom will come, since it is already present; or that the question cannot be answered, since the answer is known to God alone. For either reply we can quote supporting passages from the other teaching of Jesus. In favour of the first are such sayings as Mt. 12²⁸‖Lk. 11²⁰ (Q); Mt. 12⁴¹f.‖Lk. 11³¹f. (Q); Mt. 12⁵f. (M); in favour of the latter Mt. 24³⁷⁻⁴¹‖Lk. 17 ²⁶⁻³⁰ (Q); Mk. 13³²⁻³⁷; Mt. 24⁴³f.‖Lk. 12³⁹f. (Q). On the whole the latter view seems preferable. We must then understand Jesus to say: The Kingdom does not come in such a way that one can make a programme of its coming. There are no premonitory signs and portents which may be observed so that one could say, ' Look at this and that; it cannot be far away now.' On the contrary it comes suddenly and unexpectedly. One moment the world is just its normal self: then Lo! the Kingdom of God is among you. This interpretation has two obvious claims to acceptance. It deals with the question asked; and the reply of Jesus agrees with His genuine teaching about the final consummation as given in the Q passage which follows immediately in Lk. (17²³⁻³⁰, see above, pp. 141–144).

This interpretation of Lk. 17²⁰f. can be maintained without in any way minimising the importance of those other passages in which the Kingdom appears as a present reality at work in the world. The general view of the whole matter of the Kingdom as both present and future can best be realised in the parable of the Seed (Mk. 4²⁶⁻²⁹). There the point of the story is not the contrast between small beginnings and large results; neither has it anything to do with the length or shortness of the time between sowing and harvest. It is that a man who sows seed sets in motion natural forces which go on inevitably until they reach their consummation in the harvest. So is the Kingdom of God. The ministry of

Jesus has set in motion supernatural forces which go on inevitably until they reach their consummation. The consummated Kingdom is now present in the world as really as the harvest is present in the sown field. How the growth takes place and when it will come to full fruition—these are questions which the sower cannot answer. They are God's affair. But that heavenly forces, as real as the mysterious forces of nature, are already at work in the world moving inevitably to the great consummation—of that Jesus has no doubt whatever. The Kingdom is a present reality working towards a future consummation.

26. *THE IMPORTUNATE WIDOW* (185)

Lk. 18$^{1-8}$

18 1 And he spake a parable unto them to the end that they ought always to pray, 2 and not to faint; saying, There was in a city a judge, which feared not God, and 3 regarded not man: and there was a widow in that city; and she came oft unto him, saying, [1] Avenge me of mine adversary. 4 And he would not for a while: but afterward he said within himself, Though I fear 5 not God, nor regard man; yet because this widow troubleth me, I will avenge her, lest she [2] wear me out by her continual 6 coming. And the Lord said, Hear what 7 [3] the unrighteous judge saith. And shall not God avenge his elect, which cry to him day and night, and he is longsuffering 8 over them? I say unto you, that he will avenge them speedily. Howbeit when the Son of man cometh, shall he find [4] faith on the earth?

[1] Or, *Do me justice of*: and so in ver. 5, 7, 8.
[2] Gr. *bruise*.
[3] Gr. *the judge of unrighteousness*.
[4] Or, *the faith*.

The Evangelist's introductory note to this parable represents it as an exhortation to be instant in prayer to God. But an examination of the parable itself shows that the duty of praying is not the main point. The prayers of the righteous are taken for granted as much as the persistence of the widow in stating her claim. The true point is not that prayers should be made, but that God will answer the prayers of His servants. The object of the parable is not to encourage the habit of praying, but to induce that faith in God and His purposes of good, without which prayer cannot be anything but a formality. It is thus a word of hope and encouragement to the victims of oppression and injustice, and an integral part of the ' Gospel of the Outcast.' The message of the parable has close affinities with a striking passage in *Ecclesiasticus* (35 $^{12-20}$ $^{(14-26)}$; Charles, *Apoc. and Pseudepigr.*, i. 438 ff.), where the writer speaks of God's righteousness and His readiness to hear the cry of the oppressed:

Bribe not, for He will not receive;
And put not thy trust upon a sacrifice of extortion,
For He is a God of justice,
And with Him is no partiality.
He will not show partiality against the poor man,
And the supplications of the distressed He heareth.
He doth not ignore the cry of the fatherless,
Nor the widow, when she poureth out (her) plaint. . . .
The appeal of the lowly traverseth the skies,
And resteth not till it reach (its goal).
It shall not remove till God doth visit,

And till the righteous Judge executeth judgement.
Yea, the Lord will not tarry,
And the mighty One will not refrain Himself,
Till He smite the loins of the merciless,
And requite vengeance to the arrogant;
Till He dispossess the sceptre of pride,
And the staff of wickedness utterly cut down;
Till He render to man his due
And recompense people according to their devising;
Till He plead the cause of His people,
And rejoice them with His salvation.
[Beauteous is His favour in a time] of stress
As a rain-cloud in the season of drought.

1. The audience for this parable is, in the Lucan arrangement, the same as that of the preceding Q section (17^{22-37}), that is, the disciples (17^{22}). The Greek word (*enkakein*) translated ' faint ' is very rare. In the Greek version of the Old Testament by Symmachus it occurs four times to translate a Hebrew verb meaning to loathe, abhor, dread. Something like this appears to be the meaning here: the disciples are not to ' get fed-up ' with praying or ' be sick of praying.' Cf. 1 Thess. 5^{17}, ' Pray without ceasing.' Jewish teaching and practice did not favour incessant prayer. Three times in the day was the correct practice, based on Dan. 6^{10}. Cf. Moore, *Judaism*, ii. 221.

2 f. The character of the judge is not calculated to inspire any hope in the breast of a litigant who is not in a position to offer a bribe. Neither the laws of God nor public opinion càn stir his conscience. The widow, on the other hand, is the very type of helplessness and defencelessness. Jerusalem devastated by the Babylonians is compared to a widow (Lam. 1^1). In the Old Testament great stress is laid on the duty of treating widows and orphans aright (Exod. $22^{22 ff.}$) and on God's care for them (Ps. 68^5); and this duty is an essential part of true religion in the early Church (James 1^{27}).

4 f. The widow in the parable has no weapon but her own perseverance. She comes again and again before the judge, always with the same plea: ' Vindicate my rights against my opponent.' The situation would seem to be that the widow is the plaintiff in the case. Having failed to obtain satisfaction by other means, she appeals to the court to do her justice. The court, however, is not willing to act, and remains unwilling; so that the business becomes a war of attrition between the judge and the widow. The judge is represented as reflecting on this situation. He will not do justice out of respect for God's will nor out of regard for public opinion; but perhaps it will be best for his own convenience to grant the woman's request. The exact nature of the deciding consideration is not quite clear. The Greek of the latter part of *v.* 5 could be understood to mean that the judge fears a time when the widow, grown exasperated by the law's delays, will set about him and beat him black and blue. The verb translated ' wear me out' means properly to 'give a black eye.' It appears again in a more general sense in Paul's statement ' I buffet my body ' (1 Cor. 9^{27}). Against the

notion of such a violent climax is the fact that the judge would know how to deal with such a burst of fury. Also the Greek tenses are against this interpretation. We should probably, therefore, prefer the translation given in R.V. text and understand that the judge dreads being continually pestered by the widow, and decides to put an end to it by doing her justice.

6-8[a]. The comment of Jesus on the parable. If even an unjust judge can be induced to do justice, how much more will the righteous God, the judge of all the earth, do right. The ' elect ' of God ; the Greek word translated ' elect ' is used in the Septuagint in several senses: (a) = choice, i.e. of the best quality. In this sense the word is used of animals and things; (b) = picked, especially of picked men—the idea that is expressed by corps d'élite; (c) the chosen of God, especially Israel as God's chosen people, or great men in Israel as God's chosen servants. This third use of ' elect ' seems to belong to the period of the Exile and after. Cf. Is. 42[1], 43[20], 65[9, 15, 23]; Ps. 105[6, 43], 106[5]; 1 Chron. 16[13]; Ecclus. 46[1]. David is God's chosen (Ps. 89[3, 19]), as is Moses (Ps. 106[23]); and God made the patriarchs His elect (2 Macc. 1[25]). It is noteworthy that the idea of Israel as God's elect should appear not in the days of national greatness and prosperity, but in the period of humiliation and impotence. And it is probably significant that the term so often appears in parallelism to ' servant ' (Is. 65[9, 15]; Ps. 105[6]; 1 Chron. 16[13]). The election is not in the first instance an election to privilege, but an appointment to service. It is in line with this that we find the ' elect ' of God in parallelism with His holy ones (Wisdom 4[15]) or ' them that love Him ' (Ecclus. 47[22]) or as another name for the righteous and in contrast to the impious (Enoch 1[1, 3, 8], 5[7]). We might almost say that the mark of the elect is that they serve God by the sanctity of their lives. They are not the pampered darlings of Providence, but the corps d'élite in the army of the living God. Because they are what they are, they are foredoomed to suffering at the hands of the wicked; and in many cases the seal of election is martyrdom.

If this is the meaning of election it is easy to see why the elect cry to God day and night. We may compare the Greek text of Enoch 9[1-3]: ' Then Michael, Uriel, Raphael, and Gabriel, looking down from heaven, saw much blood being shed on the earth. And they said one to another: " The voice of them that cry upon the earth; (and their cry comes up) as far as the gates of heaven. The souls of men make their suit saying: Bring our cause before the Most High." ' See also Rev. 6[9-11] and the passage from Ecclus. quoted above.

The words ' and he is longsuffering over them ' are difficult. It is possible to take the clause as meaning that God gives a patient hearing to the cries of the elect; but that is a very lame interpretation. The elect do not want a patient hearing: they want redress. They do not want God to go on patiently listening to their outcry: they want God to take action which will make their crying unnecessary. Yet, although this interpretation is unsatisfactory, there is no other that will fit the Greek text as it stands; and we are driven to suppose that the Greek itself is a misunderstanding of the Semitic original. In the Septuagint the Greek verb here translated ' is longsuffering ' corresponds to a Hebrew, which means ' postpones (his) wrath.' In Aramaic there is a similar idiom: ' removes his wrath to a distance.' There is a Rabbinical parable based on this idiomatic phrase (p. *Taanith*, II. 65^b). A king had two legions of troops. He wondered where he should keep them, and finally decided to have them at a distance from the capital on the ground that if the civilian population became troublesome, and he had to send for the troops, there would be time for the people to come to a more reasonable frame of mind before the troops arrived. So, it is argued, God keeps His wrath at a distance in order to give Israel time to repent.

So in this case it may be supposed that the original Aramaic meant ' and He postpones the wrath, which He has on their account,' i.e. He refrains from executing His wrath on those who persecute the elect, thus giving the persecutors time to repent and amend their ways. This would give an entirely satisfactory sense. What delays the vindication of the elect is the longsuffering of God towards their foes. In this connexion we may quote another Rabbinical saying from the same passage as the parable given above. It is attributed to R. Jonathan b. Eleazar (first half of the third century A.D.). Commenting on the phrase ' postponing anger ' he remarks that in the Hebrew phrase the word for ' anger ' is not in the singular number, but in the dual. This suggests that God postpones two angers, and so leads to the conclusion that God is longsuffering not only with the righteous but with the wicked as well.

8. In *v.* 8 the answer to the question of *v.* 7 is given. Although God is patient with the oppressors of His elect, yet the vindication will come, and come quickly. The connexion of the question in *v.* 8^b with the parable is not at all clear. By some commentators it is regarded as a later editorial comment on the parable, which is taken to end with the word ' speedily.' It may be noted that in the Palestinian Syriac Lectionary *v.* 8^a ends Lesson CXV, and *v.* 8^b begins Lesson CXVI. On the assumption that the saying is genuine and that it belongs to its present context, two ways of interpreting it seem possible. First, we may take ' the coming of the Son of Man ' to mean the Parousia, as in Lk. 17$^{22-30}$ (above, pp. 141–144). In that case the Parousia will be the vindication of the elect, and the question comes to mean: ' When the Son of Man comes, will anyone be looking hopefully for that consummation? ' Alternatively ' Son of Man ' may be taken, as in Lk. 7^{34} = Mt. 11^{19} (Q), above, p. 70, as a periphrasis for the first personal pronoun. In that case the parable may be taken to show what ought to be the attitude of men. They ought to have implicit faith that God will vindicate His elect. But when one looks for such faith and hope among men, does one find it? Cf. Lk. 7^9 = Mt. 8^{10} (Q), above, p. 63, and the parable of the Great Feast (Lk. 14$^{16-24}$ (Q), above, pp. 128 ff.). In the latter parable we have the reply to the conventional piety that says, ' Blessed is he that shall eat bread in the Kingdom of God '; and the reply is in effect: ' You say that, but don't really mean it: you merely pretend to desire the Kingdom of God.' See *The Teaching of Jesus*, pp. 224 f. I still think the second line of explanation the better.

27   *THE PHARISEE AND THE PUBLICAN* (186)

LK. 18$^{9-14}$

18   9   And he spake also this parable unto certain which trusted in themselves that they were righteous, and set ^{1} all others 10 at nought: Two men went up into the temple to pray; the one a Pharisee, and 11 the other a publican. The Pharisee

stood and prayed thus with himself, God, I thank thee, that I am not as the rest of men, extortioners, unjust, adulterers, or 12 even as this publican. I fast twice in the week; I give tithes of all that I get. 13 But the publican, standing afar off, would not lift up so much as his eyes unto heaven, but smote his breast, saying,

14 God, [2] be merciful to me [3] a sinner. I say unto you, This man went down to his house justified rather than the other: for every one that exalteth himself shall be humbled; but he that humbleth himself shall be exalted.

[1] Gr. *the rest.*   [2] Or, *be propitiated.*
[3] Or, *the sinner.*

This parable obviously belongs to the ' Gospel of the Outcast.'   It is addressed to all the friends of the elder brother in the parable of the Prodigal.   According to R.V. this parable is spoken ' unto ' the people in question; but the Greek preposition may also mean ' with reference to ' or even ' against.'   Lucan usage, however, is in favour of ' unto.'   The parable is spoken to those ' who trusted in themselves that they were righteous, and set all others at nought.'   The words ' trusted in themselves ' are to be taken literally.   They do not mean ' considered themselves to be righteous '; but ' believed in themselves ' ' had faith in themselves ' ' relied upon themselves.'   The same construction appears in Lk. 11[22], where the strong man ' relied confidently on his armaments '; and, most instructively, in 2 Cor. 1[9], ' that we should not trust in ourselves, but in God.'   The mark of the people attacked in the parable is their self-confidence and self-reliance in things religious.   This consideration determines the meaning of the word ' that ' in the following clause.   The Greek word (*hoti*) may mean ' that ' or ' because.'   The latter translation is to be preferred here.   The clause gives the ground of their self-confidence.   It is not that they had a good opinion of themselves, to wit, that they were righteous; but that they really had the kind of faith in themselves and their own powers that weaker vessels are content to have in God, and that the ground of this confidence was their own achievements in piety and morality. They believed in themselves *because* they were able to live up to their own standard. And naturally they despised those who either did not acknowledge their standard or did not succeed in living up to it.

It is clear from the parable itself that the persons meant by this description are Pharisees.   Josephus describes the Pharisees (*War*, i. 110) as ' a body of Jews with the reputation of excelling the rest of their nation in the observances of religion, and as exact exponents of the laws '; and the description of Josephus is confirmed by the confession of Paul (Phil. 3[4ff.]) : ' If any other man thinketh to have confidence in the flesh (i.e. in man and things human, as opposed to God and God's grace), I yet more: circumcised the eighth day, of the stock of Israel, of the tribe of Benjamin, a Hebrew of the Hebrews; as touching the law, a Pharisee; as touching zeal, persecuting the church; as touching the righteousness which is in the law, found blameless.'

While it is clear that it is Pharisees that are meant by the description in *v.* 9, it is not certain that all Pharisees are covered by it.   That spiritual pride was a real and ever-present danger in Pharisaism is sufficiently obvious.   The danger was perceived by the great Hillel (*c.* 20 B.C.), who used to say (*Aboth* 2[5], Danby, p. 448) : ' Keep not aloof from the congregation and trust not in thyself until the day of thy death, and judge not thy fellow until thou art come to his place.'   If it be argued that such warning against a haughty, self-confident, and censorious attitude presupposes that there were some who had it (which is more than probable), it also means that there were others within the Pharisaic circle who perceived this subtle peril and strove to avoid it. We shall probably be near the truth if we think of the parable as directed not against the entire body of Pharisees, but against a certain section of them. See the discussion of the Speech against Pharisaism, above, pp. 94–105, 227–240.

10. The parable proper begins with *v.* 10. Two men, representing the two types of character, go up from the city to the temple-mount to pray. For the use of the Temple as a place of prayer see Lk. 1[10]; Acts 3[1]; Mishnah, *Tamid* 5[1] (Danby, pp. 586 f.). Besides such prayers as were incorporated in the regular daily ritual of the Temple, there were the private prayers and meditations of individuals who could use the Temple for this purpose not only at the times of the daily sacrifices, but also in the intervals between services. The two men who go up to the Temple for this purpose represent the two extremes in Judaism. The Pharisee is the type of complete devotion to the Law as the supreme standard of Jewish faith and morals. The publican represents the lowest stratum of Jewish life, those who fail miserably to live up to the religious and moral ideals of the nation.

11 f. Both men pray. Standing was the regular posture in prayer, though other attitudes were not rigidly excluded. There is great variation among the witnesses to the text at this point. The main alternatives are:

> (*a*) The Pharisee stood and prayed thus with himself.
> (*b*) The Pharisee stood and prayed thus.
> (*c*) The Pharisee stood by himself and prayed thus.

In (*a*) ' prayed with himself ' must mean that he prayed silently. Does this fit the story? We are told that the custom was to utter the words of private prayer in an undertone (Moore, *Judaism*, ii. 222 f.). The second reading is colourless, and has nothing against it—or to recommend it. The third introduces a feature that is in keeping with the rest of the parable. The Pharisee stands aloof from the common herd of worshippers, thus doing one of the three things criticised by Hillel. Intrinsically, reading (*c*) is superior to the other two. It makes a real contribution to the story. Reading (*b*) contributes nothing, and (*a*) is mere conventional detail, which fills out the picture of the Pharisee but does nothing to make it live.

The content of the Pharisee's prayer is a catalogue of his own virtues. The first and larger part of the list mentions the vices from which he abstains; the second part draws the attention of God to certain evidences of his special piety. The catalogue is introduced by a thanksgiving to God, which we must regard as sincere. There is no ground for supposing that the Pharisee is a hypocritical humbug, or that his virtues are pretended. He is a respectable God-fearing man, and what he says about himself must be taken as true. He thanks God that he has been able to abstain from a number of things that are prohibited by God Himself in His Law. The unpleasant feature in the prayer is the self-satisfied comparison which the Pharisee makes between himself and those who do not belong to his party. It is, unhappily, very easy to slip from ' There, but for the grace of God, goes John Bradford ' to ' God, I thank thee, that I am not as the rest of men '; and it would be rash to contend that Pharisees were the only people who ever made this kind of slip. The difficulty of drawing the line between the two attitudes is illustrated by the prayer which R. Nechunya b. Ha Kana (c. A.D. 70) used to offer whenever he came out of the Rabbinical College (p. *Berakhoth*, II. 7[d]):

> I give thanks before thee O Lord my God, and God of my fathers, that thou hast appointed my portion with those who sit in the College and the Synagogue, and hast not appointed my lot in the theatres and circuses. For I labour and they labour. I am keen and they are keen. I labour to inherit Paradise and they labour to inherit the pit of destruction; as it is said (Ps. 16[10]) 'Thou wilt not leave my soul to Sheol; neither wilt thou suffer thy godly one to see the pit.'

'Extortioners': cf. Is. 10[1f.]. Possibly to be distinguished from the 'unjust,' as being those who wrong their fellows while managing to keep within the letter of the law; whereas the 'unjust' break the law in their greed of gain. 'Adulterers'; see on Lk. 16[18] (Q), above, pp. 136 ff. 'Or even as this publican': better, 'or, for that matter, like this publican.' The publican may not be guilty of any specially notorious crimes; but, take him all in all, he is a despicable creature.

In *v.* 12 the Pharisee names two matters in which he goes beyond the positive commands of the Law. A regular fast day twice in the week is not prescribed in the Law; and such evidence as we have on the practice tends to show that it was a self-imposed act of piety in strict Pharisaic circles. The motives lying behind the institution are obscure. The chosen days were Monday and Thursday, probably because they satisfied the double requirement of not interfering with the Sabbath celebrations, and of being well separated from one another. According to Billerbeck (ii. 244) there is no evidence that the Jews of this period, as a whole, had a regular weekly fast, either on one day or two. Nor is there any ground for thinking that the practice of fasting twice a week was regarded as obligatory by the whole body of Pharisees. The practice was essentially a voluntary observance undertaken by individuals.

Later the two fasts were explained as days of mourning for such national calamities as the destruction of the Temple: and this explanation found its way into Christian circles. Thus in a Greek MS. quoted by Juster (i. 308 n. 2) the Jews are said to fast on Mondays because it was on a Monday that the Temple was destroyed by Nebuchadnezzar, and on Thursdays because it was on a Thursday that the Temple was destroyed by Titus.

The Church took over the two fasts in the week, but altered the days. So in the *Didache* 8[1]: 'Let not your fasts be with the hypocrites, for they fast on Mondays and Thursdays, but do you fast on Wednesdays and Fridays.' In the *Apostolic Constitutions* (vii. 23[1]) it is explained that Wednesday is a fast because on that day the betrayal of Jesus was arranged between Judas and the Jewish authorities, and Friday because it was the day of the Crucifixion. Other passages to a like effect in Juster (i. 310 n. 5).

'I give tithes of all that I get.' Here again the Pharisee goes beyond the strict legal requirement, and probably beyond the interpretations of the scribes. See notes on Lk. 11[42] (Q), above, pp. 97 f.

13. The publican is overwhelmed by the sense of his own unworthiness, and rightly so. It is a great mistake to regard the publican as a decent sort of fellow, who knew his own limitations and did not pretend to be better than he was. It is one of the marks of our time that the Pharisee and the publican have changed places; and it is the modern equivalent of the publican who may be heard thanking God that he is not like those canting humbugs, hypocrites, and killjoys, whose chief offence is that they take their religion seriously. This publican was a rotter; and he knew it. He asked for God's mercy because mercy was the only thing he dared ask for.

14ᵃ. The comment of Jesus on the story. Why does the publican go down justified rather than the Pharisee? The answer is that the decisive thing is not the past record, whether good or bad, but the present attitude towards God. Every moment before God is an opportunity to have life determined by the future rather than the past. The Pharisee asks nothing better than to go on in the way he is going. The one thing against him is that he is satisfied with life and with himself. God can do nothing for him because he lacks nothing. The publican has one point, and one only, in his favour: he is not satisfied. Where there is this heaven-born discontent, there is hope.

14ᵇ. A floating saying (it appears in Mt. 18⁴, 23¹² and Lk. 14¹¹ as well as here), which has attached itself to the parable in the course of tradition. It only serves to weaken the conclusion in v. 14ᵃ.

The remainder of this chapter consists of material derived from Mk.; and the next piece of L material is the story of Zacchæus (19¹⁻¹⁰), a fitting pendant to the parable of the Pharisee and the Publican. In the parable Jesus pillories the Pharisaic attitude to these outcasts: in the case of Zacchæus He shows by His own example the more excellent way. With this narrative the section of L material, which we have called the ' Gospel of the Outcast,' comes to an end. These L passages from 15¹–19¹⁰ contain some of our Lord's deepest thought concerning the nature of God, some of His most searching criticism of the religion of His time, and at least one perfect example of His own way with sinners.

28. THE PARABLE OF THE POUNDS (195)

LK. 19¹¹⁻²⁷

19 11 And as they heard these things, he added and spake a parable, because he was nigh to Jerusalem, and *because* they supposed that the kingdom of God was 12 immediately to appear. He said therefore, A certain nobleman went into a far country, to receive for himself a kingdom, 13 and to return. And he called ten ¹ servants of his, and gave them ten ² pounds, and said unto them, Trade ye *herewith* till 14 I come. ·But his citizens hated him, and sent an ambassage after him, saying, We 15 will not that this man reign over us. And it came to pass, when he was come back again, having received the kingdom, that he commanded these ¹ servants, unto whom he had given the money, to be

called to him, that he might know what 16 they had gained by trading. And the first came before him, saying, Lord, thy pound hath made ten pounds more. And 17 And he said unto him, Well done, thou good ³ servant: because thou wast found faithful in a very little, have thou 18 authority over ten cities. And the second came, saying, Thy pound, Lord, 19 hath made five pounds. And he said unto him also, Be thou also over five 20 cities. And ⁴ another same, saying, Lord, behold, *here is* thy pound, which I 21 kept laid up in a napkin: for I feared thee, because thou art an austere man: thou takest up that thou layedst not down, and reapest that thou didst not

22 sow. He saith unto him, Out of thine own mouth will I judge thee, thou wicked [3] servant. Thou knewest that I am an austere man, taking up that I laid not 23 down, and reaping that I did not sow; then wherefore gavest thou not my money into the bank, and [5] I at my coming should have required it with 24 interest? And he said unto them that stood by, Take away from him the pound, and give it unto him that hath 25 the ten pounds. And they said unto 26 him, Lord, he hath ten pounds. I say unto you, that unto every one that hath

shall be given; but from him that hath not, even that which he hath shall be 27 taken away from him. Howbeit these mine enemies, which would not that I should reign over them, bring hither, and slay them before me.

[1] Gr. bondservants.
[2] Mina, here translated a pound, is equal to one hundred drachmas. See ch. xv, 8.
[3] Gr. bondservant.
[4] Gr. the other.
[5] Or, I should have gone and required.

This parable has a parallel in Mt.'s parable of the Talents (Mt. 25[14-30], above pp. 245–248). There are many differences in detail between the two narratives, so many that it is difficult to suppose that the two versions can be traced back to a common written source such as Q. Indeed, it has been doubted whether they can be the same parable. The most likely solution is that we have here two versions of an original parable, which have come down through different lines of tradition and suffered modifications in the process. The most striking difference between Mt. and Lk. is the additional narrative matter peculiar to Lk., contained in vv. 12, 14, and 27. The most recent commentator on Lk. (Hauck) regards these verses as forming a separate allegory, which has been incorporated with the parable of the Pounds, and has influenced the latter in places, e.g. v. 15 ' having received the kingdom '; v. 17 ' have thou authority over ten cities '; v. 19 five cities. Harnack, noting certain similarities between the additional matter in Lk. here and the additional matter in Mt.'s version of the parable of the Great Feast (Mt. 22[1-14], above, pp. 224–227), suggested that the additions in both cases were derived from a common source. But it must be confessed that the resemblances are far outweighed by the differences.

Much more impressive is the similarity between Lk.'s additional matter and the story told by Josephus (War, II, vi. §§ 80–100; parallel in Antiquities, XVII, viii.–xi.). There we are told how Herod the Great divided his kingdom by will among his family. The bequests required the confirmation of the Roman Emperor before they could become fully valid, and accordingly Archelaus set out for Rome to obtain confirmation of the bequest to him. He was followed by an embassy of the Jews sent to protest against his appointment; and, after hearing both parties, Augustus gave Archelaus half of Herod's kingdom, with the title of Ethnarch, promising, moreover, to make him king if he proved worthy of the title. The rest was divided into two tetrarchies, which Augustus presented to two other sons of Herod, Philip and Antipas.

In view of the parable of the Talents, it seems clear that the additional matter in Lk. is really addition. But it is not like Lk. to conflate in this way, and it may be suggested that the addition of this secondary matter had already taken place before Lk. got hold of the parable.

The effect of the additions is to make the parable, as it now stands, an allegory of the Christian life in the interim between the Ascension and the Parousia. The nobleman (Christ) has departed to a distant country (heaven) to receive a kingdom. Meanwhile he entrusts the management of his affairs to his servants (Christians). His citizens (the Jews) hate him and will not have him as king (the Jews deny the Messiahship of Jesus). But in the end he receives the kingdom and returns (the Parousia) to reward his servants according to their behaviour during his absence, and to execute judgement on the rebels (at the Last Judgement). With the removal of the additional matter, we get a parable whose main purport is the same as that of the Talents.

11. The opening verse effects a connexion between the immediately preceding story of Zacchæus of Jericho—' near Jerusalem '—and the parable. The motive ascribed to Jesus—' because they supposed that the Kingdom of God was immediately to appear '—is apt to the expanded parable, but not to the original form. This fact tends to confirm the suggestion that Lk. knew the parable only in its present state, in which the coming of the Kingdom in power during the lifetime of Jesus is clearly excluded; and we may suppose that v. 11 is Lk.'s own introduction to vv. 12–27, which were already before him as a single whole in his source.

' Near to Jerusalem ': the distance from Jericho to Jerusalem is about 17 miles. See on Lk. 10³⁰, above, p. 262.

The expectation of the immediate appearance of the Kingdom is a feature also in the Marcan narrative. It underlies the request of the sons of Zebedee (Mk. 10³⁵⁻⁴⁵) and the cries of the crowd at the entry into Jerusalem (Mk. 11⁹ᶠ·). It also appears in Acts 1⁶ᶠ·. This last passage indicates clearly enough what kind of kingdom was expected to appear. It is the restoration of sovereignty to the Jewish people, or, as the crowds express it in Mk. 11¹⁰, the revival of the vanished glories of the ' Kingdom of our father David.' As against all this the expanded parable asserts (1) that the coming of the Kingdom will not take place forthwith, and (2) that when it does come it will not be a political upheaval culminating in the establishment of an Israelite Empire, but a Final Judgement in which loyalty and obedience will be rewarded and disloyalty and disobedience punished.

12, 14. The nobleman, who may originally have been Herod Archelaus, is here Jesus Himself. The departure to a distant country corresponds to the pilgrimage of Archelaus to Rome. Here it stands for the death and exaltation to heaven of Jesus. Note that in 22²² Lk. uses the same Greek verb (poreuomai—' go away ') of the death of Jesus. In Palestinian Aramaic the verb ăzal is used in the same way both of going away and of ' departing this life.' Archelaus received his kingdom from Augustus: Jesus receives His from God. (Cf. Phil. 2⁸ᶠᶠ·.) ' And to return ': the Kingship is conferred in heaven, but it is to be exercised on earth. The refusal of ' his citizens ' applies to Archelaus, whose application to Augustus was actively opposed by his own subjects. It also fits the case of Jesus, who is rejected by the ' sons of the Kingdom.' Cf. John 1¹¹, ' He came unto his own, and they that were his own received him not.' The sending of the embassy is exactly paralleled in the case of Archelaus. Fifty deputies from Palestine appeared before Augustus to oppose his claims. How this feature in the story is applied to Christ is not clear. We may perhaps compare John 19¹⁵ᶠ·: ' Pilate saith unto them, Shall I crucify your King? The chief priests answered, We have no king but Cæsar,' and the words attributed by Josephus to the Jewish embassy before Augustus (*War*, ii. 90 f.): ' They implored the Romans to take pity on the relics of Judæa and not to fling what remained of it to those who were savagely rending it in pieces, but to unite their country to Syria and to entrust the administration to governors from among themselves (i.e. Roman governors). The Jews would then show that, calumniated though they now were as factious and always at war, they knew how to obey equitable rulers ' (Thackeray's translation).

13. Archelaus before setting out for Rome had entrusted his castles and treasuries to his officers (Josephus, *War*, ii. 18 f.). With *v.* 13 the original parable may be taken to begin. The differences between Mt. and Lk. are striking. There are ten servants as against three in Mt. The distribution is equal: each servant receives one mina. In Mt. the amounts vary with the ability of the servants. The amounts entrusted are very much smaller in Lk. than in Mt.: about £4 each as against at least £1,000, £400, and £200.

Although ten servants are appointed (cf. the ten virgins, Mt. 25¹), only three of them appear in the account of the audit. On this point Lk. is in agreement with Mt. The number ten is significant in that it is ten and not twelve. The servants are not the Apostles. Further, G. Kittel has shown that in Palestine the number five was used constantly as a round number, much as we say, in a vague way, ' half a dozen.' Ten is then probably an extension of this usage, similar to our ' about a dozen.' Cf. the ten virgins (Mt. 25¹), five pairs of oxen (Lk. 14¹⁹), ten sayings by which the world was created, ten generations from Adam to Noah and from Noah to Abraham, ten temptations of Abraham, ten miracles performed for Israel in Egypt and ten at the Red Sea, ten plagues of Egypt, ten temptations with which the Israelites tempted God, ten wonders wrought by God in the Temple, ten things created on the eve of the Sabbath (*Aboth* 5¹⁻⁶, Danby, pp. 455 f.). The number ten will then suggest that the story is of Palestinian tradition. Further, since only three of the servants appear at the reckoning, it may be supposed that the number ten belongs to the additional matter. In this connexion it may also be noted that the Greek verb here translated ' trade ' also means ' to engage in State business.' These things may be indications that in *v.* 13 features from the original parable and the additional story have been conflated.

' Ten pounds,' lit. ten minas: the mina = 100 denars = rather less than £4. The whole sum entrusted to the servants is less than £40, not a large sum for a ' nobleman.' In Mt. the master hands over all his property. The smaller sums in Lk. suggest that the trust is really a test to discover which of the servants are fit for larger responsibilities.

15-19. We are not told how the servants employ themselves in the absence of the master (contrast Mt. 25¹⁶⁻¹⁸). The narrative goes straight to the return of the nobleman, now confirmed in his rank as king. His first act is to examine the conduct of his servants during his absence. The results of the investigation are different from those in Mt. There the two good servants both succeed in doubling their capital. Here the first servant shows a profit of 1,000 per cent., the second 500 per cent. Only in the case of the third servant is there agreement between Mt. and Lk. The industrious servants are rewarded by being promoted to positions of high rank and responsibility in the kingdom of their master. Here we have doubtless to recognise the influence of the additional matter on the original parable, especially when we observe that in *v.* 24 the mina of the third servant is ordered to be handed over to the first. It is not clear that a matter of £4 can mean very much to one who is now governor of ten cities.

20 f. In the verses describing the reckoning between the third servant and the master Mt. and Lk. come nearest to one another. Yet there are considerable differences in detail. In Mt. the servant buries his talent: here he wraps the money in a ' napkin.' The Greek word here translated ' napkin ' is a loan-word from the Latin *sudarium*. It is also naturalised in Aramaic. Besides this passage it occurs three times in the New Testament (John 11[44], 20[7]; Acts 19[12]). The word seems to signify some kind of scarf or neckcloth used in Palestine to protect the head and back of the neck from the heat of the sun. Billerbeck gives one Rabbinical passage from which it would appear that it was a custom to wrap up money in the folds of this garment.

' Thou art an austere man.' For ' austere ' Mt. has ' hard.' ' Austere ' is not a good rendering of the Greek word, which ' obviously means " strict, exacting," a man who expects to get blood out of a stone ' (Moulton and Milligan, *Vocab.*, p. 93*a*).

' Thou takest up where thou layedst not down.' This clause is peculiar to Lk. Perhaps a current proverbial expression for a grasping person (Plummer). Parallels are quoted from Philo and Josephus.

22 f. The unprofitable servant is judged on the terms laid down by himself. On his own showing he is not only lazy, but a fool. If he did not wish to have his own industry exploited, he could have taken steps to show a profit without any expenditure of energy on his part.

24. Those ' that stood by,' i.e. the attendants on the king, his courtiers or his bodyguard. The introductory words are absent from Mt. The description of the first servant as having ten minas is not quite correct. He has eleven: one, his original capital, and ten, his profit.

25. This verse has no parallel in Mt. It is apparently meant to prepare the way for *v.* 26 by expressing surprise at the command of *v.* 24. The first servant has ten—really eleven—minas. What does he want with more? (The fact that the first servant is now governor of ten cities seems to be forgotten.) This objection is then answered in *v.* 26. But there are certain difficulties and awkwardnesses. Who are the speakers in *v.* 25? The most natural interpretation would be that they are the attendants who have just been mentioned. Plummer argued that *v.* 25 represented the remonstrance of the audience. They have been following the story and they object to the turn given to it by Jesus at this point. Why should the servant who already has most receive more? They think that He is spoiling the parable. In that case *v.* 26 is the reply of Jesus to His critics, and not the reply of the master in the parable. This explanation is certainly attractive. But there is a further difficulty. The whole of *v.* 25 is omitted by early and important authorities for the text of Lk.; and it is accordingly rejected as an interpolation by several scholars. In any case *v.* 26 begins very abruptly after *v.* 25, without any indication of who is speaking. We should have expected

some such words as ' But he said ' or ' But he replied.' On the other hand, the omission of *v.* 25 by some of our authorities may merely be assimilation to the text of Mt.

26. The parable of the Pounds ends with *v.* 26, which has a close parallel in Mt. 25²⁹, see above, p. 248.

27. This verse belongs to the additional matter, which has been incorporated with the original parable. Unlike the other additional verses, this one has no parallel in the story of Archelaus as told by Josephus, though from what Josephus elsewhere tells us about that gentleman we might safely infer that he was quite capable of the kind of action described in this verse. For this savage treatment of defeated enemies there are numerous parallels in ancient history. The verse is doubtless meant to describe the fate that awaits the Jews who reject the Messiah. We may be horrified by the fierceness of the conclusion; but beneath the grim imagery is an equally grim fact, the fact that the coming of Jesus to the world puts every man to the test, compels every man to a decision. And that decision is no light matter. It is a matter of life and death. That is true of Christ which Wisdom says of herself (Prov. 8³⁵ᶠ·):

> Whoso findeth me findeth life,
> And shall obtain favour of the Lord.
> But he that sinneth against me wrongeth his own soul:
> All they that hate me love death.

29. *THE OFFENCE OF ENTHUSIASM* (196–197)

LK. 19³⁷⁻⁴⁰

19 37 And as he was now drawing nigh, *even* at the descent of the mount of Olives, the whole multitude of the disciples began to rejoice and praise God with a loud voice for all the [1] mighty works 38 which they had seen: saying, Blessed *is* the King that cometh in the name of the Lord: peace in heaven, and glory in the 39 highest. And some of the Pharisees from the multitude said unto him, [2] Master, 40 rebuke thy disciples. And he answered and said, I tell you that, if these shall hold their peace, the stones will cry out.

[1] Gr. *powers.*
[2] Or, *Teacher.*

Lk. 19³⁷⁻⁴⁴ would seem to be the L account of the entry into Jerusalem. Apart from a few verbal coincidences in *v.* 39, and those chiefly in a quotation from the Old Testament, the passage is quite independent of Mk. To *vv.* 39–40 we have a parallel in Mt. 21¹⁴⁻¹⁶ (M); see the discussion of this passage, above, pp. 220 f. Lk. differs from Mt. in several important particulars: time and place of the occurrence, the parties involved, and the wording of the reply of Jesus to the protesters. These differences are so great that some scholars maintain that we have in Mt. and Lk. the reports of two separate incidents. But it is more probable that we have two accounts of the same incident, which have come down through separate lines of tradition; and, on the whole, the Lucan version is freer from difficulties and probably more reliable.

37. The Lucan account locates the incident at the descent of the Mt. of Olives, i.e. at the point where the descent begins, the summit of the Hill. From

this point the pilgrims look across the Kidron valley to Jerusalem. 'Those who know the emotional potentialities of Orientals, who were here roused to great enthusiasm at beholding the longed-for holy city and by the consciousness of leading into it a Son of David who was, at the lowest estimation, a Man of God above all others, will not be astonished at the phrases used on that occasion. They suggested wishes the immediate fulfilment of which probably no one expected ' (Dalman, *Sacred Sites and Ways*, p. 257).

The multitude of disciples praise God for the mighty works which they had seen. It is objected that there have been no miracles in the story, except that of the healing of Bartimæus, since Jesus healed the ten lepers on the frontiers of Samaria and Galilee (Lk. 17^{11}). This is so; but if we may lay some weight on the word ' disciples,' we may suppose that among them there would be those who knew of or had seen other mighty works at an earlier date. There is some manu-script authority for the alternative reading, ' for all the things which they saw happening '; and perhaps this ought to be preferred, not because it is easier than the other, but because it is more likely that the colourless ' happenings ' would be altered to the more impressive ' mighty works ' than that ' mighty works ' should be reduced to ' happenings.'

38. With this verse cf. Mk. 11$^{9f.}$. The Lucan form makes the cries very definitely the plaudits offered to the Messianic King. In so doing it probably makes explicit what is implicit in the Marcan version.

39. Certain Pharisees are shocked by the display. They appeal to Jesus to stop it. It is implied that only He can quiet the enthusiasm of His followers. The complaint is made in respectful terms. They address Jesus as ' Master,' or ' Teacher,' i.e. ' Rabbi '; and that is very respectful address among Pharisees. Why do the Pharisees object to the demonstration? The answer to this question is that in accordance with their principles they could do no other. If Jesus was hailed as king, that seemed to involve at once political rebellion against Rome; and it was a settled principle with the Pharisees that the only thing that justified revolt was interference with their religion. Their attitude to the Empire in practice was the same as that of St. Paul: ' Let every soul be in subjection to the higher powers: for there is no power but of God; and the powers that be are ordained of God. Therefore he that resisteth the power, withstandeth the ordin-ance of God: and they that withstand shall receive to themselves judgement. For rulers are not a terror to the good work but to the evil.' (Rom. 13$^{1-3}$, see the whole passage.) This may be paralleled by a saying of R. Hanina, the prefect of the priests, a younger contemporary of Paul: ' Pray for the peace of the ruling power, since but for fear of it men would have swallowed up each other alive ' (*Aboth* 3^2, Danby, p. 450). On the whole question of the attitude of the Pharisees to the Roman Empire, see Moore, *Judaism*, ii. 112–118. It may, therefore, be supposed that the Pharisees, who objected on this occasion, believed that such outcry as the followers of Jesus were making was just asking for trouble.

40. In reply Jesus makes use of a proverbial expression. In Habakkuk (2^{11}) in reference to secret crimes it is said: ' The stone shall cry out of the wall, and the beam out of the timber shall answer it.' This is taken up in the Talmud (*Hagigah* 16a): ' Perhaps thou wilt say, Who witnesseth against me? The stones of a man's

house and the timbers of his house, these witness against him, as it is said, " For the stone shall cry, etc." (Hab. 2[11]).' In these cases the inanimate objects cry out against the evil deeds of men. As Jesus employs the saying they proclaim the mighty acts of God. If men were dumb, the very stones would cry out that the Kingdom of God had drawn nigh. By the ' stones ' we should probably understand the stones of the Holy City—particularly the Temple—to be meant. That inanimate objects might respond in some way to the great events of history was a common enough belief of the time. Thus at the death of Jesus the veil of the Temple is rent in twain. And Josephus (*War*, vi. 288–300) describes strange happenings in the Temple in the period preceding its destruction. The eastern gate of the inner court opened of its own accord at midnight. Voices were heard at night in the Temple; and so on. The very building seemed to be sensitive in some way to the coming disasters and to give warning of them. So also it might be argued the stones of Jerusalem would be in some way sensitive to the presence of that which is greater than the Temple and cry out, if men were insensitive and dumb.

30. *A LAMENTATION OVER JERUSALEM* (197)

LK. 19[41-44]

19 41 And when he drew nigh, he saw the 42 city and wept over it, saying, [1] If thou hadst known in this day, even thou, the things which belong unto peace! but now 43 they are hid from thine eyes.. For the days shall come upon thee, when thine enemies shall cast up a [2] bank about thee, and compass thee round, and keep 44 thee in on every side, and shall dash thee to the ground, and thy children within thee; and they shall not leave in thee one stone upon another; because thou knewest not the time of thy visitation.

[1] Or, *O that thou hadst known.*
[2] Gr. *palisade.*

The lamentation over Jerusalem comes with tremendous dramatic effect in the midst of the jubilant enthusiasm of the crowd. The passage is a prophetic oracle, which reminds us of similar prophecies in the Old Testament. We may compare the utterance of Jeremiah (Jer. 8[18ff.]):

> Incurable is my sorrow;
> My heart within me is sick.
> Hark! my people's cry of distress
>   From the land far and near:
> ' Is Yahwe not in Zion?
>   Is no King there?
> Past is the harvest, ended the fruit-time,
>   And we are not saved.'
> For the ruin of my people I mourn,
>   Horror hath seized me.
> Is there no balsam in Gilead?
>   No healer there?
> Why then does no healing come
>   For my people's hurt?

O that my head were waters,
  And my eyes a fountain of tears!
That day and night I might weep
  O'er my people's slain.
      (Skinner's translation, *Prophecy and Religion*, pp. 125 f.)

In both cases we have the prophetic sense of the inevitability of the coming catastrophe and the genuine sorrow of a tender and sympathetic nature over the sufferings that must come upon the prophet's own people. There is a similar saying of Jesus, also peculiar to Lk., in Lk. 23$^{28-31}$, below, pp. 342 f. Burney (*The Poetry of our Lord*, p. 69) found evidence of poetic form in *vv.* 43–44 of the present passage; and it is possible that the whole saying, *vv.* 42–44, was originally in poetic form. To describe these verses as a Christian composition after the event is the kind of extravagance that brings sober criticism into disrepute.

42. The force of the unfinished sentence is ' If only thou hadst known, even now, at the eleventh hour, the things that would really make for thy peace, then the future would hold something better for thee than it now does. But thou art blind, and so walking blindly to disaster.' In ' the things which belong unto peace ' there is probably a play on the Aramaic word for ' peace ' (*shĕlāmā*) and the popular etymology of the name Jerusalem as meaning ' vision of peace ' or the like. (Cf. Heb. 7$^{1f.}$.)

43 f. A prophetic description of the horrors of siege and destruction of the city. Compare Is. 29$^{1-4}$. The nature of the disasters sketched in these verses may perhaps give a clue to the nature of the failure which is their cause. Verses 43 f. depict the fate of a Jerusalem that has rebelled against Rome, a Jerusalem, that is, in which political ambition has been mistaken for zeal in the cause of God.

The first part of this passage describes the blockade of the city. The operation called ' casting up a bank ' actually took place at the siege of Jerusalem by Titus. From the account of Josephus (*War*, v. 262 ff.) it appears that the ' bank ' was an earthwork surmounted by a wooden palisade. At a later stage in the siege the place of this ' bank ' was taken by a stone wall encircling the city (*War*, v. 491 ff.), and preventing both the escape of the inhabitants and the bringing to them of supplies. When this encirclement is complete and effective the position of the defenders is truly desperate. However strong their own fortifications, however determined their resistance to the assaults of the besiegers, they must eventually succumb to famine. Then they fall an easy prey to the enemy. In *v.* 44 the sack and destruction of the city are described. The Greek verb translated ' dash thee to the ground ' means also—and originally—to ' lay level with the ground ' or ' raze to the ground.' It is probable that this original meaning is the meaning here. The city will be laid level with the ground. But this rendering obviously will not fit the following words, ' and thy children within thee.' This objection is easily met by taking the words in question as a circumstantial clause, a common Semitic idiom, describing the circumstances in which the main action takes place. What the verse says is that the city will be sacked and destroyed with its inhabitants in it. That is, they will not be allowed to evacuate the doomed city before destruction is let loose in it. The ' children ' of the city are, by another common

idiom, its inhabitants, regardless of their age.   It may be objected to this interpretation that if we translate our Greek verb by ' lay thee even with the ground,'
it is tautologous to have to add, ' And shall not leave in thee one stone upon
another.'   But, as Burney pointed out (*loc. cit.*), if these verses are poetry, it is a
case not of tautology but of parallelism; and the supposed tautology is really
another argument for the correctness of the rendering.

' They shall not leave in thee one stone upon another ': compare Mk. 13[2] and
parallels.   In Hag. 2[15] ' to lay one stone upon another ' is used for ' to build '
The opposite phrase must signify ' to demolish.'

' Because thou knewest not the time of thy visitation.'   The prime cause of the
material disaster is a moral failure; and the moral failure is essentially a failure of
religious insight.   Inability to recognise the ' time of visitation ' is the same thing
as inability to ' interpret this time ' (Lk. 12[56] Q, above, p. 121).   That is, it is the
failure to recognise that ' the Kingdom of God is come nigh unto you ' (Lk.
10[9, 11] Q, above, p. 75; Lk. 11[20]||Mt. 12[28] Q, above, p. 86).   The ministry of
Jesus and His disciples is the ' visitation.'

The Greek word translated ' visitation ' (*episkopē*) is commonly used to render
the Hebrew word *pĕḳuddāh*.   This Hebrew word stands chiefly for the visitation
of God, in which He will execute judgement upon all that is opposed to His will.
Thus in Jer. 6[15], after the arraignment of priests and prophets who deal falsely, it is
said: ' Therefore they shall fall among them that fall: at the time that I visit them
they shall be cast down, saith the Lord.'   And in Jer. 10[15], of idols, ' They are
vanity, a work of delusion: in the time of their visitation they shall perish.   Cf.
Is. 10[3], 24[22], 29[6].   The force of the word comes out clearly in *Ecclus.* 18[20]:

> Before judgement examine thyself,
> And in the hour of visitation thou shalt find forgiveness.

But the visitation, which is judgement on all unrighteousness, can also be an
occasion of grace and mercy to those who are repentant, as this last quotation
shows.   This sense for ' visitation ' appears also in *Wisdom* 3[7f.]:

> 3[1] But the souls of the righteous are in the hand of God,
> And there shall no torment touch them. . . .
> [7] And in the day of their visitation they shall shine forth,
> And as sparks in the stubble shall run to and fro.
> [8] They shall judge nations and have dominion over peoples;
> And their Lord shall be king for ever.

Similarly in *Wisdom* 4[15]:

> Grace and mercy are with His (God's) chosen
> And His visitation with His holy ones.

It is this latter sense that is the sense in our passage.   The ' visitation ' has
taken place in the mission of Jesus.   The Kingdom of God has drawn near to

Israel in grace and mercy. But Israel is rejecting this proffered mercy and going determinedly on the road that leads to disaster. This is the tragedy over which Jesus weeps.

31. *A DETACHED SAYING* (204)

LK. 20[18]

20 18 Every one that falleth on that stone shall be broken to pieces; but on whomsoever it shall fall, it will scatter him as dust.

This verse is given by the great majority of MSS. in Mt. 21[44] as well as here. But it is most probably to be regarded as an interpolation in Mt., an example of the tendency to assimilate the text of the gospels. See above, p. 224. In Lk. it appears in the parable of the Wicked Husbandmen, a passage in which Lk. is following Mk. But the verse does not appear in Mk.; and the simplest explanation is that it is an insertion by Lk. It is not, however, likely that it is an attempt by Lk. to comment on what has gone before. More probably it is detached saying, which he incorporated here in what seemed to him a suitable place.

In Mk., which is here Lk.'s source, the parable is given in 12[1-9], ending with the declaration that the owner of the vineyard will come and destroy the wicked husbandmen, and give the vineyard to others. Then Mk. adds the quotation from Ps. 118[22f.]:

> The stone which the builders rejected,
> The same was made the head of the corner:
> This was from the Lord
> And it is marvellous in our eyes (Mk. 12[10f.]).

Lk. gives the parable substantially as in Mk. (Lk. 20[9-16]). Then he adds the Psalm quotation; but gives only the first verse of it, 'The stone . . . corner' (20[17]). Then follows the verse 20[18], which has no parallel in Mk. Finally, Lk. rejoins Mk. in describing the effect of all this teaching on the leaders of the Jewish community (Lk. 20[19]‖Mk. 12[12]).

The verse added by Lk. is plainly an insertion. But it can hardly be comment on the stone which is made head of the corner. That stone is securely fixed in the building and is not likely to fall or be fallen upon. The stone in *v.* 18 is much more like the stone in Dan. 2[34, 45], or that other in Is. 8[14f.]. A still closer parallel to our verse is in the Aramaic saying, possibly a proverb, preserved in the Midrash on Esther 3[6]: ' If the stone falls on the (earthenware) pot, woe to the pot! If the pot falls on the stone, woe to the pot! In either case woe to the pot! '

Whether *v.* 18 is a genuine saying of Jesus, and if it is genuine, what He meant by it—these are questions which cannot now be answered with certainty, since we do not know the original context of the saying. All that can be said with confidence is that it probably came to Lk. as a genuine saying, and that he inserted it here in what seemed to him the most suitable context in his Gospel.

32. *THE APOCALYPTIC DISCOURSE*

This is the second apocalyptic discourse in Lk. The first, derived from Q, has already been discussed. See notes on Lk. 17²²⁻³⁷, above, pp. 141–147. This second speech (Lk. 21⁵⁻³⁶) runs parallel to Mk. 13 and Mt. 24, and the relation of Lk. to Mk. presents one of the most complicated and difficult problems in the criticism of the Gospels. The essential issue is whether Lk.'s discourse is a free rewriting of Mk. or an independent account into which Lk. has incorporated a few passages from Mk. In other words, is the substance of Lk. 21⁵⁻³⁶ derived from Mk. or L? It may be that a final solution of the problem is not possible; but at least something can be done towards making the issues clear. We begin with an analysis of Lk. 21⁵⁻³⁶, dividing the material into three classes:

(*a*) Probably derived from Mk.: *vv.* 5–11*a*, 16–17, 21*a*, 23*a*, 26*b*, 27, 29–33
(*b*) Certainly not derived from Mk.: 11*b*, 18, 25*b*, 26*a*, 28, 34–36.
(*c*) Doubtful cases: *vv.* 12–15, 19, 20, 21*b*, 22, 23*b*, 24, 25*a*.

On the basis of this classification two theories are possible:

(1) The groundwork of the discourse is (*a*) + (*c*); and (*a*) + (*c*) is the Marcan apocalypse revised and in part rewritten by Lk. To this groundwork the Evangelist has added the fragments collected under the heading (*b*).

(2) The groundwork is (*b*) + (*c*), which may be regarded as the L version of the apocalyptic discourse. Into this discourse Lk has incorporated selected passages from Mk., namely those grouped under (*a*).

Both theories have the support of distinguished scholars. Those who uphold theory (1) have to maintain that Mk. has been severely edited and rewritten by Lk. in view of what happened at the siege and destruction of Jerusalem. Against this is the fact that in our study of the documents up to this point we have found little reason to think that Lk. was addicted to the practice of rewriting his sources. Further, there are observations in detail which tell against the hypothesis of Lucan rewriting.

(i) MK. 13¹¹	LK. 21¹⁴⁻¹⁵
And when they lead you to judgement, and deliver you up, be not anxious beforehand what ye shall speak: but whatsoever shall be given you in that hour, that speak ye: for it is not ye that speak, but the Holy Ghost.	Settle it therefore in your hearts, not to meditate beforehand how to answer: for I will give you a mouth and wisdom, which all your adversaries shall not be able to withstand or to gainsay.

Cf. Lk. 12¹¹⁻¹² Q (above, p. 110).

The word 'spirit' is a favourite word with Lk. It is not likely that he would have altered it in this case, especially in view of Lk. 12¹¹f., where he gives the Q form of the saying without alteration.

(ii) The result of the supposed editorial rewriting of Mk. in Lk. 21²⁰⁻²⁴ is to produce something that looks extremely like poetry (see notes on this passage). It is not usual for editorial revision to turn prose into verse.

The analysis of Lk. 21⁵⁻³⁶ must begin with *vv.* 5-7, a passage commonly regarded as derived from Mk. 13¹⁻⁴.

MK. 13[1-4]

LK. 21[5-7] (Huck § 213)

13 1 And as he went forth out of the temple, one of his disciples saith unto him, [1] Master, behold, what manner of stones 2 and what manner of buildings! And Jesus said unto him, Seest thou these great buildings? there shall not be left here one stone upon another, which shall not be thrown down. 3 And as he sat on the mount of Olives over against the temple, Peter and James and John and Andrew asked him privately, 4 Tell us, when shall these things be? and what *shall be* the sign when these things are all about to be accomplished?

[1] Or, *Teacher.*

21 5 And as some spake of the temple, how it was adorned with goodly stones and 6 offerings, he said, As for these things which ye behold, the days will come, in which there shall not be left here one stone upon another, that shall not be thrown down. 7 And they asked him, saying, [1] Master, when therefore shall these things be? and what *shall be* the sign when these things are about to come to pass?

[1] Or, *Teacher.*

There is no doubt that Mk. and Lk. here give the same thing—a prophecy by Jesus of the destruction of the Temple. But there is one striking difference. In Mk. the prophecy is given in reply to a remark by one of His disciples; and the whole of the following apocalyptic address is a private communication to Peter, James, John, and Andrew. In Lk. the persons who comment on the grandeur of the Temple, and so lead up to the prediction of its fall, are undefined. But in *v.* 7 it becomes clear that they are not disciples. For they go on to address Jesus as 'Teacher' (*didaskale*). Now in Lk. the disciples never address Jesus as *didaskale*. They use the more honorific terms 'Lord' (*kurie*) or 'Master' (*epistata*). It is only those outside the circle of the disciples who call Jesus 'Teacher.' (See Burkitt, *Gospel History and its Transmission*, p. 114.) We must therefore suppose that Lk. has altered a conversation between Jesus and His disciples into a public declaration.

.But this supposition is more than difficult in view of what immediately follows in Lk. For, whatever we may think of *vv.* 8–11, there cannot be the least doubt that *vv.* 12–19 must have been spoken to disciples and not to the Jewish populace; and this fact must have been as obvious to Lk. as it is to us. On the hypothesis of Lucan editing of Mk. we are thus led to the position that Lk. made a quite pointless alteration in Mk., and one which immediately involved him in making a public speech out of what was obviously a private conversation. This seems unlikely.

Further, the Lucan passages *vv.* 8–11, 12–19 do not seem to deal with the question put in *v.* 7. For the question put concerns the destruction of the Temple and that only. The answer is not given till *vv.* 20–24. It is thus natural to suppose that originally Lk. 21[5-7] was followed immediately by 21[20-24], and that the intervening passages have been inserted, probably at an earlier stage in the tradition than the composition of Lk. Now it is highly probable that Mk. 13 contains an early apocalyptic passage, which has been incorporated bodily into the chapter. It is to be noted that the question in Mk. 13[4] appears to be a double one: when will the destruction of Jerusalem take place, and what will be the sign of the end of the existing world order? The Marcan form of the question prepares the way for a passage dealing with both topics in a way that the Lucan question does not. The passage thus introduced is the so-called 'Little Apocalypse,' which may be supposed to be represented by Mk. 13$^{5-31}$. (See my *Teaching of Jesus*, p. 262, n. 1.) If, as is likely, this little apocalypse was in circulation before Mk. was written, it may well have influenced the formation of the L material into its present shape. This would be the more likely if, as Hölscher maintains, the substance of Mk.'s little apocalypse (Mk. 13$^{7f.,\ 12,\ 14-20,}$ $^{24-27}$) was composed in A.D. 40 under stress of the threatened profanation of the Temple by Caligula.

I am therefore inclined to think that Lk. 21$^{5-36}$ is, in the main, a solid block of L material whose arrangement—and, to a considerable extent, its wording also—has been determined by the pre-Marcan 'little apocalypse.' No explanation is free from difficulties; and I am not confident that this hypothesis is a final solution of the problem. I only put it forward in default of a better.

MK. 13$^{5-8}$	LK. 21$^{8-11}$ (Huck § 214)
13 5 And Jesus began to say unto them, Take heed that no man lead you astray. 6 Many shall come in my name, saying, I am *he*; and shall lead many astray. 7 And when ye shall hear of wars and rumours of wars, be not troubled: *these things* must needs come to pass; but the 8 end is not yet. For nation shall rise against nation, and kingdom against kingdom: there shall be earthquakes in divers places; there shall be famines: these things are the beginning of travail.	21 8 And he said, Take heed that ye be not led astray: for many shall come in my name, saying, I am *he*; and, The time is 9 at hand: go ye not after them. And when ye shall hear of wars and tumults, be not terrified: for these things must needs come to pass first; but the end is not immediately. 10 Then said he unto them, Nation shall rise against nation, and kingdom 11 against kingdom: and there shall be great earthquakes, and in divers places famines and pestilences; and there shall be terrors and great signs from heaven.

These verses, both in Mk. and Lk., I take to be derived from the 'little apocalypse.' It is difficult to suppose that the events enumerated here are indications that Jerusalem is about to be destroyed. They seem rather to be the premonitory signs of the final consummation. Mk. and Lk. run parallel for the most part. The order of events is: (*a*) appearance of false messiahs; (*b*) wars and disturbances—the break-up of the social order; (*c*) earthquakes, famines, pestilences, etc.—the break-up of the order of nature. According to Mk. these are the birth-pangs of the new age. But these premonitory signs do not lead up to anything immediately; for the next section in both Mk. and Lk. describes persecution of the disciples, and after that comes the account of the distresses in Judæa (Mk.) or the siege and destruction of Jerusalem (Lk.). Now in *v.* 11 Lk. has a sentence which has no parallel in Mk.: ' and there shall be terrors and great signs from heaven.' The natural continuation of this is in Lk. 21^{25}: ' And there shall be signs in sun and moon and stars.' We should therefore naturally suppose that Lk. 21$^{8-11,\ 25-28}$ belong together, and that the whole passage has to do with the final consummation.

8. The Marcan parallel announces the rise of bogus messiahs. Lk. has a small addition. Besides the pretenders who say ' I am he,' there are others who announce that the time is at hand. These may be the false prophets who appear along with false Christs in Mk. 13^{22}. The injunction ' Go ye not after them ' has no parallel in Mk. Cf. Lk. 17^{23} (Q), above, p. 142.

9–11. According to Mk. there will be wars and rumours of wars, or perhaps wars (at home) and news of wars (in other lands). Lk. has wars and tumults. The Greek word translated 'tumults' stands for confusion and anarchy. It is war accompanied by a general break-down of civil order. This might well cause terror; but those who are forewarned will recognise in this upheaval a necessary stage in the passing of the old order. At the same time they will not be unduly elated, for there are still worse convulsions to come. There will be a period of world-wide war in which all nations and kingdoms will be involved. (The Lucan 'Then said he unto them,' which starts a new paragraph, is not an improvement on Mk. It is probably secondary.) This universal strife will be accompanied by convulsions of the natural order, earthquakes, famines, pestilences. The pestilences have no parallel in Mk., and look like an addition in Greek for the sake of the word-play on famines (*līmoi*) and pestilences (*loimoi*). The collocation of the two words is as old as Hesiod. The end of v. 11 is peculiar to Lk. Where Mk. has 'these things are the beginnings of travail,' Lk. has instead ' and there shall be terrors and great signs from heaven.' The 'terrors' are, most likely, strange and unnatural events on earth, prodigies. Such things are described by Josephus (*War*, vi. 288 ff.). He relates, for example, how a cow brought for sacrifice gave birth to a lamb in the middle of the Temple court. By great signs from heaven are meant such things as Josephus mentions (§ 289): ' A star resembling a sword stood over the city, and a comet which continued for a year.' Cf. 4 *Ezra* 5⁴ (Box's translation).

> Then shall the sun suddenly shine forth by night
> and the moon by day:
> And blood shall trickle forth from wood,
> and the stone utter its voice:
> The peoples shall be in commotion,
> the outgoings (?) (of the stars) shall change.

The description in Lk. 21⁸⁻¹¹ seems to be leading up to the final consummation; but the story is interrupted by the introduction of a fresh topic.

(a) THE PERSECUTION OF THE DISCIPLES (215)

MK. 13⁹⁻¹³	LK. 21¹²⁻¹⁹
13 9 But take ye heed to yourselves: for they shall deliver you up to councils; and in synagogues shall ye be beaten; and before governors and kings shall ye stand for 10 my sake, for a testimony unto them. And the gospel must first be preached unto all 11 the nations. And when they lead you *to judgement*, and deliver you up, be not anxious beforehand what ye shall speak: but whatsoever shall be given you in that hour, that speak ye: for it is not ye that 12 speak, but the Holy Ghost. And brother shall deliver up brother to death, and the father his child; and children shall rise up against parents, and ¹ cause them to	21 12 But before all these things, they shall lay their hands on you, and shall persecute you, delivering you up to the synagogues and prisons, ¹ bringing you before kings and governors for my name's 13 sake. It shall turn unto you for a testi-14 mony. Settle it therefore in your hearts, not to meditate beforehand how to 15 answer: for I will give you a mouth and wisdom, which all your adversaries shall not be able to withstand or to gainsay. 16 But ye shall be delivered up even by parents, and brethren, and kinsfolk, and friends; and *some* of you ² shall they cause 17 to be put to death. And ye shall be

13 be put to death. And ye shall be hated of all men for my name's sake: but he that endureth to the end, the same shall be saved.[1]

¹ Or, *put them to death.*

hated of all men for my name's sake. 18 And not a hair of your head shall perish. 19 In your patience ye shall win your[3] souls.

¹ Gr. you *being brought.*
² Or, *shall they put to death.*
³ Or, *lives.*

The break in the narration is marked in Mk. by the words, ' But take ye heed to yourselves,' and in Lk., still more emphatically, by the words, ' But before all these things.' In what follows Mk. and Lk. are parallel in substance but very far apart in wording. And the differences in language are not easily explained as revision on the part of Lk. Reasons have already been given above (p. 323) for thinking that *v.* 14 of Lk. is not a rewriting of *v.* 11 of Mk. It is unlikely also that *v.* 12 of Lk. is a rewriting by Lk. of *v.* 9 of Mk. The Greek construction in Lk. *v.* 12 is, as Creed justly notes, very awkward: so awkward that it is scarcely credible that Lk., the stylist of the Synoptics, could have produced it out of the clear statement of Mk.

The impression left by a comparison of Mk. and Lk. in this passage is that of two independent versions of the same original; and the question arises whether the original may not be the ' Little Apocalypse ' in its pre-Marcan state, and perhaps in Aramaic.

12. Lk. has additional matter at the beginning of the verse: ' they shall lay their hands on you and persecute you ': and he omits the notice of the flogging, which appears in the corresponding verse in Mk. There does not seem to be any reason why he should have suppressed the beatings, since he himself records one in Acts 5⁴⁰.

13–15. The disciples will have to face the hostility both of Jew and Gentile authorities. They will be accused of heresy in the synagogues and of sedition before the civil rulers. (Cf. 2 Cor. 11²⁴ᶠ·, where Paul states that he had received five synagogue floggings and three Roman scourgings with rods.) That which is heresy to orthodox Judaism and sedition to kings and governors is the preaching of Jesus as Lord and Christ (Acts 2³⁶). But all this persecution will provide opportunity for the disciples to bear witness to the truth: and that not merely what they think true, but a truth divinely revealed, whose very wording will be inspired. It is for this reason that the disciples are told not to prepare beforehand the speeches to be made. The speeches will be provided from above; and they will be unanswerable and irresistible. In *vv.* 14 f. the wording of Lk. is almost totally different from Mk.

The Greek word translated ' meditate ' in *v.* 14 occurs only here in the Greek Bible. It occurs in Aristophanes of ' preparing ' a speech, and again of ' rehearsing ' a dance for a subsequent performance. The word evidently signifies more than ' meditation ' about the matter of what is to be said. It is careful preparation of the actual words and even gestures.

16, 17. The hostility aroused against the disciples will cut across all human ties. This is the other side of the saying that he who does not ' hate ' his relatives cannot be a disciple. It is more than likely that they will hate him. And in the case of some of the disciples this hatred will not be satisfied by anything short of their death. This hatred aroused by the name of Jesus will be universal.

In *vv.* 16 f. Lk. comes very close to Mk. in wording; indeed *v.* 17 agrees word for word with *v.* 13 of Mk. This close agreement in the middle of so much diversity is very striking; and even those who maintain the general independence of Lk. in this chapter admit that *vv.* 16 f. are probably inserted from Mk. There are two facts which seem to support this view. First, the whole passage, up to this point, suggests a successful defence by the disciples. They will be able to speak in such a way that their opponents will be overwhelmed. And this confident tone is as clearly present in *vv.* 18 f. Verses 16 f. seem somewhat foreign to this context. Secondly, the prophecy at the end of *v.* 16: ' Some of you they shall put to death ' is not consistent with *v.* 18: ' Not a hair of your head shall perish.' It is therefore quite possible that *vv.* 16 f. have been inserted from Mk. into their present context by Lk. It may be added that the omission of *vv.* 16 f. leaves a perfectly good connexion between *vv.* 15 and 18.

18. This verse has no parallel in Mk. There is, however, a similar saying in Q (Lk. 12⁷‖Mt. 10³⁰), see above, pp. 107 f. For the form of the expression cf. 1 Sam. 14⁴⁵; Acts 27³⁴. In both cases it is a way of saying emphatically that this human life will be preserved, not that the ultimate salvation of the persons concerned will be secured. The factual parallel in the Old Testament is such a story as that of the three faithful Jews in Dan. 3. They stand fast in their faith and suffer persecution for it; but even the fiery furnace cannot touch them. ' The fire had no power upon their bodies, nor was the hair of their head singed ' (Dan. 3²⁷).

19. This verse says the same as *v.* 13ᵇ in Mk., but in almost entirely different words. Endurance during the period of trial will have its reward. The time of persecution will pass and the day of vindication will come. And the faithful disciples will be there to see it.

If we omit *vv.* 16 f., the general impression made by the whole passage is that the disciples will meet with violent opposition and persecution; but that, by supernatural aid, they will be able to triumph over it and endure to the day of their vindication. They will be God's representatives against an evil world; and God will look after His own, and bring them through to ultimate victory. The text of the whole discourse might well be the saying (Lk. 12³²): ' Fear not, little flock; for it is your Father's good pleasure to give you the kingdom.'

After these digressions we return to the question raised at the beginning of the discourse in *v.* 7: when shall these things be and what will be the sign that they are coming to pass?—' these things ' being the destruction of the Temple.

(b) THE FALL OF JERUSALEM (216)

MK. 13¹⁴⁻²⁰	LK. 21²⁰⁻²⁴
13 14 But when ye see the abomination of desolation standing where he ought not (let him that readeth understand), then let them that are in Judæa flee unto the 15 mountains: and let him that is on the housetop not go down, nor enter in, to 16 take anything out of his house: and let him that is in the field not return back to 17 take his cloke. But woe unto them that are with child and to them that give suck	21 20 But when ye see Jerusalem compassed with armies, then know that her desola- 21 tion is at hand. Then let them that are in Judæa flee unto the mountains; and let them that are in the midst of her depart out; and let not them that are in 22 the country enter therein. For these are days of vengeance, that all things which 23 are written may be fulfilled. Woe unto them that are with child and to them

18 in those days! And pray ye that it be 19 not in the winter. For those days shall be tribulation, such as there hath not been the like from the beginning of the creation which God created until now, 20 and never shall be. And except the Lord had shortened the days, no flesh would have been saved: but for the elect's sake, whom he chose, he shortened the days.

that give suck in those days! for there shall be great distress upon the [1] land, 24 and wrath unto this people. And they shall fall by the edge of the sword, and shall be led captive into all the nations: and Jerusalem shall be trodden down of the Gentiles, until the times of the Gentiles be fulfilled.

[1] Or, earth.

This passage in Lk. raises the question of dependence on Mk. in an acute form. At two points there is word for word agreement with Mk.; in the first clause of *v.* 21, and in the first half of *v.* 23. The rest of the passage has hardly a word in common with Mk. A theory of dependence of Lk. on Mk. requires us to suppose that, with the exception of these two short pieces, Lk. has completely rewritten Mk., taking pains not to use any words already used by Mk. Not only so: we have also to suppose that Lk. has succeeded in throwing his rewriting into poetic form:

> But when ye see Jerusalem compassed with armies
> Then know that her desolation is at hand.
> Let them that are in the midst of her depart out;
> And let not them that are in the country enter therein.
> For these are days of vengeance,
> That all things that are written may be fulfilled.
> For there shall be great distress upon the land,
> And wrath unto this people.
> And they shall fall by the edge of the sword,
> And shall be led captive into all the nations:
> And Jerusalem shall be trodden down of the Gentiles,
> Until the times of the Gentiles be fulfilled.

It is much simpler to suppose that this poetical passage is independent of Mk., and that Lk. has incorporated into it the two short pieces from Mk. The general similarity in thought between Mk. and Lk. could then be explained by the hypothesis that we have in the two gospels two independent versions of the pre-Marcan 'Little Apocalypse.'

20. The difference between Mk. and Lk. is usually explained as due to the fact that Lk. has rewritten Mk. in the light of what happened in A.D. 70. But this is going a little too fast. It is more likely that Mk. 13[14] has been rewritten in the light of what happened in A.D. 40, when the Emperor Caligula decided to have his statue set up in the Temple at Jerusalem. Josephus tells us (*War*, ii. 184 f., Thackeray's translation):

'The insolence with which the emperor Gaius (Caligula) defied fortune surpassed all bounds: he wished to be considered a god and to be hailed as such, he cut off the flower of the nobility of his country, and his impiety extended even to Judæa. In fact, he sent Petronius with an army to Jerusalem to instal in the sanctuary statues of himself; in the event of the Jews refusing to admit them, his orders were to put the recalcitrants to death and to reduce the whole nation to slavery.'

The remarkable phrase used in Mk.—' the abomination of desolation '—is used in the book of Daniel (9^{27}, 11^{31}, 12^{11}) and in 1 *Macc.* (1^{54}, cf. 1^{59}, 6^{7}) to describe a similar profanation of the Temple, the erection therein of an altar (and statue?) to Olympian Zeus in 168 B.C. Any Jewish Christian reading Mk. 13^{14} would naturally interpret the ' abomination of desolation ' as meaning a new profanation of the Temple similar to that which had already occurred. And so, in fact, did early Christian interpreters. Thus Hippolytus says: ' The " abomination of desolation " is the image of the emperor which he set up in Jerusalem.' He also denies that the words refer to the events of A.D. 70. ' This was not fulfilled in the siege of Vespasian. There was in this nothing new; wars and sieges have often taken place.'

Further, the verses which follow in Mk. are very appropriate advice in case of an approaching siege. The best thing the inhabitants can do is to get out of the city before the investment is complete. But it is not specially relevant to a profanation of the Temple. The inhabitants do not mend matters nor improve their own case by fleeing from the city.

In view of these considerations I am inclined to think that the original form of this oracle predicted the destruction of Jerusalem in general terms, and that in Mk. and Lk. we have two independent versions of the prediction. The Marcan version has been modified to meet the crisis of A.D. 40, while the Lucan has escaped this editing, and gives the prediction in something like its original form. If Lk. 21^{20} is the answer to the question in Lk. 21^{7}, it may be thought to be a somewhat unsatisfactory reply. ' When will these things be and what will be the sign that they are about to happen? ' ' When you see Jerusalem surrounded by armies.' This is not very informative; but compare Lk. 17^{37} (Q): ' And they answering say unto him, Where, Lord? And he said unto them, Where the body is, thither will the eagles also be gathered together.'

21. The first clause of the verse is copied word for word from Mk. That it is an addition is clear from what follows. For ' Let them that are in the midst of her depart out; and let not them that are in the country enter therein ' must refer to Jerusalem. The reference to the inhabitants of Judæa thus breaks the sense. Except for this insertion the verse is entirely independent of Mk. It is to be noted that the two clauses peculiar to Lk. are in close parallelism. The motive for flight is obvious. It is the only way to escape the horrors of a siege.

22. And there need be no expectation that there will be a Divine intervention in favour of the city. The besieging armies are the instruments of Divine judgement. Jerusalem is doomed, and her fate is the fulfilment of what is written in Scriptures, of all the prophecies uttered against the rebellious nation. Cf. Hos. 9^{7}; Jer. 5^{29}, $26^{4ff.}$; Dan. 9^{26}.

23. The first half of this verse again agrees word for word with Mk. 13^{17}; and again it can be removed without detriment to the sense. It is to be noted that Lk. does not insert Mk. 13^{18}: ' And pray ye that it be not in the winter.' The omission may be an indication that Lk. is writing after A.D. 70; for, as a matter of fact, the siege took place in the summer (April to September). The latter half of *v.* 23 is again independent of Mk. in wording, though there are similarities of thought in Mk. 13^{19}. The Lucan form is in parallelism. The R.V. text

' land ' is to be preferred to the mg. ' earth.' The reference is to the land and people of Israel, not to the earth and its inhabitants in general. The ' wrath ' does not occur elsewhere in the teaching of Jesus in the Synoptics. It does, however, appear in the preaching of John the Baptist (Lk. 3⁷||Mt. 3⁷ Q).

24. The ' wrath ' will work itself out in three particulars: the slaughter of part of the population, the carrying away captive of the rest, and the total destruction of the city. For ' treading down ' as a figure for desolation and destruction, see Dan. 8¹³; 1 Macc. 9⁴⁵, ⁵¹, 4⁶⁰; Rev. 11⁸. The period set for this desolation of Jerusalem is ' until the times of the Gentiles be fulfilled.' The meaning of the phrase is uncertain. It may mean merely the period during which the Gentiles are to be permitted to do their worst to Jerusalem (cf. Dan. 8¹³f., 12⁵⁻¹³), or it may be the period allowed to the Gentiles in which they may themselves turn to God (cf. Mk. 13¹⁰; Rom. 11²⁵). It is, in any case, a limited period; and it is not to be followed by the restoration of Jerusalem. As the text of Lk. now stands the expiration of this period is to be followed by—

(c) THE GREAT CONSUMMATION (219

MK. 13²⁴⁻²⁷	LK. 21²⁵⁻²⁸
13 24 But in those days, after that tribulation, the sun shall be darkened, and the 25 moon shall not give her light, and the stars shall be falling from heaven, and the powers that are in the heavens shall 26 be shaken. And then shall they see the Son of man coming in clouds with great 27 power and glory. And then shall he send forth the angels, and shall gather together his elect from the four winds, from the uttermost part of the earth to the uttermost part of heaven.	21 25 And there shall be signs in sun and moon and stars; and upon the earth distress of nations, in perplexity for the roaring of 26 the sea and the billows; men ¹ fainting for fear, and for expectation of the things which are coming on ² the world: for the powers of the heavens shall be shaken. 27 And then shall they see the Son of man coming in a cloud with power and great 28 glory. But when these things begin to come to pass, look up, and lift up your heads; because your redemption draweth nigh.

¹ Or, expiring.
² Gr. the inhabited earth.

There is nothing here in Lk. corresponding to Mk. 13²¹⁻²³. Lk. 21²⁵ seems to resume the discourse that was broken off at v. 11, which ends with the words, ' and there shall be terrors and great signs from heaven.' This might well be continued by ' in sun and moon and stars.' The words at the beginning of v. 25, ' And there shall be signs,' might then be regarded as a necessary addition in order to make a fresh start. The alternative is to regard Lk. 21²⁵ᵃ as an abbreviated version of Mk. 13²⁴, ²⁵ᵃ. There is nothing in Mk. corresponding to vv. 25ᵇ and 26ᵃ of Lk.: ' and upon the earth . . . things which are coming on the world.' Lk. 21²⁶ᵇ ²⁷, ' for the powers . . . great glory ' is an insertion from Mk., which makes nonsense of the following verse (28) in Lk. For v. 28 is a message of hope. It says in effect: The darkest hour is the hour before the dawn. When the whole world seems to be falling to pieces about you, then you may be sure that a new world is coming to birth. But all this is out of place after v. 27. For with the coming of the Son of Man the redemption has come. Faith has given place to sight. The removal of the insertion from Mk. removes this difficulty, and gives a perfect sense. The whole world will be in a state of chaos, nations in perplexity, men terrified to death of what may happen next. When you see these things you—and you alone—will be able to hold up your heads, because you know that they are the signs that your vindication is at hand.

25 f. These verses describe tremendous convulsions in the order of nature. The whole natural world is affected. The signs in the heavenly bodies are mentioned by Lk. In Mk. they are more fully described. On the other hand, Lk. describes the upheaval of the sea which is not mentioned at all in Mk. For the imagery, cf. Ps. 65⁷ᶠ·. Behind the description may lie the Semitic horror of the sea, which comes to its sharpest expression in Rev. 21¹: ' And I saw a new heaven and a new earth: for the first heaven and the first earth are passed away; and the sea is no more.' But it is more probable that ' the roaring of the sea and the billows ' describes the world reverting to primeval chaos. See the full collection of material in Dodd's *The Bible and the Greeks*, pp. 105 ff. The Greek word translated ' perplexity ' has a fairly wide range of meanings. ' Perplexity ' is hardly strong enough to describe the condition which is portrayed in this verse. It is more than mere puzzlement: it is the bewildered despair of men who find that there is nothing reliable or safe in the world any more. In *v.* 26 ' fainting ' is preferable to ' expiring.' The men are terrified to death but not dying of terror. They have no hope but only the expectation that there is still worse to come upon the world. It is the whole inhabited earth that is involved in these calamities, not as in *v.* 23 the land of Israel.

28. In the midst of this helpless terror the disciples will be calm and hopeful. They know the meaning of these disasters. It is the old order breaking up to make way for the new: and the more rapid the process of dissolution, the nearer the coming of their deliverance.

26ᵇ, 27. The additional matter inserted from Mk. is a description, in terms borrowed from the book of Daniel 7¹³, of the final consummation, which is also the ' redemption ' of the faithful. The interpretation given in the book of Daniel itself (7²⁷) is that the ' Son of Man ' is ' the people of the saints of the Most High.' If we apply the Danielic interpretation to the Danielic figure in its new context, the coming of the ' Son of Man ' with power and great glory ought to mean the triumphant vindication of the faithful disciples. But this is not the usual interpretation. The coming of the Son of Man is held to be the return of the risen and glorified Christ at the Second Advent. That is, it is not itself the vindication of the saints but a preliminary thereto. For a discussion of the whole question of the interpretation of the phrase ' Son of Man ' in the Synoptic Gospels see my *Teaching of Jesus*, pp. 211–234.

(d) THE PARABLE OF THE FIG TREE (220)

MK. 13²⁸⁻²⁹	LK. 21²⁹⁻³¹
13 28 Now from the fig tree learn her parable: when her branch is now become tender, and putteth forth its leaves, ye 29 know that the summer is nigh; even so ye also, when ye see these things coming to pass, know ye that ¹ he is nigh, *even* at the doors.	21 29 And he spake to them a parable: Behold the fig tree, and all the trees: 30 when they now shoot forth, ye see it and know of your own selves that the summer 31 is now nigh. Even so ye also, when ye see these things coming to pass, know ye that the kingdom of God is nigh.

¹ Or, *it*.

This parable is given in much the same terms by Mk. and Lk.   It is reasonable to suppose that it has been taken over by Lk. from Mk.   The parable is an excellent illustration of the piece of teaching just given concerning the end.   As the shooting forth of the leaves is an indication of the approach of summer, so the terrible experiences, through which the disciples must pass, will be an indication that the consummated Kingdom of God is at hand.

29 f. Lk. has provided the parable with an introduction.   He has also added the words, ' and all the trees.'   The fig is not the only tree to advertise the approach of summer, even if it does so before most.   The description of the bursting of the tree into leaf is fuller in Mk.   Lk. adds the words ' of yourselves ' to ' know.'   Those who see these things happening do not need anyone to tell them that summer is now near.   Their own common sense will tell them.   Cf. Lk. 12^{57}, Q.

31. The application.   When you see ' these things,' i.e. the calamities described in the previous section—not, however, the events described in vv. 26^{b}, 27—know that the Kingdom of God (Lk. supplies the subject of the clause) is near.   Lk. omits the words of Mk, ' at the doors.'

In all that has hitherto been said the original question has not been precisely answered.   The discourse gives indications from which the disciples may infer that the destruction of Jerusalem is about to take place or that the coming of the Kingdom in power is at hand; but the questioners have not been given any date at which they may be on the look-out for premonitory signs.   The next section in Lk. contains two sayings taken from Mk.; and in one of these a terminus is fixed.   The other saying is, in its present context, apparently meant as a strong confirmation of the preceding prophecies.   Mk. has a third saying, which is not reproduced by Lk. (Mk. 13^{32}).

(e) Two Sayings (221)

MK. 13^{30-31}	LK. 21^{32-33}
13 30 Verily I say unto you, This generation shall not pass away, until all these things 31 be accomplished. Heaven and earth shall pass away: but my words shall not pass away.	21 32 Verily I say unto you, This generation shall not pass away, till all things be 33 accomplished. Heaven and earth shall pass away: but my words shall not pass away.

32. This saying gives a limit within which the prophecies are to be fulfilled. It is in substantial agreement with another saying (Mk. 9^{1}) : ' Verily I say unto you, There be some here of them that stand by, which shall in no wise taste of death, till they see the kingdom of God come with power.'   It is quite clear that in the primitive Church this was really believed, and that the accomplishment of all things and the coming of the Kingdom with power were related to the return of the risen and glorified Christ.   The position of Mk. 13^{30} and Lk. 21^{32} makes it clear that the reference of ' all these things ' or ' all things ' is to the whole of the preceding complex of predictions, including persecution of the disciples, the destruction of Jerusalem, and the consummation of the Kingdom.   But is this the original sense of the saying?   When it is considered that the eschatological discourse is a complex of predictions, one might be tempted to argue that perhaps the saying did not originally apply to all, and to suggest that its reference is, let us say, only to the fall of Jerusalem.   So far as Lk. is concerned, this view would be

supported by the fact that the original question in *v.* 7 appears to apply only to the fall of Jerusalem. On the other hand the saying in Mk. 9¹ refers definitely to the coming of the Kingdom with power. It is, therefore, more likely that in the present case the saying (Mk. 13³⁰‖Lk. 21³²) is meant to cover all the predictions in the discourse, and in particular that of the final redemption.

This view creates difficulty; for the final consummation did not come in the lifetime of the first generation of disciples. But it is to be noted that, in the nature of the case, it was a difficulty that would be felt more acutely in the first century, when the expectation was a living thing, than in the twentieth. And the Church of the first century survived the disappointment of its expectations. The case of St. Paul is instructive. From first to last he believes in the Parousia as the consummation of all things and the fulfilment of the Christian hope. But as time goes on he seems to become less interested in the question whether he will live to see it. And the reason is plain. In the earliest formulation of his eschatology the essence of the final consummation is given not in the creation of a new and better world but in the fact that we shall be for ever with the Lord (1 Thess. 4¹⁷). That and nothing else is the complete fulfilment of the Christian hope. But by the time that Philippians comes to be written Paul is convinced that this same thing can be achieved in another way, by death—' to depart and be with Christ; for it is very far better ' (Phil. 1²³). Once this point is reached it ceases to be a matter of great personal moment whether or not the Parousia will occur in the lifetime of Paul or any other believer. If it does so, well and good: if not, that which is its crowning mercy will be found on the other side of the gate of death.

33. Here we have another saying whose connexion with the foregoing would seem to depend on verbal links more than on any continuity of thought. The saying is to be compared with that on the Law (Mt. 5¹⁸; Lk. 16¹⁷, above, pp. 135, 154). And it is probable that we should take this saying as having to do with the validity of the teaching of Jesus as a whole rather than with the smaller matter of the correctness of the predictions in the apocalyptic discourse. Doubtless the intention of the compiler was to give this word as a guarantee of the prophecies contained in the discourse; but we may doubt whether that is the original sense of the verse. More probably Jesus is claiming for His teaching as a whole an eternal validity. It is valid not only in the present age, but also for the age to come. The greatness of the claim is realised when we consider that it was a debated question among the Rabbis whether the sacred Law would continue in full force in the world to come. The saying in effect puts the teaching of Jesus on a higher level of authority than the Law. We have here the most striking example of that ' authority ' in Jesus which so amazed His hearers, an authority which rests on His assurance of knowing the Father and the Father's will.

(f) CLOSING ADMONITIONS (223)

LK. 21³⁴⁻³⁶

21 34 But take heed to yourselves, lest haply your hearts be overcharged with surfeiting, and drunkenness, and cares of this life, and that day come on you suddenly 35 as a snare: for *so* shall it come upon all them that dwell on the face of all the 36 earth. But watch ye at every season, making supplication, that ye may prevail to escape all these things that shall come to pass, and to stand before the Son of man.

This final exhortation is independent of Mk.; and, if we are right in regarding *vv.* 29–33 as inserted from Mk., it ought to be the continuation of *v.* 28. It may be noted that in that case we have a better connexion than the existing one. For *v.* 28 is a message of hope and encouragement. In the midst of disaster and despair the disciples are to be full of confidence. But this confidence is not to degenerate into carelessness. The elect dare not presume on their election. The worldly may say: ' Let us eat and drink, for tomorrow we die '; but woe to the disciples if they say: ' Let us eat and drink, for tomorrow comes the redemption.'

There are important parallels to this passage in 1 Thess. 5^{1-11} (cf. Rom. 13^{13}):

5 1 But concerning the times and the seasons, brethren, ye have no need that 2 aught be written unto you. For yourselves know perfectly that the day of the Lord so 3 cometh as a thief in the night. When they are saying, Peace and safety, then sudden destruction cometh upon them, as travail upon a woman with child; and 4 they shall in no wise escape. But ye, brethren, are not in darkness, that that 5 day should overtake you [1] as a thief: for ye are all sons of light, and sons of the day: 6 we are not of the night, nor of darkness; so then let us not sleep, as do the rest, but let 7 us watch and be sober. For they that sleep sleep in the night; and they that be 8 drunken are drunken in the night. But let us, since we are of the day, be sober, putting on the breastplate of faith and love; and for a helmet, the hope of salva-9 tion. For God appointed us not unto wrath, but unto the obtaining of salvation 10 through our Lord Jesus Christ, who died for us, that, whether we [2] wake or sleep, we should live together with him. Where-11 fore [3] exhort one another, and build each other up, even as also ye do.

[1] Some ancient authorities read *as thieves.*
[2] Or, *watch.*
[3] Or, *comfort.*

vv. 1–3. Cf. Lk. $21^{34f.}$.

v. 7. Cf. Lk. 21^{34a}.

vv. 8–10. Cf. Lk. 21^{36}.

34. ' Lest haply your hearts be overcharged.' ' Heart ' is here, as in the Old Testament, the inner man, the soul as the seat of thought, will, and feeling. The soul becomes dull, heavy, insensitive, stupefied by self-indulgence and worldly cares. The Greek word rendered ' surfeiting ' (*kraipalē*) is most commonly used to describe the condition following on a drunken bout. It is ' the morning after the night before.' ' Drunkenness ' (*methē*) is ' the night before.' ' The cares of this life ' are, one may suppose, the ancient equivalent of ' a hard day at the office.' And between the ' hard day at the office ' and the ' lively evening at the night-club ' and the ' morning after,' the soul has little chance to be anything but dull and stupid, insensitive to great issues, and unprepared for crisis.

35. The crisis, when it comes, will be sudden, as sudden as the springing of a trap. For the figure cf. Is. $24^{17f.}$. And it will come upon all the inhabitants of the world without exception. The mere name of ' disciple ' will confer no immunity. Cf. Rom. 14^{10}; 2 Cor. 5^{10}.

36. It is therefore all the more necessary that disciples should be spiritually alert, fortifying themselves against the coming trials by prayer, or, in Paul's words, ' putting on the breastplate of faith and love; and for a helmet, the hope of salvation.' Only so will they be able to pass safely through the impending troubles and to face the judgement with confidence. To stand before the Son of Man could be the same as to ' stand in the judgement ' (Ps. 1⁵), i.e. to secure a favourable verdict in the judgement. Otherwise it may mean to stand in the presence of the Son of Man as acknowledged disciples and servants. Cf. Lk. 12⁸.

In considering the discourse as a whole there are two important facts to be borne in mind. The first is that it presents a very different picture of the last days from that given in Q. In the Q statement (Lk. 17²²⁻³⁰, above, pp. 141–144), the end of the existing order is a bolt from the blue. Here it is the climax of a long series of catastrophes. The second fact is that the discourse here is obviously a complex of predictions dealing with the fate of Jerusalem, the persecution of the disciples, and the termination of the whole existing world-order. These different prophecies have been woven into a single discourse. The natural conclusion to be drawn from these facts is that the simple straightforward account in Q is the original, and that the discourse in Mk. 13 and Lk. 21 is a later compilation.

What is the purpose of this compilation? One motive appears fairly clearly, and more clearly in Mk. than in Lk. ' The end is not yet ' (13⁷); ' these things are the *beginning* of travail ' (13⁸); the Gospel must first be preached unto all the nations ' (13¹⁰); ' he that endureth *to the end*, the same shall be saved ' (13¹³); ' in those days, *after* that tribulation ' (13²⁴). There are also traces in Lk.: ' the end is not immediately ' (21⁹); ' Jerusalem shall be trodden down . . . until the times of the Gentiles be fulfilled ' (21²⁴). The effect of all these little touches is to postpone the final consummation; and this is the effect also of the arrangement of the discourse. Persecutions, wars, the destruction of Jerusalem, natural catastrophes —these things are not so much stages leading up to the consummation as means of postponing it. The burden of the discourse is: ' Be ready for the coming of the Kingdom at any time; but don't expect it yet.'

Now we know that in the middle of the first century, some twenty years after the Crucifixion, the Church of Thessalonica was troubled about this question of the Parousia; and in 2 Thess. 2¹⁻¹² an explanation is offered why the great redemption must be delayed. The ' man of sin ' must first be revealed, who will sit ' in the temple of God, setting himself forth as God ' (cf. Mk. 13¹⁴). The genuine Parousia must be preceded by a Satanic Parousia, the last great fling of the forces of evil. The end is not yet.

It is likely that if such questions arose in the young community at Thessalonica, they could still more easily arise in the Palestinian churches, where Christians had been awaiting the Parousia for a matter of twenty years. It is indeed possible that such questions arose in Palestine before they arose in the Gentile churches. If they were not raised within the community, they would almost certainly be raised by opponents outside. It is at least possible that what we call the ' Little Apocalypse ' was put together in order to furnish an answer to these questionings. It is not necessary to suppose that the whole thing is an invention. Jesus undoubtedly taught that His disciples must undergo persecution. It is reasonably certain that

He prophesied the downfall of Jerusalem and the Temple.   And He had something to say about the final consummation.   That which is new in the apocalyptic
discourse is not the matter, but the way in which it is put together, the way in
which persecutions of disciples and tribulations in Judæa are used to push the final
consummation into the future.

The discussion of Mk. 13[14-20] and Lk. 21[20-24] suggests that the form of the ' Little
Apocalypse' incorporated in Mk. was already in existence about A.D. 40; and the
general conclusion to which our consideration of the whole discourse leads is that
Mk. and Lk. offer two versions of this Palestinian document.

33. RANK IN THE KINGDOM OF GOD (237b)

LK. 22[24-30]

22 24   And there arose also a contention
among them, which of them is accounted
25 to be [1] greatest.   And he said unto them,
The kings of the Gentiles have lordship
over them; and they that have authority
26 over them are called Benefactors.   But
ye *shall* not *be* so: but he that is the
greater among you, let him become as
the younger; and he that is chief, as he
27 that doth serve.   For whether is greater,
he that [2] sitteth at meat, or he that
serveth? is not he that [2] sitteth at meat?
but I am in the midst of you as he that

28 serveth.   But ye are they which have
continued with me in my temptations;
29 and [3] I appoint unto you a kingdom, even
30 as my Father appointed unto me, that
ye may eat and drink at my table in my
kingdom; and ye shall sit on thrones
judging the twelve tribes of Israel.

[1] Gr. *greater.*
[2] Gr. *reclineth.*
[3] Or, *I appoint unto you, even as my
Father appointed unto me a kingdom, that ye
may eat and drink, &c.*

This passage falls into three parts: (*a*) the dispute among the disciples and the
comment of Jesus (*vv.* 24–26); (*b*) a further saying in parabolic form (*v.* 27); (*c*) a
promise to the Twelve (*vv.* 28–30).   To (*a*) there is a parallel in Mk. 10[42-45].   The
sons of Zebedee have tried to steal a march on the other disciples and secure for
themselves the chief places in the coming Kingdom.   The ten are naturally
incensed at this; and Jesus rebukes the whole company in terms very similar to
vv. 25–26 in this passage.   Lk. in chapter 18, where he is following Mk., omits the
story about the sons of Zebedee, although he has the incidents immediately preceding and following it.   This suggests that Lk. already has another version of the
dispute and the saying of Jesus, probably already connected with the Passion
story, and that he drops the Marcan account in favour of his own, namely that
which he gives here.   Another incident which has some points of contact with the
present passage is Mk. 9[33-37].   To this there is a parallel in Lk. 9[46-48].   There is no
parallel to (*b*) in the Synoptics; but it is significant that in John 13 we have the
story of how Jesus, at the Last Supper, did in fact perform the duty of a servant for
the disciples, and afterwards set His act before them as an example to be followed.
The third part (*c*) has a parallel in Mt. 19[28] (M), see above, pp. 216 f.   We
should probably regard the whole passage *vv.* 24–30 as independent of Mk. and
derived from Lk.'s special source.

The Lucan account differs from the Marcan in making the narrative framework of the sayings quite vague and general.   In Mk. the dispute takes place on
the road to Jerusalem; and the story as told by Mk. could hardly be fitted into the
account of the Last Supper without violence.   The Lucan framework is so vague

that the incident could be fitted in almost anywhere. Why does Lk. put it here? It may be conjectured that the determining factor is the material which follows in (b) and (c). If there was a tradition that Jesus had washed the disciples' feet at the Last Supper, v. 28 would be very appropriate in its present context. And, in any case, the promise of places at the Messianic feast would be appropriate in an account of the Last Supper. In that case we might suppose that (b) and (c) are the elements which have determined the placing of the passage; and from that it would follow that the whole passage was already in existence as a single unit when Lk. put it into its present place in his narrative. There is great dramatic, even tragic, power in the way in which the dispute is brought into the story of the last meal of Jesus and the disciples. Nevertheless the narrative setting of Mk. seems inherently more probable.

24. For the introductory formula compare Lk. 9^{46}: 'And there arose a reasoning among them, which of them should be greatest.' This is Lk.'s abbreviated version of Mk. 9^{33f}. It is possible that Lk.'s introduction here is a similar condensation of a narrative that was originally more detailed. It was natural that there should be such disputes. The Gospel narratives make it plain that the Twelve were not equal in seniority. Some would seem to be of longer standing as disciples than others. And there certainly was an inner circle within the group: Peter, James, and John, with Andrew sometimes added. The fact that Jesus took this inner circle most fully into His confidence may well have given them a sense of their own importance. And it is to be noted that it is two of the inner circle who try to overreach the rest in the story told in Mk. 10.

25 f. The reply of Jesus is similar to that in Mk. 10^{42ff}. The way of the world is contrasted with the way of the Kingdom. In the heathen world ambition and pushfulness are natural, and he who is most domineering is treated with the greatest respect. Kings make themselves masters over their people, not merely in the sense that they keep order and good government in their territories, but also and primarily in the sense that the king is master and the rest of the people his servants. Those who show the greatest ability in bending the wills of others to serve their own purposes assume or are given the title of ' Benefactors.' The Greek word Euergetēs (Benefactor) was, in fact, assumed as a title by Ptolemy III of Egypt and by the Seleucid king Antiochus VII (Bevan, The House of Seleucus, ii. 237). The title was also occasionally conferred by the cities of the ancient world on outstanding men. The practice is somewhat similar to that of conferring the honorary freedom of a city in modern times. It was not necessary that the recipient of the honour should actually have bestowed any benefit on the city in question, so long as he was sufficiently great and powerful.

The way of the disciples is to be the opposite of this. The Lucan form of the saying is slightly different from that in Mk. Mk.'s version suggests that the way to greatness is the way of service. The only kind of primacy attainable in the community is that which comes of being most perfectly the servant of others. Lk.'s statement, on the other hand, seems to imply that there are in fact differences of rank. Some are by nature leaders. But they are not to give themselves airs on that account. Leadership is a form of service, not a kind of privilege.

27. A parable peculiar to Lk. It makes the same contrast as the previous

verses. The way of the world is to make a sharp distinction between those who wait and those who are waited upon. The logical issue of this is that he is greatest who sits while all others stand in attendance upon him. That is the way of the world. What is the way of the community of the followers of Jesus? There is no question who is chief in this circle. Jesus Himself is the acknowledged leader and head of the group. But He does not sit to be waited on. He stands among His followers as the servant of all. It is evident that such a saying as this would come with tremendous force, if it followed upon the washing of the disciples' feet (John 13).

28 ff. The concluding saying of the group has a parallel in Mt. 19²⁸ (above, pp. 216 f.). The similarities in wording between the two forms are confined to the concluding words about sitting on thrones judging the twelve tribes of Israel. It should be noted that Mt. has ' twelve thrones,' whereas Lk. has only ' thrones.' Now there is a serious difficulty about the saying as Lk. gives it here. Is it conceivable that Jesus should have made this prediction concerning the Twelve at this point, when He knew that one of them was on the point of betraying Him? The fact that Lk. has omitted the ' twelve ' before ' thrones ' may be an indication that he was not unaware of this difficulty.

The saying is clearly a farewell-saying. It looks back over the period of the Ministry to praise the faithfulness of the Twelve in difficult and trying times. They have shared the trials of Jesus: they shall also share His future glory. Cf. Rom. 8¹⁷. The construction of *v.* 29 is awkward, but the general sense seems to be clear enough, God has assigned the Kingdom to Jesus; and He assigns a share in it to His disciples. This share includes both the joy of the Kingdom—represented under the figure of feasting at the table of the Messiah—and its privileges and responsibilities—represented by the sitting upon thrones and judging. For a parallel to this way of thinking of the duties and rewards of the disciples compare Lk.'s parable of the Pounds (19¹¹⁻²⁷, above, pp. 312–317).

34. *EXHORTATION TO PETER* (237c)

LK. 22³¹⁻³³

22 31 Simon, Simon, behold, Satan ¹ asked to have you, that he might sift you as 32 wheat: but I made supplication for thee, that thy faith fail not: and do thou, when once thou hast turned again, 33 stablish thy brethren. And he said unto him, Lord, with thee I am ready to go 34 both to prison and to death. And he said, I tell thee, Peter, the cock shall not crow this day, until thou shalt thrice deny that thou knowest me.

¹ Or, *obtained you by asking.*

The complete paragraph in Lk., as it now stands, contains *vv.* 31–34. But *v.* 34 is most probably derived from Mk., as are also the verses (59ᵇ–62) which relate the fulfilment of the prediction in *v.* 34. It does not seem that the special source of Lk. contained the story of Peter's denial. Note that in *v.* 31 the apostle is addressed as Simon, whereas in *v.* 34 he is called Peter. Verses 31–33 are a self-contained unit, without *v.* 34; and the purport of them is not to foretell Peter's denial. What they do say is that all the disciples will be tried to the uttermost and that all will fail under the test; but that Peter will be the first to recover and restore the brethren. That Peter was, in fact, the first to see the

Risen Lord is attested by Paul (1 Cor. 15[5]), and it is implied in Lk. 24[34]: ' The Lord is risen indeed, and hath appeared to Simon '—note that the name Simon is used here. Elsewhere the first appearance is to Mary Magdalene either alone or along with another of the women followers of Jesus. The question then arises whether the saying is not a prophecy after the event, which puts into the mouth of Jesus a prediction of what actually happened. Against such a view is the fact that Peter was not the only person to have the vision of the Risen Christ. The Easter faith did not depend on his testimony alone. Further, it seems only natural that Jesus, knowing that His life on earth was nearing its end, and that the end would be of a kind that would be likely to shatter the faith of His followers, should look among them for one who would be most likely to come through the experience. And of the Twelve Peter seemed to Him the one of whom most could be expected.

31. The double vocative is characteristic of Lk. (Cf. 10[41], 13[34]—proper names—and 8[24]; also 7[14], where the true text repeats the vocative, ' Young man.') It is also a common Jewish usage. The picture of Satan desiring to put the disciples to the test is reminiscent of the Prologue to the book of Job. The similarity was noticed by Tertullian (De Fuga ii.). Both in Job and in Zech. 3[1ff.] Satan appears as the accuser, whose purpose it is to bring the faults and weaknesses of men to the light of day. From that it is an easy step to incite men to sin in order to have something to expose. This idea appears in the Testaments of the XII Patriarchs (Benjamin 3[3]): ' Fear ye the Lord, and love your neighbour; and even though the spirits of Beliar (= Satan) claim you to afflict you with every evil, yet shall they not have dominion over you.' The Greek word here rendered ' claim ' is the same as that translated ' asked to have ' in R.V. The sifting doubtless stands for severe trial of the faith and constancy of the disciples. And it is to be applied to all of them. Primarily it is the shameful death of their Master that is thought of; but the danger of hatred and persecution directed against the followers is also a reality.

32. While Satan appears as the adversary, Jesus is the advocate for His followers. His intercession is above all for Peter. If Peter can come through this trial, he will be the rallying-point for the rest. It is not expected that Peter will come through unscathed. His faith will be shaken; but Jesus believes that, in answer to His prayers, it will not completely fail. Peter may desert with the rest; but he will return; and when he returns he will strengthen the others.

33. But Peter has more confidence in himself. There is no need to speak of his turning back, for he will not fall away. He is ready to face imprisonment or death with Jesus.

If the analysis of the passage given above is correct, there is no reply to this bold claim. And there need not be. The event will show whether or not it can be fulfilled.

35. THEN AND NOW (237d)

LK. 22[35-38]

22 35 And he said unto them, When I sent you forth without purse, and wallet, and shoes, lacked ye anything? And they

36 said, Nothing. And he said unto them, But now, he that hath a purse, let him take it, and likewise a wallet: [1] and he

that hath none, let him sell his cloke, and
37 buy a sword. For I say unto you, that
this which is written must be fulfilled in
me, And he was reckoned with transgressors: for that which concerneth me hath
38 [2] fulfilment. And they said, Lord, be-

hold, here are two swords. And he said
unto them, It is enough.

[1] Or, *and he that hath no sword, let him
sell his cloke, and buy one.*
[2] Gr. *end.*

This short dialogue throws a brilliant light on the tragedy of the Ministry. It goes with the Q lamentation over Jerusalem (Lk. 13[34 f.]||Mt. 23[37-39]); and, like that elegy, it is full of bitter disillusionment. The grim irony of *v.* 36 is the utterance of a broken heart. Jesus looks back on the earlier days when He sent the disciples out on the Mission journey. Then they could rely on the goodwill of the people. Now they cannot. Then they could expect hospitality and a friendly welcome. Now nobody will give them a crust or a copper, and he who kills them will think he does God a service. The ' friend of publicans and sinners ' will be ' reckoned with transgressors,' and His life will end in defeat and ignominy. Jesus Himself has already accepted this necessity and found its meaning in the prophecies concerning the Servant of Jehovah. With His faith in God and conviction that His whole career has been ordered in accordance with God's will, there is only one way left of making sense of it all; and that is that the suffering and death of God's Servant will accomplish what His life of devoted service has failed to accomplish; that those who could not recognise the Anointed of God as He went about doing good will recognise Him on the Cross.

The disciples cannot see this. They are aware of the growing hostility of the people; but the irony of the saying about buying a sword is lost upon them. They see in it a token that the Master is at last going to rouse Himself to action. If He is for fighting, they are with Him. And they have two swords. They are ready to die like men. They are not ready to be led ' as a lamb that is led to the slaughter.'

They and He are at cross purposes; and Jesus breaks off the conversation. He must die alone.

35. The verse refers back to the Mission of the disciples (Lk. 10), and the list of things not carried by the disciples on that occasion tallies exactly with that given in 10[4] (see above, p. 74). Those were happy days. The missioners had returned with joy (10[17]). Their work had been successful and the people had been friendly to them. They took no provision with them, yet they lacked nothing.

36. The comment of Jesus on all that is that it is no longer possible. If such a mission were undertaken now, the missioners would have to carry provisions and money, and a sword would be more useful than a cloak. The translation given in R.V. mg. is preferable to that in the text. It is exceedingly unlikely either that this verse is meant to prepare the way for the story of the armed resistance at the arrest of Jesus (22[49 f.]), or that Jesus is thinking of a situation in which He will perish but the disciples will succeed in cutting their way out. The verse has nothing to say directly on the question whether armed resistance to injustice and evil is ever justifiable. It is simply a vivid pictorial way of describing the complete change which has come about in the temper and attitude of the Jewish people since the days of the disciples' Mission. The disciples understood the saying literally and so missed the point; but that is no reason why we should follow their example.

37. In any case armed resistance would be of no use to Jesus; for His fate is already determined. He finds the true meaning of His own career in the poem of the Suffering Servant of Jehovah (Is. 53); and if that prophecy is to be the interpretation of His life, He must be ' reckoned with transgressors ' (Is. 53¹²). If, as is likely, the quotation is allusive, we ought to take into account the whole verse of Isaiah, especially: ' He poured out his soul unto death, and was numbered with the transgressors: yet he bare the sin of many, and made intercession for the transgressors.' This verse of Lk. is ' the sole unambiguous Synoptic reference to the Isaianic Servant passages; a most significant fact, considering the importance of these passages to the earliest Christian apologetic ' (Easton).

The last clause of the verse is difficult. The Greek phrase translated ' that which concerneth me ' (or, taking the variant reading, ' those things concerning me ') is most easily understood, on the analogy of similar phrases in Lk. 24¹⁹, ²⁷; Acts 1⁸; Phil. 1²⁷, as meaning ' my story,' i.e. my career, my life. The marginal ' hath end ' is better than ' hath fulfilment.' The whole clause thus seems to mean: ' For in truth my life is at an end.' That is, events are moving inevitably in one direction for Jesus. There can only be one end to His Ministry; and that is the end foreshadowed in the fifty-third chapter of Isaiah.

38. But the disciples are not prepared to accept defeat of this sort. There has been talk of swords, and that they can understand. It is not too late; and a decisive stroke might yet turn the tables in favour of the Master. They have devotion to Him. They are ready to hazard their lives in His defence. They hate the thought that He should be brought to shame and death (cf. Mk. 8³²ᶠ.‖ Mt. 16²²ᶠ.). Jesus does not rebuke them. Nor does He try to explain further. He breaks off the conversation. The words ' It is enough ' can scarcely refer to the swords. Two swords would not be enough. More probably we have here a Semitic idiom analogous to our ' That will do ' to put a stop to a conversation. There is such an idiom in Biblical Hebrew, e.g. Dt. 3²⁶; and Rabbinical Hebrew has a similar idiom (Gen. R., ed. Theodor, p. 200 ll. 6 ff.). The effect of ' It is enough ' is thus to put the closure on any further talk about armed resistance. Jesus must fulfil the rôle of the Servant. He has done it throughout the Ministry —it is significant that we naturally call it the Ministry—and He will play the part through to its tragic end. To fight against it is not just attempting to defy destiny. It is rejecting what for Jesus is the revealed will of God. With that the die is cast. Only God can now save Him from the Cross. In the light of this it is possible to understand a little better the prayer in Gethsemane (Mk. 14³⁶), and perhaps also the cry of dereliction (Mk. 15³⁴).

36. *THE FATE OF JERUSALEM* (248)

LK. 23²⁷⁻³¹

23 27 And there followed him a great multitude of the people, and of women who 28 bewailed and lamented him. But Jesus turning unto them said, Daughters of Jerusalem, weep not for me, but weep for 29 yourselves, and for your children. For behold, the days are coming, in which they shall say, Blessed are the barren, and the wombs that never bare, and the 30 breasts that never gave suck. Then shall they begin to say to the mountains, Fall 31 on us; and to the hills, Cover us. For if they do these things in the green tree, what shall be done in the dry?

27. This incident is placed by Lk. in the account of the procession from the court to the place of crucifixion. The usual crowd, drawn by curiosity, is in attendance. Among them are women, who moved to sympathy for the victim raise a lamentation over him, beating their breasts and wailing. Dalman (*Jesus—Jeshua*, p. 193) quotes a Rabbinical passage in illustration (*Sifre Dt.* § 308): ' When a man goes out to be crucified, his father weeps for him; his mother weeps for him and beats (her breast) for him; and the one says " Woe is me "; and the other says " Woe is me." But the real woe is to him who goes out to be crucified.' The Greek word translated ' bewailed ' in R.V. is properly to beat oneself in token of grief.

28. The women lament the fate of Jesus. They raise the death-wail over Him in anticipation. He in His turn raises, as it were, the death-wail over Jerusalem in anticipation. The Holy City is doomed, and those who weep for Jesus might well weep for themselves if they knew what the future held in store for them. The address ' Daughters of Jerusalem ' occurs in the Old Testament (Song of Songs 1⁵; cf. Is. 3¹⁶, ' Daughters of Zion '). ' Weep not for me ' is not a prohibition except in grammatical form. The effect of the whole sentence is: If you only knew, you have better cause to weep for yourselves and your children than for me. For the form of the saying cf. Lk. 10²⁰.

29, 30. Verse 29 gives the reason why the women should weep for themselves rather than for Jesus. The phrase ' Behold, the days are coming ' is a common introductory formula of prophetic oracles in the Old Testament. The future is such that what among Jewish women was a reproach and humiliation will be looked upon as a blessing. The childless woman will suffer; but she will not have the added torture of seeing her children suffer too. What the sufferings will be is not stated. But they will be so terrible that people will pray for some convulsion of nature to overwhelm them and put them out of their misery. The words are borrowed from the Old Testament (Hos. 10⁸).

31. This verse is not a continuation of *v.* 30. It is most probably a proverbial saying with which Jesus ends what He has to say. Its purport appears to be: If crucifixion is the fate of one who has obeyed the will of God in all things, what will be the fate of those who flout the will of God at all points? We may compare the story related of Jose ben Joezer (2nd cent. B.C.). The Rabbi was being taken out to be crucified, and his nephew rode on horseback beside him mocking him. The nephew said to him: ' See my horse on which my master (the King) mounts me; and see your horse (the Cross) on which your master (God) mounts you!' The Rabbi replied: ' If such things (as you enjoy) come to those who offend Him (God), how much more will come to those who do His will.' The nephew said: ' And has any man done His will more than you?' (and yet you are crucified). He replied: ' If such things (as crucifixion) happen to those who do His will, how much more (and worse will happen) to those who offend Him.' A similar thought is expressed in 1 Pet. 4¹⁷ᶠ·: ' For the time is come for judgement to begin at the house of God: and if it begin first at us, what shall be the end of them that obey not the gospel of God? And if the righteous is scarcely saved, where shall the ungodly and sinner appear? '

EPILOGUE

It is scarcely possible to sum up the teaching in a few sentences; and any attempt to do so would inevitably produce a one-sided and distorted picture. For the teaching is not the Gospel, and Jesus is more than an inspired teacher of religion and morals. He was not called Saviour, Lord, and Christ by the early Church for being a great teacher or even an inspired prophet. The teaching is indissolubly bound up with the life and ministry of Jesus; and, as we have seen again and again, much of the teaching is only intelligible in its connexion with the ministry. The life and work of Jesus, His teaching, the mission of the disciples, the Cross and Resurrection, are all of a piece. For Jesus the teaching is an essential part of His life-work; but it is not the whole. The whole is the manifestation of the Kingdom of God as a present reality. Origen was right when he called Jesus *autobasileia*—the Kingdom itself.

This gives the fundamental explanation of our Lord's attitude to the Jewish Law, whether written or oral. He is not trying to effect a reformation of the theory and practice of Pharisaic Judaism, much less indulging in carping criticism of established institutions. He represents the Kingdom of God; and what He claims is that where the requirements of the Kingdom clash with the requirements of the Law, the former take precedence. That and nothing more; but it is an epoch-making claim.

It explains the paradoxes of the teaching and the life of Jesus.

His hearers were amazed by the authority with which He spoke. He dominated the crowds, and He was, without ever striving for mastery, easily the Master of His band of disciples. Yet He constantly insisted that He was the servant of all, and as constantly demonstrated the genuineness of that strange claim. The secret of His mastery and His service alike is that He was first and supremely the Servant of Jehovah. He sought first the Kingdom of God; and other things were added to Him.

The religious authorities were horrified by the freedom with which He criticised doctrines and practices hallowed by centuries of pious observance. Yet He was wont to go to the Synagogue on the Sabbath; and He enjoined the healed leper to do what Moses commanded in the matter of his healing. The explanation of this seeming inconsistency lies in the fact that the claims of the Kingdom of God take precedence of the requirements of the Law. But only the claims of the Kingdom: not private taste or fancy or convenience.

Respectable people were scandalised by the freedom and familiarity of His intercourse with the disreputable. He was nicknamed ' Friend of publicans and sinners.' Yet the quality of the friendship was determined by Him, not by the publicans and sinners. The friendship is a manifestation of the Kingdom of God: and one element in the conception of the Kingdom is that there is more joy in heaven over one sinner that repents than over ninety-nine righteous persons who do not need to repent. Not that God takes no pleasure in the righteous; but that the repentance of the sinner is the triumph of the Kingdom.

The rank and file of the Jewish nation were estranged in the end by His lack of patriotism. Yet He wept over the impending fate of Jerusalem; and He was executed as a political agitator along with two rebels against Rome. Again the explanation is in terms of the Kingdom of God, whose claims outweigh the claims of the Roman Empire *and* the claims of the ' Kingdom of our father David.'

If we ask what is this Kingdom of God that so dominates the life and words of Jesus and rides roughshod over established belief and practice, challenging all constituted authorities, the only answer is that it is the realisation of God's will in the world. It is God's will being done on earth as it is done in heaven. But what then is this will of God ? For Pharisaic Judaism it was holiness and righteousness as revealed in the Law. For those Jews who nourished their souls on the Apocalyptic literature, there was added an intenser assurance of a Divine power that would destroy evil and vindicate righteousness, and that right early. For many the Kingdom of God meant the downfall of Rome and the exaltation of Israel to world-dominion. For Jesus the will of God is primarily the forgiving, reconciling, redeeming love of God. And being what it is, it must express itself in a Divine act for men rather than in a Divine demand upon men; though this demand follows inevitably upon the act.

The essence of the Gospel is that Jesus—His life and death and victory over death, His ministry, His teaching—Jesus is the divine act, the fulfilment of God's redemptive purpose, the incarnation of the Kingdom of God. The ministry of Jesus is no mere prelude to the coming of the Kingdom, nor even a preparation for it: it *is* the Kingdom at work in the world. His ethic is no mere ' interim ethic ' to bridge the gap between the present and the future: it is the will of God which, whenever and wherever the Kingdom comes, is done on earth as it is in heaven. God was in Christ reconciling the world unto Himself. It is probable that the key to the teaching and the ministry of Jesus, and indeed to the whole New Testament, lies in a single phrase, which expresses, as perfectly as words can, the supreme interest of our Lord, that for which He lived and died, for which He endured hardship, loneliness, and obloquy, that to which He gave His whole undivided devotion—not ' the Law and the Prophets,' not ' the Kingdom of our father David,' but ' the Kingdom of my Father.'

SELECT BIBLIOGRAPHY

The following list does not give all the works consulted in the preparation of this commentary. Its purpose is rather to indicate the books which will be most useful to the student who wishes to go farther in the study of the subject.

The most convenient text is A. Huck's *Synopse der drei ersten Evangelien* (8th ed., 1931). This gives the Greek text of the Synoptic Gospels in parallel columns, with excellent cross-references. It has also an appendix containing the parallels from John. The text given is that of Tischendorf, and there is a useful *apparatus criticus.*

The standard Grammar of New Testament Greek, for English readers, is that begun by J. H. Moulton and now being completed by W. F. Howard.

For serious study of the text two works are indispensable: Moulton and Geden's *Concordance to the New Testament,* and Hatch and Redpath's *Concordance to the Septuagint.* Of dictionaries, the best combination in English is the *Greek-English Lexicon of the New Testament,* by Grimm and Thayer, supplemented by Moulton and Milligan's *Vocabulary of the Greek Testament.* If these are not available, there is the excellent *Manual Greek Lexicon of the New Testament* by Abbott-Smith. In German, W. Bauer's *Wörterbuch zum Neuen Testament* is altogether admirable. Another dictionary of the greatest importance is the *Theologisches Wörterbuch zum N.T.* edited by G. Kittel. It is being published in parts (Vols. I and II have already been published) and, when complete, will be a great encyclopædia of New Testament theology.

The most important documents illustrating the Jewish background of early Christianity are available in English translations. The extra-canonical Jewish books are collected in Charles's *Apocrypha and Pseudepigrapha of the Old Testament.* There is an excellent translation of the *Mishnah* by H. Danby. And the works of Philo and Josephus are in process of publication in the Loeb series. The history of the Jewish people during this period can be studied in E. R. Bevan's brilliant sketch, *Jerusalem under the High-Priests.* The fullest treatment is in Schürer's *Geschichte des Jüdischen Volkes im Zeitalter Jesu Christi* (4th ed.), and there is much important material in *Les Juifs dans l'Empire Romain,* by J. Juster. The finest account of the Jewish religion is G. F. Moore's *Judaism.*

For the study of the Synoptic Problem the reader is referred to Streeter's *The Four Gospels,* Stanton's *The Gospels as Historical Documents* (Pt. II), and—an indispensable tool—*Horae Synopticae,* by Sir J. C. Hawkins. Very important for the study of Q is Harnack's *Sprüche und Reden Jesu* (English translation, *The Sayings of Jesus*). A new solution of the Synoptic Problem is expounded in Bussmann's *Synoptische Studien.* Whether this theory is satisfactory remains to be seen; but there is much acute observation in Bussmann's three volumes.

In recent years there has been a determined attempt to get behind the documents embodied in the Gospels, and to study the material as it may have taken shape in oral tradition. A good introduction to this special line of research is furnished by V. Taylor's *The Formation of the Gospel Tradition.* The works of the leading representatives of the Form-critical school are accessible—in the main—only to those who read German; but what is perhaps the most important of them, the second edition of *Die Formgeschichte des Evangeliums,* by M. Dibelius, has recently been translated under the title *From Tradition to Gospel.* In this connexion mention may be made of Burney's demonstration, in *The Poetry of our Lord,* that much of the teaching of Jesus was delivered in poetic form.

Works devoted to the interpretation of the Gospels are legion. Here we can take account only of those which have a direct bearing on the teaching and of commentaries on the Gospels of Mt. and Lk.

The completest collection of material for the illustration of the teaching from the Jewish literature is Billerbeck's great *Kommentar zum N.T. aus Talmud und Midrasch.* Billerbeck gives a vast quantity of material from Jewish sources translated into German; and the task of the user of the commentary is to select from the store what is really relevant. In English we have the *Studies in Pharisaism and the Gospels,* by I. Abrahams, and C. G. Montefiore's two works: his Commentary on the Synoptic Gospels and his *Rabbinic Literature and Gospel Teachings.* Most important are Dalman's two books, both translated: *The*

Words of Jesus and *Jesus-Jeshua*. Schlatter's *Der Evangelist Matthäus* also contains much valuable Jewish material, especially from Josephus; and my *Teaching of Jesus* is an attempt to interpret the teaching on its Jewish background.

Of commentaries Wettstein's (1751) has yet to be superseded as a collection of illustrative material from Greek and Latin authors; and Bengel's *Gnomon* cannot be superseded. Of modern commentators in German Wellhausen is most stimulating and suggestive. J. Weiss (in Vol. I of *Die Schriften des Neuen Testaments*) did for German readers what the present work is designed to do for English readers. Among the most useful of German commentaries on the Synoptic Gospels are Klostermann's in Lietzmann's *Handbuch zum N.T.* (*Mt.* 2nd ed., 1927; *Lk.* 2nd ed., 1929). Zahn's big commentaries on Mt. and Lk. are learned and conservative. In English McNeile's commentary on Mt. and Plummer's on Lk. contain a great deal of useful information. A more recent commentary on Lk., which takes account of the newer research, is that of J. M. Creed.

In addition to the books mentioned there is much to be learned from the text-books of New Testament Theology and from the various ' Lives ' of Jesus. Two other books that must be mentioned are Otto's *Reich Gottes und Menschensohn*, a work which may well prove to be a turning-point in the study of the Gospels, and *The Parables of the Kingdom* by C. H. Dodd.

Finally, a few books of a supplementary nature: Dalman's exhaustive study of the topography of the Gospels is now available in English under the title, *Sacred Sites and Ways*. The student of the New Testament must also study the early Christian literature which was not included in the Canon. The collection known as *The Apostolic Fathers* is available with text and translation in the Loeb series (Kirsopp Lake); and the apocryphal Gospels, Acts, and Epistles have been brought together in translation by the foremost English authority on the subject in *The Apocryphal New Testament*, translated by M. R. James.

ADDENDA TO BIBLIOGRAPHY

Four volumes of the *Theologisches Wörterbuch* have now been published.

The Jewish background of early Christianity : add *Judaism and Christianity* (Vol. I, *The Age of Transition* ; Vol. II, *The Contact of Pharisaism with other Cultures* ; Vol. III, *Law and Religion*). L. Finkelstein, *The Pharisees* is a fresh and in many ways illuminating study of its subject. Most valuable for the understanding of Rabbinic Judaism is *A Rabbinic Anthology*, by C. G. Montefiore and H. Loewe.

To Dalman's two works dealing with the original language of the Christian tradition, we can now add an excellent treatise by M. Black, *An Aramaic Approach to the Gospels and Acts*.

Of general works useful to a student of the Teaching I should mention W. A. Curtis, *Jesus Christ the Teacher*, and W. Manson, *Jesus the Messiah*. J. W. Bowman's *The Intention of Jesus* breaks new ground. Otto's *Reich Gottes und Menschensohn* has been translated with the title *The Kingdom of God and the Son of Man*. Of the highest importance for the understanding of the New Testament in general, and the teaching of Jesus in particular, is O. Cullmann's *Christus und die Zeit*.

To the supplementary works should be added : for topography, Abel's *Géographie de la Palestine* ; and for social and economic conditions, Dalman, *Arbeit und Sitte in Palästina* ; J. Jeremias, *Jerusalem zur Zeit Jesu*. There is much valuable material in the later volumes of the Cambridge Ancient History

Additional Notes

16 ff. For a fuller discussion of Papias' statement about Matthew see my article in the *Bulletin of the John Rylands Library* XXIX (1946), 392–428.

37. last paragraph. Cf. E. Brunner, *The Divine Imperative*, 55.

51. On Lk. 6²⁹ ᶠ· Origen (*De Princ.* IV. 18 = *Philocalia* I, 19(18), ed. J. A. Robinson, p. 26) saw the point about a right-handed blow landing on the left cheek, but had not the Rabbinic clue to the puzzle.

52. l. 14. For Act 15²⁸ read Acts 15²⁹.

78 ff. On Lk. 10²¹ ᶠ· see Wm. Manson, *Jesus the Messiah*, 71–76.

86 f. On Lk. 11²¹ ᶠ· see E. G. Selwyn, *The First Epistle of St. Peter*, 457 f.

97, n. 1. For the fuller discussion of the name Pharisee see my article in the *Bulletin of the John Rylands Library* XXII (1938), 144–59.

101. On Lk. 11⁴⁷ ᶠ· cf. R. B. Y. Scott, *The Relevance of the Prophets*, 150 f.

115 f. On Lk. 12³⁵ cf. I Pet. 1¹³ with Selwyn's note and my review of Selwyn in *J.T.S.* XLVII (1946), 221. The possibility that the writer of the Epistle was acquainted with Q may be worth further investigation.
On Lk. 12³⁷ see T. F. Glasson, *The Second Advent*, 95.

118. On Lk. 12⁴⁶ see F. C. Burkitt, *Jesus Christ, an Historical Outline*, 72 f. ; J. R. Harris, *The Gospel of the Twelve Apostles*, p. 27, l. 13 ; E. Littmann in *Z.N.W.* XXXIV (1935), 24.

126 f. On Lk. 13³⁴ cf. the *Koran* ii. 81 (Bell's translation I, p. 12).

132. On Lk. 14³⁴ ᶠ· see L. Köhler, *Kleine Lichter*, No. 20.

135. On Lk. 16¹⁷ see E. Robertson, *The Text of the Old Testament and the Methods of Textual Criticism* (*Lectiones* I. 10 f.)

143. On Lk. 17²⁶, ²⁸, an interesting parallel is in the *Mishnah, Ta'anith* I, 7, dealing with fasting to get rain in time of drought. It says, ' If these days (of fasting) passed by and their prayers were not answered, they must give themselves but little to business, building or planting, betrothals or marriages, or greetings one to another, as becomes men that suffer God's displeasure ' (*tr.* Danby, p. 195).

The words of our poem with their description of such activities in full swing may be taken to indicate that the people concerned feel sure that *they* are not under God's displeasure, a confidence rudely shattered in the cases cited from the O.T., and to be as rudely shattered on the day of the Son of Man. And this goes to show that the day of the Son of Man is, like the prophetic ' day of the Lord ', to be a day of judgement.

150. Cf. A. N. Wilder, *Eschatology and Ethics in the Teaching of Jesus*, 120 ' The ethics called for in the Beatitudes are not so much ethics of obedience as ethics of grace.' Similarly M. Dibelius, *Jesus*, 90 f.

153. On Mt. 5¹⁶ J. Jeremias (*Z.N.W.* XXXV (1936), 78) suggests that ' good works ' here is equivalent to the Rabbinic *gĕmīlūth ḥăsādīm*—the mutual regard and practical kindness of members of the community. In that case the light shines clearly when non-Christians are forced to say, ' See how these Christians love one another.'

155. On Mt. 5²³ f. see J. Jeremias in *Z.N.W.* XXXVI (1937), 150–4.

158. On Oaths and Vows see Danby, *Mishnah*, 264 n. 1 ; S. Lieberman, *Greek in Jewish Palestine*, 115–43. For a parallel to ' the great King ' as a name for God, cf. the *Testament of Abraham* ed. M. R. James in *Texts and Studies* II. 2., p. 78 l. 31.

159. On Mt. 5³⁸ see D. Daube in *J.T.S.* XLV (1944), 177–87, and *Studies in Biblical Law* 102–53 ; L. Finkelstein in *Harvard Theological Review* XVI (1923), 59.

167. The Lord's Prayer. See L. S. Thornton, *The Common Life in the Body of Christ*, 358–68 ; Harnack, *Erforschtes und Erlebtes*, 24–35 ; E. F. Scott, *Man and Society in the New Testament*, 87. On Mt. 6[11] see E. Littmann in *Z.N.W.* XXXIV (1935), 29 f. ; M. Black in *J.T.S.* XLII (1941), 186–9. On Mt. 6[13] see T. W. Manson in *Asking them Questions* II, 128–32.

174. On Mt. 7[6] cf. *Const. Apost.* VII, 25 (ed. Funk I, 412) ; Theodoret on Philippians 3[2] (ed. C. Marriott II, 58) ; and Swete's note in his edition of Theodore of Mopsuestia on the Minor Epistles of St. Paul, I, 231.

175. On the two ways see Conington's *Persius*, p. 60 ; H. Preisker in *Z.N.W.* XX (1921), 204 ; W. Jaeger, *Paideia*[2] I, 105 f. ; A. J. Festugière, *L'Idéal religieux des Grecs et l'Evangile*, 80 n. 9.

185. On Mt. 11[28–30] cf. G. Kittel, *Lexicographia Sacra*, 26, ' The terminology first receives its real character when *He* speaks of " *My* yoke." ' Note that it is ' I will *give* you rest ', and not ' I will put you in the way of finding it for yourselves.' See D. Edwards, *Jesus, the Gospel Portrait*, 40.

192 f. On the Wheat and Tares cf. A. D. Nock, *St. Paul*, 60.

199. On Mt. 15[13]. ' Planting ' as a name for Israel appears in Frey's *Corpus Inscr. Iudaicarum* I, No. 72, where Julia Irene Arista is said to have kept the Jewish faith—*fidem sationis*.

214. On Mt. 18[31], the Greek word translated ' told ' is the regular term for the report of an official to his superior. Cf. *P. Haun*, I, 77.

221. On Mt. 21[14] J. Jeremias, *Jerusalem zur Zeit Jesu*, II A. 34, places this scene in the Court of the Gentiles.

247. On Mt. 25[27]. This verse played a part in the development of the Church's teaching on the taking of interest. For an account of this with references to the relevant texts, see Bright, *Notes on the Canons of the First Four General Councils*, 56–9.

255. On the Lucan itinerary see W. Gasse, ' Zum Reisebericht des Lukas ' in *Z.N.W.* XXXIV (1935), 293–9 ; C. C. McCown, ' The Geography of Luke's Central Section ' in *J.B.L.* LVII, Pt. 1 (1938), 51–66.

262. On Lk. 10[31], ' The owners of the lands of Jericho were, to a large extent, priests of the upper classes.' L. Finkelstein, *The Pharisees*, II, 655 n. 103. Jacob Mann in *J.Q.R.* (N.S.) VI (1915–16) 415–22, suggested that the priest was a Sadducee, who, believing the man to be dead, would not defile himself by touching the corpse. The suggestion is discussed by Billerbeck (*Komm.* II, 183), Jeremias (*Jerusalem* II B, 9 n. 1), and Finkelstein (*Pharisees*, II, 645), without reaching any very definite conclusion. The idea that a woman or a Samaritan might perform services which would be hardly proper for an observant male Jew is tacitly rejected in *T. Shabbath*, XV, 15 (Zuckermandel 134). See H. Loewe in *Judaism and Christianity—the Age of Transition*, 166 n. 1.

268 f. For a probable application of the saying about outward and inward cleansing in later Christian liturgical practice, see R. H. Connolly, *The So-called Egyptian Church Order*, 84, 89–94. The order of baptism provides not only for the external application of the water, but also for a cup of water to be drunk by the baptized person. Of this cup Dom Connolly says (p. 90), ' Its purpose is to signify the cleansing of the inner, as well as the outer, man by baptism : " ut et interior homo, quod est animale, similia consequantur sicut et corpus ".'

276. On Lk. 13[32] an interesting parallel to the use of the word ' fox ' here is to be found in an article by Bruno Meissner, ' Sprichwörter bei Asarhaddon ', in *Archiv für Orientforschung* X, 6 (1936), 362. A proverbial saying runs, ' Whither can the fox go when the sun is up ? ' ; which means that the petty potentate, who works by stealth under cover of darkness, cannot do anything effective when it comes to facing the great king in broad daylight. So the underhand dealings of the Grand Duke Herod Antipas are condemned to futility in face of the intervention of the Great King.

ADDITIONAL NOTES

282. On the parable of the Lost Sheep see E. F. Scott, *Man and Society in the New Testament*, 100.

292 ff. On Lk. 16¹⁻⁹. On the alteration of documents see O. Roller's article ' Das Buch mit sieben Siegeln,' in *Z.N.W.* XXXVI (1937), 98–113. According to Roller these were *chirographa* (cf. Col. 2¹⁴ f.) acknowledgements of indebtedness written by the debtors themselves and handed over to the creditor. They were thus secured against alteration or falsification, unless an ' unjust steward ' gave opportunity to tamper with them. For the writing of the bond by, or at the dictation of, the debtor, see Cowley, *Aramaic Papyri*, No. 10 (456 B.C.), a bond for a loan of money ; P. Ryl. Gk. 173 (a) (A.D. 99) ; 175 (A.D. 168) ; P. Fay 89 (A.D. 9).

For the Jewish law regarding the preparation of such *chirographa* see the Mishnah *Baba Bathra* X, 3 (Danby, p. 380) : ' They may write a bond for the debtor even if the creditor is not with him, but they may not write a bond for the creditor unless the debtor is with him ; and the debtor must pay the fee.' Similarly in the *Koran* II, 282, it is laid down that the document must be written at the dictation of the debtor, who is exhorted to ' show piety towards Allah his Lord, and not diminish aught thereof ' (i.e. of the debt). See Bell's translation I, 41 f.

For examples of altered documents see Lieberman, *Greek in Jewish Palestine*, 26 f. ; E. H. H. Minns in *Journal of Hellenic Studies* XXXV (1915), 28 f.

295. On Lk. 16¹⁴ f. For the transference to the Pharisees of matter which was originally concerned with other Jewish parties, see Lauterbach's essay in *Hebrew Union College Annual* VI (1929), 74 f.

The view that it is the Sadducees who are attacked here is confirmed by the following passages :

(*a*) *Enoch* 102¹⁰ ' See now ! they who justify themselves, how great has been their downfall,' etc. Cf. the newly recovered Greek text ed. C. Bonner, *Studies and Documents* VIII, 63.

(*b*) *Assumption of Moses* VII, 3, ' et regnabunt de his homines pestilentiosi et impii, *dicentes se esse iustos.*'

In both these cases Charles argues, rightly I think, that the persons referred to are Sadducees.

(*c*) Aucher and Moesinger, *S. Ephraemi Evangelii Expositio*, 188. ' Saducaei diebus Ioannis inchoarunt, *velut iustos a populo se separantes.*'

296. On the parable of Dives and Lazarus see J. Jeremias in *Theol. Wörterbuch zum N.T.* I, 146–50.

303 f. On Lk. 17²¹, ' The kingdom of God only comes at all because in Christ it is already " amongst us ".' P. Tillich in *The Kingdom of God and History*, 142. See also Otto, *The Kingdom of God and the Son of Man*, 131–7 ; K. L. Schmidt in *Theol. Wb.* I, 587 ; Dibelius, *Jesus*, 62 f. ; J. Héring, *Le Royaume de Dieu et sa Venue*, 42 f.

319 ff. On Lk. 19⁴¹⁻⁴⁴ see T. F. Glasson, *The Second Advent*, 94.

323 ff. On the apocalyptic discourse in Lk. 21 see H. H. Rowley, *The Relevance of Apocalyptic*, 120.

343. On Lk. 23²⁷. It is only the women who mourn.

Index of Scriptural References